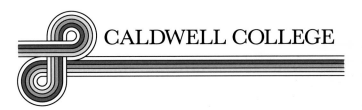

Public Papers of
the Secretaries-General of
the United Nations

VOLUME V

DAG
HAMMARSKJÖLD

1960–1961

Public Papers of

the Secretaries-General of

the United Nations

VOLUME V

DAG HAMMARSKJÖLD

1960–1961

Selected and Edited with Commentary by

ANDREW W. CORDIER

AND

WILDER FOOTE

COLUMBIA UNIVERSITY PRESS

1975

NEW YORK AND LONDON

ANDREW W. CORDIER has served as Dean of the School of International Affairs at Columbia University 1962-1972 and as President of the University 1968-1970. From the beginning of the United Nations until 1962 Dr. Cordier was Executive Assistant to the Secretary-General with the rank of Under-Secretary. During the entire period he also had the top Secretariat responsibility for General Assembly affairs.

WILDER FOOTE served in the United Nations Secretariat from its early days until December 1960 as Director of Press and Publications and acted as spokesman to the press for Secretaries-General Trygve Lie and Dag Hammarskjöld. Later he was a Research Associate in the School of International Affairs, Columbia University.

Library of Congress Cataloging in Publication Data   (Revised)

Cordier, Andrew Wellington, 1901-   comp.
  Public papers of the Secretaries-General of the
United Nations.

  Includes bibliographical references and indexes.
  CONTENTS: v. 1. Trygve Lie: 1946-53.—v. 2. Dag
Hammarskjöld: 1953-1956.—v. 3. Dag Hammarskjöld:
1956-1957. [etc.]
  1. United Nations—Collected works.   I. Foote, Wilder, joint comp.
II. Lie, Trygve, 1896-1968.
III. Hammarskjöld, Dag, 1905-1961.   IV. Title.
JX1977.C62   341.23'2   68-8873
ISBN 0-231-03633-7 (v.2)

This volume is dedicated to my colleague, Wilder Foote. He died on February 14, 1975, just as he had completed work on the volumes in this series for which he was responsible. I am deeply indebted to him both for his friendship over the years and for the wisdom and experience he brought to our collaboration on these volumes.

ANDREW W. CORDIER

April 23, 1975

Editors' Note on the Series

THE ROLE OF THE Secretary-General in the political life and constitutional development of the United Nations since 1945 has far exceeded the expectations of those who wrote the Charter. This has enhanced the historical significance of their public papers. These include many texts that are valuable and often indispensable as source materials in study of the Organization as a whole, of the office of Secretary-General in particular, and of the place of both in world affairs.

It is important that such papers be readily available to scholars and specialists in international affairs. In practice their accessibility has been severely limited. Some of the public papers of the Secretaries-General are included in the official documentation and some are not. In the former category are periodic and special reports to United Nations organs, proposals, and statements at meetings of the General Assembly, the Security Council, the other councils, committees, and commissions, and certain communications to governments. Not included in the official records are various other communications to governments, the Secretary-General's addresses outside the United Nations, statements to the press, press conference transcripts, radio and television broadcasts, and contributions to magazines and books. Most of the texts in this second category were issued as press releases, none as official documents.

More or less comprehensive collections of the official documents are maintained by depository libraries designated by the United Nations and located in most of the countries of the world. After more than twenty-five years it is not surprising that the volume of this documentation is immense. The record of what successive Secretaries-General have spoken or written in the official proceedings is widely dispersed throughout a great mass of records. Furthermore, it is necessary to go to the press releases for the public papers in the second category described above. The Dag Hammarskjöld Library at United Nations Headquarters maintains a comprehensive collection of press releases but it has not been the practice to include them in the deposit of official documentation in the depository libraries. Yet the press releases are usually the only source of a very important part of the public record—the Secretary-General's speeches to other groups and organizations and his press statements and press conferences. Successive Secretaries-General have frequently used these for historically significant and revealing statements.

Thus the present series of volumes of the public papers of the Secretaries-General has been undertaken to meet a real need. The project has been made possibly by a grant from the Ford Foundation to the School of International Affairs of Columbia University. The series will include all texts believed by the editors to be essential or most likely to be useful in study and research about the United Nations. These have been assembled from official, semiofficial, and nonofficial sources. The texts selected for the printed series are reproduced in full except where otherwise indicated. The styles of spelling and capitalization, which were variable in the official documents and press releases, have generally been reproduced as they were in the originals. Dates have been conformed throughout to the month-day-year style. The texts are arranged for the most part in chronological order corresponding to the sequence of events to which they are related. Commentary recalling the contemporary context and giving other background for the texts is provided whenever this seems useful. The full collections at Columbia University and the Dag Hammarskjöld Library are open to scholars wishing to consult them.

It should also be explained that the official records of the United Nations include many reports issued in the name of the Secretary-General that may more correctly be classified with the records of the organs requesting them. Such reports are factual accounts of developments or programs without personal commitments of policy or principle by the Secretary-General. There are a few borderline cases, but in general reports of this nature have not been considered as belonging with the public papers of the Secretaries-General.

Acknowledgments

THE SERIES of volumes of *Public Papers of the Secretaries-General of the United Nations* has been made possible by a grant from the Ford Foundation to the School of International Affairs of Columbia University. The editors are deeply grateful for this financial assistance.

The task of assembling the texts has been greatly facilitated by various officers serving in the United Nations Secretariat, especially those in the Dag Hammarskjöld Library and in the Public Inquiries Unit at United Nations Headquarters. Their willing cooperation is much appreciated.

Our editorial and research assistant, Alice Smith, has rendered indispensable and devoted service in assembling texts, researching the background of events for use in the commentary, finding and checking sources and references, reading proof, and supervising the transcription and reproduction of both texts and commentary. In the later stages, her successor, Charlotte Carpenter, provided invaluable service in preparing the manuscript for publication and in reading and checking the proofs. Both Miss Smith and Miss Carpenter have had many years of rich experience in the Secretariat of the United Nations.

A special word of appreciation is also due to the School of International Affairs' very helpful and efficient Xeroxing service.

Finally, the editors are grateful to Max Harrelson, chief of the United Nations bureau of the Associated Press from 1950 to 1972 and thereafter a Research Associate in the School of International Affairs, who read the manuscript of volume V and made helpful comments.

Contents

1961

*Public Papers of
the Secretaries-General of
the United Nations*

VOLUME V

DAG
HAMMARSKJÖLD

1960-1961

Note

In the course of the decade following the events recorded in this volume European names of places and a number of persons in the Congo were changed to African names. Thus, the Republic of the Congo itself was renamed the Republic of Zaïre, Leopoldville became Kinshasa, Elisabethville Lubumbashi and General Joseph Mobutu (who became President in 1965) Mobutu Sese Seko. All names in this volume are given only as they appeared in the official records of the time.

Introduction to This Volume of the Public Papers of Dag Hammarskjöld

I

THIS IS THE FOURTH and last of the Dag Hammarskjöld volumes in the series of *Public Papers of the Secretaries-General of the United Nations.* It begins with Hammarskjöld's response in July 1960 to the call for help from the Congo and ends with his death on September 17, 1961, in an airplane crash on his last mission to that country.

During this period he was engaged in unremitting struggle with the challenges and trials of the Congo operation itself and soon also of the simultaneous campaign of the Soviet Union to force his resignation and to replace the office of Secretary-General by a three-man directorate with a built-in veto—the "troika." These issues so dominated the final fourteen months of Hammarskjöld's service to the United Nations that the documentary source material and accompanying commentary in this volume are, with a few exceptions to be noted later, wholly taken up by them. The changed circumstances in which the Secretary-General found himself also caused him to take part in the debates of the Security Council and the General Assembly much more frequently than before and in a style often markedly in contrast with his previous custom.

Though he had of course freely expressed his views in private talks with delegates during such previous crises as the Suez and Lebanon affairs, his public interventions in the debate had usually been carefully nonpartisan and expressed in the restrained diplomatic language that was his rule. In the Congo operation his situation quickly became quite different from those previous experiences. From late August 1960 onward he came under heavy, abusive and repetitive public attacks from the Soviet side and met, as well, recurrent criticisms and misunderstandings from various other quarters. Time and again he felt it necessary to explain and defend his policies and his actions. In these interventions he tended more and more to speak like a responsible minister under attack in a parliamentary debate, mincing no words in reply to his accusers and often infusing his appeals for political and moral support from the Member states with an emotion and eloquence rarely revealed before that time. Thus the reader will find in this volume, along with Hammarskjöld's many reports and diplomatic notes during the Congo operation, the texts of more than forty interventions by the Secretary-General in successive Security Council and General Assembly debates on the Congo during 1960 and 1961.

Though he was often placed on the defensive and also suffered many setbacks both inside and outside the Congo, he succeeded in maintaining a level of political support among the Members that was strong and representative enough to enable him to carry on the Congo operation in accordance with the basic principles he evoked and defended. When he died the ultimate result was still in doubt but hope for its eventual success remained very much alive, and the office of Secretary-General itself had been preserved intact from the attempt to destroy it.

The decisions and events of the period from July to October 1960 inexorably determined the framework within which the Secretary-General had to carry on the struggle in the months that followed. Therefore it seems useful to devote these introductory paragraphs mainly to a consideration of the circumstances in which Hammarskjöld took and held the lead in the Congo affair and how the Soviet Union's attitude toward his role rapidly evolved from acquiescence to savage and implacable hostility.

II

The Secretary-General had returned from his African journey early in 1960 more convinced than ever that the United Nations could fill a modest but influential role in helping the weak and inexperienced new African Member states to find their way in world affairs and to grow in national strength, thus reducing the temptations offered by weakness to great power interventions from outside the continent or to ambitious adventurers from among their midst. He was thinking primarily in terms of expert development and administrative assistance and of what he called the "moral support" that the United Nations could provide to small countries in a world where naked power too often called the tune (volume IV of this series, page 528).

The year before when responding in a more general context to a press conference question about the capabilities and limitations of the United Nations, he had said: "The policy line, as I see it, is that the UN simply must respond to those demands which may be put to it. If we feel that those demands go beyond the present capacity, from my point of view that in itself is not a reason why I, for my part, would say no, because I do not know the exact capacity of this machine. It did take the very steep hill of Suez; it may take other and even steeper hills. . . . My policy attitude remains . . . the UN should respond and have confidence in its strength" (volume IV of this series, April 2, 1959 press conference, page 344).

The Belgian Congo was territorially the largest and one of the richest in resources of the European colonies in Africa to gain independence in 1960. It was also one of the least well prepared for self-government. Hammarskjöld had in mind the "moral support" and the "modest" technical assistance that United Nations resources would permit when he sent a high-level Secretariat mission to Leopoldville for the Independence Day ceremonies on June 30 and for follow-up discussions with the new central government headed by President Joseph Kasavubu and Prime Minister Patrice Lumumba. When Congolese soldiers unexpectedly began a series of mutinies against their Belgian officers, the first request for UN aid was indeed for "technical assistance in the field of security administration"— in other words, expert help in reorganizing and restoring discipline to the Congolese army.

Within hours this approach was overtaken by a succession of disastrous actions and reactions. Unruly soldiers ran amok, assaulting or threatening Belgians and other Europeans whom the new government desperately needed to help administer the public services and maintain the economy. A panic flight of Europeans by the thousands began and insistent demands were made for the immediate return of Belgian troops to protect the whites in the meantime. The troops returned, against the wishes of the Congo's central government and in violation of Belgium's treaty commitments. In Katanga, however, the Congo's richest province and home of the Union Minière, the provincial leader, Moïse Tshombé, invited and welcomed the return of the Belgian soldiers and promptly proclaimed the secession and independence of his province.

These moves provoked more bloodshed, thus accelerating the exodus of European civilians and further embittering relations between Belgium and the great majority of Congolese, who saw their colonial masters returning by force less than two weeks after independence and protecting secession as well. The central government began addressing frantic appeals in many directions for troops to help them deal with the Belgian "aggression"—to the United States, to the Soviet Union, to Ghana and Guinea in Africa, as well as to the United Nations Secretary-General.

To Hammarskjöld the situation was one to which, as he had said in 1959, the "UN simply must respond . . . with confidence in its strength" despite all the grave risks, both those that could readily be foreseen and those still unforeseeable. Unless the Belgian troops were promptly withdrawn the pressures for forceful outside interventions on one side and the other were likely to escalate rapidly beyond control, leading to a Spanish Civil War type of conflict.

Immediate action to establish in the Congo a United Nations force large enough to maintain law and order was expected to lead to the rapid and peaceful withdrawal of the Belgian troops in a way similar to the British and French withdrawal from Suez after the establishment of UNEF in 1956. The UN Force would then remain as the main protection of civil order only long enough to allow for the retraining of the Congolese army to take over the task. Meanwhile the administrative and public services of the government were to be reestablished with the help of a substantial United Nations civil assistance program while the competing political factions, including Tshombé's, were encouraged to work out their differences by peaceful and constitutional means, preserving also the territorial integrity and unity of the Congo.

These were the goals. That many of them remained beyond reach during the rest of Hammarskjöld's life does not detract from the validity of the effort. And the most immediate and essential aim—forestalling a civil war with external involvement in the heart of Africa by getting there first with a strong United Nations presence—was indeed accomplished.

III

Sensing the gravity of the crisis in the Congo, on July 13 the Secretary-General seized the initiative, acting under Article 99 of the Charter for the first time. The fact that the Security Council adopted its Congo resolutions of July 14 and 22 and August 9 without a dissenting vote gave a most misleading impression of the solidity of support—or even of understanding—for the principles which the Secretary-General believed should guide the operation. Nevertheless, Hammarskjöld estimated that the area of common interest among the Members, narrow and tentative though it was, might give him sufficient room if he acted fast and decisively enough.

Before the Security Council met the Secretary-General had first made sure of solid African support for his initiative. The African governments were outraged by the Belgian military intervention and alarmed by the encouragement thus given to secession in Katanga. They demanded immediate withdrawal and were ready to give military assistance to the Congo government under United Nations auspices. There was strong sentiment among them for an all-African force under African command but they acceded to Hammarskjöld's insistence that a UN force, while mainly African in this instance, must include representation from other continents as well because of the universal character of the Organization.

The Soviet Union gave all-out verbal support to the African complaint against Belgium and "its NATO allies." It would doubtless have preferred an independent African initiative to which it could give assistance on a direct bilateral basis and it was also constitutionally opposed to an executive role for the Secretary-General in any UN force. However, it had abstained when the Assembly voted for UNEF in 1956 because Egypt had already agreed to the Force. This time it did not wish to oppose a proposal backed by all the Africans and most Asians as well.

The Western powers considered the Belgian intervention justified by the provocations but thought it wise to help extricate their ally before greater complications ensued. Thus they were willing to accept the idea of a UN force that would take over from the Belgian troops as soon as it could be deployed in sufficient numbers to uphold civil order and the security of persons, especially of the Europeans who had so far been the principal victims of violence.

With this background, it proved possible to win adoption of a resolution authorizing a UN force in the early hours of July 14 by a vote of 8 to none, with Britain, France, and Nationalist China abstaining. The resolution also called for the withdrawal of Belgian troops, but without setting a time limit. As to the mandate of the force, the wording of the operative paragraph was ambiguous unless read together with the Secretary-General's recommendations for action given in his opening statement to the Council.

The Congolese leaders had requested a UN force to "protect" the nation against Belgian "aggression." The Secretary-General's recommendation to the Council, however, was for a UN Force to take over the task of maintaining public order as "a stop-gap arrangement," thus facilitating the peaceful withdrawal of the Belgian troops. He had also informed the Council that if it acted affirmatively on his recommendation he would be guided by the principles set forth in his 1958 "Summary Study" of the UNEF experience (see volume IV of this series), and he specifically mentioned three of these principles—the UN Force would not be authorized to use force except in self-defense, nor to take any action "which would make them a party to internal conflicts," and troops of the Council's permanent members would be excluded.

Four days later his first report to the Security Council spelled out in more detail these and related principles that he believed should govern the mandate of the UN Force. In particular he stressed that the Force, though there to assist the Congolese government, was not under that government's orders but exclusively under United Nations command. It could not, he wrote, be used in joint operations with that government, nor "to enforce any specific political solution of pending problems or to influence the political balance decisive to such a solution." The Security Council's second Congo resolution, adopted unanimously on July 22, included a paragraph in which the Council "commends" the Secretary-General for the "prompt action" taken "and for his first report," thus implicitly endorsing the principles set forth in that report.

While there was no direct reference to Katanga the resolution called upon "all States" not to "undermine the territorial integrity and political independence" of the Congo as a whole, and to refrain from any action which might impede the exercise of the central government's authority and the restoration of law and order. Belgium should implement "speedily" the July 14 call for withdrawal of its troops.

Once again language that was sometimes ambiguous had been employed to secure maximum support. The Soviet Union voted for the resolution and Lumumba at first welcomed it as progress, but neither ever really accepted the basic policy line enunciated by the Secretary-General and supported by the majority. Before the vote the Soviet delegate had proposed a three-day deadline for total Belgian withdrawal and warned that stronger measures might soon be necessary, whether by the United Nations or by "the peace-loving States" to support the Congo against Western "imperialist aggression." The volatile and impatient Lumumba had repeatedly called for an immediate UN invasion of Katanga to end the secession by force, and had threatened to turn to the Soviet Union for help if the UN failed to act. Some of the African governments, too, with their special sensitivity to the danger of secessionist movements, believed that the United Nations should move more forcefully on Katanga.

The Secretary-General was working against time and he knew it. By August 1 the UN Force numbered over 11,000 from eight countries, six of them African, with more on the way. The Force was being deployed in every province where it had been possible to secure Belgian cooperation in withdrawal, and this meant everywhere except in Katanga.

Meanwhile Hammarskjöld had continued to report fully and frequently to the Security Council by means of oral and written reports and a stream of addenda to the latter. These concerned not only the progress of deployment but elaborated also on the constitutional and political principles involved. If the Council's resolutions were sometimes ambiguous on the mandate of the Force, it is hard to see how anyone who read these documents at that time, or rereads them now, could be in any doubt about how Hammarskjöld saw his duty and the mandate.

The Secretary-General was now ready to move on Katanga, but *not* by forceful means. Unless the Council acted under Article 42 that would be against the law of the Charter. It was also against his strongly held personal conviction that the United Nations should so act as to help Africans *not* to fight Africans, rather than the reverse. Nor should it intervene on one side or the other in internal disputes.

In Katanga Tshombé and his supporters threatened to oppose by force the entry of UN troops, fearing the collapse of his régime if the Belgians withdrew. Belgium, in turn, while professing its willingness to withdraw its troops from Katanga also if UN troops came in and could guarantee order, covertly encouraged Tshombé to hold out. In the meantime its troops stayed on. Thus, at a critical moment, the honest cooperation of Belgium was withheld and the behind-the-scenes diplomatic support for Hammarskjöld's plan that was needed from Belgium's NATO allies, especially from Britain and France, was found wanting or was lukewarm at best. Western Europe had a big economic stake in Katanga and there was growing sympathy for the violent opposition of Tshombé's European supporters there to the central government and especially to Lumumba.

After Tshombé rudely rebuffed a first attempt to arrange for the peaceful entry of the UN Force Hammarskjöld returned to the Security Council and succeeded on August 9 in obtaining a resolution explicitly invoking Articles 25 and 49 of the Charter, thus making compliance mandatory under Chapter VII. This resolution called for the "immediate" withdrawal of Belgian troops from Katanga, declared that the entry of the

UN Force into Katanga was necessary and reaffirmed that the UN Force "will not be a party to or in any way intervene in or be used to influence the outcome of any internal conflict, constitutional or otherwise." The resolution carried by 9 votes to none, with France and Italy abstaining. For the third and last time the Soviet Union and the United States voted together in the affirmative but Soviet criticism of the Secretary General's policies with respect to Katanga and Belgium was becoming sharper and more direct.

Four days later Hammarskjöld personally achieved the peaceful entry of the UN Force into Katanga by a bold stroke, bringing with him for his talks with Tshombé an advance guard of two Swedish UN companies and a copy of a memorandum of his interpretation of the paragraph in the August 9 resolution just quoted above. He had this interpretation circulated as a Security Council document the same day. It was based mainly on the policy of neutrality between the government and rebel groups that was followed by the United Nations Observation Group in Lebanon in 1958.

Having received this pledge of noninterference in his dispute with the central government Tshombé accepted the deployment of the UN Force in Katanga. This removed the last excuse for the continued presence of Belgian troops and the regulars were, in fact, fully withdrawn in a short time, though there were some further attempts at delay and evasive maneuvers.

Hammarskjöld considered deployment of the UN Force in Katanga to constitute in itself a strong affirmation of the unity and territorial integrity of the Congo and a denial of the legitimacy of secession. This and the withdrawal of the Belgian troops on whose presence Tshombé had depended should, he thought, ease the fears of the central government and also improve the chances for working toward a peaceful resolution of the constitutional and political conflict. Almost immediately the ground was cut from under these assumptions.

In Leopoldville Lumumba turned furiously against Hammarskjöld because he had shut the door to the use of UN troops to subdue Tshombé. In Katanga, though the regular troops were leaving it was soon discovered that Belgian assistance continued, in the form of individually seconded or recruited military personnel and civilian advisers, shipment of arms and lavish financing from Belgian banking and the Union Minière resources.

The central government of the Congo was in disarray, public services were broken down and the Congolese Army (ANC) still undisciplined, unpaid, and divided into factions. Nevertheless, Lumumba decided to attempt an immediate invasion of Katanga on his own, using units of the ANC personally loyal to him. For such an attempt he needed transport planes to ferry the troops. He secretly asked for and received these from the Soviet Union, without consulting President Kasavubu or the more moderate members of his coalition cabinet. The invasion attempt never reached Katanga for the ANC units became bogged down in tribal clashes in neighboring Kasai province, but the dispatch of the Soviet transport planes constituted a unilateral intervention so serious as to signal a Soviet decision to break definitively with United Nations policy in the Congo.

Since the Soviet Union had voted for all three resolutions on the Congo the offensive it now launched in the Security Council and the General Assembly had to be directed mainly against the Secretary-General himself, who was charged with favoring the "Western colonialists" and with many other "sins" in the execution of the resolutions.

The Soviet intervention on Lumumba's side hardened the growing Western distrust of the latter's intentions into outright hostility. Many of the more moderate members of the Congolese government were also turning against him because of his extreme stands and failures to consult, though he remained a charismatic figure with something of a national following. These reactions combined to produce early in September successive moves by President Kasavubu and General Mobutu, the ANC chief of staff, to deprive Lumumba of office, moves that were contrary to UN efforts in support of reconciliation and legitimacy but were encouraged and welcomed by Western governments. When civil war threatened to erupt the United Nations temporarily shut down the radio station and the airfields until things calmed down. Soon afterward Kasavubu and Mobutu proceeded to expel the Soviet and Czech diplomatic missions despite UN attempts to dissuade them. All these developments became additional subjects for controversy.

There were two inconclusive Congo debates in the Security Council during the latter part of August and first part of September. These were marked by increasingly abusive attacks by the Soviet Union on Hammarskjöld's policies and conduct. Although Ghana and Guinea were openly unhappy about the refusal to use force in Katanga or to intervene on Lumumba's side during the government crisis in Leopoldville, and other left-leaning African and Asian states also had reservations about some of his policies, the confidence of the African-Asian bloc as a whole in Hammarskjöld's leadership remained generally quite solid. When the question was transferred to an emergency session of the General Assembly the Soviet Union's campaign against the Secretary-General suffered a sharp setback. An Afro-Asian resolution affirming a convincing measure of support for Hammarskjöld was adopted by 77 votes to none, with only the Soviet bloc, France, and South Africa abstaining. However, the Soviet Union was not to be deterred, and Khrushchev promptly carried the campaign a fateful step further in his speeches at the "summit" session of the General Assembly on September 23 and October 3.

IV

It is not yet clear exactly when it was that the Soviet Union decided to link a demand for Hammarskjöld's resignation with a proposal to replace the office of Secretary-General by a three-man directorate composed of one representative each of the Western powers, the Communist states and the neutralist, or "third world" countries, each with a veto on the other two. The decision may have come quite late in the game, without sufficiently careful consideration. In any event Hammarskjöld's position in the ensuing David versus Goliath struggle that stirred the admiration of so much of the world was greatly strengthened thereby.

The "troika," or something like it, was not a new idea. At the United Nations Conference on International Organization, held in San Francisco in 1945, the Soviet Union had worked in vain for a representative collegium in some form to run the Secretariat. Having lost that contest it had defended on most occasions a very conservative view of the functions and powers of the Secretary-General. With its minority position in the Organization and perceptions influenced by its ideology the USSR was always uncomfortable with the concept of the international civil servant as set forth in Article 100 of the Charter and uneasy about an executive who, once elected, was not subject to administrative veto in the conduct of his responsibilities for the next five years.

The Summit Assembly was mainly the result of Khrushchev's personal promotion. Early in August he had announced his intention of coming in person with new Soviet proposals on disarmament and he had urged other Heads of Government to join him in the debate. More than thirty others, including all the best known Member government leaders of the time except De Gaulle, decided that they should come, although a good many had little enthusiasm for the exercise. Khrushchev conceived of it as an ideal opportunity for a dramatic demonstration to the countries of the "third world" of the Soviet Union's peaceful intentions and its championship of their cause against the Western "colonialists." With sixteen more newly independent African countries due for admission to United Nations membership and the developing crisis over UN policy in the Congo the center of interest had shifted from disarmament by the time Khrushchev spoke on September 23, though a major part of his address was given over to presenting the Soviet disarmament plan.

The Soviet leader accused the Western "colonialists" of "doing their dirty work in the Congo through the Secretary-General and his staff." The Assembly, he said, "should call Mr. Hammarskjöld to order and ensure that he does not misuse the position of the Secretary-General." Later in the speech, when discussing Soviet disarmament proposals, he said that disarmament would require establishing United Nations armed forces to keep the peace and that United Nations machinery should be revised beforehand to ensure the impartial use of such forces. He then declared that "conditions have clearly matured to the point where the post of Secretary-General, who alone directs the staff and alone interprets and executes the decisions of the Security Council and the sessions of the General Assembly, should be abolished," in favor of a tripartite executive—the "troika."

Hammarskjöld responded with the first of his two eloquent replies to Khrushchev, pointing out that the Assembly was now being confronted with a question "not of a man but of an institution" and with a challenge to the fundamental principles of Article 100 of the Charter (pp. 196-98).

Khrushchev renewed his attack in abusive terms during a speech on the issue of Chinese representation on October 1 and then on October 3 for the first time explicitly called on Hammarskjöld to resign. That afternoon the Secretary-General replied in a short speech that to resign now would, because of the Soviet stand on the "troika," be to "throw the Organization to the winds." He "had no right to do so" and would remain in his post as long as those nations for whom the United Nations was of decisive importance wished him to stay. His statement evoked the greatest spontaneous ovation in United Nations history (pp. 199-201).

The violence and personally abusive nature of Khrushchev's attacks upon the Secretary-General's conduct and integrity shocked and angered the Asian and African representatives whom the Soviet leader was trying to impress. Nor did his "troika" proposal, as he had presented it, win any direct support outside of the Soviet bloc. After his return home, however, Soviet bloc representatives kept renewing the offensive at every opportunity on both fronts—for the "troika" and against the principles applied in the Congo operation. They sensed possibilities for making inroads in both directions if they kept up the pressure.

Some "third-world" leaders, especially in the more radical nations, were attracted by the idea of special representation for their views and interests. Thus trial balloons were floated by Nehru and Nkrumah suggesting the creation of a tripartite consultative council to advise the Secretary-General or the appointment of three deputy Secretaries-General, though no formal proposals were tabled. In the Fifth (Administrative and Budgetary) Committee Soviet representatives also hammered away at the theme that Westerners dominated the Secretariat from top to bottom and advocated drastic measures aimed at securing equal representation with the West for the Communist bloc and the neutralist states.

The advocacy of a Secretariat that would represent three major ideological and power groupings in the world was a gross distortion of the desirability of wide geographical distribution and would strike at the very heart of the exclusively international obligations of the Secretariat as defined in Article 100 of the Charter. Hammarskjöld considered it necessary time and again to come to the defense of this concept in the face of incessant Soviet pounding and recurrent signs of weakness on the issue among some of the other Member states.

In the Congo the difficulties and differences encountered by the United Nations continued to mount in number and in intensity, providing the Soviet bloc with many opportunities to renew their attacks on Hammarskjöld's conduct of the operation and to exploit and exacerbate the splits that developed both within the Congo and among the African and Asian members. These attacks, and the Secretary-General's responses, being all out in the open, tended to obscure the difficulties that also developed during this time over certain acts and policies of Belgium and its Western allies with which Hammarskjöld sharply disagreed.

V

The remaining months of Hammarskjöld's service to the United Nations were devoted to a constantly renewed struggle amidst storms of adversity to keep the Congo operation afloat, to maintain its guiding principles intact and to preserve the integrity and independence of the office of

Secretary-General. The full story is too long and complex to summarize in a few paragraphs but it may be followed in detail and step-by-step in the documentation and commentary included in this volume. Here we shall simply mention the main trends in the development.

The period from October 1960 to the spring of 1961 was a time when almost everything seemed to be going from bad to worse, both in the Congo and in New York. In the Congo there was no central government worthy of the name for the United Nations to work with, and anarchy and disintegration proceeded apace. In Katanga the defiance and hostility to United Nations aims of both Tshombé and Belgium became more open. In New York the Western powers succeeded in winning a split vote to seat an Assembly delegation named by Kasavubu against Hammarskjöld's advice to leave the seat open, thus giving African members more time to work for a reconciliation between the warring Congolese political factions. After this setback Lumumba attempted to flee from his enemies in Leopoldville to his political base in Stanleyville in order to establish there a rival central government to the Kasavubu-Mobutu régime. He was arrested en route and soon thereafter sent as a prisoner to Katanga, where he was promptly murdered with Tshombé's connivance.

Lumumba's arrest and death sharply intensified the feeling in some "third-world" countries that the United Nations should have intervened earlier on his side against both Kasavubu in Leopoldville and Tshombé in Katanga. Morocco, Guinea, and several other African and Asian states had already threatened to withdraw their contingents from the UN Force on this issue and now proceeded to do so. The Soviet Union moved to exploit the emotions that had been aroused with new and even more violent attacks on Hammarskjöld who along with the Western powers, was accused of complicity in the assassination. Again his immediate resignation was demanded during successive Security Council and General Assembly debates and again it was necessary for Hammarskjöld to defend his policies and his actions in both Council and Assembly. Once again the Soviet drive to force his resignation failed to make headway. However, there were also various failures by other Member states to assure responsible and consistent political and financial backing at the levels required if the Congo operation were to surmount its many difficulties. The Secretary-General did not hesitate in his interventions to appeal for greater support in these respects.

The tide began to turn in the spring of 1961. Nehru was persuaded to contribute an Indian brigade to the UN Congo Force, which in succeeding months was built up to its maximum strength of 20,000 men despite earlier withdrawals. In Leopoldville Kasavubu moved on from a long period of hostility toward the UN operation to an attitude of full cooperation. He had been angered by the Secretary-General's refusal to recognize the legitimacy of the shadow cabinets of the Mobutu period and had even for a while tried an alliance with Tshombé, which soon turned sour. Now he gave his support to UN efforts to promote reconciliation among the various political leaders and the reconvening of parliament under UN protection so that a coalition government could be constitutionally installed. In August the parliament confirmed a new coalition cabinet headed by Cyrille Adoula that included Antoine Gizenga, Lumumba's successor, as well as members of all the other factions except Tshombé's. The latter had at first agreed to participate but then backed down.

Hammarskjöld returned to the Congo in September on Adoula's invitation and with hopes that during his visit he might help to persuade Tshombé to a more moderate course vis-à-vis both the United Nations and the new central government. However Tshombé's mercenaries and the UN Force became involved in serious fighting in Katanga while the Secretary-General was en route from New York to Leopoldville. He immediately engaged in efforts to negotiate a cease-fire and was on his way to talk to Tshombé about it when he was killed in the crash of his plane during the night of September 17.

Around the world his death evoked an extraordinary outpouring of grief and expressions of respect for the rare quality of his character and the dedication, courage and skill with which he had served the cause of peace.

VI

In addition to the documentation and commentary that are strictly part of the Congo story this volume includes three related texts of enduring significance for the history and development of the United Nations. These are the introductions to the 1960 and 1961 Annual Reports of the Secretary-General and his lecture at Oxford on May 30, 1961, "The International Civil Servant in Law and in Fact." The Oxford lecture and the 1961 Introduction in particular present a carefully reasoned case for the concept of the Organization as "a dynamic instrument of governments" for executive action in support of peace that is served by a Secretary-

General and Secretariat responsible only to the Organization as a whole and goes well beyond a mere conference machinery.

Mention may also be made of his mission to South Africa and of the Bizerta affair, the only important political initiatives outside the Congo operation that were undertaken by the Secretary-General during this period. His intervention in Bizerta was not successful because it met a hostile reception from General De Gaulle, who also strongly disapproved of the UN operation in the Congo.

Finally, and on quite a different level, the reader will find in this volume the text of Hammarskjöld's moving words during the 1960 United Nations Day concert when the Philadelphia Orchestra played Beethoven's Ninth Symphony, "this enormous confession of faith in the victorious human spirit and in human brotherhood, a confession valid for all times." Eleven months later the Orchestra returned to the General Assembly Hall to play the Ninth Symphony in a memorial ceremony for Hammarskjöld and for those who had died with him, and his voice was heard again in a recording of his 1960 remarks.

ANDREW W. CORDIER
and WILDER FOOTE

September 1974

❦ 1960 ❧

THE UNITED NATIONS OPERATION IN
THE CONGO BEGINS

THE HASTILY IMPROVISED ARRANGEMENTS under which the Congo became independent from Belgium collapsed with catastrophic suddenness only a few days
after the ceremonies of Independence Day on July 1, 1960. The succession of
events between July 1 and 13 and the background for them have been extensively
recorded in various accounts.[1] Here it is sufficient to mention key factors in the
development of those events.

Belgium had provided this vast colonial territory—which was over seventy
times the size of Belgium and richly endowed in natural resources—with one of
the most efficient and extensive administrations in Africa. It was also one of the
most paternalistic and exploitative. When independence came, there were 10,000
Belgian civil servants who held virtually all the responsible jobs in the public
services. The Congolese army, then called the Force publique, had 1,000 officers,
all white Belgians, and 24,000 other ranks, all black Africans. Control of the
economy of the country—mining, industry, agricultural enterprises—was in the
hands of large Western European corporations with huge investments to defend.
The handful of Congolese university graduates did not include a single doctor or
engineer. The small politically active Congolese leadership group had almost no
experience in, or preparation for, the responsibilities of self-government. The first
legislative elections ever held in the Congo took place in May 1960 and the first
central government, with Joseph Kasavubu as President and Patrice Lumumba as
Prime Minister, took office only a week before independence. There was little
sense of national identity among the people. Tribal loyalties, often clashing with
each other, predominated.

In such unfavorable circumstances the odds against an orderly transition from
colony to nationhood were very heavy. For there to be any chance at all it was
vital that the Belgian civil servants stay on in loyal service to the new government
while Congolese gained the training and experience to succeed them in the administration. It was equally vital that the Force publique prove itself competent

---

[1] See especially Catherine Hoskyns, *The Congo since Independence,* (London: Oxford University Press, 1965), pp. 1–105.

and disciplined in the maintenance of public order. Almost immediately both these expectations were shattered by events.

The Congolese soldiers thought independence should bring with it a real beginning at least of Africanization of the officers' corps of the army, but the Belgian commander, General Emile Janssens, had firmly resisted and the new government did not at first press the issue. Beginning on July 5 this led to a series of mutinies in garrisons throughout the country. The officers lost control and armed bands of mutinous soldiers roamed the streets, expressing in brutal violence long-suppressed resentments and a desire to visit humiliation upon the white Europeans who had been their masters for so long. Many Belgians were manhandled and some women were raped.

Reports of such outrages, often exaggerated, spread panic among the Belgians and other Europeans. A mass exodus began and there were calls for the return of Belgian troops. The terms of the treaty between Belgium and the Congo provided that Belgian troops should return only by request of the Congolese government. Lumumba and Kasavubu refused to take this course and sought to bring the situation under control by negotiating with the mutineers for the Africanization of command of the army which the soldiers were calling for. An agreement was reached at Leopoldville and the political leaders then set out by air to seek similar results in other cities where mutinies and disorder were occurring.

While Kasavubu and Lumumba were on this mission the Belgian government decided that military intervention had become necessary, even without the consent of the central Congolese government. Paratroops were flown in on July 10 to Elisabethville, the capital of Katanga province, and in the following days to other major centers. There followed more fighting, loss of life, and ugly incidents which further stimulated the mass flight of Belgian civilians.

Katanga was dominated by the great international company—Union Minière du Haut Katanga—and was by far the wealthiest province of the Congo. The Belgians there felt much closer to Rhodesia than to Leopoldville and especially disliked the centralized form of government under which the Congo had become independent. These attitudes were shared by Moïse Tshombé, the provincial president and strongest political figure in Katanga. He had requested the Belgian paratroops on July 10. The next day he proclaimed the independence of Katanga, alleging that the central government was "neo-Communist." On July 12, when Kasavubu and Lumumba attempted to land at Elisabethville airport in the course of their tour of provincial capitals they were refused permission and had to return to Luluabourg, the capital of Kasai province.

Thus, less than a fortnight after independence, the new republic was falling apart in conflict and chaos. Like others familiar with Belgium's failure to prepare the ground for independence, Hammarskjöld had been anxious about what might happen, though he had not anticipated such a rapid and all-embracing collapse. Ralph Bunche, who had represented him at the Independence Day ceremonies, had stayed on to discuss plans for United Nations technical assistance and to demonstrate that "moral support" for the new African nations of which the Secretary-General had spoken earlier in the year on his return from his tour of Africa (see volume IV of this series).

In the developing chaos little progress on planning had been possible, but on July 10 Bunche met with members of the cabinet, which decided to ask the United Nations for military advisers, experts, and technicians to help in making the Force publique once again into a disciplined army capable of maintaining law and order but with an African, not a Belgian, officer corps. Bunche reported the cabinet's decision by telephone. Hammarskjöld had just arrived in Geneva for the ministerial level meeting of the Economic and Social Council. He decided to return to New York the next evening after making his opening statement to the Council (see volume IV of this series) and he asked Cordier to arrange a meeting on July 12 with representatives of the African Member states to discuss a request from the Congo for "technical assistance in the field of security administration."

The Secretary-General met on July 12, as planned, with the heads of the delegations of Ethiopia, Ghana, Guinea, Liberia, Libya, Morocco, Sudan, Tunisia, and the United Arab Republic, but the rush of events in the Congo during the day quickly deprived the technical assistance approach of immediate practical significance. The secession of Katanga and the seizure by Belgian paratroops of the port of Matadi in bloody fighting on July 11 had turned the Congolese leaders decisively against the Belgians. They decided they must have immediate military assistance from other quarters to preserve the independence and integrity of the country.

In Leopoldville on July 12 the vice-premier, Antoine Gizenga, acting in the absence of Kasavubu and Lumumba, inquired of U.S. Ambassador Claude Timberlake if the United States would send a force of three thousand men. This inquiry was not pursued after a special mission sent by President Kwame Nkrumah of Ghana advised against it and urged the government to turn to the United Nations instead. This was also the United States position. Soon after word of Gizenga's approach reached United Nations Headquarters a cablegram arrived from Kasavubu and Lumumba requesting the "urgent dispatch by the United Nations of military assistance." The message originated in Luluabourg where the two leaders had returned after being refused permission to land at Elisabethville. The text was as follows:

I. *Telegram dated July 12, 1960, from the President and the Prime Minister of the Republic of the Congo to the Secretary-General*[2]

The Government of the Republic of the Congo requests urgent dispatch by the United Nations of military assistance. This request is justified by the dispatch to the Congo of metropolitan Belgian troops in violation of the treaty of friendship signed between Belgium and the Republic of the Congo on June 29, 1960. Under the terms of that treaty, Belgian troops may only intervene on the express request of the Congolese government. No such request was ever made by the Government of the Republic of the Congo and

[2] Security Council Official Records, Fifteenth Year, Supplement for July, August, and September 1960, document S/4382.

we therefore regard the unsolicited Belgian action as an act of aggression against our country.

The real cause of most of the disturbances can be found in colonialist machinations. We accuse the Belgian government of having carefully prepared the secession of Katanga with a view to maintaining a hold on our country. The government, supported by the Congolese people, refuses to accept a *fait accompli* resulting from a conspiracy between Belgian imperialists and a small group of Katanga leaders. The overwhelming majority of the Katanga population is opposed to secession, which means the disguised perpetuation of the colonialist régime. The essential purpose of the requested military aid is to protect the national territory of the Congo against the present external aggression which is a threat to international peace. We strongly stress the extremely urgent need for the dispatch of United Nations troops to the Congo.

Joseph Kasavubu
President of the Republic of the Congo and
Supreme Commander of the National Army

Patrice Lumumba
Prime Minister and Minister of National Defence

The next morning, July 13, brought news of the occupation by returning Belgian troops of the Leopoldville airport and the European sector of the city where the government buildings were located. Belgian units were also landing at other key centers in the country. Lumumba told Bunche that Ghana was being asked to send troops at once, pending the arrival of a UN force. Kasavubu and Lumumba arrived in Kindu from Luluabourg and sent from there cables to Brussels breaking off diplomatic relations with Belgium, and to Khrushchev telling him they might have to call on the Soviet Union for help. They also sent a second cable to the Secretary-General which read as follows:

II. *Telegram dated July 13, 1960, from the President and the Prime Minister of the Republic of the Congo to the Secretary-General*[3]

In connection with military assistance requested of the United Nations by the Republic of the Congo, the Chief of State and the Prime Minister of the Congo make the following clarification: (1) the purpose of the aid requested is not to restore the internal situation in Congo but rather to protect the national territory against acts of aggression committed by Belgian metropolitan troops. (2) The request for assistance relates only to a United Nations force consisting of military personnel from neutral countries and not from the United States as reported by certain radio stations. (3) If the assistance requested is not received without delay the Republic of the Congo will be obliged to appeal to the Bandung treaty powers. (4) The aid has been re-

---

[3] Ibid.

quested by the Republic of the Congo in the exercise of its sovereign rights and not in agreement with Belgium as reported.

Joseph Kasavubu
President of the Republic of the Congo

Patrice Lumumba
Prime Minister and Minister of National Defence

The wording of this message reflected fear that a United Nations force might collaborate with the Belgian troops, an idea which was attracting support in Belgium.

It had earlier been arranged that the members of the Security Council would meet for luncheon in Hammarskjöld's office suite for preliminary discussion of the crisis. Now the Secretary-General decided that he should proceed at once on the first step even before this consultation. He addressed a letter to the President of the Security Council formally invoking Article 99 of the Charter for the first time and requesting a meeting at 8:30 that night (first following text). During and after the luncheon he presented his ideas on how the United Nations might respond to the crisis and his belief that an effective response was of extreme urgency. The Council members asked questions but voiced no opposition to Hammarskjöld's general approach. When the Council met that evening the way had been prepared in intensive private discussions with both Council members and African representatives. Hammarskjöld was the first speaker after adoption of the agenda (second following text).

---

1. Letter to the President of the Security Council

NEW YORK   JULY 13, 1960

I WISH TO INFORM you that I have to bring to the attention of the Security Council a matter which, in my opinion, may threaten the maintenance of international peace and security. Thus, I request you to call an urgent

Security Council Official Records, Fifteenth Year, Supplement for July, August, and September 1960, document S/4381.

meeting of the Security Council to hear a report of the Secretary-General on a demand for United Nations action in relation to the Republic of the Congo.

May I suggest that the meeting is called for tonight at 8:30 p.m.

DAG HAMMARSKJÖLD
Secretary-General of the United Nations

2. Opening Statement in the Security Council

NEW YORK   JULY 13, 1960

THE REASON FOR my request, under Article 99 of the Charter, for an immediate meeting of the Security Council is the situation which has arisen in the newly independent Republic of the Congo.

The difficulties which have developed in the Congo are well known to all members of the Council. They are connected with the maintenance of order in the country and the protection of life. But the difficulties have an important international bearing as they are of a nature that cannot be disregarded by other countries.

I have received three communications from the Government of the Congo. They are all three known to the members of the Security Council.

One is a request for urgent technical assistance in the field of adminis-tration, aiming especially at assistance in developing the security admin-istration of the country. This request is within the limits of the compe-tence of the Secretary-General and I have sent it informally to the members of the Security Council, only because of its bearing on the gen-eral problem.

The other two communications are both related to a request for mili-tary assistance from the United Nations. One is the formal request, the other one is a clarification of this request and of the intentions of the Government of the Republic of the Congo. Both these communications have been circulated in a Security Council document.

As all three documents are known to you, I have no reason to analyse

Security Council Official Records, Fifteenth Year, 873rd meeting.

them here. I can address myself directly to the demands for action, their relationship, and their significance for the maintenance of international peace and security.

It is a matter of course that the only sound and lasting solution to the problem which has arisen is that the regular instruments of the government, in the first place its security administration, are rendered capable of taking care of the situation. I understand the request for technical assistance to have been sent with this in view. My reaction, already communicated to the Government of the Congo, is entirely positive. A technical-assistance office is being established and a resident representative appointed. I will submit to the Government of the Congo today or tomorrow detailed proposals for implementation of my acceptance of the request. In formulating my proposals regarding technical assistance experts in the field of security administration, I have had the advantage of consulting the heads of a number of delegations of African Member states.

Keeping firmly in mind what I have just characterized as the sound and lasting solution, which I hope we will effectively further through the steps on which I have decided at the request of the Government, we must, on the other hand, realistically recognize that this work will take some time and that therefore there is an intermediary period during which the Government may find it difficult to operate in the security field with all the needed efficiency. Irrespective of what we can do in order to shorten this intermediary or transitional period, we must therefore face the problem of what, if anything, should be our assistance to the government pending satisfactory results on the technical assistance line.

As is well known, the Belgian government has in the Congo troops stated by the government to be maintained there in protection of life and for the maintenance of order. It is not for the Secretary-General to pronounce himself on this action and its legal and political aspects, but I must conclude from the communications received from the Government of the Congo that the presence of these troops is a source of internal, and potentially also of international, tension. In these circumstances, the presence of the Belgian troops cannot be accepted as a satisfactory stopgap arrangement pending the reestablishment of order through the national security force.

It is in this light that I personally wish to see the request for military assistance, which has been addressed to me by the Government of the Congo. Although I am fully aware of all the problems, difficulties, and even risks involved, I find that the stopgap arrangement envisaged by the

Government of the Congo is preferable to any other formula. It is, therefore, my conclusion that the United Nations should accede to the request of the Government of the Congo, and, in consequence, I strongly recommend to the Council to authorize the Secretary-General to take the necessary steps, in consultation with the Government of the Congo, to provide the government with military assistance during the period which may have to pass before, through the efforts of the government with the technical assistance of the United Nations, the national security forces are able to fully meet their tasks. It would be understood that were the United Nations to act as proposed, the Belgian government would see its way to a withdrawal.

Were the Security Council to act on my recommendation, I would base my actions on the principles which were set out in my report to the General Assembly on the conclusions drawn from previous experiences in the field. It follows that the United Nations Force would not be authorized to action beyond self-defence. It follows further that they may not take any action which would make them a party to internal conflicts in the country. Finally, the selection of personnel should be such as to avoid complications because of the nationalities used. In the prevailing situation this does not, in my view, exclude the use of units from African states, while, on the other hand, it does exclude recourse to troops from any of the permanent members of the Security Council. May I add that in fact it would be my intention to get, in the first place, assistance from African nations.

In conclusion, I must invite the Council to act with the utmost speed. A decision in principle reached today would be of the highest value. I would welcome consultations followed by renewed meetings for a fuller elaboration of the mandate which I recommend to the Security Council to give to me now. As a matter of course I would report to the Council as appropriate on any action taken on the basis of the authorization which I hope the Council will give me tonight.

AFTER THE SECRETARY-GENERAL had spoken, a request by Belgium's permanent representative, Walter Loridan, to be seated at the table caused a complication that might have prevented the Council from reaching a decision that night. The Belgian request was in order, but there was no representative of the Republic of the Congo as yet in New York. Arkady Sobolev for the USSR and Mongi Slim for Tunisia, the Council's only African member, at first objected to seating the

Belgian delegate until the Congo's representative was also present, while Western delegates thought Belgium should be given an opportunity to speak before a decision was reached. Hammarskjöld then made the following compromise suggestion (next following text).

---

3. *Second Statement in the Security Council*

NEW YORK　　　　　JULY 13, 1960

AS THIS MEETING has been convened at my request, I hope that the members of the Council will permit me to intervene at this stage. I do not, I think, presume too much if I say that as my request for this meeting was based on demands from the Government of the Congo, I am the one who is closest to speaking for the Government of the Congo at this table.

I can say with certainty, understanding the situation in the country, on the basis of the very full reports which we have received, that the Government of the Congo would be the first one to regret if, out of a gesture to them, a decision on their demands would be delayed. It cannot be a question of a delay of a few hours; it is a question of delay of a few days and I would say, in all seriousness, that we have not got them.

May I add a suggestion. I have indicated in my initial statement that I foresee several meetings of the Security Council on this issue. If the Security Council were to take a positive decision, I would be necessarily under the obligation to keep the Council currently informed on developments and on action taken. I foresee that on the basis of such reports, the Council may wish to meet again. I ask myself if a decision now on an invitation to the two parties—if we talk about parties—could not be interpreted in this sense: We recognize that one of the parties has no representative here, but the invitation is cabled to the Government on the understanding that in forthcoming meetings of the Council the first decision would be followed up and they would have their place at the table. What would then happen is only that they would not be able to speak here at the table tonight. But they have spoken through their two cables which are before the Council and I feel that their legitimate interests are best

Security Council Official Records, Fifteenth Year, 873rd meeting.

safeguarded if on the one side they get a speedy decision and, on the other hand, they will have the opportunity to be heard and to speak at later occasions when the Council is likely to consider the same question.

IT WAS THEN quickly agreed that invitations to Belgium and the Congo be extended simultaneously (to the latter by telephone) and that Loridan could be seated that night on the understanding that he would not speak until all Council members had been heard.

Mongi Slim of Tunisia introduced the following draft resolution:

The Security Council,

Considering the report of the Secretary-General on a request for United Nations action in relation to the Republic of the Congo,

Considering the request for military assistance addressed to the Secretary-General by the President and the Prime Minister of the Republic of the Congo (S/4382),

1. *Calls upon* the Government of Belgium to withdraw its troops from the territory of the Republic of the Congo;

2. *Decides* to authorize the Secretary-General to take the necessary steps, in consultation with the Government of the Republic of the Congo, to provide the government with such military assistance as may be necessary until, through the efforts of the Congolese government with the technical assistance of the United Nations, the national security forces may be able, in the opinion of the government, to meet fully their tasks;

3. *Requests* the Secretary-General to report to the Security Council as appropriate. [1]

The Western powers—France, Great Britain, the United States, and Italy—were not happy with the call for Belgian withdrawal as phrased in the first operative paragraph. Although Belgium was not explicitly condemned for sending in its troops and no time limit was set for withdrawal, the implication of censure was there. Indeed, when introducing his resolution Mongi Slim declared that the disorders and acts of violence against Belgians and other Europeans in the Congo, however regrettable, did not justify the unilateral Belgian intervention undertaken in violation of treaty commitments and against the wishes of the Congolese government. He characterized the intervention as "without any doubt an aggressive act which can be justified by nothing." [2]

The Western powers, on the other hand, tended to view the Belgian intervention as legally and morally justified to protect lives and property. They supported the proposal for a UN force which could take over from the Belgians the task of maintaining law and order, but the Belgians should remain until the United

---

[1] Security Council Official Records, Fifteenth Year, Supplement for July, August, and September 1960, document S/4387.

[2] Ibid., Fifteenth Year, 873rd meeting.

Nations had put in place a force strong enough to do the job. The resolution was silent on such a linkage, though it had been suggested—in deliberately imprecise language—in Hammarskjöld's opening statement when he said "It would be understood that were the United Nations to act as proposed, the Belgian government would see its way to a withdrawal."

The Soviet Union was also dissatisfied with the references to Belgium in the resolution, not because they were too strong but because, in its view, they were too weak. Sobolev declared that the resolution should include a condemnation of Belgium for "armed aggression," that the call for withdrawal should include the word "immediately," and that withdrawal should be unconditional, not linked in any way with the arrival of a UN force.

The African Member states were united in their condemnation of the Belgian intervention, and the moderate language about withdrawal in the Tunisian resolution was as far as they were willing to go to meet the Western position. Mongi Slim stood firm against all pressures to drop or amend the withdrawal paragraph or to make any other changes in his resolution. To the West, including Belgium, quick establishment of a UN force was of higher priority than the offending paragraph. On the other side the Soviet Union, which presented itself as a champion of African independence from Western colonialism, was not in a good position to veto, as too weak, a resolution introduced by Africa's representative on the Security Council.

Sobolev did press to a vote his amendments calling for condemnation and immediate withdrawal. These were defeated by 7 votes to 2 (USSR and Poland), with 2 abstentions (Ecuador and Tunisia). He also introduced a third amendment which would limit the composition of the force to contingents from African states. This was a proposal to which Nkrumah and some other African leaders were sympathetic but it went against Hammarskjöld's view that a United Nations force, while rightly in this instance mainly African, should also include some contingents from other parts of the world to reflect the universal character of the Organization. On this amendment there were 5 votes against, 4 in favor, and 2 abstentions, Tunisia and Ceylon joining the USSR and Poland in the affirmative.

Just before the Tunisian resolution was put to the vote Armand Bérard of France requested that the vote be paragraph by paragraph, hoping by this means to eliminate the withdrawal paragraph, but Slim insisted, as was his right, that the resolution be voted on as a whole. It carried by 8 votes to none, with 3 abstentions. The United States and the USSR both voted for the resolution, along with Argentina, Ceylon, Ecuador, Italy, Poland, and Tunisia. France and the United Kingdom abstained, joined by Nationalist China. When they explained their votes Lodge and Sobolev gave opposing interpretations of the resolution. Lodge said the resolution made Belgian withdrawal contingent upon creation and deployment of the UN Force. Sobolev said the resolution should be interpreted as calling for immediate and unconditional Belgian withdrawal.

The Council adjourned at 3:25 a.m. on July 14. Hammarskjöld returned to his office and, with his closest advisers and staff, immediately took steps to organize with all possible speed the most difficult, complex, and dangerous mission ever handed to the Secretary-General. He appointed, as Supreme Commander of the

UN Force in the Congo, Major-General Carl C. von Horn, the Swedish general who had been serving as Chief of Staff of the UN Truce Supervision Organization in Palestine since March 1958. Stüre Linnér, who had just been appointed resident representative for UN technical assistance, was made chief of civilian operations. Both of these men served under Ralph Bunche, the Secretary-General's personal representative in the Congo. Hammarskjöld sent an immediate appeal for troops to Morocco, Tunisia, Ghana, Guinea, and Mali and a general appeal for military or other contributions to the chiefs of state of all African nations north of the Congo. Requests for airlift assistance went to the United States, the United Kingdom, and the USSR.

The pace was remarkably swift. U.S. transport planes arrived with the first Tunisian contigent on July 15, the day after the Security Council had acted, and these were soon followed by troops from Ghana, Ethiopia, and Morocco. By July 18, when the Secretary-General made his first report to the Security Council (next following text), thirty-five hundred UN troops had reached Leopoldville and more were on the way. By this same date, however, the situation in the Congo had become more ominous than ever. About twenty-five thousand Belgian and other European civilians had by now fled the country, thus paralyzing the Congo's entire administrative structure and all its public services. On the other hand, ten thousand Belgian soldiers had returned to hold the airports and other key points in all the Congo's major cities. On July 17 the Katanga provincial assembly formally approved Tshombé's declaration of independence. In Belgium there was strong and growing support for Tshombé, though the Belgian government withheld recognition of his régime. It seemed to Lumumba that Belgium was moving to undermine the independence and destroy the unity of the country before United Nations action could be effective. He and Kasavubu sent word to Bunche threatening to appeal for help to the Soviet Union unless Belgian troops left the Congo in twenty-four hours. It was the first of several such ultimatums in the days to come.

The Congolese leaders were not the only ones who did not understand the principles of the mandate for the UN Force and the limitations upon its freedom of action. Hammarskjöld thus devoted the first part of the following report to the Security Council to a careful analysis of the mandate and the governing principles as he saw them. This was followed by an account of his stewardship to date.

4. First Report on Assistance to the Republic of the Congo

NEW YORK   JULY 18, 1960

1. BY THE RESOLUTION ADOPTED by the Security Council at its 873rd meeting on July 13-14, 1960, the Council, after considering the report from the Secretary-General and the request for military assistance (S/ 4382) addressed to the Secretary-General by the President and the Prime Minister of the Republic of the Congo, authorized the Secretary-General "to take the necessary steps, in consultation with the Government of the Republic of the Congo, to provide the government with such military assistance as may be necessary until, through the efforts of the Congolese government with the technical assistance of the United Nations, the national security forces may be able, in the opinion of the government, to meet fully their tasks." The Council also "called upon the Government of Belgium to withdraw its troops from the territory of the Republic of the Congo." The Security Council requested the Secretary-General to report to the Council as appropriate.

2. This first progress report on the implementation of the resolution of the Security Council is submitted with reference to this request.

The mandate

3. The resolution of the Security Council was adopted in response to my initial statement to the Council (873rd meeting, paras. 18-29). Therefore, that statement may be regarded as a basic document on the interpretation of the mandate. In the statement I made clear my view of the main purpose of the introduction of a United Nations force in the Congo as well as of the relationship between this action and withdrawal of Belgian troops. I also stated in general terms what legal principles in my view should apply to the operation.

Security Council Official Records, Fifteenth Year, Supplement for July, August, and September 1960, documents S/4389 and Add. 1.

4. However, even with these explanations of my intentions and of my interpretation of the situations, important points were left open for an interpretation in practice. In submitting this first progress report, I want not only to bring to the knowledge of the Council what so far has been achieved, but also what lines I have followed concerning the implementation of the authorization.

5. I indicated as a "sound and lasting solution" to the difficulties which had arisen in the Congo the re-establishment of the instruments of the government for the maintenance of order. It was implied in my presentation that it was the breakdown of those instruments which had created a situation which through its consequences represented a threat to peace and security justifying United Nations intervention on the basis of the explicit request of the Government of the Republic of the Congo. Thus the two main elements, from the legal point of view, were on the one hand this request, and on the other hand, the implied finding that the circumstances to which I referred were such as to justify United Nations action under the Charter. Whether or not it was also held that the United Nations faced a conflict between two parties, was, under these circumstances, in my view, legally not essential for the justification of the action. However, I pointed out that, on the basis of the interpretation I had given, it would be understood that, were the United Nations to act as I proposed, the Belgian government "would see its way to a withdrawal," and the Council itself called upon the Belgian government to withdraw its troops.

6. In order to assist the Government of the Republic of the Congo to re-establish its administration, specifically in the field of security, certain decisions had already been taken by me in response to a general appeal from the government. However, they could yield results only after a certain time and in the meanwhile there was a need for a stopgap arrangement, established by the United Nations in consultation with the government, no preferable alternative arrangements being available for the intermediate period which might have to pass until, in the words of the resolution, "the national security forces may be able, in the opinion of the government, to meet fully their tasks." Thus, the Force introduced is to be regarded as a temporary security force, present in the Republic of the Congo with the consent of the government for the time and the purpose indicated.

7. Although the United Nations Force under the resolution is dispatched to the Congo at the request of the government and will be present in the Congo with its consent, and although it may be considered as

serving as an arm of the government for the maintenance of order and protection of life—tasks which naturally belong to the national authorities and which will pass to such authorities as soon as, in the view of the government, they are sufficiently firmly established—the Force is necessarily under the exclusive command of the United Nations, vested in the Secretary-General under the control of the Security Council. This is in accordance with the principles generally applied by the Organization. The Force is thus not under the orders of the government nor can it, as I pointed out in my statement to the Council, be permitted to become a party to any internal conflict. A departure from this principle would seriously endanger the impartiality of the United Nations and of the operation.

8. Another principle which I consider as generally applicable and, therefore, as basic also to the present operation, is that, while, on its side, the host government, when exercising its sovereign right with regard to the presence of the Force, should be guided by good faith in the interpretation of the purpose of the Force, the United Nations, on its side, should be understood to be determined by similar good faith in the interpretation of the purpose when it considers the question of the maintenance of the Force in the host country. This principle is reflected in the final phrase of the relevant paragraph of the resolution authorizing the Secretary-General to provide the Government of the Republic of the Congo with United Nations military assistance.

9. From this basic understanding regarding the presence of a United Nations Force in the country it follows that the United Nations activity should have freedom of movement within its area of operations and all such facilities regarding access to that area and communications as are necessary for a successful accomplishment of the task. A further elaboration of this rule obviously requires an agreement with the government, i.e. specifying what is to be considered the area of operations.

10. Regarding the composition of the Force, there is another general principle which, in the light of previous experience, I find it necessary to apply. In the report to which I referred in my statement to the Security Council, it is stated that "while the United Nations must reserve for itself the authority to decide on the composition of such (military) elements, it is obvious that the host country, in giving its consent, cannot be indifferent to the composition of those elements." The report continues:

In order to limit the scope of possible differences of opinion, the United Nations in recent operations has followed two principles: not to include units from any of the permanent members of the Security Council; and not to include units from any country which, because of its geographical position or for other reasons, might be considered as possibly having a special interest in the situation which has called for the operation. . . . It would seem desirable to accept the formula . . . to the effect that, while it is for the United Nations alone to decide on the composition of military elements sent to a country, the United Nations should, in deciding on composition, take fully into account the view of the host government as one of the most serious factors which should guide the recruitment of the personnel. Usually, this is likely to mean that serious objections by the host country against participation by a specific contributing country in the United Nations operation will determine the action of the Organization. However, were the United Nations for good reasons to find that course inadvisable, it would remain free to pursue its own line, and any resulting conflict would have to be resolved on a political rather than on a legal basis.

I recommended, in the report quoted, that this principle should be considered applicable to all United Nations operations of the present kind. The problem is in this particular case covered by the request for consultations with the Congo government. In my statement to the Council I pointed out that, while I consider that the aforementioned principle excludes military units in the Force from any of the permanent members of the Security Council, I, in fact, had the "intention to get, in the first place, assistance from African nations."

11. Among other principles which I consider essential to this operation, I may mention the following.

12. The authority granted to the United Nations Force cannot be exercised within the Congo either in competition with representatives of the host government or in cooperation with them in any joint operation. This naturally applies *a fortiori* to representatives and military units of other governments than the host government. Thus, the United Nations operation must be separate and distinct from activities by any national authorities.

13. Likewise, it follows from the rule that the United Nations units must not become parties in internal conflicts, that they cannot be used to enforce any specific political solution of pending problems or to influence the political balance decisive to such a solution. Apart from the general reasons for this principle, there is the specific one, that it is only on this basis that the United Nations can expect to be able to draw on Member countries for contributions in men and material.

14. To all United Nations personnel used in the present operation the basic rules of the United Nations for international service should be con-

sidered as applicable, particularly as regards full loyalty to the aims of the Organization and abstention from actions in relation to their country of origin which might deprive the operation of its international character and create a situation of dual loyalty.

15. In my initial statement I recalled the rule applied in previous United Nations operations to the effect that the military units would be entitled to act only in self-defence. In amplification of this statement I would like to quote the following passage from the report to which I referred: ". . . men engaged in the operation may never take the initiative in the use of armed force, but are entitled to respond with force to an attack with arms, including attempts to use force to make them withdraw from positions which they occupy under orders from the commander," acting under the authority of the Security Council and with the scope of its resolution. "The basic element involved is clearly the prohibition against any *initiative* in the use of armed force."

The composition of the Force

16. Before reporting on the steps taken for the building up of the Force and on the agreements reached with a number of governments regarding contributions to the Force, I wish to make some general observations.

17. As stated to the Security Council on July 13, 1960, the ultimate solution to the problem that has arisen in the Congo has to be found by the Republic of the Congo itself, with the assistance of the United Nations. In the same spirit I believe that, to the extent that the Republic of the Congo needs international assistance, such assistance should, within the framework of the United Nations, in the first instance be given by its sister African nations, as an act of African solidarity. However, this natural reliance on regional solidarity for the solution of a problem of this kind should be qualified by an element of universality natural—and indeed essential—to any United Nations operation. Therefore, while the Force, in my view, should be built around a hard core of military units from African states, it should also, to the extent which might be found practical, include units from other areas which meet the general conditions for the composition of a United Nations Force to which I have referred above.

18. Thus, in my view, the present operation is, in the first place, a manifestation of the willingness and ability of the African states to help within the framework of the United Nations, of which I have found the most convincing evidence in the course of this effort. Elements from other

regions, included in the Force, may be considered an assistance given, in the spirit of the Charter, to the African community of nations by nations of those other regions. With this approach, the present operation should serve to strengthen the African community of nations and to strengthen also their ties, within the United Nations, with the world community. It would be wholly unjustified to interpret the United Nations action in the sense that nations from outside the region step into the Congo situation, using the United Nations as their instrumentality, because of the incapability of the Congo and of the African states themselves to make the basic contribution to the solution of the problem.

19. My efforts to build up the Force have been guided by this interpretation of the United Nations operation. For that reason I have, in the first place, appealed to African states for troops, addressing myself in the second stage to other nations meeting the conditions which are generally applicable, and continuing my efforts to activate further African units to the extent necessary. While the requests for troops so far presented by me, or offers of troops accepted by me, follow the patterns just stated, I have already in the first stage addressed a series of appeals for support in such fields as logistics, signals, material, aircraft, and specialized personnel to those countries which are most likely to provide them at very short notice, irrespective of their geographical position.

20. Apart from being influenced by the factors which I have explained above, I have, naturally, been guided by considerations of availability of troops, language, and geographical distribution within the region.

21. Even before the decision of the Security Council I was informed by the Republic of Ghana that it had responded favourably to an urgent demand from the Government of the Republic of the Congo for military assistance and that it wanted this assistance to be integrated in the general United Nations effort which the government anticipated, after having been informed of the convening of the Security Council and of my proposals to the Council. Likewise, the Governments of Guinea, Morocco, and Tunisia informed me at this early stage of their willingness to put, forthwith, military units at the disposal of the United Nations. These offers have been accepted and the troops have been or will be airlifted to the Congo as quickly as practicable. Some short delays have been unavoidable for logistic reasons or because of the necessity to stagger the airlifts.

22. Immediately after the end of the meeting of the Security Council, in the morning of July 14, 1960, I addressed appeals for assistance to the

chiefs of state of all African member nations north of the Congo and of the Federation of Mali, either asking directly for troops or, where language difficulties could be foreseen, asking for an immediate discussion with their permanent representatives at the United Nations about the best form in which the country concerned could render help. A full account of the results of this appeal and of arrangements made will be given in the following paragraphs. At this point I wish to state that I immediately accepted an offer of troops also from Ethiopia, thus getting in the first setup of the Force adequate representation from North Africa, West Africa, and East Africa. As will be clear from the detailed report on arrangements made, the five countries specifically mentioned provide the Force with an initial strength of seven battalions, numbering more than four thousand men.

23. I have received promises of additional battalions from several French-speaking African countries, as well as from some English-speaking nations in Africa. An offer from the Federation of Mali has been accepted and will be activated at a somewhat later stage. In the light of the general approach to which I referred above, I am activating the other offers as necessary.

24. Following the pattern which I have previously explained, I have, with the establishment of an initial Force of seven battalions from five African countries, completed a first phase of the building up of the Force. For a second phase I have appealed for assistance in the form of troops from three European, one Asian, and one Latin American country, meeting the general conditions applying to a United Nations Force. In one of these cases, Sweden, I have asked and received permission, on a temporary basis, to transfer the Swedish battalion of the United Nations Emergency Force (UNEF) in Gaza to the Congo by an airlift which is likely to be carried out on Wednesday, July 20, thus bringing the total strength up to eight battalions.

25. As regards assistance in other forms, I have reached agreement on the sending of police companies from a number of African states. I have also appealed for aircraft, heavy equipment, and specialized personnel from some of those countries. Apart from its other contribution, Ghana has undertaken to provide the Force with two military medical units.

26. Requests for heavy material and aircraft as well as for signals and other parts of the logistic support have been addressed to a number of non-African States; as regards signals, a special difficulty has been created by the fact that the personnel should, if at all possible, be bilingual, having a knowledge of both French and English.

27. Appeals for assistance with air transport have been addressed to three non-African nations.

28. The response to all these various appeals has been favourable.

29. I have appointed Major-General Carl von Horn, Sweden, Supreme Commander of the Force. As chief of staff of the United Nations Truce Supervision Organization for three years, General von Horn has already had considerable experience as a senior military representative of the United Nations. He will be assisted by a small personal staff of officers drawn from the group under his command in Jerusalem. I have directed a request to India to make available to me a senior officer as military adviser in the executive office of the Secretary-General.

30. In broad outline, this completes the picture of the geographical distribution sought for the Force in implementation of the decision of the Security Council on the basis of the principles outlined above. It reflects my wish to give to the African community of nations the central position which in this case is their due, while maintaining the universal character of a United Nations operation. As the composition of the Force is still not completed, I can in the following stages make such adjustments as the Security Council may find desirable, but I wish to express my hope that the steps so far taken on the basis of the authority given to me by the Council will meet with the approval of the Council.

State of implementation of the Council's decision

31. I now turn to the detailed information which, at the present moment, can be given to the Council regarding the implementation of its decision.

32. At the time of writing of this report, about 3,500 troops in addition to substantial equipment from four of the contributing countries have arrived in Leopoldville. The 3,500 consist of 460 troops from Ethiopia, 770 troops from Ghana, 1,250 troops from Morocco, and 1,020 troops from Tunisia. Each of the battalions is well equipped. As stated above, offers have also been accepted from the Republic of Guinea and the Federation of Mali. Groups of some 700 men will be airlifted later this week from Guinea.

33. On July 20, 635 men of the Swedish battalion in UNEF will be airlifted to Leopoldville to serve for one month in the Congo; a small rear party of the battalion will remain in Gaza. Meanwhile, arrangements are being made for the airlifting of other contingents for the Force, including police units, hospital units, and signals and logistics personnel.

34. As it is essential that troops should be deployed at many points throughout the country, the Force will have to be built up to a level considerably higher than that attained so far.

35. The Ethiopian troops were airlifted by their own air force. The airlifting of the balance of the Force has been made possible by assistance granted at my request from the United Kingdom and United States governments. The British government has provided aircraft to transport elements of the contingent of Ghana, while thirty-three aircraft of the United States Air Force have been used to transport the Tunisian and Moroccan contingents and to assist in the later stages of the transportation of the contingent from Ghana.

36. To meet the requirements of reconnaissance and mobility within such a large country as the Congo, troop-carrying trucks, aircraft of the DC-3 type, small reconnaissance aircraft, and helicopters are being contributed by Member countries as part of the equipment of the Force.

37. Since United Nations contingents began to arrive before the arrival of the commander and because of the generally unsettled situation in the country, on July 15, I appointed Mr. Ralph J. Bunche, my special representative in the Congo, as commander *ad interim* of the Force with immediate effect. On July 16, he deployed United Nations units to the radio station, power station, Harvard Boulevard, and the European sector of Leopoldville. On July 17, he deployed further units at Stanleyville, Matadi, Thysville, and Coquilhatville.

38. The arrival of the troops of the United Nations Force in Leopoldville has already had a salutary effect and the growing recognition of its role as a Force for the restoration of peace and order will contribute to its increasing effectiveness.

39. General von Horn took over the command of the Force on the morning of July 18. He is continuing with all possible speed to deploy units at strategic points and in critical areas of tension. Because of the major task which confronts the supreme commander in taking over the command of the Force in its organization at its inception, he has been authorized to use for a short period limited numbers of officers who have been selected from the United Nations Truce Supervision Organization in Jerusalem to assist in connection with the programme of technical assistance in the field of security administration.

40. The general disorder combined with the breakdown of transportation and public services led to a threatened food shortage which it was necessary to avert. Consequently, at the request of the Government of the

Congo, I made appeals to the Governments of Canada, Denmark, France, India, Italy, the Union of Soviet Socialist Republics, the United Kingdom of Great Britain and Northern Ireland, and the United States of America for food. The response to this appeal has been generous. The contributions so far pledged are from Canada, Denmark, France, India, the Soviet Union, the United Kingdom, and the United States. A contribution has also been offered by Switzerland.

41. Some of this food is being flown into Leopoldville at the present time by United States, British, Canadian, and Soviet aircraft. In addition, the Swiss government has responded to my request to provide Swiss aircraft to assist in the transport of food and other supplies. Some of the food is being concentrated in the United Nations depot at Pisa awaiting airlift to Leopoldville. A further staging point and depot for this and other purposes connected with the United Nations operations in the Congo has been established at Kano, Nigeria, as assistance granted by the Government of Nigeria.

42. The Secretariat is in touch with twenty-seven countries for contributions to the establishment of the United Nations Force or to the food supplies in response to my appeal. I am deeply gratified with the generous response which has made possible the early activation of United Nations influence. It is hoped that the Force can be brought up to its necessary strength and effectiveness with no loss of the quickness of action that has so encouragingly characterized the development of the Force in the period since the Security Council met on July 13-14.

Withdrawal of Belgian troops

43. As recalled above, the resolution of the Security Council refers also to the withdrawal of Belgian troops. Both at Headquarters and in Leopoldville, we remain in close touch with this aspect of the problems covered by the resolution.

44. I have been informed by my representative in Leopoldville that he has received from the Belgian ambassador a letter according to which instructions have been given to the Belgian commander in the Congo to the effect that Belgian military interventions should be limited to what is called for by the security needs of Belgian nationals and that in all other matters the Belgian command has been advised to abide by the instructions of the military command of the United Nations Forces. The letter further states that in case of grave and imminent danger the Belgian

forces will continue to take the necessary security measures, but that in each case they will immediately refer the matter to the military command of the United Nations. The Belgian military command, according to the letter, has been ordered to impose strict discipline upon its forces in the Congo, and has been told to cooperate to the fullest extent when any request is made to it by the United Nations.

45. My representative in Leopoldville has also been informed that, following the arrival of United Nations Forces, Belgian units amounting to one company and one platoon left Leopoldville on July 17, 1960. They are being kept at the disposal of the Commander of the Belgian metropolitan forces to answer calls of help where there are no United Nations troops available.

46. I wish to draw the attention of the Council to the fact that this statement refers to the situation as at July 17, 1960. Discussions are continuing and I shall report separately on the development.

DOCUMENT S/4389/ADD.I

July 19, 1960

I have received today, July 19, 1960, from my special representative in the Republic of the Congo the following statement based on a meeting this morning between him and the Belgian ambassador, the Belgian Army Chief of Staff, and the Commanding General Gheysen.

1. In a statement made on July 16, 1960, the Ambassador of Belgium informed me as follows: "Consequent upon the arrival of United Nations troops the first contingents of the Belgian armed forces left Leopoldville this afternoon." I have since been informed that these troops have returned to their bases.

2. The United Nations is now in a position to guarantee that contingents of the United Nations Force, drawn from both European and African countries, will arrive this week in sufficient numbers to ensure order and protect the entire population, European and African. The complete protection of all sectors of the population is the primary and most immediate purpose of the United Nations operation here.

3. In the light of this assurance and the request made by General von Horn and myself, it has been decided that the Belgian forces will begin to withdraw completely from the Leopoldville area and return to their bases on Wednesday, July 20. This withdrawal operation should be completed by 6 p.m. on Saturday, July 23, 1960.

4. The Ndjili airfield will also be placed under United Nations control. A flight unit of about forty persons in charge of air transport and an administrative unit of about forty persons of all grades will remain temporarily at the airfield to ensure the maintenance of the Belgian aircraft transporting men, supplies, and equipment, and to deal with evacuees.

5. Everyone may be confident that the United Nations Force is assuming the responsibility of ensuring respect for the law and the maintenance of public order in the most conscientious manner and that it will take whatever steps may be necessary to carry out this task.

Editors' note—Addenda 2,3, and 4 to the Secretary-General's report of July 18 (S/4389) have been omitted. Dated July 19, 20, and 26 respectively, they give additional information on offers of contingents and on deployment of the Force as this became available. Addendum 5, dated July 29, gives the text of the basic agreement with the Government of the Republic of the Congo on the presence and functioning of the United Nations Force in the Congo (see section 6 below). Addendum 6, dated July 31, summarizes the composition and deployment of the Force as of that date (see section 7 below).

THE SECURITY COUNCIL was called into session in the evening of July 20 to consider the Secretary-General's report and to hear the Belgian foreign minister, Pierre Wigny, and Thomas Kanza, the Congo's minister delegate at the United Nations, who had just reached New York. A few years before, Kanza had been the first of the very few young Congolese who were enabled to go abroad for a university education. His father, Daniel Kanza, had been imprisoned by the Belgians, along with Kasavubu and Lumumba, during the 1959 agitation for independence.

Hammarskjöld spoke first (next following text). In his report he had gone to some lengths to explain why the United Nations Force could not use force except in self-defense, could not become a party to any internal political conflict, and could not be used to enforce any particular solution of such a conflict or "to influence the political balance decisive for such a solution."

Faced by the secession of Katanga and the continuing Belgian military intervention, the Congolese leaders, and other African governments as well, disliked these restrictions. Now, in his opening statement to the Council it may be noted that the Secretary-General sought to balance these negatives by a positive statement of principle on Katanga. Both the area of operations mandated for the United Nations Force and the Council's call for withdrawal of Belgian troops applied to the whole of the Republic of the Congo, and that meant Katanga as well as the rest of the country. Furthermore, Hammarskjöld explicitly invited the Council to clarify and strengthen his mandate on withdrawal.

5. Statement in the Security Council Introducing His Report

NEW YORK   JULY 20, 1960

IN INTRODUCING THE REPORT to which you, Mr. President, have just referred, I can be very brief.

One week has passed since the Security Council adopted its resolution regarding military assistance to the Republic of the Congo and a withdrawal of Belgian troops.

The development up to Monday morning has been covered in my first report to the Council. I have later issued three addenda which indicate, on the one side, that the Force has now been brought up to twelve African battalions and two European battalions, one of which, however, is there only on a temporary basis; I have not specified the other and numerous military units of a smaller size and of specialized character which, thanks to the help of various Member states, we are bringing into the Congo. The addenda also show where we stood as of yesterday regarding the question of Belgian withdrawal.

I want to use this opportunity to pay a sincere tribute to all those countries, who—sometimes with considerable sacrifice—have hastened to give their assistance to the United Nations. It is a most encouraging experience and marks a major step forward in international cooperation. Short of such a response, from African countries and non-African countries alike, no efforts of the United Nations would have been of any avail. Now we are in a position to look with hope, if not yet with absolute confidence, at the future. We have got off to a most promising start, but we have in no way passed the corner.

As regards the military operation, we have brought the Force up to a strength which, for the moment, should serve as a satisfactory basis for our continued effort to assist the Government of the Republic. I do in no way exclude a major expansion of the Force, but such an expansion

Security Council Official Records, Fifteenth Year, 877th meeting.

would have to take into account a series of considerations which should be studied in the breathing spell which we may have at the present before approaching Member governments with new requests.

In this situation, after having concentrated on getting sufficient manpower, we now devote our attention to all the essential and supporting services which are needed in the field of equipment, signals, supplies, health, and administration. We are happy to have with us at present General Alexander, who came to New York today after discussions with the representatives of the Congo government and with our representatives, bringing fresh evaluations of the needs of the Force.

I need not point out to the members of the Council the difficulties which confront those who are responsible for the moulding of the Force into a proper unit and for its deployment and use. The enterprise is far bigger and far more complicated than the United Nations Emergency Force, many more nations being involved, a multilingual basis to be used, military units with very different traditions to cooperate, and a vast area to be covered. However, I have full confidence in our men on the spot and I am sure that they will be able to count on continued and full cooperation from the Congo authorities, obviously a necessary condition for the success of this effort which has been started at the request of the Government of the Republic of the Congo.

In the civilian field, we face not only the major administrative problem to which I referred in my statement to the Security Council last Wednesday, but also problems in the fields of food and fuel supplies, and in particular, most recently, in the field of health.

You know about the main line which we pursue in the field of administration and you know what starts I have made. However, in the past week, during which I had hoped to make progress regarding administration, I have for obvious reasons instead had to put all the resources of the Secretariat into the establishment of the United Nations Force in the Congo. To the extent the military operation can be considered as in hand, we will again concentrate on the administrative problem.

In the field of food, considerable quantities have been put at our disposal in response to appeals addressed to various Governments. They have been and are being airlifted to the Leopoldville area which is the region of particular concern in this report.

As regards fuel, one of the main concerns is to get the supply running normally again. We are doing what we can to achieve this aim. In this context I wish to mention that tonight or tomorrow General Wheeler, well-known from the Suez Canal clearance, will go to Leopoldville to organize the necessary work in order to prevent the silting of the Congo River.

In the field of health, I am in personal contact with Dr. Candau, Director-General of the World Health Organization, whom I have asked, in collaboration with the International Red Cross, to do his utmost in order to stage a crash operation serving to forestall developing dangers. The necessary spraying in the Leopoldville area has not taken place for weeks. There is a great question mark as regards the water control. There has been an exodus of doctors and nurses which has stripped the city of necessary medical services. I need not point out what this may come to mean unless quick measures are taken. Although I know that the World Health Organization will do anything in its power to help, I would appreciate it if the Council, as a result of the debate or in its resolution, would give his work the desirable backing, addressing itself, in fact, to all of those specialized agencies which will have a task to fulfil in support of the United Nations action.

Let me now turn to the question of withdrawal. In the first instance I refer to my report and its addendum 1 of yesterday. You find in the report an indication that in due time there will have to be established, by agreement with the Government of the Congo, an area of operation for the United Nations Force, as well as certain other conditions for its contribution to the maintenance of satisfactory conditions in the country. On this point, I would like to stress that, in one important respect, there cannot, from my viewpoint, exist any hesitation as regards what is the area of operation. The resolution of the Security Council, in response to the appeal from the Government of the Congo, clearly applies to the whole of the Territory of the Republic as it existed when the Security Council, only a few days earlier, recommended the Congo for admission as a Member of the United Nations. Thus, in my view, the United Nations Force, under the resolution and on the basis of the request of the Government of the Congo, is entitled to access to all parts of the territory in fulfilment of its duties.

I may mention here that, in reply to a communication to me from Mr. Tshombé, President of the Provincial Government of Katanga, I have made it clear that actions of the United Nations through the Secretary-General, in respects covered by the resolution, must, in view of the legal circumstances which he has to take into account, be considered by him as actions referring to the Republic of the Congo as an entity.

I should recall that I said both in my initial statement and in my first report that the United Nations Force cannot be a party to any internal conflict nor can the United Nations Force intervene in a domestic conflict.

Although the Security Council did not, as it has done in previous cases, authorize or request the Secretary-General to take specific steps for the implementation of withdrawal—apart, of course, from the establishment of the Force—my representatives in the Congo have taken the initiatives they have found indicated for the coordination of the implementation of the Security Council decision on the Force with implementation of its decision on withdrawal. Although I do not consider it necessary, a clarification of my mandate on this point may be found useful by the Council. Such a clarification, if made, might aim at establishing the substance of my mandate on this point and the aim of the Council as regards the implementation of the call for a withdrawal.

Through the decision of the Security Council of last Wednesday, the United Nations has embarked on its biggest single effort under United Nations colours, organized and directed by the United Nations itself. I already had reason to pay a tribute to Member governments for what they have done to render the task of the Organization possible. May I say here and now that I will have—as a spokesman for the Security Council and on behalf of the United Nations—to ask for much, much more from Member nations, in the military field as well as in the civilian field. There should not be any hesitation, because we are at a turn of the road where our attitude will be of decisive significance, I believe, not only for the future of this Organization, but also for the future of Africa. And Africa may well, in present circumstances, mean the world. I know these are very strong words, but I hope that this Council and the Members of this Organization know that I do not use strong words unless they are supported by strong convictions.

AFTER HAMMARSKJÖLD'S STATEMENT the Council listened to an exchange of speeches by Kanza and Wigny that were highly charged with emotion on both sides. However, Kanza played down the significance of Lumumba's threat to ask for Soviet assistance if Belgian troops were not immediately withdrawn and replaced by the United Nations Force. The Government of the Congo, though impatient, still had confidence in the United Nations, he said, and the word "immediate" might be understood to mean "as soon as possible." Wigny, for his part, reaffirmed in general terms the Belgian commitment to withdraw its troops as soon as and to the extent that the United Nations Force ensured order and the security of persons, though his failure to mention Katanga left ambiguous Belgium's position on that secessionist province.

There was also a cold-war exchange between Ambassador Lodge and Vasily V. Kuznetsov, First Deputy Foreign Minister, who had come from Moscow to speak for the Soviet Union. Kuznetsov introduced a draft resolution calling for Belgian withdrawal within three days. In the course of a speech denouncing Western "colonialism" he said that if "the aggression" continued, more effective measures would be necessary, both by the United Nations and by "the peace-loving States" that sympathized with the Congo's cause.

Lodge replied immediately. He first pointed out that the United States had demonstrated its full support for the United Nations operation not only in words but by such practical assistance as providing the airlift for most of the UN troops and large quantities of equipment, supplies, and food as well. He then warned: "With other United Nations members we will do whatever may be necessary to prevent the intrusion of any military forces not requested by the United Nations." [1]

The next day Mongi Slim, Africa's spokesman on the Security Council, again introduced a draft resolution that responded very closely to the line the Secretary-General had proposed in his report and in his opening statement to the Council. This time the Council's Asian member, Ceylon, represented by Sir Claude Corea, was a cosponsor. The resolution (145 [1960]) as it was adopted that night without substantive alteration, read as follows:

The Security Council,
  Having considered the first report by the Secretary-General (S/4389 and *Add.* 1–3) on the implementation of Security Council resolution S/4387 of July 14, 1960,
  Appreciating the work of the Secretary-General and the support so readily and so speedily given to him by all Member States invited by him to give assistance,
  Noting that, as stated by the Secretary-General, the arrival of the troops of the United Nations Force in Leopoldville has already had a salutary effect,
  Recognizing that an urgent need still exists to continue and to increase such efforts,
  Considering that the complete restoration of law and order in the Republic of the Congo would effectively contribute to the maintenance of international peace and security,
  Recognizing that the Security Council recommended the admission of the Republic of the Congo to membership in the United Nations as a unit,
  1. *Calls upon* the Government of Belgium to implement speedily the Security Council resolution of July 14, 1960 on the withdrawal of its troops, and authorizes the Secretary-General to take all necessary action to this effect;

[1] Security Council Official Records, Fifteenth Year, 877th meeting.

2. *Requests* all States to refrain from any action which might tend to impede the restoration of law and order and the exercise by the Government of the Congo of its authority and also to refrain from any action which might undermine the territorial integrity and the political independence of the Republic of the Congo;

3. *Commends* the Secretary-General for the prompt action he has taken to carry out resolution S/4387 of the Security Council, and for his first report;

4. *Invites* the specialized agencies of the United Nations to render to the Secretary-General such assistance as he may require;

5. *Requests* the Secretary-General to report further to the Security Council as appropriate.

The ensuing debate, during the afternoon and evening meetings of the Council, provided an overwhelming demonstration of support for the Secretary-General's conduct of the operation and his declared intentions for the future, though there were nuances in their attitudes toward Belgium's conduct between the sponsors of the resolution and the Western powers—also between the sponsors themselves as reflected in the speeches of Slim and Corea. Wigny of Belgium and Kanza of the Congo also approved, though with differing accents. Kuznetsov did not join in praise of the Secretary-General, but he did not press his own resolution to a vote and joined the ten other Council members in unanimous support for the resolution of Tunisia and Ceylon. The vote came on July 22, just after midnight.

Kuznetsov was a man who used moderate language in representing the Soviet position. Thus, the cumulative significance of certain statements he had made in the course of the debate did not at the time attract as much attention as they deserved. He criticized the Secretary-General specifically on two counts—for permitting the presence of U.S. military men in Leopoldville (though they were only the twenty or so administrative and technical personnel required for the Leopoldville end of the airlift), and for allegedly failing to provide prompt airlift for the UN contingent from Guinea (which was regarded in the West as having a "leftist" régime).

In response to Lodge's warning against any assistance to the Congo outside the United Nations, Kuznetsov had the following to say:

> Since a particular group of States is dominant in the United Nations, that means: without the knowledge and the consent of the United States. Is not this going much too far? If the United States representative thinks that by speaking in this way he can influence the Soviet Union's attitude, or possibly intimidate the Soviet Union, he is very gravely mistaken. In this context I should like to explain the attitude of the Soviet Union. The USSR responds to all appeals when it is a question of helping peoples who are struggling for their liberation.[2]

Finally, Kuznetsov declared that the July 14 resolution and the July 22 resolution, for both of which the USSR had voted, "should not . . . be considered as a

---

[2] Ibid., 879th meeting.

precedent for the future." The United Nations had no right to assume responsibility for domestic law and order within a country, he said, but "the United Nations Force must also be entrusted with the task of safeguarding the territorial integrity of the Republic of the Congo."

Thus, Kuznetsov placed on the record a basis for future opposition to the UN Congo operation. Nevertheless, Hammarskjöld felt the unanimous vote on a strong resolution had given the enterprise a fair chance. As the meeting ended with a warm tribute from the Council's president, José Correa of Ecuador, he spoke as follows:

"Mr. President, the generous words which you have just addressed to me are in fact addressed to all those who in the service of the United Nations have worked for its aim in assistance to the Congo. The spirit and hope which have inspired us during the past week will not fail. They have been strengthened by the unanimity that has given this effort its special weight and power."[3]

The volatile Patrice Lumumba welcomed the Security Council's action and announced that Russian aid would no longer be necessary. Almost immediately he left Leopoldville for New York, Washington, and Ottawa, accompanied by a large delegation of Congolese officials. His trip had two purposes. First, he wished to explain personally to Hammarskjöld and to United Nations delegates why he considered it so urgent to get the Belgians out of Katanga and to restore the central government's authority there—using force if necessary—before the secessionist régime had time to consolidate its position. Second, he hoped to obtain direct bilateral financial and technical aid from the United States, as well as French-speaking experts from Canada, to supplement the program being organized by the United Nations with the specialized agencies.

The talks between Hammarskjöld and Lumumba and their advisers on July 24 and 25, though difficult at times, on the whole went well. The Secretary-General carefully explained the Council's intention—and his own—to bring the UN Force into Katanga as soon as possible and to secure the evacuation of the Belgian units there, but this had to be done by peaceful means. The UN Force could not, under the existing mandate, fight its way in, nor could it be used to end Katanga's secession by force. This did not satisfy Lumumba, but he did not, at the moment, attempt to force the issue. On questions of United Nations economic and technical assistance understandings were reached in such areas of top priority as the restoration of communications and transport facilities, health service needs, the reopening of schools, and the government's financial difficulties, including the absence of funds to meet payrolls.

On July 26 the Secretary-General left for Leopoldville. On the way he stopped over in Brussels for a day of strenuous behind-the-scenes efforts to persuade the Belgian government to urge upon Tshombé acceptance of the peaceful entry of United Nations troops and the simultaneous withdrawal of Belgian troops from the province. He met strong Belgian resistance on both counts. On July 28

---

[3] Ibid.

Hammarskjöld arrived in Leopoldville and was given a friendly welcome by Vice-Premier Gizenga and other members of the government (Lumumba was in Washington).

Meanwhile negotiation had been completed of a basic agreement on the presence and functioning of the UN Force in the Congo, employing a "good faith" formula similar to the UNEF agreement with Egypt (see volume III of this series). This was communicated to the Security Council as addendum 5 to Hammarskjöld's first report (next following text). Two days later the UN Congo Force reached a strength of over 11,000 men and deployment was proceeding rapidly in all parts of the Republic of the Congo except Katanga. This was reported to the Council on July 31 in addendum 6 to the report (second following text).

6. Basic Agreement on the Presence and Functioning of the United Nations Force in the Congo

NEW YORK   JULY 29, 1960

WITH REFERENCE TO PARAGRAPHS 7 to 9 of my report of July 18, on the implementation of Security Council resolution S/4387 of July 14, 1960, I have the honour to circulate the following duly initialled basic agreement with the government of the Republic of the Congo.

1. The government of the Republic of the Congo states that, in the exercise of its sovereign rights with respect to any question concerning the presence and functioning of the United Nations Force in the Congo, it will be guided, in good faith, by the fact that it has requested military assistance from the United Nations and by its acceptance of the resolutions of the Security Council of July 14 and 22, 1960; it likewise states that it will ensure the freedom of movement of the Force in the interior of the country and will accord the requisite privileges and immunities to all personnel associated with the activities of the Force.

2. The United Nations takes note of this statement of the government of the Republic of the Congo and states that, with regard to the activities

Security Council Official Records, Fifteenth Year, Supplement for July, August, and September 1960, document S/4389/Add.5.

of the United Nations Force in the Congo, it will be guided, in good faith, by the task assigned to the Force in the aforementioned resolutions; in particular the United Nations reaffirms, considering it to be in accordance with the wishes of the government of the Republic of the Congo, that it is prepared to maintain the United Nations Force in the Congo until such time as it deems the latter's task to have been fully accomplished.

3. The government of the Republic of the Congo and the Secretary-General state their intention to proceed immediately, in the light of paragraphs 1 and 2 above, to explore jointly specific aspects of the functioning of the United Nations Force in the Congo, notably with respect to its deployment, the question of its lines of communication and supply, its lodging, and its provisioning; the government of the Republic of the Congo, confirming its intention to facilitate the functioning of the United Nations Force in the Congo, and the United Nations have agreed to work together to hasten the implementation of the guiding principles laid down in consequence of the work of joint exploration on the basis of the resolutions of the Security Council.

4. The foregoing provisions shall likewise be applicable, as appropriate, to the nonmilitary aspects of the United Nations operations in the Congo.

---

7. Summary of Composition and Deployment of the United Nations Force in the Congo

NEW YORK   JULY 31, 1960

---

1. IN THE FOURTH ADDENDUM, dated July 26, 1960, to my report to the Security Council of July 18, I summarized the strength of the United Nations Force actually on duty in the Republic of the Congo as at midnight July 25-26, I also indicated the points in the Republic of the Congo where units of the Force were deployed.

Security Council Official Records, Supplement for July, August, and September 1960, document S/4389/Add. 6.

2. In the present addendum I summarize the strength of the United Nations Force actually on duty in the Republic of the Congo as at July 31 and indicate the key points at which units of the United Nations Force are deployed. For the convenience of the members of the Council, a map is attached showing the points of deployment as well as the nationality of the unit deployed at each point. In addition to all of the points mentioned it may be noted that all the units are fanning out hour by hour to other locations from the central points indicated on this map.

Contingents of the United Nations Force in the Republic of the Congo

Ethiopian battalions: Stanleyville, Bumba, Aketi, Paulis, Watsa, Maituru, Bunia.

Ghanaian battalions: Leopoldville.

Guinean battalion: Banningville, Nioki, Mushie, and Inongo.

Irish battalion: Kindu, Kasongo, Goma.

Liberian battalion: Libenge, Gemena.

Moroccan battalions: Matadi, Boma, Thysville, Popokabaka, Kenge, Kikwit, Coquilhatville, and Boende.

Swedish battalion: Leopoldville.

Tunisian battalions: Luluabourg, Port-Francqui, Tshikapa, Kanda-Kanda, and Lusambo.

3. Units of the following countries are now on duty in the Republic of the Congo in the strength indicated:

Ethiopia	1,860
Ghana	2,412
Guinea	741
Ireland	678
Liberia	225
Morocco	2,465
Sweden	623
Tunisia	2,151

Total 11,155

4. In addition, an advance party of the battalion contributed by the Federation of Mali has arrived, and the balance, totalling 564 men, is due this week. Some sixty pilots manning the United Nations airlift in the Republic of the Congo have been provided by Argentina, Brazil, Ethi-

opia, India, Norway, Sweden, and Yugoslavia. Small groups of officers from the United Nations Truce Supervision Organization and UNEF are serving temporarily with the Force.

Editors' note—The map is included at the end of the Security Council Supplement for July, August, and September 1960.

IN LEOPOLDVILLE Hammarskjöld encountered first-hand the chaos of emotions compounded of shock, hysteria, anger, impatience, fear, and suspicion that prevailed within the central government of the Congo as well as in the country at large. In the course of a single month these inexperienced, ill-prepared men had, in rapid succession, first welcomed with pride the status of equality among nations that independence had at last brought to the Congo; then struggled with sudden mutinies in their own Belgian-trained army; then experienced the return, without their consent, of the troops of their colonial masters and the pell-mell flight of almost all the Belgian civil servants upon whose help in running the country they had depended; and finally watched helplessly as the Belgians in Katanga encouraged and supported the secession of by far their richest province. They had turned to the United Nations for help and the United Nations was responding with unprecedented speed, but they were impatient, their expectations were unrealistic and they had little or no understanding of the considerations which it was necessary for the Organization—and the Secretary-General—to take into account.

Hammarskjöld worked hard while in Leopoldville, both in private conversations and in public statements, to increase their understanding of and strengthen their confidence in what the United Nations was trying to do. He had an uphill job. In the midst of a hospitable government reception given to him on July 31 Antoine Gizenga, acting in Lumumba's absence, suddenly launched into a speech bitterly critical of the United Nations for not having already disarmed the Belgian troops and moved into Katanga to end the secession. The Secretary-General refused to be drawn into debate of specific questions which belonged in the Security Council and instead responded with a plea for trust and a general explanation of the United Nations approach and its value to the Congo (first following text). The next day he spoke in similar vein at a dinner he gave for President Kasavubu (second following text).

Statement at Dinner Given by the Vice-Premier of the Republic of the Congo, Antoine Gizenga

LEOPOLDVILLE, THE CONGO   JULY 31, 1960

(UNOFFICIAL TRANSLATION FROM FRENCH)

First of all, Mr. Vice-Premier, allow me to thank you sincerely for the generous and hospitable welcome that you and your colleagues have given here, in Leopoldville, not only to me but also to the United Nations as a whole. I have greatly appreciated your generous words of good wishes and gratitude.

This is a delightful place and in this delightful place, tonight, I feel very far from the Security Council. Just the same, let me speak for a short time on the purposes and principles of the United Nations. There is a phrase which we often repeat at the United Nations: peace with justice. Allow me tonight to change the order of the words—that is to say, justice with peace. I think you all understand that, by changing the order of words which we ordinarily use at the United Nations, I do not want to lean on history.

I have found at the United Nations that history is important to explain attitudes, but history can enchain us, and what is important is to work for the future of peoples; and men are happiest when they have the strength and the courage to rid themselves, not of their great national memories, but of their resentments and of their unhappy memories. That gives them new strength, makes them more productive, makes them better workers, not only for the progress of their country, but for world peace.

It is for that reason that, as Secretary-General, I have a certain tendency to be antihistoric, to be as far as possible—I and my associates—creators. Creation, that is to succeed in building something new, something built on human values which exist everywhere and which can always be saved if we have the courage to do so and to rid ourselves of our bonds.

All this applies not only to my Congolese friends, to the people of the Congo and to the new Republic of the Congo; it applies everywhere in the world. It also applies to the United Nations itself.

UN Press Release, SG/937-CO/34, August 2, 1960.

You have, Mr. Vice-Premier, mentioned many cases, many subjects which have been discussed in the Security Council. I have already said that tonight it is difficult for me to direct my attention to questions which have their proper place of debate, discussion, and judgment so far from us.

If I speak of the future, it is of the future indicated by the Security Council. It is to speak of the wishes which have been so well expressed in the resolutions of this Council. We desire peace in the Congo. We desire calm in the Congo. We desire independence for the Congo, and we offer to the Republic of the Congo all the assistance of which the United Nations and its affiliated agencies are capable.

I am here as the representative of this family, of the Organization itself, and of the Security Council. We have begun conversations which I have found fruitful and encouraging. We have found during these discussions and talks difficult points where there is a reconciliation to be made—a reconciliation not of objectives but of views regarding methods and evaluations. I am sure that it will be reached. It will be reached on the basis posed in the course of our meetings and conversations here. I am sure that the Congo, within the United Nations, will find all that we desire for the Republic, all that moved and inspired the Security Council in its resolutions.

The United Nations is an organization for peace, or, as I said before, for justice with peace. Do not expect from us actions which might jeopardize the future happiness of those we wish to help. We do not want to assume such a responsibility and we shall not, Ladies and Gentlemen, act in a manner which goes against our convictions, which were based on thorough study of the problems of the country and its people, and which were guided by the views expressed by their representatives. We will not abandon a line of action which, in our eyes, tries to meet our responsibilities toward the community of nations and toward the peoples whom we serve.

I believe this is the promise, the best promise that I can give to the representatives of the Republic of the Congo. I make it happily. I make it joyfully because I have been received by you as a friend and I think now that you know you have in me an associate and a friend. And that goes beyond professional duty; it goes to my heart.

I believe that, if we serve justice with peace, without forgetting that we have more than a brain with thoughts, ambitions, and purposes, but also a heart which is first of all concerned with human values and with the happiness of man, then we shall reach our goal.

It is on this basis that I desire now, as do all of you, happiness, progress, peace and justice for our friends of the Congo, for the people of the Congo, for the young Republic of the Congo. Therefore I ask you all to join with me in a toast to peace and to the Republic of the Congo.

Statement at Dinner for President Joseph Kasavubu
of the Republic of the Congo
LEOPOLDVILLE, THE CONGO   AUGUST 1, 1960

(UNOFFICIAL TRANSLATION FROM FRENCH)

It is a privilege and an honor for us, the representatives of the United Nations, to receive you among us in Congolese territory, in a manifestation of the close cooperation established by your government with the United Nations, acting on the basis of your request, for the time judged necessary, to reach the defined objective. Cooperation is always based on confidence. And confidence is strengthened by the experience of happy cooperation.

Franklin D. Roosevelt, during the dark times of a great world depression, told his compatriots that they had nothing to fear but fear itself. In a variation on his phraseology and in the same sense I would like to say that in our cooperation the only thing we should mistrust is mistrust itself.

Our relations are of recent date, but through the intensive nature of the contacts established we already know each other well enough to be sure that there exists a firm harmony regarding the objectives of our efforts, the relations between the United Nations organization and the republic as one of its future members, and the role of the United Nations as a disinterested servant of the interests of the Republic of the Congo.

Through assistance determined in volume and in form by your needs, as evaluated by yourselves, we shall try to fill the gaps and to give you support. But we wish to do this only to the degree necessary and until the creative forces of the people and nation of the Congo, by their own vitality and their own resources, have taken care of your needs.

In a time of trouble and under conditions of a complication rare in modern history, it is natural that sometimes misunderstandings develop under the pressure of intense emotions and of the difficulty of seeing clearly the play of factors of which international politics must take account. It is on these points, above all, that one must "mistrust mistrust" as something that sours relations, weakens common effort, and corrodes the very structure of society.

UN Press Release SG/936-CO/33, August 2, 1960.

Gentlemen, you have a great task, the task of giving the Congolese people and the Congolese nation a life in peace and unity.

You have entered into today's world and into the framework of the great international family with a will to follow a straight line dictated by the interest of the people in creating for themselves a destiny correspond-ing to their traditions and their ideology. Considering the prime impor-tance of the harmonious integration of the republic into the great interna-tional family, a part of the great task you have to face will be to explain to your people what the United Nations is—what its ideals and its objec-tives are—and that you can all find in it impartial support in your difficul-ties.

One does not create a great nation overnight. One does not create understanding of the role of the nation in the international community in a few hours. The close cooperation that has been established gives you an extraordinary chance to promote the integration of the Congolese people in today's world, as you find it represented here now by the United Na-tions.

You know that the action of the United Nations on your behalf was voted with unanimity by the members of the Security Council. In this you can see an indication of your road into the future. A world divided on that which concerns the Congo would weaken you. A world of unity maintained behind you would give the Congo more strength and more security.

At each step, at each turning of the road, there are risks of division created by a wrong choice of direction. I am sure you wish to avoid such wrong choices. You certainly wish to avoid divisions among the people but certainly also about the Congolese people. In your effort to find the right direction, you can regard the standard of the United Nations as a symbol of a world united in your support which gives you a voice in these councils, a voice that will allow you to make your national contribution to the international cooperation represented by this standard.

We are at the beginning of a long road. The road is your road. During the first difficult steps, we shall be happy to go with you hand in hand. But after the first steps, when you feel sure of your strength and of your direction, you will walk alone, not abandoned by the United Nations, of course, but with the same relationship to the Organization as that enjoyed by all the other Members, with a voice in its meetings, taking advantage of the experience gained by the work of the Organization and protected by the equilibrium to which all efforts of the United Nations are directed in the interests of the ultimate peace that we all hope to see established.

In ending these few words, permit me, Mr. President, to address to you again our best wishes and to give you again the assurance of our assistance, which is guided only by the objectives and principles of the United Nations Charter and which, for that reason, remains always free of any particularistic influence of groups or of ideology.

ON THE SAME DAY that Hammarskjöld hosted the dinner in Leopoldville in honor of Kasavubu, Patrice Lumumba stopped at UN Headquarters on his way back to Africa from Washington and Ottawa. His requests for bilateral financial and technical aid had been rebuffed in both capitals—all assistance must be channeled through the United Nations. He had also received from Gizenga an account of the bloody Belgian attack a week before upon Congolese troops loyal to the central government in the Kolwezi barracks at Elisabethville.

When Lumumba talked with Cordier on August 1 he was in a hostile and frustrated state of mind, quite different from his attitude on July 25. He brought a letter addressed, not to the Secretary-General, but to the President of the Security Council, complaining of the continued presence of Belgian troops in Katanga and charging that no United Nations troops had yet entered the province "because this is opposed by the Belgian government solely in order to strengthen the secession movement it has instigated." As Lumumba requested, this letter was circulated as a Security Council document.[1]

Cordier told Lumumba he was quite mistaken about Hammarskjöld's attitude. The United Nations must go into Katanga and the Belgian troops must withdraw completely as soon as possible, but it was imperative to achieve these results by peaceful means, not by force, and to maintain the unanimity of the Council. The Secretary-General was continuing to press the Belgian government very hard to give its cooperation in the application of the July 22 resolution to Katanga. Contrary to Lumumba's complaints, Brussels thought Hammarskjöld was being unfair to Belgium and much too favorable to the position of the central government of the Congo. Cordier counseled patience for a few more days to give the peaceful approach a chance to prevail.

Lumumba, however, decided to visit Tunisia, Morocco, Guinea, Ghana, Liberia, and Togoland on the way home, seeking pledges of military support for the forcible expulsion of the Belgians from Katanga and an end to the secession. Most of the African leaders remained loyal to the United Nations approach but the governments of Kwame Nkrumah in Ghana and Sékou Touré in Guinea both indicated a readiness to join Lumumba's government in the use of force if the United Nations should fail to get the Belgians out and keep Katanga in.

---

[1] Security Council Official Records, Fifteenth Year, Supplement for July, August, and September 1960, document S/4414.

UNITED NATIONS ENTRY INTO
KATANGA

ON AUGUST 1 the Secretary-General made another effort to persuade the Belgian government to give him the help he needed for a peaceful entry of UN troops into Katanga. He sent Heinrich Wieschhoff, his chief Secretariat specialist on Africa, to Brussels with an urgent private appeal and warning for Pierre Wigny, the Belgian foreign minister. The warning was of a threatened breakdown in the whole United Nations effort and the danger of a widening war if steps were not quickly taken to apply the Security Council's July 22 resolution to Katanga. The appeal was for a public declaration by the Belgian government of its intention to do its part in implementing that decision. If this seemed too difficult in the present state of Belgian public opinion, then at the very least he asked the Belgian government to accept a statement by himself to the effect that he had been assured of Belgium's intention to abide by the resolution as interpreted by the Secretary-General. The best that Wieschhoff could obtain was a private commitment not to oppose execution of the resolution, but no public statement to this effect would be given.

The Secretary-General's second report to the Security Council, dated August 6, gives his account of what followed between August 2 and 6 when he attempted in vain to arrange a peaceful entry for UN troops into Katanga and therefore decided to return to the Security Council with a request for further action to strengthen his hand (first following text).

1. Second Report on the Implementation of the Security Council Resolutions of July 14 and 22 on the Congo

NEW YORK   AUGUST 6, 1960

1. IN ITS RESOLUTION of July 14, 1960 (S/4387), the Security Council called upon the Government of Belgium to withdraw its troops from the

Security Council Official Records, Fifteenth Year, Supplement for July, August, and September 1960, document S/4417.

territory of the Republic of the Congo and decided to authorize the Secretary-General to take the necessary steps, in consultation with the Government of the Republic of the Congo, to provide the Government with such military assistance, as might be necessary, until, through the efforts of the Congolese government with the technical assistance of the United Nations, the national security forces might be able, in the opinion of the government, to meet fully their tasks.

2. When the Council met again on July 20 (877th meeting) to consider my first report (S/4389 and Add.1-3) on the implementation of that resolution, I stated as my interpretation that the resolution clearly applied to the whole of the territory of the Republic as it existed when the Security Council only a few days earlier recommended the Congo for admission as a member of the United Nations. Thus, the United Nations Force, under the resolution and on the basis of the request of the Government of the Congo, was entitled to access to all parts of the territory in fulfilment of its duties. I also mentioned in this context that in reply to a communication from Mr. Tshombé, President of the provincial government of Katanga, I had made it clear that actions of the United Nations through the Secretary-General, in respects covered by the resolution, must in view of the legal circumstances which the Secretary-General has to take into account be considered by him as actions referring to the Republic of the Congo as an entity. I also recalled to Mr. Tshombé that I had said in my initial statement (873rd meeting) and in my first report that the United Nations Force could not be a party to or intervene in any internal conflict.

3. There was no objection raised against this interpretation during the course of the meeting and the interpretation was confirmed in the second resolution of the Security Council of July 22 (S/4405). This resolution called upon the Government of Belgium to implement speedily the Security Council resolution of July 14, 1960 on the withdrawal of its troops, and authorized the Secretary-General to take all necessary action to this effect and requested all states to refrain from any action which might tend to impede the restoration of law and order and the exercise by the Government of the Congo of its authority and also to refrain from any action which might undermine the territorial integrity and the political independence of the Republic of the Congo.

4. In a statement on August 2 to the Congolese Cabinet Committee for cooperation with the United Nations, I emphasized that the resolutions of the Security Council did not leave any room for doubt as to the legal

situation; the call to the Belgian government applied equally to Katanga province, as did the instructions given to the Secretary-General to send United Nations troops. I stated:

The eleven days which have passed since this latter resolution, and which represent the duration of my personal mandate, have witnessed important developments, which demonstrate the effectiveness of the instrument which the governments of the world possess in the United Nations for the maintenance of peace with justice. I have spent five days here with you, in talks with the central government, prepared for by discussions with the Prime Minister of the government in New York. We now have at our disposal a military force, under the flag of the United Nations in the Congo, of more than 11,000 men. These troops are deployed throughout the vast territory of the Congo, with one exception, Katanga. All the Belgian troops have withdrawn from all regions in Congolese territory where there are now United Nations troops. The deployment of the United Nations troops was carried out despite the enormous practical difficulties raised by the vast distances to be covered, the lack of communications, and the absence of any preparations for supply. The United Nations has surely done the impossible, and its efforts have been crowned with success. There remains the question of Katanga province. As I have already told you, the Security Council's second resolution leaves no room for doubt as regards the legal situation; the call to the Belgian government applied equally to Katanga province, as do the instructions given to the Secretary-General to send United Nations troops. Now the time has come to give effect to the Security Council's resolutions in Katanga also. I have the assurance that the interpretation of the situation which I have given here is accepted by the Belgian government, and that the Belgian government does not oppose the execution of these resolutions in the sense in which I have interpreted them to you. Thus the United Nations is faced with no problem of Belgian opposition. Accordingly, there remains only a practical problem. The United Nations military force is a modest one for the great task confronting it in the Congo. We are still awaiting a battalion from Mali and a battalion from Guinea, which, according to my plans and according to the agreements concluded with the governments in question, ought by now to have been at their posts. There are also other battalions to come which, I trust, will arrive a little later to give the United Nations Force its full effectiveness. There still remain to be completed and consolidated the lines of communication and supply which have been established. Despite the difficulties imposed on us by circumstances beyond anyone's control, we do not wish to delay for one moment the establishment of United Nations security control over the entire territory. And I should like to tell you now how that is to be done, according to the present plan. On Friday (August 5) I am going to send my assistant, Mr. Bunche, to Elisabethville with the necessary staff; there he will begin the initial negotiations concerning the withdrawal of Belgian troops to their bases, as the first step towards the full implementation of the Security Council resolutions so far as concerns Katanga. Mr. Bunche will be followed on the next day, i.e. Saturday August 6, by the first United Nations military units; and the withdrawal of Belgian troops from the place of deployment of the United

Nations troops is to commence immediately. As you see, the situation is quite clear: the obligations and rights laid down by the Security Council with full and prompt application to the entire territory of the Congo are meeting no opposition from any government. The plans are fixed and on Friday on his return we shall make the necessary arrangements on the spot as regards the procedure for the withdrawal of the Belgian troops from Katanga also. As speedily as possible the commencement of these negotiations will be followed by the entry of the United Nations troops, which should thus take place towards the end of this week. Only about two weeks after the Security Council's final decision entrusting to me the task of carrying out its will, the United Nations troops will thus be in control of the security of the entire territory of a united Congo.

5. On August 2 the minister for foreign affairs of Belgium, Mr. Wigny, referred to the position of the Belgian government regarding Katanga as follows:

The Belgian government wishes to clarify the policy which it has adopted and is pursuing steadfastly in Central Africa.

It recalls, at the outset, that the Congo achieved independence on June 30 in friendship and harmony with Belgium. That was a conclusive fact which Belgium will respect.

Later, Belgian troops were obliged to intervene solely in order to save the lives of fellow-countrymen who were in great danger, lacking any of the protection which a state must afford to private individuals.

This intervention implies no interference in the internal affairs of the Congo. It is temporary in nature.

These rescue duties come to an end as soon as United Nations troops arrive in a given region to take over and, at the same time, to assume responsibility for the safety of individuals.

Belgian troops are already being withdrawn to their bases and repatriated to Belgium. The Belgian government is grateful to the United Nations for having undertaken speedily and effectively a mission of public welfare.

There thus arises the problem of Katanga. Persistent requests are being made to the Belgian government to define its attitude. This attitude has never varied. The Belgian troops went to Katanga at the request of the authorities in order to ensure—there as elsewhere—the safety of individuals; they are refraining from any interference in internal affairs.

The Belgian government is, however, obliged to face facts. The first of them is that in this area law and order prevail and everyone is at work. The second is that the Katanga government, while proclaiming the independence of the province, has at the same time proposed the reconstitution of the Congo as a federation. The third fact is that the many European technicians who keep the economic life of the area going and, consequently, ensure the daily bread of the masses of the population, are very much alarmed and are resolved to leave the country if there is any danger of the anarchy now ravaging other parts of the Congo spreading to Katanga.

6. On August 3, I received through the Belgian diplomatic mission in Leopoldville a message from Mr. Tshombé the text of which follows:

The Katanga government is unanimous in its determination to resist by every means the Lumumba government, its illegal representative . . . and the dispatch of United Nations forces to Katanga. Their arrival would set off a general uprising in Katanga. The Katanga government is ready to explain its position to Mr. Bunche. It begs a meeting with him at Elisabethville not later than tomorrow before calamitous incidents occur. Responsibility would rest solely on the United Nations. With reference to its earlier declaration, the government of Katanga declares its readiness to consider any formula of cooperation with other sovereign states of the former Belgian Congo.

On August 4, I requested the Belgian Mission to transmit to Mr. Tshombé the following reply:

The Secretary-General acknowledges receipt of a message received from Mr. Tshombé. He notes that according to this message the dispatch of United Nations troops to Katanga will be resisted and that the arrival of these troops will set off a general uprising in Katanga. The Secretary-General wishes to draw attention to Article 25 of the United Nations Charter, as also to Article 49, which Articles confer on the Security Council an authority applicable directly to governments, and *a fortiori* to subordinate territorial nongovernmental authorities of Member nations. The same obligations must be regarded as applicable by analogy to nations which, like the Republic of the Congo, have been recommended for admission to the United Nations. Resistance by a Member government to a Security Council decision has legal consequences laid down in the Charter. These sanctions necessarily apply also to the subordinate territorial organs of a nation to which the Charter rules apply. The Secretary-General has already transmitted the text of an interpretative statement which he made to the Security Council, which makes it clear that the Security Council's resolutions apply to the entire territory of the Congo. The Secretary-General's position was unanimously approved by the Security Council. The conclusions to be drawn from this and from the Charter rules for the Congo are obvious. The Secretary-General trusts that in the light of these observations the intentions indicated in the message will be considered with full knowledge of their extremely serious character. He hopes also that the situation will be clarified before the arrival of the United Nations troops, in such a way as to provide every assurance that the entry of these military elements does not represent any interference in the internal affairs of the Republic of the Congo, including its provinces, or impede or modify in any way the free exercise of rights to act, in legal and democratic forms, in favour of one or another solution of such constitutional problems as may in due time arise for the Congolese people.

Before concluding this message, the Secretary-General wishes also to draw attention to the following principles, which apply to this operation as to any paramilitary operation of the United Nations. (i) The troops are under the sole command and the sole control of the United Nations. (ii) The troops are not permitted to interfere in the internal affairs of the country in which they are deployed. They cannot be used in order to impose any particular political solution of pending problems, or to exert any influence on a balance of political forces which may be decisive for such a solution. (iii) United Nations military units are not entitled to act except in self-defence. This rule categorically prohibits the troops participating in the operation from taking the initiative of resorting to armed force, but permits them to reply by force to an armed attack, in particular to any attempts to resort to force which might be made with the object of compelling them to evacuate positions which they occupy on the orders of their commander. If the position of refusal to accept the application of the Security Council decisions is maintained, despite the pertinent observations here made, the Secretary-General will request the immediate calling of the Security Council, which, undoubtedly, will not fail to take as a matter of urgency such measures as may be necessary.

7. In the afternoon of August 3, I was informed that the "Conseil du Cabinet du Vice-Premier Ministre" had "decided" that Mr. Bunche, on his mission to Katanga, should be accompanied by those gentlemen representing the central government, to be escorted by twenty soldiers of Ghanaian nationality.

I replied that a similar proposal had already been rejected by me in an earlier meeting with the full cabinet and had not been repeated when I announced my decision to send Mr. Bunche to Katanga. I continued: "In this respect I have to tell you again that the mission of Mr. Bunche is purely a United Nations mission, the character of which should not be compromised by the arrangements made."

I rejected also the proposal for military escort, noting that military dispositions regarding the Force were under the sole authority of the Secretary-General and, under him, the Commander, and that the plans did not foresee any military escort for Mr. Bunche and his party.

Later, the same evening, the Vice-Prime Minister announced to me that he had found it necessary to add to the team of Mr. Bunche also one journalist. I rejected the proposal, pointing out that the Secretary-General alone could determine the composition of a United Nations mission.

8. In the morning of August 4, Mr. Bunche left Leopoldville for Elisabethville. I had issued the following instructions to Mr. Bunche for his mission:

The general plan for the entry of units of the United Nations Force into Katanga is outlined in my statement of August 2. You are also aware of the detailed planning for the military operation which will mean that in the course of August 6, 1960, units of three national contingents of the United Nations Force will arrive in Elisabethville, unless other orders were to be given through the commander.

You are also aware of the legal basis on which this action is taken. I annex to this letter the following documents establishing our legal right to move United Nations troops into Katanga:

(a) Record of the 877th meeting of the Security Council, held on July 20-21, 1960 (see statement of the Secretary-General, paragraphs 3-19);

(b) Resolutions of the Security Council of July 14 and 22, 1960 (S/4387 and S/4405);

(c) A memorandum regarding the interpretation of the withdrawal clauses in resolution of the Security Council of July 22, 1960 (this memorandum has been informally communicated to the Belgian government);

(d) My reply to a message received on August 3, 1960, from Mr. Tshombé (para. 6 above).

Your task is to discuss with the appropriate Belgian authorities the modalities for the withdrawal of Belgian troops and their replacement by troops of the United Nations Force, which will be charged with maintenance of security also in this part of the territory of the Republic of the Congo.

You are entitled through the Belgian authorities to have such contact with leaders of the European community and with Mr. Tshombé and other representatives of the population as you may find necessary in order to prepare the ground for the withdrawal of the Belgian and the entry of United Nations troops, with maintenance of peace and order. You should if necessary give those authorities information on the legal basis of the United Nations action and of the consequences of resistance.

In the light of declarations made to me by the Government of Belgium, both orally and in writing, later also in an official statement, I know that no opposition will be offered by Belgian authorities or forces. Disorder may all the same develop, either at the instigation of local leaders or spontaneously. As regards spontaneous demonstrations, the same rules apply as those we have agreed upon for similar occurrences in other parts of the territory. In the case of resistance by force, or firm indications that such resistance would be made at the instigation of local leaders, you should immediately communicate with me and give me an appraisal of the situation.

Should you arrive at the conclusion that resistance by force represents a serious risk in view of the attitude of leaders, and that for that reason you have to advise against the entry of United Nations troops, I shall, upon receipt of your report, ask for the immediate convening of the Security Council to which I shall present a complete report on what has occurred, with a request for instructions.

Thus it is for you to judge whether intentions indicated by Katanga authorities in the message received through the Belgian diplomatic mission today, to the effect that active resistance will be offered against the entry of United Nations troops, are maintained in a way which might force the United Nations military units to action involving a possible risk of lives. Were you to consider that to be the case, I trust that you will take appropriate initiatives in relation to me giving me sufficient time to activate the Security Council before further action is taken.

It is obviously the purpose of the contacts with the Belgian authorities, and through them possibly with local representatives, to see to it that the aims of the Security Council are speedily achieved, but without frictions which would introduce, unnecessarily, serious complications in a situation already fraught with difficulties, or which would compromise the impartial attitude and pacific status of a United Nations Force.

Wishing you all the luck in your assignment, I express my hope that this operation will be carried through without friction, to the benefit not only of the people of the Congo, including all those who live in Katanga, irrespective of race or nationality, but also of peace and stability, with justice, for all.

9. According to my announcement on Tuesday, August 2, Mr. Bunche and his collaborators were to have gone to Katanga on Friday, August 5, to be followed on Saturday, August 6, by United Nations military units. As circumstances made it possible to go earlier, Mr. Bunche went instead on Thursday, August 4, without any change in the plans to send troops on August 6.

In Elisabethville, Mr. Bunche undertook the task defined in his instructions, on the basis of the decisions of the Security Council.

Mr. Bunche returned to Leopoldville on Friday afternoon, August 5, and reported to me. His conclusions are summed up as follows:

Thus my recommendation to stop the Katanga operations is based on:

(i) The unqualified and unyielding opposition of Mr. Tshombé, his ministers and the grand chiefs, to the coming of United Nations troops; their repeated warnings that the United Nations troops would be opposed by all the force Katangans could bring to bear (the last such warning being at 11 a.m. on August 5); and the demand that their position be conveyed to you fully and personally, since in their view the United Nations would have to bear the responsibility for the disaster that would occur if United Nations troops tried to enter Katanga;

(ii) The tangible evidence of opposition to the arrival of United Nations troops, in the press, in the calls for "mobilization," in the long columns of new recruits for the army marching in the streets, in the appeal to the "warriors" and the possibility of a trap being prepared at Jadotville, should elements of the Force land there;

(iii) The quite convincing evidence of fanatical opposition at the airport on the morning of August 5 where I was able to avert most serious trouble only with the greatest difficulty;

(iv) The fact that preparations for the operations were not based on an assumption of an arrival likely to encounter armed opposition and that such a contingency would make necessary much different planning if the operation were to be carried out successfully.

10. It is thus clear that the entry of United Nations military units into Katanga would have had to be achieved by the use of force.

In my first report to the Security Council, commended by the Council in its resolution of July 22, it was stated as one of the principles for the operation of the Force that military units would be entitled to act only in self-defence. This statement was amplified by the following interpretation: ". . . men engaged in the operation may never take the initiative in the use of armed force, but are entitled to respond with force to an attack with arms, including attempts to use force to make them withdraw from positions which they occupy under orders from the commander." Therefore, the Force is not entitled to such military initiative and action as, in view of what has now been made clear, would be necessary for an implementation of the Security Council decisions.

I now have to ask for instructions from the Security Council and for such decisions as the Council may find appropriate in order to achieve integrally its aims.

On the one hand, the Council resolutions regarding withdrawal and the sending of United Nations military units obviously are intended to apply to the whole territory of the Congo as recommended for admission to the United Nations. In implementation of my mandate under the resolution of July 22, this, therefore, has been the way in which I have understood my instructions, and this also has been the direction in which I have operated, with all the speed and efficiency which circumstances have permitted. On the other hand, it is now also clear that, as stated above, the aims of the resolutions cannot be achieved by the use of the United Nations Force, as its mandate has been defined. If the Council, as it is assumed, wishes to maintain its objectives, the Council must, therefore, either change the character of the Force, which appears to me to be impossible, both for constitutional reasons and in view of the commitments to the contributing governments, or resort to other methods which would enable me to carry through the implementation of its resolution without going beyond my instructions as regards the Force.

The difficulty which the Council faces in the case of Katanga does not have its root in the Belgian attitude regarding the problem as stated to me, as the Belgian government acquiesces in the Security Council decisions and therefore undoubtedly will instruct its military elements in the province to act in accordance with the resolutions as implemented by the United Nations Force, if that has not yet been done.

Nor is the problem a desire on the part of the authorities of the province to secede from the Republic of the Congo. The question is a constitutional one with strong undercurrents of individual and collective political aims. The problem for those resisting the United Nations Force in

Katanga may be stated in these terms: Will United Nations participation in security control in Katanga submit the province to the immediate control and authority of the central government against its wishes? They consider this seriously to jeopardize their possibility to work for other constitutional solutions than a strictly unitarian one, e.g. some kind of federal structure providing for a higher degree of provincial self-government than now foreseen. The spokesmen for this attitude reject the unitarian formula as incompatible with the interests of the whole Congo people and as imposed from outside.

This is an internal political problem to which the United Nations as an organization obviously cannot be a party. Nor would the entry of the United Nations Force in Katanga mean any taking of sides in the conflict to which I have just referred. Nor should it be permitted to shift the weights between personalities or groups or schools of thought in a way which would prejudge the solution of the internal political problem. I believe all this can be avoided if the United Nations maintains firmly its aim and acts with clarity and tact, but the question is not one which can be taken lightly. The Security Council may wish to clarify its views on the matter and to lay down such rules for the United Nations operation as would serve to separate effectively questions of a peaceful and democratic development in the constitutional field from any questions relating to the presence of the United Nations Force.

Were the Council to do so, it might well open the door to a speedy implementation of its previous resolutions, also as regards Katanga. In this respect, it obviously has not been possible for me, in my efforts to give effect to the resolutions, to go beyond the firm statements of the principle of neutrality of the United Nations and of its actions in relation to all conflicts of an essentially domestic nature, which are found in the documents reproduced in this report and which reflect the policy approved by the Security Council.

2. Exchange of Messages with Sékou Touré on Use of Guinea's Troops in Katanga

NEW YORK   AUGUST 7, 1960

I APPEND HERETO an exchange of telegrams with the President of the Republic of Guinea.

I. Telegram dated August 6, 1960, from the President of the Republic of Guinea to the Secretary-General

I have the honour to approach you on behalf of my government and to urge the immediate use of our troops in Katanga. If this proposal were not accepted, my government would place them under the direct authority of the Congolese government.

SÉKOU TOURÉ
President of the Republic of Guinea

II. Telegram dated August 6, 1960, from the Secretary-General to the President of the Republic of Guinea

I have received your telegram in which you urge the use of your troops for entering Katanga. As you know, the question of the entry of United Nations troops into Katanga will be considered tomorrow by the Security Council. You will also have noted that no decision has been taken on my part to the effect that the United Nations troops should not enter Katanga, provided naturally that this can be done under the terms of reference established by the Security Council. You will also appreciate that no decision has been taken on the final composition of the contingents of the United Nations Force in Katanga.

DAG HAMMARSKJÖLD
Secretary-General of the United Nations

Security Council Official Records, Fifteenth Year, Supplement for July, August, and September 1960, document S/4417/Add.1/Rev.1.

III. Telegram dated August, 7, 1960, from the President of the Republic of Guinea to the Secretary-General

In reassuring you of our confidence, we venture to urge that, in view of the unfortunate turn events have taken in the Congo, a turn which threatens to discredit the authority of the highest organ of the independent nations of the world, you take steps to ensure the faithful and immediate implementation of the Security Council resolutions providing for the complete evacuation of Belgian troops from the Congo and safeguarding the territorial integrity of that state. The intervention of the United Nations will result either in its triumph or in a failure which would seriously endanger the future of the international Organization and the fate of world peace. All the African peoples are highly sensitive to the manner in which the United Nations fulfils the historic role it is called upon to play in securing victory for freedom and the integrity of nations.

SÉKOU TOURÉ
President of the Republic of Guinea

IV. Telegram dated August 7, 1960, from the Secretary-General to the President of the Republic of Guinea

I have received your telegram of today's date for which I am most grateful. Your appeal to us, and to me personally, "to ensure the faithful and immediate implementation of the Security Council resolutions providing for the complete evacuation of Belgian troops from the Congo and safeguarding the territorial integrity of that State" is one which, I can assure you, is in keeping with my own wishes and efforts. That is why I myself have appealed to the Security Council to reach early agreement on a resolution which would strengthen my hand, while clarifying the obligations and rights involved. The strongest support we can have in this great test of the instrument of the independent nations of the world—the United Nations—is the confidence and solidarity of the African Member states, acting with a common purpose, that of maintaining Africa in peace and free of all interference alien to the African world.

DAG HAMMARSKJÖLD
Secretary-General of the United Nations

Editors' note—Document S/4417/Add. 2 gives the texts of letters exchanged with Antoine Gizenga about his request that members of the central government accompany Ralph Bunche to Katanga. These are adequately summarized in paragraph 7 of the Secretary-General's report (S/4417), and Add. 2 is therefore omitted. See below exchange of messages with Tshombé dated August 10 (S/4417/Add. 3 and 4) and accompanying commentary; memorandum on civilian operations dated August 11 (Add. 5); and interpretation of the Security Council's third resolution on the Congo dated August 12 (Add. 6).

IN GHANA PRESIDENT KWAME NKRUMAH issued a long statement blaming Belgium for promoting the secession of Katanga and for preventing the introduction of UN troops which included the following passage:

> Ghana, for one, certainly, and I believe also all of the other African states, would not tolerate the construction in the centre of Africa of a puppet state maintained by Belgian troops and designed to fit the needs of an international mining concern. If no United Nations solution is forthcoming, Ghana would lend such armed assistance as the Republic of the Congo might request. Ghana would provide this assistance even though it meant that Ghana and the Congo had to fight alone against Belgian troops and other forces maintained and supplied from Belgium.[1]

Nkrumah's statement was circulated as a Security Council document before the Council met on August 8, as were two Soviet government statements dated July 31 and August 6, and a telegram from Patrice Lumumba.

The first Soviet statement declared that if "the aggression" against the Congo continued, "the Soviet government will not hesitate to take resolute measures to rebuff the aggressors who, as has now become perfectly clear, are in fact acting with the encouragement of all the colonialist Powers of NATO."[2] There was also a promise of continuing economic and technical aid with no mention of channeling such aid through the United Nations. The August 6 statement did not criticize the Secretary-General by name but had harsh words for the alleged delinquencies of the UN "command" in the Congo. Unless this "command" provided the military assistance needed by the central government to expel the Belgians and end the secession, "it should be replaced by a new command," using troops from countries prepared to join in such "resolute and effective action."[3]

Lumumba requested the Security Council to send a group of observers composed of representatives of India, Ceylon, Ghana, Ethiopia, Morocco, Guinea, the United Arab Republic, Afghanistan, Indonesia, and Burma "to ensure, on the spot and without delay, the strict application" of the Council's decisions.[4] These developments formed part of the background for the Secretary-General's opening statement in the Council (next following text).

---

[1] Security Council Official Records, Fifteenth Year, Supplement for July, August, and September 1960, document S/4420.

[2] Ibid., document S/4416.

[3] Ibid., document S/4418.

[4] Ibid., document S/4421.

3. *First Statement in the Security Council Introducing His Second Report*

NEW YORK   AUGUST 8, 1960

I REGRET that it has been necessary for me to call again the attention of the Security Council to the problem we are facing in the Congo. I would have hoped that through full, active, and immediate cooperation of all those concerned we would by now have reached a more advanced stage in the implementation of the Security Council resolutions than we have, and I would have hoped that we would not have come to what temporarily may appear as a deadlock, requiring the consideration of the Council. I said "temporarily" because I am firmly convinced that we shall achieve the aims of the resolutions even if it will have required somewhat more time and also, perhaps, a somewhat different balance of means for their implementation than originally envisaged.

I said that I would have hoped for active support from all those concerned. Such support has only partly been forthcoming, and I must note that a lack of support has been registered from quarters which I might have expected to act differently. Let me be specific.

Mr. Tshombé and the Katanga authorities for which he carries responsibility have taken the stand which I register in the report. This means that they have introduced an unexpected element of organized military opposition by Congolese forces against the entry of the United Nations Force. Such opposition would require military initiative from the United Nations Force to which I would not be entitled to resort short of a formal authorization of the Council, even in that case naturally using only contingents representing governments which would accept such a new stand by the Council.

In this situation I note that, while there is no opposition from the Belgian government and those representing the Belgian government, their stand has been summed up by the Prime Minister of Belgium as being one of "submission" to the Security Council resolutions and to the entrance of the United Nations Force. I read "submission" to mean only absence of active resistance and that naturally presents us with a serious problem, especially in a situation like the one now created by Mr. Tshombé.

The central government, in its turn, has shown great impatience. When I presented to them the reasons why, while acting with the utmost speed, I could not responsibly act more speedily, from many quarters the reaction has been one of distrust which may well be spread through the population—indeed, there are signs that it has begun to do so—thus creating a most harmful atmosphere against the major effort of the United Nations in active support of the Republic of the Congo. This dangerous tendency of sowing distrust has not been without support from other quarters outside the Congo.

Finally, it does not help the United Nations effort if it has to live under a threat of any one—or more—contributing governments taking matters in its, or their, own hands, breaking away from the United Nations Force and pursuing a unilateral policy.

These are the main difficulties as we have encountered them, and I do not excuse myself for stating them here plainly and simply.

I am, however, more convinced than ever that this effort must and can be carried to a successful conclusion.

By a "successful conclusion" I mean a conclusion preserving the unity of the Congo people, while protecting the democratic rights of everybody to let his influence bear, in democratic forms, on the final constitution for the Republic to be determined only by the Congolese people themselves.

I further mean by that term the speediest possible withdrawal of Belgian troops in accordance with the Security Council resolutions, as the presence of those troops now is the main cause of continued danger, a withdrawal that must be complete and unconditional; once the end in this respect is definitely in hand—and that should be possible immediately—methods and timetables are practical matters which must be considered in the light of, for example, the fact that a Congolese population of some fifteen thousand depends economically on the Kamina base and that, therefore, with the return of Belgian troops from the base to Belgium, immediate arrangements must be made by the United Nations for the maintenance of this big population.

Finally, I mean by a satisfactory solution one which will permit the Congolese people to choose freely its political orientation in our world of today, independent of any foreign elements the presence and role of which would mean that through the Congo we might get conflicts extraneous to the African world introduced on the continent.

I do not hesitate to say that the speediest possible—I would even say immediate—achievement of such a solution of the Congo problem is a question of peace or war, and when saying peace or war I do not limit my perspective to the Congo. A delay now, hesitation now, efforts to safeguard national or group interests now in a way that would hamper the United Nations effort, would risk values immeasurably greater than any of those which such action may be intended to protect. This applies to all parties, first of all to the one to which the Security Council has addressed its appeal.

The Charter states in several articles the obligations of Member nations in relation to the Organization in a situation like the present one. I have mentioned them in the reply to Mr. Tshombé's *démarche* which is published in my report, but I want here and now to quote them in full. The first one is Article 25, which says: "The Members of the United Nations agree to accept and carry out the decisions of the Security Council in accordance with the present Charter." The other one is Article 49, which says: "The Members of the United Nations shall join in affording mutual assistance in carrying out the measures decided upon by the Security Council."

Could there be a more explicit basis for my hope that we may now count on active support, in the ways which emerge from what I have said, from the governments directly concerned? Could there be a more explicit basis also for my expectation that local authorities will now adjust themselves to the obligations which their country has incurred?

However, I want to go one step further and quote also Article 40 of the Charter, which speaks about actions taken by the Security Council in protection of peace and security, first of all, by certain so-called "provisional measures." It is stated in the Article: "Such provisional measures shall be without prejudice to the rights, claims, or position of the parties concerned. The Security Council shall duly take account of failure to comply with such provisional measures."

Please, permit me here to remind you also of Article 41: "The Security Council may decide what measures not involving the use of armed force are to be employed to give effect to its decisions, and it may call upon the Members of the United Nations to apply such measures."

The resolutions of the Security Council of July 14 and July 22 were not explicitly adopted under Chapter VII, but they were passed on the basis of an initiative under Article 99. For that reason I have felt entitled to quote three articles under Chapter VII, and I repeat what I have already said in this respect: in a perspective which may well be short rather than long, the problem facing the Congo is one of peace or war—and not only in the Congo.

In my second report I have given, in broad terms, my views as to the direction in which the Security Council may now take useful action. The Council should, for the sake of clarity, reaffirm its aims and demands as stated in the previous resolutions. It may wish to clarify its views on the methods to be used and on the time-limits which should be our target. It may also wish to state explicitly what so far has been only implied, that is to say, that its resolutions apply fully and in all parts also to Katanga. It should, in my view, request the immediate and active support by all Member governments, no one excluded. It should also find its way to formulate principles for the United Nations presence, which, in accordance with the purposes and principles of the Charter, would safeguard democratic rights and protect the spokesmen of all different political views within the large entity of the Congo so as to make it possible for them to make their voice heard in democratic forms; this is not any easy matter, because it will require a sensitive development of the United Nations activities, but I am sure it can be done, and I feel strongly that the United Nations would have failed in its mission if it maintained order while permitting democratic principles to be violated.

Thus, I envisage a result which guarantees the speedy and complete withdrawal of the Belgian troops and through which the basic unity of the whole Congo without delay is made manifest in the presence of the United Nations all over its territory; in which, further, safeguards are given for every direction of political opinion to make its voice heard and to bring its will to bear in democratic forms on the final solution of the constitutional development of the Congo—to be determined solely by the people of the Congo; and in which, finally, unanimity would be maintained, among Africans and non-Africans alike, here in the United Nations so that this United Nations operation remains unambiguously and actively supported by all the Members of the Organization in full understanding of its vital necessity, its clear aims, and the laws of impartiality and justice under which it has to be developed.

I have held it necessary and in accordance with the intentions of the Council that everywhere in the Congo the withdrawal of Belgian troops should be immediately followed, or even preceded, by the entry of United Nations troops, shouldering the responsibility for the maintenance of security and order. So it has been everywhere outside Katanga.

In Katanga this principle has led to the development of a vicious circle. The entry of United Nations troops is obstructed and, correspondingly, the withdrawal of the Belgian troops is rendered impossible if the principle is to be maintained that, at the withdrawal, the responsibility for security must be taken over at once by United Nations troops. However, the opposition to the United Nations is raised in the shadow of the continued presence of the Belgian troops.

This vicious circle must be broken; further delays in the entry of United Nations troops, due to armed opposition, can in my view not any longer be permitted to delay the withdrawal of the Belgian troops. If, at the withdrawal of Belgian troops, the United Nations troops are not in the area because of such opposition, it is for those who oppose the entry of the United Nations troops, or who support or encourage this obstruction, to carry the full responsibility for what may develop in the vacuum which they have forced upon us.

One final word about the situation of some of those private interests which are involved in the present situation. I think of Europeans who work in Katanga. There is no need for me to assure them that the United Nations has not come to the region in order to "take over" or put others in their place. There should not be any need for me to explain that the United Nations action is their best hope for the future, as their work will have to be in harmony with the interest of the people among whom they live and whom they ultimately serve, and must be under the protection of security, maintained in forms which guarantee the rights of all.

In a state of emotion irrational reactions are to be expected and we should have understanding and sympathy for those who see themselves as being threatened. However, is it too much to expect that the people to whom I refer may lift themselves above their emotions, see present-day realities as they are and see, for that reason, in the United Nations their only valid support if they wish to continue a work to which they have devoted so much of their best efforts? Surely, others who are more remote from the heat of present conflicts—and I think in the first place of the Belgian government itself—should be able to help in creating the right atmosphere and the right understanding of the United Nations operation; if so, I believe that even the present unrest and worry may be overcome and also that the United Nations will not encounter further resistance in its efforts from those to whom this assistance should bring satisfaction and not fear.

The initiative now lies with the members of the Council and with the Council itself. After having listened to the views and reactions in the debate on which you now embark, I may be able to assist with more concrete suggestions adjusted to the line of thinking which emerges from the debate.

I cannot end without stressing once again the extreme seriousness with which I regard, and with which I have treated, the present situation. To the best of my understanding I have acted as swiftly as has been humanly possible and in strict accordance with the principles and purposes of the Charter. Whatever views may be held on this or that aspect of the actions for which I shoulder personal responsibility, I hope that there will be no doubt about the aims that have guided me, about the will to give the utmost of what this Organization is capable of doing in the implementation of your resolutions in the service of world peace.

JUSTIN BOMBOKO, minister for foreign affairs, a young university graduate like Kanza, spoke for the Congo, although the deputy prime minister, Antoine Gizenga, was also a member of the delegation present for the Council session. In contrast to Gizenga (and Lumumba) Bomboko praised "the Secretary-General . . . and his collaborators for the way and the spirit in which they have undertaken and carried out the delicate tasks entrusted to them." The Congo's "impatience and sense of urgency" was not a sign of mistrust of the United Nations, he said, but of Belgium, which he accused of responsibility for promoting and supporting the attempted secession of Katanga.[1] Belgium's foreign minister, Pierre Wigny, repeated his earlier denials of any Belgian responsibility for Tshombé's stand. Belgian troops would not resist entry of the United Nations Force into Katanga, but it was up to the Secretary-General, not Belgium, to persuade Tshombé not to resist and to assure the public safety that would permit Belgian troop withdrawal.

Once again Africa's spokesman on the Security Council, Mongi Slim of Tunisia, introduced a draft resolution fully in accord with Hammarskjöld's approach, just as he had done on July 14 and 22. And for the second time Sir Claude Corea of Ceylon, the Council's only nonpermanent Asian member, joined in sponsoring the draft resolution. It read as follows:

The Security Council,
    Recalling its resolution of July 22, 1960 (S/4405), *inter alia,* calling upon the Government of Belgium to implement speedily the Security Council reso-

---

[1] Security Council Official Records, Fifteenth Year, 885th meeting.

lution of July 14 (S/4387) on the withdrawal of its troops and authorizing the Secretary-General to take all necessary action to this effect,

Having noted the second report of the Secretary-General (S/4417) on the implementation of the aforesaid two resolutions and his statement before the Council,

Having considered the statements made by the representatives of Belgium and the Republic of the Congo to this Council at this meeting,

Noting with satisfaction the progress made by the United Nations in carrying out the Security Council resolutions in respect of the territory of the Republic of the Congo other than the province of Katanga,

Noting, however, that the United Nations had been prevented from implementing the aforesaid resolutions in the province of Katanga although it was ready, and in fact attempted, to do so,

Recognizing that the withdrawal of Belgian troops from the province of Katanga will be a positive contribution to and essential for the proper implementation of the Council resolutions,

1. *Confirms* the authority given to the Secretary-General by the Security Council resolutions of July 14 and July 22, 1960, and requests him to continue to carry out the responsibility placed on him thereby;

2. *Calls upon* the Government of Belgium to withdraw immediately its troops from the province of Katanga under speedy modalities determined by the Secretary-General and to assist in every possible way the implementation of the Council's resolutions;

3. *Declares* that the entry of the United Nations Force into the province of Katanga is necessary for the full implementation of the Council's resolution;

4. *Reaffirms* that the United Nations Force in the Congo will not be a party to or in any way intervene in or be used to influence the outcome of any internal conflict, constitutional or otherwise;

5. *Calls upon* all Member states, in accordance with Articles 25 and 49 of the Charter of the United Nations, to accept and carry out the decisions of the Security Council and to afford mutual assistance in carrying out measures decided upon by the Council;

6. *Requests* the Secretary-General to implement this resolution and to report further to the Council as appropriate.[2]

For the Soviet Union V.V. Kuznetsov introduced a draft resolution declaring that the Security Council "*imposes* (emphasis added) on the Secretary-General the obligation to take decisive measures, without hesitating to use any means to that end, to remove the Belgian troops from the territory of the Congo and to put an end to acts directed against the territorial integrity of the Republic of the Congo."[3]

Kuznetsov supported the stands of Ghana, Guinea, and Lumumba, criticized the "United Nations command" for not going into Katanga and the Secretary-General for being too gentle with Belgium in his report. However, he also said:

[2] Ibid., Supplement for July, August, and September 1960, document S/4426.
[3] Ibid., Fifteenth Year, 885th meeting.

"We naturally pay due tribute to the energy shown and the efforts made by the Secretary-General and his assistants in the Secretariat in connection with events in the Congo."[4] His own language in general was more moderate than that used in the government statements emanating from Moscow but in a later intervention he repeated the threat made on July 31 that "in the event of the aggression against the Congo continuing . . . the Soviet government will not hesitate to take resolute measures to rebuff the aggressors who, as has now become perfectly clear, are in fact acting with the encouragement of all the colonialist Powers of NATO."[5]

The Secretary-General's second statement in the debate (next following text) followed Kuznetsov's opening speech.

[4] Ibid.
[5] Ibid., 886th meeting.

---

4. Second Statement in the Security Council

NEW YORK   AUGUST 8, 1960

I AM SORRY THAT the representative of the Soviet Union is not present, because I should like to make a couple of comments on his intervention. However, I am sure that it will be reported to him, and in such circumstances he will certainly excuse me if I begin my observations even without his presence.

I am certain that the representative of the Soviet Union is as anxious as I am to keep the record straight and that for that reason he will understand if I use this opportunity to correct what I think are a couple of misunderstandings and also correct a couple of statements which I believe are based on misinformation.

The representative of the Soviet Union mentioned first that we had been disarming the national military units. On that point, I can refer him to the statement made earlier in the present meeting by the Foreign Minister of the Republic of the Congo, when he said: "To enable the United Nations troops to carry out their mission, the military command of the National Army, in agreement with the Congolese government, has called on the Congolese soldiers to lay down their arms wherever United Nations forces were present."

Security Council Official Records, Fifteenth Year, 885th meeting.

That is to say, it is a decision by the sovereign Government of the Congo, not a decision by me or by the United Nations command, and I think that should be on record.

Further, the representative of the Soviet Union said that there had been conflicts between our forces and the national forces and the population. Again, I would just simply refer to the statement of Mr. Bomboko, when he said, on the one side, "Everywhere the United Nations forces have been given a most friendly reception by the people of the Republic," and when he further said, "Everywhere, as you see, the United Nations forces entered the Congo without meeting any resistance on the part of either our soldiers or our people."

If I then turn to what I believe to be misunderstandings—understandable, but in any event misleading—the first one I should like to mention is the authority of the command and the authority of the Secretary-General.

The order to stop the entry of the United Nations forces into Katanga was given by me, not by the command, as the command is under instructions of the Secretary-General acting on the authority of the Security Council. The command would have taken any kind of order which I gave. I have reported the matter in my report to the Security Council and I would shoulder, naturally, full responsibility if the Security Council were to find that my order was wrong.

I have already explained why I gave the order. There are limits to my authority and those limits are found in the first report, which was in fact commended by the Security Council with the concurring vote of the Soviet delegation. In that first report I spelled out the legal position and competence of the United Nations Force and even stated at some length the reasons why the Force should not take any military initiative and should be regarded in that respect as limited to action in self-defence. I do not remember having heard any objection to that interpretation of its status, functions, and competence; and that being the case, I would certainly have acted beyond my competence as established by the Security Council if I had, with open eyes, given an order, or rather, confirmed an order which would have meant that our forces would have been forced to military initiative.

In that context I should like to mention another aspect. The representative of the Soviet Union expressed a sincere wish to help the Congolese people. That wish is certainly shared by everybody, and for me it is a guiding inspiration. I do not believe, personally, that we help the Congolese people by actions in which Africans kill Africans, or Congolese kill Congolese, and that will remain my guiding principle for the future.

It was also said that the Force should assist the central government. Yes, certainly, in the maintenance of order, but not as a political instrument. That has never been the intention and it goes against the very principles on which the Force has been established—again stated in the draft resolution which has been presented to us in the first place by the representative of Tunisia who, I believe, may here be regarded as speaking for the whole African group.

There was also reference to the proposal of Mr. Lumumba that observers should be sent to the Congo—observers of the withdrawal, observers of our activities. I do not see in that any vote of distrust or any expression of lack of confidence, but I see in it a proposal which has a certain value, a value which must be judged in the light of practical needs.

I should like to draw attention to the fact that the deputy supreme commander is a general from Morocco; that the chief of staff is a general from Ethiopia; that the chief liaison officer is a general from Ghana, and that the chief liaison officer between the staff on the spot and Headquarters is a general from India. I wonder, in those circumstances, if observers from those same countries, perhaps with an addition or two, could make a useful contribution.

I think that this is all I need to say. It is not for the Secretary-General to engage in the debate of the Council; his role is simply to give information and to express his reactions as regards his own action, and for that reason I leave aside what has been said in this intervention, to which I referred, or in other interventions.

FOR THE UNITED STATES Lodge gave his unqualified support to the resolution sponsored by Tunisia and Ceylon and to the Secretary-General's policy line. The representatives of the Western European members—the United Kingdom, France and Italy—also spoke in support of the Secretary-General, but thought that some of the language of the resolution was too harsh with Belgium and placed too much emphasis on immediate withdrawal. Sir Pierson Dixon, for example, asked the Secretary-General how he would interpret his responsibilities under the second operative paragraph. Hammarskjöld's third intervention (next following text) was in response to that enquiry.

5. *Third Statement in the Security Council*

NEW YORK   AUGUST 8, 1960

THE REPRESENTATIVE OF THE United Kingdom asked me how I would interpret the phrase "speedy modalities determined by the Secretary-General." It may be natural if I hesitate a little bit to venture an interpretation at this stage of the debate.

For me, necessarily, the main interpretative document will be my own statement this morning, to which I regard this draft resolution as a reply. But I think perhaps that, in that light, I can risk an attempt to explain how I look at the position.

I read the phrase "speedy modalities" as a recognition of the need for me—and I repeat "for me"—so to implement the request for immediate withdrawal addressed to the Government of Belgium as to provide for an orderly development within the limits of the possible as determined also by factors over which others than we are the masters and, of course, with due regard to the overriding needs of the situation.

Thus I read the phrase quoted by the representative of the United Kingdom as entitling me, *inter alia,* to have regard to the concern expressed by this very Council that there should be effective and continued maintenance of law and order. This will not slow down the withdrawal provided that, as the Security Council has a right to expect the Belgian government and Mr. Tshombé—and those who may support him—give their full and immediate cooperation. There are also other related considerations which must influence me in determining the modalities. May it suffice to remind the Council of what I said this morning regarding the problem presented by the fifteen thousand Congolese who depend on the Kamina base. Together, such considerations as those mentioned will, on my side, necessitate the establishment of speedy timetables which, with a background in the obligation of the Belgian government established by the proposed resolution, are determined by the possibilities, the responsibilities, and the aims of the United Nations.

Security Council Official Records, Fifteenth Year, 886th meeting.

JUST BEFORE the debate came to an end in the early morning hours of August 9 Sir Claude Corea of Ceylon gave the Secretary-General an opportunity to make a much needed clarification of some loosely drafted language in his report which had been used during the debate to indicate an endorsement of the Belgian position going well beyond what he had intended (next following text).

6. Fourth Statement in the Security Council

NEW YORK   AUGUST 9, 1960

THE REPRESENTATIVE OF CEYLON has drawn attention to two statements of mine, one in the second report and the other in the statement I made this morning. The first one covers a phrase which has been very much quoted here today—but practically always, I must say, quoted incompletely. "The difficulty which the Council faces in the case of the Katanga does not have its root in the Belgian attitude" is only the beginning of the sentence. Two things follow. First of all, it speaks of "the Belgian attitude . . . as stated to me." And then there follows an explanation: "as the Belgian government acquiesces in the Security Council decisions and therefore undoubtedly will"—in the future tense—"instruct its military elements in the Province to act in accordance with the resolutions as implemented by the United Nations Force."

That is to say, what I wanted to bring out was the fact that the Belgian policy line, to be implemented by action, did not present us with a problem; there was nothing new to expect from that side.

The other statement, the one in my intervention this morning, refers to the situation *de facto,* as of today: "the presence of those troops now is the main cause of continued danger."

I think that the representative of Ceylon will see the connection between the two statements.

Security Council Official Records, Fifteenth Year, 886th meeting.

WHEN THE RESOLUTION was put to the vote the result was 9 votes to none, with 2 abstentions (France and Italy). Thus, for the third time since July 13 the Council acted on the Congo operation without a dissenting vote. For the third time, also, the United States and the Soviet Union voted together in the affirmative though with very different interpretations of what the resolution meant. This time the resolution explicitly invoked Articles 25 and 49, which made compliance with its terms mandatory under Chapter VII of the Charter. The Council adjourned at 4:25 a.m.

7. Exchange of Messages with Tshombé on Entry of the United Nations Force Into Katanga

AUGUST 10, 1960

RIGHT AFTER the Security Council had acted on August 9 the Secretary-General asked Wigny, Lumumba, and Tshombé respectively for assurances that Belgium, the central government of the Congo and the provincial government of Katanga understood and would accept the mandatory requirements of the August 9 resolution and agree to cooperate. Wigny gave an evasively affirmative oral response, subject to consultation after his return to Brussels. Lumumba replied affirmatively on August 10. He welcomed the Council's resolution but added that he awaited the arrival of the Secretary-General "to determine together with him all the measures to be taken to implement the decisions of the Security Council" and that he "would soon enter Katanga with all the members of my government." [1]

Hammarskjöld's message to Tshombé arrived after the latter had sent a cable of his own proposing discussions on the question of UN entry into Katanga. The Secretary-General then sent a second cable on August 10 announcing his intention to arrive on August 12 accompanied by the Deputy Supreme Commander of the UN Force and two companies of the Swedish battalion. The text of this cable and Tshombé's response giving "assurance that you and your party will be received in an orderly manner and with the highest courtesy" follow. [2]

Security Council Official Records, Fifteenth Year, Supplement for July, August, and September 1960, document S/4417/Add. 4.

[1] Security Council Official Records, Supplement for July, August, and September 1960, Fifteeenth Year, document S/4417/Add. 3.

[2] Ibid., document S/4417/Add.4.

(a) Telegram from the Secretary-General to the provincial government of Katanga

I have received your telegram of August 9, 1960, in which you express the desire to study with a delegation from the United Nations the problem which exists in Katanga within the framework of the resolutions of the Security Council. You must have received my telegram of the same date in which I requested you to give me the assurance that you would accept the obligations which are incumbent upon you, as upon all others, under the terms of the resolution of August 9 (S/4426). I regret that I have not yet received a reply from you and such an assurance. Nevertheless, in order to bring about a general pacification as speedily as possible, I propose to discuss personally with you the modalities of the deployment of the United Nations troops in Katanga. There can be no question of conditions or of an agreement, since such arrangements would be contrary to the constitutional rules which determine our relations, but for practical reasons and in view of our desire to contribute to a peaceful development with protection for the democratic rights of all, I feel that it is urgent to have a frank exchange of views with you by which I may be guided in my instructions to my representatives and by which you may be given assurances concerning the rights which the United Nations protects. I expect to arrive at Elisabethville on Friday, August 12, accompanied by General Kettani of Morocco, Deputy Supreme Commander of the United Nations Force, General Rikhye of India, Military Adviser to the Secretary-General for operations in the Congo, civilian advisers from United Nations Headquarters, and two companies of the Swedish battalion, all the military to be in uniform but with the understanding that they will be under my exclusive personal authority and will have only the right of legitimate self-defence in the event—which I rule out as inconceivable—that they are attacked. I am convinced that under the arrangement which I propose it will be possible to eliminate without delay the causes of the armed conflict which is still a threat to all of us. In these conditions I have no doubt that you will share my views as expressed above. I should appreciate an immediate reply inasmuch as it will be necessary for me to leave New York this evening if I am to reach you at the proper time.

DAG HAMMARSKJÖLD
Secretary-General of the United Nations

(b) Telegram from the President of the provincial government of Katanga to the Secretary-General

I have received your telegram of August 10 suggesting a frank exchange of views between us and announcing your arrival on August 12 with two generals, civilian advisers, and two Swedish companies under your personal and exclusive authority. I agree with you that by having such a meeting and acquainting yourself with the real situation, you will be enabled to give your representatives such instructions as will obviate all difficulties and ensure respect for the territorial sovereignty of my government and the free exercise of its rights. I can give you the assurance that you and your party will be received in an orderly manner and with the highest courtesy.

M. TSHOMBÉ
President of the provincial government of Katanga

HAMMARSKJÖLD left for the Congo at midnight on August 10. Before reaching Leopoldville late in the evening of August 11 his plane stopped briefly at Accra. This was announced as a refueling stop, but President Kwame Nkrumah of Ghana met briefly with him at the airport. The Secretary-General received a renewed assurance of Ghana's cooperation in the United Nations Force under the August 9 resolution but the worth of this assurance was put in question by Nkrumah's strong opposition to any United Nations dealings with Tshombé's provincial government and his insistence that the Katanga gendarmerie should be disarmed.[3]

On the way to Leopoldville Hammarskjöld wrote out his interpretation of paragraph 4 of the August 9 resolution, basing himself mainly on the precedent of the United Nations operation in Lebanon in 1958 (see volume IV of this series). When he left Leopoldville early the next morning (August 12) on his flight to Elisabethville he had a copy of this memorandum with him for use in his talks with Tshombé. Ralph Bunche handed another copy to Lumumba that same day.

Before leaving New York Hammarskjöld had told Gizenga and Bomboko of his plan to go to Elisabethville and he felt the central government had thus been sufficiently informed of his intentions. In Leopoldville he deliberately had no contact with Lumumba before proceeding to Katanga. Lumumba could be expected to attempt by any available means to make Hammarskjöld's expedition a joint one with the Central Government and thus perhaps destroy the very basis for the UN breakthrough into Katanga that the Secretary-General had devised.

The Secretary-General's interpretative memorandum was also circulated as a Security Council document (next following text).

---

[3] Nkrumah's position was set forth in a policy statement issued in Accra on August 11 and circulated six days later as a Security Council document (S/4427).

8. Interpretation of Paragraph 4 of the Security Council's Third Resolution on the Congo

LEOPOLDVILLE, THE CONGO   AUGUST 12, 1960

THE SECRETARY-GENERAL, with reference to the Security Council resolution of August 9, 1960 (S/4426), has the honour to inform the Council of the interpretation which he has given to the central government of the Republic of the Congo, as well as to the provincial government of Katanga, of operative paragraph 4 of the resolution.

Memorandum on implementation of the Security Council resolution of August 9, 1960, operative paragraph 4

1. Operative paragraph 4 of the resolution of the Security Council of August 9 reads: "*Reaffirms* that the United Nations Force in the Congo will not be a party to or in any way intervene in or be used to influence the outcome of any internal conflict, constitutional or otherwise." The paragraph has to be read together with operative paragraph 3, which reads: "*Declares* that the entry of the United Nations Force into the Province of Katanga is necessary for the full implementation of this resolution."

2. Guidance for the interpretation of operative paragraph 4 can be found in the attitudes upheld by the Security Council in previous cases where elements of an internal nature have been mixed. The stand of the Security Council in those cases has been consistent. It most clearly emerges from the policy maintained in the case of Lebanon which, therefore, will be analysed here in the first instance.

3. In the Lebanese question, as considered by the Security Council in the summer of 1958, there was a conflict between the constitutional President, Mr. Chamoun, and a group of insurgents, among them Mr. Kar-

Security Council Official Records, Fifteenth Year, Supplement for July, August, and September 1960, document S/4417/Add. 6.

ame, later prime minister of the republic. The government called for United Nations assistance, alleging that a rebellion was fomented from abroad and supported actively by the introduction of volunteers and arms across the border. The request of the government was in the first place that the United Nations should send observers to report on intervention from abroad; however, no clear distinction was made on the part of the government between such observation activities and active assistance from the United Nations in the form of troops for sealing off the border. The Security Council responded by requesting the Secretary-General to dispatch an observer group, which, in fact, at the height of the crisis numbered some five hundred officers. This group of observers was deployed on the side held by the Government as well as on the other side. The observers passed freely between the parts into which the country was divided through civil war. It was perfectly clear that the Security Council considered itself as concerned solely with the possibility of intervention from outside in assistance to the rebels. All observation activities were limited to that problem and the Security Council never raised the question of intervention in support of the constitutional government or in support of the other party. It is clear from the record that had the government side asked for United Nations assistance for protection either in its effort to stop the rebellion or, for example, in an effort to blockade the rebel-held territory, the United Nations would have refused to cooperate. Naturally, the same would have been true of a similar approach from the rebel side in relation to the government side.

4. The importance of this example for the interpretation of operative paragraph 4 of the resolution of August 9 is obvious. There is reason to underscore especially the words in the paragraph that the Force will not "in any way . . . be used to influence the outcome of any internal conflict, constitutional or otherwise." This is, in fact, the first expression in a resolution of the Security Council under Chapter VII of the Charter of the principle applied and approved in the case of Lebanon.

5. As another example of the doctrine upheld by the Security Council, there may be cited its attitude in the Hungarian case, where decisions were directed solely against the intervention of foreign troops in support of the government, without any stand being taken on the relationship between the government and the insurgents.

6. Applied to the situation in Katanga, this means that the United

Nations is directly concerned with the attitude taken by the provincial government of Katanga to the extent that it may be based on the presence of Belgian troops, or as being, for its effectiveness, influenced by that presence. It should, in this context, be noted that the same resolution, of August 9, 1960, which reaffirmed the principle of nonintervention, put the main emphasis on the withdrawal of Belgian troops. Therefore, in the application of operative paragraph 4, as seen in the light of precedents, it can be concluded that if the Belgian troops were withdrawn and if, pending full withdrawal, a Belgian assurance were given to the Secretary-General that the Belgian troops would in no way "intervene in or be used to influence the outcome of" the conflict between the provincial government and the central government—that is to say, that they would remain completely inactive during the phasing out—the question between the provincial government and the central government would be one in which the United Nations would in no sense be a party and on which it could in no sense exert an influence. It might be held that the United Nations is duty bound to uphold the Fundamental Law as the legal constitution and, therefore, should assist the central government in exercising its power in Katanga. However, the United Nations has to observe that, *de facto,* the provincial government is in active opposition—once a Belgian assurance of nonintervention and withdrawal has been given—using only its own military means in order to achieve certain political aims.

7. The view that the United Nations should support the central government, as it functions under the provisional Fundamental Law, and as it is the party which has asked for assistance, is contradicted by the stand maintained in the case of Lebanon, where both those conditions were met and yet the United Nations stood aside and had to stand aside.

8. Applying the line pursued by the Security Council in the Lebanese case to the interpretation of operative paragraph 4, it follows that the United Nations Force cannot be used on behalf of the central government to subdue or to force the provincial government to a specific line of action. It further follows that United Nations facilities cannot be used, for example to transport civilian or military representatives, under the authority of the central government, to Katanga against the decision of the Katanga provincial government. It further follows that the United Nations Force has no duty, or right, to protect civilian or military personnel representing the Central Government, arriving in Katanga, beyond what follows from its general duty to maintain law and order. It finally follows

that the United Nations, naturally, on the other hand, has no right to forbid the central government to take any action which by its own means, in accordance with the purposes and principles of the Charter, it can carry through in relation to Katanga. All these conclusions necessarily apply, *mutatis mutandis,* as regards the provincial government in its relations with the central government.

9. The policy line stated here, in interpretation of operative paragraph 4, represents a unilateral declaration of interpretation by the Secretary-General. It can be contested before the Security Council. And it can be changed by the Security Council through an explanation of its intentions in the resolution of August 9. The finding is not subject to agreement or negotiation.

10. The Secretary-General presents his findings, as to the significance of the operative paragraph in question, to the central government and to the provincial government. If, as expected, the provincial government, on the basis of this declaration, were to admit the free deployment of the United Nations Force in Katanga, but if, on the other hand, the finding and its consequences were to be challenged before the Security Council by others, and the Council were to disapprove of the finding, this would obviously mean a change of assumptions for the actions of the provincial government which would justify a reconsideration of its stand, having been taken in good faith on the basis of the interpretation given by the Secretary-General.

11. Were the findings of the Secretary-General, as regards operative paragraph 4, to be challenged either by the central or by the provincial government, the Secretary-General would immediately report to the Security Council with a request that it consider the interpretation and pronounce itself on its validity. Naturally, the Secretary-General in this context would draw the attention of the Council to its previous stand, and strongly recommend its confirmation of this interpretation.

THERE WERE SECOND THOUGHTS in Tshombé's entourage about the entry of the two Swedish companies of the United Nations Force. When Hammarskjöld's plane approached the Elisabethville airfield, followed by four DC-4's carrying the Swedish soldiers, the control tower told the pilot the troops could not land. The Secretary-General immediately sent a radio message to Tshombé, who was on hand to receive him, that unless permission was given in five minutes for the troops to land all five planes would return to Leopoldville. This got results. Tshombé claimed it was all a misunderstanding and the peaceful entry of the vanguard of United Nations troops into Katanga was accomplished.

Hammarskjöld made his memorandum the basis for his discussions with Tshombé and refused to recognize the latter's right to impose any conditions for the presence and functioning of the United Nations Force in Katanga. Meanwhile Generals Kettani and Rikhye and the staff officers accompanying them held parallel talks with the Belgian military representatives on the withdrawal of the Belgian troops. The successful outcome of these talks was announced in Elisabethville at 3 p.m. on August 13 in the following *communiqués*:

(1)

At the end of the discussions between the Secretary-General of the United Nations and the authorities of the Katanga, the following press release has been issued:

The participants in the talks have made a *tour d'horizon* regarding the problems arising under the Security Council resolutions of July 14, July 22, and August 9. In that context special attention has been given to the modalities for the deployment of the UN Force within the Katanga in accordance with the resolutions. Note has been taken of the principle of noninterference in internal affairs which applies to the activities of such a force and which has been explicitly stated by the Security Council regarding the operation in the Congo in its resolution of August 9.

The Secretary-General has in this context explained the report which he presented on August 12 to the Security Council in elaboration of the principle of noninterference as applied to any UN presence.[1]

(2)

The military representatives who accompany the Secretary-General have made arrangements for the speedy deployment of the UN Force and discussed with the Belgian military representatives immediate withdrawal of the Belgian troops to the bases on arrival of the UN contingents.

Two Swedish companies are already on the spot, having come with the Secretary-General yesterday. The rest of the first contingent of the UN Force will arrive at Elisabethville as well as at other places Monday and Tuesday, August 15 and 16; an advance party to provide for necessary preparations will arrive in Elisabethville tomorrow.

The Secretary-General will leave Elisabethville tomorrow with several members of his party. On his way to Leopoldville he will stop over in Kamina for a first hand acquaintance with the situation and for discussions regarding the modalities for the Belgian withdrawal from the bases.[2]

---

[1] UN Press Release CO/47.
[2] UN Press Release CO/46.

Following further discussions between military representatives of the United Nations and Belgium, the following additional press *communiqué* was issued:

After discussions between the military representatives of the United Nations and of Belgium, it has been decided that the relief of the Belgian troops in the Katanga by United Nations troops will begin today Saturday August 13, 1960 at 5 p.m. local time. From that hour, guard duties and the protection of the airport at Elisabethville will be carried out by Swedish elements of the United Nations Force.[3]

[3] Ibid.

Memorandum on the Organization of the United Nations Civilian Operation in the Republic of the Congo

NEW YORK   AUGUST 11, 1960

A PLAN OF OPERATIONS for the civilian assistance to be provided by the United Nations and the specialized agencies to the Government of the Republic of the Congo was agreed in its essentials early in August despite the pervasive political turmoil and is outlined in the following memorandum circulated as a Security Council document. Kuznetsov visited Cordier on August 16, just before Hammarskjöld's return to Headquarters, to enter a vigorous protest against both the plan for civilian operations and the Secretary-General's interpretation of paragraph 4 of the August 9 resolution. This Soviet position was reaffirmed in strong terms when the Security Council reconvened on August 21.

---

1. WHEN THE SECURITY COUNCIL adopted its resolutions on the United Nations operation in the Congo, it conceived the civilian part of the operation and the military part as interrelated and mutually supporting elements of the assistance. The essential and long-term contribution would be in the civilian field but it required the establishment of order and security. For that reason, the United Nations Force was organized and sent to the Congo pending the reorganization of the national army and police at the same time as steps were taken for the building up of a large-scale civilian assistance activity. The Security Council reflected the latter element of its approach and the basic unity of the operation in its resolution of July 22, 1960 (S/4405), when it invited the "specialized agencies of the United Nations to render to the Secretary-General such assistance as he may require."

2. The basic and necessary unity of the civilian and military operations and the ensuing necessity for centralized organization and leadership within the United Nations family naturally in no way detracts from the

Security Council Official Records, Fifteenth Year, Supplement for July, August, and September 1960, document S/4417/Add. 5.

authority and competence of the specialized agencies. It does, however, introduce a factor which the specialized agencies may be expected to take into account in their own planning; at the same time, the resolution quoted above adds a new obligation for the specialized agencies to render assistance to the United Nations as requested; this follows from the fact that the Security Council decision under Chapter VII of the Charter is mandatory in relation to governments, and therefore necessarily mandatory also in relation to governmental organizations.

3. As regards the development of the civilian activities, they can be based on the traditional pattern and methods of technical assistance and the programme for the provision of operational, executive, and administrative personnel (OPEX), but they must go further. The United Nations must in the situation now facing the Congo go beyond the time-honoured forms for technical assistance in order to do what is necessary, but it has to do it in forms which do not in any way infringe upon the sovereignty of the country or hamper the speedy development of the national administration.

4. The formula suggested, approved by the Government of the Republic of the Congo and, in part, already implemented, is the following. A distinction is made between, on the one side, technical assistance proper, which is in principle on a technical and advisory level, with the experts having the normal relationship to the national government and national administration, and, on the other side, activities on a level of higher administrative responsibility, for which the experts employed must receive a new and so far untried status.

5. The introduction of this latter group into ministries and administrations, in a way accepted for regular technical assistance, might lead to misunderstandings or to a slowing down of the growth of the national administration and false assumptions of responsibilities. The experts chosen for the task and forming the group will be attached to the chief of the United Nations civilian operation, Mr. Stüre Linnér (who is also the resident representative of the Technical Assistance Board), as his consultants, each one having his own and specific administrative responsibility for all activities within the range of his expertise.

6. Thus, the chief of the civilian activities—who in rank and authority will be the opposite number to the Supreme Commander of the United Nations Force as chief of the military activities—will have at his disposal, and be the chairman of, a "consultative group" composed of the senior experts with the responsibilities outlined above in relation to the technical

assistance operations in the various fields which are covered by their respective activities.

7. The members of the consultative group, the status of which has just been defined, would carry the title of consultants to the chief of the civilian operation. They would, however, in accordance with a promise given to the government, be available at the call of the government to give advice on various problems and provide the government with such studies as it may request for the planning of its activities and its decisions.

8. Thus, the consultants, without being accredited to the ministries and having formally functions only within the United Nations orbit, would *de facto* be able to serve, with senior responsibility, at the request of the government, the various ministries and departments. But—and that has to be repeated—they will fulfil the latter function on an *ad hoc* basis and at the specific request of the government.

9. After consultations with the Government of the Republic of the Congo it has been decided that the following fields will have to be covered by the consultants, members of the consultative group:

(*a*) Agriculture;

(*b*) Communications;

(*c*) Education;

(*d*) Finance;

(*e*) Foreign trade;

(*f*) Health;

(*g*) Instruction (national security forces);

(*h*) Labour market;

(*i*) Magistrature;

(*j*) Natural resources and industry;

(*k*) Public administration.

10. It will be observed that in this list certain areas are within the responsibility of one or more specialized agencies. Thus, agriculture corresponds to the field of the Food and Agriculture Organization of the United Nations (FAO), communications correspond to the field of the International Telecommunication Union (ITU), the Universal Postal Union (UPU), the International Civil Aviation Organization (ICAO) and the World Meteorological Organization (WMO) and education to the field of the United Nations Educational, Scientific and Cultural Organization (UNESCO). Health corresponds to the field of the World Health Organization (WHO) and finally, the labour market corresponds to the field of activity of the International Labour Organisation (ILO). In addi-

tion, finance, in part, is a field in which consultations are carried on with the International Bank for Reconstruction and Development (IBRD) and the International Monetary Fund (IMF). In the other cases, the activities are exclusively within the field of the United Nations itself.

11. In order to organize this administrative system in a way which fully reflects the constitutional situation and thus avoids any interference with the activities of the specialized agencies or infringement upon their competence, while reflecting their added responsibilities, the following line has been chosen.

12. The specialized agency concerned appoints a local representative of such seniority as to correspond to the duties which he will have in the field, taking fully into account, on the one side, the scope of the operation, on the other side, his senior responsibilities as adviser to the government at its request. Naturally, the local representative appointed by the specialized agency remains in the regular relationship to his agency and under its authority. Such representatives have already been appointed in several cases and that has in all cases been done in consultation with the United Nations. The Secretary-General, in turn, appoints the local representative of the specialized agency as consultant and member of the consultative group, thus adding to the representative's normal responsibilities, providing for full integration with the other activities and reflecting in an adequate form the basic unity of the total operation. In cases where several agencies are concerned, the appointments have been made by the United Nations in close consultation with the agencies.

13. The activities of the specialized agencies will profit from the fact that they can act under the security provided by the United Nations Force and use the services provided by the United Nations administration and the United Nations communication system and, finally, seek guidance from the head of the whole United Nations operation in the Congo, who has the position of political adviser and personal representative of the Secretary-General; naturally such consultation should take place through the chief of the civilian operation. These advantages obviously add a further reason for the administrative arrangements to which reference has just been made.

14. The Secretary-General has been approached by the Government of the Republic of the Congo with a request for assistance at the earliest possible moment for the establishment of plans for its administrative and economic activities. Special stress has been put on the problem of unemployment. The Secretary-General has likewise been approached by a

number of Member governments with requests for early indication of the needs for technical assistance experts in the various fields with specification as to number and qualifications. These requests indicate a first major task of the consultative group, under the chairmanship of the chief of the civilian operation. It is to be hoped that the group can start its work early next week.

15. The Secretary-General is reluctant to embark on a diffuse programme whose effectiveness would be doubtful until the consultative group has had an opportunity to advise on what is wanted. A number of appointments were necessary to cope with the emergency and these have been, or are being, made. These apart, it is desirable to follow as orderly a course as possible and the consultative group will give its first attention to setting up necessary surveys and working teams to report to it.

16. All posts approved by the Secretary-General will be financed from United Nations funds. This would, of course, not preclude the specialized agencies from financing activities under their regular programmes. It is assumed, however, that such projects would first be the subject of consultation with the chief of the United Nations civilian operation in the Congo and would be coordinated with the total programme outlined by the government of the Republic of the Congo.

17. Ordinarily, the procedure will be that, subject to due approval by, or consultation with, the Government of the Republic of the Congo, the Secretary-General will sanction a number of posts in specified areas of activity; the specialized agencies will then proceed to recruit, contract with, and pay personnel against reimbursement by the United Nations. Until the situation is clearer, the United Nations policy is to grant initial contracts for outside experts only on a short-term basis, namely six months as a maximum. Conditions of service will be in accordance with the rules applicable to technical assistance personnel.

18. The United Nations will reimburse the specialized agencies on the basis of their "extra costs" in respect of all seconded agency staff and technical assistance experts employed by the agencies in posts approved by the United Nations to participate in the United Nations Congo operation on the following basis:

(a) The United Nations will reimburse the agencies for salaries and related costs in respect of any temporary assistance staff required to be employed as replacements for the agencies' regular staff assigned to the Congo.

(b) The United Nations will reimburse the agencies for salaries and related costs in respect of all agreed technical assistance experts employed specifically to participate in the United Nations Congo operation.

(c) The United Nations will reimburse the agencies for transportation and travel subsistence costs incurred in connection with travel to and from the Republic of the Congo for their seconded regular staff and technical assistance experts, but not for any dependants of such personnel.

(d) The United Nations will reimburse the agencies for any extra costs they may incur in connection with death, disability, or illness to their staff members and technical assistance experts employed in the Congo operation.

19. United Nations financial responsibility must be limited to the costs in connection with posts for which it has given advance agreement. United Nations agreement will stipulate the number of posts authorized and may indicate the approximate grade and level contemplated.

20. The Chief Administrative Officer of the United Nations Force in the Congo will provide all administrative services for such personnel, including payment of emoluments and allowances payable in the Republic of the Congo.

LUMUMBA BREAKS WITH
HAMMARSKJÖLD

WHEN THE SECRETARY-GENERAL returned to Leopoldville from Katanga on the evening of August 14 he addressed a letter to Justin Bomboko, the foreign minister, expressing his wish to report to "the Government of the Republic of the Congo" on his mission. He had received no reply to this request but thought Lumumba and Gizenga had accepted his invitation to talk things over when at noon on August 15 the first of three letters arrived in rapid succession from a furious Lumumba. The prime minister totally rejected Hammarskjöld's interpretation of the August 9 resolution, accused him of siding with the Belgians and Tshombé by the manner of his entry into Katanga and made the following demands, among others:

1. To entrust the task of guarding all the airfields of the Republic to troops of the National Army and the Congolese police in place of United Nations troops.

2. To send immediately to Katanga Moroccan, Guinean, Ghanaian, Ethiopian, Malian, Tunisian, Sudanese, Liberian, and Congolese troops.

3. To put aircraft at the disposal of the Government of the Republic for the transportation of Congolese troops and civilians engaged in restoring order throughout the country.

4. To proceed immediately to seize all arms and ammunition distributed by the Belgians in Katanga to the partisans of the rebel government, whether Congolese or foreign, and to put at the disposal of the Government of the Republic the arms and ammunition so seized, as they are the property of the Government.

5. To withdraw all non-African troops from Katanga immediately.

I hope that you will signify your agreement to the foregoing. If my government does not receive satisfaction it will be obliged to take other steps.[1]

Hammarskjöld replied that the dispute would have to be submitted to the Security Council. If his offers to talk things over and report to the government were not accepted, he planned to leave for New York that evening.

In the course of this correspondence Lumumba included a denunciation of Hammarskjöld for his "manoeuvers in sending to Katanga only troops from Sweden—a country which is known by public opinion to have special affinities with the Belgian royal family."[2] He concluded with the following statement:

[1] Security Council Official Records, Fifteenth Year, Supplement for July, August, and September 1960, document S/4417/Add. 7.

[2] Ibid. (*Editors note:* King Baudouin of Belgium was the son of King Leopold and the former Princess Astrid of Sweden).

In view of all the foregoing, the government and people of the Congo have lost their confidence in the Secretary-General of the United Nations. Accordingly, we request the Security Council today to send immediately to the Congo a group of observers representing the following countries: Morocco, Tunisia, Ethiopia, Ghana, Guinea, the United Arab Republic, Sudan, Ceylon, Liberia, Mali, Burma, India, Afghanistan, and Lebanon. The task of these observers will be to ensure the immediate and entire application of the Security Council resolutions of July 14 and 22 and August 9, 1960. I earnestly hope that the Security Council, in which we place our full confidence, will grant our legitimate request. A delegation of the government will accompany you, in order to express its views to the Security Council. I would therefore ask you kindly to delay your departure by twenty-four hours in order to permit our delegation to travel on the same aircraft."[3]

Hammarskjöld replied that Lumumba's letters with their demands and denunciations would all be circulated as Security Council documents. He declined the proposal to accommodate Lumumba's delegation in his plane but promised that the Council would not meet until after the Congo's representatives had arrived.

The Council was not able to meet until August 21. In the meantime Lumumba declared a state of emergency and secretly appealed to the Soviet Union for transport planes and trucks which would enable units of the Armée nationale congolaise (ANC), formerly the *Force publique,* to attempt an invasion of Katanga. The hysteria which now marked many of his public denunciations of the policies pursued by the Secretary-General resulted in two ugly incidents involving United Nations personnel on August 17 and 18. In one of these unruly ANC soldiers suddenly attacked and seized Canadian members of the UN Force at the Leopoldville airport, in response to rumors that they were Belgian paratroopers in disguise. Hammarskjöld immediately addressed the following *note verbale* to the government (first following text).

[3] Ibid.

---

1. Protest to Government of the Congo Concerning Hostile Incidents

NEW YORK   AUGUST 18, 1960

---

1. THE SECRETARY-GENERAL PRESENTS his compliments to the Government of the Republic of the Congo and has the honour to present the following formal and serious protest.

Security Council Official Records, Fifteenth Year, Supplement for July, August, and September 1960, document S/4417/Add. 8, annex II.

2. The Secretary-General has been informed about the incident which took place this morning when units of the Congolese National Army at the Ndjili Airport interfered with an Indian aircraft in the United Nations service and searched and manhandled Canadian personnel working for the United Nations under the United Nations command. It was only through the intervention of Generals Iyassou of Ethiopia and Rikhye of India that worse consequences from this interference than those which occurred did not take place.

3. The Secretary-General has further received a report on the treatment of United Nations security personnel when, on Wednesday, August 17, they tried to deliver a letter to the prime minister from the personal representative of the Secretary-General, Mr. Bunche. They were detained, searched and under threat of being shot, worse developments than those that occurred being stopped only by the interference of a noncommissioned officer of the United Nations guard.

4. It must be apparent to the government that unlawful acts like the ones described here and which, under all circumstances, would be highly reprehensible, must be regarded as even more serious when directed against the United Nations and its representatives, acting in the Congo at the request of the government.

5. The government has stated its intention of complying with the mandatory decision of the Security Council calling for full cooperation by all Member governments under Article 49 of the Charter. The government has further, through a basic agreement regarding the presence of the United Nations Force, bound itself to the obligation to pursue its policy in relation to the Force on the basis of good faith as regards all conditions relating to its presence.

6. Continued occurrences of the type reported would lead to conditions which would render the work of the United Nations in assistance of the Congo practically impossible. Such a development might therefore make it necessary for the Secretary-General to submit to the Security Council for reconsideration all the United Nations activities in the Congo. In these circumstances the Secretary-General expects that the government will immediately take all measures necessary to forestall the recurrence of any such incidents as those to which this protest refers.

7. The Secretary-General wishes to point out that the United Nations has put its resources at the disposal of the Republic of the Congo in the form and to the extent that such a service to the Republic of the Congo serves the overriding purpose of maintaining international peace and security. That purpose was the basis for the decision of the Security Council

and the further development of the United Nations activities will be determined by it.

ON JULY 19 Col. Joseph Mobutu, chief of staff of the Armée nationale congolaise, sent to Ralph Bunche a letter of regret on behalf of the Congolese Army for the Ndjili airport incident, and requested him to offer apologies also to the Canadian government and the officers who had been assaulted.[1] Strong disciplinary measures had been taken against the Congolese soldiers involved. Lumumba and Gizenga, however, excused the soldiers and repeated the myth about Belgians returning under UN disguise.

Also on the table before the Security Council session began on Sunday, August 21, were two more Soviet government statements, both dated August 20.[2] These gave full support to Lumumba's complaints and termed Hammarskjöld's plan for the United Nations civilian operation entirely unacceptable because the predominance of experts from the United States and its allies indicated apparent intention "to turn the abortive Belgian intervention into an American one camouflaged under the United Nations flag." Lumumba also sent a letter to the President of the Security Council reaffirming the position he had taken on August 15.[3]

Finally the Secretary-General brought the Council up to date on the strength and deployment of the United Nations Force in the Congo in a final addendum to his report of August 6. There were now 14,500 men on duty, including contingents from Ethiopia, Ghana, Guinea, Ireland, Liberia, Mali, Morocco, Sudan, Sweden, and Tunisia, with another 500 men from the United Arab Republic due to arrive in a day or two and a battalion from Indonesia expected when transportation could be arranged. Units were now deployed at scores of centers located in all the provinces of the republic.[4]

The Secretary-General was the first speaker when the Council convened at 12:30 p.m. and he gave an extensive oral report on developments which minced no words (next following text).

---

[1] Security Council Official Records, Fifteenth Year, Supplement for July, August, and September 1960, document S/4449.
[2] Ibid., documents S/4446 and S/4450.
[3] Ibid., document S/4448.
[4] Ibid., document S/4417/Add. 10.

2. *Opening Statement in the Security Council*

NEW YORK   AUGUST 21, 1960

AT THE MOMENT WHEN the unity of the territory of the Congo and the people of the Congo was manifested by the establishment all over the Republic of the presence of the United Nations Force under a unified command, at the moment when the United Nations Force was deployed in strength in Katanga, at the moment when the Belgian withdrawal was under way even from the Kamina base, the actions and attitudes of the United Nations, and in particular of its Secretary-General, came under severe criticism from the prime minister of the Congo. This criticism was followed by a series of actions against officials in the service of the United Nations which, whatever the immediate cause might have been for those actions, gave an impression of deep distrust and hostility fomented for political ends. They were of a nature to call for a formal and serious protest. If continued, they may create such great difficulties for all the United Nations activities in the Congo that they may finally force me to raise the question of a reconsideration of those activities by the competent United Nations organs.

Recently, we have had to register a number of unprecedented allegations in communications addressed to me or stated in press conferences, and also various complaints raised on a level on which I do not believe the Security Council would wish to pursue this matter. However, the Council should, in my view, give the numerous statements to which I am referring a careful study. They are both causes and symptoms of a deterioration for which I cannot find any valid substantive reasons.

I can understand susceptibilities and tensions developing in a difficult situation and I take them fully into account. I can understand also how in a state of disintegration those who are supposed to be the agents of the law may be the first to break it. However, whatever the explanation of the actions and reactions to which I have referred, they have created for the

Security Council Official Records, Fifteenth Year, 887th meeting.

United Nations a most delicate position in which the very dignity of the Organization and of the governments which it represents sometimes has been put in question.

In order to carry out my mandate, I have been forced to act with great firmness in relation to many parties. One of them has been the central government itself. I do not believe that I have ever failed in courtesy. On the other hand, I do not excuse myself for having stated clearly the prin- ciples of the Charter and for having acted independently on their basis, mindful of the dignity of the Organization—and to have done so whether it suited all those we are trying to help or not. Nor have I forgotten that the ultimate purpose of the United Nations services to the Republic of the Congo is to protect international peace and security, and that, to the extent that the difficulties facing the Republic are not of a nature to endanger international peace, they are not of our concern.

In the *note verbale* which I had to address to the Government of the Republic of the Congo three days ago, I said:

> The Secretary-General wishes to point out that the United Nations has put its resources at the disposal of the Republic of the Congo in the form and to the extent such a service to the Republic of the Congo serves the overriding purpose of maintaining international peace and security. That purpose was the basis for the decision of the Security Council and the further development of the United Nations activities will be determined by it.

Is it because the Government of the Republic has not understood this, is it because of frustration at the discovery of the limits this principle puts on the ways in which the United Nations can serve in the Congo, that we are now blamed? However, also, the Congo belongs to a world in which its people must integrate themselves on a basis of equal rights and equal duties with others, following the law which is above us all.

I shall now turn to the questions of substance which are facing us. First, a word about my contact with Mr. Tshombé.

The first time the possibility of a personal contact with him was raised was during my first visit to Leopoldville, when, presiding over a meeting of the Council of Ministers, the vice-prime minister asked me whether I would consider establishing such a contact. My reply was that I, for my part, had no objection, but that I would be guided by the reaction of the Council of Ministers. It emerged from the discussion that, at that stage, the Council of Ministers preferred that such a contact, in preparation of the entry of the United Nations Force, were established not be me per- sonally, but by Mr. Bunche as my personal representative. This, however, was not for any reasons of principle but in order to reduce the risk that the contact be exploited in propaganda, as indicating a recognition by me of a special Katanga problem. Thus, the question of the United Nations contact with Mr. Tshombé, which was recognized as desirable, was then regarded as a question of form and presentation. The question arose in this form, if I understood the situation correctly, in large part because of the ambiguity regarding Katanga which still might be said to be found in the resolutions of the Security Council.

Later, when I announced the departure of Mr. Bunche, it is true that "le Conseil du cabinet du Vice-Premier Ministre" asked for the inclusion of three representatives of the government in Mr. Bunche's party, and that this request was later repeated from the same source. However, as appears from documents circulated to the Council, the request which, if accepted, would have changed fundamentally the character of Mr. Bunche's contact with Mr. Tshombé, was, once I had rejected it, not endorsed by the Council of Ministers.

For reasons known to the Council, the mission of Mr. Bunche did not succeed. The effort showed us that an attempt to move the United Nations troops into Katanga, in the situation then prevailing and as envisaged, would meet with organized armed resistance.

In the Security Council discussion on the Katanga problem the words "vicious circle" were used (886th meeting), to characterize the situation facing the United Nations. The term was adequate in view of this armed resistance against landings of United Nations troops, combined with the fact that the entry of United Nations troops was a condition for the withdrawal of Belgian troops, and that the withdrawal of Belgian troops, in turn, seemed to be the condition for the breaking of the armed resistance.

I arrived, after the meeting of the Security Council, at the conclusion that two things were necessary in order to break the vicious circle without falling back on whatever assistance might eventually be forthcoming from the Belgian side. The first one was not to separate the civilian approach from the military one. The second one was to make the civilian approach on a level where the full weight of the United Nations was brought to bear on the issue, this irrespective of any objections as to form. An approach of the type thus indicated by previous experiences was facilitated by the fact that the new Security Council resolution (S/4426) had eliminated all ambiguity and that, therefore, no question of presentation should any longer exist in the way which had hampered us at the previous stage.

In these circumstances, I felt that we had to try to achieve a speedy withdrawal of Belgian troops by staging a breakthrough for the United Nations Force into Katanga with token units accompanying me personally. All other lines of action seemed more uncertain and definitely slower in their effect.

This decision being reached, keeping in reserve the possibility of Belgian assistance at our entry as a less promising alternative that I might fall back on if the attempt failed, I approached, the day after the Security Council had adopted its resolution, Mr. Tshombé along the line mentioned. As appears from a memorandum circulated to the Security Council, I immediately briefed the Congolese delegation about my plan, without, in the first instance, giving the details, but later giving full information about the approach and its necessary timetable. I did so without meeting any objections from their side. This seemed to me natural in view of the circumstances, the previous reasons for hesitation being eliminated by the Security Council and the previous experience showing that nothing short of what I tried to do was likely to succeed in a sufficiently near future.

I followed through on my plan with all the speed necessary in view of the fact that every delay might reduce the chances of success. The approach worked, and, at present, the Security Council resolution is being fully implemented in Katanga. The way in which I operated is being criticized by spokesmen of the Republic of the Congo as contrary to the aims pursued. Let me ask, what were then their aims: the speediest possible withdrawal of Belgian troops while order and security were maintained by the United Nations troops? If so, my approach proved to be adequate. Or was it something different?

As is well known to the Council, I had made it clear to the provincial authorities, before my visit to Elisabethville, that there could be no agreements nor any talk about conditions. Once the presence of the United Nations Force in Katanga was an established fact, I had only to explain its function, rights, and duties as stated by me already before my visit in the memorandum circulated as Addendum No. 6 to my second report; it may here be noted that this memorandum was handed to the prime minister of the Republic of the Congo before I used it in my own talks in Katanga.

There is another point which may merit some short observations. Immediately on my return from Elisabethville, on the evening of August 14, I sought contact with the central government and sent to the minister for foreign affairs a letter requesting an opportunity to report to the government. That letter was received by the minister for foreign affairs soon after midnight on August 15. Between 11 and 12 o'clock the same morning, I invited the prime minister and the deputy prime minister to come to my office and see me in the afternoon of the same day, and the invitation was accepted. At noon, I received the letter in which the prime minister presented his criticism of my stand and of the United Nations action. You are well acquainted with this letter which has been circulated as a Security Council document.

I shall not comment on the rest of the somewhat lively correspondence of that day beyond saying that I kept my plans open until 10 p.m. that evening, without having received any reply to my request for a meeting with the government and without having received the guests whom I had invited and whose invitation I had not cancelled.

I am sorry to have taken even a few minutes of the time of the Council with what may look like trivialities. I have not done so in order to criticize anything which has or has not been done by the spokesmen of the government. My only reason is that the data are necessary as comments to the correspondence which I have had to circulate to the Council and, thus, form part of the record on which the Security Council will have to base its evaluation of the problems facing the United Nations in this matter.

After these clarifications which I think should dispose of all the marginal issues which have been raised in these recent days, I wish to turn to the two matters which rightly can claim the attention of the Council. The first one is the question of the Belgian withdrawal; the second one is the question of the mandate of the United Nations Force in relation to the internal conflict which had developed in the Congo.

Before the breakthrough into Katanga, all Belgian troops were already withdrawn from the five other provinces of the Republic of the Congo, except for the Kitona base in the province of Leopoldville. In the ten days between Mr. Bunche's visit and mine, Belgian troops in Katanga had been reduced from 8,600 to 3,600, out of which latter number 1,000 are technicians essential to civilian activities in Kamina. The withdrawal started in Elisabethville the day after the arrival of the first United Nations troops, that is to say, Saturday, August 13. It has continued in and from Katanga, including Kamina, throughout the past week, and the

withdrawal of the remaining combat troops is going on at a pace determined solely by the availability of air transport. It is going on in the same
way also from Kitona, where 500 technicians are placed presenting the
same practical problem as the technicians in Kamina.

I have received the formal assurance of the Belgian government of
completion of the withdrawal of all combat troops within, at the most,
eight days. The question to which the Council has given primary consideration in the case of the Congo, that is to say the withdrawal of the
Belgian troops, can thus be now regarded as definitely resolved. Some
delay in the evacuation from Kamina and Kitona of noncombat personnel should not be attributed to Belgian resistance to the move, but results
from the responsibility, which will now be that of the United Nations, of
assisting the country in the maintenance of the substantial Congolese
population so fully dependent on the bases for the security of their work
and income. Whatever Belgian noncombat personnel may have to be
retained for some time at the bases, I anticipate that, in less than a week,
the last soldiers will have left.

It is recognized, of course, that there may be certain problems resulting
from any delay in the departure of even the noncombat Belgian personnel. Having particularly in mind the reality of suspicion as a potent fact
in the society, the United Nations should undertake to ensure that the
bases will in no way be used and that the personnel retained in them will
not engage in political or propaganda activities of any kind, and that
there will be no interference in the internal affairs of the State.

I should perhaps at this point add a footnote on the legal situation as
regards the bases. Many legal and economic interests are involved, and,
for that reason, negotiations concerning the handing-over of the bases to
the Republic of the Congo were foreseen in the General Treaty of Friendship, Assistance, and Co-operation of June 29, 1960. Obviously, the temporary takeover by the United Nations of the bases, in assistance to the
country, does not mean that the United Nations has resolved or taken a
stand on these various legal problems. The temporary United Nations
administration, on the contrary, must be established with the clear understanding that all rights involved are reserved for later negotiation. Thus,
in the language of the Charter, this administration must be regarded as a
provisional measure without prejudice to the rights or claims of the parties concerned. If we had had to wait for the necessary negotiations before the temporary take-over, it would have delayed the withdrawal of
Belgian troops in a way which was not acceptable. The formula indicated

thus is the only one which, in the circumstances, can resolve the immediate problem.

Indeed, with this short summary of the Belgian withdrawal, and with the resulting vacuum filled by the United Nations, we should be entitled to regard the chapter of the Congo story which describes the situation as one of a threat to international peace and security as being close to the end. This is said in the firm expectation, of course, that we need not envisage a risk from any new developments in the Congo outside the framework firmly established by the Security Council and contrary to the attitude on action by foreign troops that the Council has taken in this as in other cases. It is said also in the firm expectation that the Government of the Republic will take such measures as are within its power to assist the United Nations Force in carrying out the Council's decision and, thus, helping to bring about the order and stability necessary to avoid future eruptions.

Other chapters are to unfold, but they relate to the construction of the state and the laying of foundations for a balanced political, economic, and social life for the people. In the long run, they are more important than the chapter which has come to an end, but they are only indirectly within the sphere of the responsibility of the Security Council, whatever importance they may have for the United Nations in its effort to help Africa to achieve its rightful place in our political and economic world of today.

With the short reference which I have just made to the problems really facing the United Nations in the Congo, it is with some hesitation that I turn to the legal question concerning the functions and authority of the United Nations Force. I do so not because I can regard it as a matter to which the Security Council should give attention equal to the one required by the question of withdrawal, but in order to see to it that the record of the United Nations is kept straight.

Before I turn to that task, I would, with your permission, give an indication of my intentions on a practical problem, closely related to the withdrawal of Belgian troops and to the deployment of the United Nations Force.

The distinguished representative of the Soviet Union, at a recent meeting of the Security Council, raised the question of an advisory committee. I have given further thought to his idea. I should now welcome a more formal and regular arrangement for the current and highly useful consultations which I have with the countries contributing units to the United

Nations Force. If that would not meet with any objection from the Council, it would therefore be my intention to invite the representatives of those countries to serve as members of an advisory committee to the Secretary-General personally, following the pattern established by the advisory committee functioning for the United Nations Emergency Force in the Middle East.

In its resolution of August 9, 1960, the Security Council declared, in operative paragraph 3, that: ". . . the entry of the United Nations Force into the Province of Katanga is necessary for the full implementation of this resolution." It further reaffirmed, in operative paragraph 4: ". . . that the United Nations Force in the Congo will not be a party to or in any way intervene in or be used to influence the outcome of any internal conflict, constitutional or otherwise."

I have later circulated as Addendum No. 6 to my second report a memorandum on the implementation of operative paragraph 4 of the said resolution.

In a letter from the prime minister of the Republic of the Congo, dated August 14, 1960, and—as already mentioned—received at noon the following day, the interpretation given by me in that memorandum has been challenged. This challenge is based mainly on an interpretation of the resolution of the Security Council of July 14, 1960, that is the first resolution and in particular on the words in that resolution authorizing the Secretary-General "to provide the Government (of the Republic of the Congo) with such military assistance as may be necessary"; attention is also given to the phrase that steps should be taken "in consultation with" the government.

Although the interpretation I have given to operative paragraph 4 of the resolution of August 9 seems to me to be incontestable in the light of the Charter, of the debate preceding the adoption of the resolution of July 14, of the relevant paragraphs of my first report as "commended" by the Security Council, and by the following debates and resolutions, in particular the resolution of August 9, as well as in the light of previous Security Council and General Assembly practices, the argument now put forward requires an analysis.

In the light of the legal history of the matter, I do not see any reason for the Security Council to confirm my interpretation of the functions of the United Nations Force in the respect now challenged. Should, on the other hand, any member of the Council be at variance with my interpretation on the basis indicated by the prime minister of the Republic of the

Congo, or on any other basis, I am sure that they may wish to give expression, in a draft resolution, to what they consider to be the right interpretation.

After these introductory observations on the legal problem, I shall now go into an evaluation of the arguments used in criticism of my interpretation.

The reason given for the consent to send military assistance to the Congo, which is to be found in the resolution of July 14 and which was presented by the Secretary-General without contradiction from the Council, may be summed up as follows. Order and security in the Congo had broken down. The way in which they were maintained was not acceptable, as the presence of Belgian troops was a source of internal and international tension. The withdrawal of Belgian troops and the introduction of the United Nations Force, pending the reestablishment of order and security by normal means, were therefore indicated in order to overcome a situation which represented a threat to peace and security.

Although reference had been made in the Security Council to the claim of independence by the provincial authorities of Katanga, there is nothing in the record leading up to the resolution which indicates that the Council, when discussing such military assistance "as may be necessary" intended that such assistance be used to subdue the revolt in the province of Katanga. It would indeed have been necessary, as a minimum, that the Council should state explicitly such an intention, if the Secretary-General were expected to act in a way contrary to his express statement that United Nations forces in the Republic of the Congo could "not take any action which would make them a party to internal conflicts in the country." This statement, it is emphasized, was not challenged by any member of the Council in the debate which preceded the adoption of the resolution of July 14, 1960. Certainly, the Council cannot be deemed to have instructed the Secretary-General, without stating so explicitly, to act beyond the scope of his own request or contrary to the specific limitation regarding nonintervention in internal conflicts which he stated to the Council. Moreover, in the light of the domestic jurisdiction limitation of the Charter, it must be assumed that the Council would not authorize the Secretary-General to intervene with armed troops in an internal conflict, when the Council had not specifically adopted enforcement measures under Articles 41 and 42 of Chapter VII of the Charter.

This interpretation is further borne out by my subsequent reports and the debates and resolutions of the Council. Before the meeting of the

Security Council resulting in the adoption of the resolution of July 22 I had presented to the Council my first report containing also an elaboration of the principles determining the actions of the United Nations Force. From this report the following paragraph should be quoted in full:

Although the United Nations Force under the resolution is dispatched to the Congo at the request of the government and will be present in the Congo with its consent, and although it may be considered as serving as an arm of the Government for the maintenance of order and protection of life—tasks which naturally belong to the national authorities and which will pass to such authorities as soon as, in the view of the government, they are sufficiently firmly established—the Force is necessarily under the exclusive command of the United Nations, vested in the Secretary-General under the control of the Security Council. This is in accordance with the principles generally applied by the Organization. The Force is thus not under the orders of the government, nor can it, as I pointed out in my statement to the Council (873rd meeting), be permitted to become a party to any internal conflict. A departure from this principle would seriously endanger the impartiality of the United Nations and of the operation.

Also the following paragraph in this report should be quoted:

The authority granted to the United Nations Force cannot be exercised within the Congo either in competition with representatives of the host government or in cooperation with them in any joint operation. This naturally applies *a fortiori* to representatives and military units of other governments than the host government. Thus, the United Nations operation must be separate and distinct from activities by any national authorities.

Significantly, no representative dissented from the principle of nonintervention thus asserted by me, and my report was "commended," as I recall, by the Council in its resolution of July 22. It must therefore be concluded that the Council endorsed the principles which the Secretary-General set forth in that report.

Finally, it should be noted that, in operative paragraph 4 of the resolution of August 9, the Council "reaffirms" that the United Nations Force would not be used to influence the outcome of any internal conflict. The use of the word "reaffirms" shows that the Council was expressly stating what had previously been the understanding of the earlier resolutions and, in this sense operative paragraph 4 of the resolution of August 9 must be considered as decisive in interpreting the military assistance "as may be necessary" referred to in the resolution of July 14.

In the development leading up to the resolution of July 22, it was I who gave the interpretation that the two steps explicitly requested by the Council referred to the whole of the territory of the Republic of the

Congo on the formal ground that this territory was so established earlier in the month when the republic had been recommended by the Council for admission to the United Nations.

This interpretation of mine was confirmed by the Council in the last paragraph of the preamble of its resolution of July 22, still, however, without any precision as to how the Council regarded the conflict between local authorities in Katanga and the central government. There is nothing in the debate nor in the arguments given in favour of the new resolution which went beyond the two purposes for the United Nations military operation as stated and recognized, that is to say, the maintenance of order and security by the United Nations troops combined with the withdrawal of Belgian troops, the former being the means to the latter as a main political end. Had it, at this stage, become the intention of the Council that the troops should be used for the further purpose of subduing the rebellion, it would, as already noted, have been obvious that this would have had to be explicitly said.

It was not until in my introductory statement in the debate leading up to the resolution of August 9 that the issue of Katanga was presented for decision, and it was then so presented in order to arrive at the reaffirmation of the right of the United Nations Force to enter Katanga and the obligation of the Belgian troops to leave Katanga. It was made clear in my own statements and in those of a majority of the members of the Council that, given the withdrawal of the Belgian troops from Katanga, the conflict between the central government and the provincial authorities was an internal matter, constitutional or otherwise. Neither in my presentation nor from the sponsors or supporters of the resolution did it emerge that United Nations troops—in contradiction to the whole history of the case up to that stage—would be introduced in order to impose the authority of the central government on the rebellious provincial leaders. On the contrary, the current of thought characterizing the debate was that the United Nations Force could not and should not force its way into Katanga, but should arrive there on a basis of acceptance by the Katanga authorities of the Security Council decisions as worded. It is for that reason characteristic that operative paragraph 3, which requested the presence of United Nations troops in Katanga, was combined with operative paragraph 4, "reaffirming" that the Force would not "be used to influence the outcome of any internal conflict, constitutional or otherwise." Why should that have been said in this context, if not in order to make it clear that the presence of the United Nations troops in Katanga, as requested, was not intended to be an instrument to be used to influence the conflict of the provincial authorities with the central government?

I repeat what I have already said: I do not ask for a confirmation by the Security Council of the obvious. Whatever the development within the Council, I would have achieved the aim of my request of the Security Council to convene at this stage, that aim being solely, in the light of the views presented by the Prime Minister of the Republic of the Congo, to arrive at a clarification of the attitude of the Council.

In concluding, let me look at the future. The Belgian chapter in the history of the Congo in its earlier forms is ended. The United Nations, thus manifesting the unity of the territory and the people, is all over the area in charge of order and security, creating an umbrella under which the people of the Congo should be able to find its way to peace and to create the forms of government and administration under which it wishes to live. Can the United Nations do more? Yes, in one respect: by putting its technical resources at the disposal of the people of the Congo in assistance in the enormous tasks it is facing. But apart from the protection which the United Nations gives to normal civilian life, its contribution cannot go beyond assistance to the people. The decisions will have to be those of the people, the choices will be theirs and the creation of a political structure which will provide a stable and constructive government, must be theirs. It must be theirs to find, along the road of reconciliation, compromise, and agreement, marked by willingness to put the interests of the nation above the interests of groups, areas, or individuals.

Is it too much to expect that it will be understood that a period of utter crisis and disintegration is one in which those who work for their personal benefit are acting against the interest of the people of the country, while those who work for the interest of the people of the country will find that they themselves have profited by their self-oblivion in submission to the common cause?

The United Nations stands ready to help also in the creative process to which I referred, but it can help only to the extent that it is requested to help and to the extent that it meets with a confidence rising above considerations of nationality and race which are contrary to the very spirit of universality, fundamental to the Charter, a spirit in which, alone, Africa—and the Congo as one part of Africa—can find its rightful place in the international community of nations.

In the perspective just outlined, the tensions of the moment disappear and even the Belgian intervention and the Security Council counteraction are reduced to an episode. This meeting of the Security Council would rise above the reasons which have made it necessary if we were to look towards the real problems of the future. The needs of the moment may falsify our perspectives. It seems to me to be time to look ahead and to brush aside those conflicts and divergencies of views and emotions, which for too long have delayed a concentrated effort to mold the people of the Congo into a happy and prosperous state, adding to the stability and progress of Africa and thereby contributing to the peace of the world.

THIS TIME it was Antoine Gizenga, instead of the more moderate Bomboko, who represented the Congolese government before the Security Council. Gizenga repeated the demands Lumumba had made in his letters to the Secretary-General and the President of the Council, and complained that "if the resolutions of the Security Council continue to be badly interpreted, this will not lead to the liberation of the Congo but to the effective reconquest of the country."[1] His complaints included the fantasies about Belgian paratroopers disguising themselves as United Nations officials. Belgians were also stealing UN identity cards, Gizenga asserted, and he added a new version of Lumumba's complaint against the Secretary-General for bringing only Swedish members of the UN Force with him when he flew to Elisabethville on August 12. He had done this at Tshombé's bidding, Gizenga charged, not knowing that the purpose was to permit Belgians to disguise themselves as part of the Swedish contingent. After Gizenga spoke, Hammarskjöld made the brief comments that follow.

[1] Security Council Official Records, Fifteenth Year, 887th meeting.

---

3. Second Statement During Council Debate

NEW YORK   AUGUST 21, 1960

AS THE REPRESENTATIVE OF the Republic of the Congo has asked for the right later on to be permitted to give a "mise au point" of this or that statement of mine, it may not be considered inappropriate if I myself exercise that same right at this stage of the debate. I shall not take up the

Security Council Official Records, Fifteenth Year, 888th meeting.

time of the Council by such a "mise au point" of all the various points which might call for it in the statement of the representative of the Republic of the Congo, as in fact most of them have been covered by what I have already said myself. However, there are a few points which may merit the attention of the Council.

It was said that the supreme commander of the United Nations Force had gone to Katanga under certain conditions which were described by the representative of the Republic of the Congo. This obviously refers to the first stage and to Dr. Bunche, who as you know, is my personal representative. I have already told the Council under what circumstances Dr. Bunche's contact came about. I have no reason to discuss the way in which Mr. Tshombé later presented the situation to the press. If he gave publicity to the fact that I intended to go to the Security Council if our entry was not permitted, he certainly did not reveal anything in his favour.

The representative of the Republic of the Congo also complained that I brought the matter back to the Security Council at that stage without consulting his government. May I remind him of the fact that the relations between the Secretary-General and the Council are not to be interfered with by any government. In this case, the criticism seems all the more unnecessary, as I went to the Security Council in the best interest of the central government of the Congo.

It would be useless to state again that I neither negotiated nor had any agreement with Mr. Tshombé. In fact, he never even presented his so-called conditions to the United Nations.

The representative of the Republic of the Congo also enumerated certain steps which he qualified as "maladresses." There are only two which I think merit comment here. First, I can assure the representative that the discipline of the Swedish army is such that no people in disguise are able to figure as members of the Swedish troops. Secondly, if I used two Swedish companies as my personal support at the Katanga breakthrough, while, as he knows, the troops following the vanguard had an overwhelming majority of Africans, it was simply because I wanted to reduce the risks of a failure of the breakthrough to an absolute minimum by establishing an identity between myself and the troops.

It would be tempting to go into the questions of the armband and of the identity card of Mr. Dieu, but I shall abstain because they cannot be considered relevant to the serious matter which is under consideration by the Council.

Naturally, I reserve my right to ask to speak again not in order to engage in any polemics but in order to avoid that the debate of the Security Council be deviated by misinformation.

THE NEXT TWO SPEAKERS were Caba Sory of Guinea, who had requested an opportunity to make a statement, and V.V. Kuznetsov of the USSR. On instructions from Sékou Touré, Caba Sory gave Guinea's support to Lumumba's demands though refraining from direct personal criticism of the Secretary-General. Kuznetsov repeated the Soviet Union's rejection of Hammarskjöld's interpretation of paragraph 4 of the August 9 resolution and its opposition to his plan for civilian assistance to the Congo. He alleged that UN troops had orders to fire if Congolese soldiers attempted to enter the airport at Leopoldville, blamed Hammarskjöld for introducing soldiers from Canada, "an ally of Belgium under NATO," against the wishes of the Congolese government and demanded their immediate withdrawal. In general, Kuznetsov reaffirmed Soviet backing for all of Lumumba's demands. In view of later developments it may especially be noted that he declared that the Congolese army should be given control of all airports and seaports and that the United Nations should provide to the government of the Congo "aircraft for transporting Congolese to any part of its territory where their presence is considered necessary."[1]

The Secretary-General responded immediately (next following text).

[1] Security Council Official Records, Fifteenth Year, 888th meeting.

---

4. Third Statement During Council Debate

NEW YORK   AUGUST 21, 1960

IN MY LAST INTERVENTION I said that I had no intention, nor is it my right, to engage in polemics; and I will not do so. But I do believe that it might be helpful to the members of the Council if I presented a few clarifications on points which seem to have been overlooked or misunderstood.

First of all, as to the military situation. The representative of the Soviet Union seemed to understand that there were 3,600 troops at Kamina on

Security Council Official Records, Fifteenth Year, 888th meeting.

a certain date, the 17th, and he asked what other troops there might be around. The latest information we have—the exact information—which I could not use in my speech this morning, is as follows: in Katanga, 1,700; in Kamina, 600; in Kitona, 300—a sum total of 2,600 combat troops. That covers the whole field, and for that reason there is no gap which need give rise to any question.

Attention was drawn to the unfortunate incident at the Leopoldville airfield the other day, and it was stressed that Canadians were involved. That is true. But the unfortunate happenings were directed just as much against Moroccans and Indians; that is to say, I cannot find that the situation, as such, indicates any specially bad position for the Canadians.

I would, in this context, like to draw the attention of the Council to document S/4449, which is a letter from the chief of staff of the Congolese national army. I shall read just two paragraphs from it:

> We deeply regret that clear instructions were not given to the company on duty at the airport in time to prevent the deplorable incident which has just occurred at Ndjili. We hope that it will be possible in the future to station liaison officers here—preferably French-speaking—so that they may cooperate with the Congolese military authorities in controlling traffic at the Leopoldville airport.
>
> We have in any case taken strong measures to deal with the Congolese soldiers responsible for the Ndjili incident.

This is a letter to Dr. Bunche from the chief of staff of the Congolese national army.

The Security Council has also before it a document which should clarify the question about instructions and from which I should like to read out the following paragraph. This is a quotation from the comments made by Dr. Bunche on the situation as regards the right of the troops in the field:

> Again, in its directive on "protection of internal security," the United Nations command states that "the principal purpose of the United Nations Force in the Congo as defined in the proposal to the Security Council is to assist the government in maintaining law and order. In pursuing this purpose, the United Nations operation in the Congo should exhaust all possible peaceful means of keeping order before any resort to force. Every effort should be exerted to avoid harm to anyone, since public reaction to the employment of force by United Nations personnel might well prove disastrous to the success of the entire United Nations operation.
>
> "Firing, even in self-defence, should be resorted to only in extreme instances. Any effort to disarm members of the United Nations Force is to be regarded as a legitimate cause for self-defence. This principle should be interpreted in the light of the overriding force of principle."

I think that this quotation makes it perfectly clear that we have applied a most restrictive interpretation of the right of self-defence. I believe also that the incident at the airport shows that this is practised, because indeed there was no resort to armed force.

Another point is the question of the composition of the Force. An observation has been made that Canada, as a NATO power, is a less desirable country, if I may express it that way. The Council will remember that in the basic report which it had before it at the meetings of July 21 and 22, I discussed this question of composition and I applied the rule which was approved previously to the case of the United Nations Emergency Force in the United Arab Republic. That rule was simply that forces from any of the permanent members of the Security Council should be excluded, and I read "forces" in a very extensive sense, that is to say, it includes units or higher command of any kind. Beyond that, the Security Council has not given me any guidance as to composition.

There is also another rule, and that is that no country which can be considered as having a direct interest in the conflict should be permitted to send forces. In this peculiar and specific situation, this has not, in my view, limited my choice. For practical reasons it is, in the Canadian case, a question of signals—I had to get good technicians, preferably bilingual. I could not find them in any other country than Canada. I regret that for reasons which are outside my control, for example, a request to the Polish government to furnish a solid military medical unit has not led to any result. In any event, I do not look at membership in either NATO or the Warsaw Pact or any other grouping of that kind as excluding a country from participating in the operation. And I wish, of course, to maintain a balanced geographic composition at all events. I can in this context mention that the countries with which we are at present having negotiations concerning added battalions are the United Arab Republic, Indonesia, and Sudan; as regards smaller units, India, Ceylon, and Burma. I think that clearly indicates that I move in the area where the considerations which here gave rise to some worry do not apply.

I turn now to another matter. There was obviously a feeling that I was, as it was said, acting openly against the Security Council decisions. I must say that that observation worries me a little bit. At the same time, it gives me some consolation because, quite frankly, I had the impression that I had to a certain extent overburdened the Security Council by coming back to it and asking for this and that kind of clarification and amplification. Certainly I have tried to keep very closely in touch with the opinion of the Council.

Another point was that I granted the same position to Mr. Tshombé and the local authorities in Katanga as to the central government. That is not so. The United Nations and the Secretary-General negotiate solely with sovereign governments and not with private persons or local authorities. There is a very distinct difference, constitutional in law and in fact, as regards our relations to the two groupings mentioned.

As regards the question whether the line we have been following does not in fact mean that we come to support Mr. Tshombé, I can draw attention to one thing which, if I remember correctly, was said in the document circulated as addendum 6 to my second report: We cannot, we will not, and we have no right to raise any resistance to any move made by the central government to assert its authority in Katanga. The other thing is that we cannot lend our active support, contrary to the principles announced here on a couple of occasions, to efforts of the central government. The two things should be kept apart. It should not be concluded from the fact that we cannot lend active support to the central government that we lend any kind of support to the other party, strengthen its hand, or resist any moves from the central government.

I come now to a somewhat difficult question of law and the position of the Security Council. I do not want here in any way to argue. I have already said that I do not want to go into any kind of polemics. Let me simply point out that the Security Council has asked me to implement the resolution. Implementation obviously means interpretation in the first instance. I gave an interpretation and that interpretation was challenged. I have referred the matter back to the Security Council. I have the right to expect guidance. That guidance can be given in many forms. But it should be obvious that if the Security Council says nothing I have no other choice than to follow my conviction.

I turn now to the broader field of civilian activities which was raised and on which I should like to present some information. Members of the Council will have seen document S/4447 regarding the matter. As is clear from that document, these people whom we have introduced as consultants have indeed a new and untried status. But as I say, this latter status is, in relation to the national administration, a weaker one than that of technical assistance in the conventional sense. They are in fact our internal administrators for the United Nations operation, the contact of which with the government is regular technical assistance. Under such circumstances, I do not feel that there is any reason for me to clarify that these men cannot have and will not have any executive authority or responsibility.

On this point I can give the Council a rather interesting example of how the matter is handled by the central government. I have to translate from a document in French which we have received today:

After an exchange of views which has taken place between Mr. Kabangui, minister of planning and economic co-ordination, especially charged by the Government of the Congo with relations with the United Nations, and Mr. Stüre Linner, chief of the civilian operations of the United Nations, it has been decided to create a commission which should visit the provinces of Kasai, Kivu, the Orientale province, and that of l'Equateur.

This mixed commission is composed as follows:

Representing the central government: Mr. Kabangi, minister of planning and economic co-ordination; Mr. Lutula, minister of agriculture; Mr. Mussampa, chef de cabinet in the ministry of the middle classes; Mr. Kambo, chef de cabinet in the ministry of work; Mr. Kambuy, secretary in the ministry of health; Mr. Sokomy, chef de cabinet in the ministry of agriculture; Professor Verhagen, chef de cabinet in the ministry of planning.

On the United Nations side and on the side of specialized agencies there are only four representatives. There is Mr. David from the United Nations; he is Haitian. Mr. Sundaram from the International Telecommunication Union; if I am correctly informed he is an Indian or perhaps a Ceylonese. Then there is Dr. Kesteven from the Food and Agriculture Organization and Dr. Soliman from the World Health Organization.

This represents the kind of cooperation we have in mind. It represents the way in which our consultants are used by the central government. I do feel that, even without going into any details of the work of this special commission, it clearly indicates that that arrangement is one which has been welcomed in practice by the central government.

I agree with the representative of the Soviet Union that the geographical distribution is not satisfactory. Nor is it satisfactory here. In the Secretariat we have fifteen years back of us. In this operation we have five weeks, and five very hectic weeks. We have had to try to find people who were good technical experts, reasonably fluent in French, and who at least had good English. We had further to rely very heavily upon the recruitment arranged by the specialized agencies. We could not possibly take care of all matters from here. The result is not what I would like to see and things will certainly be adjusted as time passes. I think I can assure the Council that to the extent that technicians with the proper background and schooling are available from various areas, they will be recruited in such a way as at least to give us a reasonable approach to the desirable geographical distribution.

This whole civilian operation is basically a technical assistance operation and should, of course, follow the rules applied for technical assistance, also as regards decisions. That means that the Economic and Social Council, the Third Committee, and the General Assembly will have to deal with the matter. It is not within the range of the direct responsibilities of the Security Council.

The other arrangement, that is to say the consultant arrangement, is, as I said, an arrangement which refers to the way in which we secretariat-wise organize our work. For good or for bad I have had to assume the responsibility for that under Article 101 of the Charter.

In various interventions, reference has been made to the question of some kind of group, and it was mentioned that I now seemed to favour a group of observers, or whatever they should be called, to be sent to the Congo. I want to make it clear that that is not what I proposed. I proposed a parallel to the Advisory Committee established in the case of the United Nations Emergency Force; that is to say, an advisory committee meeting with the Secretary-General, it may be here or, in some cases, it may be in the Congo. But to station it in the Congo when I have to be here either for the Security Council or for the General Assembly would deprive me of the advantages of current consultation.

There is one point which has also been raised in some interventions, and that is the question of national governments' wishes as regards the employment of their troops. I think it must be clear that military operations of this kind have to be under a unified command exercising its authority and its judgement as best it can. If we were to try to meet desires expressed by the very many participating governments, then I think that operation would very soon come to a deadlock.

For that reason, while on the one side we naturally listen carefully to, and seriously consider, the wishes expressed by governments, it would be against the efficiency of the whole operation if it were considered necessary for us to take their wishes into account when they run counter to other considerations of a military and technical nature.

Mr. President, my last point is only to remind you that when we come to the question of Kamina and Kitona there are two problems. One is the problem of withdrawal of combat troops, and I repeat what I said in my initial statement. I have the formal assurance of the Government of Belgium that all soldiers will be out of the Congo within less than eight days.

What remain are technicians in Kamina and Kitona, and out of a sense of responsibility for the Congolese who depend for their livelihood and for their lives upon the activities of those two bases, I cannot ask for the withdrawal of those people short of being able to put others in their place, and I beg you to understand that that is not an easy operation.

[The PRESIDENT (translated from French): The Secretary-General has asked for the floor in order to make a correction.]

Mr. President, I apologize to the Council, but I made a mistake on one of the points on which I wished to give information. I said that we had requested a military medical unit from Poland. This was not the case. We have requested one ordnance company, to establish a base ordnance depot at Leopoldville, and five forward detachments or brigades; and further one veterinary team consisting of one hygiene officer and two assistants. The first point is obviously an important one; it is a purely military outfit.

The Polish government, to its own regret and to my regret, was not able to meet our demand, pointing out, among other things, that for the time being they had to take into consideration the fact that the recent floods in Poland required the mobilization of all available means to remove their disastrous results.

WITH THE EXCEPTION of the Soviet Union and Poland the members of the Security Council endorsed the course followed by the Secretary-General. Mongi Slim of Tunisia and Sir Claude Corea of Ceylon, the spokesmen for Africa and Asia on the Council, did not falter in maintaining their complete support for Hammarskjöld's conduct of the Congo operation. Among the African states only Guinea at this point had given unreserved endorsement of Lumumba's program, without joining in his attacks on Hammarskjöld. The West maintained its support of the Secretary-General, though Britain and France thought he tended to press the Belgians too hard on withdrawal. Before the last of three successive meetings of the Council ended shortly before 2 a.m. on August 22, Kuznetsov announced he would not press for a vote on a draft resolution he had introduced to send to the Congo a group of representatives of the countries contributing to the UN Force in order to oversee the operation on the spot. No other resolution was introduced. Kuznetsov knew he would lose on any attempt to challenge the Secretary-General's interpretation of his mandate and the latter's supporters naturally refrained from attempting a resolution endorsing his stand that would invite a Soviet veto.

Introduction to the Fifteenth Annual Report

NEW YORK   AUGUST 31, 1960

SOMEHOW HAMMARSKJÖLD FOUND TIME in the midst of dealing hour by hour with all the crises and complexities of the Congo operation to produce, in the Introduction to the fifteenth Annual Report of the Secretary-General, a policy statement of such sound historical perspective that its message is for the most part as valid and as applicable to international affairs in the 1970s as it was when he wrote it in August 1960.

I

On January 1, 1960, the former trust territory of the Cameroons under French administration became independent. For the first time a territory previously under United Nations trusteeship became an independent state by itself, thus giving full effect to the objective stated in Article 76 b of the Charter that the United Nations shall "promote the political, economic, social, and educational advancement of the inhabitants of the Trust Territories, and their progressive development towards self-government or independence. . . ."

The event which thus marked the first day of 1960 has been followed by the accession to independence by many more African states, among them two additional trust territories, the Togolese Republic and the Republic of Somalia. By the time the General Assembly meets, fourteen African states will have been recommended by the Security Council for admission as new members of the United Nations. It can confidently be expected that the Federation of Nigeria will apply for membership soon after the opening of the General Assembly; the admission of all these new states would bring the number of African Member states of the United Nations from ten at the end of 1959 to twenty-five at the fifteenth session of the General Assembly.

Another new member has also been recommended for admission; I have in mind Cyprus, the independence of which has brought to an end a

General Assembly Official Records, Fifteenth Session, Supplement No. 1A (A/4390/ Add.1).

long-standing conflict considered at several sessions of the General Assembly.

It is not only the development into independence and into membership in the United Nations of a great number of African states which, for the Organization, characterizes the year 1960, so symbolically inaugurated by the independence of an African trust territory. The developments in the Republic of the Congo have engaged the United Nations in the greatest single task which it has had to handle by its own means and on its own conditions.

In these circumstances it may be appropriate for this introduction to the Annual Report of the Secretary-General to the General Assembly to give attention, in the first place, to the problem of Africa and its importance for the international community.

Historically, Africa is not a unit. While North Africa and parts of East and West Africa have significant traditional links to the Mediterranean, to Islam or even to Southern Asia, West, East, and Central Africa south of the Sahara have received a significant impact from different European colonial administrations, varying in length and intensity, linking them, however tenuously, to institutions of a few European countries. The southern part of the continent has a development of its own, which finds but few parallels in the rest of Africa.

Not only have these diverse influences in Africa's past relations with the outside world led to divisions on the continent, but the manner and form in which colonial rule has been exercised have tended to accentuate these divisions. There are great differences between the evolution in areas formerly under British control and those formerly under French control, and there are even greater differences between these areas and the territories which were administered by Belgium. This applies to language, to certain traditions established, to legal ideas transmitted, and particularly to the ways in which political development for these territories was conceived and advanced.

The differences thus superimposed by recent history are reinforced by underlying diversities of race and national history. In these respects, Africa is much less homogeneous than South or South-East Asia, not to speak of Europe or Latin America. There are not only basic differences between the Arabs and Berbers living in the northern part of the continent and Africans south of the Sahara, but among the latter the impact of the environment, and of the great distances and difficulties of communication, has tended to create populations with very distinct differences in attitude and approach which are deeper and wider than tribal differences existing in other parts of the continent.

Finally, in Africa the first beginnings can now be seen of those conflicts between ideologies and interests which split the world. Africa is still, in comparison with other areas, a virgin territory which many have found reason to believe can or should be won for their aims and interests.

It is in the face of all this that the United Nations has, in the great task which it is facing in the Congo, appealed to "African solidarity within the framework of the United Nations". As the developments have shown, this is not a mere phrase; it applies to something which has become a reality. It is my firm conviction that the African states cannot render themselves and their peoples a greater service than to foster this solidarity. Likewise, I am convinced that the United Nations cannot render its new African Member states and the whole community of nations in Africa a greater service than to assist them, within the framework of their own efforts, to mould their new national and regional life, now that they enter the community of nations, in ways that will give Africa its rightful place on the international scene.

It is for the African states themselves to define the elements which establish the basis for African solidarity. It is also for them to find and define the aims which this regional community should pursue. But, also, for one not belonging to the region, it is possible, in the light of experiences, especially as they have evolved during the Congo crisis, to give some general indications.

There are negative elements in the picture, only too natural in the light of history. I have in mind the strong anticolonialism which has created a marked resistance against any suspected attempt to interfere or to impose from outside a will foreign to the will of the peoples. There are, of course, also elements of racism, just as understandable in the light of experience, which, however, are strongly rejected by forward-looking, responsible leaders. It is a mistake to see in any of these reactions a hostility in principle against peoples of other races or regions. Expressed in positive terms, as it should be, the attitude is one of willingness to cooperate with the rest of the world and one of eagerness to integrate into the rest of the world, combined, however, with a firm rejection of any attempts by others to turn the efforts of the African states to achieve this cooperation and integration into subjection, be it political, economic, or ideological.

Reactions from the outside have been mixed. There are those who try to maintain what history has already judged. There are those who try to put in place of the past new and more subtle forms of predominance and influence. There are, on the other hand, also those for whom independence is an end in itself, irrespective of whether or not, in the form in which it can be offered, it serves the best interest of the people. There are, finally, those who, using these various reactions and counter reactions, try to manipulate them for their own ends.

The attitude of the United Nations in this situation seems to me to be clear; it follows from the aims of the Charter. The Organization must further and support policies aiming at independence, not only in the constitutional sense but in every sense of the word, protecting the possibilities of the African peoples to choose their own way without undue influences being exercised and without attempts to abuse the situation. This must be true in all fields—the political, the economic, as well as the ideological— if independence is to have a real meaning. Working for these purposes, the United Nations can build on the confidence of the best and most responsible elements of all the countries of the continent. As a universal organization neutral in the Big Power struggles over ideology and influence in the world, subordinated to the common will of the Member governments and free from any aspirations of its own to power and influence over any group or nation, the United Nations can render service which can be received without suspicion and which can be absorbed without influencing the free choice of the peoples.

These possibilities of the United Nations create a corresponding responsibility. If the Organization is willing and able to face its duties, it will have given the new nations of Africa the framework of which they are in need during the first and sensitive years of independence. It will also be helping the African world, in solidarity, to determine its own political personality in the setting of universality as represented by the United Nations. If it faces these tasks and succeeds in them, it will make a vitally necessary contribution to international peace and to a more stable world.

In spite of all the divisions mentioned, African solidarity is a fact. Its growth is something that rightly should be hailed by other regions and by all nations, whatever the legacy of past relationships and whatever immediate political aims may seem to be countered by the growth of such solidarity.

The African states have realized that to grow into independence means to grow into interdependence. But to grow into interdependence means also to assume international responsibility and such international responsibility must be based on national responsibility. The contribution made from independent Member states in Africa to the Congo operation has shown that African solidarity within the framework of the United Nations can build on a strong sense of national responsibility, radiating into the international sphere and creating the interdependence in which independence can yield its most rewarding results.

II

The African developments are putting the United Nations to a test both as regards the functions of its parliamentary institutions and as regards the efficiency and strength of its executive capacity.

The considerable increase in the membership of the United Nations stemming from a region with short independent experience in international politics has led to doubts regarding the possibility of the General Assembly and its committees to work expeditiously and in a way which truly reflects considered world opinion. In this context the question of the voting system has again been raised.

In previous reports to the General Assembly I have touched on this problem, indicating as my conviction that there is no practical alternative in keeping with the basic tenets of the Charter to the present system of equal votes for all sovereign Member states. Naturally it may be said that the irrationality of such a system is demonstrated when a new voting balance can be achieved through a sudden expansion of the number of Members by some 20 percent. However, this fails to take into account realities to which reference has likewise been made in previous reports.

The General Assembly is a body which reflects in its decisions on major questions the results of long and careful negotiations and consideration. During this process, common lines are elaborated and compromises reached which give to the decisions the character of a confirmation of a negotiated approach rather than of a solution achieved through the mechanics of voting. Furthermore, the background of the decisions of the General Assembly, which, of course, anyway have the character of recommendations, should be analysed in order to arrive at a true evaluation of their significance. A voting victory or a voting defeat may be of short-lived significance. What is regarded as responsible world opinion as reflected in the voting and in the debates is in many respects more important than any formally registered result.

There is in the views expressed in favour of weighted voting an implied lack of confidence in the seriousness and responsibility with which newly independent states are likely to take their stands. Such a lack of confidence is not warranted by the history of the United Nations and must be rejected as contrary to facts. Neither size, nor wealth, nor age is historically to be regarded as a guarantee for the quality of the international policy pursued by any nation.

It is my conviction that the addition of a great number of new Member states will widen the perspectives, enrich the debate and bring the United Nations closer to present-day realities. I also believe that this development will exercise a sound influence in the direction of a democratization of proceedings by lessening the influence of firm groupings with firm engagements.

However, the widened membership does create certain practical problems. It may tend to lengthen debates, and it may make the General Assembly proceedings seem too cumbersome in cases where speed and efficiency are of the essence. For that reason, the development directs attention again to the possibilities for improving the methods applied in the parliamentary institutions of the Organization. Thus, I feel that Member nations may wish to consider a greater role for the General Committee, so that it can assume a wider responsibility for the conduct of the work of the General Assembly and eventually ease the burden of the Assembly and its substantive committees.

If and when the question of Charter revision comes up for consideration, the evolution of the General Assembly also is likely to add weight to the question of the role, composition, and procedures of the Security Council.

During the Suez and Hungary crises, a development took place through which increased responsibilities were temporarily transferred from the Security Council to the General Assembly. Since it is difficult for the General Assembly to act expeditiously if it is required to engage in detailed consideration of complicated legal and technical problems, the Assembly found that the most adequate way to meet the challenges which it had to face was to entrust the Secretary-General with wide executive tasks on the basis of mandates of a general nature.

Especially in the Suez crisis, when all the executive work was entrusted to the Secretary-General, this put the Secretariat to a severe test. However, it proved possible, in close interplay between the General Assembly and the Secretary-General, assisted by the Advisory Committee appointed by the General Assembly, to work smoothly and swiftly towards a speedy achievement of the established aims. The value and possibilities of the Secretariat as an executive organ were thus proved, a fact which has in significant ways influenced later developments.

Without going into detail, I wish to recall that in the Lebanon crisis the General Assembly came into the picture only at a very late stage, while executive action in the earlier phases of the crisis was guided by the Security Council, which for the purpose availed itself of the services of the Secretary-General. Likewise, the first part of the Laos crisis was entirely in the hands of the Security Council.

This year has seen a further return of the Security Council to its central role as the organ of the United Nations which carries primary responsibility for peace and security. Thus, the question of South Africa and especially the question of the Congo have been major tasks with which the Council has been exclusively seized. The reason for this return to the Security Council from the General Assembly is, naturally, that both these questions have been of a nature which has to a degree placed them outside the conflicts between the main power blocs. The shift of the emphasis back from the General Assembly to the Security Council has, however, not led to a change of working methods, as the Council, following the recent procedures of the Assembly, has used the services of the Secretariat and the Secretary-General as its main executive agent.

The Congo crisis has put the Secretariat under the heaviest strain which it has ever had to face. The organization of a sizable military force under very difficult geographical and physical conditions, the creation of the necessary administrative framework for the military operation, and the development of a far-reaching civilian programme to meet the most urgent needs of the country's economy have proved possible thanks only to the unstinting willingness of all Secretariat members to assume added burdens and the availability of a great number of people of a sufficiently general background to take up new assignments, sometimes far beyond and far different from their normal professional work. I wish on this point to pay a tribute to all those members of the Secretariat who have made the Congo operation possible.

The activities entrusted to the Secretariat by the Security Council in the case of the Congo have been widespread and have required an unusual combination of elements which normally would have required a much bigger and more specialized machinery than the one of which the United Nations disposes. The interplay between parliamentary operations in the United Nations, political action, diplomatic negotiation, military operations, and administrative measures has been subtle and exacting. To the extent that it may be said to have worked and to have led to the desired results, it bears witness of a flexibility in the organization of the work of the United Nations which is encouraging for the future.

Naturally, however, the experiences have demonstrated also weaknesses in the organization of the Secretariat. It does not dispose of a sufficient number of highly qualified senior officials for all the tasks that now have to be met—in spite of the feelings sometimes voiced that the Organization is "top-heavy." There is, generally speaking, within the Secretariat not enough of a diplomatic tradition or staff with training in political and diplomatic field activities to meet the needs which have developed over the years. And it is, finally, a considerable weakness that the Secretariat has not in its ranks a highly qualified military expertise which is able, on a current basis, to maintain a state of preparedness for the kind of situation which the Organization has suddenly had to face. It is, of course, not my intention that in these various respects the Secretariat should be normally organized so as to be able to meet without difficulty or added strain a crisis of the Congo type. What I have in mind is only that it is desirable to have within the Secretariat a nucleus which can be switched over to the present type of task with full knowledge of the requirements and proper preparation, while leaving the normal work of the Organization intact because of the availability of sufficient second-line reserves.

I have mentioned the need for some strengthening of the Secretariat on the military side. This, in the light of recent experience, would be my reply, as regards actions by the United Nations, to those who have found in the Congo developments new reasons for the organization of a standing United Nations force. As I have already clarified my views on this problem in earlier reports to the General Assembly, I have no reason to go into the matter in any detail here. It should, however, be stressed that the Congo experience has strengthened my conviction that the organization of a standing United Nations force would represent an unnecessary and impractical measure, especially in view of the fact that every new situation and crisis which the Organization will have to face is likely to present new problems as to the best adjustment of the composition of a force, its equipment, its training, and its organization.

It is an entirely different matter if governments, in a position and willing to do so, would maintain a state of preparedness so as to be able to meet possible demands from the United Nations. And it is also an en-

tirely different matter, for the Organization itself, to have a state of preparedness with considerable flexibility and in the hands of a qualified
staff which quickly and smoothly can adjust their plans to new situations
and assist the Secretary-General in the crucially important first stages of
the execution of a decision by the main organs to set up a United Nations
force, whatever its type or task.

The value of such preparedness can be seen from the fact that the
organization of the United Nations Force in the Congo was considerably
facilitated by the fact that it was possible for the Secretary-General to
draw on the experience of the United Nations Emergency Force in Gaza
and on the conclusions regarding various questions of principle and law
which had been reached on the basis of that experience. The Congo
operation being far more complicated and far bigger than the Gaza operation, it is likely that it will lead to a new series of valuable experiences
which should be fully utilized by the United Nations, by appropriate
informal planning within the administration.

III

On various points the preceding observations have touched upon the
ideological conflicts and the conflicts of power which divide our world of
today. .

There is no reason to elaborate here the way in which these major
conflicts have influenced proceedings within the United Nations and even
the constitutional pattern which has developed in practice. One word
may, however, be said about the possibilities of substantive action by the
United Nations in a split world.

Fundamental though the differences splitting our world are, the areas
which are not committed in the major conflicts are still considerable.
Whether the countries concerned call themselves noncommitted, neutral,
neutralist, or something else, they have all found it not to be in harmony
with their role and interests in world politics to tie their policies, in a
general sense, to any one of the blocs or to any specific line of action
supported by one of the sides in the major conflict. The reasons for such
attitudes vary. That, however, is less important in this special context
than the fact that conflicts arising within the noncommitted areas offer
opportunities for solutions which avoid an aggravation of Big Power differences and can remain uninfluenced by them. There is thus a field
within which international conflicts may be faced and solved with such

harmony between the power blocs as was anticipated as a condition for Security Council action in San Francisco. Agreement may be achieved because of a mutual interest among the Big Powers to avoid having a regional or local conflict drawn into the sphere of bloc politics.

With its constitution and structure, it is extremely difficult for the United Nations to exercise an influence on problems which are clearly and definitely within the orbit of present day conflicts between power blocs. If a specific conflict is within that orbit, it can be assumed that the Security Council is rendered inactive, and it may be feared that even positions taken by the General Assembly would follow lines strongly influenced by considerations only indirectly related to the concrete difficulty under consideration. Whatever the attitude of the General Assembly and the Security Council, it is in such cases also practically impossible for the Secretary-General to operate effectively with the means put at his disposal, short of risking seriously to impair the usefulness of his office for the Organization in all the other cases for which the services of the United Nations Secretariat are needed.

This clearly defines the main field of useful activity of the United Nations in its efforts to prevent conflicts or to solve conflicts. Those efforts must aim at keeping newly arising conflicts outside the sphere of bloc differences. Further, in the case of conflicts on the margin of, or inside, the sphere of bloc differences, the United Nations should seek to bring such conflicts out of this sphere through solutions aiming, in the first instance, at their strict localization. In doing so, the Organization and its agents have to lay down a policy line, but this will then not be for one party against another, but for the general purpose of avoiding an extension or achieving a reduction of the area into which the bloc conflicts penetrate.

Experience indicates that the preventive diplomacy, to which the efforts of the United Nations must thus to a large extent be directed, is of special significance in cases where the original conflict may be said either to be the result of, or to imply risks for, the creation of a power vacuum between the main blocs. Preventive action in such cases must in the first place aim at filling the vacuum so that it will not provoke action from any of the major parties, the initiative for which might be taken for preventive purposes but might in turn lead to counteraction from the other side. The ways in which a vacuum can be filled by the United Nations so as to forestall such initiatives differ from case to case, but they have this in common: temporarily, and pending the filling of a vacuum by normal means, the United Nations enters the picture on the basis of its noncommitment to any power bloc, so as to provide to the extent possible a guarantee in relation to all parties against initiatives from others.

The special need and the special possibilities for what I here call preventive United Nations diplomacy have been demonstrated in several recent cases, such as Suez and Gaza, Lebanon and Jordan, Laos, and the Congo.

A study of the records of the conflicts to which I have just referred shows how it has been possible to use the means and methods of the United Nations for the purposes I have indicated. In all cases, whatever the immediate reason for the United Nations initiative, the Organization has moved so as to forestall developments which might draw the specific conflict, openly or actively, into the sphere of power bloc differences. It has done so by introducing itself into the picture, sometimes with very modest means, sometimes in strength, so as to eliminate a political, economic and social, or military vacuum.

The view expressed here as to the special possibilities and responsibilities of the Organization in situations of a vacuum has reached an unusually clear expression in the case of the Congo. There, the main argument presented for United Nations intervention was the breakdown of law and order, the rejection of the attempt to maintain order by foreign troops, and the introduction of the United Nations Force so as to create the basis for the withdrawal of the foreign troops and for the forestalling of initiatives to introduce any other foreign troops into the territory with the obvious risks for widening international conflict which would ensue.

Whether the Congo operation is characterized as a case of preventive diplomacy, or as a move in order to fill a vacuum and to forestall the international risks created by the development of such a vacuum, or as a policy aimed at the localization of a conflict with potentially wide international repercussions, is not essential. Whatever the description, the political reality remains. It is a policy which is justified by the wish of the international community to avoid this important area being split by bloc conflicts. It is a policy rendered possible by the fact that both blocs have an interest in avoiding such an extension of the area of conflict because of the threatening consequences, were the localization of the conflict to fail.

Those who look with impatience at present-day efforts by the United Nations to resolve major international problems are inclined to neglect, or to misread, the significance of the efforts which can be made by the United Nations in the field of practical politics in order to guide the international community in a direction of growing stability. They see the incapacity of the United Nations to resolve the major bloc conflicts as an argument against the very form of international cooperation which the Organization represents. In doing so, they forget what the Organization has achieved and can achieve, through its activities regarding conflicts which are initially only on the margin of, or outside, the bloc conflicts, but which, unless solved or localized, might widen the bloc conflicts and seriously aggravate them. Thus the Organization in fact also exercises a most important, though indirect, influence on the conflicts between the power blocs by preventing the widening of the geographical and political area covered by these conflicts and by providing for solutions whenever the interests of all parties in a localization of conflict can be mobilized in favour of its efforts.

The Organization in this way also makes a significant contribution in the direction of an ultimate solution of the differences between the power blocs, as it is obvious that it is a condition for an improvement in the situation that the area to which those differences apply, as a minimum requirement, is not permitted to expand and, so far as possible, is reduced.

It is with this background that the initiative for United Nations intervention in the Congo conflict was taken under Article 99 of the Charter, for the first time applied fully, according to its letter and in the spirit in which it must have been drafted. It is also in this light that one has to view the fact that not only the first but also the subsequent decisions in the Security Council regarding the Congo have been taken by votes in which the power bloc conflicts have not been reflected.

These observations are of special interest when we turn to the consideration of questions regarding which the power bloc interests openly clash. I have in mind especially disarmament. In general terms, it is not surprising that, in the case of problems so deeply related to the security of many nations and to the predominant powers within the different blocs, negotiations have presented extraordinary difficulties. On the other hand, it is also evident that there is a latitude within which a shared interest in avoiding an aggravation of the situation overrides the specific security interests of any one party and within which, for that reason, agreement may be possible.

De facto, we have seen such an agreement developing in the field of nuclear tests. I believe that there are also other questions within the field of disarmament regarding which success is possible for new efforts to reach agreement, on at least so much of a common de facto policy as is indicated by the mutual interest to avoid a widening of the substantive basis for the present day race towards a world crisis. Approached in this way, disarmament seems to offer important possibilities, still incompletely explored, of a gradual reduction of the area in which clashing security interests so far have rendered formal agreement impossible.

There is no contradiction between this application to the disarmament problem of the philosophy and practices successfully tried by the United Nations in specific conflicts and the view that there can be no solution to the disarmament problem short of the acceptance of total disarmament under satisfactory control by both sides. The pragmatic approach and the, so to say, global one are not at variance, for it is obvious that efforts to avoid a widening of the field of conflict and to reduce the area in which concrete agreement for the moment is impossible should at all events be integrated into a wider, more far-reaching plan under which the security interests of the parties can be balanced out against each other in ways that will make it possible for the parties to reach the ideal target of total disarmament.

It is certainly not productive to approach the disarmament problem solely on a pragmatic basis, without integration of the steps taken into a plan ultimately aiming at full disarmament. Likewise, however, it seems unrealistic to approach the total problem oblivious of the fact that all political experience and all previous negotiation show that the road to progress lies in the direction of efforts to contain and reduce the area of disagreement by mobilizing such common interests as may exist and as may override other and special interests tending in the opposite direction.

The Members of the General Assembly will excuse me for presenting these general observations on a problem to which the Assembly has devoted so much attention. I have done so only because it seems to me that the experiences from other political fields in which the United Nations has acted with success have a bearing also on a field like this one where, so far, the Organization has failed to achieve results.

IV

The responsibilities and possibilities of the Organization in the exercise of preventive diplomacy apply also to the economic sphere. Far less dramatic in their impact as the economic activities must be, they are of decisive long-term significance for the welfare of the international community. In the end, the United Nations is likely to be judged not so much by the criterion of how successfully it has overcome this or that crisis as by the significance of its total contribution towards building the kind of world community in which such crises will no longer be inevitable.

This aim, naturally, cannot be reached overnight, nor can it be considerably furthered by any institutional or constitutional reforms of the United Nations. It cannot even be achieved by the political resolution of the conflicts which today divide the major powers. Essential though such a political resolution would be, it would not by itself ensure stability and peace in the face of the dangerous economic and social vacuum created and maintained by the enormous gap which separates countries at different stages of development.

In the enduring task of bridging the gulf between countries, all Member nations, whether developed or underdeveloped, whether in the East or the West, have a common interest. This common interest is recognized by everyone. It is clearly stated in the Charter of the United Nations, in which countries pledge themselves to take joint and separate action in cooperation with the Organization to promote "higher standards of living, full employment and conditions of economic and social progress and development." It is reflected in all of the debates of the Economic and Social Council as well as of the General Assembly on the relevant items. It has borne fruit in a host of activities within the United Nations and its sister institutions. And yet, in considering the rate of progress that has been made in relation to the task that remains to be achieved, it is difficult to escape a feeling of disappointment.

It is true that the mere recognition of the community of interest in the economic development of underdeveloped countries itself represents a major step forward. And the expressions of common interest in economic development are no lip service. The achievements of the United Nations family in the economic and social field, as generously supported by Member governments, demonstrates their seriousness. However, it must, in the context of a newly emerging Africa, be registered, in a spirit of candid realism, that the rate of achievement is not at all commensurate with the needs.

The coincidence of interest in the economic field stems from the economic interdependence of the world community. The degree of interdependence has been increasing rapidly, partly as the inevitable outcome of an accelerating rate of advance in science and technology, partly owing to the emergence of the countries of the continents of Asia and of Africa to independence and full participation in the affairs of the world at large, but, to a significant degree, also as a result of economic forces making for a growing integration of the world community.

For the first time in history, the concept of a world economy has come to take on a significant meaning not only for the student of economics but also for the statesman and the layman.

Unfortunately, this growing interdependence has recently been reflected much less in efforts and activities within the United Nations than outside it. The United Nations can welcome regional arrangements among neighbouring or like-minded countries; as long as such arrangements are so designed as to reinforce rather than to supplant the common effort towards establishing conditions of economic and social progress, they have an important role to play. A real danger arises, however, when such regional arrangements are so envisaged as to make them fall within the sphere of bloc conflict. In that case, efforts which properly should embody and be supported by a common interest may instead lead to a weakening of the uniting force of that interest and aggravate the split. This, obviously, is the reverse of the major purpose and function of the United Nations in its efforts to provide for a growing measure of political stability.

Just as it is clearly within the interests of the entire world community to prevent the widening of the area of conflict in cases of political crises, so it must be in the interests of all constantly to seek to widen rather than to restrict the area of coincidence of economic interest within the United Nations. Unless this is done, the entire world, and not just one or the other side, is bound to lose. As I noted in my statement to the Economic and Social Council at its thirtieth session, "the United Nations Organization remains the only universal agency in which countries with widely differing political institutions and at different stages of economic development may exchange views, share their problems and experiences, probe each other's reactions to policies of mutual interest, and initiate collective action."

It was this recognition of the growing area of coincidence of economic interest which was at the basis of my proposal and of the Council's decision that it hold its thirtieth session at the ministerial level in order to undertake, at the beginning of a new decade, a broad examination of the direction to be taken by the United Nations to meet the challenge of both national and collective responsibility for economic growth and development.

At its thirteenth session, the General Assembly adopted resolution 1316 (XIII) calling upon Member states to undertake a review of accomplishments to date and to chart their future courses of cooperative action for the purpose of giving further impetus to the economic development of the less developed countries. At the national level also, many countries, both developed and underdeveloped, have found it useful to establish long-term plans for economic growth as guidelines for economic policy, and others have established national commissions on economic and social goals and policies.

In the light of these events, and in the light of the changes that have taken place in the national economic and political landscape since the Charter was first signed, it was my belief that the Economic and Social Council might usefully explore the question of the desirability and feasibility of some United Nations undertaking to chart the future course of cooperative action to implement the economic and social objectives of the Charter.

A common stand has not yet been reached on the possibility or advisability of harmonizing and coordinating national economic policies. Even the idea of regular and systematic consultation with a view to achieving fuller knowledge of the facts and the issues is new. In view of the very modest and very recent progress in harmonization of national economic policies, even within regional groupings of like-minded countries, it is not surprising that no consensus on the possibility or desirability of harmonizing or coordinating national economic policies within the framework of the United Nations should as yet exist.

And yet, though the objective is not within immediate reach, and though I do not wish to underestimate the obstacles, the importance of a harmonization of national economic development policies within the United Nations must be stressed. Even though the session at the ministerial level did not produce the results that some may have hoped, it did represent a beginning. It did lead to a useful exchange of views. It did provide an opportunity for contacts between ministers in charge of economic questions, some of whom have only limited alternative possibilities of making such direct contacts. It did lead to at least one important step looking towards better coordination in the future of policies of economic projections. Thus, this meeting, with its achievements—and its shortcomings—may be regarded as opening the door to new efforts to explore and utilize for common ends the wide area of common economic interests, at the same time as it demonstrates the difficulties we encounter and the early stage of evolution at which we still find ourselves.

Until now, the economic analyses undertaken by the Secretariat and consequently the debates within the Economic and Social Council and the General Assembly have been concerned essentially with past and present trends. Now, with the programme of work in economic projections initiated by the Council, we may hope that, as we succeed in ascertaining the constituent elements of policies of economic growth, the Organization will be able to make an important contribution towards widening the bounds of the area of coincidence of interest within the United Nations, thus helping to harmonize decisions of Governments in the field of national policy and in the promotion of rapid and stable economic development for all.

V

In the Introduction to my Report to the General Assembly at its fourteenth session I discussed the role of the United Nations. In that context I said: "The work of today within and for the United Nations is a work through which the basis may be laid for increasingly satisfactory forms of international cooperation and for a future international system of law and order, for which the world is not yet ripe." I continued:

It has so often been said that the world of today is one which requires organized international cooperation on a basis of universality that one repeats it with hesitation. However, there are reasons to do so. It still seems sometimes to be forgotten that—whatever views may be held about the United Nations as an institution—the principle of organized international cooperation on a basis of universality which is at present reflected in this Organization is one which has emerged from bitter experiences and should now be considered as firmly established.

In the previous parts of this Introduction I have tried to outline my views on some specific problems arising for the Organization at the present juncture, which may well, in the perspective of history, come to be regarded as a turning point. Especially, I have wished to draw the attention of the Members to the scope for possible diplomatic and political action by the Organization in a split world and to the desirability of the widening of that scope by patient and persistent action, using as the lever the community of interests which is created by the desire of everybody to limit the area of conflict, to reduce the risk of conflicts, and to create a basis for joint action for solution, or at least localization, of conflicts.

Recent developments—reflected in a revolutionary technical evolution of arms for destruction, in the entry of new major regions of the world in full strength into international politics, and in new and world-wide economic interdependence—have given to the Organization, and what it represents as an instrument in the hands of Member governments, greatly increased responsibilities, but also increased usefulness.

The Organization and its activities can be viewed on different levels. It provides Member governments with a highly developed, continuously operating conference and negotiation machinery. However, to a growing extent it has provided them also with an effective executive organ for joint action. In this latter respect, the evolution has taken a course somewhat different from the one envisaged in San Francisco, but, as recent developments have shown, the departure as to methods is not considerable and the conformity as to aims is complete. Finally, the Organization is also the embodiment of an ideal and the symbol of an approach to international life which recognizes the common interest of all in the rejection of the use of force, in any form, as a means for settling international disputes and in adherence to the principles of law, justice, and human rights.

The Organization has often in the past been faced, and is likely in its continued work again and again to be faced, with situations in which a compromise with these last-mentioned principles might seem to facilitate the achievement of results in negotiations or to promise an easier success for the Organization in its executive efforts to resolve a problem. It is for the Members themselves to judge to what extent the Organization, in particular cases, has accepted such compromises and to what extent it has remained faithful to the principles and ideals which it embodies.

It is my firm conviction that any result bought at the price of a compromise with the principles and ideals of the Organization, either by yielding to force, by disregard of justice, by neglect of common interests, or by contempt for human rights, is bought at too high a price. That is so because a compromise with its principles and purposes weakens the Organization in a way representing a definite loss for the future that cannot be balanced by any immediate advantage achieved.

The United Nations has increasingly become the main platform—and the main protector of the interests—of those many nations who feel themselves strong as members of the international family but who are weak in isolation. Thus, an increasing number of nations have come to look to the United Nations for leadership and support in ways somewhat different from those natural in the light of traditional international diplomacy. They look to the Organization as a spokesman and as an agent for principles which give them strength in an international concert in which other voices can mobilize all the weight of armed force, wealth, an historical role, and that influence which is the other side of a special responsibility for peace and security. Therefore, a weakening of the Organization, resulting from an attempt to achieve results at the cost of principles, is a loss not only for the future but also immediately in respect of the significance of the Organization for the vast majority of nations and in respect of their confidence in the Organization on which its strength in our present-day world ultimately depends.

There are in the Charter elements of a thinking which, I believe, belongs to an earlier period in the development of the world community. I have in mind especially the concept that the permanent members of the Security Council should not only, as is natural, be recognized as carrying special responsibility for peace and security, but that, further, these permanent members, working together, should represent a kind of "built-in" directing group for the world community as organized in the United Nations.

The fifteen years which have passed since the founding of the United Nations have witnessed a different development. In the first place, we have seen a split among the permanent members which, in fact, has created the major war risk of today and considerably hampered the development of the Organization. But, further, we have experienced a growth into independence of a majority of states of two great continents, with other interests, other traditions, and other concepts of international politics than those of the countries of Europe and the Americas. Who can deny that today the countries of Asia or the countries of Africa, acting in a common spirit, represent powerful elements in the international community, in their ways as important as any of the Big Powers, although lacking in their military and economic potential?

The United Nations is an organic creation of the political situation facing our generation. At the same time, however, the international community has, so to say, come to political self-consciousness in the Organization and, therefore, can use it in a meaningful way in order to influence those very circumstances of which the Organization is a creation.

It is impossible for anyone to say where the international community is heading and how the United Nations will change in the further course of the evolution of international politics. But it can safely be said that international cooperation will become increasingly essential for the maintenance of peace, progress, and international justice. It can also safely be said that if the United Nations firmly adheres to its principles and purposes, with flexibility and intelligent adjustment to needs as regards procedure, Members engaged in this cooperation will increasingly turn to the Organization for assistance. Therefore, they will find it increasingly necessary to maintain its strength as an instrument for the world community in their efforts to reduce those areas of major conflict where the Organization so far has been powerless, as well as in efforts to resolve problems, arising outside or on the margin of these areas, in a spirit reflecting the overriding common interest.

This concept of the role and of the future of the United Nations may go beyond the conventional thinking which sees in the Organization only, or mainly, a machinery for negotiation, but I am convinced of its realism and I am convinced also that the Organization and its Member nations would act rightly and wisely if they acted consistently with this concept in mind, even if temporarily it may seem to point out a road full of risks and of difficulties which they may doubt that the Organization is yet strong enough to overcome.

August 31, 1960

DAG HAMMARSKJÖLD
Secretary-General

BELGIUM AND THE USSR ACT TO CIRCUMVENT UNITED NATIONS POLICY

THE FIRST TWO of the following texts reflect the Secretary-General's increasing disillusion with the delays in completing the Belgian withdrawal from Katanga and the growing evidence that he had been misinformed—even deceived—about the military assistance that Belgium was continuing to provide to Tshombé's provincial government. The third text, the *note verbale* of September 5 addressed to the USSR, enquired pointedly about Soviet transport planes and trucks which had apparently been provided directly to the central government of the Congo as military assistance instead of going through United Nations channels. This enquiry was prompted by the following developments:

Soon after August 15 Prime Minister Lumumba, seeing that all his efforts to obtain military help from the UN Force in the reconquest of Katanga had been rebuffed, decided to make the attempt on his own, using units of the ANC loyal to him. To provide the necessary transport the Soviet Union, in response to his appeal, secretly made available fifteen Ilyushin transport planes as well as one-hundred trucks, the latter originally promised to the United Nations Operation in the Congo in July. The plan of campaign, if it can be called that, was to ferry Armée Nationale Congolaise troops into the province of Kasai, first to Lulua-bourg and then to Bakwanga in South Kasai, as the first steps to an invasion of Katanga proper.

In Kasai there had long been periodic feuding between Lulua and Baluba tribesmen. Tribal fighting had broken out again in August and the Baluba leader, Albert Kalonji, had declared South Kasai an autonomous state. Its capital was Bakwanga, a center for diamond mines owned by a sister company of the Union Minière, and Kalonji had promptly gone to Elisabethville, seeking help from Tshombé. On August 26 Ilyushin planes brought in ANC troops from Lulua-bourg, who proceeded to occupy Bakwanga without difficulty. Unpaid for two months and without rations or any other supplies of their own the government troops then started looting and requisitioning at random and became involved on the side of the Luluas in savage attacks on the Balubas, including massacres of civilians.

The Soviet delegation did not reply to Hammarskjöld's *note verbale* until September 10, when it flatly denied that the Secretary-General had any right to control assistance rendered by any state at the request of the Congolese government and claimed the Ilyushins were, in any case, civil aircraft, operated by civilian crews.

1. Third Report to the Security Council—Belgium Delays Withdrawals

NEW YORK   AUGUST 30, 1960

1. ACCORDING TO FORMAL ASSURANCES received by the Secretary-General from the Government of Belgium, and reported by him to the Security Council at its 887th meeting on August 21, 1960, all Belgian combat troops were to have left the Congo at the latest at 2400 hours on August 29. The letters of assurance are annexed to the present report (annexes I and II).

2. The situation prevailing at the expiry of the term indicated by the Government of Belgium for the withdrawal emerges from the following three annexed documents:

Note verbale from the Secretary-General to the permanent representative of Belgium, dated August 29, 1960 (annex III);

Letter from the permanent representative of Belgium to the Secretary-General, dated August 30, 1960 (annex IV);

Note verbale from the Secretary-General to the permanent representative of Belgium, dated August 30, 1960 (annex V).

3. At the withdrawal of Belgian combat troops from Kamina, the United Nations, in accordance with the statement of the Secretary-General at the aforementioned meeting of the Security Council, has taken over full responsibility for the administration of the base, without prejudice to the rights and claims of the parties concerned. In doing so, the United Nations naturally must exercise exclusive authority as administrator as regards the base, as any other line would put in question or impair the impartiality of the Organization which in this case acts as caretaker for all legitimate interests involved in accordance with recognized principles of law. The temporary administration established by the United Nations is regarded as a provisional measure in the sense of Article 40 of the

Security Council Official Records, Fifteenth Year, Supplement for July, August, and September 1960, document S/4475.

Charter, necessary under the mandate given to the Secretary-General for the achievement of the withdrawal of Belgian troops "under speedy modalities determined by the Secretary-General."

4. The same arrangements apply to the Kitona base.

5. In view of the impossibility to assemble and organize on short notice an experienced staff for the maintenance of the bases and of the employment of the population dependent on them, the Secretary-General has called upon the Belgium government to put the necessary number of technicians, in a civilian capacity, at the disposal of the Organization as technical assistance for the temporary administration of the bases.

6. Under the rules which the Organization must maintain as regards the territory of the bases, no military or civilian personnel will be permitted to come to, or stay at, the bases other than those serving the purposes of the United Nations in its administration of the bases and for its assistance to the Republic of the Congo.

ANNEX I
Letter Dated August 20, 1960, from the Representative of Belgium to the Secretary-General

I have the honour to confirm my letter of today's date concerning the withdrawal of Belgian troops from bases in the Congo.

The Belgian government has instructed me to inform you that the Kitona and Kamina bases will be evacuated except for experts.

It is understood that these bases cannot be abandoned and the express conditions which the Belgian government attaches to their evacuation is that they are to be occupied by United Nations troops.

The withdrawal will be effected within a maximum period of eight days. The Belgian government will probably find it necessary to accept the help of the United States Air Forces as offered through you; this help will be accepted subject to confirmation by my government.

The number of experts required for essential services is one thousand at the maximum for Kamina and five hundred for Kitona.

The resolutions adopted by the Security Council concerning the military personnel are thus implemented, the final disposition of the bases being a matter for further negotiation.

WALTER LORIDAN
Permanent Representative of Belgium
to the United Nations

ANNEX II

Letter Dated August 24, 1960, from the Representative of Belgium to the Secretary-General

I have the honour to refer to my letter of August 20, [annex I] in which I informed you that the withdrawal of Belgian troops from the Congo would be effected within a maximum period of eight days.

Acting upon the request made to me yesterday by your aide Mr. Wieschhoff, I am in a position to confirm to you, on behalf of my government, that the Belgian troops will in fact have withdrawn from the Congo before 2400 hours, August 29.

I wish to add that the small contingent of Belgian troops still at Albertville (Katanga) will be evacuated before today is over. The help of the United States aircraft offered Belgium through your intermediary will be required to effect the total withdrawal of the troops.

The Belgian government requests your support in enabling the Sabena aircraft which are in the Congo to be used for transportation into the interior of the Congo.

WALTER LORIDAN
Permanent Representative of Belgium
to the United Nations

P.S. As I signed this letter I learned that the Belgian troops have left Albertville.

ANNEX III

Note Verbale of August 29, 1960, from the Secretary-General to the Representative of Belgium

The Secretary-General presents his compliments to the Permanent Representative of the Belgian government to the United Nations and wishes to draw his attention to the following facts:

In a letter dated August 20 [annex I] the representative gave the Secretary-General the assurance that the withdrawal of the Belgian troops would be effected within a maximum period of eight days. Subsequently, in a letter dated August 24 [annex II], the representative confirmed, on behalf of his government, that the Belgian troops would in fact have left the Congo before 2400 hours on August 29.

In reply to a request addressed to the Secretary-General's representative at Elisabethville for precise information concerning the situation prevailing in Katanga at 2400 hours on August 29, the Secretary-General has just been informed as follows:

> Because of communication difficulties, details concerning the situation at Albertville and Kamina have not been received. It appears, however, that one company and troops of the Headquarters staff are still at Elisabethville and that a like number of troops are at Kamina, awaiting their departure. Also, the rear-guard of a paratroop battalion at Albertville expects to embark tomorrow morning.

The Secretary-General wishes to draw the Government's attention to this information, which he hopes is unfounded. He would be grateful if the government would give him precise information concerning the situation prevailing at the expiry of the term indicated by the representative for the evacuation of the troops.

ANNEX IV
Letter Dated August 30, 1960, from the Representative of Belgium to the Secretary-General

I have the honour to inform you that the withdrawal of Belgian troops in the Congo has been completed with the sole exception of some members of the First Paratroop Battalion who are in transit at Albertville, awaiting a vessel which should arrive at any moment to transport them to Usumbura. Instructions have been issued to the effect that, should it be necessary and in order to avoid any delay, they should be evacuated by air. Thus the withdrawal of Belgian troops from the Congo has in effect been completed.

I shall not fail to inform you as soon as I have been advised of the departure of the last troops.

WALTER LORIDAN
Permanent Representative of Belgium
to the United Nations

ANNEX V
Note Verbale *of August 30, 1960, from the Secretary-General to the Representative of Belgium*

The Secretary-General of the United Nations presents his compliments to the Permanent Representative of Belgium to the United Nations and wishes to inform him as follows:

In a *note verbale* dated August 29, 1960, [annex III] the Secretary-General expressed the desire to receive from the Belgian government precise information concerning the situation with regard to the evacuation of Belgian troops at the expiry of the term indicated in its letters of August 20 and 24 [annexes I and II] for their evacuation.

In reply to that note the Secretary-General has today received a letter [annex IV] informing him that the withdrawal of Belgian troops from the Congo has been completed with the sole exception of some members of the First Paratroop Battalion who are in transit at Albertville awaiting a vessel which should arrive at any moment to transport them to Usumbura. The withdrawal of Belgian troops from the Congo, the representative states, has thus in effect been completed.

The Secretary-General has, however, just received a report from his representatives who arrived at Kamina today, August 30, at 1430 hours local time. At that time, Belgian combat troops consisting of one 400-man battalion of paratroopers, one 120-man company of airfield guards and one school of aviation comprising fifty instructors and students had not yet been evacuated. The Secretary-General's representatives have been informed that it is proposed to evacuate seventy men on the evening of August 30 and thirty-nine men on August 31 by air and that the rest are to be evacuated by rail on September 1 and 2 and subsequently by ship from Albertville on September 3 and 4.

The Secretary-General expresses his surprise at finding that there is a marked difference between the information received from Brussels and the facts observed on the scene. He finds it necessary to stress that the presence of large Belgian military units, contrary to the assurances given by the Belgian government, is certain to arouse sharp criticism. The United Nations based itself on the assurances received and did everything to facilitate the evacuation. As the evacuation has, nevertheless, not yet been completed the Secretary-General deems it necessary to submit a formal protest to the Belgian government requesting that the evacuation of Belgian troops which are still in the Congo should be effected immediately.

The Secretary-General considers it necessary to submit a report to the Security Council concerning the situation.

2. Communications Protesting Belgium's Actions in Katanga

(a) Note verbale *dated September 4, 1960*

The Secretary-General of the United Nations presents his compliments to the Permanent Representative of Belgium to the United Nations and has the honour to draw his attention to the following.

It will be recalled that in operative paragraph 2 of its resolution of July 22, 1960 [S/4405], the Security Council *"Requests* all States to refrain from any action which might tend to impede the restoration of law and order and the exercise by the Government of Congo of its authority. . . ."

According to information received by the Secretary-General, officers of Belgian nationality are at the present time attached to Katanga forces and other groups in armed conflict with the Central Government of the Republic of the Congo. The minister of foreign affairs of Belgium has orally explained to the Secretary-General that these officers are under neither the authority nor the disciplinary control of the Belgian government. In view of the circumstances, however, the situation can be interpreted in the sense that the Belgian government has at least permitted persons connected with its military services under a "technical assistance" programme to give help to forces fighting the Government of the Congo. If that is so, the situation is essentially different from that in which private individuals volunteer for service in a foreign army. In this case, if the prevalent interpretation of the situation is correct, officers of the Belgian army who had been serving in the Force publique under "technical assistance" to the Congo have now entered the ranks of the Katanga forces or of other groups. In view of customary military regulations, it may be assumed that this transfer (whether the officers have been "detached" or have "resigned") could not have occurred without the assent in one form or another of the Belgian military authorities; at all events, it would be

Security Council Official Records, Fifteenth Year, Supplement for July, August, and September 1960, document S/4482/Add.3.

hard to believe that officers of the Belgian army have severed their connection with that Army in order to enroll in provincial forces fighting in the Congo without having obtained the approval of their military superiors and without having thereby made certain that they could rejoin the Belgian army, if necessary with a loss in rank or seniority.

In the circumstances, the Secretary-General would wish, having regard to the Security Council's resolution of July 22, 1960, to be informed of the conditions under which the Belgian officers are serving in the Katanga forces and other military or paramilitary groups in armed conflict with the central government. He would like the information supplied to deal with all the points mentioned above: assent of the Belgian military authorities, status of the persons concerned during their service in the Katanga forces, conditions of reinstatement in the Belgian forces, and their need for the assent of the Belgian authorities in order to continue to serve in the Katanga forces without losing their rights to rejoin the Belgian army in any capacity.

(b) Note verbale *dated September 8, 1960*

The Secretary-General of the United Nations presents his compliments to the Permanent Representative of Belgium to the United Nations and has the honour to draw his attention to the following.

Confirmed reports have been received to the effect that a cargo of weapons, marked "Belgian weapons" or something similar, the weight of which is estimated at nine tons, was unloaded at Elisabethville airport yesterday from a DC-7 civil aircraft of the Sabena Airlines.

The Secretary-General wishes to draw this report to the immediate attention of the Belgian government in order to ascertain whether it is true that the Belgian government has thus sent, or authorized the sending of, weapons from Belgium to the provincial authorities at Elisabethville. Should this be the case, the Secretary-General would consider it necessary to make a formal serious protest against the delivery, which is contrary to the letter and spirit of the Security Council resolution of July 22, 1960 [S/4405], paragraph 2 of which reads as follows: "*Requests* all States to refrain from any action which might tend to impede the restoration of law and order and the exercise by the Government of Congo of its authority and also to refrain from any action which might undermine the territorial integrity and the political independence of the Republic of the Congo."

The Secretary-General considers it necessary to emphasize that this decision is binding under Articles 25 and 49 of the Charter, which were expressly invoked by the Security Council in its resolution of August 9, 1960 [S/4426], paragraph 5, which "calls upon all Member States, in accordance with Articles 25 and 49 of the Charter of the United Nations, to accept and carry out the decisions of the Security Council and to afford mutual assistance in carrying out measures decided upon by the Council."

---

3. Note Verbale *to USSR About Soviet Planes and Trucks Supplied Direct to Congo Government*

NEW YORK   SEPTEMBER 5, 1960

THE SECRETARY-GENERAL of the United Nations presents his compliments to the delegation of the Union of Soviet Socialist Republics and wishes to draw its attention to the following observations and questions.

In a letter from the permanent representative of the Union of Soviet Socialist Republics of July 19, 1960 (S/4398), the representative, on the instruction of his government, expressed a protest against the sending of United States troop units to the Republic of the Congo on any pretext and insisted on their immediate withdrawal from the Republic of the Congo.

Later, in a *note verbale* of July 23, the Government of the USSR informed the Secretary-General that it had given its consent to the temporary utilization of the five Soviet aircraft IL-18, assigned to the Government of Ghana for the transport of Ghanaian troops, also for the transport to Leopoldville, the capital of the Republic of the Congo, and other points in the Congo of motor transport, communications equipment, food supplies, and other freight being sent by the Government of Ghana for the purpose of rendering the necessary assistance to the Government of the Congo.

In reply to this last-mentioned *note verbale* the Secretary-General sent

Security Council Official Records, Fifteenth Year, Supplement for July, August, and September 1960, document S/4503.

to the permanent representative a *note verbale* in which he stated that, in accordance with principles approved by the Security Council and maintained by the Secretary-General, no transports of troops and material are undertaken by units from permanent members of the Security Council from one point within the territory of the Congo to the other, directly for the United Nations Force or indirectly for the Force in the service of a government participating in the Force with its own national contingent. The Secretary-General added that he understood that no such transports were envisaged by the USSR offer as reported in the *note verbale* of July 23. To this reply from the Secretary-General no reaction has been received from the delegation of the USSR.

According to information available to the Secretary-General, a certain number of planes, type IL-14, have been put directly at the disposal of the Government of the Republic of the Congo by the Government of the USSR, presumably with crews, technicians, ground personnel, etc. It is reported today from Luluabourg that ten of these planes, coming from Stanleyville, arrived at Luluabourg carrying Congolese troops to reinforce the Congolese force, in the Bakwanga area. According to the report, the troops carried amounted to two hundred, the planes returning to Stanleyville supposedly in order to transport further reinforcements. The crews of the planes are reported as being in civilian clothes.

In the light of the views earlier expressed by the Soviet Union and the principles maintained by the United Nations for its own operation, the Secretary-General would appreciate being informed about the nationality and status of the crews of the troop-carrying planes, which presumably are now under the control of the Congolese government. The significance of this information will be appreciated in view of the precedent that may be created.

Addressing himself to the representative of the USSR, the Secretary-General would wish to recall the *note verbale* received by him, on July 22, 1960, from the Government of the USSR regarding the provision of trucks for the armed forces directed to the Congo in accordance with the decision of the Security Council. According to the note, one hundred Soviet trucks GAZ-63, sets of spare parts for them, and one automobile repair shop have been provided by the Soviet Government in accordance with the decision of the Security Council. The Secretary-General, not being informed about the delivery of these trucks to the appropriate United Nations authorities in the Congo, would appreciate information regarding the status of the undertaking thus entered into by the Soviet government under the Security Council resolution.

CENTRAL GOVERNMENT OF THE CONGO FALLS APART

BESIDES THE TROUBLES caused by Soviet planes for Lumumba and Belgian military assistance to Tshombé with which the immediately preceding texts and commentary are concerned, certain other developments preceding the submission of the Secretary-General's fourth report to the Security Council should be mentioned.

One of these was the succession to Ralph Bunche as the Secretary-General's personal representative in the Congo. It had originally been intended that Bunche would return to Headquarters early in August with the Secretary-General on the latter's return from his intended mission to South Africa, which had to be postponed (see volume IV of this series). Hammarskjöld then requested Prime Minister Nehru of India to make Ambassador Rajeshwar Dayal available as Bunche's successor in Leopoldville. Dayal, a former permanent representative of India to the United Nations and currently India's high commissioner in Pakistan, had been seconded to the United Nations once before, as a member of the United Nations Observation Group in Lebanon in 1958 (see volume IV of this series).

On August 20, after Nehru had consented to release him for the new assignment, Dayal's appointment was announced. However, he would not be able to assume his functions until September 8. Lumumba was now refusing to talk with Bunche and the latter was anxious to be relieved, so Hammarskjöld sent Cordier out at the end of August to hold the fort as his special representative in the interim. Cordier had been working day and night as the Secretary-General's closest associate and right-hand man at Headquarters on all matters relating to the Congo since the crisis first erupted on July 12.

Another development was the establishment of the Advisory Committee on the Congo in accordance with the intention Hammarskjöld had expressed to the Security Council on August 21. Like the UNEF Advisory Committee it was composed of the permanent representatives of nations contributing units to the UN Force in the Congo, with the Secretary-General serving as chairman. Its initial membership included representatives of Canada, Ethiopia, Ghana, Guinea, India, Indonesia, Ireland, Liberia, the Federation of Mali, Morocco, Pakistan, Sudan, Sweden, Tunisia, and the United Arab Republic. It met for the first time on August 24 and continued to meet frequently thereafter. As with the UNEF Advisory Committee no votes were taken. At the end of each meeting Hammarskjöld summed up the discussion with a statement of the degree of consensus he thought had emerged. The Secretary-General had, of course, consulted widely and frequently from the beginning of the Congo operation, but the Congo Advisory Committee provided a regularly scheduled group procedure that helped to clear misunderstandings and to cope with the differences that had already begun to emerge among the African members and were soon to become more serious.

Two of the most influential African delegates—Mongi Slim of Tunisia and Alex Quaison-Sackey of Ghana—went to Leopoldville for the Pan-African Conference which met from August 25 to 30 at the invitation of the Congo government. Lumumba had hoped to win promises of African military support for his attack on Katanga, but received none except from Guinea. The African govenments agreed on the importance of ending the Katanga secession and maintaining the unity of the Congo, but they were virtually unanimous in their resolve to stay with the United Nations approach and in their disapproval of Lumumba's behavior toward Hammarskjöld and ONUC. Many also saw Lumumba's resort to Soviet transport for his Katanga venture as increasing the danger of Great Power interventions from both sides. They urged negotiation and compromise as the right way to strengthen both the political unity of the Congo and the working relationships with ONUC and offered their good offices in both respects.

Lumumba was not responsive to these counsels of moderation. On August 27 he flew off to Stanleyville, the capital of Orientale province, the center of his political strength and the take-off point for the Soviet planes brought in to ferry ANC units into South Kasai. A large crowd was at the airport awaiting Lumumba's arrival when two U.S. transports carrying bilingual signals personnel and communications equipment from Canada for the UN Force landed in succession. At first the crowd was friendly. Then someone shouted "paratroopers" and the rumor spread like a flash-fire that the Belgians had come back to arrest Lumumba. There was a wild melee joined by some ANC soldiers and the Americans and Canadians were severely mauled and beaten before Ethiopian UN troops managed to rescue them. This incident, following others in recent days, further angered the West and indicated rapidly rising risks for the safety of ONUC personnel, both civilian and military. Lumumba returned to Leopoldville determined to pursue the course he had chosen and the massacres of Balubas in Kasai continued.

When Cordier took over from Bunche in Leopoldville on August 30 the status of the United Nations operation in the Congo in both its international and internal aspects may be summed up as follows:

On the international level the Soviet Union had followed up its previous verbal support for Lumumba's policies by sending him transport planes and trucks. This was a definitive commitment to one side in what could now easily develop into a spreading and very bloody civil war. In retrospect it probably also signalled the Soviet decision to break openly with United Nations policy and therefore with the Secretary-General. Since the Soviet Union had voted for all three Security Council resolutions on the Congo, while interpreting their provisions in a sense quite different from the position of the majority—and of Hammarskjöld—this made the latter inevitably the main target of such a shift in Soviet tactics.

On the Western side Belgium, behind a façade of equivocations and evasions, had continued to strengthen Tshombé with arms and seconded military personnel. The West, with its sympathy for an ally's predicament and its strong economic and financial interests in Katanga, had not pressed Belgium very hard to live up to the Security Council resolutions. Now the open Soviet intervention on Lumumba's side could well provoke countermoves by the West and pose the danger of escalation of the civil war into a Korean-type conflict.

Meanwhile the internal breakdown of government and administration at all levels in the Congo had gone from bad to worse. Lumumba was ill-suited by temperament to head a coalition cabinet. During August his extreme reactions, his failures to consult colleagues not committed personally to him, his break with ONUC and turn to the Soviet Union for aid, his total lack of interest in efforts to bring some order into the administrative chaos—all these combined to turn many of the more moderate political leaders against him. By the time Cordier arrived the breakdown of the Congolese political consensus on which the Kasavuba-Lumumba government had rested was far advanced and this was interacting with the simultaneous breakdown of the equally tenuous East-West consensus on the United Nations operation. Ranged on one side were Lumumba and Gizenga; on the other, such figures as President Kasavubu, Foreign Minister Bomboko, Joseph Iléo, President of the Senate, and Cyrille Adoula, leader of the trade union movement.

During the Pan-African Conference, African delegates like Mongi Slim had sought to encourage the various factions to reestablish the working coalition of June 30. This also was one of Cordier's endeavors in his consultations with Congolese leaders after his arrival. He tried, in vain, however, to make personal contact with Lumumba. The Western embassies followed a quite different line. They had now turned definitely against Lumumba for having become, in their eyes, an instrument for Soviet penetration as well as a promoter of civil war and they privately encouraged Kasavubu and others to act against him.

Leopoldville was rife with rumors of plots and counterplots in the first days of September. The sequence of events is described in the commentary that follows the Secretary-General's fourth report to the Security Council (the next following text). This report, although dated September 7, does not refer to these events. It resulted from Hammarskjöld's decision to place before the Council at this time a proposal for a $100 million program of financial assistance to the Republic of the Congo, financed by voluntary contributions to a United Nations fund. The Secretary-General requested the Council to make an urgent appeal for contributions to such a fund. He also asked the Council to urge the Congolese to resolve their internal conflicts by peaceful means and to reaffirm its stand against unilateral interventions by Member states. Hammarskjöld had been horrified by the massacres of Baluba tribesmen in which ANC troops in South Kasai had participated. He saw this as approaching the crime of genocide and suggested the Council might redefine the mandate of the UN Force to give it authority in such circumstances temporarily to disarm Congolese soldiers so engaged.

1. Fourth Report to the Security Council

NEW YORK   SEPTEMBER 7, 1960

1. INTERNATIONAL FINANCIAL AID to the Republic of the Congo is a matter of such urgency that I have decided that it is necessary to place it before the Security Council now, however rough and uncertain may be the estimates that I can make at this time. It was inevitable that, in the conditions which prevailed during the first weeks of independence, efforts undertaken in the Congo by the United Nations under the Security Council's decisions should have mainly concentrated on the military aspects of assistance. The results of action previously initiated, however, may very soon be put in jeopardy, or even nullified, unless certain steps are now taken to stabilize the financial position of the Congolese government and to lay the foundation for the future growth of the Congo economy. The immediate provision of financial assistance on a large scale is required if a stable public administration is to be reconstructed, if business activity is to be revitalized, and if employment is to be found for a substantial part of the scores of thousands of Congolese who have lost their jobs as a direct consequence of events since independence. The attainment of these objectives has a direct and important bearing on the restoration of peace and security and the responsibilities of the Security Council are thereby invoked.

2. Although, even on the very tentative estimate now possible, the sums required may appear large, it must be emphasized that they are no more than sufficient to assure the limited objectives just stated. This financial assistance is not designed to set up a permanent régime of external subsidy to the Congo; it is put forward with the expectation and intention that the Republic should be able to pay its own way both currently and for development purposes in the near future. If the economic and administrative fabric can be kept intact, the country will be enabled to move forward again.

Security Council Official Records, Fifteenth Year, Supplement for July, August, and September 1960, document S/4482.

3. With a rapid decrease in the treasury balance of the Congo Government and tax collections brought to a very low level by the collapse of the administrative services and by civil strife, with foreign exchange proceeds from exports being immobilized, with monetary reserves reduced from the equivalent of $75 million on June 30 to $35 million on August 15—part of which is the property of Ruanda-Urundi—the government will very soon be unable to meet its monthly bills, except through dangerous inflationary devices, and economic activity would have to come to a virtual standstill.

4. Estimates of the needs of the Congo economy, with respect to the probable level of cash transactions on government and balance-of-payments accounts must, by necessity, be extremely hazardous. They have to be based on calculations with respect to factors involving the rate of revival in governmental and business activities which, in turn, depend very largely upon the restoration of public security and confidence. In addition, there is no clear basis for making assumptions regarding borrowing opportunities and possible arrangements on the debt service. The basic assumptions are that the republic will remain a single economic unit and that its tax structure will, within a reasonable period, regain the level of potential yields written into the 1960 budget. The economic infrastructure, fortunately, is relatively intact.

5. In regard to 1960, an estimate made in June, before independence, forecast a deficit of $100 million for the second half of the year (over and above a realized deficit of $34 million in the first six months). A later estimate made in mid-August at the request of the United Nations, which took account of the deterioration in the economic situation but assumed that the Government of the Congo would reestablish public services and undertake public works designed to absorb unemployment at a reasonable pace, raised the estimated deficit for the current six months to about $125 million. The volume of international transactions consistent with this level of government activity and with the assumed pace of recovery in the private sector of the economy is expected to produce an unfavourable balance of payments of the order of $100 million. If certain arrangements can be made regarding the consolidated public debt, these estimated deficits might be reduced by about $20 million each.

6. Even in the three weeks which have passed since the mid-August estimate was framed, the continuance of unsettled conditions in the Congo and the consequent low level of economic activity will have affected the estimate. As soon as more stable conditions prevail, I propose to

present a revised estimate to the Security Council. By that time there may also be better information about the shape of the financial settlement likely to be reached between the Congo and Belgium, on which negotiations have already started under the aegis and with the good offices of the United Nations. In the meantime, it would be realistic to anticipate that assistance in the same amount as mentioned above will be needed for the calendar year 1961 and that this temporary assistance can be phased out at a substantially lower level in 1962, by which time it is expected that this international finance will have enabled the great economic potential of the Congo to get to work. Thus, as stated above, this programme of assistance is not intended to initiate a permanent régime of external subsidy, but is rather a relatively short-term effort designed to set the Congo on the road to becoming a source of economic strength once more. Despite the uncertainties, I have thought it appropriate to attempt some estimate of the ultimate order of magnitude of the international financial assistance required. Another compelling reason for doing so now is the time required by the parliamentary processes of some Member states in sanctioning appropriations for this purpose. At this time, therefore, I propose that the Security Council appeal to Member governments for urgent voluntary contributions to a United Nations Fund for the Congo to be used under United Nations control for the purposes indicated in this report. Immediate financial support from Member states is needed in the sum of $100 million, in convertible currencies. Without such assistance and support, the Government of the Congo cannot develop a programme to cover the internal expenditures (including such public works as are required to reduce unemployment), to restore essential imports, and to allow such remittances as will encourage foreign technicians to work in the country.

7. I therefore seek the establishment, within the United Nations, of an international account, into which would be directed the contributions of all countries willing to help in the restoration of economic life in the Congo, and to carry on its public services, including education, health, and internal security, at such levels as are possible and reasonable. In view of the Security Council's recognition of the responsibility of the international community for the restoration of peace and order in the Congo, it would appear logical that this financial assistance be channelled through the United Nations.

8. The formulation of a minimum set of rules and regulations will no doubt be required, if funds are to reach the level mentioned, but it is

hoped that the Security Council will authorize the establishment of the account and invite contributions to it without waiting for the completion of legal and administrative steps which require the intervention of the General Assembly. Pending the establishment of such a minimum set of rules, the forms in which control over the use of the fund should be exercised may be determined by the Secretary-General.

9. In deciding, in fulfilment of its primary duty to maintain peace and security, to dispatch to the Republic of the Congo the United Nations Force, the Security Council made only the first move necessary in order to stabilize the country and to protect peace in Africa. The very considerable efforts of a great number of Member countries, assisted by the Organization, in order to forestall a further disintegration of the country with all the serious consequences such a development would entail, would be of no avail unless parallel and consecutive steps were to be taken in order to rebuild the national life. Members of the Security Council have already taken note of the contributions of the United Nations in the field of technical assistance and of the general framework established, in consultation with the government, for United Nations civilian activities in its assistance. Above, I have raised the question how to meet, on a preliminary basis, the imperative financial needs of the country which have to be covered if the Organization is to succeed in this major peace effort.

10. However, neither the military and civilian operations, nor the financial assistance for which I now suggest that the Council make an urgent appeal, would serve their purpose, if Member nations and the United Nations cannot count on full cooperation from all responsible quarters within the Republic of the Congo itself. As is well known, the people and the country have been torn by internal strife, centering around constitutional problems but reaching further, and deeper, and being linked also to tribal differences and claims. These conflicts, which so far have completely stymied all efforts to reestablish normal life, must speedily be brought to an end if disintegration is not to continue in spite of all efforts made from the outside to achieve a stabilization. And they must be brought to an end by peaceful means. I therefore consider it necessary that, to the same ultimate end as the one that would be served by the financial fund, the Council now urge the parties concerned, within the Congo, to seek by peaceful means a solution to their internal problems, keeping in mind that such solutions should aim at the conservation and consolidation of the unity and integrity of the country.

11. The internal conflicts, which have become increasingly grave in the

last few weeks and even days, have taken on a particularly serious aspect due to the fact that parties have relied on and obtained certain assistance from the outside, contrary to the spirit of the Security Council resolutions and tending to reintroduce elements of the very kind which the Security Council wished to eliminate when it requested the immediate withdrawal of Belgian troops. The conflicts have further led to considerable losses of human lives and to continued danger for human lives in forms which sometimes have been of great brutality, contrary to the principles established and maintained by the United Nations.

12. In view of this dual aggravating aspect of the internal conflicts, I consider it essential, as part of the widened and intensified effort for which I appeal in this report, that the Security Council reaffirm its request to all states to refrain from any action which might tend to impede the restoration of law and order or to aggravate differences, and that it clarify, in appropriate terms, the mandate of the United Nations Force. In the first respect, special emphasis should be placed on the interest of all to assist towards a peaceful solution of the conflicts, aiming at overcoming present threats to the unity and integrity of the country without further disruption and threats to civilian life. In the second respect, emphasis now should be put on the protection of the lives of the civilian population in the spirit of the Declaration of Human Rights and the Convention on the Prevention and Punishment of the Crime of Genocide. This may necessitate a temporary disarming of military units which, in view of present circumstances, are an obstacle to the reestablishment of law and order in the interest of the people and the stability of the nation.

13. In ending, I wish to stress the consistency of my proposals with the spirit and letter of the Security Council's previous actions in the case of the Congo. My suggestions are parts of one carefully developed and balanced operation, reflecting its adjustment to current developments and experiences. The operation, naturally, remains entirely nonpartisan, guided only by the interests of the people of the Congo in peace and stability within a united nation, the integrity of which is protected against all and safeguarded also by the elimination of the war threat which a continued disintegration would sharpen.

THE SECURITY COUNCIL did not meet to consider the Secretary-General's report until September 9. In the meantime the political conflict in Leopoldville had rapidly evolved into a crisis of major proportions—for the Congo and for the United Nations.

By September 3 Kasavubu had decided on how to move against Lumumba. Under the constitution there were two ways in which the latter could be lawfully dismissed as prime minister—a vote of censure by the Parliament or an order by the president countersigned by at least one minister in the cabinet. Since Lumumba had so far retained the support of a majority of the Parliament, Kasavubu chose the second alternative. Cordier first learned of Kasavubu's intentions on September 3 when the president called him to his office. Cordier immediately told Kasavubu that the United Nations could not be associated in any way with his proposed move and warned him as well that it would be likely to bring a violent reaction. Kasavubu asked Cordier to order UN soldiers to close the Parliament and agree to arrest some twenty-five unnamed persons. Cordier refused and again reminded the president that the United Nations could not take sides in internal political disputes.

There was no further word from Kasavubu about his intentions on September 4, but that evening Joseph Iléo, the president of the Senate, came to visit Cordier with four tribal leaders of the Kasai Balubas. Iléo and the Baluba leaders were fearful that reinforcement by air of ANC units hostile to the Balubas would lead to worse tribal massacres in South Kasai and might soon endanger the Balubas in the Leopoldville area as well.

The next afternoon, September 5, when Cordier called on Kasavubu at the latter's request, the president informed him that he planned to announce the dismissal of Lumumba that evening over the Leopoldville radio. His decree dismissing Lumumba and six of his ministers was countersigned by the foreign minister, Justin Bomboko, and by Albert Delvaux, minister resident to Belgium. He accused Lumumba of arbitrary actions that were involving the country in civil war and announced the appointment of Joseph Iléo, as the new prime minister. Within the hour Lumumba was on the air with a denunciation of Kasavubu's decree as illegal and a declaration that he, as prime minister, was now dismissing Kasavubu as president. Lumumba appealed in inflammatory language to the army and to the people to come to his support, and his speech was repeated three times during the night.

Prior to the events of the evening of September 5, Cordier had received instructions from the Secretary-General giving him wide discretion to act without further consultation should he be faced by a governmental collapse and the imminent threat of large-scale violence. Hammarskjöld had even added what he termed an "irresponsible observation" to the effect that "people on the spot might commit themselves to what the Secretary-General could not justify doing himself—taking the risk of being disowned when it no longer mattered."

It was evident that the situation in Leopoldville was like a tinder-box which might at any moment burst into uncontrollable riot and civil strife. The local ANC garrison was unruly, unpaid for two months and divided into pro- and anti-Lumumba factions. The Soviet planes that had arrived at Stanleyville to ferry pro-Lumumba ANC soldiers into South Kasai could also be used to bring them to Leopoldville if Lumumba chose to attempt a military showdown. The radio war that Kasavubu and Lumumba had begun was likely soon to bring excitable crowds into the streets.

The strength of the United Nations Force in Leopoldville was strictly limited. Cordier saw to it that units were deployed at key points and their commanders alerted that it might be necessary to use force to defend their positions against attack. The Moroccan general, Ben Hammou Kettani, deputy supreme commander of ONUC, had previously been appointed to serve also as military advisor to the prime minister at Lumumba's request. His mission was to restore order and discipline to the ANC. He now renewed his advice to Lumumbu—and Mobutu—to keep the ANC out of the political struggle. What was already happening or anticipated in South Kasai did nothing to encourage hope that Lumumba would heed this advice.

During the night of September 5-6 the situation was appraised as so dangerous as to call for emergency measures to reduce the risks of a sudden and potentially disastrous turn of events. Cordier consulted extensively with the military and civilian chiefs of ONUC. In the light of subsequent controversy the nationalities of the participating ONUC officers may be noted—Swedish, Moroccan, Ethiopian, Indian, and Ghanaian. They agreed that all the airfields in the Congo should be temporarily closed to all but UN traffic and that the Leopoldville radio station should be temporarily shut down. These measures would immobilize the ANC outside Leopoldville and end incitements to the people to take to the streets. They would be lifted as soon as the risks to public order subsided to manageable proportions. Cordier discussed these steps with Dayal, who had just arrived. He then ordered them into effect on his personal responsibility and without prior consultation with the Secretary-General. This was in line with the instructions and advice Hammarskjöld had given to him for an emergency situation.

At their request UN guards were provided or strengthened for both Kasavubu and Lumumba at their respective residences, for various other personalities and to safeguard Parliament against mutinous ANC soldiers.

On September 6, Cordier asked the Secretary-General to provide at once $1 million to supply food and pay for the restless ANC in Leopoldville and elsewhere, who had received neither pay nor rations for two months. Hammarskjöld replied the next day that the money would be transferred on September 9 to the Banque du Congo to be disbursed through General Kettani as a measure in aid of law and order. Because of this prospect Lundula, Mobutu, and other ANC commanders joined in opposing an earlier order by Lumumba to attack UN troops guarding the airport and later in the day the prime minister told General Kettani he approved the arrangements for paying the ANC and even claimed credit for himself calling off the planned attack. The payments began on September 10. Lumumba, at his first meeting that day with Dayal, who had taken over from Cordier on September 8, alternated threats of immediate resort to force with expressions of thanks for United Nations financial assistance and offers on full cooperation.

Before Cordier left Leopoldville he had agreed that Jean David, a Haitian member of the United Nations staff on leave as an assistant to Kasavubu, might try to effect a reconciliation between the president and the prime minister, but

David's efforts, like all others, were not successful. Between September 6 and 8 Lumumba first claimed the support of a majority of his cabinet for a declaration that Kasavubu was guilty of high treason and then went to Parliament, which voted against both Kasavubu's dismissal of Lumumba and Lumumba's dismissal of Kasavubu. The president was unhappy that the United Nations was not supporting him against Lumumba. He had himself asked the United Nations to assume full responsibility for law and order throughout the Congo and to close the airports to all but ONUC traffic but he was insulted at being excluded, as Lumumba was, from the Leopoldville radio station. The United States ambassador, Claude Timberlake, also was bitterly disappointed that the United Nations was not supporting Kasavubu against Lumumba and scolded Cordier for his neutral stance. Earlier Timberlake had outraged Cordier by repeatedly telling him the United Nations should "fight it out."

2. Opening Statement in the Security Council

NEW YORK　　　SEPTEMBER 9, 1960

THE SECURITY COUNCIL met during the evening of September 9 at the Secretary-General's request to consider his fourth report. Before the Secretary-General made his opening statement the Council discussed and voted down a proposal by Kuznetsov to accept an invitation from Lumumba for the Council to meet in Leopoldville instead of New York.[1] Hammarskjöld then made the statement that follows, defending the closing of the airports and radio station as temporary but necessary emergency measures, and asking the Council to declare explicitly that all assistance to the Republic of the Congo be channeled only through the United Nations.

FOR THE FIFTH TIME, the Security Council is considering the case of the Congo. On each of the previous four occasions, note having been taken of information received and experiences gathered, the debate has brought the Council closer to the realities of the problem. On this fifth occasion I have wished, through my fourth report, to assist the Council in going one

Security Council Official Records, Fifteenth Year, 896th meeting.

[1] Security Council Official Records, Fifteenth Year, Supplement for July, August, and September 1960, document S/4485.

step further in the same direction. It is in this spirit that I would like to introduce to you my report with a few observations necessary for an appraisal of the true character of the vast problem in which the United Nations has had to engage itself in order to forestall the worst.

Members will have gathered from the report that, in spite of the great natural resources of the country, the financial situation is one of bankruptcy. True, there are financial assets, but they are hopelessly insufficient. And with a complete disruption of civilian and economic life, where are the new revenues, where the foreign exchange, where the taxes, where the customs duties? We face a nation with a budget with all the necessary outlays and nothing to cover them—and with few or no efforts made to cover them. Examples of where this leads can easily be given. Let me mention only one. Among the troops sent down by the Prime Minister to Kasai, some units have not had any pay for two months and they have no food, with the result that they disobey orders and loot from the civilian population under circumstances which I need not describe.

In this situation spokesmen of the central government speak about the assistance rendered by the international community through the United Nations as if it were an imposition and treat the Organization as if they had all rights and no obligations. They seem to believe that the independence of the Republic of the Congo, in the sense of the international sovereignty of the state which everybody respects, means independence also in a substantive sense of the word which, in our interdependent world of today, is unreal even for a country living by its own means and able to provide for its own security and administration.

A government without financial means is dependent on those who help it to meet its needs. It may depend financially on another state, or group of states, and thereby tie its fate to that of the donors. Or it may depend on the international community in its entirety, represented by the United Nations, and so remain free. There is no third alternative this side of a complete breakdown of the state through inflation or a speedy disintegration of all social and economic services.

These are the hard facts against which the Security Council has to consider my main proposal in the fourth report. These are the hard facts which should be remembered when the relations of the United Nations with the central government are discussed.

Money provided for the financing of the elementary services for which the Government of the Congo is responsible to its people is obviously money lost, however great the need and imperative the political reasons for granting it, if nothing is done to restore national life to law and order, so that economic activities can get under way again, taxes can be collected, foreign exchange accumulated, and state revenue developed.

Surely, when the Security Council decided on assistance to the country, it did so in the firm expectation that nothing would be left undone by the authorities in the Congo in order fully to utilize the assistance given and to provide all these authorities could provide in order to reestablish order and get the life of the community reintegrated. We now hear that it is the United Nations that has worked against such efforts by the authorities, and in such circumstances it may be permissible, also on this point, to say a word about the realities. Let me take a recent example which has the added advantage that it, at the same time, explains certain actions by the United Nations about which members may wish to be informed.

On the evening of September 5 the chief of state, President Kasavubu, announced that he had revoked the mandate of Prime Minister Lumumba and charged the president of the Senate, Mr. Iléo, with the task of forming a new cabinet. According to what has been made public, the decree dismissing the prime minister was countersigned by two cabinet ministers.

I do not want to analyse the complicated constitution and the complicated constitutional situation, but let me register as a fact that, according to the constitution, the president has the right to revoke the mandate of the prime minister and that his decisions are effective when countersigned by constitutionally responsible ministers. However, Prime Minister Lumumba at once declared over the radio that he had dismissed the chief of state because the chief of state had acted illegally. This view was also expressed by the prime minister in a letter to my representatives in the Congo in which he further developed his legal theses.

According to Mr. Lumumba's interpretation, the constitution gave the Council of Ministers all power, if the president were incapacitated. However, the constitution does not entitle the prime minister under any circumstances to dismiss the chief of state—least of all, of course, for an action to which the chief of state is explicitly entitled by the constitution.

In this situation—where there was on the one side a chief of state whom the United Nations must recognize and whom the statements of the prime minister had not deprived of his rights, but where there was, on the other side, a cabinet which continued in being, but the chief of which had put himself in sharp opposition to the chief of state—the instructions to our representatives in the Congo were to avoid any action by which,

directly or indirectly, openly or by implication, they would pass judgement on the stand taken by either one of the parties in the conflict. I think
that what I have said about the constitutional situation is enough fully to
justify this stand.

When the constitutional crisis broke out, the atmosphere was already
tense, and all experience showed that, subjected to the fire of propaganda,
the population was highly excitable. With whom could the United Nations representatives consult in this situation without taking sides? In the
light of what I have said, the answer is obvious: they had to act on their
own responsibility, within their general mandate, in order to meet the
emergency which they were facing. Let me repeat it, there was nobody,
really nobody, with whom they could consult without prejudging the
constitutional issue.

Leopoldville is a fairly big city. In the city there were supporters of
both protagonists in the constitutional conflict. The members of the
Council have seen ample evidence of this in the newspapers. Were this
population to be worked up by a radio war between the protagonists, the
consequences would be unforeseeable. A popular uprising, with fights
between parties, could easily present the United Nations Force with a
problem far exceeding its powers. Such an eventuality had to be fore-
stalled and, therefore, as an emergency measure under its mandate, for
the maintenance of law and order, the United Nations representatives
closed the radio station. They also closed the airports for all but United
Nations operations, so as to be certain that the United Nations would be
able to operate in fulfilment of its mandate, whatever happened.

The two far-reaching steps of an emergency nature which were taken
by the United Nations representatives were, as I have already said, not
preceded by a consultation with the authorities. Nor could they have
been. But further, they were not preceded by any reference of the matter
to me, because of the extreme urgency of the problem our people were
facing on the spot. This latter fact throws, in my view, considerable light
on the character of a situation which it is easy to sit in New York and
discuss in terms of protocol, but which it requires wisdom and courage to
handle when you are at the front. Anyway, it should be clear that the
steps taken cannot be discussed in terms of partisanship, colonialism, or
anticolonialism.

As I said, I was not consulted, but I fully endorse the action taken and
I have not seen any reason so far to revise the decisions of my representatives. Naturally, I assume full personal responsibility for what has been

done on my behalf, and I do it convinced of the wisdom of the actions and of their complete accordance with the spirit and the letter of the Security Council decisions, adjusted to a situation of unique complication and, of course, utterly unforeseeable when the resolutions of the Council were adopted.

It was my hope, after the votes taken in the House of Representatives and in the Senate, and with the resulting pressure for a reconciliation of differences and a compromise solution, that matters would become stabilized and that, therefore, the two steps by the United Nations which I have explained and which were taken solely in order to face an immediate emergency and naturally only as temporary safeguards, could be cancelled, and that thus the airports and the radio station could have been opened without delay. However, the situation remains such that I feel that I have to submit the question of the closing of the airports and the closing of the national radio to the Security Council for its consideration and instruction. It seems to me that those who are critical of the emergency measures should be the first to recognize the urgency of this consideration. If, before the Security Council reaches a decision, the situation were to develop in such a way that on the spot these various measures could be cancelled, I would of course be the first one to welcome such a development.

I was led to the description of the United Nations role in the recent crisis—a role of utter discretion and impartiality—by the need to illustrate the kind of conflicts with which we are faced in our efforts to help build the new country. The episode gives also an example—though, of course, an extreme one—of our difficulties in implementing the wish of the Security Council that in fulfilment of its mandate of July 14 we should act in consultation with the central government. In the United Nations we have rich experiences of such consultations in all parts of the world and for all purposes within the sphere of the United Nations responsibilities. So far, we have never had any difficulties which have not been easily overcome. But then, when a matter had been arranged with a responsible minister, his word was honoured by the government. Or, when we had helped the responsible ministers to favourable results in a negotiation, we were not accused of plotting against the government and worse. When we had, correctly, informed the foreign minister about our moves, we were not said to have neglected the government. We have now gathered new experiences. That, however, is insignificant in comparison with the fact that, while we had to wait for reactions on which we could build, life did not stand still and urgent action was required and finally had to be taken—in the very interest of those for whose support we had appealed in vain.

I feel that another example of the realities of domestic conflicts and domestic difficulties at this stage may be in order. Information which has reached us from the United Nations and International Red Cross personnel in the Kasai region indicates that the personnel of the Armée nationale congolaise have engaged in slaughter not only of combatants but also of defenceless civilians. In the Bakwanga region, for example, hundreds of Balubas were reported killed on August 29 and 30, according to World Health Organization and Red Cross officials who visited the area at that time. One shocking incident that was widely reported is that of the massacre on August 31, 1960, by troops from the Armée nationale congolaise, using machetes, of seventy Balubas including women and children who had taken refuge in a mission school. Other reports indicate that villages have been pillaged and burnt and their inhabitants, men, women, and children, killed. United Nations officials were informed that unarmed persons were deliberately killed simply on the ground that they were Balubas.

These actions obviously cannot be viewed merely as examples of internal political conflict. They involve a most flagrant violation of elementary human rights and have the characteristics of the crime of genocide since they appear to be directed toward the extermination of a specific ethnic group, the Balubas.

I have, as regards developments in the Kasai region, already referred to the status of part of the military units of the Armée nationale congolaise. It should here be added that there is evidence that the soldiers have broken away from their command, which has been unable to control their actions. Whatever the motives for bringing the troops to the region, and whatever role they may have been intended to play in the domestic conflict, they have, of course, through such undisciplined actions, and once the authorities have lost control, ceased to be parts of a responsible army. Should it be supposed that the duty of the United Nations to observe strict neutrality in the domestic conflicts and to assist the central government means that the United Nations cannot take action in such cases?

So far, I have described some of the realities facing the United Nations in the provinces held by the central government. Some may draw the conclusion that I take sides by giving a dark picture of one side while, by my silence, whitewashing the other. Let me therefore add that the difficulties the United Nations encounters on the Katanga side may be different in type but are no less serious, whether caused by the attitude of the authorities in Elisabethville or by their supporters.

As regards specifically the problems which have arisen between the United Nations and the Belgian government, I can refer to various documents which have been circulated. As regards the authorities in Katanga, we have in important cases not been able to enforce the rules which flow from the general obligations of the United Nations in the Congo. Specifically, I have had emphatically to protest against the import of arms, contrary to the letter and spirit of the Security Council resolutions. I deplore the continued use of foreign elements in the forces organized in Katanga. I have strongly protested against the way in which the authorities in Elisabethville, by bringing the situation to a point of acute crisis, broke through the general United Nations policy of closing the airports at the time of the conflict between the president and the prime minister, in a way that, whatever their reasons for this act of defiance of the United Nations, put the United Nations effort in serious jeopardy.

The Council will, from what I have said, understand why I have found it necessary to link together in the fourth report the question of the necessary and most urgent financial assistance to the government with the general problem of law and order in the country and the attitude of the authorities. If United Nations action, military and civilian, or financial, is to have any sense beyond the immediate moment, if its continuation is to be defensible, the domestic conflicts must be resolved with a sense of responsibility, on the part of the leaders, not only to the nation but also to the international community which cannot be supposed to be willing to foot the bill for political ineptitude and irresponsibility.

The domestic problems must be solved, and they must be solved by peaceful means. I am personally firmly convinced that such solutions are within reach if all the parties were fully to show responsibility, to subordinate themselves to the higher interests of the people, and to act within the limits of the Constitution. For the world community to ask for such attitudes is not to ask for too much.

It may be said that, irrespective of how the authorities in the Congo operate and how the domestic situation develops, the United Nations operation must continue. I believe that this is true, because of the great risks which exist for the spreading of the Congo crisis over Africa, and even more widely, were a continued disintegration of order, economy, and civilian life to be permitted. But to use such an argument as a reason why the international community should continue to keep the country afloat without proper contributions from the leaders of that country would be for those leaders to resort to a policy which in other fields of life has a name which I will not repeat.

One final point. I have talked in the report also about the aggravating elements introduced into the picture by interference from outside. Technical assistance—a term well known to the United Nations—has in the Congo, indeed, come to take on a new significance. I have already referred to Belgian assistance in Katanga. But the Belgians are not alone. There are others who follow a similar line, though they justify their policy by a reference to the fact that assistance is given to the constitutional government of the country. Admittedly, there is a difference, but these latter actions are not covered by explicit requests in the Security Council decisions. I think, however, it should be recognized that this is no longer a question of form and legal justification, but a question of very hard realities, where the use to which the assistance is put is more important than the heading in an export list under which it is registered, or the status of the one to whom it is addressed.

News has been published today to the effect that a national detachment within the United Nations Force has stated that it wants to pull out from the Force until the United Nations "ceases its flagrant interference in internal Congolese affairs." I believe this news to be misleading, but it prompts me to recall the following statement from my first report on the question of the Congo, as commended by the Security Council: "The authority granted to the United Nations Force cannot be exercised within the Congo either in competition with representatives of the host government or in cooperation with them in any joint operation. This naturally applies *a fortiori* to representatives and military units of other governments than the host government." Were a national contingent to leave the United Nations Force, they would have to be regarded as foreign troops introduced into the Congo, and the Security Council would have to consider their continued presence in the Congo, as well as its consequences for the United Nations operation, in this light.

I believe that the Security Council has now come to a point where it must take a clear line as regards all assistance to the Congo. I believe it will achieve its aims only if it requests now that such assistance should be channeled through the United Nations, and only through the United Nations. It would, thereby, solve the problem of military assistance to Katanga, and it would also solve the problem of abuse of technical assistance in other parts of the Congo, thus at the same time serving the vital interest in a localization of the conflict and the interest in a peaceful solution of the domestic problems of the Congo, without any interference from outside influencing the outcome. Thus, and only thus, could it justify its appeal to Member states for the funds now so desperately needed by the Congo, whether the need is seen by the leaders of the country or not.

I said at the beginning that I wished, through my fourth report and through my oral introduction to it, to bring the debate yet one step closer to realities. There may still be many steps to go before the facts are clearly before the Council and fully grasped. I hope the Council will not have to take these steps but, if so, there should be no hesitation in identifying clearly what has come to represent a threat to peace and security.

LATER IN THE EVENING the Yugoslav representative, Dobrivoje Vidic, who had been instructed by Tito to request a Council meeting on the Congo crisis, made a statement which was moderately critical of the "UN command" for not giving better "cooperation" to the central government in dealing with the Katanga and Kasai secessionist movements and for taking such steps as closing the airfields and radio station. Before the meeting adjourned soon after midnight the Secretary-General made the following preliminary reply.

---

3. Second Statement During Security Council Debate

NEW YORK   SEPTEMBER 10, 1960

AT THIS LATE HOUR I will not take up any of the very many points made by the representative of Yugoslavia. I would also like to have an opportunity to read the text. There are, however, two points which I would like to put on record.

The representative of Yugoslavia addressed a criticism against the

Security Council Official Records, Fifteenth Year, 896th meeting.

United Nations command. The command had, according to him, not implemented correctly the resolutions of the Security Council. The address is mistaken, because the command has acted under my instructions, and if there are any mistakes in the interpretation of the resolutions they are mine.

That leads me to the second point. On August 21 this Council discussed problems which were closely related to the ones raised now by the representative of Yugoslavia. On that occasion I made a careful analysis of the interpretation which had been given to me in a letter from Prime Minister Lumumba. My analysis stands, and I would invite the representative of Yugoslavia to study it. From that it appears that you cannot base an interpretation of the mandate of the Force solely on the resolution of July 14, because the Council itself has interpreted that resolution, especially in its resolution of August 9. For that reason, the resolution of July 14, especially the paragraph quoted by the representative, has to be read in its proper context of related resolutions. That is what I have done, and my interpretation has in fact been discussed at this table at a later meeting which did not result in any resolution at all. My conclusion from that later meeting was that my interpretation was approved by the majority of the Council.

WHEN THE COUNCIL reconvened in the afternoon of September 10 it was informed of a request from the Central Government of the Congo, transmitted through Dayal, for a postponement until its delegation could arrive.[1] During the course of the meeting further messages arrived from Kasavubu denouncing Lumumba as a usurper and declaring the new cabinet headed by Joseph Iléo to be the only lawful government.[2] Just before Hammarskjöld made the statement that follows a lengthy cable arrived from Lumumba asserting that Kasavubu had acted illegally and protesting strongly against the Secretary-General's interpretation of the Congo's constitution and his "interference" in the internal affairs of the country.[3]

The discussion in the Council was mainly procedural and there was a general inclination to delay further debate until the Congo could be represented. However, the Western delegates supported the stand taken by Mongi Slim and Sir

---

[1] Security Council Official Records, Fifteenth Year, Supplement for July, August, and September 1960, document S/4496.
[2] Ibid., documents S/4500 and S/4502.
[3] Ibid., document S/4498.

Claude Corea, urging an appeal by the President of the Council (Ambassador Ortona of Italy) against any action in the Congo of such a nature as to aggravate an already critical situation, pending the resumption of the Council's debate. After hearing this appeal the Council adjourned until Monday afternoon, September 12.

---

4. Third Statement During Security Council Debate

NEW YORK   SEPTEMBER 10, 1960

I BELIEVE THAT A FEW clarifications might be useful to the members of the Council at this stage.

The representative of the Soviet Union expressed some concern about the fact that the request for a postponement of the consideration by the Security Council of the present item had been passed through the channel of the special representative of the Secretary-General in Leopoldville. I got the impression that he felt that this was in some way humiliating to the government. I would like to explain the situation.

We receive communications from the government in very many ways, and if they are received by telegram they are just as welcome and will be treated here in exactly the same way as if they are passed through our representative in Leopoldville. However, more and more the central government has chosen to go through our representative. I suppose they consider this to be more practical, and it is, because our line of communication is much more rapid than theirs. I think that in this case especially they found it convenient because it was an oral message, and under such circumstances they obviously gain time by picking up the telephone instead of typing a telegram and going to a post office in order to send it. So I do not think there is any reason to read into this transmittal anything but a practical choice by the central government, and I am very happy if we can render them assistance in this very simple way, whatever their considerations may be.

The representative of Ceylon felt that somehow Ambassador Dayal of India, who is now the representative in Leopoldville, had taken a stand

Security Council Official Records, Fifteenth Year, 897th meeting.

on the constitutional issue by transmitting this telegram. Most certainly that is not the case. It follows from what I have already said that we function in this case like a telegraph office, and he would be the first to acknowledge and recognize the validity of the instruction which I told you about yesterday, that our representatives are to avoid any action by which directly or indirectly, openly or by implication, they would pass judgement on the stand taken by either one of the parties in the constitutional conflict. Thus nothing at all can be read into this transmittal of the message, as regards a stand by Ambassador Dayal on the constitutional issue.

The representative of the Soviet Union directed a question to his colleagues, and it is for his colleagues, obviously, to reply. The question was whether there was some intention to widen the powers of the Secretary-General or to give him a mandate that would carry us further than the mandates which you find in the Security Council resolutions as debated here and as interpreted by the Security Council. As I said, it is definitely for the members of the Council to reply to that question, but I think that it might be of interest to the representative of the Soviet Union if I were to remind him of what I have asked for.

First of all—and that is the overriding consideration—I have asked for money. I have asked for money because I do not feel happy if, as Secretary-General, I have to advance money, in consultation with the prime minister, out of United Nations funds in order to make it possible for the government to pay salaries—not the salaries of the Cabinet, but the salaries of the servants of the Cabinet. I think this matter must be straightened out, and there is one way to straighten it out: that is, by an appeal to the governments of Member states, to which I have no doubt they will respond with the generosity which they have so often demonstrated.

The other point I raised yesterday with a sense of urgency was the point about airports and the radio. I told the Council under what circumstances that decision had been taken. I told the Council that, for my part, I would be happy to see it reversed as soon as possible but that, frankly, I did not feel that the situation was such that I should take the responsibility upon myself, with all the consequences that move might have.

The members of the Council are in a position to judge for themselves. They have before them communications from two authorities in the country, from two authorities that are still in sharp opposition to each other. I have referred my responsibility, as I think I should, to the Security Council, and I think that the Security Council should shoulder its responsibility.

I can imagine that some members of the Council may question the attitude I take on the constitutional issue. In fact, the members of the Council will have before them in a few minutes, I think, a letter from Mr. Lumumba—that letter, too, transmitted through Mr. Dayal—which challenges what I said yesterday and challenges it in, let me say, vigorous terms. However, in that very letter, Mr. Lumumba himself describes the constitutional situation, and I should like to quote one sentence from his letter. He is describing what the situation is after the debate on these issues in the Parliament. Perhaps I may be permitted to quote it in French: [Continued in French] "In their interpretation the Congolese legislative chambers further state that the government headed by Prime Minister Patrice Lumumba and the head of state, Mr. Kasavubu, having been separately invested with office by Parliament, the latter alone has the power to dismiss one or the other." [Continued in English] This letter is signed by Mr. Lumumba, and I think that the quotation I have given shows that Mr. Lumumba himself acknowledges that his decision that Mr. Kasavubu is no longer president is not valid.

All the same, I can see that members may ask why letters from a head of state have been circulated to the Security Council. That leads me to a question of procedure and protocol which I think it is just as well to put on record. The rule has been that the Secretary-General communicates with the foreign minister. If he does not communicate with the foreign minister, he communicates with the head of state. For him to communicate with the prime minister is the exception. I should like to add just one thing: Practically the whole correspondence regarding the setting up of the United Nations Force has been a correspondence with the heads of state of the African countries concerned. I think that that disposes of any doubt as to the propriety of circulating these various communications from Mr. Kasavubu.

BEFORE THE COUNCIL met again on September 12 Deputy Foreign Minister Valerian Zorin arrived to replace Kuznetsov as the Soviet representative. He had instructions to open a direct frontal attack upon the Secretary-General in line with the following quotation from a new Soviet government statement:

One can hardly help but be struck by the unseemly role assumed in regard to the Congo by United Nations Secretary-General Hammarskjöld. It can

properly be said that the events in the Congo and the part played by the
United Nations representatives in the implementation of the relevant resolutions of the Security Council were a serious test of the impartiality of the
United Nations organism; and it must be said quite bluntly that the senior
official of this organism—the Secretary-General—has failed to display the
minimum of impartiality required of him in the situation which has arisen. In
the over-all workings of the United Nations organism, its chief has proved to
be the very component which is functioning most unashamedly on the side of
the colonialists, thus compromising the United Nations in the eyes of the
world.[1]

Messages arrived from Leopoldville announcing that rival delegations representing the Congo were on their way—Thomas Kanza by appointment of
Lumumba and Foreign Minister Justin Bomboko by appointment of Kasavubu
and Iléo. The Security Council met only long enough for Zorin to be formally
seated and then adjourned until September 14. In Leopoldville, meanwhile, Dayal
had managed to win commitments from both Kasavubu and Lumumba to refrain
from inflammatory statements over the radio and from leaders of the Senate and
Chamber that Parliament would take steps "to ensure that the radio station is not
used for purposes contrary to peace and public order."[2] On these assurances the
radio station resumed normal broadcasting on September 12 and the airfields
were also reopened for "all civilian, humanitarian, and peaceful purposes" on
September 13.
   On that same day, however, Lumumba sent forty armed men to the radio
station in an attempt to arrest Jean Bolikango, who had been named minister of
defense in Iléo's cabinet, while he was broadcasting an appeal for national unity.[3]
This attempt, which failed, followed a similar incident the day before, when
Lumumba was temporarily arrested by *gendarmerie* and then released by the
army command. Later on September 13 Lumumba sent, through Dayal, a message addressed jointly to the President of the Security Council, the Secretary-
General, Thomas Kanza and the chairman of the Afro-Asian group in the United
Nations. Because of the "aggression" perpetrated against him Lumumba demanded the immediate dispatch of twenty aircraft with crews, a large quantity of
arms and ammunition and a powerful radio transmitter to enable the government
to reach the people. If these requests were refused, Lumumba concluded, "the
government will be obliged to seek such assistance elsewhere."[4]
   There were many other signs of spreading fear and panic, as well as of irrationality, which frustrated all efforts by Dayal and others to calm things down and
encourage reconciliation. The ANC Commander, General Lundula, put himself
under UN protection. Colonel Mobutu, the chief of staff, took his family for safe-
keeping to the home of General Kettani and later told Dayal he intended to

[1] Security Council Official Records, Fifteenth Year, Supplement for July, August, and
September 1960, document S/4497.
[2] Ibid., document S/4505/Add.1.
[3] Ibid., document S/4505/Add.2.
[4] Ibid., document S/4507.

resign because of political interference with the army. Dayal refused Iléo's request to resume UN operation of the radio station and the next day heard that Lumumba now wished him to strengthen the UN guard at both the radio station and the airport!

At a joint session of Parliament on September 13—with many members absent—a resolution was voted granting full powers to Lumumba, but under the supervision of a parliamentary commission. This commission the next day produced a suggestion for a new compromise cabinet retaining Lumumba as prime minister but with Cyrille Adoula replacing Gizenga as vice prime minister. Nothing came of this proposal and Kasavubu proceeded to prorogue Parliament for a month. Both the joint session of Parliament and Kasavubu's ordinance were of questionable legality under the constitution.

In New York the Security Council met three times on September 14. The first two meetings were occupied with questions of which Congolese delegation to seat or whether to seat neither one. In so utterly confused a situation most delegates favored holding back until matters were further clarified. A proposal to seat Lumumba's delegate, Thomas Kanza, received the affirmative votes of only the USSR, Poland, and Ceylon. All the other representatives abstained. No proposal to seat Bomboko was put to a vote.

At the third meeting of the Council that evening, Zorin delivered a long and sharply critical attack upon the Secretary-General and the manner in which the United Nations Operation in the Congo was being conducted. Khrushchev was on his way across the Atlantic in the ship *Baltika* to attend the General Assembly session and had radioed to the *London Daily Express* a statement published on September 13 that included much criticism of Hammarskjöld. Zorin quoted liberally from Khrushchev's remarks, including the following indication of the Chairman's intentions at the coming Assembly session:

> The decisive moment has now come for the United Nations to choose the proper course. We should like to hope that the forthcoming session of the General Assembly will state its opinion on the tremendously important question of the Congo and that the United Nations will adopt the appropriate policy, in keeping with the interests of the people struggling for independence and freedom rather than with the interests of the colonialists.[5]

The Secretary-General made an immediate response to Zorin's speech (first following text).

---

[5] Ibid., Fifteenth Year, 901st meeting.

5. *Fourth Statement During Security Council Debate*

NEW YORK   SEPTEMBER 14, 1960

THE MEMBERS OF THE COUNCIL have listened to a long speech. The hour is late. It is therefore with hesitation that I use my right of reply. However, I find it difficult not to do so in view of the line followed by the representative of the Soviet Union. I maintain the rule in the debates of the various organs of the United Nations, including the Security Council, not to enter into the debate, but to limit myself to explanations and clarifications of facts. I think that the members of the Council will understand if, in view of the circumstances tonight, I depart for a few minutes from that rule.

The representative of the Soviet Union said himself, and quoted both from the Soviet government and from Mr. Khrushchev's statements to the effect that I was the conscious tool of imperialist plans and consciously served the interests of colonialists. I understand that the spokesman of the Soviet Union in this respect feels that he voiced the opinion of the peoples of Africa and Asia, for which the Soviet Union regards itself an interpreter.

I am sure that these peoples will have followed and will study with the greatest interest the statements of the representative of the Soviet Union. They are able to form their own opinion. I have no doubt that they will express it, and I would deem their reactions to be those of the peoples directly interested and with direct and complete knowledge of my activities both in the Congo and through the years in Asia and Africa.

My record is on the table of the Security Council and of the United Nations with such completeness that there is no need for me to add anything or to explain anything. I stand by it, and that is all I have to say.

Thus I do not feel it necessary myself to go, for example, to *The Wall Street Journal,* and I would not recommend anybody to do so on an issue

Security Council Official Records, Fifteenth Year, 901st meeting.

about which that paper cannot speak with any inside knowledge or authority. The representative of the Soviet Union called its reaction characteristic. Maybe it is characteristic of the paper: I rarely see it, so I really could not tell. Anyway, what was quoted is not characteristic of the way the United Nations and its Secretary-General meet their duties.

It was mentioned that for the first two months my personal representative in the Congo was an American, but it was omitted that this was the natural function of the person in question in view of the position he holds in the United Nations Secretariat, and also because of his unmatched personal record of fighting for the interest of the African peoples and for minorities.

It was also mentioned that for some ten days or a fortnight my executive assistant, an American, was in Leopoldville, but it was not mentioned that the present personal representative, who will be staying there until further notice, is an Indian.

I could not escape the impression that it was the opinion of the distinguished speaker that the fourth report was not complete, that I was hiding something. I felt that I went, perhaps, to the opposite extreme. The members of the Council do not, I think, believe that I am less outspoken and less sincere in what I say about the United Nations activities than in what I say about those of others. Anyway, I failed to hear any example of incompleteness which was correct and which supported the allegation.

In reference to the fourth report it was mentioned that I considered it desirable that all assistance should be channelled through the United Nations, but it was not mentioned that this has a background in the first report, which was commended by the Council with the concurring vote of the Soviet Union. It was mentioned that I pointed out in the fourth report that the protection of civilian life in cases of serious infringements upon human rights might render necessary the temporary disarming of military units, but it was not mentioned that, as is clearly stated in the text, what I had in mind were groups which had broken loose from their command and turned to irresponsible marauding. And especially it was not mentioned that the main purpose of the report is to provide funds for the country, the treasury of which had monetary reserves for two weeks at the day of independence, and at the present has and for a considerable future will have no possibility of covering its regular expenses for essential services to the people.

Thus the presentation of the case against me, and allegedly for the Congo, was somewhat incomplete, but it was also, alas, badly informed.

We have never disarmed any units of the Congolese army. Not we, but the command of the Congolese army, ordered a cease fire in Kasai. It is, according to our reports, at the request of that command that we placed observers at the border. I do not know of any case where United Nations troops have opposed the regular army of the Republic of the Congo. On the contrary, there has been a daily and close cooperation between the command of the Congolese forces and the command of the United Nations Force, consolidated by the fact that the deputy supreme commander of the United Nations Force, General Kettani, of Morocco, at the request of Mr. Lumumba, is chief military adviser to the Congolese army. Speaking of General Kettani, I may again draw to the attention of the Council, and especially to the attention of the representative of the Soviet Union, the fact that this United Nations command, which is now said to represent a colonizing element, apart from the supreme commander, who is from a country which never had any colonies, consists of one Moroccan and one Ethiopian general, at present assisted by an Indian general. But, of course, in official statements I have recently seen it hinted that even some African countries have now turned colonizers. I begin, quite frankly, to feel uncertain about what this word means in modern political terminology.

To a large extent the speech to which we listened covered all the ground thoroughly debated by the Council before Mr. Zorin arrived here. Thus the Council has, as you all remember, devoted a long meeting to the question of Katanga. There have also been long discussions about consultations, and about just those complaints which were now quoted again. In this context it was mentioned that once one of my representatives did not come when he was summoned by the prime minister. The case is, in fact, a good illustration of the problem of consultation. My representative had tried for eight days to see the prime minister without result, but finally, on the night of September 5, he was summoned for four o'clock in the morning. If he was not available then I do not blame him.

A lot was said about the Belgian withdrawal, and there was, I think, an innuendo that somehow I had been misleading the Council. I note in this context only that the basis for all the statements made by the distinguished representative, with one single exception, I believe, was to be found in documents published by myself. And is it forgotten that I have been the first to condemn delays in withdrawal?

Another criticism was based on the fact that, according to the resolution of July 14, it is for the government only to decide when the troops shall be withdrawn. Obviously it was felt that I now somehow had reserved that right to myself. I have not. But the Security Council may wish to remember not only Article 2, paragraph 2, of the Charter and the first report commended by it at its meeting on July 22, but also the basic agreement concluded with the Government of the Congo. All these three documents bind the Government of the Congo to a good faith interpretation of the purposes of the United Nations measures.

But really I cannot continue this list of clarifications or corrections. There are other and much more serious subjects to be considered tonight by the Council. Let me only, in concluding, say that among a total of 127 civilian experts 87 are from countries which by no stretch of the imagination can be linked with NATO. And after that, of the Force—now, I think, some 18,000 men—some 500 are from NATO countries, and half of that number we have had to take because Poland did not find it possible to help us.

The United Nations is engaged in a major effort to give life and substance to the independence of the Republic of the Congo. No misunderstandings, no misinformation, no misinterpretations of the actions of the United Nations Organization should be permitted to hamper an operation the importance of which, I know, is fully appreciated by all those African countries which, with great efforts of their own, support the work of the United Nations in the Congo and, indeed, seem to me to deserve better than to be told that they are misled.

DURING THE EVENING of September 14 in Leopoldville Colonel Mobutu announced that the Army had decided to "neutralize" the president, the two rival cabinets and the Parliament until December 31, 1960. This was not a military coup d'état, Mobutu said, but a move to give the political leaders time to cope with their difficulties in a calmer atmosphere. He would rely on the United Nations for assistance and intended to set up a collège des universitaires (composed of both young graduates and students) to administer the governmental services on a temporary basis. In an apparently offhand reply to a question he gave the Soviet and Czech diplomatic missions forty-eight hours to leave the country, lock, stock, and barrel.

Lumumba and Kasavubu were apparently both taken by surprise. When Lumumba went to the principal ANC camp to find Mobutu his life was threatened by riotous Baluba soldiers whose relatives had suffered in Kasai. For hours a hard-pressed Ghana contingent of UN troops held off the Balubas and it required Dayal's personal intervention to extricate the prime minister and return him safely to his residence. The next day Lumumba issued a press statement demanding the total withdrawal of all UN personnel. If they failed to leave within eight days the Soviet Union would come to his aid and expel them by force.

Kasavubu, on the other hand, quickly decided to give Mobutu his support. Dayal urged the president in the strongest terms to rescind the order expelling Soviet bloc personnel, but Kasavubu refused, and the Soviet and Czech missions departed on September 17. This incident further hardened Soviet hostility to Hammarskjöld and ONUC, for Khrushchev wrongly believed the United Nations was implicated.

In New York the Security Council met five more times during September 15 and 16. The United States tabled a draft resolution responsive to the Secretary-General's recommendations. This drew support from the West. The Soviet Union's draft resolution called for removal of the United Nations command for "gross violations" of the Security Council resolutions. In addition to Yugoslavia, the African governments of Ethiopia, Ghana, Guinea, Liberia, Morocco, and the United Arab Republic all requested permission to participate in the Council's debate. Their representatives reflected in their speeches a general suspicion that the Western powers had instigated the successive Kasavubu and Mobutu coups and a tendency to see Lumumba, despite his obvious faults, as a genuinely nationalist African leader deserving of more support than he had received. Only Guinea's representative, however, endorsed without reservation Lumumba's demands and even he did not criticize the Secretary-General, though referring to "errors" committed by his representatives. The others stressed the need for better cooperation between ONUC and the Congo leaders and for the latter to try harder to reconcile the differences among themselves.

The Afro-Asian members of the Council, Mongi Slim of Tunisia and Sir Claude Corea of Ceylon, again came to the support of the Secretary-General's interpretation and conduct of his mandate under the Council's resolutions and of the recommendations in his fourth report. They also urged the appointment of a good offices or conciliation committee drawn from the Congo Advisory Committee's membership to help the Congo leaders settle their differences. At the final Council meeting during the night of September 16 Slim and Corea once again joined in submitting a draft resolution supported by the African and Asian states. Before that happened Hammarskjöld made his last intervention in the debate (next following text), impelled by a speech of the Polish representative, Bohdan Lewandowski, repeating some of Zorin's charges that his actions had favored the West.

6. *Fifth Statement During Security Council Debate*

NEW YORK   SEPTEMBER 16, 1960

I AM SURE THE REPRESENTATIVE of Poland will understand me if, for the record, I give a few clarifications. I would also like to give the Council members some additional information.

First, a word about the Katanga debate, to which I referred in my reply the other day to the representative of Yugoslavia. As the members will remember, the situation was as follows. I had given a certain interpretation to my mandate from the Security Council. That interpretation was challenged by the prime minister of the Republic of the Congo, and challenged also at the table by his spokesman. The challenge was not taken up by any delegation. There was only one draft resolution on the table and that draft resolution was concerned with another matter: the sending of a group of observers to the Congo. Even that resolution was withdrawn.

I leave it, naturally, to the Council and to the members of the Council to interpret what such a situation means in parliamentary language and as to its legal effect. I have my own interpretation; but I repeat, it is obviously for the Council itself to interpret what happened.

The representative of Poland said that assistance had been refused contrary to the resolutions. That was a point on which he was not specific. He did not give any example and for that reason I find it difficult to explain what were our motives if such a case had arisen. I can, however, guess that he may have in mind one or two cases where assistance was refused to the government, but that was because their demands were contrary to the resolutions and I do not believe that either the representative of Poland or any other member of the Council would expect me to let the Government of the Congo overrule the Security Council.

I have no reason and no right even to comment in any way on any of the draft resolutions on the table, but one specific point in the draft resolution of the United States of America was mentioned by the representative of Poland which in fact raises a problem I had raised in the fourth report. That is the question of so-called conditions for economic aid. Let me reply with a simple question: Does the representative of Poland believe that we shall have any voluntary contributions unless the donors know that the way in which the money is spent is under some kind of control?

I then come to a point which has been mentioned several times, but which I have to mention again. If I understood correctly and heard correctly, the representative of Poland said that we handed over the radio to the rebels. According to a message dated September 11 from my special representative, the radio control was abandoned on the basis of a declaration from the vice-president of the Senate and the president of the House of Representatives which reads as follows: "Parliament will assume responsibility for the supervision of broadcasts and will take steps to ensure that the radio station is not used for purposes contrary to peace and public order."

If the situation has to be described as a handing over to anybody, it was thus a case of the handing over of the radio station to Parliament, represented by Mr. Kasongo and Mr. Okito, and I do not believe that the representative of Poland regards them as rebels.

Another case which was presented in a way which makes it a bit difficult to reply properly was the one about an alleged threat to the safety of the prime minister from the United Nations Force. It may be that the representative of Poland had in mind an incident of last Sunday when, contrary to his promise, the prime minister came himself to the radio station with some soldiers and those soldiers drew their guns and threatened our people. Anyway, I think we can leave that aside and note the later and interesting event of yesterday, when the life of the prime minister was saved, I dare say, by those very troops which are here criticized. It happened, as you know, at Camp Leopold.

Here I should like to bring to the attention of the members of the Security Council a telegram which I have just received from President Kasavubu, which has a bearing, an important bearing, on the question of impartiality and the question of threats to the life of the prime minister or others. This telegram will be circulated as a document, coming as it does from the president, but I should like to read it here, and I shall permit myself to read it in French as so far I have no translation. This is the text of the telegram:

[Later English translation]

I have the honour to lodge a vigorous protest against United Nations interference in the internal and, more particularly, the judicial affairs of the

Congo. Former Prime Minister Lumumba has just been arrested by the Congolese army on a warrant of arrest legally issued by the *"Procureur général,"* but Ghanaian troops of the United Nations Force are preventing the Congolese army from bringing him before an examining magistrate.

I think that some members might say: "Well, here we really have an example of *ingérence dans les affaires intérieures."* It is now said even by President Kasavubu.

That leads me to end this intervention by quoting a paragraph from a report received from Ambassador Dayal. Ambassador Dayal took over responsibility eight days ago; he has no responsibility for what happened before that time. As we all know, he is a man of very great independence and he would not have hesitated to take another line if he had disapproved of action taken by his predecessors. This is what he says:

It has been made clear, times without number, that the United Nations is here to help but not to intervene, to advise but not to order, to conciliate but not to take sides. We are holding ourselves scrupulously aloof. We have refused to take any position if it could even remotely be considered as an act of intervention. But how can the duty of maintaining law and order be discharged without taking specific action where necessary? That is the problem which faces us daily and which is yet to be solved. It is to the great credit of the United Nations Forces that, despite innumerable provocations and humiliations, they have throughout the country not used force in any situation.

In such circumstances, and with this—I dare say—impartial and trustworthy testimony, is it not a bit unnecessary to talk about this or that interest which our measures have been intended to serve apart from and contrary to the United Nations' own purposes?

THE TEXT of the draft resolution introduced by Ceylon and Tunisia during the night meeting of September 16 was as follows:

The Security Council,

Recalling its resolutions of July 14 and 22 and of August 9, 1960 (S/4387, S/4405, S/4426),

Having considered the fourth report of the Secretary-General of September 7, 1960 (S/4482),

Taking note of the unsatisfactory economic and political situation that continues in the Republic of the Congo,

Considering that, with a view to preserving the territorial integrity and independence of the Congo and to protecting and advancing the welfare of its people and to safeguarding international peace, it is essential for the United Nations to continue to assist the Congo,

1. *Reaffirms* its resolutions of July 14 and 22 and of August 9 and urges the Secretary-General to continue to give vigorous implementation to them;

2. *Calls upon* all Congolese within the Republic of the Congo to seek a speedy solution by peaceful means of all their internal conflicts for the unity and integrity of the Congo;

3. *Reaffirms* that the United Nations Force should continue to act to restore and maintain law and order as necessary for the maintenance of international peace and security;

4. *Appeals* to all Member governments for urgent voluntary contributions to a United Nations Fund for the Congo to be used under United Nations control and in consultation with the Central Government of the Congo for the purpose of rendering the fullest possible assistance to achieve the aforementioned objectives;

5. *Reaffirms* specifically:

(a) Its request to all states to refrain from any action which might tend to impede the restoration of law and order and the exercise by the Government of the Congo of its authority and also to refrain from any action which might undermine the territorial integrity and the political independence of the Republic of the Congo and decides that no assistance for military purposes be sent to the Congo except as part of the United Nations action;

(b) Its call to all Member states, in accordance with Articles 25 and 49 of the Charter of the United Nations, to accept and carry out the decisions of the Security Council and to afford mutual assistance in carrying out measures decided upon by the Council.[1]

The sponsors hoped that the Soviet Union might decide to abstain in order to avoid using the veto against a resolution supported by the African and Asian Members. They had, in fact, omitted a paragraph endorsing a conciliation committee to help resolve the Congo's internal political differences, because Soviet opposition to such an effort had been made plain. Zorin offered several amendments, most of which were unacceptable to the sponsors. After the Soviet's own resolution had been defeated by 7 votes to 2, with Ceylon and Tunisia abstaining, the Soviet amendments to the draft resolution of Ceylon and Tunisia were all voted down. The resolution then received eight affirmative votes but the Soviet Union and Poland both voted "no", and the draft resolution was thus defeated by a Soviet veto. France abstained.

The United States did not press its own draft resolution to a vote. Instead Ambassador James J. Wadsworth, the United States representative in Lodge's absence, proposed that the General Assembly be called into emergency special session. This was voted over Zorin's protests and the Assembly convened on the evening of September 17.

[1] Security Council Official Records, Supplement for July, August, and September 1960, document S/4523.

ACTION ON THE CONGO BY EMERGENCY SPECIAL SESSION OF THE GENERAL ASSEMBLY

THE EMERGENCY SPECIAL SESSION of the General Assembly was called to order in the evening of September 17, less than twenty-four hours after the Security Council had voted to convoke it. Zorin was one of the first speakers and repeated the attack he had made in the Council upon the Secretary-General's conduct of the Congo operation, using at times even sharper language. This caused Hammarskjöld to make the following immediate and brief comment, in which he raised the possibility of his resignation.

---

1. First Statement in the Assembly After Soviet Attack on His Policies

NEW YORK   SEPTEMBER 17, 1960

THE REPRESENTATIVE OF THE Soviet Union has seen fit to make again the strong personal attack upon me which he made in the Security Council. I replied in the Security Council, and I have no reason to repeat my reply here; the records of the Security Council are available to all representatives. The representative of the Soviet Union also saw fit to repeat a series of specific allegations which I refuted in the Security Council, and again I refer to the record. I wish, however, Mr. President, to reserve my right to return to the matter once I have read the text of the speech. The representative of the Soviet Union used strong language which, quite frankly, I do not know how to interpret. The General Assembly knows me well enough to realize that I would not wish to serve one day beyond the point at which such continued service would be, and would be considered to be, in the best interests of this Organization.

General Assembly Official Records, Fourth Emergency Special Session, 858th plenary meeting.

DURING THE NEXT MEETING of the Assembly, in the afternoon of Sunday, September 18, Hammarskjöld spoke again after listening to a series of speeches by Soviet bloc delegates that repeated the misstatements and distortions which he had time and again shown to be false and which the Council itself, by the record of the resolutions it had adopted and the stands taken in its debates, had repudiated (next following text).

2. Second Statement During Debate

NEW YORK   SEPTEMBER 18, 1960

THE UNITED NATIONS OPERATION in the Congo has been going on for a little bit more than two months, but our memories are short and, what is worse, our memories are selective and often erroneous. For that reason I may be excused for repeating things which have been said in reports to the Security Council, which have been said orally by me to the Security Council, and which have been in other ways published to Members of the Organization. I excuse myself for such repetition. It is rendered necessary by the fact that so many errors in the way of writing history also have been repeated.

Let me start with Katanga, which has been mentioned here by several speakers. It has been said that the breakthrough in Katanga and what I did personally in that context was done without consultation with the central government. I have told the Security Council that before going to Katanga I consulted the delegation here in New York. And the Assembly will remember that that delegation included the vice-prime minister, the foreign minister, the minister for United Nations affairs and two other members of the Cabinet. But obviously consultation with the central government means consultation with Mr. Lumumba. In all other cases about which I know, consultation with responsible, constitutionally responsible members of the Cabinet concerning a certain question covers the whole need for consultation with the government.

General Assembly Official Records, Fourth Emergency Special Session, 859th plenary meeting.

The talks with Mr. Tshombé were indeed necessary. We may have our views on this or that legal aspect, but we cannot deny facts. A very short time before the Katanga breakthrough, Mr. Tshombé, with the forces at his disposal, had stopped the United Nations Force from entering Katanga. It was obviously the view of the Security Council members when the matter was discussed that we should not use force to get into Katanga. It would in fact have been against the rules established for the United Nations Force. Well, what means remained in such circumstances other than to negotiate one's way in, and in such negotiations you do not recognize any constitutional position, you do not recognize any rights, you recognize a situation *de facto*.

On my return to Leopoldville, it was not I who refused to see the prime minister. It was the prime minister who showed very clearly that he had no interest in seeing me, as my first act was to ask for a meeting with the government, a meeting to which I was never invited. Here in New York the matter was discussed, as you will remember, by the Security Council. At that meeting the views of the central government were amply explained by a spokesman for that government, in fact, the vice-prime minister. That was, it seems to me, the occasion when all the criticisms so eloquently exposed here today and yesterday and also in the Security Council of the interpretation of the resolutions as regards Katanga could have been properly voiced. I feel for that reason that very much of what has been said is properly addressed to the Security Council. That does not mean that I hold that they were wrong; I mean that they were right, but they took the responsibility, they discussed the issue and there it stands.

It has also been said that we have not been helping the government. Well there are ways and ways of helping a government. There are ways which are in keeping with the rules of the United Nations; there are ways which are not in keeping with such rules. No sovereign government, as an act of sovereignty, can turn the United Nations Force into a national force which it uses for its own purposes. That is what I refused to do, and if that is wrong I do not understand the Charter and I do not understand the rules applied to the United Nations Force.

Another point made is that there have not been any consultations. Those who say so obviously build entirely on the repeated allegations to that effect which have been received from the prime minister. It would have been very interesting if we had had before us a complete diary of the consultations which have taken place, because, in fact, they have been of an unusual intensity. I wonder if in any other case the contact between a

United Nations mission and the government in question has been so intense as in this one—in spite of very great difficulties.

In the civilian field there is very good cooperation indeed with several responsible ministers. That is never mentioned. We have gone quite far in the development of all sorts of practical activities in close consultation and in close agreement with the respective responsible ministers. That is never mentioned. I wonder again what is meant by consultation. Is it consultation with the government, with constitutionally responsible ministers, or is it something else?

In the military field, it should be obvious to everybody that we do not act in a kind of independence, as a state within a state, as some people seem to think. It should be obvious already, from the fact that it was the deputy supreme commander who was invited by the prime minister to be chief military adviser as regards the Armée nationale congolaise and who, after that invitation, which was accepted and approved by me, has certainly been in daily, and I would say even hourly contact with the authorities on the Congolese side. Certainly, even if it does not follow a specific channel, it is what in all other contexts is to be regarded as consultation.

I would go further, and say we have had not only consultation, we have had, in the respect to which I referred, cooperation. It has been said in that context that there has been nothing of the kind, that in fact we have challenged every day, every hour, the authority of the government. I think that it would perhaps be more just to those who have had to carry the burden in the Congo if we said that in their work they have been challenged every day, every hour, and in spite of that we have had these consultations to which I have referred, we have had that cooperation. It may seem contradictory, but I think all of you can find the explanation if you wish.

It has also been said that the United Nations Force is the predominant power in the country. No, that is not so, that cannot be so, that should not be so. There is an Armée nationale congolaise, which is the instrument of the government, but we cannot dictate how that force works, in what direction it works, for the government or against the government. It is, however, the army of the government in the country. We are not anything more than what was said and desired by the Security Council and by the government itself.

One small specific point may deserve mention. There was a reference to a statement of mine in a report dated August 6 to the effect that the

Belgian attitude regarding withdrawal as stated to me was not the obstacle. The quotation was correct and complete, but my accent was on some words which were overlooked—the Belgian attitude "as stated to me." "As stated to me" means of course, the stand in principle, and that remains true. If, later on, it has proved that the Belgian authorities have implemented it in a way which I deplore and protest against, that is another matter. The attitude and principle as stated at that time did not represent the obstacle. The implementation, to a certain extent, did.

One final point, and I think this is the only one in regard to which I would like to refer to a speech made yesterday. It was said that the Secretary-General has all powers to implement the Belgian withdrawal. All powers! The Security Council itself has not resorted to any decision regarding enforcement measures. They have never invoked Article 41 or Article 42 of the Charter. So much less have they delegated to the Secretary-General any right to take any decision on enforcement measures. The power of the Secretary-General in such circumstances resides exclusively in the moral and legal weight of the decisions of the Security Council itself. If that weight in this case, in the view of some, has proved insufficient, it seems to me to be not the first case in the history of the United Nations.

WITH MONGI SLIM of Tunisia, Sir Claude Corea of Ceylon and Alex Quaison-Sackey of Ghana once again leading the way the African and Asian members now proceeded to provide a convincing demonstration of support for the Secretary-General's position and to cut the ground right out from under the Soviet's tactical position. No less than seventeen Afro-Asians joined in sponsoring a draft resolution (A/L.292/Rev. 1) based on the one vetoed by the Soviet Union in the Security Council. They were Ceylon, Ghana, Guinea, Indonesia, Iraq, Jordan, Lebanon, Liberia, Libya, Morocco, Nepal, Saudi Arabia, Sudan, Tunisia, the United Arab Republic, and Yemen. The draft resolution was introduced during the evening meeting on Sunday, September 18, and read as follows:

The General Assembly,

Having considered the situation in the Republic of the Congo,

Taking note of the resolutions of July 14, July 22, and August 9, 1960, of the Security Council,

Taking into account the unsatisfactory economic and political conditions that continue in the Republic of the Congo,

Considering that, with a view to preserving the unity, territorial integrity and political independence of the Congo, to protecting and advancing the welfare of its people, and to safeguarding international peace, it is essential for the United Nations to continue to assist the Central Government of the Congo,

1. *Fully supports* the resolutions of July 14 and 22 and August 9, 1960, of the Security Council;

2. *Requests* the Secretary-General to continue to take vigorous action in accordance with the terms of the aforesaid resolutions and to assist the Central Government of the Congo in the restoration and maintenance of law and order throughout the territory of the Republic of the Congo and to safeguard its unity, territorial integrity and political independence in the interests of international peace and security;

3. *Appeals* to all Congolese within the Republic of the Congo to seek a speedy solution by peaceful means of all their internal conflicts for the unity and integrity of the Congo, with the assistance, as appropriate, of Asian and African representatives appointed by the Advisory Committee on the Congo, in consultation with the Secretary-General, for the purpose of conciliation;

4. *Appeals* to all Member governments for urgent voluntary contributions to a United Nations Fund for the Congo to be used under United Nations control and in consultation with the Central Government for the purpose of rendering the fullest possible assistance to achieve the objective mentioned in the preamble;

5. *Requests:*

(a) All states to refrain from any action which might tend to impede the restoration of law and order and the exercise by the Government of the Republic of the Congo of its authority and also to refrain from any action which might undermine the unity, territorial integrity and the political independence of the Republic of the Congo;

(b) All Member states, in accordance with Articles 25 and 49 of the Charter of the United Nations, to accept and carry out the decisions of the Security Council and to afford mutual assistance in carrying out measures decided upon by the Security Council;

6. Without prejudice to the sovereign rights of the Republic of the Congo, *calls upon* all states to refrain from the direct and indirect provision of arms or other materials of war and military personnel and other assistance for military purposes in the Congo during the temporary period of military assistance through the United Nations, except upon the request of the United Nations through the Secretary-General for carrying out the purposes of this resolution and of the resolutions of July 14 and 22 and August 9, 1960 of the Security Council.

Zorin introduced a Soviet draft resolution that, among other provisions, noted "that the failure of the Secretary-General and the United Nations command to implement" the Security Council's resolutions on the Congo "has resulted in the disorganization of the economy, the aggravation of the political situation in the country and the removal of the legitimate government and Parliament."[1] The

[1] General Assembly Official Records, Fourth Emergency Special Session, Annexes, document A/L.293.

debate during morning, afternoon, and evening meetings of the Assembly on September 19 produced no support whatever for this resolution outside the Soviet bloc.

Zorin then tried the tactic of proposing amendments to the Afro-Asian draft. Sir Claude Corea and Quaison-Sackey, speaking for the sponsors, responded by asking Zorin not to press his amendments on the ground that the draft resolution as it stood resulted from a laborious compromise that would be upset if any changes were permitted. Zorin ended by agreeing not to ask for a vote on either his amendments or on the Soviet draft resolution. The Afro-Asian draft resolution was then adopted by 70 votes to none, with 11 abstentions (resolution 1474 (ES-IV)). Those abstaining included the Soviet bloc, France and the Union of South Africa. The Secretary-General then made the brief statement that follows.

---

3. Concluding Statement After Adoption of Afro-Asian Resolution

NEW YORK   SEPTEMBER 19, 1960

MAY I BE PERMITTED to say one word with regard to the resolution just adopted.

In a report to the Security Council on September 9, 1960, I proposed that the Council appeal for financial support for the Republic of the Congo. Owing to well-known circumstances the Security Council did not reach a positive decision on this matter. Knowing the desperate needs of the Republic of the Congo, I am deeply gratified indeed by the decision which has now been taken by the General Assembly on this subject. Members will undoubtedly bring this appeal to the notice of their governments. They will, certainly, permit me to do the same, stressing the urgency of the appeal. I am sure that governments will respond with their usual generosity. It must give the Congo and its people special satisfaction that, whatever differences of opinion have been reflected in the debates, there has been full agreement on the substance of this specific proposal.

Having taken the floor, I may, perhaps, add that I have carefully noted

General Assembly Official Records, Fourth Emergency Special Session, 863rd plenary meeting.

the explanations given by the sponsors of the text of their draft resolution. These explanations will provide helpful guidance for its implementation.

I have been happy indeed to note the correspondence between the attitude reflected in the resolution and that of the Secretariat as presented most recently in the fourth report. I believe that I am right in finding in this fact evidence of a fundamental and encouraging agreement with and within the African world regarding the aims and the very philosophy of this major United Nations operation.

THE SUMMIT ASSEMBLY AND THE
COLLISION WITH KHRUSHCHEV

NEVER BEFORE had the General Assembly attracted so many heads of government or heads of state as came to the fifteenth annual session which opened on September 20. There were thirty-two of them and they included, among others, Khrushchev, Eisenhower, Harold Macmillan, Nehru, Tito, Nasser, Castro, Nkrumah, Touré, Sukarno, Gomulka, János Kádár, Podgorny, King Hussein, King Frederick IX of Denmark, Prince Sihanouk of Cambodia, Diefenbaker of Canada, Menzies of Australia, and Walter Nash of New Zealand.

Directly or indirectly Khrushchev was mainly responsible for bringing together such an extraordinary assemblage. After the U-2 incident he had broken up the Paris Summit Conference and reinvigorated cold war attitudes and rhetoric toward the West. In the other direction his troubles with the Chinese Communist party and government were coming to a head, though still mainly hidden from view, and a vigorous display of Soviet ideological and political influence vis-à-vis the "third world" was called for. No less than sixteen newly independent African nations would become Members of the United Nations at this Assembly. "Third world" leaders like Nehru were worried by the revival of the cold war and attracted by possibilities for moving to mend the East-West breach at a summit assembly.

At the beginning of August Khrushchev had proposed that heads of government come to the Assembly for a full-dress debate on disarmament. As the difficulties in the Congo grew worse he sought to exploit all openings for increasing Soviet influence in Africa, presenting the Soviet Union as the principal protector and friend of the new countries against Western "colonialism." The Western powers were much less than enthusiastic about what they saw as a major propaganda exercise by Khrushchev but, with the exception of De Gaulle, they decided they could not afford to stand aside.

President Eisenhower, whose term in the White House would be ending in four months, spoke on the opening day of the general debate, September 22. He gave strong support to the United Nations program in the Congo and to the Secretary-General's conduct of it and sharply criticized the Soviet Union for its attacks, but his address in general struck a moderate and constructive note in the typical Eisenhower manner.

The next day Khrushchev responded with a long and violently worded denunciation of Eisenhower, of Hammarskjöld and of "the colonialists" who "have been doing their dirty work in the Congo through the Secretary-General of the United Nations and his staff." He told the Assembly that "it should call Mr. Hammarskjöld to order and ensure that he does not misuse the position of the

Secretary-General but carries out his functions in strict accordance with the provisions of the United Nations Charter and the decisions of the Security Council."[1]

Khrushchev had come to the Assembly armed with revised Soviet proposals for "general and complete disarmament." He devoted a good part of his address to these proposals, noting that both East and West recognized the need to follow up disarmament agreements with United Nations armed forces to keep the peace as decided by the Security Council. To ensure the impartial use of such forces United Nations machinery should be revised beforehand.

"Conditions have clearly matured," he said, "to the point where the post of Secretary-General, who alone directs the staff and alone interprets and executes the decisions of the Security Council and the sessions of the General Assembly, should be abolished."[2]

The executive body of the United Nations should not consist of one person— the Secretary-General—but of three persons representative, respectively, of the following groups: the Western powers, the socialist states and the neutralist states.

This proposal for a tripartite executive instantly became known as the "troika." It would have introduced the power of veto into the day-to-day administrative and executive functions of the Secretariat, for the "troika" would function only by unanimous agreement. The plan revived in a new form an old Soviet preference for a collegium to run the Secretariat. At the San Francisco conference in 1945 Molotov had first proposed that the Secretary-General and four deputy secretaries-general be elected for two-year terms, with the Secretary-General not eligible for reelection. The idea was to rotate the top post among the five permanent members of the Security Council. Soon afterward the sponsoring great powers actually proposed to the conference a modified version which provided for a three-year term and made the Secretary-General eligible for reelection but his four deputies were still to be elected by the Assembly on the recommendation of the Security Council, where the veto applied. Fortunately all but the Soviet Union had soon thought better of the idea and the concept prevailed of a single elected official heading a Secretariat with exclusively international responsibilities (see also volume II of this series, pp. 191-192).

Khrushchev's speech had now carried matters beyond the question of Hammarskjöld's conduct of the Congo operation to an attack upon the office of Secretary-General itself and upon the basic principles which should guide the conduct of that office. This was a challenge that could lead to gravely undermining the future effectiveness of the United Nations itself. When the general debate resumed on Monday, September 26, the Secretary-General was the first speaker (first following text).

---

[1] General Assembly Official Records, Fifteenth Session, 869th plenary meeting.
[2] Ibid.

1. Statement of Reply to Khrushchev and Others During General Debate

NEW YORK   SEPTEMBER 26, 1960

WHEN I ASKED FOR the privilege of exercising my right of reply at this stage of the general debate, it was not because I wanted to use this opportunity to correct any factual mistakes or misrepresentations. That should be unnecessary in the light of the very full debates in the Security Council and at the very recent emergency special session of the General Assembly. At any rate, such a clarification of facts and such other observations as may be called for may more usefully come at a later stage when a wider ground may have been covered by interventions in this debate. Naturally, I reserve my right to such an intervention, if necessary and in due time.

I should like, however, in this context to draw the urgent attention of delegations to the first progress report on the situation in the Congo, circulated just a few days ago. This paper, submitted by Ambassador Dayal as document S/4531, will, I am sure, be found very helpful by those who want to get a balanced picture of the realities with which the Organization is dealing.

My reason for taking the floor is now another one. I felt that, before the debate goes any further, it would be appropriate for me to make clear to the Assembly what, in my view, is and is not the problem before the Assembly in certain respects on which the Secretary-General has been addressed by some speakers.

In those respects the General Assembly is facing a question not of any specific actions but of the principles guiding United Nations activities. In those respects it is a question not of a man but of an institution.

Just one week ago the General Assembly adopted resolution 1474 (ESS-IV) regarding the Congo operation. It did so after a thorough debate and a full presentation of facts. As that is the situation it may well be

General Assembly Official Records, Fifteenth Session, 871st plenary meeting.

asked why those same facts should now be brought out again in the Assembly as a basis for new and far-reaching conclusions, perhaps involving even a question of confidence.

The question before the General Assembly is no longer one of certain actions but one of the principles guiding them. Time and again the United Nations has had to face situations in which a wrong move might have tended to throw the weight of the Organization over in favour of this or that specific party in a conflict of a primarily domestic character. To permit that to happen is indeed to intervene in domestic affairs contrary to the letter and the spirit of the Charter.

To avoid doing so is to be true to the letter and spirit of the Charter, whatever disappointment it might cause those who might have thought that they could add to their political weight by drawing the United Nations over to their side.

This is, of course, the basic reason for the principle spelled out at the very first stage of the Congo operation, and approved by the Security Council, to the effect that the United Nations Force is not under the orders of a government requesting its assistance and cannot be permitted to become a party to any internal conflict, be it one in which the government is engaged or not. It is common experience that nothing, in the heat of emotion, is regarded as more partial by one who takes himself the position of a party than strict impartiality.

Further, as I have said, this is a question not of a man but of an institution. Use whatever words you like, independence, impartiality, objectivity—they all describe essential aspects of what, without exception, must be the attitude of the Secretary-General. Such an attitude, which has found its clear and decisive expression in Article 100 of the Charter, may at any stage become an obstacle for those who work for certain political aims which would be better served or more easily achieved if the Secretary-General compromised with this attitude. But if he did, how gravely he would then betray the trust of all those for whom the strict maintenance of such an attitude is their best protection in the world-wide fight for power and influence. Thus, if the office of the Secretary-General becomes a stumbling block for anyone, be it an individual, a group, or a government, because the incumbent stands by the basic principle which must guide his whole activity, and if, for that reason, he comes under criticism, such criticism strikes at the very office and the concepts on which it is based. I would rather see that office break on strict adherence to the principle of independence, impartiality, and objectivity than drift on the basis of compromise. That is the choice daily facing the Secretary-General. It is also the choice now openly facing the General Assembly, both in substance and in form. I believe that all those whose interests are safeguarded by the United Nations will realize that the choice is not one of the convenience of the moment but one which is decisive for the future, their future.

One last word. Sometimes one gets the impression that the Congo operation is looked at as being in the hands of the Secretary-General, as somehow distinct from the United Nations. No: this is your operation, gentlemen. And this is true whether you represent the African and Asian Member countries, which carry the main burden for the Force and for its command, or speak and act for other parts of the world. There is nothing in the Charter which puts responsibility of this kind on the shoulders of the Secretary-General or makes him the independent master of such an operation. It was the Security Council which, without any dissenting vote, gave this mandate to the Secretary-General on July 14. It was the Security Council which, on July 22, commended his report on the principles that should be applied. It was the Security Council, on August 9, which, again without any dissenting vote, confirmed the authority given to the Secretary-General. Again, just a week ago, the General Assembly, without any dissenting vote, requested the Secretary-General to continue to take vigorous action. Indeed, as I said, this is your operation, gentlemen. It is for you to indicate what you want to have done. As the agent of the Organization I am grateful for any positive advice, but if no such positive advice is forthcoming—as happened in the Security Council on August 21, when my line of implementation had been challenged from outside—then I have no choice but to follow my own conviction, guided by the principles to which I have just referred.

KHRUSHCHEV RENEWED his attack on the Secretary-General during a speech on the issue of Chinese representation on October 1 and again on the morning of October 3. On the second occasion he explicitly called upon Hammarskjöld to resign. At the beginning of the afternoon session the Secretary-General made his famous reply—a speech that evoked a tremendous standing ovation from the overwhelming majority of delegates that continued for several minutes (first following text). Throughout most of the non-Communist world he unexpectedly became a popular hero—a David against a Goliath or, more correctly, one man standing up to a juggernaut.

2. *"I Shall Remain in My Post . . ."—Second Statement of Reply*

NEW YORK   OCTOBER 3, 1960

The head of the Soviet delegation to the General Assembly this morning, in exercising his right of reply, said, among other things, that the present Secretary-General has always been biased against the socialist countries, that he has used the United Nations to support the colonial forces fighting the Congolese government and parliament in order to impose "a new yoke on the Congo"; and, finally, that if I myself "cannot muster the courage to resign, in, let us say, a chivalrous way, we [the Soviet Union] shall draw the inevitable conclusions from the situation." In support of his challenge the representative of the Soviet Union said that there is no room for a man who has "violated the elementary principles of justice in such an important post as that of Secretary-General."

Later on he found reason to say to the representatives at this session that they should not "be deluded by the high-flown words used here" by me in "an attempt to justify the bloody crimes committed against the people of the Congo."

The General Assembly can rightly expect an immediate reply from my side to a statement so directly addressed to me regarding a matter of such potential significance.

The Assembly has witnessed over the last weeks how historical truth is established. Once an allegation has been repeated a few times it is no longer an allegation, it is an established fact even if no evidence has been brought out to support it. However, facts are facts and the true facts are there for whomsoever cares for truth. Those who invoke history will certainly be heard by history. And they will have to accept its verdict as it will be pronounced on the basis of the facts by men free of mind and firm in their conviction that only on a scrutiny of truth can a future of peace be built.

General Assembly Official Records, Fifteenth Session, 883rd plenary meeting.

I have no reason to defend myself or my colleagues against the accusations and judgements to which you have listened. Let me say only this: that you, all of you, are the judges. No single party can claim that authority. I am sure that you will be guided by truth and justice. In particular, let those who know what the United Nations has done and is doing in the Congo, and those who are not pursuing aims proper only to themselves, pass judgement on our actions there. Let the countries which have liberated themselves in the last fifteen years speak for themselves.

I regret that the intervention to which I found it necessary to reply has again tended to personalize an issue which, as I have said, in my view is not a question of a man but of an institution. The man does not count; the institution does. A weak or nonexistent executive would mean that the United Nations would no longer be able to serve as an effective instrument for active protection of the interests of those many Members who need such protection. The man holding the responsibility as chief executive should leave if he weakens the executive. He should stay if this is necessary for its maintenance. This and only this seems to be the substantive criterion that has to be applied.

I said the other day that I would not wish to continue to serve as Secretary-General one day longer than such continued service was considered to be in the best interests of the Organization. The statement this morning seems to indicate that the Soviet Union finds it impossible to work with the present Secretary-General. This may seem to provide a strong reason why I should resign. However, the Soviet Union has also made it clear that if the present Secretary-General were to resign now, it would not wish to elect a new incumbent but insist on an arrangement which—and this is my firm conviction based on broad experience—would make it impossible to maintain an effective executive. By resigning I would, therefore, at the present difficult and dangerous juncture throw the Organization to the winds. I have no right to do so because I have a responsibility to all those Member states for which the Organization is of decisive importance—a responsibility which overrides all other considerations.

It is not the Soviet Union or indeed any other Big Powers which need the United Nations for their protection. It is all the others. In this sense, the Organization is first of all their Organization and I deeply believe in the wisdom with which they will be able to use it and guide it. I shall remain in my post during the term of office as a servant of the Organization in the interest of all those other nations as long as they wish me to do so. [Here the speech was interrupted for several minutes by a standing ovation.]

In this context the representative of the Soviet Union spoke of courage. It is very easy to resign. It is not so easy to stay on. It is very easy to bow to the wish of a Big Power. It is another matter to resist. As is well known to all members of this Assembly I have done so before on many occasions and in many directions. If it is the wish of those nations who see in the Organization their best protection in the present world, I shall now do so again.

THE VIOLENCE and vituperation of Khrushchev's assault upon the Secretary-General had shocked and angered the Asian and African delegates with whom the Soviet leader had hoped to make headway against the West. While he maintained the substance of his demands—that Hammarskjöld resign and be replaced by a "troika"—he toned down his language somewhat before he left for home on October 13. His farewell remarks in the Assembly that day included the following passage:

I should like to ask the Assembly to bear with me a little longer so that I may revert once again to the question of the Secretary-General of the United Nations. I am not making war on Mr. Hammarskjöld personally. I have met him and we have had very pleasant conversations. I consider that Mr. Hammarskjöld is in my debt, because he exploited me, when he was our guest on the Black Sea. I took him around in a rowboat and he has not paid off that debt; he has not done the same for me.[1]

It was not a question of personalities, Khrushchev continued, but he was a Communist and Hammarskjöld a representative of big capital who acted in the interests of a certain group of states. To these remarks the Secretary-General made the following brief reply.

[1] General Assembly Official Records, Fifteenth Session, 904th plenary meeting.

3. Third Statement of Reply

NEW YORK　　　　OCTOBER 13, 1960

I ask the indulgence of the General Assembly in order to say just a few words to the spokesman of the Soviet Union. I do so because he addressed me so personally.

I was very happy to hear that Mr. Khrushchev has good memories of the time when I had the honour to be rowed by him on the Black Sea. I have not, as he said, been able to reply in kind. But my promise to do so stands, and I hope the day will come when he can avail himself of this offer. For if he did I am sure that he would discover that I know how to row—following only my own compass.

General Assembly Official Records, Fifteenth Session, 904th plenary meeting.

ON THE FINAL DAY of the general debate Hammarskjöld spoke once more—this time not attempting to straighten out all the confusions, misstatements and distortions about the Congo but to bring the attention of the delegates back to the fundamental realities of the United Nations effort to help that country despite all the obstacles encountered (first following text).

4. Statement on United Nations Operation in the Congo at End of General Debate

NEW YORK　　　　OCTOBER 17, 1960

In my first intervention during the general debate I reserved my right to ask for the floor at a later stage for such clarifications and comments as

General Assembly Official Records, Fifteenth Session, 906th plenary meeting.

might seem indicated. I thank the president, for giving me this opportunity of saying a few words at this final stage of the debate.

The president of the Republic of Guinea said in his speech the other day:

> Let us regard the Congo as a part of the life of our human race and consider the fate reserved for millions of men, women, and children. Let there be less discussion of Mr. Lumumba, Mr. Kasavubu, Mr. Mobutu, Mr. Iléo and others, and let there be serious efforts to find for this problem a just solution which will serve the cause of a people who desire only well-being, peace and progress.

Much has been said in this debate regarding the Congo (Leopoldville), its problems and the United Nations effort in support of the independence, integrity, peace, and progress of the Congo. Much has been said which has been ill-founded. Whether this has been the result of misinformation, of an emotional engagement, or of tactical considerations but flimsily related to the interests of the Congo, I leave to others to consider. Following the statement of President Sékou Touré which I have just quoted, I would, instead of taking up the Assembly's time with setting straight a record mainly concerned with basically superficial and temporary problems, wish to fill out the picture of the General Assembly by talking about what has not been mentioned: the needs of the people of the Congo and the work of the United Nations in assistance of the authorities whose responsibility it is to meet those needs.

In the confusing fights and conflicts which have now been going on for more than three months in the Congo among political dignitaries of that country, an impression has grown that few have realized that to lead and govern is not a privilege to be sought but a burden of responsibility to be assumed.

It is not those names which we read about in the papers which are tied to the painstaking daily efforts to maintain a minimum of order, to keep an administration—on a minimum level—running, to forestall epidemics and cure disease, to keep the transport system working, to feed the hungriest, to see to it that the many workers for the state are in a position to pay for the necessities of their families. No, that work has been undertaken by many who are nameless, by Congolese officials who are never mentioned and whose names will probably never be known to the world. They have chosen to serve instead of to rule, they have chosen to subordinate themselves instead of searching for power. May I pay tribute to these men and to what they have done to give life and sense to the independence of the Congo. It is those with whom the United Nations has had to work, it is those we have been able to consult, those we have tried to assist.

In doing so, we have been accused of serving the interest of foreign elements, of working hand in hand with imperialists and of impeding the legitimate authorities. We have been accused of substituting ourselves for those authorities, of seeking power for the United Nations in the Congo and of reinstituting some kind of colonialism. Let nobody be misled. Those many men, from very many nations in Africa, Asia, Europe, and the trans-Atlantic countries who are serving the United Nations in the Congo, why are they there? They have left their families. They do not solicit merits for future advancement in the home countries to which they want to return. They work against the heaviest odds under a continuous nerve strain, they have endless working days, they do not know whether all that they do will not be swept aside one of these days by new waves of political unrest. And yet, they give the best they can. May I pay them a tribute as pioneers for that growing group of men all over the world who regard service to the fellow members of the community of mankind as a reward in itself, giving sense to their efforts and to their life—guided by faith in a better future and maintaining the strict norms of behaviour which the Charter requests of an international civil servant? Blame them for their shortcomings, if you will; say that they should do more, if you believe that you are entitled to say so; criticize this or that decision they have taken because in your perspective another decision might have been better, but do not throw doubt on their honesty and seriousness, do not impugn their motives and, especially, do not try to depict them as enemies of the very cause—the well-being of the Congolese people in a life of peace and true independence—for which they are giving so much and, in worldly terms, as individuals, receiving little or nothing.

I wish to say this as an act of justice, necessary if this Organization is to live up to the moral standards it professes and if it is to be able to count in the future on the services of those for whom those standards are a creed which it is their duty to uphold in practical action.

Much of the debate has had as its obvious background this or that specific United Nations emergency step with supposed political implications—or even supposed motives. The listener may have got the impression that what the United Nations is doing in the Congo is really crystallized and summed up in those few actions. In my perspective they are details in a vast pattern of activity; important though they may be in themselves, they are only highly publicized events which have occurred when, in the course of the political complications of the situation, the activities of the Organization, because of the principles which it must maintain, momentarily may seem to have collided with some specific party interest.

With the collapse and disintegration of the Congolese national army as a stabilizing factor, there are now instead, on an emergency basis, close to twenty thousand men of the United Nations Force in the Congo, found necessary to maintain a minimum assurance for the life of the people and, thus, carrying a burden normally assumed by the national security forces. This complicated operation, rendered possible very largely through the generosity and sacrifices of other African states, is also heavily dependent on a highly qualified cadre of officers of very many nations and on highly developed and costly technical services. The Force could not be there without one of the biggest airlifts in history, which we could arrange only by drawing on the resources of the most powerful countries in the world. The Force is serviced by technicians with the most qualified technical schooling and machinery available. And yet it is feeble in relation to its own tasks. Indeed, this is a strange background for statements to the effect that the Force should and could be withdrawn or that its tasks could be taken over by the national security forces or by a few of the units now making up part of it.

But the activities of the Force are, I hope, a quickly passing phase in the United Nations effort to give to the Congo its full and real independence and to reestablish its integrity. Already now, and increasingly so, the civilian operation is of decisive importance. And in that civilian operation what has been achieved has required the services of all the agencies in the United Nations to their full capacity.

In the vastness of the Congo, where so much movement depends on air services, everything would have been grounded in the last three months but for the air traffic control, the radio and navigation aids, the weather forecasting and telecommunications provided by the International Civil Aviation Organization, the International Telecommunications Union, and the World Meterological Organization. Even the food and milk so generously provided by Member states for supply to children and refugees—when supplies were not interrupted by political disturbances—have been largely carried in United Nations aircraft to countrywide distribution points where local authorities and the Red Cross took over. The early breakdown of surface transport which caused local shortages of food has been overcome by United Nations personnel, who saw to the dredging of the river and reopening of the ocean port, who moved pilots by helicopter to increase their effective working hours, who reactivated the oil pipelines between port and capital, and who are supervising workshops and maintenance of harbours and railways. Some of these engineers have been diverted to the preparation of a programme of public works for the relief of unemployment. International Labour Office programmes are dealing with a number of crucial labour and social security fields. Hospitals, abandoned by their medical staff, have been quickly restored to use by medical units provided by Red Cross societies of many countries, and the elementary health services have been maintained by the World Health Organization. Plans and actions for the reopening of schools and the organization of secondary and technical education have largely depended on the activities of the United Nations Educational, Scientific, and Cultural Organization.

Plans for maintaining agricultural services are being developed through the Food and Agriculture Organization. Research institutions of continental value, whose prestige is world-wide, are being protected and maintained through the United Nations. Plans are being drawn for the training of tomorrow's doctors, teachers, and civil servants, so that the Congo may make the maximum use of its reservoir of youth, its greatest and most durable asset. All these vitally essential services are rendered under the United Nations flag, thus eliminating any risks that they create a dependence of the Congo on any specific foreign powers or that outside elements be permitted to establish what might develop into vested interests in the country. They, thereby, effectively help in establishing and strengthening its true independence.

You may ask where, then, the government and the administration are to be found in this picture. I think I have already given the reply. We have tried to consult to all the extent there was anybody who could be consulted—and who paid any attention to the needs. We have cooperated on a continuous basis of great intimacy with a number of central government officials. We have avoided taking decisions for which we could not get authoritative approval, but when a specific situation reached the stage of acute crisis, requiring immediate counteraction, and when we could not find those whose support we wished to have, we have had to act as responsible human beings facing a desperate emergency. You try to save a drowning man without prior authorization and even if he resists you; you do not let him go even when he tries to strangle you. I do not believe that any one would wish the Organization to follow other rules than those you apply to yourself when faced with such a situation.

I said in the Congo, some time ago, that the birth of an independent Congo had come to coincide with the birth of true cooperation of the United Nations family of agencies in the service of a Member nation. As a spokesman for all these administrations, I can say that we are proud that we have been permitted to serve in this way, but I should add that we shall be even prouder when, through all the joint efforts, the stage has been reached when our services are no longer necessary in the Congo and when we can leave the country solely and fully in the good hands of its own people, with its independence, peace, and prosperity safeguarded by its own means.

Of course, the end of all political effort must be the well-being of the individual in a life of safety and freedom. In the case of the Congo, as elsewhere, the means to this end are in the first place the independence, peace, integrity, and prosperity of the country. In turn, this goal requires the maintenance and progress of economic life, the functioning of a good judiciary system, a soundly working administration, all under the responsibility of a government, stable thanks to its firm roots in the free will of the people, expressed and developed in democratic forms. This is the perspective in which the effort of the United Nations must be seen. This perspective should determine our judgement and give us the sense of proportion necessary if we are to avoid substituting the means for the ends and the interests of the man or the group for those of the people.

WHEN KHRUSHCHEV left for Moscow he had not won any direct support outside the Soviet bloc for replacing the office of Secretary-General by a tripartite executive. Among the Asian-Africans U Thant of Burma was an especially strong defender of the Secretary-General's position and of Hammarskjöld personally. However there were signs that future inroads might be possible among some states committed to a neutralist foreign policy and anxious to promote negotiation and compromise between the West and the Soviet bloc.

This anxiety had led Nehru, Sukarno, Nasser, Tito, and Nkrumah early in the session to join in an abortive appeal to Khrushchev and Eisenhower to renew their contacts. The attempt was not itself related to the "troika" proposal but it reflected a general disposition among the more leftward-leaning neutralist governments toward reaching some accommodation with Soviet views. Also the idea of giving formal recognition to neutralism as a third force in the United Nations had its attractions. Thus Nehru talked of a "consultative council" to advise the Secretary-General, and Nkrumah suggested appointment of three deputy secretaries-general, though neither put these forward as formal proposals.

Such reactions encouraged the Soviet delegation to pursue the "troika" approach. On October 17 the Soviet representative in the Fifth (Administrative and Budgetary) Committee, A. A. Roshchin, accused the Secretary-General of deliberately favoring the West—in particular the United States—in the composition and administration of the Secretariat, especially at the higher levels and in field operations. The Secretariat, he declared, should represent equally the three groups of Member states—the socialist states, the neutralist states, and the United States and its allies. As an interim measure, all recruitment from North America and Western Europe should be immediately discontinued.

The next day this brought the following response from the Secretary-General (see also his further statement in the Fifth Committee on November 21).

---

5. *Statement of Reply in the Fifth Committee to Soviet Attack on His Personnel Policies*

NEW YORK   OCTOBER 18, 1960

As I have already indicated, I hope later on, during the general debate on the budget, to have an opportunity to revert to the main financial and budgetary problems this year facing the United Nations. It is therefore with hesitation that I intervene at this stage. However, such an intervention has been rendered necessary by a statement made here yesterday by the delegate of the USSR, obviously as part of a follow-up of an operation forcefully started by Mr. Khrushchev in the General Assembly. I am certain that members of the Committee can easily see for themselves the fallacies in the arguments presented as evidence of my allegedly biased attitude, but it may be appropriate that the one attacked puts briefly on record his views on the arguments presented.

The Committee will later have to study the question of geographical distribution and will then be able to base its debate on a full presentation of statistics showing the development. It will not be the first time that the Committee considers this important part of Secretariat policies, but it

UN Press Release SG/971. For the summary record, see General Assembly Official Records, Fifteenth Session, Fifth Committee, 769th meeting.

certainly will be the first time that it will do so being faced with a flat allegation that the universally recognized lack of balance in the composition of the Secretariat is the expression of a conscious and partial policy. In the light of all previous studies of the matter, the Committee should be able to see for itself why the composition is as it is.

The staff is to an overwhelming extent employed in a form providing for career service. For that and other practical reasons the composition I inherited when I came here seven and a half years ago was, on the whole, a *fait accompli* in which I could make changes only to the extent that openings presented themselves for a correction when officers resigned because of age or for other reasons.

As I engaged in a policy of stabilizing the staff—after an initial reduction within the limits of the possible—those openings were very restricted, and no revolutionary changes in the composition could be achieved. I have stuck to a rule which goes back to the Charter and the staff regulations, and which is solidly based in common decency as regards fulfillment of contractual obligations in good faith, to the effect that people should not be fired for nationality reasons in order to provide possibilities for the United Nations to arrive at another geographical balance. I would not believe that the Assembly would wish to depart from this rule, whatever the purpose.

What are the bases for recruitment, and what are the bases for the choice of people to be sent on missions or to be given special assignments? The Charter, which in this case should guide us, talks in the first instance about "the necessity of securing the highest standards of efficiency, competence, and integrity." It adds—in Article 101, paragraph 3—that "due regard shall be paid to the importance of recruiting the staff on as wide a geographical basis as possible." Thus, when the spokesman of the USSR starts out from the primary request that, under all circumstances, three groups should be balanced within the Secretariat, he is at variance with the criteria established in the Charter.

The Charter talks about "efficiency, competence, and integrity" as the decisive elements. Of those three criteria I would put integrity first. To me, integrity means that the officials should have only one loyalty in the performance of their duties, and that is the one to the United Nations. Those who do not see their job in that light or who are forced to act on the basis of a different standard, may still be useful in a United Nations operation, but the difference of the rules of integrity which they apply can never be forgotten by the chief executive—and that is true whatever their nationality!

If a man meets the criterion of integrity, I would, thereafter, rank competence and efficiency equal. The United Nations official must be willing to give all his time to the job, if so required. And he must be able to do so in an efficient way, being able to adjust himself to true teamwork with people who may have very different notions than he himself has carried with him when he came to the United Nations. And competence—competence means not only to have reasonably good training in this or that professional field. It means to be able to put this training to full use in the international field.

Applying these Charter criteria, I have found it easier to recruit from some parts of the world than from others. And if this has been reflected in the composition of missions which have had to be organized in a very short time, I do not present any excuse for it. I have to add one thing: to accuse people who serve this Organization in the true spirit of the Charter, with an integrity beyond praise and a loyalty which does not suffer any reservation, to accuse such people of being the spokesmen of one power bloc or another because of their passports, is a slight to men and women who deserve much better.

Another practical observation. I get from this or that country lists of candidates. We pick out those who seem to fit to the vacancies which develop and, then, it happens—too often in some cases—that after a short time of employment, without any prewarning, those recruited go home again or, maybe, are withdrawn. In fact, it is in some cases difficult to keep such a pace in recruitment as to balance the pace of withdrawal in a way which leads to a continuous and desirable increase of the group concerned.

Finally, on this point, one overriding consideration. With means which are very limited indeed in relation to the tasks, if you compare the situation with that maintained by most national administrations, I must have one thing in mind: that the Secretariat, in spite of all difficulties, should be able to do its job and do it in a way which will stand up to the critics of the future as well as to the honest critics of today. To compromise with that aim in order to smooth the way momentarily is to betray the trust which we all of us carry in the Secretariat, we whose task it has become to be the caretakers of this experiment in international cooperation which will lay the basis for similar efforts in the future. With this in mind I must first of all look for the man and only in second place at the statistics. Is it not time for others too to apply qualitative instead of quantitative criteria?

The other main point in the intervention of the delegate of the Soviet Union was concerned with the various United Nations missions. Again I find him at variance with the Charter, and seriously so. On this point I would not like to go into any criticism but I want to make it clear what his proposals mean as an expression of a philosophy regarding the United Nations.

They mean first of all that he has chosen to forget Article 99 and what follows from that Article. If the Secretary-General is entitled to draw the attention of the Security Council to threats to peace and security, has he to rely on reports in the press or from this or that government? Has he to take the word of Moscow or Washington? No, certainly not. He has to find out for himself and that may mean, as in the case of the criticised journey to Laos last November, that he has to go himself. To deny the Secretary-General the right to such personal fact-finding, is in fact to erase from the Charter Article 99. Rob that Article of its content, if you feel that this is the right thing to do, but then, do not expect anybody with a sense of his responsibilities to assume the duties of a Secretary-General under the Charter.

But the standpoint of the spokesman of the Soviet Union means more. The mission to Laos of the personal representative of the Secretary-General, charged with the coordination of widespread and important practical activities in the social and economic fields, was arranged at the request of the chief of state and his legitimate government. It has been endorsed by succeeding governments, including the present one. Obviously, the criticism means that the Secretary-General would not be allowed to respond to a practical request of a government, and all legitimate authorities of a country, unless such a move had the approval of the Security Council, under the unanimity rule, or by the General Assembly, which may not be in session when the need arises. Those countries who wish to have the independent assistance of the United Nations, in the modest forms possible for the Secretary-General and without running into the stormy weather of a major international political debate, will certainly be interested in this attitude of the delegate of the Soviet Union.

What is true of Laos is true of Guinea. At the moment when that was a most unpopular move in parts of the world which the Soviet delegate alleges that I represent, I offered President Sékou Touré our practical assistance. He and his government wanted it, accepted it, and used it. Certainly, the party directly concerned in this case will also be most interested to hear that I acted illegally in helping them.

It is useless to continue the list. It is not because we want to interfere that we take on ourselves the burden to help a government at its request and within the field that administratively is under the authority of the Secretary-General. We do it, and I have done it, because I believe that this is part of the duties of the Organization. The delegate of the Soviet Union seems to hold another view. Let him say so clearly and test his view against the view of those who look to the United Nations for support. There is reason to ponder why this role of the United Nations is now considered to be so objectionable.

I should, before leaving this subject, draw the attention of the Committee to one thing. Technical assistance missions of the regular kind, which to my knowledge so far has not been subject to criticism such as the one now raised, can be and have been of very different types. It may be a question of a few technical experts on the margin, or it may be a question of, at the other extreme, highly qualified experts used by the government as advisers in their central planning. In the first case, a sharp distinction is obviously drawn between a technical assistance mission and a mission having some kind of political impact. In the second case, the technical assistance mission may be of political significance but in a way entirely under the control of the government. Various governments have in the past sought such more qualified technical assistance and various governments have received it. Is that also to be considered illegal? And is it to be considered illegal if the resident representative in a regular technical assistance mission frequently is called in by the cabinet for discussions and, maybe, has direct access also to the chief of state? But if that is not the case, what is then the difference between a technical assistance mission and a special representative of the kind against which objections are now raised and of which you find examples in Laos and Guinea? Or is the present line of criticism based on the view that governments should not ask for, receive, and accept technical assistance which is more than marginal and which may strengthen their hand so as to make them more independent of bilateral arrangements from whatever source and for whatever reasons they may be offered?

It would seem that the full-scale attack on certain policies to which the Committee listened yesterday could with greater justification have taken place in some other body of the United Nations where it could have been based on my introductions to the annual reports to the General Assembly for the two years 1958–1959 and 1959–1960. The principles I apply and the aims I pursue have been fully spelled out in those documents, and spelled out in a way which would make it clear what this difference of views is really all about. I would ask the members of the Committee to read page 3 in the English text of the introduction to the Annual Report of last year, and to read section III of the Introduction to the Annual Report of this year.[1] I would have liked to quote here the relevant passages, but I will not take more time than necessary from the Committee and the important tasks which it has in fields different from the one covered by the political parts of the statement to which I am giving my comments.

If I am to draw my general conclusions from the observations made in the statement of yesterday, it would be, as I have already said, that technical assistance should be reduced to marginal expert work and that the Secretary-General should forget the responsibilities and needs which flow from Article 99 and serve only as chief administrator of a Secretariat technically assisting a vast conference machinery. This would mean that the United Nations organization should be reduced to the role of a framework for public multilateral negotiations and robbed of its possibilities of action in the preservation of peace in prevention of such conflicts as might come before the various organs of the United Nations.

The United Nations is the instrument of its Member governments, and those governments decide the destiny of the Organization. They can choose the line which slowly has been emerging in response to current needs over the last few years, or they can choose to fall back on the pattern of the League of Nations or of the most conservative interpreters of the Charter of the present Organization. The Secretariat as a body will certainly loyally accept the role for the Organization chosen by its Members, but it should be understood that every member of the Secretariat serves in accordance with his own conscience and that the best may withdraw if they were to feel that they can have no faith in the line along which the Organization is permitted to survive.

---

[1] See volume IV of this series, pp. 451–52, and pp. 130–34 of this volume.

PROTESTS AND APPEALS DIRECTED TO THE GOVERNMENT OF BELGIUM AND TO TSHOMBÉ

THE FOLLOWING *notes verbales* of October 8, 19, and 29 addressed by the Secretary-General to the Government of Belgium, together with his letter of October 8 to Tshombé, were not circulated until November 2, when they were included as part B of Dayal's second progress report to the Secretary-General covering developments in the Congo from September 21 to the end of October.[1] Dayal's first progress report[2] had been submitted on September 21. It may be noted that after Dayal became his special representative in the Congo on September 8, the Secretary-General discontinued his own reports during this period and instead circulated, without comment, Dayal's reports to him.

Both the Belgian government and Tshombé made sharply negative replies to Hammarskjöld's appeals addressed to them in the following texts.

1. Note Verbale *to the Representative of Belgium*

NEW YORK   OCTOBER 8, 1960

THE SECRETARY-GENERAL OF the United Nations presents his compliments to the Permanent Representative of Belgium to the United Nations and has the honour to state that, having regard to the resolution adopted by the General Assembly on September 20, 1960 (1474 ES-IV), and after

Security Council Official Records, Fifteenth Year, Supplement for October, November, and December 1960, document S/4557, section B.

[1] Security Council Official Records, Fifteenth Year, Supplement for October, November, and December 1960, document S/4557, part B.
[2] Ibid., Supplement for July, August, and September 1960, document S/4531.

careful study of the conditions at present prevailing in the Congo, he is more convinced than ever that it is absolutely essential that no technical or financial aid should be furnished to any of the authorities in the Congo except through the United Nations. He accordingly concludes that the unilateral assistance which the Belgian government is continuing to furnish to the authorities in both Katanga and South Kasai is not in conformity with the requirements of the General Assembly, in particular with those set out in paragraph 5 (a) of the resolution, and is in fact impeding the restoration of normal political and economic conditions in the Republic of the Congo.

On the basis of this conclusion, the Secretary-General would request the Belgian government to withdraw all the military, paramilitary, or civil personnel which it has placed at the disposal of the authorities in the Congo and henceforth to follow the example of many other states by channelling all aid to the Congo, or to any authorities in the Congo, through the United Nations.

The Secretary-General is convinced that only acceptance of these requests can prevent the occurrence of events in the Congo that may result in the country becoming the theatre of a conflict of world-wide dimensions which would be fraught with the utmost danger for the country itself.

The Secretary-General wishes to inform the Belgian government that he has sent a personal message to Mr. Tshombé, a copy of which is attached for information.

---

2. Note Verbale *to the Representative of Belgium*

NEW YORK   OCTOBER 19, 1960

REFERRING TO THE *note verbale* that he had the honour to address to the Permanent Representative of Belgium on October 14, 1960,[1] the Secretary-General wishes to inform the Permanent Representative that, ac-

---

[1] This is the date of transmission of the *note verbale* of October 8. The delay was caused by the necessity of ensuring that the text was communicated at one and the same time to the representative of Belgium and to Mr. Tshombé, president of the provincial government of Katanga.

cording to recent reports from his Special Representative at Leopoldville, 114 Belgian officers and 117 other ranks are still serving in the gendarmerie of the Katanga authorities and 58 Belgian officers are at present in the service of the Katanga police. It further appears from these reports that all the key positions in Katanga, in both civil affairs and security, are either directly in the hands of Belgian officials or under the control of Belgian advisers attached to Congolese officials. Such is the situation at the moment, although the Belgian technical assistance mission was apparently withdrawn on October 13, 1960.

With regard to the would-be autonomous state of South Kasai, the reports continue to assert that Colonel Crèvecoeur wears Belgian uniform in the exercise of his duties and is assisted by a Belgian officer, Colonel Levaureg, and that they are both engaged in training new military units in the service of the authorities of south Katanga. In this connection, it is stated that chief medical officer de Forminière, who is of Belgian nationality, serves as medical inspector for these military units.

It is also reported that light military equipment is transported from Katanga to Kabinda through the Mwene-Ditu district and that a Belgian business man is supporting this arms traffic.

The Secretary-General also wishes to draw the attention of the Permanent Representative of Belgium to some recent reports according to which a recruiting agency for the Congo has been set up in Brussels under the direction of Professor Lacroix and with the support of Professor Verhagen, both of the University of Lovanium. The object of this agency is apparently to send an ever increasing number of Belgian officials to the Congo, many of whom have already taken up their duties at what is called the Collège des Commissaires. Several cases in which these Belgian experts have seriously hampered the implementation of the United Nations technical assistance programme have already been reported to the United Nations authorities in the Congo. Some of these experts have even deliberately delayed the submission of requests from the Congolese authorities for United Nations technical assistance.

It is clear that the employment of Belgian experts by the Congolese authorities and the activities of these experts, which are often directed against the United Nations, cannot fail to give rise to serious disputes, especially in view of the unstable political situation at present prevailing in the Congo. In this connection, the Secretary-General feels it is his duty to point out that the agreements entered into between Belgian technicians and the various Congolese authorities are not approved by any government or any authority that can rightly claim to be the legitimate central government of the Congo.

3. Note Verbale *to the Representative of Belgium*

NEW YORK   OCTOBER 29, 1960

THE SECRETARY-GENERAL PRESENTS his compliments to the Permanent Representative of Belgium to the United Nations and has the honour to inform him that the Secretary-General's Special Representative in the Congo has just notified him officially that under an agreement between the Belgian authorities and Colonel Mobutu, thirty-seven members of the Congolese national army have been sent to Belgium to receive military training in Belgian military schools. The Secretary-General wishes also to draw the attention of the representative of Belgium to the report, confirmed today by the local representative of the United Nations at Elisabethville, that forty-seven cadets of the so-called Katanga army have been sent from Katanga to Belgian military schools for the same purpose.

The Secretary-General, being responsible for taking such action as may be appropriate to ensure the implementation of the General Assembly resolution of September 20, is obliged to draw the attention of the Belgian government, as a matter of urgency, to the fact that these arrangements for military training are contrary to the letter and spirit of paragraph 6 of that resolution, in which the General Assembly called upon all states to refrain from the direct and indirect provision of arms or other materials of war and military personnel and "other assistance for military purposes in the Congo" during the temporary period of military assistance through the United Nations, except upon the request of the United Nations through the Secretary-General for carrying out the purposes of that resolution and of the resolutions of July 14 and 22 and of August 9, 1960, of the Security Council [S/4387, S/4405 and S/4426].

In this connection, it should be noted that the aforesaid arrangements have not been entered into with any legal authority of the Republic of the Congo recognized as such by the General Assembly or the Security Council.

The Secretary-General requests the Belgian government to give urgent consideration to the question and to inform him of the measures it intends to take to ensure the implementation of the provisions of the above-mentioned resolution.

---

4. Letter to Mr. Tshombé, President of the Provincial Government of Katanga

NEW YORK   OCTOBER 8, 1960

AS YOU ARE UNDOUBTEDLY AWARE, the situation in the Congo, in view of the reciprocal influence of internal and international reactions, is evolving in the direction of an increasing danger. The withdrawal of Belgian troops from the whole of the territory, including Katanga, to a certain extent reduced the dangers for a time, but we are now witnessing a recrudescence of tension. In the light of the discussion in the General Assembly, you cannot have failed to realize that the shadow of an armed conflict is once more hanging over the country.

The dangers, as they appear at present, seem in my opinion to derive from three factors: the confused and disquieting situation which still prevails at Leopoldville, the continued presence of a considerable number of Belgian nationals—soldiers, paramilitary personnel, and civilians—and, lastly, the unresolved constitutional conflict, threatening the unity of the Congo, which is symbolized by the name Katanga. Among these factors, I regard the last two as of crucial importance, even from the standpoint of the first: that is to say that, if we could fully circumscribe the Belgian factor and eliminate it and if we could lay the groundwork for a reconciliation between Katanga and the rest of the territory of the Republic of the Congo, the situation at Leopoldville might very well be rectified. The way towards a pacification of the country would thus be opened.

Taking the above into account, I am submitting certain requests to the Belgians of which I wish to inform you without delay. These requests are based on the General Assembly resolution of September 20, 1960, with which your are of course fully acquainted. My requests to the Belgian government are twofold in nature. Firstly, the Belgians would withdraw all the military, paramilitary, and civilian personnel they have placed at the disposal of the authorities in the Congo and, secondly, they would henceforth follow the example given by the great Western powers, and above all by the United States, in channelling any assistance to the Congo, or to any authorities in the Congo, through the United Nations. I am convinced that only the acceptance of these two requests can prevent the occurrence of events in the Congo that may result in the country becoming the theatre of a conflict of world-wide dimensions which would be fraught with the utmost danger for the country itself.

You will fully realize that if the Belgians also withdrew all their technicians, under whatever title they are now serving in the Congo, and if, in addition, they channelled all their assistance through the United Nations, the result would be a situation in which all the parties in the Congo would have to give urgent reconsideration to their policies regarding the future of the country. I am certain that, with that in view, you yourself would wish to review your policy, in view of the fact that Katanga might find itself cut off from all outside assistance, with the exception of what you could receive within the framework of the assistance furnished through the United Nations to the Republic of the Congo. It should also be clear that the possibilities that the United Nations has of preventing ill-considered action on the part of those who are at present responsible for the employment of most of the population of Eville would disappear if an agreement concerning future policy were not made along the lines I have just indicated.

Of course, your reaction to the situation which will result from the attitude adopted by the United Nations will be influenced by what takes place at Leopoldville. I leave it to you to appraise the situation in that town and its implications for your policy. What is essential is that, in the present situation, your cooperation may be decisive for the future of the country. I know your patriotism and consequently I do not doubt that you will follow the development of the situation and allow yourself to be guided in the last analysis by concern for the strength and integrity of the Republic of the Congo.

Beyond the national and local perspectives which command attention, when the present policies are examined in the light of the attitude of the United Nations and the development of the situation in the Congo, there are international considerations to be taken into account. We have barely avoided certain major dangers of war, which, had they materialized, would have torn the Congo apart, with disastrous consequences for Katanga as well. The nature of those dangers has changed to a certain extent, but their gravity has not decreased. I would be lacking in candour if I did not tell you that unless the Katanga problem—which is a part of the larger problem of the Congo—is very soon resolved in a spirit of conciliation and unity, the resistance the United Nations could offer to a radical split on a world scale, which would carve up the whole of Africa and the Congo, might be irremediably weakened. You are undoubtedly aware that I would not address a warning of this kind to you if I did not sincerely think that the dangers are real and immediate.

If you should think that these considerations do not provide an accurate picture of the present situation and that therefore you yourself cannot initiate any action in the direction of reconciliation and in favour of the unity which now seems called for, I should like you to have a conversation with one of my personal representatives at Leopoldville, either Mr. Dayal or General Rikhye, which would enable you to examine the situation together and thus to lay a solid foundation upon which you could give the problem further study along the lines I have indicated.

BESIDES THE COMPLAINTS about the activities of Belgian military personnel and technicians in violation of the Assembly's September 20 resolution, Dayal's November 2 report was highly critical of the increased confusion and breakdown of law and order that followed Mobutu's military coup. ONUC maintained day-to-day contacts on practical and technical matters with Mobutu's College of Commissioners and its officials, but did not, he said, recognize the Mobutu régime as the legitimate central government. In the confused situation that prevailed only two institutions remained that clearly derived sanction from the constitution—the *Loi fondamentale*. These were the office of the chief of state and the Parliament. If the army could be brought under some measure of control and other lawless elements subdued, Dayal wrote, "it would open the way to the leaders of the country to seek peaceful solutions through the medium of these two institutions. . . . there is a chance of a single government of conciliation, representing all the principal interests, emerging."

Dayal's report received a bad reception from the Western powers. They preferred the Kasavubu-Mobutu régime, unconstitutional and inefficient as it was, to risking the return of Lumumba. They opposed for that reason reconvening the Parliament, where Lumumba had so far maintained majority support. On Dayal's orders the UN guard at Lumumba's residence had also refused to permit the army to enter for the purpose of arresting Lumumba, who had parliamentary immunity. Even the United States government, which had hitherto backed

Hammarskjöld all the way on his Congo policies, criticized his views on the constitutional situation and on Belgium's activities and the stands taken by Dayal in Leopoldville.

The question of legitimacy was now brought to the General Assembly for decision. Guinea first proposed seating Lumumba's representatives on October 10. Then, on October 28, Ceylon, Ghana, India, Indonesia, Mali, Morocco, and the United Arab Republic joined Guinea in sponsoring a revised draft resolution to seat Lumumba's delegation and requesting the Secretary-General to take action to ensure the security of a meeting of the Congolese parliament. There were immediate countermoves from Kasavubu's supporters, led by the United States. The President flew to New York to address the Assembly on November 8 in his capacity as chief of state. He announced the names of a delegation headed by himself, asked that they be seated immediately and declared that he had sole authority under the constitution to appoint the Congo's representatives to the Assembly.

The Ghana delegation responded by circulating a letter signed by the president of the Chamber and acting president of the Senate of the Congolese Parliament asserting the legality of the Lumumba government and that the chief of state had no authority to speak for the Congo before the United Nations. Hammarskjöld thought both the United States and Lumumba's Afro-Asian supporters were making a grave mistake in pushing for a decision. Whichever way it went it could only complicate efforts at conciliation among the rival leaders. The United States, however, was determined to go ahead and it soon became evident that its all-out diplomatic campaign had mobilized the necessary votes. Too late Lumumba's Afro-Asian sponsors sought to postpone a decision on the ground that it might hamper the work of the Conciliation Commission appointed by the Congo Advisory Committee on November 5. Kasavubu's delegation was seated by a vote of 53 to 24, with 19 abstentions, on November 22.

The Conciliation Commission consisted of representatives of Ethiopia, the Federation of Malaya, Ghana, Guinea, India, Indonesia, Liberia, Mali, Morocco, Nigeria, Pakistan, Senegal, Sudan, Tunisia, and the United Arab Republic. Jaja Wachuku of Nigeria was elected chairman. The Commission's original intention was to go to Leopoldville on November 26, but at Kasavubu's request the departure was postponed.

Second Interim Report to the Security Council Under the Council's Resolution on South Africa

NEW YORK   OCTOBER 11, 1960

As WE HAVE noted earlier, the Congo crisis caused postponement of the planned visit to the Union of South Africa by the Secretary-General under his mandate from the Security Council. The presence at the Assembly of Eric H. Louw, South Africa's foreign minister, provided an opportunity to reschedule the visit for January 1961.

---

1. By MY INTERIM REPORT to the Security Council dated April 19, 1960, [S/4305] I informed the Council that I had accepted a proposal of the Government of the Union of South Africa that preliminary consultations between the prime minister and minister of external affairs and myself should be held in London after the conclusion of the Commonwealth Prime Ministers' Conference, probably in early May 1960. I further informed the Security Council that these preliminary discussions were to be preparatory to a visit to the Union of South Africa at the end of July or beginning of August.

2. During the preliminary discussions in London, which took place on May 13 and 14, 1960, it was agreed between the Secretary-General and the minister of external affairs of the Union of South Africa that the basis for future discussions would flow from paragraph 5 of the first interim report, which reads as follows:

The consultations rendered necessary by the provisions of paragraph 5 of the Security Council's resolution of April 1, 1960, will be undertaken on the basis of the authority of the Secretary-General under the Charter. It is agreed between the Government of the Union of South Africa and myself that consent of the Union government to discuss the Security Council's resolution with the Secretary-General would not require prior recognition from the Union government of the United Nations authority.

Security Council Official Records, Fifteenth Year, Supplement for October, November, and December 1960, document S/4551.

3. During these exploratory discussions, agreement was reached on the character and course of the further consultations to take place in Pretoria.

4. It was also agreed that during the contemplated visit to the Union of South Africa, while consultation throughout would be with the Union government, no restrictive rules were to be imposed on the Secretary-General.

5. Due to circumstances resulting from the mandate given to me by the Security Council by resolutions S/4387, S/4405, and S/4426 dated July 14 and 22 and August 9, 1960, in connection with the United Nations operation in the Republic of the Congo (Leopoldville), I have been unable to visit the Union of South Africa as envisaged in the interim report. On four occasions, precise plans were made for the visit, but on each occasion it became necessary first to postpone, then finally to cancel those plans, owing to developments in the Republic of the Congo.

6. During a meeting at Headquarters with the minister of external affairs of the Union of South Africa on September 28, 1960, a new invitation was extended to me by the prime minister of the Union government to visit the Union early in January 1961.

7. It would be my hope to arrange for the visit at the time suggested for the purpose of the requested consultations with the prime minister of the Union of South Africa. In this connection, it would be my intention to explore with the prime minister the possibility of arrangements which would provide for appropriate safeguards of human rights, with adequate contact with the United Nations.

Remarks at United Nations Day Concert

NEW YORK   OCTOBER 24, 1960

THIS WAS the last of the talks given by Dag Hammarskjöld at the annual United Nations Day concerts. A recording made at the time was repeated eleven months later during the memorial ceremony in the General Assembly Hall for him and those who had died with him in the airplane crash at Ndola on September 18, 1961. The Philadelphia Orchestra returned on that occasion to play again Beethoven's Ninth Symphony as a tribute to the Secretary-General.

IT IS THE TRADITION that the Organization marks United Nations Day with a concert including the final movement of Beethoven's Ninth Symphony. Today we shall, for the first time in this hall, listen to the symphony in its entirety.

It is difficult to say anything knowing that the words spoken will be followed by this enormous confession of faith in the victorious human spirit and in human brotherhood, a confession valid for all times and with a depth and wealth of expression never surpassed. However, this concert is in celebration of United Nations Day and it has been felt that a few words may remind us of the purpose for which we have assembled.

When the Ninth Symphony opens we enter a drama full of harsh conflict and dark threats. But the composer leads us on, and in the beginning of the last movement we hear again the various themes repeated, now as a bridge toward a final synthesis. A moment of silence and a new theme is introduced, the theme of reconciliation and joy in reconciliation. A human voice is raised in rejection of all that has preceded and we enter the dreamt kingdom of peace. New voices join the first and mix in a jubilant assertion of life and all that it gives us when we meet it, joined in faith and human solidarity.

On his road from conflict and emotion to reconciliation in this final hymn of praise, Beethoven has given us a confession and a credo which we, who work within and for this Organization, may well make our own.

UN Press Release SG/973.

We take part in the continuous fight between conflicting interests and ideologies which so far has marked the history of mankind, but we may never lose our faith that the first movements one day will be followed by the fourth movement. In that faith we strive to bring order and purity into chaos and anarchy. Inspired by that faith we try to impose the laws of the human mind and of the integrity of the human will on the dramatic evolution in which we are all engaged and in which we all carry our responsibility.

The road of Beethoven in his Ninth Symphony is also the road followed by the authors of the Preamble of the Charter. It begins with the recognition of the threat under which we all live, speaking as it does of the need to save succeeding generations from the scourge of war which has brought untold sorrow to mankind. It moves on to a reaffirmation of faith in the dignity and worth of the human person. And it ends with the promise to practice tolerance and live together in peace with one another as good neighbors and to unite our strength to maintain peace.

This year, the fifteenth in the life of the Organization, is putting it to new tests. Experience has shown how far we are from the end which inspired the Charter. We are indeed still in the first movements. But no matter how deep the shadows may be, how sharp the conflicts, how tense the mistrust reflected in what is said and done in our world of today as reflected in this hall and in this house, we are not permitted to forget that we have too much in common, too great a sharing of interests and too much that we might lose together, for ourselves and for succeeding generations, ever to weaken in our efforts to surmount the difficulties and not to turn the simple human values, which are our common heritage, into the firm foundation on which we may unite our strength and live together in peace.

May this be enough as a reminder of the significance of this day. And may now the symphony develop its themes, uniting us in its recognition of fear and its confession of faith.

In ending, may I express the gratitude of the Organization, and of all of us, to Mr. Ormandy and to the Philadelphia Orchestra for coming to us today and for helping us to celebrate this fifteenth United Nations Day.

Statement in the Fifth Committee on the Financial Crisis and His Policies

NEW YORK   NOVEMBER 21, 1960

THE MAIN PURPOSE of the following statement in the Fifth Committee was an appeal to the Member governments to face up to their responsibility to provide adequate and assured financing for programs like ONUC which they themselves had decided were necessary to the maintenance of international peace and security. Hammarskjöld also used the occasion to respond again on various points to the relentless campaign waged by the Soviet bloc against his past and present conduct of the office of Secretary-General. As we have previously noted, this campaign was aimed also at undermining the very concept of a Secretariat with purely international responsibilities and replacing it by a Secretariat representing the ideologies and interests of three groups of Member states—the Western states, the socialist states, and the "neutral" states.

THE FIFTH COMMITTEE has devoted considerable time to a general discussion of the 1961 budget estimates and personnel problems facing it. In the course of the general debate much has been said which represents constructive criticism and helpful suggestions. But much has also been said which has but a faint relation to the real problems which the General Assembly will have to resolve, far as it has been from realities and coloured as it has been by purposes extraneous to a serious consideration of problems of this Committee. I do not think that it would be a useful exercise for me to prolong the discussion on the terms of such misrepresentations as those to which I refer, tempting though it is to put the record straight. I believe those misrepresentations belong to a sphere of argument through which the members of this Committee will easily find their way without any assistance from my side.

The real problems are of a different nature. Will this Organization face the economic consequences of its own actions and how will it be done?

General Assembly Official Records, Fifteenth Session, Annexes, agenda item 50, document A/C.5/843. For the summary record, see ibid., Fifteenth Session, Fifth Committee, 796th meeting.

Further, if it is not willing to face the financial consequences of its own decisions, is it then prepared to change its substantive policies? There is no third alternative. It must be remembered that it is not the Secretariat which carries the responsibility for costs caused by steps taken by the General Assembly or the Security Council. Nor is it the Secretariat which has the right to change the substantive policy if Member nations are not willing to shoulder the financial consequences of the stands they have taken.

However, before entering upon the facts which confront the Fifth Committee and the General Assembly with the choice to which I have just referred, I feel that there are a couple of points arising out of the general debate on which clarifications from my side are necessary. The first and most important one refers to the assertion that I have been misleading the General Assembly in saying that a stabilization policy has been pursued in earlier years, and that the budget proposal for next year represents a first modest departure from such a policy. Instead, I have been said to have pursued a lavish and extravagant spending policy.

Quite apart from the fact that this criticism, if it were true, hits the Advisory Committee on Administrative and Budgetary Questions and the Fifth Committee, just as hard as it hits the Secretariat, the statements referred to, for factual reasons, certainly deserve your most serious attention. I circulated this morning to the members of the Committee a memorandum [A/C.5/842] with a full analysis of the budget and the budget development from which the Members will be able to draw their own conclusions. I have done so because I do not wish to leave any uncertainty in the minds of the governments of Member states, while, on the other hand, I would not have liked to burden you here with such a detailed exposition of facts and figures as would be required for a complete refutation of the criticism. I shall only quote a few data from which you can draw your own conclusions.

The total number of the professional posts approved in the 1954 budget—the first one for which I was responsible—was 1,648. On a strictly comparable basis the same figure for 1960 is lower than the one approved for 1954. Leaving aside the requirements of the Economic Commission for Africa, my budget proposals for 1961 show an increase over the comparable 1954 establishment of twenty-eight professional staff for a total of 1,676 posts as compared to the figure of 1,648. I think that the comparative figures amply justify my claim that the professional establishment has been remarkably stable over the period in question and the significance of this fact is all the greater in view of the parallel increase in membership and the increase in tasks to be handled by the Secretariat. Whether or not the figure for 1961 will exceed that for 1954 within the modest limit mentioned, will of course depend on the Fifth Committee's final judgement as to what is required to meet the substantive demands formulated by the General Assembly itself.

If we turn from this decisive comparison of the establishment in 1960 and 1961 with the establishment in 1954 to the development of the budget figures, these figures may seem to contradict the comparison just made as they show a considerable increase in staff costs and certain other expenditure. I shall not burden the debate with an analysis of the figures as such an analysis has been made available in detail in the memorandum to which I referred. Suffice it to say that an overwhelming part of the cost increase is what, in budgetary language, is called automatic and explained by annual increments, salary adjustments, and similar factors. There has been no extravagant expenditure or uncalled for expansion as would indeed have been most unlikely in view of the close scrutiny to which both the Advisory Committee and this Committee have submitted the budget estimates each year.

One short word may also be said about the Laos mission, as it has attracted some special attention. It has been charged that we use a staff of twenty-eight persons at an expenditure of some $260,000 for assistance planned at a level of only $213,000. The point has already been made here in the Committee that the 1960 expenditure includes costs which will be of a nonrecurrent character, for example, accommodation, communications, equipment, etc. The following added facts, however, should be put on record. First, the figure quoted for the planned assistance is very misleading and falls far short of the total scope of the operation which has to be handled. It is difficult to give an exact figure that may be taken as the correct measure of the scope of the work. An analysis of the situation has, however, been included in the memorandum circulated. It should also be observed that, apart from the chief, the staff of the mission consists only of a principal secretary and an administrative officer, three secretaries, and three field service staff. The rest mentioned in the figures just quoted are local recruits who serve as drivers, messengers, maintenance men, etc. As this shows, the professional establishment is very modest and certainly not out of proportion in relation to the tasks which have to be handled. Finally, it should be noted that the establishment, as well as the individual men and women concerned, have been specifically requested and approved by the Royal Government of Laos. This last-mentioned fact takes us beyond the field of purely administrative considerations and into a wider and more important area: should the United Nations, even on the modest level established in this case, fail to render the government of a Member state, in desperate need of assistance, the help that it specifically requests in order, at long last, to get its economic development under way in support of its young independence? Similar corrections as those made here in relation to Laos are given in the memorandum regarding the mission to Guinea.

When I take the floor at this stage of the development of the work of the Fifth Committee, it is difficult to bypass entirely the question just debated, that is, geographical distribution. I will, however, limit myself to a couple of observations of principle, leaving aside questions of statistics and similar matters covered in the report.

Under the provision in the Charter that "due regard" should be paid to wide geographical distribution, a line of thinking seems now to be slipping into the debate which, I am convinced, is entirely foreign to the philosophy of the Charter. Geographic distribution means geographic distribution and nothing but that. The phrase has to be seen in conjunction with the Charter demand for full and exclusive loyalty of the international civil servants to the Organization, the other side of this demand being that United Nations officials should sever all their ties of interest in or loyalty to their home country.

Thus, geographic distribution cannot mean a balanced representation of interests or ideologies. Were another view to be held and the development of the Secretariat to be determined by it, it would represent a basic departure from the Charter concept. The Secretariat is international in the way in which it fulfils its functions, not because of its geographic composition but because of the attitudes of the members of the Secretariat and the truly international spirit in which they fulfil their tasks—if that had not been the view, the Charter would certainly have made wide geographic representation a primary consideration, instead of subordinating it to a demand for integrity.

There may be members of the Secretariat of the United Nations and of the secretariats of other international organizations, who tend to regard themselves as spokesmen for their country's interests or for this or that ideology and, in consequence, may feel that they are entitled to be influenced by what they are told to be or believe to be their country's interests, and may likewise feel entitled to serve as informal channels of information. There may be such staff members, but if there are, they would be endangering the international character of the Secretariat, from whatever geographic area they come.

I am concerned about the implications of the present discussion of geographic distribution because those implications may confuse the views as to what constitutes the international character of the Secretariat and, within the Secretariat itself, may foster the false idea that anyone is there as an informal representative of a country or a group, or of interests or ideologies, and that any staff member is entitled to regard himself as being in a special relationship to any outside interests or views. I have said before in this Committee that those who in their functions recognize other loyalties than the one to the Organization can certainly be used by the Organization, but that their usefulness is subject to restrictions. While, as I have stated on many occasions in the past, the application of the principle of wide geographic distribution needs improvement, it would be a bad day for the Organization if, against the clear line of the Charter, such an attitude became the norm or was even sanctioned by the General Assembly, as may happen through the introduction of a demand that geographic distribution should provide for a balanced representation of groups, interests, and ideologies.

Let me now turn to the crucial question of the financial status of the United Nations. I wish first of all to draw attention to the cash outlook.

Cash and investments on hand at October 31, 1960 amounted to approximately $9.4 million—$7.65 million in the general fund and $1.75 million in the special account of the United Nations Emergency Force (UNEF). These amounts do not include certain held-in-trust and other payables, e.g. Suez Canal surcharge collections, residual assets of the United Nations Korean Reconstruction Agency (UNKRA), and voluntary contributions received for the United Nations Fund for the Congo.

Projecting to the end of the year as optimistically as possible, it is estimated that likely receipts of contributions to the regular budget may amount to $5.85 million and to UNEF to $100,000. Expenditure likely to be incurred from November 1, to December 31, inclusive on these accounts (i.e., regular budget and UNEF) are estimated at $9.1 million and $6.85 million, respectively.

Thus it is foreseen that without making any allowance for further ONUC remittances and expenditures subsequent to October 31, 1960, there will be a cash deficit by December 31, of approximately $500,000. This amount compares to a cash balance of January 1, 1960, of $16.5

million. The outlook, however, is somewhat worse than these estimates would indicate, in so far as it will be necessary to maintain bank balances of not less than $3 to $4 million in the general fund and the UNEF account. Minimum requirements at the year end, apart altogether from those relating to ONUC, will therefore exceed cash availabilities by not less than $4 to $5 million.

Up to and including November 18, 1960 total disbursements for the Congo operations (expenditure at New York plus remittances to the Congo) amounted to approximately $15 million. It is difficult to estimate the extent to which further cash expenditure or remittances in connection with the Congo operations will take place between now and December 31. The 1960 supplementary estimates for ONUC amount to $66,625,000. I believe it would be prudent to assume that perhaps some $25 to 30 million of obligations will need to be liquidated in 1960, involving further cash requirements by December 31 of say $10 to $15 million.

On the basis of year-end requirements only, we must therefore find ways and means of supplementing available cash resources by not less than $20 million.

This, however, is not the full extent of the problem, since financing will need to be assured for the regular budget as well as for UNEF and ONUC in 1961.

So far as the regular budget is concerned, it might be helpful if at this point, I were to attempt a forecast of the level at which contributions are likely to be assessed in 1961. On the basis of the estimates already approved in first reading, and others which, though yet to be considered, appear reasonably firm, total budgetary expenditures (apart from UNEF and the Congo) of approximately $74 million gross can be foreseen. This figure, I should add, would allow for an increased provision for technical programmes for economic development and for an expanded programme for the provision of operational, executive, and administrative personnel (OPEX). Miscellaneous income and the 1959 balance on surplus account could reduce the gross total to about $67.8 million. To this should be added the supplementary estimates for 1960 already approved by the Fifth Committee or which are still to be considered—let us say in the amount of $2.5 million (excluding whatever sum may be assessed for the Congo). We thus reach a total of some $70.3 million as an assessment base for 1961, against which there will be offsetting credits from staff-assessment income estimated at $6.9 million. (The comparable 1959 figures were $58.3 million and $6.3 million, respectively.)

To sum up, therefore, the present outlook is that the Organization will begin the 1961 financial year with a virtually empty treasury; with arrears of assessed contributions totalling approximately $31 million ($8.5 million on the regular budget and $22.5 million on the UNEF budget); and, at the same time, the necessity of financing normal budgetry disbursements amounting to some $5 million a month, UNEF expenditure of about $1.5 million a month, and substantially larger monthly requirements for ONUC (perhaps of the order of $10 million monthly for such period as the Force and its supporting services must be maintained at their present strength). There can be no assurance, moreover, even with some further improvement in dates of payment, that more than 10 per cent of budget assessments will be paid by the end of the first quarter or more than 23 per cent to 25 per cent during the first half-year.

The figures and estimates I have given, though approximate only, will, I hope, clearly indicate the gravity of the situation. True, immediate requirements can be met to a rather limited and temporary extent, by borrowing, at interest, from special accounts in the Secretary-General's custody. This, however, does not, and cannot solve the problem. It can only prolong the Organization's solvency for a few weeks or for a month or two. If, pending receipt of the 1961 contributions, essential activities are to be maintained and obligations fulfilled, funds will have to be provided and provided quickly, either through substantial voluntary contributions, advances from governments, or borrowings from other sources.

These observations on the cash position lead to the question of the financing of the Congo operation, our main financial burden at the moment. As Members are aware, this question includes two parts: one refers to the United Nations budget proper and is reflected in the request for appropriations amounting to a round figure of $66 million for the remainder of 1960, together with whatever financial arrangements may be made for the maintenance of the Force thereafter; the other one refers to the budget and trade deficit of the Republic of the Congo and is covered by the appeal for voluntary contributions to a United Nations Fund for the Congo to an amount of $100 million. Contributions pledged to the Fund so far amount only to some $12.5 million.

Obviously, the Organization is facing here a crucial question. The United Nations operation in the Congo has been considered vitally necessary both by the Security Council and the General Assembly. This essential operation involves costs of the order indicated by the figures quoted. But while unanimity has prevailed regarding the political decisions giving rise to these outlays and expenditures, considerable hesitation is facing us when it comes to the question of voluntary contributions and of assessments on the budget.

The Secretariat finds itself in a difficult position. On the one hand, it has to pursue "vigorously" the policy decided upon by the General Assembly and the Security Council. On the other hand, it is continuously fighting against the financial difficulties with which these decisions under present circumstances face the Organization. Of course, the Organization cannot have it both ways. It must either pursue its policy, as represented by the presence of the Force in the Congo, and make appropriate and speedy arrangements for covering the cost, or it must take the initial steps to liquidate the military operation and so reverse its policy. This choice must be squarely faced, and faced at such time as to prevent financial considerations from casting a shadow of uncertainty over the political steps. Is it out of order in this context to remind the Members of the fact that according to estimates quoted this autumn here in the United Nations, current armament costs in the world amount daily to some $320 million? It may be felt by Members that the cost of peace is high, but what is it in comparison to the cost for the preparation of war—not to speak about war itself. Permit me on this point to say that I feel strongly that future generations would never understand it if financial considerations of the order which we have before us led the Organization and its Member nations to abandon or weaken a policy, the significance of which for the maintenance of peace cannot be doubted.

What I have said applies to the United Nations Force in the Congo as well as to the activities temporarily to be financed from the United Nations Fund for the Congo. As regards civilian activities, the Organization is equally facing a choice. It cannot on the one hand assume responsibilities for assistance to the Congo, aiming at giving substance to the independence of the country and at avoiding such bilateral arrangements as, for the time being and in present circumstances, at least a majority of the Members regard as dangerous for the future and for that reason undesirable, while on the other hand it works with such modest means as not to be able to do more than to keep the head of the Congolese economic life above water. At this time, owing to lack of means, commitments against the United Nations Fund for the Congo are limited to the most urgent emergency operations of assuring health protection and health services, the continued operation of airports and essential communications, the institution of a public works programme in certain areas of the most acute unemployment, emergency recruitment of school teachers needed for the Congolese elementary school system, and technical training. The needs are vastly more extensive. Every vacuum needs to be filled. If no steps are taken by the United Nations to fill, under its flag, the vacuum that exists today in the Congo, it will inexorably be filled in other ways as pressures become irresistible.

If I try to make a forecast, I do not for the present see any likely prospects of receiving contributions of more than say another $15 million above the present level. United Nations commitments represented by the activities for the restoration of public services and economic life in the Congo should, I think, be limited to the amount which we have good reason to believe will, in fact, be attainable. Further, the present rate of expenditure for reimbursement to specialized agencies and direct disbursements must be kept within the cash on hand. However, if the purposes of the United Nations Fund for the Congo are to be served to the minimum extent needed, the rate of disbursements must increase. In these circumstances a much higher rate of pledges and a much faster rate of contribution payments must take place within the near future. Were such an improvement not to materialize, how then could the Organization and its Members continue to justify a stand which reduces or excludes the possibilities of immediate bilateral assistance—whatever its source and consequences—outside the United Nations framework?

The points to which I have drawn attention here are very serious. They have tended to be overshadowed in the current discussion by much more limited considerations. In the political field, specifically, they have tended to be overshadowed by problems which, whatever their significance, will mean less for the well-being of the people of the Congo and for the effort of the United Nations to maintain peace than the financial and economic decisions which the governments of Member states must take in the knowledge that they will thereby be setting the limits for present and future United Nations activities.

I am sure that when Members consider among themselves and in this Committee the measures that might be adopted, the useful comment offered by the Advisory Committee in paragraphs 63 to 68 of its report will not be overlooked. I may perhaps conclude my remarks by referring to one among the possible remedial measures noted by the Committee, namely, the establishment of a peace and security fund to be financed perhaps in part from the regular budget, in part by voluntary contributions, and possibly also by advances from Member states.

I propose, at this point, to say only a few words on this subject, limiting myself to such questions as the need for a fund of this kind, and its scope and use. It would obviously be premature to touch upon the "mechanics" of the fund, or the method of financing.

Since the earliest days, Member states have recognized the need for authority and cash provision to meet urgent expenditure for the maintenance of peace and security. Thus, for the year 1947, the Secretary-General was authorized by the General Assembly to advance, on his certification, up to $3 million for "combined unforeseen and extraordinary expenses." For 1948 the amount was reduced to $2 million, and the definition of purpose amended to read "maintenance of peace and security and economic rehabilitation"—this being futher amended for 1949 by the insertion of the qualifying word "urgent" before "economic rehabilitation."

Throughout the years since 1948 this figure of $2 million has remained unaltered despite progressive increases in the level of the Working Capital Fund, and despite a radical change in the nature and scope of the demands made on the fund. For, while the Working Capital Fund has served continuously through the years to finance unbudgeted expenditure, both without and with the prior concurrence of the Advisory Committee, in recent years the volume of such expenditure has grown enormously. There is the further consideration that the financing of the regular budget today constitutes a far heavier drain on the Working Capital Fund than in earlier years. In 1948, for example, the budget total stood at $34 million, the Working Capital Fund at $20 million; in 1960, the corresponding figures are $63 million and $25 million.

The obvious definition of the purpose of the proposed fund would be to finance those expenditures which are clearly related to the maintenance of peace and security. Conditions governing the use of such a fund might provide, for example, (a) for expenditure within limits authorized by the General Assembly (or perhaps, provisionally, by the Security Council) for specific purposes; and (b) for additional expenditure within a prescribed amount, for other unforeseen or extraordinary expenses (within the ambit of the fund) on the certification of need by the Secretary-General, expenditure above that limit being incurred only with prior concurrence of the Advisory Committee.

I believe that you would not wish me to go further in outlining tentative arrangements for a fund which, as I have said, is only one among several possible measures for strengthening our resources. For my part, I would in any case wish first to hear the views of the members of this Committee before attempting to frame specific proposals.

I am convinced, nevertheless, that some arrangement along the lines I have suggested and to which attention has been called by the Advisory Committee, is indispensable if the solvency of the Organization is to be preserved and its capacity to respond promptly and effectively to the demands placed upon it in fulfilment of the basic purposes of the Charter is not to be permanently frustrated.

THE FIFTH COMMITTEE was badly divided on the issue of paying for the Congo operation. The Advisory Committee on Administrative and Budgetary Questions estimated total 1960 requirements at $60 million. This figure was reduced to $48.5 million after the United States announced it would waive reimbursement of over $10 million for the costs of its airlift services, provided the Committee voted to recognize that Article 17, paragraph 2, of the Charter applied to expenses for the Congo operation "and that the assessment thereof against Member states creates binding legal obligations on such States to pay their assessed shares." On the same condition the United Kingdom and Canada waived reimbursement of nearly $1.2 million for their combined air transport costs and the United States offered an additional voluntary cash contribution of $3.5 to $4.0 million to be used to reduce assessments against Member states with a limited capacity to pay.

Pakistan, Senegal and Tunisia joined in sponsoring a draft resolution appropriating $48.5 million and including in its preamble the reference to Article 17 already quoted. That paragraph was put to a separate roll-call vote. It was adopted by 40 votes to 27, with 17 abstentions. A slim plurality of the Asian-African members voted in favor, but no fewer than 12, including India, joined the Soviet bloc and France in voting "no." The nay votes and abstentions together outnumbered the affirmative votes. The resolution as a whole was adopted by 45 votes to 15, with 25 abstentions (resolution 1583 (XV)). This time five of the Arab members and Portugal joined the Soviet bloc in the negative and France joined the abstainers.

The Fifth Committee also approved a resolution authorizing the Secretary-General to spend up to $24 million for the Congo operation during the first three months of 1961 and requesting him to submit 1961 cost estimates by March 1, 1961. Both resolutions were adopted by the Assembly in a plenary meeting on December 20 just before the Assembly recessed its fifteenth session until March. The plenary vote on the 1960 Congo costs had been 46 to 17, with 24 abstentions. The vote on the authorization for the first three months of 1961 was 39 to 11, with 44 abstentions (resolution 1590 (XV)). This vote reflected the erosion of Afro-Asian support for ONUC that had occurred during December.

THE ARREST OF LUMUMBA AND ITS AFTERMATH

1. Letters to President Kasavubu

(a) Letter dated December 3, 1960

SINCE EARLY SEPTEMBER soldiers of the United Nations Force had maintained a security guard at Lumumba's residence at the latter's request. Similar guard units were maintained at the residences of Kasavubu and other political and military leaders of various persuasions. The UN soldiers were there to guard the leaders while in their homes against forcible entry, assault, or seizure by some hostile faction. In the case of Lumumba, as with the others, the guards neither interfered with his coming and going nor provided protection when he was outside his residence. Since early October when an ANC attempt to arrest Lumumba had been balked by the UN guards, the ANC had maintained an outer ring of soldiers loyal to Mobutu surrounding Lumumba's residence, while the UN soldiers continued their protective duties within this outer circle.

On the night of November 27, when Kasavubu's supporters were celebrating the return of the president from New York after his victory in the Assembly, a closed black limousine left Lumumba's residence and passed through an inattentive outer ANC guard without difficulty. The UN soldiers did not see who was inside the car but an inspection of the residence confirmed that Lumumba was gone. On December 1 Mobutu's men caught up with him in Kasai. He was arrested, beaten up, and returned to Leopoldville the next day. Several of his leading supporters in Parliament, who had accompanied him, were also arrested and Kasavubu announced his intention to bring Lumumba to trial on charges of serious crimes against the security of the State.

It was apparent that Lumumba had decided to flee to Stanleyville, his political base, where Gizenga had preceded him in October, with the intention of establishing his government there as the rightful government of the Congo in opposition to Kasavubu and Mobutu.

Lumumba's arrest caused strong protests from the Asian and African states. It

Security Council Official Records, Fifteenth Year, Supplement for October, November, and December 1960, document S/4571, annexes I and II.

was a heavy blow to Hammarskjöld's hopes to encourage conciliation among the Congolese factions and it also provided a favorable occasion for a violent renewal by the Soviet Union of its attacks upon the Secretary-General. Hammarskjöld immediately dispatched two letters to President Kasavubu appealing for legality and reminding him of his own recent statements in support of a political settlement among the leaders of all groups, including Lumumba (first following texts).

I have learnt about the arrest of Mr. Lumumba and note that according to newspaper reports Mr. Lumumba has now been brought to Leopoldville "for trial."

A great number of delegations have approached me expressing their grave concern that a situation might develop in which action against Mr. Lumumba would be taken contrary to recognized rules of law and order and outside the framework of due process of law. It is felt that such a development—which it is widely trusted would be entirely against your intentions and views—would put seriously in jeopardy the international prestige of the Republic of the Congo and mean a most serious blow to principles to be upheld by the United Nations and by its Members. In view of the cooperation established between the Congo and the United Nations and in view of our personal contacts, I have considered it my duty to bring these views to your urgent attention. I feel entitled to do so especially as the United Nations has been entrusted by you to assist in upholding law and order in the Congo.

To the views of a number of delegations which I have thus felt I should bring to your attention, you will permit me to add my own reaction. Trusting your wisdom and fair-mindedness, I feel sure that you share my view as to the imperative need for the young republic firmly to uphold those general principles by which it wishes to live and to which it has put its signature when it became a Member of the United Nations. This is of special significance now, when you personally are the recognized head of the Congo delegation to the United Nations. I feel therefore that you will use your decisive influence to see to it that in the further developments due process of law is observed taking into account the special circumstances which, in the view of large sectors of international opinion, characterize Mr. Lumumba's status. In saying this I do not, of course, in any way wish to express an opinion on any internal problems in the Congo or to exercise any influence on how those problems should be solved; as in many other cases during my term of office as Secretary-General, I have only wished, faithful to the principles of the Charter of the United Nations, to emphasize those principles as the only basis on which a fruitful national and international cooperation in our present world can be built. The sad cases of departures from those principles which we have had to witness in the past do not change anything in their significance in each new situation in which a country and its government have to decide on an issue to which those principles apply.

(b) Letter dated December 5, 1960

I should like to refer to my letter to you of December 3, 1960, and to the approaches made to me on behalf of numerous delegations to the General Assembly of the United Nations, including the entire group of African-Asian delegations, expressing their grave concern at reports which have figured in the world press concerning the arrest and detention of Mr. Patrice Lumumba.

As I stressed in my previous letter, it is obviously not for me to seek to influence in any way the solution of any internal political problem of the Republic of the Congo. However, I know you would wish me to elaborate on the points which have given rise to special disquiet at a time when the attention of the world is so strongly focused upon the Congo and upon the scope of the effort which the international community, in the first place your African sister nations, can furnish by way of further assistance.

I am sure you will already have given your closest examination to the effect upon world opinion of any departure from the observance of the principles of the United Nations Charter concerning "respect for human rights and for fundamental freedoms for all." This respect is reflected in the provisions of the Fundamental Law on the structures of the Congo and on public liberties in the Congo, as well as in the Universal Declaration of Human Rights.

In this connection may I be permitted to note that Mr. Lumumba and others who recently have been seized and are now detained are members of one or the other Chamber of Parliament. According to available information, persons in that position may not be prosecuted or arrested in any penal matter without prior compliance with the parliamentary procedures provided in Article 66 of the Fundamental Law on the structures of the Congo. You will in this context, regarding the exception made in that article for arrest in *le cas de flagrant délit,* note the interpretation given to that formula according to universal principles of law. Inasmuch as the principle of parliamentary immunity exists throughout the world as a means of protecting not the private interests of the individual but rather the structure of parliamentary democracy, world public opinion will be certain to give to this point great attention, without regard to the political positions of the various personages detained.

It has been widely noted with appreciation that you have pronounced yourself in favour of an amicable and nation-wide settlement of the Congolese political crisis, to embrace all the leading political figures including, according to reported public statements by you, Mr. Lumumba. I am sure that you are in a better position than I am to evaluate the full significance for such a solution of any action taken in the present case.

Approaching you again, I wish to invite your attention also to the reports of a number of independent eyewitnesses, which give ground for fearing that the detainees, in particular Mr. Lumumba, have suffered physical violence and degrading treatment. In making various efforts to use its good offices for the freeing from illegal detention of Mr. Songolo and other parliamentarians, to our great regret still held in Stanleyville, the United Nations has suggested that the International Red Cross be asked to examine the detained persons and their places and conditions of detention and otherwise to obtain the necessary assurances for their safety. It is natural for me to propose for your serious and urgent consideration that immediate recourse should be had to the same procedure in the case of Mr. Lumumba and other detainees.

In my previous letter, representing the immediate and serious reaction of myself and the great number of delegates who had approached me regarding the matter, I made a strong appeal for application of due process of law, as generally understood in law. I felt sure that it was your own wish and intention to apply the rules of such due process which, as you know, applies to every stage of police action or legal action, including arrest and detention. Of special importance in this context is the concept of due process of law as developed in general recognized law and the fundamental law of public liberties. I refer in particular to the questions of the necessity for and legality of the warrant of arrest, the requirements that the detainee be informed, within twenty-four hours at the latest, of the reasons for his arrest and of the formal charges in detail entered against him, that he shall not be prosecuted except in the cases provided for by legislation and in accordance with the procedures in force at the time when the offence was perpetrated, that he may have counsel of his own choice, and further, that he shall be entitled in full equality to a fair and public hearing by an independent and impartial tribunal in the determination of any criminal charge against him.

PRESIDENT KASAVUBU and Justin Bomboko, who now served as commissioner-general for foreign affairs, both signed a reply to the Secretary-General dated December 7.[1] They gave no ground. Everything was Lumumba's fault, he had committed grave crimes and had been justly arrested and detained. The Afro-Asian delegations should stop their agitation in his behalf, for the Congolese resented such outside interventions "and the serious effects which they will undoubtedly have on public opinion will only make it very difficult to ensure that the proceedings take place in regular form."

As for the request that the International Red Cross be permitted to check on Lumumba's condition, the reply asserted that two physicians had found him to be "in a satisfactory state of health" and asked "What more, then, is desired. . . . Must we in turn investigate the treatment the members of the opposition in Ghana are receiving, ascertain what has become of General Naguib in Egypt, and recall the victims of the Hungarian insurrection?" Such provocative language had all the earmarks of ghost writing by the Belgian advisers who had been brought back in large numbers by the Mobutu régime after the United Nations' refusal to recognize the legitimacy of the College of Commissioners. Dayal had complained in his November 2 report about the hostility toward the United Nations of many of these Belgian officials.

The arrest of Lumumba and Kasavubu's defiant response, coming so soon after the success of the ill-conceived Western-led drive to seat Kasavubu's delegation in the General Assembly, constituted a disastrous set-back for Hammarskjöld's desperate efforts to restore and maintain African solidarity behind ONUC and played right into the hands of the Soviet campaign to split the Africans apart.

The USSR called for an immediate meeting of the Security Council and circulated another Soviet government statement pinning the blame on Hammarskjöld for what had happened and demanding that ONUC should free Lumumba by force, disarm Mobutu's "bands of terrorists" and expel all Belgian officials and soldiers from the Congo.[2] The left-leaning African governments also thought ONUC should have prevented Lumumba's arrest and should now act to free him. They were joined by some Asians. The rest of the Asians and Africans, except for a few of the former French colonies, were also outraged by Lumumba's arrest and the behaviour of the Kasavubu-Mobutu régime, but did not, in general, join in criticism of the Secretary-General or advocate resort to force by the United Nations.

[1] Security Council Official Records, Fifteenth Year, Supplement for October, November, and December 1960, document S/4571, annex I.
[2] Ibid., document S/4573.

At the beginning of the debate in the Security Council on December 7 the Secretary-General reaffirmed once again, in the light of the latest crisis, the mandate, the principles, and the constitutional limitations governing the United Nations operation in the Congo as they had been defined in the resolutions adopted by the Council and Assembly and by the Charter itself (first following text).

---

2. *Opening Statement in the Security Council*

NEW YORK   DECEMBER 7, 1960

Mr. President, the Council has before it a statement by the delegation of the Union of Soviet Socialist Republics circulated at its request. In this statement the delegation raises in fact the whole problem presented by the present situation in the Congo and especially the question of the role of the United Nations in the country.

The other new document before the Council, transmitted by the Secretary-General, treats exclusively with the arrest and detention of Mr. Lumumba.

It may in the circumstances be appropriate for the Secretary-General to present at this initial stage of the debate his comments on the problems raised, regarding which he carries special responsibilities in relation to the Council. The President mentioned the wish he expressed informally to me yesterday for a report on all United Nations action in the Congo. I did not understand that as a formal request, and also, for reasons of time, it is obvious that such a report could not be presented at this juncture.

The United Nations sent troops and civilian technicians to the Congo for clearly defined Charter aims and under clearly defined Charter principles.

The aim was to protect life and property within the Congo, in danger after the breakdown of the national security system, so as to eliminate the reasons given for the Belgian military intervention and thereby to reduce what internationally had to be regarded as a serious threat to peace and security.

Security Council Official Records, Fifteenth Year, 913th meeting.

The principles were that the Organization, in the pursuit of this aim, should maintain a position of strict neutrality in relation to all domestic problems of a political nature into which the Organization under the Charter had no right to interfere. This meant that neither the United Nations Force nor the civilian operation could be used by any person or faction in pursuit of his or their political aims; thus, the United Nations Force was not to be an instrument for anybody in order to exert his political authority. This further meant that the United Nations and its representatives had no right to further any specific political solutions of domestic problems of the Congo, such problems having to be resolved solely by the Congolese themselves in accordance with their own free will and in democratic forms.

The aims and the principles thus defined have been strictly maintained by me and my collaborators all through the operation. There have been no shifts in policy or changes of approach. Nor have we been "lackeys" of anybody or shown "servility" to any interest.

Of course, we have been accused of all this, and from all sides, although the terminology may have varied. What is more natural? By maintaining our aim, and by being faithful to the principles of the United Nations, we were bound to cause disappointment to those who have wished to abuse the Organization, and we were bound to be regarded also as enemies or obstacles by those who found that the very neutrality of the United Nations represented an obstacle to their aims. It is indeed common experience to everyone who has tried to pursue a line of independence and objectivity in human affairs that he comes under criticism from those who believe that they would have had a greater chance to success for their own special aims if it had not been for this attitude.

Thus nobody should be surprised by the attacks which in rich measure have been directed against the United Nations operation, in succession, by leading personalities in the Congo of various factions and by public opinion or governments from the East to the West. And nobody should, from that criticism, or from the way its centre has shifted from one point to the other, permit himself to draw the conclusion that the United Nations policy has shifted. Nor should anybody permit himself to look at any one criticism, thus voiced, as objective in the sense that it is wholly detached from political aims or pressures. That does not mean, of course, that I claim any infallibility for what the United Nations has done in the Congo—naturally, mistakes have been made—but what I do claim is that such possible mistakes have not reflected any change of policy implying a departure from the aims and principles proper to the Organization. It should be a reason for reflection that the very day the Soviet Union repeats its well-known criticism against the Secretary-General and his representatives we are under equally heavy criticism from people whom the Soviet Union in the same document characterizes as those to whom we show servile subservience.

All the misunderstandings, all the wilful misrepresentations, all the efforts to make what is done now suspected could be treated lightly as part of a political game in which, I believe, the players themselves must regard all these various statements only as moves and not as statements of fact, if it were not for their effect on this Organization and its authority. I believe, and many believe with me, that this Organization in all its frailty represents the sole approach which may give us a chance to reduce the risk that the constant frictions—large and small—which characterize the life of our present-day world, build up to a tension easily triggered into a clash in which we would all be engulfed. I also believe that it is essential, for the growth of a human society in which the dignity of the human being will be respected, that every effort is made to make this step in the direction of an organized world community a success. In these circumstances I may be excused if I express the deepest worry at seeing the way in which this Organization is abused in words and abused as an instrument for purposes contrary to the Charter.

We have been accused of servility in relation to the West, of softness in relation to the East, of supporting this or that man in the Congo whom one group or another on the world scene has chosen to make its symbol, or for assisting another man to whom another group has chosen to tie their hopes for the success of interests which they wish to safeguard. However, this is no excessive price to be paid for avoiding the thing for which no one in my position should be forgiven: to compromise, in any political interest, with the aims and principles of this Organization. It has not been done and it will not be done with my knowledge or acquiescence. I can only repeat what I said in the General Assembly, that I would rather like to see the office of the Secretary-General break on this principle than drift on compromise. May these observations be accepted as a reply to the criticism of the Secretariat which we find repeated in the Soviet statement, and also as a reply to all those who now criticize us so freely for the very opposite reasons.

After these initial observations which have pressed themselves on me in the light of recent developments I would wish to remind you all, in the first place, of what is the mandate of the United Nations Force.

To understand the position of the United Nations in the Congo in the light of current problems, it is necessary to recall once again the precise terms of the mandate of the United Nations Force as laid down by the Security Council in its resolutions of July and August 1960, and the circumstances which led to these decisions. The original resolution of July 14, 1960, authorized the Secretary-General:

. . . to take the necessary steps, in consultation with the Government of the Republic of the Congo, to provide the government with such military assistance as may be necessary until, through the efforts of the Congolese government with the technical assistance of the United Nations, the national security forces may be able, in the opinion of the government, to meet fully their tasks.

This resolution did not specifically state that the United Nations Force was to maintain law and order, but it was clear from the context that this would be its essential function. The legal justification for the Council decision was the threat to peace and security which arose as a result of the intervention of Belgian troops in the Congo; this intervention, in turn, occurred purportedly because of the widespread internal disorders in the country. Consequently, to bring about the withdrawal of the Belgian troops, it was considered necessary, in response to the request of the Government of the Republic of the Congo, to introduce United Nations troops to assist the restoration of internal order and security.

It should be recalled that at this initial stage there was no United Nations concern with the constitutional issues or political institutions of the Congo. The task of the United Nations Force was a police task—that is, to protect lives and property against violence and disorder. It was made clear in the Council, at that time, almost as a matter of course, that, in accordance with established United Nations principles, the Force could not take any action that would make it a party to internal conflict in the country.

It was after the adoption of the first two resolutions by the Security Council that internal conflict and political rivalry gave rise to the demands that the United Nations Force take action against competing political groups on the basis of constitutional provisions. I need hardly recall to you the debates that took place in the Security Council as a result of this problem, but it is perhaps useful to remind you that the Council did not see fit to modify the original mandate of the Force and that it adopted on August 9 a specific injunction reaffirming the principle that the Force should not "be used to influence the outcome of any internal conflict, constitutional or otherwise."

The records of both the Security Council and the General Assembly contain abundant references to the emphasis which the great majority of Member states have placed on this principle.

It is possible to argue in a purely theoretical way that the maintenance of law and order may embrace the enforcement of basic constitutional law, but it is hardly possible to reconcile this point of view with the actual decisions taken by the Security Council. For there can be no doubt that if the United Nations Force were employed to "enforce the Constitution," it would involve the United Nations in coercive action against competing political factions to a degree that was clearly excluded from the scope of its mandate. Moreover, as several delegates have observed, such forcible intervention in internal constitutional and political conflict could not be considered as compatible with the basic principles of Article 2 of the Charter relating to sovereign equality and nonintervention in domestic jurisdiction.

From the legal standpoint, therefore, the only conclusion open to the Secretary-General was to apply the mandate of the Force with full regard to the provisions of the Council resolutions; that is, to avoid employing the Force so as to favour any political group or to influence the outcome of the constitutional controversy, but at the same time to assist in preserving law and order in the basic sense of protecting the lives and property of the inhabitants of the Republic of the Congo. As events have shown, this task has been a delicate and complex one, and not always attainable. Ambassador Dayal's reports have vividly revealed the difficulties in concrete situations. Thus, the Force has exercised its military power to protect political leaders of various factions from outright violence, even though such acts of protection have given rise to vigorous objection from the opposing side as being interference in political events. On the other hand, it has been considered beyond the scope of the mandate for the United Nations to interpose its Force against the national Congolese army acting under the authority of a chief of state whose representatives now have been accepted by the General Assembly.

However, it may be noted that the restrictions imposed on the United Nations in respect to its forcible intervention in constitutional matters do not, in my view, prelude representations by the Secretary-General or his representatives on matters which fall within the concern of the United

Nations in the light of its role in the Congo. Thus, since the Force has been requested to assume functions in regard to law and order, there is a legal basis and justification for the Secretary-General to concern himself with the observance of elementary and generally accepted human rights. It is on this basis that the Secretary-General and his special representative have made representations to the Congolese authorities to apply due process of law as that concept is generally understood. Similarly, the decisions of the United Nations have furnished a basis for the Secretary-General to appeal for an amicable settlement of internal political conflicts in the interests of the unity and integrity of the Congo.

But appeals of this kind based on the moral authority of the United Nations are sharply distinguishable from the use of United Nations armed force in purely internal conflicts; it is the latter that has been clearly excluded by the resolutions of the Security Council and, indeed, by the principles of the Charter.

What I have said here about the mandate given to me and through me to the United Nations Force in the Congo is all too often forgotten or perhaps wilfully neglected or distorted. We could simply not do or have done the things which you have seen presented as our clear obligation. Criticism would have been justified if we had done what is now requested, by going beyond the clear mandate of the Security Council. But instead we are attacked for having remained within its limits. Why were the critics not, at an earlier stage, interested in widening the mandate, as their comments now indicate, including a disarming of the Armée nationale congolaise? Are they really willing to do so now, irrespective of what further changes may come about in the Congo?

The United Nations operation in the Congo was begun after the mutiny in the Congo's security force, the Force publique, and after the calling into action of Belgian troops from their Congo bases and their taking it upon themselves to restore security in the territory against the will of the central government. The purpose of the United Nations was the establishment in the Congo of an agency for the maintenance of protection of life and security which the security forces of the Congo could no longer undertake and which should not be undertaken on a bilateral basis because of the international implications of such an arrangement.

As a result of the rapid build-up of United Nations forces, thanks to the full cooperation of the contributing states of the United Nations—in particular of those African states which it is now claimed I have tried to keep out—I announced to the Security Council on August 21, 1960, that Belgian forces had been withdrawn from the Congo, except for those then remaining at the bases of Kamina and Kitona, forces which did not then present an immediate security problem. During the month of August, the United Nations forces had been able to establish in most regions of the Congo a degree of security which made possible if not the resumption of normal activities, at least the maintenance of minimum services for the civilian population.

This favourable result was to no small degree due to the speedy introduction into the Congo of a civilian operation which reestablished the main lifelines of the country and which has maintained at least minimum services for the civilian population. It is noteworthy that, even though normal economic activities were far from satisfactory, life has continued on a minimum basis of normalcy due to the various forms of assistance rendered by the United Nations.

In spite of all difficulties encountered, also, as you will remember, in relation to the central government of Mr. Lumumba, there thus appeared in those days of late August and early September a reasonable prospect that, aside from the special problem affecting Katanga, the basis for revitalization of the country had been laid. It is true that the number of United Nations troops employed was not sufficient to cover all the vast areas of the Congo to the fullest satisfaction, particularly areas affected by large-scale tribal fighting and areas of isolated economic activities, but the prospect for a possible consolidation appeared to have been established.

It should be noted that, throughout the early months of the United Nations operation in the Congo, the Congolese security force, restyled as the Armée nationale congolaise, remained for the most part inactive and, in several instances, units of the Armée nationale congolaise had, by agreement with the United Nations, voluntarily disarmed themselves. It is important to stress that, during this period, the central government in Leopoldville, although not in complete control of the country as a whole, even aside from Katanga, was at least claiming to maintain a semblance of a central authority.

This situation changed rapidly in late August and early September, when major disputes developed between the various factions which had composed the coalition government of Mr. Lumumba. These disputes led to a quick disintegration of the government, culminating in the declaration of the dismissal of Mr. Lumumba as prime minister by the president of the republic, Mr. Kasavubu. This disintegration of the central government was accompanied by, and is perhaps even a result of, the emergence of units within the Armée nationale congolaise loyal to individual political leaders who began to feud with each other. This situation was on the verge of developing into a major civil war, had it not been for the quick intervention by the United Nations which neutralized, to the greatest degree in its power, the warring factions without, however, interfering directly or indirectly in the political struggle which continued to be waged among the political leaders.

It was during this period that United Nations forces were protecting all major installations vital to the maintenance of minimum civilian activities and thereby guaranteeing normalcy of life, as well as those installations which were vital to the security both of the Congolese and of the United Nations.

The development of private armies loyal to individual political leaders within the Armée nationale congolaise led in September to the emergence of Colonel Mobutu as a military leader in the Leopoldville area. It is difficult to see how this emergence of a more consolidated Armée nationale congolaise in the Leopoldville and surrounding area could be possible without some outside technical and financial assistance. This development has led to the creation of authorities which have no basis in the constitution of the Congo. The Armée nationale congolaise under Colonel Mobutu and the other authorities now holding control in Leopoldville have on many occasions directly and aggressively challenged the United Nations military forces, as well as the United Nations civilian operation, restricting on many occasions the task of the United Nations to maintain law and order, with which it was charged by the resolutions of the Security Council.

It should be noted that this challenge to the United Nations Force has in no way been limited to the Leopoldville area and to the section of the Armée nationale congolaise which is under the control of Colonel Mobutu but has, in the course of the last months, also been presented in other parts of the country, such as Orientale Province and, of course, Katanga where other private armies appear to owe individual allegiance to other political leaders. Thus the function entrusted to the United Nations Force, namely, to preserve law and order throughout the country, has been challenged to such a degree that all too often conflicts between the Armée nationale congolaise and its commands and that of the United Nations have occurred.

Increased political breakdown in the centre, as well as in the provinces, has been accompanied by a process which has brought, so tragically, old tribal disputes into the political arena. This is particularly exemplified in the struggle between various ethnic groups in Southern Kasai and Northern Katanga. These struggles have made it necessary for the United Nations to concentrate heavily on the reestablishment of law and order in those areas, and in many instances the United Nations has been made the target of attacks because, mistakenly, the United Nations has come to be identified with one side or the other in tribal disputes which have led to considerable loss of life, both on the side of the United Nations and of the Congolese.

Thus it must be stated that while the original objectives of the United Nations, namely, the elimination of Belgian military forces, has been achieved and the establishment of peace and order throughout the territory appeared some two months ago to be close to realization, the change in the political alignments both in Leopoldville and in the provinces has given an entirely new and different setting for the operation of the United Nations.

Among all the things that are said now about the United Nations operation in the Congo, there is one which tends to recur even on the lips of commentators who have a positive attitude to the United Nations effort and wish to give it a fair judgement. That is that the operation has failed or is facing failure. This is dangerous criticism. Of course the logical conclusion would be that the operation should be liquidated, not because it represents an obstacle to such and such specific interests for which the critics make themselves the spokesmen, but because it is no longer of value. This pessimistic judgement, therefore, merits close scrutiny.

From what I have said it is clear that the combined aims of the operation were to achieve the withdrawal of Belgian troops from the territory of the Congo and to maintain proper protection for life and property. I excuse myself for repeating this, but I think it is necessary to keep this constantly before our eyes. The first aim was, as I have recalled, achieved before the end of August and those who remember the Suez operation would not regard a delay of five weeks in the accomplishment of such a task as a failure.

The second aim was, as I said a moment ago, reasonably well achieved at about the same time as the last Belgian troops departed. That, in the wake of the serious disturbances in the month of July and under the impact of secessionist movements, tribal warfare should have occurred, did not mean any failure of the United Nations operation. On the contrary, short of this operation the situation would probably have got entirely out of hand. Further, through combined military and diplomatic efforts, a pacification was achieved in the most sensitive regions much preferable to the repression which had characterized previous efforts by others and this in fact dragged on into the period of United Nations responsibility.

During the same period a very valuable ground was laid for technical assistance so framed as to promote a maximum of independent Congolese activities while saving the main lifelines of the Congo economy. Short of that technical assistance and short of the speed with which it was staged, the Congo civilian life would in various areas have been threatened with a complete breakdown after the speedy full-scale exodus of practically all Belgian technicians.

Why then, in the light of these achievements during the first month and a half of the United Nations operation—and what I have said leaves out what the operation meant for the reduction of the threat to international peace and security—why then talk about the failure of the operation?

This judgement must refer exclusively to the period from early September onwards and seems based on the idea that it was for the United Nations to create a stable government within the framework of the Constitution.

It follows from what I have said above that such a task was completely foreign to all those in this Council who in July voted for the United Nations operation. It also follows from the Charter itself that this could never have been the task of the United Nations, as solely the people of the Congo itself, and its leaders, were able and entitled to try to create such a government. The duty of the United Nations could not be anything but to unburden the authorities of the immediate responsibility for the protection of life and security and to eliminate foreign military intervention so as, in those respects, to create a framework within which the people of the Congo could find its way to a stable government, enjoying adequate nationwide authority.

What is now laid at the doorstep of the United Nations as a failure is the failure of the political leaders of the Congo and of its people to take advantage of the unparalleled international assistance for the creation of normal political life within the country. These are harsh words and I hesitate to pronounce them but I do believe that this Organization is too often and too easily used as a whipping horse by those who wish to unburden themselves of their own responsibilities—this Organization which, however, represents values and hopes which go beyond that of any single man, any single political group, and—why not—any single country. Putting responsibility for later developments where it properly lies, I do not wish to criticize any individual or to pass judgement, I only wish to fulfil my duty to this Organization which, in the best interest of all its Member nations, also has a claim to fair judgement and to justice.

What could perhaps be said about the United Nations and its role during the past few months is that developments have shown that the means available to the United Nations have been insufficient for the creation of a stable political life in the Congo. Of course, that is true and how could it be otherwise unless Members were willing to entrust to the United Nations tasks falling within the range of a kind of control aiming at the development of stable political institutions. It seems to me typical of the confusion of the present situation that while some Members of the Organization without mentioning the word, in fact, accuse us for not having taken steps falling within that sphere of ideas—as for example the disarming of the army—others have tried to discredit the Organization by innuendos to the effect that we are striving for some kind of trusteeship. The first kind of criticism seems to me to be as out of place as the second type of accusation. How could the United Nations take steps against a Member nation representing infringements of its sovereignty? And why should this Organization—and especially anybody in the Secretariat—have any wish to move in that direction? The Organization should indeed not be accused of doing what it is not permitted to do and it should not be discredited by implying that it is trying to do something it can have no wish to do.

The real problem in the present situation is not one of failure but one of what the true functions are of the United Nations in the changed situation. This is a question which certainly requires the most serious consideration, and the reply to which should determine whether the United Nations should continue its Congo operation or not, and in what form to do it.

In trying to give some comments on this problem I should like to start out from the security situation. The United Nations went into the Congo because the Force publique was not capable of protecting life and property, that is, in that sense, of maintaining law and order. That was so not only because of the acute crisis through which the Force publique was passing after the mutiny in early July but also because of the fact that, whatever the quality of the soldiers, it was an army for all practical purposes without experienced officers after the Belgians departed. In consultation with the governmental authorities and at their request, the United Nations during the first period made serious efforts to help to reorganize the Force publique, now called the Armée nationale. With increasing political involvement of the army, these efforts came to nought.

Therefore, the situation as to the cadres of the army is not very different now from what it was at the time of the crisis. In these circumstances I cannot see how the need which existed in July can now have disappeared. My negative evaluation is confirmed by our experiences of the tribal warfare and by what we see of fighting between factions of the army owing allegiance to different leaders or tribes.

If this is true—and I believe it is—the original reasons for the United Nations military presence are still valid, if we are to avoid chaos and anarchy rendering impossible not only the technical assistance activities of the United Nations, modest though they are, but also civilian activities by others who may have been invited by this or that authority to come to the Congo, as well as normal political leadership itself. Withdraw the United Nations Force and, it is my fear, everything would crumble, short of a substitute being created for the Force from the outside, thus putting us back from denationalized multilateral assistance to bilateral assistance with all that this means.

It has been said, as we see it done in the Soviet statement, that in pursuing its activities the United Nations is "screening" developments contrary to the aims of the Organization. The conclusion from this thought might be that the United Nations should now withdraw in spite of the objections I have mentioned. Whatever may be said, I find it difficult to believe that anyone, on serious and responsible afterthought, would be willing to stand for that conclusion in view of the possible consequences of such a move at the present juncture.

Apart from the specific argumentation which I have just rejected as a reason for withdrawal, it is for obvious reasons desirable that the United Nations Force be withdrawn as quickly as possible. But this has to be done in a responsible way, leaving a legacy of order to the people of the Congo with which they can maintain a peaceful life. That requires renewed and serious efforts to put the army in such a shape as to make it capable of taking care of the situation itself. However, if the United Nations is to be able to contribute to such a result—a result which the Council once envisaged and which was the aim of the representatives of the Congo themselves—it obviously cannot be under circumstances in which the army plays a political role outside the Constitution and overriding democratic rules of government.

I have permitted myself at this stage to outline the problem and to point out in what direction a study of it indicates that further considerations of the United Nations operation must move. Pending more definite conclusions, I feel that we have to stand by the mandate already laid down, interpreted strictly in accordance with the principles of the Charter but adjusted to the peculiar circumstances at present prevailing in the Congo. This adjustment unavoidably leads to a serious curtailment for the present of our activities and to great restraint as regards the assistance we can grant. However, just as only the Congo people can find and create the forms in which it wants to be governed, so only the Congo people can open the doors which have to be opened if United Nations assistance is to make its full contribution. The fact that such a full contribution under present circumstances is not possible, and the fact that the United Nations cannot itself open the doors, is, in my view, not a reason for any talk about failure or for liquidation of an operation the imperative international reasons for which remain.

In this statement I have said nothing directly about the deplorable incident which I understand to be the direct cause for the Soviet demand for a Security Council meeting. However, the facts are known: it is for everybody to put them into the total perspective of the tragic and confused history of the Congo after its independence. I have therefore limited myself to comments on the background against which those incidents have to be seen both in terms of the changes over the months in the situation in the Congo and in terms of the United Nations mandate and the United Nations role in the Congo.

THE SECURITY COUNCIL debate continued through seven more meetings. Deputy Foreign Minister Zorin, whose turn it was to be President of the Council, submitted a draft resolution embodying the demands in the Soviet government's December 6 statement for the release of Lumumba, the disarming of Mobutu's soldiers and the expulsion of the Belgians.[1] The United States, the United Kingdom, Italy, and Argentina joined in sponsoring a draft resolution urging that "no measures contrary to recognized rules of law and order" be taken against anyone arrested or imprisoned and supporting permission for the Red Cross to check on the treatment and condition of such prisoners and to obtain "the necessary assurances for their safety."[2] The sponsors of this draft, however, gave support during the debate to Kasavubu's legal right to arrest and detain Lumumba. They did not ask for Lumumba's release, only that he and others receive humane and equitable treatment. Ambassador Wadsworth in particular, made no effort to disguise United States relief that Lumumba was in custody.

For the United Arab Republic its foreign minister, Mahmoud Fawzi, spoke in unreserved support of Lumumba and of the Soviet draft resolution and announced that the United Arab Republic contingent would be withdrawn unless ONUC policies were changed. He carefully put the blame on the Western powers, not on Hammarskjöld, for what had gone wrong and recalled with "nostalgia . . . the noble, courageous, alert, and imaginative stand and action of the United Nations as a whole and of the Secretariat, with Mr. Hammarskjöld at its head" at the time of Suez.[3] These kind words did little, in the context of the relentless Soviet offensive against Hammarskjöld, to mitigate the bitter impact of Fawzi's support for Zorin's resolution.

The representatives of Yugoslavia, Guinea, and Indonesia also announced plans to withdraw their contingents from the UN Force and Morocco's representative indicated that his country might do likewise "if the United Nations does not modify its conduct in the Congo."[4] This was also the position of Ceylon. Sir Claude Corea sought to show that it would be constitutional under the Charter and the Council's resolutions for ONUC forcibly to disarm units of the ANC now serving as "private armies" to Mobutu or rival leaders. For Tunisia Mongi Slim did not go so far, but thought the Council should authorize the Secretary-General to "demand"—and he emphasized the word—that the Congolese leaders restore legality to the country.

All the Asian and Arab representatives called for the release of Lumumba and other political figures from detention and a reconvening of Parliament, with ONUC providing security. They shared a tendency to evade the constitutional questions and to emphasize *what* should be done, with little regard for the *how*. The atmosphere was made to order for Zorin and he returned to the attack again and again. The Secretary-General spoke briefly on three occasions to correct misstatements and distortions of the record. These interventions during the 915th, 917th and 919th meetings, on December 8, 10, and 12, are not reproduced, since the position he defended is fully expressed in the following statement made near the close of the debate.

[1] Security Council Official Records, Fifteenth Year, Supplement for October, November, and December 1960, document S/4579.
[2] Ibid., document S/4578/Rev. 1.
[3] Ibid., Fifteenth Year, 916th meeting.
[4] Ibid., 917th meeting.

3. Concluding Statement in the Security Council

NEW YORK　　　　DECEMBER 13, 1960

IN MY STATEMENT TO the Council on December 7, I said: "Withdraw the United Nations Force and, it is my fear, everything would crumble, short of a substitute being created for the Force from the outside, thus putting us back from denationalized multilateral assistance to bilateral assistance with all that this means." I stated as my opinion that, therefore, the imperative international reasons for the United Nations operation remained valid.

In the light of later developments I feel that there is reason to elaborate on what I then said. The evaluation that follows has the full support of Mr. Dayal and his senior colleagues in the Congo.

If the United Nations operations were, for whatever reason, to be forced out of the Congo, I am convinced that the counsequence would be immediate civil war, degenerating into tribal conflicts fought in the most uninhibited manner. And such a situation could last for years. It would also mean the complete disintegration of whatever fabric of national unity still remains, as it can be foreseen that the country would be disrupted into fragments. Of course, the economic life of the country in such circumstances would be totally paralysed. I believe it can be safely anticipated that the outside world would not stand aside in such a situation, but that assistance of a military nature, in one guise or another, would be forthcoming from the different factions. If and when that were to happen, the world would be facing a confused Spanish-war situation, with fighting going on all over the prostrate body of the Congo and pursued for nebulous and conflicting aims. Could such a situation be contained? And if not contained, how would it influence peace and war in the world? I need not elaborate on this point as I am sure that nobody doubts what perspectives would be opened.

These, gentlemen, are the stakes: these are the stakes for the people of the Congo, and for other nations—in Africa or outside, contributing to

Security Council Official Records, Fifteenth Year, 920th meeting.

the Force or not. These are the stakes for the United Nations and what it represents.

In these circumstances it seems obvious that the United Nations operation must continue. It is, however, necessary to consider under what circumstances it can continue. It cannot continue if it is being pushed around by various leaders and factions in the Congo, able to activate, against the United Nations, this or that member country, or group of member countries, willing, for whatever reason, to keep the operation under a fire of criticism and suspicion. It cannot continue if it is enfeebled from within by divisions, or by withdrawals, or by a lack of financial and material support, depriving it of its weight as a serious and authoritative factor in the local situation. Were any of these possible, or indeed threatening, situations to develop, the United Nations would find itself in an untenable position: it would, on the one side, be forced to remain in operation in the Congo, with the sense of responsibility which must guide the actions of the Organization, while on the other hand, it would be reduced to a situation of emasculated passivity. The Organization might still stop complete chaos from developing in the Congo but it might itself quickly get corroded, saddled as it would be with grave responsibilities, while powerless to act beyond the insufficient capabilities open to it in view of the actions of its own Member nations.

From some speeches in the Council a listener might have been tempted to draw the conclusion that he was attending a lawsuit against the Organization by its own Members, with the Secretary-General and his collaborators in the dock. Thus, strong statements have been made regarding the responsibility of the Secretariat—as well as that, of course, of the Belgians and other foreign powers alleged to be supporting them. But few words have been heard about the responsibility of those major organs of the United Nations which have formulated the mandate and which, if the interpretation of the mandate now put forward by the critics were correct, would at least have had the responsibility to state it explicitly—not to speak about their obvious responsibility, in such circumstances, to provide the executive organs with the means by which such a broader mandate could be handled.

Nor have we, from the same quarters, heard anything about any responsibility for the political leaders in the Congo. On the contrary, when I referred to their responsibility, the comments were that this showed a colonialist attitude. May I ask: who shows respect for a political leader, the one who, like I did, counts on his ability and therefore on his responsibility—in a critical sense or not—or the one who, like my critics in this context, seems to regard the leader as outside any consideration of responsibility?

This would be unimportant if it were not for the desperate need for an unemotional, unpolitical, clearheaded analysis of the sickness from which the Congo is suffering; short of such an analysis, how can this body hope to find a remedy? Certainly, the sickness is not cured by even the most eloquent descriptions of this or that symptom, neglecting to take all the factors into account, neglecting also to analyse the sequel of cause and effect and, therefore, never reaching a balanced consideration of remedies.

Before indicating in what direction I personally see need for action, I would like to mention a few facts which merit attention.

First of all, the economic situation remains desperate. It may be that, as a spokesman of Belgium said on a television interview the other day, Belgium left the Congo "a portfolio of $750 million." However, to the best of my knowledge those means are not, at present, available to the Congo. Instead the Treasury remains depleted so that the United Nations has had to try to meet the most desperate budgetary needs, to the extent that this was possible for political reasons, and the question can legitimately be asked, from where are the salaries for the Commissariat and their advisers and the troops financed, the United Nations not being in the picture in a way which provides an explanation.

Two months passed before the so-called *coup d'état,* with the then functioning Central Government under Mr. Lumumba carrying the responsibility. What was done? Was there any improvement? Were, for example, the unemployed cared for? The negative replies are known to all. Since then, another three months have passed, and the questions can be repeated—on the whole with the same replies. Today we are facing a situation where, for example, between 250,000 and 300,000 people are actually starving in the South Kasai, with an estimated 200 people dying daily from sheer starvation. This is an extreme case, but it is significant and it does show that there may be greater problems from the point of view of human rights than those which get the greatest publicity. However, these various problems are not unrelated. Responsibility is not a question of political terminology or rhetoric. It is a question of fact and if the facts are not seen now they will remain on record all the same.

The question for the United Nations in this latter context is a simple one. Is it less important to bring help to a quarter of a million people starving, than to find what the proper constitutional framework for such consultation would be, as would formally entitle the United Nations to that action? Yet, I know that if we take such action—as we should and will—we may come to be accused of supporting this or that faction, or of acting outside a mandate requesting consultation with a nonfunctioning Central Government. In parenthesis I wish to inform the Council that I have requested a full report on the situation in Kasai to which I have just referred, and that this report will be circulated to the Members of the Organization for their urgent consideration.

A second point I wish to mention is this one. In two *démarches* dated October 8, but completed only some few days later, I approached the Government of Belgium and Mr. Tshombé personally. In my communications which have been circulated to the Members of the United Nations I gave my interpretation of operative paragraph 5 (*a*) in the General Assembly resolution of September 20. On the basis of that paragraph, I pressed for the elimination of the Belgian political element in Katanga and for a switch-over from the bilateral assistance from Belgium, which had been requested by the authorities of Katanga and by various others claiming to be speaking for the Congo, to assistance within the framework of the United Nations operation. My stand was met from the Belgian side with the most emphatic criticism. However, I am certain of the correctness of my interpretation of the intentions of the General Assembly, and back of the General Assembly, the Security Council. But so far my *démarches* have received no formal support from any one of those two organs. Admittedly, I have not asked for such support but the lack of it should be noted and on record when criticism is voiced against my policy in relation to Belgium.

The comments voiced have run along other lines. It is said that our *démarches* have been only formal or that we have not gone far enough, or, as the representative of the Soviet Union said tonight, have not been followed up. In this context—beyond reminding you of the fact that no support has been forthcoming for my interpretation of the General Assembly decision—I would like to draw your attention to what I said in the Fifth Committee. Unless the United Nations disposes of the necessary funds, how can the United Nations insist on withdrawal of technicians provided on a bilateral basis to meet essential needs, and to claim that either those technicians should be employed under the United Nations flag or that the United Nations should in other forms provide the necessary assistance? If multilateral assistance cannot be provided, it is difficult to go to a country and request, for this or that political reason, that they should not ask for, or receive, bilateral assistance which is badly needed—and offered. Therefore, regarding the question of the Belgian return, I have to remind you, both of my stand as made clear two months ago, and of the fact that neither formally nor economically has that stand so far received any support from within the Organization.

Members will recall that Belgium has transmitted a *note verbale* with comments on the second progress report of the Secretary-General's special representative in the Congo. I have already said concerning this document that I have no factual confirmed information, of relevance to this debate, to add to the Dayal report. Obviously, the Secretary-General is not in a position where he is entitled to express guesses or fears and— as Mr. Krishna Menon pointed out—we neither do nor could maintain an intelligence service. I may, however, be permitted to express my hope that the Belgians show the first and most essential quality of friendship; that in their actions they put the interests of the Congo before their own interests, and also that they realize that a people, like an individual, has problems into which especially a friend knows that he should not permit himself to intrude.

At the end of the Belgian government's observations it is said: "In a spirit of mutual understanding, the Belgian government also proposed to the Secretary-General, in its note of October 28, that a special envoy should be sent to New York to clear up any misunderstandings between the Secretary-General and the Belgian government. That offer still stands." That offer still stands and it has not, as rumoured, been rejected, but I have said that I want to know on what assumptions such contact could come about. It seems to me that, if it is on the assumption warranted by statements of the Belgian government, to the effect that the Belgians returning do so on the basis of individual arrangements, outside the responsibility of the Belgian government, the question raised by the Belgian return should be discussed between United Nations representatives and Congolese authorities, not with the Belgian government. On the other hand, if, directly or indirectly, the Belgian government recognizes responsibility for this return, I have set out what I understand to be the line of principle established by the United Nations on these questions. As already recalled, my interpretation has been rejected by the Belgian government. As, obviously, I cannot discuss on any basis other than the one laid down by the General Assembly and the Security Council, interpreted to the best of my understanding of the intentions, it is difficult to see, also on this assumption, how in those circumstances the suggested contact could be useful.

Another point. Without reopening the legal discussion, I have to make a few observations regarding the stand of the General Assembly and the Security Council on the basis on which this operation functions.

In interventions in the course of this debate in the Council, I have pointed out that the Council has never explicitly referred to the Charter Article on the basis of which it took action in the Congo. In particular, it is significant that the Council did not invoke Articles 41 and 42 of Chapter VII, which provide for enforcement measures and which would override the domestic jurisdiction limitation of Article 2 (7). I mention this as one of the reasons why some far-reaching interpretations of the mandate of the Force, to which we have listened here, are, quite frankly, difficult to understand. Those interpretations would require at least that the Security Council had clearly taken enforcement measures under Articles 41 and 42. In fact, I may recall to the Council that, on August 21, I pointed this out in the following statement: " . . . in the light of the domestic jurisdiction limitation of the Charter, it must be assumed that the Council would not authorize the Secretary-General to intervene with armed troops in an internal conflict, when the Council had not specifically adopted enforcement measures under Articles 41 and 42 of Chapter VII." Members may remember that no one in the Council raised any question about this statement.

It is true that, in its resolution of August 9, the Council referred to Articles 25 and 49 as the basis for the legal obligation imposed on the states concerned by the Council's action, but this is certainly not the same as invoking enforcement measures.

My own view, which I have expressed to the Council, is that the resolutions may be considered as implicitly taken under Article 40 and, in that sense, as based on an implicit finding under Article 39. But what I should like to emphasize is that neither the Council nor the Assembly has ever endorsed this interpretation, much less put such endorsement in a resolution. What is even more certain is that the Council in no way directed that we go beyond the legal basis of Article 40 and into the coercive action covered by Articles 41 and 42. Certainly the Organization, as represented by the Security Council and the General Assembly, must consider its responsibility as an executive organ to take carefully into account the limits on its authority as indicated by the facts which I have just recalled.

I said before, and I have to repeat it, that the criticism voiced in this debate has been directed mainly against the Secretariat, without much effort to see what has been the basis on which the Secretariat was acting or could act and what, therefore, was the responsibility of the Security Council itself. As members will remember, it has been said that the aims of the operation have been distorted by me, and in proof of that, a quotation was made from the telegrams from Mr. Kasavubu and Mr. Lumumba. These telegrams were what provoked me to action under Article 99. The resolution of July 14, was in response to my proposals and the main operative paragraph was in fact, for all practical purposes, a quote from my statement. I believe that it is, in these circumstances, appropriate to ask those who talk about distortion to look again at my proposal as being at least of equal significance as the cables which, by the way, did not even figure on the agenda.

A few speakers have, with opposite intentions, referred to the discussion of the mandate in the Security Council which took place on the basis of my report of August 12. I have little to add to what was said on that point by the representative of Tunisia, but it might be worth recalling that not only did no member of the Council put forward any proposal for a clarification of the mandate as a result of the challenge from the Congo of my interpretation, but the same situation was facing the fourth emergency special session, and the resolution resulting from the debate of the Assembly—which had before it all the documents relevant to the discussion about the mandate—asked the Secretary-General to continue vigorously his action, without questioning the mandate. The resolution was passed, as will be recalled, with 70 votes in favor and none against, and it must, from the point of view of the executive organ, be considered as concluding the debate of the substance of the mandate in favour of the stand taken by myself. Of course, this leaves any member free to ask for a revision of the mandate or a clarification, but I believe that it does not entitle members to say that I have misinterpreted or distorted the mandate in the past.

Members have also heard criticism of our "lack of courage to give candid information." The reply is simply that there is no information which I have felt the slightest reason to withhold in protection of the Secretariat, but some information which I have not found it in order to put to the Council, following normal diplomatic rules as regards interests of various Member nations. Nor, of course, do we apply to the Congo case new rules as to the circulation of documents. Papers which would never be circulated in other cases, because of their character, or because of their origin, should not be circulated in this case either, unless explicitly requested by Members.

I must now turn for a moment to the statement of the representative of the Soviet Union to which we just listened. As he kindly asked me "not to take offence," I shall treat it with "chivalry."

The representative of the Soviet Union said that there was no need for the United States to send any troops, as the United Nations staff in the area was to such a great extent from NATO countries. He obviously found some difficulty with the fact that those in responsible positions were not from NATO countries, but he got round it by talking about their dependence on subordinates and the possibility of errors. I would not like to burden the Council with a detailed discussion of the setup in the Congo, but I should like to draw attention to two fundamental facts which seem to be overlooked by the representative of the Soviet Union.

The first one is that servants of the United Nations who are loyal to their oath of service accept one undivided loyalty—and that one is to the United Nations. Therefore they cannot be treated as, and are not, representatives of any national interests. I am proud of the fact that the majority of members of the Secretariat show this single-mindedness, and I am sorry, but I must regard it as an affront to the staff to believe that, for example, somebody who happens to have a Norwegian passport is a kind of emissary of NATO. But different countries, or different organizations, may have different ideas on this point, and maybe I should not be surprised by the fact that the distinguished representative overlooked this character of the international Secretariat. I am more surprised that he accepts as a matter of course the dependence of the policy-making senior staff on their subordinates. I can assure him that in that respect we, in the United Nations, have established a discipline which is satisfactory, although, of course, perhaps not so far-reaching as that achieved in some countries. The representative referred to Mr. Dayal and to General Kettani in person. I am afraid that they will read his comments with some surprise.

Mr. Zorin dealt also at length with the way in which my short observations to the representative of Ceylon the other day had, according to the Soviet representative, shown my partiality. If Mr. Zorin does not see the difference between using the normal means at our disposal, mainly diplomatic, in order to forestall a move about which we had, generously, been prewarned; a move to the effect that what Mr. Zorin called "the legitimate provincial authorities," within forty-eight hours intended to take some one thousand or more hostages and perhaps execute a few of them unless we met certain demands of theirs—I say, if he does not see the difference between that and the use of military initiative to liberate somebody who has been arrested, then I find it difficult to discuss, because it is then obvious that we do not speak exactly the same language.

I was interested to note the reference to "the legitimate provincial authorities" in view of the fact that the provincial president in Orientale Province has been arrested, by supporters of Lumumba and the competence of whatever authority there may remain in power, according to the Loi fondamentale, is strictly limited to normal police activities. May it be that a double standard should, in this case, be applied to the interpretation of the Loi fondamentale?

I can assure Mr. Zorin that, if an evacuation of Europeans takes place in Orientale Province, it will not be by United Nations planes, as we have no such planes available in this case, any more than we had in the case to which Mr. Zorin referred. We are very short on the transport side in general, and will be even more so, for our most elementary needs, if some of the now-threatening withdrawals come about.

As regards the point which I made to the representative of Ceylon, concerning the legal rights of the Security Council when it came to liberation—I repeat liberation—of Mr. Lumumba, or disarming the forces, or recalling Parliament, the representative of the Soviet Union overlooked what I thought I made perfectly clear. I repeat that the Secretary-General can use, and has used, all diplomatic means at his disposal, to achieve results in line with the resolutions of the Security Council. What I pointed out to the representative of Ceylon concerned another matter: the limits to the possibility of the Security Council to decide on the use of military force—that is to say to take military initiative—in order to liberate a person, held on the authority of the chief of state, or to do the same in order to disarm military units under the orders of the chief of state, or to threaten to do the same in order to enforce the convening of a parliament which should be convened by the chief of state. The distinction between the use of force and the use of persuasion is fundamental, and it should be obvious that it is not possible to conduct a useful discussion if it is blurred.

Needless to say there is no contradiction between quotations from the "Dayal report" to which we listened and what I said. But I am afraid it would not be fair to the Council to burden it with a detailed discussion at this moment of that matter.

Let me end this rejoinder to the statement by noting the very far-reaching interpretation that Mr. Zorin obviously puts on Chapter VII of the Charter and perhaps also his lack of interest in the constitutional aspect when it comes to the question of the authority of the chief of state.

One final remark. The representative of the Soviet Union interpreted the attitude of those countries who have announced their wish to withdraw as expressing the wish to avoid to "sully their fair name." What about all those African and Asian states who do not intend to withdraw?

For the rest, I do not believe that, on the whole, it would be in keeping with the seriousness of the situation and with the aims of this debate to enter upon all the various points made in supposed support of the thesis that the Secretariat has not been doing its duty. However, there are a few specific points on which you may rightly expect me to comment.

The spokesman of the Republic of the Congo (Leopoldville) asked me two direct questions in clarification of something I said on December 10 regarding the restraint which present conditions impose on the United Nations. In order to simplify the matter, let us forget for the moment about the political role of the army and let me ask the question whether the representative does not consider it natural that, once units of the Armée nationale congolaise have engaged in a series of hostile acts against the United Nations Force—taking, for example, military initiative in attacking units of that Force acting under orders strictly in line with its mandate, and further, taking at gun's point matériel of the Force, without fully restoring it even after protests and complaints—we have to reconsider our continued assistance. He will also remember that not only Colonel Mobutu, but also some commissioners, in public statements have made the strongest attacks on the United Nations Force, as if it were a hostile element.

The representative also sought a clarification of what I said about the budget. I can use the same example. Once the army in Leopoldville had openly turned against the United Nations, as it did for a while at least, as well as taking upon itself a role in purely political contexts, it would be difficult for the United Nations to justify contributions to the salaries of that same army, without running counter to the injunction from the General Assembly and the Security Council that the United Nations should not lend its support to any political factions. We sincerely want to use all the means put at our disposal for the benefit of the Congolese people, and we shall do so, but we have to do it in such a form so as to avoid that this indirectly means an engagement in internal problems to which we must not be a party.

We have heard in this debate an eyewitness account of one who was present at the penultimate and the last meetings of the Congolese parliament. It may interest the Council if I note here other eyewitness accounts that add to this description. These latter eyewitnesses stated that in the Hall of the Chamber of Deputies there were some scores of the Armée nationale congolaise present—then loyal to Mr. Lumumba—during the debate and the voting. They were fully armed with rifles and submachine guns. During this tense period in Leopoldville United Nations troops, by request, were stationed next to and outside the Parliament building, to prevent incidents. They did not at any time prevent anyone from entering the building nor did they enter it themselves. After the two meetings had taken place in the two chambers on successive days elements of the Armée nationale obstructed entry to the building.

Referring to certain alleged policies and actions on our part in a manner which I have already had reason to correct, one speaker talked about a *logique des attitudes* of the United Nations. Indeed I hope that there is such a *logique des attitudes* on our side—although in a different sense than the one the honourable speaker had in mind. On the other hand, I note that there is also in certain quarters a *logique des interprétations,* in the sense that everything that may be turned into an argument for the thesis that we act in favour of certain interests is brought out, while everything else seems to be forgotten. This *logique des interprétations* goes very far when, for example, it is said that we are those who confirmed the secession of Katanga, while the truth of the matter is, that the fact that we got the United Nations Force into Katanga under the central leadership of a command in Leopoldville, thus giving emphatic expression to the unity of the Congo and creating the conditions for the withdrawal of troops under Belgian command from Katanga, is, to my knowledge, the most marked setback for secessionist policies in Katanga which has come about during these five months.

Mr. Krishna Menon, in his speech on December 10, made the important point that changing situations may call for a change in reactions; what the Secretary-General said several months ago, as he stated, may not be what he would say today. I certainly agree with this pragmatic attitude as long as it is not a question of principles. But agreeing with the stand of Mr. Krishna Menon, I would ask you if the same does not apply also in other respects, that is to say, for example, whether what was true about a certain person and his position in July may not be untrue in December? Neither as regards attitudes of the United Nations, nor as regards the evaluation of the facts of the situation in the Congo, is any immobility permissible. I say this because it is of decisive significance for the judgement of the future policies of the United Nations. Obviously such policies must start out from the facts, whatever our attitude to those facts and how much we may disapprove or approve of them. The principles remain, but the actions must translate those principles in the terms of today's situation.

Where do we get with such an approach? I shall try to state it as briefly as possible. I have already expressed my opinion that the United Nations operations must continue, and this is true both of the military and of the civilian field. I have further stated that this is not possible, unless conditions are maintained under which operations can continue, without making the United Nations a hostage of such or such factions or powers, or a dumb witness of developments contrary to the aims of the Organization and therefore leading to the corrosion of the Organization.

This means—outside the framework of all the resolutions—that I must appeal to Members to avoid using the United Nations and its operation in the Congo as a pawn in games for unrelated purposes.

But further—and within the range of the resolutions—I would ask the Security Council to clarify the mandate if it is its collective view that an extension is necessary beyond the present one, as so far interpreted, and I would then ask the Council, if it does so, to provide me and my collaborators with the means by which such a wider mandate could be fulfilled, keeping carefully in mind the limits put by the Charter on the authority of the Council. I would further invite the Council to consider such arrangements as would mean that Member nations would assume formally their part of the responsibility for the policy pursued from day to day in the Congo. This does not mean that the operations of the Secretary-General or his special representative should be put under some kind of stultifying control of a parliamentary body; conditions do not permit such a policy. Nor does it mean, from my side, any reservations as regards the extremely useful activities of the Advisory Committee, the members of which, however, do not carry any formal responsibility for the policy pursued. Nor does it mean any reservations as to the most valuable contribution that the Conciliation Commission, or its forerunners—already on their way—might give to the development of a sound policy. What I have in mind is: there are daily decisions, involving interpretations in detail of the extent of our power, which I and my collaborators now have had to take alone for five months. Representatives of the Council or the General Assembly might well shoulder on behalf of the General Assembly or the Council the fair share of the responsibility of these organs for current interpretations of the mandate.

Were the Council to define its stand clearly in the respects to which I have referred, and were, as I hope, countries who now have announced a wish to withdraw to reconsider their attitude in the light of this development, I believe that we may look forward with increased confidence. Were that not to happen, we would continue to do our best on the Secretariat side, knowing, however, that we would still be weakened by ambiguities and that our efficiency might continue to be reduced by a political war waged around our activities.

MONGI SLIM and Sir Claude Corea again attempted to draft a compromise resolution that would at the same time satisfy the Afro-Asians, be acceptable to the West and avoid a Soviet veto, but the task was impossible in the prevailing atmosphere. The West's "humanitarian" resolution was vetoed by the Soviet Union on a vote of 7 to 3, with one abstention. Ceylon joined the Soviet Union and Poland in the negative and Tunisia abstained. The Soviet resolution was then defeated by 8 votes to 2, with Ceylon abstaining and Tunisia joining the Western majority. Poland then proposed a brief draft resolution requesting the Secretary-General "to undertake the necessary measures in order to obtain the immediate release of Patrice Lumumba and all persons who are now under arrest or detention despite their parliamentary immunity."[1] This was defeated by 6 votes to 3, with 2 abstentions. Ceylon again joined the Soviet Union and Poland in the affirmative, while Argentina, one of the sponsors of the Western draft, joined Tunisia in abstaining. Thus the series of Council meetings ended in deadlock.

Meanwhile, in the Congo, the arrest of Lumumba had led to new developments at Stanleyville, the center of Lumumba's strength and the capital of Orientale Province, where, as we have seen, some of his ministers and parliamentary supporters had begun to gather. The first reaction in Stanleyville to his arrest had been a series of threats by the provincial authorities to arrest all Belgians in Orientale if Lumumba were not released within forty-eight hours. These threats and reports that some arrests and beatings had already taken place alarmed the

[1] Security Council Official Records, Fifteenth Year, 920th meeting.

European community who numbered between 800 and 1,000 in Stanleyville and an equal number in the rest of the province.

In response to requests for protection from violence the United Nations representatives decided to place under UN guard a school building capable of accommodating five hundred persons to serve as a refuge for those desiring to use it. Dayal also sent a formal note of protest to the provincial authorities.

A few days later Antoine Gizenga proclaimed "the reestablishment of the legal government of the Republic of the Congo" with its temporary capital at Stanleyville. Thus, when the Assembly debate resumed on December 16 there were competing governments claiming authority over all or parts of the Congo in Leopoldville, Stanleyville, Elisabethville, and South Kasai.

Zorin led off the Assembly debate with a long speech that followed the same lines of attack he had used in the Security Council. His distortion of the United Nations actions in providing a refuge for the threatened Europeans in Stanleyville while failing to rescue Lumumba provoked the Secretary-General to his first intervention in the debate, warning the Assembly to be on guard against "inverted racialism" (first following text).

---

4. *First Statement in the General Assembly's Resumed Debate on the Congo*

NEW YORK   DECEMBER 16, 1960

I HOPE LATER ON in this debate to revert to various points made which require fuller comments or rejoinders, but there is one matter which has been raised here on which I feel that I should make some comments immediately in exercise of my right of reply.

The matter was first raised by the representative of the Soviet Union, but it reappeared later on in other statements. I have in mind the alleged differences of treatment of the population, or certain fractions of the population, in Stanleyville, and of Mr. Lumumba.

However, before going on to that matter, I must remind the General Assembly of the background. We have just listened to an impassioned speech in which it was said that our mandate was quite complete, that that mandate obviously permitted us to disarm and "to deal with Colonel

General Assembly Official Records, Fifteenth Session, 950th plenary meeting.

Mobutu." I would like to ask the honourable Assembly if it or the Security Council has ever permitted me, or the Force, to take the initiative in military action.

Under the Charter, such an initiative requires a decision on enforcement measures, when it is a question of international affairs. The minimum, in the case of a national affair, is of course the same, if you regard the Charter as authorizing such military initiative in the national field at all. Anyway, I repeat my question: Has any mandate been given which authorizes military initiative in the Congo? My reply is "no," and anybody who cares to go to the record can see that that is the case.

The Force has the right of self-defence in a position which it holds under orders in the maintenance of its mandate. It cannot attack units of any kind.

Now, in the case which arose in Stanleyville, there was a threat to a certain group of the population which was transmitted to us beforehand. Those of the population, who assembled at certain houses where we were in a proper position, were promised that we would, so to say, protect those houses. That would require only acts of self-defence. It would be acts under the mandate; they do not require any military initiative at all. We did it, for example, at the Ghana Embassy in Leopoldville and we have done it on several other occasions. We did it in the case of Mr. Lumumba, when Mr. Lumumba asked us for protection at his residence. We replied, "Yes, we can protect you at your residence, but we cannot protect you wherever you may be." Now, Mr. Lumumba left his house, and went out into the country. We had no idea even where he was. He was arrested; an action from our side, either at the place of arrest or later on in Leopoldville, would have meant that we should have ordered the units of the United Nations Force to attack the units on the other side.

You may say that we should have done it. That is a judgement which anyone is free to make. But I must repeat my question: Where do you find authorization for us to attack those units through military initiative?

I said in the Security Council on December 13 that I found it frankly quite difficult to discuss the matter if it is impossible to see the distinction between situations which in no respect can be compared.

On the whole I think that this is really all that I should say on this occasion. However, I should like to add one general observation. When the representative of the Soviet Union spoke of this case of a threat to take hostages in what may be an incipient civil war, hostages who have absolutely nothing to do with it, he used the terminology it was a question of administrative measure of the Stanleyville authorities with regard to the Belgians, and later on he said that I was prepared to take immediate and effective measures to defend the Belgians. The aim of that terminology and of this way of characterizing the operation is obvious. I think that the Members of the General Assembly should be on guard against what I would call inverted racialism.

I know that this whole question of the mandate has become one on which one can speak very freely. We heard a statement today to the effect that I have been requested to take necessary action, and it was pointed out that "necessary" was the word, and not "legal." Should I read that as meaning that I could take what I considered to be necessary illegal action? I do not think so. Anyway, if that is the case, I will not do it.

THE AFRO-ASIAN Members most dissatisfied and impatient with the constitutional and policy restraints upon the use of force by the United Nations in the Congo were divided among those now determined to pull out of ONUC and go it alone, and those who preferred to seek instead a change in ONUC policies. India and Ghana were among those most active in supporting the latter view, which finally prevailed after intensive discussions in the Afro-Asian caucuses. Ceylon, Ghana, India, Indonesia, Iraq, Morocco, the United Arab Republic, and Yugoslavia joined in introducing a draft resolution calling for more forceful and interventionist action.

Operative paragraph 1 declared that "the United Nations must henceforth implement its mandate fully" to prevent breaches of peace and security and to restore and maintain law and order and the inviolability of persons. The phraseology implied that previous policies had been too restrictive and passive. The resolution also called for the immediate release of all political prisoners, the convening of Parliament and measures to prevent armed units and personnel from interfering in the political life of the country. Belgium was reprimanded for disregard of previous UN resolutions, and the immediate withdrawal of all Belgian military and civilian technicians and advisers was demanded. The draft resolution also called for a decision by the Assembly to appoint a standing delegation to go to Leopoldville and function in close cooperation with the UN special representative there. Finally it recommended that all economic and financial assistance should be supplied only through the United Nations.[1]

With the exception of the last two provisions the draft resolution tended to confuse ends with means and, with respect to the latter, leaned toward enforcement measures that would be constitutional only if ordered by the Security Council under Chapter VII of the Charter. In such respects it was unacceptable to a majority of the Assembly.

[1] General Assembly Official Records, Fifteenth Session, Annexes, agenda item 85, document A/L.331/Rev. 1.

Hammarskjöld did not speak directly on the draft resolution but in the statement that follows he made plain his continued opposition to any forceful intervention in the Congo's internal affairs. The aims stated in the draft, he said, must be pursued "by the normal political and diplomatic means of persuasion and advice, not by the use of force or intimidation." The Secretary-General also used the occasion to focus the Assembly's attention once again on the Soviet purpose to exploit differences over the Congo operation in order to gain support for its campaign to undermine the Secretariat's capacity to function in world affairs as an instrument for action owing loyalty only to the Charter and the world community as a whole.

---

5. Second Statement in the Assembly

NEW YORK   DECEMBER 17, 1960

THE ITEM TO WHICH this debate refers is called "The situation in the Congo." I do not believe that anybody is in doubt that for some the real issue might better have been called "The situation in the United Nations." The discussion of this question was opened in September during the general debate, and from then on it has been continued, overtly and covertly, in all the organs of the United Nations here at Headquarters.

The methods used in the interventions concerning this question have been new to the United Nations, and have given this discussion a significance going beyond the underlying problems of the administrative structure of the Organization or of the relative influence of this or that group. They have done so because they have brought us to a point where many may have been tempted to ask whether facts, or truth, or law no longer count, and whether it is possible to debate without respect for some basic rules of debate as developed in parliamentary life, either as regards form or as regards substance. If questions regarding the intellectual integrity of the discussion can be asked, it means that we are facing a great threat to this Organization and its stature. Popular or not, proper for me or not, I feel it is my duty to voice concern.

For reasons made clear to the Members of the Assembly in September, a concerted and consistent effort has been made in order to create conditions for a radical change of the administrative structure of the Organiza-

General Assembly Official Records, Fifteenth Session, 953rd plenary meeting.

tion and, with that in view, to corrode whatever confidence there may be among Members in the integrity of the Secretariat. No argument has been left untried. It would be vain to try to make a catalogue of all the misrepresentations of facts to which the Members have had to listen, or demands which could not be realized, or proposals for which those putting them forward would not be willing to share in the responsibility in action, and all the distortions of the actions of the representatives of the Organization. And yet if such a catalogue is not made, and if every point is not dealt with by me, you will undoubtedly hear again that the criticisms of the Secretariat must be correct as they have not been countered.

In spite of this, I will not repeat what I have said already on most of the points raised, although the attacks to which my observations have been the reply have been repeated in the current debate, in the obvious hope that by repetition they will create conviction. I shall limit myself to a few points which seem to represent innovations.

The representative of the Soviet Union said in his intervention at the 949th meeting that the Secretary-General has been acting against demands for the convening of the Congo parliament, and now has even some doubts of the legality of that organ. The representative has no basis for such a statement. The facts are that I have been working consistently for the reestablishment of Parliament in its proper position and that the flimsy basis that Mr. Zorin may believe that he can invoke, in support of his second allegation, is simply that I pointed out in the Security Council the obvious fact that we, the United Nations, cannot ourselves convene Parliament, nor put military forces as a sanction behind a suggestion to the proper authorities to convene Parliament.

Further, the representative of the Soviet Union told the General Assembly that I have acted against the Conciliation Commission. Fortunately, in this case the verbatim records of the meetings of the Advisory Committee are there, and the eighteen members of that Committee sit in this Assembly. The records show, and the members can tell, that there is no basis whatsoever for what Mr. Zorin said. But that is not sufficient. It has been said, and if I do not here present evidence showing that what is said is false I assume it is supposed to be accepted as the truth. Even if I took up the time of the Assembly with such a detailed refutation, I am sure we should soon have the same allegation repeated.

But more revealing than the statement to which I have referred, as an example of the way in which the question of the Congo is now discussed by a certain group, is the statement of the representative of Hungary to which we listened yesterday. I might take other examples, but, with the permission of the Members, I should like to give some special attention to that intervention.

Let me start out with a quotation from Mr. Peter's speech here yesterday—a quotation to which I suppose that a number of Members will have given all the attention it merits. The representative said: "Speaking from a human and moral point of view, it is absolutely impossible to understand what the psychological motivation may be of a person's attitude when there is not the slightest sign of self-examination when confronted with an enormously grave situation partly or entirely provoked by actions under his command."[1] It seems to me that the representative feels that we have now reached a stage in a certain modern ritual where it is time for a confession, to be followed by repentance and judgement.

With this background of concern about my supposed unwillingness to evaluate the actions of the Secretariat, the representative of Hungary wished to help me and presented eight points indicating our grave omissions. Let me repeat them and comment on them in order.

First, the representative of Hungary says that at the very beginning the Secretary-General did not clarify in his first proposals to the Security Council for what purpose, with what limitation, he was taking the responsibility for military action in the Congo. May I remind the representative of the fact that I did not ask for any powers. The responsibility was put on me by the Security Council, which supposedly itself had formed an idea about what exactly was expected, and certainly was capable of expressing it. Let me further remind him of the fact that exactly those points which later on proved controversial—for example, nonintervention and limitation of military action to self-defence—were made very clear by me both in my very first presentation of the problem to the Security Council on July 13 and, later on, in the first report the same month. The Security Council acted with that background, and its action must have involved the approval of the principles I outlined as it formally endorsed my report. Thus the first point of the representative of Hungary has no substance for those who care about the history of the case.

The second point of the representative of Hungary is that the Secretary-General when he supposedly realized that actions within the scope as he originally imagined it could not meet the situation, did not report to the Security Council nor ask for new instructions. I believe the members of the Security Council can confirm that it has been exactly the other way

[1] General Assembly Official Records, Fifteenth Session, 950th plenary meeting.

around, and that at every doubtful point during the decisive phases of this operation I brought the matter back to the Security Council for its consideration.

Thirdly, it is said that I did not inform Mr. Kasavubu early in September that the United Nations could not continue its assistance any longer unless the Loi fondamentale was observed and, further, that I did not inform the Security Council about the entirely new situation devolving from the move of Mr. Kasavubu at that time. Certainly, the representative does realize that the Secretary-General has no right to threaten with the cancellation of an operation decided by the Security Council. Certainly, the representative also remembers that Mr. Kasavubu's step was taken on September 5 and that I reported in writing and orally on the situation in the course of the same week. However, as this does not fit into the picture it is left out, obviously in the hope that nobody will remember.

Fourthly, the Secretary-General has not complied with Article 99 of the Charter as he has not initiated meetings of the General Assembly or the Security Council as the situation grew more dangerous. I will not enter upon any constitutional discussion with the representative, but he has here presented a new interpretation of Article 99, especially as regards the situation when the General Assembly is in session, forgetting that the initiative of the Secretary-General is subsidiary and that his duty under Article 99, in the prevailing situation, has been fulfilled when, by reports and documentation, he has fully provided the Members with the facts, giving them a chance to judge for themselves.

Fifthly, it is said that the Secretary-General has omitted to report in due time regarding several serious aspects, and as an example—the only one quoted—it is said that only at the last meeting of the Security Council did he report on the fact that in South Kasai some two hundred persons were dying daily from starvation. If the representative had asked me before making that statement I could have told him that that piece of disturbing news was received the very same day it was reported to the Security Council.

The sixth point is that, as the Secretary-General has not asked for the necessary clarification of his mandate, he has become an autonomous organ of the United Nations, being himself above the legal organs. I have to refer the delegations to the record and to what I said under point two: it just is not so.

The seventh point is that I have neglected the views of the Member states which undertook responsibility for the situation in the Congo by providing military units. Can it be that the representative is unaware of the fact that all of those Member governments are represented in the Advisory Committee, which has had meetings at least every week at which so far—with one single exception—agreement has been reached on actions to be taken, and at which every member has been free to raise whatever point he wanted. The single exception was when, at the last meeting, the representative of Guinea took a stand against the sending of a vanguard of the Conciliation Commission to the Congo.

The eighth and last point made by the representative is that I am requesting Member states to continue their undertakings, sharing in the responsibility for a situation created mainly by failures of the Secretariat. Certainly, if I had not requested them to continue, that would also—and with justification—have been listed as an omission.

What is interesting in the eight points of sins of omission and commission allegedly committed by me is less their lack of substance than the fact that, by implication, they exclude even the possibility of any responsibility of the Security Council and its members, or of the General Assembly and its Members, or of anybody in the Congo. Everything is left at the doorstep of the Secretariat. The concentration on my activities is such that for a moment even the imperialists and colonialists seem to fade out of the picture. Why? Those who remember some things said in this hall in September and early October and who have followed the interventions of a certain group of countries all through the General Assembly—in a follow-up of the operation started in the general debate—know the reply. As I have not been willing to pave the way for reforms of the Secretariat, desired by a certain party, by resigning "so to say, in a chivalrous manner," the desired result has to be achieved in a way the least weakness of which is that it is not chivalrous. I said at the beginning that this debate has for some been basically one about the United Nations. In what sense this is true is clear from what I have recalled here about some of the arguments used.

On an entirely different level from the points to which I have found it necessary to refer, by way of illustration of a trend in the present debate, is the open or implied question directed to me regarding the way in which I look at the present need for United Nations action in order to achieve what, from the beginning and all through the operation, has been the aim to which the Organization wished to contribute: stable and peaceful political conditions in the Congo, with its integrity safeguarded against all actions from outside—irrespective of the source—and with its sovereignty upheld by the subordination to the wish of the authorities of the Congo of all assistance given. To state and restate this obvious aim, in a more or less detailed form and with more or less specific indications of this or that aspect, is neither to indicate how the aim is to be achieved nor to provide the means for its achievement. These distinctions must be made.

First, as regards the aim: nobody has come out in opposition to the aim as I have here brought it again to the Assembly's attention. Some have, however, acted in various ways so as to endanger the possibilities of achieving it. This is true of parties both outside and inside the Congo. It is anybody's guess whether those who have acted in this way have done it wilfully, with aims of their own in mind, or not.

Secondly, with this aim, the United Nations has decided on certain military and civilian assistance to the Republic of the Congo and charged the Secretary-General with executive responsibility. The mandate of the United Nations representatives has been to work for the aim within the legal limits set by the Charter, and by the decisions of the Security Council and the General Assembly, to the extent rendered possible by the means put at the disposal of the executive organ. Certainly the mandate has never been understood as being the achievement of the aim, irrespective of the legal limits set for the United Nations actions and irrespective of the adequacy of the means provided.

Thirdly, as regards the means: the main instrument provided has been the United Nations Force set up by the Security Council without explicit reference to Article 39 or 40 and, *a fortiori,* without basing itself on Article 41 or 42. As at early stages I brought this, both in substance and in form, to the attention of the Security Council, there can not have been any misunderstanding on this point. It follows from this, and it was stated at the very beginning of the operation—and approved by the Security Council—that the Force was not entitled to take military action unless in self-defence or to protect life and property, and that it could not be used as an instrument for solutions of domestic political problems, constitutional or otherwise.

The discussion of principle which has characterized the development of the question here at the United Nations has tended to confuse the aim with the mandate and also to reinterpret the question of the means in terms of the mandate, irrespective of legal considerations. For that reason, during the most recent series of meetings of the Security Council, I asked for a clarification of the Council's interpretation of the mandate and a provision of means corresponding to the mandate, if it were the case that the Council felt that the mandate should be widened beyond what I have said above and beyond what present means permit. In that context I reminded the Council of the fact that such a clarification and possible expansion of the mandate and of the means had to proceed strictly within the limits set by the Charter. I added that I felt that it would be fair for the Security Council or the General Assembly, in an appropriate form, to share in the responsibility for the carrying out from day to day of the mandate and, of course, also in the decisions on the use of the means. Thus, I myself did not ask for a widening of the mandate or for new means, but I did ask the Council to do away with the ambiguities which had arisen, mainly through the discussion around the Council table. The only new point I brought in myself was the suggestion for an arrangement for an appropriate sharing of responsibilities, and I have noted with encouragement that this idea was taken up by the foreign minister of the United Arab Republic.

If I did not ask for a widened mandate or for new means, it was because I do not believe that it is by such new means, within the limits set by the Charter, that the present problem of the Congo can be solved. This is so for two reasons. First, I reject everything that would have a touch of control or direction of the Congo's internal affairs—noting with some surprise that proposals in that direction have been made from highly authoritative African sources—and, second, I do not believe that the use of military initiative, or pressure, is the way to bring about the political structure, in terms of persons and institutions, which at present is the first need of the Congo. The United Nations can help in such a direction, but that is by the normal political and diplomatic means of persuasion and advice, not by the use of force or intimidation.

Nor, of course, can widened means, of the kind on which the Security Council and the General Assembly may decide, resolve the problems presented by various forms of external support or intervention—although a solution, especially to the question of support to the Armée nationale congolaise is probably vital to the future of the United Nations Force— such political moves naturally having to be made, also by the organs of the United Nations, on a political level and by political means. For example, an influx of technicians, considered not to be desirable, can be counteracted by attempts to exercise direct influence on the country from which they come and on those in the Congo who have hired them, but I do not believe that we have the right to break individual contracts nor to use our military means for the arrest and deportation of individuals, at least not short of a direct request to that effect from such authorities as unquestionably would be entitled to take such actions themselves.

These question marks as regards the usefulness of a wider mandate or new means should not be construed as a negative attitude from my side on decisions by the General Assembly by which the Assembly morally and politically would strengthen the hand of its representatives in their efforts to work, by peaceful and legal means, for the aim we all should have in common. On the contrary, such a strengthening is highly desirable as the authority of the United Nations has been challenged from many quarters, although for opposite reasons. In case of such strengthened authority, which might find one of its expressions in the sharing of responsibilities that I have mentioned as desirable, I would envisage the future, in brief, as follows.

The overriding consideration must be one of, on the one side, return to constitutionality and, on the other side, national reconciliation. With this background I feel that the United Nations should exercise its influence in favour of the restoration of Parliament to its proper position in the constitutional system, facilitating by available means its resumption of action. Combined with that, I feel that it is necessary to work in the direction of a reduction of the army to its constitutional place as a subordinate instrument for the national executive in the maintenance of law and order.

This—which highlights the importance of an elimination of foreign support in money or men—indicates the necessity for the reestablishment of a civilian government which must have constitutional legitimacy and a sufficient basis to command nation-wide authority and which, further, must have a minimum degree of inner cohesion achieved by reconciliation and compromise between various factions and leaders, as normal in political life. The key position and responsibility of the chief of state in such a development as the one indicated here is obvious, but it would be improper for me to comment on it beyond this simple statement.

Naturally, the development I envisage would require the establishment of a certain balance between various factions in Congolese political life, a balance which in the stormy first months has been tipped for some time in one direction and at other times just as one-sidedly in other directions. The secessionist tendencies must in this context be broken if we are to be entitled to hope for future stability in the area.

What can the Organization and its Members do to further a development of this kind? First there is the obvious duty for all Members, as stated already by the General Assembly in its resolution of September 20, to abstain from everything that would counteract the desired development. This applies both to comments on the situation in the Congo, to actions in relation to various parties in the Congo, and to actions in the Congo itself.

Secondly, the General Assembly itself can, as I have said, in various ways strengthen the hand of the Organization in support of progress in the direction envisaged, but for reasons already mentioned I do not feel that it can do so by such concrete measures as, whatever their legality, would represent a direct interference by pressure of force in favour of any specific solutions in terms of persons or parties. Therefore, a formal decision of the Assembly would in a large part have to represent an effort to advise and to guide by an expression of world opinion as regards various elements appearing to be necessary as part of a situation corresponding to the ultimate aim of the Organization.

Thirdly, Members know that the presiding officers of the Conciliation Commission have gone to Leopoldville. I firmly believe in their possibility and later in the possibility of the Commission itself, to help towards the aims of the Organization. Naturally, I do, and will do what I can for that same purpose, but the contribution of the Commission and its forerunners is an important new element in our assistance.

I believe that I should in this intervention say also a word about the civilian operation.

References have been made to the need of assisting the Congo government in the civilian field and of channelling all technical assistance through the United Nations. In this connection, the request for the withdrawal of Belgian civilians has been strongly voiced. Those who have followed my various reports on the Congo operation will no doubt recall that I have repeatedly urged that personnel for the Congo should be channelled through United Nations agencies and that unilateral and competitive assistance can only lead to the most undesirable consequences. This is a matter of record.

Some statistics may be helpful in placing this problem in its proper perspective. Prior to independence, there were employed in the administrative apparatus of the Congo more than seven thousand Belgians, most of whom left after the events of early July. An assessment of the needs of the Congo government for non-Congolese staff, within the same category, which has recently been undertaken by Mr. Gardiner, a Ghana citizen who was for a while seconded from the Economic Commission for Africa to Leopoldville, indicated that the number of Belgians employed was high and that some 1,800 non-Congolese would be necessary to assist the Congolese in managing their own affairs, until some Congolese will have been trained. Most of these 1,800 are in the categories of technicians, but about 10 percent of those required, that is to say, some 180 persons, would have to be assigned to posts which could be regarded as on the policy-making level, posts which would be sufficiently sensitive to be filled only by persons of impartiality and utmost integrity, ready to serve the interests of an independent Congo only.

Of 1,800 posts required, only a fraction are presently filled. The United Nations maintains 233 technicians, including 76 International Red Cross personnel. Belgian technicians are estimated at a low figure of 320, but it may be anything up to 970; it is impossible at present to secure more reliable information. It is even more difficult to state how large the number of Belgians is serving in the category of "policy-making" positions. Staff recruited for these levels by the United Nations amounts so far to only some 25.

It must be obvious that the lack of technical services has a significant impact on the political crisis in the Congo, and it is even more obvious that as long as the non-Congolese staff on the policy level is not exclusively concerned with the fostering of the interests of the Congo, the political crisis is likely to be aggravated. I need not repeat here my deep conviction that the United Nations contribution could be most significant, provided that the Organization is willing to shoulder, at least temporarily, through the Congo Fund and by other means, the responsibility for underwriting adequately the civilian programme which has been initiated. It is obviously not sufficient to request the withdrawal of technicians provided outside the United Nations framework, if no steps are suggested as to how the gap created by such withdrawals can be filled by the United Nations itself.

Even the very modest civilian operation which the situation in the Congo has so far made possible could not be maintained in the country short of the degree of protection of life and property achieved through the United Nations Force. But that Force might have to be discontinued, as I pointed out in the Security Council, either because of political developments in and around the country or because of withdrawals of such magnitude as to render the remainder of the Force ineffective. Thus, a reasonably stable solution to the domestic problems of the Congo, the attitude of Member governments to the Force, the maintenance of protection of life and property within the country, and the maintenance of the badly needed technical assistance under United Nations auspices are all linked together into a whole of which no one part can be jeopardized without endangering all the others.

From early September, and even more so from the time of the debate on the representation of the Congo in the General Assembly, this Assembly has been deeply divided. This same split characterizes also the group of African Members. In the earlier stages the operation had the unanimous support of the Security Council, the General Assembly, and the African group. This change is not of the making of the Secretariat. Is it permissible to overlook its dangerous influence on the effort of the Organization to help the people of the Congo to find and break its own way to a situation giving full substance to its independence?

THE UNITED STATES and the United Kingdom introduced a draft resolution[1] requesting the Secretary-General to continue his efforts to ensure that no foreign military or paramilitary personnel were introduced or remained in the Congo in violation of earlier resolutions adopted by the Security Council or General Assembly. With due regard for paragraph 4 of the Council's August 9 resolution (that the UN Force "will not be a party to or in any way intervene in or be used to influence the outcome of any internal conflict, constitutional or otherwise"), the Secretary-General was also requested to do everything possible to assist the President in establishing conditions in which Parliament could meet and function in security and freedom.

The draft resolution also repeated parts of the West's "humanitarian" resolution that had been vetoed in the Security Council and expressed hope for the success of the Conciliation Commission's efforts to resolve by peaceful means the Congo's internal conflicts and preserve the country's unity and integrity. There was no call for the release of political prisoners or for the recall of Belgian civilian advisers and technicians. These omissions, plus the designation of Kasavubu as the man to be helped in efforts to reactivate Parliament, gave the resolution too much of a Western flavor for the Africans, and for most Asians as well.

The prospects were poor for a constructive outcome of the debate. Before it came to an end Hammarskjöld felt he should put the Assembly on notice about his intentions should he receive no further guidance. He also gave warning that, should an all-out civil-war situation develop, despite his best efforts, he saw no alternative to a withdrawal of the UN Force (first following text).

[1] General Assembly Official Records, Fifteenth Session, Annexes, agenda item 85, document A/L.332.

6. *Third Statement in the Assembly*

NEW YORK   DECEMBER 19, 1960

IN MY STATEMENT IN THE General Assembly at the 953rd meeting, I said that the United Nations Force and its operations might have to be discontinued either because of political developments in and around the country or because of withdrawals of such magnitude as to render the remainder of the Force ineffective. Previously, in the Security Council I had made clear the grave risk that a withdrawal now of the United Nations would lead to a Spanish War situation. Further I have stated, in the General Assembly, that a withdrawal would necessitate also a liquidation of the United Nations civilian operation.

Before the General Assembly proceeds to a vote on the drafts before it, and later adjourns, depriving us of the possibility of such further suggestions to the Assembly as may be called for in view of developments in the Congo in a near future, I have felt that I have now to elaborate one aspect of the conditions under which I would consider myself forced to propose a withdrawal of the United Nations Force. I excuse myself, Mr. President, for burdening the debate of the Assembly with these further observations, but the question seems to me so important as to justify this additional intervention. I promise you it will be a short one.

In the Security Council I drew, as I recalled, attention to the possibility that, following a United Nations withdrawal, a situation of civil war would develop, with direct or indirect engagement of outside powers being practically inevitable. What about the position of the United Nations if such a situation were to develop while the Force is still there— something which, naturally, cannot be excluded if one side or the other were to take the initiative to an offensive in oblivion of the overriding interests of the country as a whole and in disregard of the United Nations.

One thing is obvious: it is the duty of the United Nations by all means to try to forestall such a development. This is nothing new; we have

General Assembly Official Records, Fifteenth Session, 957th plenary meeting.

consistently tried to do so, especially, so far, giving attention to steps that seem to have been taken in the direction of a build-up of the armed forces with outside assistance. In continued efforts to forestall the major risk I have just mentioned, in a situation of increased danger, reflected in actions in the country, I believe that the mandate to protect life and property and to act in self-defence may be given—let me call it—an "emergency interpretation," stretching the possibility of preventive action beyond what under other circumstances would be reasonable and permissible. That is to say, the mandate, unless changed or clarified, necessarily remains as determined from the beginning, but its implementation should be adjusted to the seriousness of the threat that the United Nations tries to stem.

However, also the most energetic action by the United Nations, within the formal limits of its mandate, even if it were adjusted to emergency needs stretching our rights beyond the normal, may not be successful in forestalling a change of the situation into one of acute civil war with the grave overtones to which I have referred. If that happens, what should thereafter be the policy of the United Nations? A taking of sides obviously would be impermissible under the general rules applied, and a standing aside which in other circumstances might seem to correspond best with the principles of the United Nations operation would, in the situation considered here, be likely to place the United Nations and its Force in an untenable position, being so to say in the role of a passive witness to developments diametrically opposed to those which the Organization wishes to further.

Should then the United Nations try to interpose itself? That seems to be what should follow from the general rule of noninterference, as the alternative of complete passivity would have to be ruled out. Is such interposition possible with maintenance of the proper role for the Organization? In situations of much lesser scope and without the same overtones the Force has, to a limited extent, locally interposed itself and has succeeded in doing so without compromising its basic position. However, in the situation envisaged here the chance to pursue such a policy would be very slight indeed. Practically every act of interposition in such a situation might lend itself to the interpretation that it was taken in order to help one side or the other—and that not only locally but in an international sense, due to the support that may be given from the outside to the various parties in the Congo. Also this would represent an impossible position for the United Nations. My conclusion is that, just as I have had to exclude the taking of sides or passivity, I anticipate that it would be impossible to pursue a policy of interposition. Therefore, were a situation for the United Nations of the kind I have described to develop, I would have to put up to the Security Council the question whether the United Nations Force should not withdraw.

Stated in other terms, the problem to which I refer can be explained as follows: The United Nations went in on a basis which at least gave the Organization a fair chance that it could assist in stabilizing conditions in the Congo without becoming a party either to domestic conflict or—what would have been even more serious—to an international conflict. It could therefore also rely on troops from a number of countries neutral in the world-wide conflict and neutral in the controversies dividing the Congo.

We have suffered from increasing difficulties because of the way in which the conflicts dividing the country have developed, especially early in September, and again quite recently. We have suffered from those conflicts especially because of an involvement of other countries in them, directly or indirectly. There is naturally a point where the sharpening of those conflicts and the weight of foreign involvement become such, that neither the participating member nations nor the Organization itself should continue because continuation would contribute little to an improvement of the situation but risk to compromise the position both of participating nations and of the Organization as a whole. We are in my view not there, but we might easily get there through irresponsible moves, nationally or internationally. It should be clearly understood that the result of such moves may well be a decision of the Security Council on the withdrawal of the United Nations, with the resulting fundamental change in the position of parties in the country who may have felt that they could play it safely in the shadow of the Organization.

I hope indeed such a crisis will not develop, as it would mean the failure of a great effort to keep the cold war in its sharper forms out of Africa, and the failure also to stabilize the situation in the Congo through such means as the Charter makes available to the Organization. Everything should be done by the Organization and its representatives to forestall such a crisis, but if our efforts are of no avail it is better for the future of this Organization to look the situation in the eye and to draw the conclusions.

I have a couple of times referred to the desirability of a sharing of responsibility between representatives of the main organs and the Secretary-General. I hope everybody understands that, under present circumstances, decisions of the type which we have to take daily, and in particular decisions of the kind which might be forced upon us in an emergency like the one to which I have referred as a possibility, go beyond what reasonably should be put on the shoulders of any one man and his collaborators. If my suggestion were not to meet with any further response, it would, to my regret, leave me only the possibility to continue to rely on the Advisory Committee, which, with all its high competence, has after all only limited authority. I would naturally look for assistance, in particular, from the representatives of the Committee who have gone or will go to the Congo.

In concluding I wish to remind the General Assembly also of what I have said about the way in which I envisage the future in the Congo if circumstances permit our Congolese friends and us to continue our work under peaceful conditions. If I get no other guidance from the Assembly I hope it will be understood that these views will be what I would personally try to further within the limits of our resources.

WHEN THE AFRO-ASIAN draft resolution was put to a vote on December 20 it went down to defeat by 42 votes to 28, with 27 abstentions. Seventeen African and Asian states joined the Soviet bloc in the affirmative and twenty-one others abstained. The West voted solidly in the negative.

The United States-United Kingdom draft resolution then failed by a single vote to win the necessary two-thirds margin. There were 43 affirmative votes, 22 against and 32 abstentions. Not a single African state voted with the West and only seven Asian states, all of whom—like Japan, Thailand, and Nationalist China—were closely tied to the West. Eleven Africans and Asians voted against the West and twenty-two others abstained. A shift of just one of the negative votes to an abstention would have carried the Western resolution but such a victory would have been worth little because of the great number of nay votes and abstentions that were recorded.

Zorin warned that since the authority of the United Nations had been "gravely impaired . . . the peace-loving states will naturally seek other ways of ensuring peace in Africa." He indicated considerable satisfaction in the fact that the peoples of the world would find, in a study of the treatment of the situation in the Republic of the Congo in the United Nations, an excellent lesson for "they can now see more clearly . . . who really is in favor of eliminating the colonial system in all its forms, and who is attempting by hook or by crook to preserve colonialism." In the end, he predicted, "the people of the Congo, with the support of all peace-loving peoples, will triumph in the struggle against the colonialists."[1]

For his part the Secretary-General spoke in the following terms (first following text).

[1] General Assembly Official Records, Fifteenth Session, 959th plenary meeting.

7. *Concluding Statement in the Assembly*

NEW YORK   DECEMBER 20, 1960

JUST AS A SHORT TIME AGO the Security Council, so now after a long debate the General Assembly has failed to reach a positive decision regarding the problem of the Congo, further developing the stand of the Organization as already defined. The most serious aspect of this dual failure is what it reveals of the present split within the Organization on this issue of vital significance.

Naturally, the operation will be continued under the previous decisions with all energy, within the limits of the law, with an adjustment—to the best of our understanding—of the implementation of our mandate to the needs, and with aims which, in spite of all, I believe remain common, at least, to the vast majority of Member states. However, the outcome here, as it now stands, has not given us the moral or political support of which the operation is in need.

May I hope that in spite of the division of opinion, the representatives of the Organization may count on the continued good cooperation which they have enjoyed in the past from those countries which have shown their willingness to shoulder responsibility in the matter, and that those same countries in cooperation also outside the formal framework of the United Nations, will act in support of a final solution of our problem in a way which fully reflects the seriousness of the situation, will provide us with the necessary means, and will do all that in other respects is possible in order to neutralize the loss we may have suffered.

General Assembly Official Records, Fifteenth Session, 958th plenary meeting.

One thing should be firmly on record; the previous resolutions on the Congo remain fully valid, and so do, to the full, all the obligations they impose on all Member nations. This is of special importance, retroactively as well as for the next future, in respect of the request for abstention from bilateral action as ruled out by this Assembly on September 20, 1960.

HAMMARSKJÖLD WROTE to Kasavubu immediately after the Assembly recessed. His review of the outcome pointed out that, despite sharp differences on some questions, a very large majority of Members voting for one resolution or the other were agreed in their concern for the welfare of political prisoners, in their desire for a reconvening of Parliament, for cooperation with the Conciliation Commission's efforts to bring an end to internal political strife and against bilateral interventions on one side or the other. His letter, although sent on December 21, was not distributed to delegates in a public document until January 1, 1961.

---

8. Letter to President Kasavubu

NEW YORK   DECEMBER 21, 1960

YOU HAVE NO DOUBT been informed by your representative at the United Nations concerning the consideration which the General Assembly has been giving to the question of the Congo in the course of the last few days. I am sure that the draft resolutions which have been submitted by the United States and the United Kingdom, on the one hand, and by Ceylon, Ghana, India, Indonesia, Iraq, Morocco, United Arab Republic, and Yugoslavia on the other hand, have been brought to your attention. I must also assume that you have been informed concerning the various interventions which I have made during the discussion. If this should not be the case, I shall ask Mr. Dayal to submit these texts to you for your perusal.

Security Council Official Records, Sixteenth Year, Supplement for January, February and March 1961, document S/4606, January 1, 1961.

As is by now well known to you, neither of the two resolutions referred to above has been adopted by the General Assembly by the required majorities and consequently the resolutions which had previously been adopted by the Security Council and by the fourth emergency special session of the General Assembly remain operative. I permit myself to draw your attention to excerpts of the statement which I made to the General Assembly following the indecisive votes on the draft resolutions:

... the General Assembly has failed to reach a positive decision regarding the problem of the Congo, further developing the stand of the Organization as already defined. ...

Naturally, the operation will be continued under the previous decisions with all energy, within the limits of the law, with an adjustment—to the best of our understanding—of the implementation of our mandate to the needs, and with aims which, in spite of all, I believe remain common, at least, to the vast majority of Member states.

One thing should be firmly on record: the previous resolutions on the Congo remain fully valid, and so do, to the full, all the obligations they impose on all Member nations. This is of special importance, retroactively as well as for the immediate future, in respect of the request for abstention from bilateral action as ruled out by this Assembly on September 20, 1960.

Although the General Assembly did not come to a definitive decision, it is important to emphasize that there is in the Assembly a strong concern about the recent developments in the Republic of the Congo, particularly regarding the manner in which the relationship between the United Nations and the authorities of the Republic of the Congo has been developing in recent months. You will perhaps permit me to point out that this concern is quite considerable among those groups of states which previously had taken a rather positive attitude with regard to your representation in the United Nations. This is predominantly expressed in the draft resolution sponsored by the United Kingdom and the United States which, except for one vote, might have been adopted by the General Assembly.

It should be noted that this draft resolution requests me, as the Secretary-General of the United Nations, to continue to discharge the mandate which was originally entrusted to me by the Security Council and, in particular, asks me to continue to use the presence and the machinery of the United Nations to assist the Republic of the Congo in the restoration and maintenance of law and order throughout its territory.

This draft resolution requests the Secretary-General *inter alia* to do everything possible to assist the chief of state of the Republic of the

Congo in establishing conditions in which the Parliament could meet and in which it could function in security and freedom from outside interference.

This latter request for the convening of Parliament and for the taking of the necessary protective measures was more forcefully expressed in the eight-power draft resolution and therefore I may fairly state that, even though the Assembly was in disagreement in regard to what steps should be taken, the overwhelming majority of the members is strongly of the opinion that the convening of Parliament and the return to democratic practices is a matter of great urgency. This, as you well know, is a view which I have held for a long time. Although this view may not have found the formal endorsement of the General Assembly, it should nevertheless be regarded by you as the strong conviction of almost all Member states. I can therefore only hope that you, by virtue of the powers invested in you, will see your way clear to convoke Parliament at an early date and I, for my part, can assure you full cooperation in providing security to the members of Parliament.

Another paragraph of the United Kingdom-United States draft resolution which should not be lightly dismissed declares that any violation of human rights against persons held prisoners or under arrest anywhere in the Congo would be inconsistent with the purposes of the United Nations. Again in regard to this matter, which so clearly refers to the recent arrests of political personalities, the draft resolution of the eight powers is much more direct in that it urges the immediate release of all political prisoners under detention and particularly of those enjoying parliamentary immunity. While recognizing that both resolutions approach this problem from a different point of view, there is an unmistakable undercurrent in both of them which, having regard to the Congo's relations to other Members of the United Nations, would merit in my opinion your most urgent attention. I am quite certain that as long as "due process of law," as indicated in my letter of December 3, 1960, has not been fully applied, this question will remain a major irritant in the relations between the Congo and many other Member states. In this connection, it should be noted that the draft resolution of the United Kingdom and the United States expresses the hope that the International Committee of the Red Cross should be allowed to examine detained prisoners throughout the Republic of the Congo.

This same draft resolution also expresses the hope that the forthcoming round-table conference, to be convened by you as the chief of state, as well as the visit, for the purpose of conciliation, to the Republic of the Congo by certain representatives appointed by the Advisory Committee on the Congo, will help to resolve internal conflicts by peaceful means and to preserve the unity and integrity of the Congo. I need not restate the great importance which I have attached to the task of the Conciliation Commission in assisting the Congo in arriving at a satisfactory solution of its internal difficulties. I remain of the hope that I can count on your full cooperation enabling this Commission to become a helpful agency in securing reconciliation and permitting it to assist the political leaders of the Congo in settling their disputes in the interest of maintaining the country's unity.

You will no doubt wish to note that the draft resolution of the United Kingdom and the United States also requests the Secretary-General to continue his vigorous efforts to ensure that no foreign military or para-military personnel are introduced into the Republic of the Congo and calls, as did the General Assembly resolution of September 20, 1960, upon all states to refrain from direct and indirect provision of arms or other materials of war and military personnel and other assistance for military purposes in the Congo while the United Nations provides military assistance. The draft resolution specifically states that the provision of arms and war material and personnel can only be given at the request of the United Nations through the Secretary-General. The importance of this is obvious and clearly outlines the philosophy of the sponsors concerning the role which the United Nations is to play. I may add at this point that the Government of Belgium voted in favour of this resolution, a fact which may be of some significance if viewed against some of the difficulties which the United Nations recently encountered.

Finally, and perhaps most significantly, the draft resolution also requests all Congolese to lend practical cooperation to the United Nations in order that the purposes that guide the United Nations operation in the Congo can be fruitfully achieved.

It may be of interest to you to note that the eight-power draft resolution urged *inter alia* that measures be taken forthwith to prevent armed units and personnel in the Congo from any interference in the political life of the country as well as from obtaining any material or other support from abroad. The vote for the resolution containing this paragraph was not too sizeable, but it reflects a widespread critical reaction caused by the difficulties which have characterized the recent relationship between the United Nations and the Armée nationale congolaise; you find the same reaction in some of my statements which echoed a conviction I have also met among many of those who voted against the said resolution.

This brief analysis of the draft resolutions which were before the General Assembly indicates quite clearly that the overwhelming membership of the United Nations, including those who have made contributions to the United Nations operation in the Congo, continue to exhibit the same interest in the welfare of the Congo as they have in the past. They are, however, much concerned about the impact which the internal affairs of the Congo may have upon the world at large and they obviously do not wish, at this time, to disassociate the United Nations from the affairs of the Republic of the Congo for fear that a withdrawal of United Nations contingents would not only pave the way for civil war, with inestimable international implications, but that such a withdrawal might even lead to a conflagration of wider scope.

In this connection, I must draw to your attention the great concern which the recent developments in the Congo have given me and which in general terms I conveyed to the General Assembly, namely my concern about a developing civil war involving various sections of the Congo and its unavoidable effect upon the presence of the United Nations Force. It is quite obvious that if such a development should take place, the United Nations, being by its mandate prohibited from taking sides in any internal conflict, would be placed in an untenable position since it would have to stand aside in the developments which are so clearly opposed to those which the United Nations has attempted to foster in the Congo. I sincerely trust that no situation will develop which would give me no choice but to recommend to the Security Council that it authorize the withdrawal of the United Nations Force from the Republic of the Congo; thus throwing on the authorities of the Congo the full responsibility of maintaining law and order, unaided by the United Nations and without the possibility of recourse from other military assistance from outside; in view of the extremely grave risks involved in such assistance at the present juncture. I am certain, Mr. President, that you share my view that this renders military moves activating the problem of a United Nations withdrawal most inadvisable.

I am personally convinced that you yourself see these difficulties and that it is your solemn determination to use your influence for a peaceful solution of the Congo's internal problems. The basis for such a solution must quite clearly be the unreserved acceptance of a United Nations Force by the Congolese authorities and the noninterference in the performance of its tasks to maintain peace and order. Events such as those which have recently taken place at Kitona and Bukavu are, of course, intolerable. There is no excuse for the arbitrary action taken by the Armée nationale congolaise against the United Nations Force and the time has come when you as head of state must make an unequivocal declaration in order to enable us to continue. I am deeply convinced that it is imperative to reach a clear understanding concerning the conditions under which the United Nations can usefully remain and serve in the Congo.

At this time, when the unity of the Congo is likely to be threatened more than ever before, I felt it my duty to bring these matters to your urgent attention.

DAG HAMMARSKJÖLD
Secretary-General of the United Nations

THE REFERENCES at the end of the letter to recent incidents at Kitona and Bukavu concerned actions by units of the ANC, first, to seize control from the United Nations of the military base at Kitona and, second, to arrest and mistreat Austrian medical and hospital personnel who had just arrived at Bukavu on a UN assignment. The Kitona action was soon nullified and a gruding apology was forthcoming for the Bukavu incident.

Remarks at Unveiling of Portrait of Trygve Lie

NEW YORK   NOVEMBER 21, 1960

IT WAS A COINCIDENCE that Trygve Lie was in New York for the presentation of his portrait on the same day that Hammarskjöld, this time in the Fifth Committee (p. 226), was called upon for one of his frequent replies to the recurrent attacks upon him and his office by the Soviet Union. It had been fashionable in the earlier Hammarskjöld days for some in the inner circle to criticize Lie for staying on after his stand on Korea made him a Soviet target. Hammarskjöld himself, when fresh on the job, had rejected, sometimes in rather critical terms, Lie's description of the task of Secretary-General as "the most impossible job in the world" (see, for example, volume II of this series, p. 41). Now, however, he quite gracefully modified that earlier judgment in the light of his own experience.

BASING YOURSELF ON YOUR personal experiences and referring to that chronicle of the first seven years of the life of this Organization which we have in Mr. Lie's memoirs, you, Mr. Ambassador,[1] have reminded us of the growth of this Organization and of the difficulties it had to encounter during the time when Mr. Lie was its Secretary-General. And you, many of the others here present, senior members of the Secretariat during the time of Mr. Lie's Secretary-Generalship, have also personally an experience that naturally I cannot match. In these circumstances there is no reason for me to go back to those formative years in the life of the Organization.

In the development of an experiment of international cooperation like this one, every day counts, every action, yes, even every word counts in establishing the record on which the final outcome will be judged. What has happened in the last few years has therefore as its background the events and the moves that preceded the present period. We reap what was sown and we add to the history our own successes and our own failures. It is necessary that we keep the perspective clear and look always at the life of the Organization in its organic entirety.

Source: Unnumbered typescript.

[1] Sievert A. Nielsen, Permanent Representative of Norway, who made the presentation.

It is therefore fitting that the first seven years of this Organization be commemorated by this generous gift to the United Nations of a portrait of Mr. Lie in which his countrymen have taken the initiative, and which I have now the honor to receive from the hands of the representative of the Government of Norway.

It is always difficult in public to speak as man to man, especially, I may add, for a Scandinavian for whom this kind of approach, in the language of this Organization, is slightly "out of order." However, let me say to you, Mr. Lie, that this picture of my distinguished predecessor will, in the light of my own experiences, always remind me of all the difficulties you had to encounter and to overcome in what, on my arrival to New York in the spring of 1953, you yourself called "the most impossible job in the world."

Statement at the Human Rights Day Concert

NEW YORK   DECEMBER 10, 1960

THE FOLLOWING STATEMENT provides a fitting year-end commentary for the travails of 1960.

ONCE AGAIN, on this twelfth anniversary, we honor the proclamation by the General Assembly of the United Nations of the Universal Declaration of Human Rights.

In doing so, we pay honor also to those in East and West who, in past generations, have asserted the inherent dignity of man against the acts of inhumanity which all our ancestors have witnessed and we also witness in this century.

Human rights—their counterpart is human obligations. In celebrating Human Rights Day we should remember that no declarations on human rights, nor even any conventions or laws protecting human rights, are sufficient for their purpose unless we recognize, as a personal responsibility, respect in word and deed for the dignity of the human being.

A great German philosopher formulated the underlying principle when he said that the basic rule of ethics is never to treat man as a means but always as an end.[1] In less paradoxical forms the same thought is common to all the great religions represented in this Organization. And yet, we witness daily actions which may slip through the network of general statements and of law, but yet brutally reflect man's cruelty to man, and men's abuse of men. We witness it on a national level and we witness it on the international level.

The General Assembly is now engaged in a debate on the colonial issue. It is significant for the present international revolution. The prog-

UN Press Release SG/984.

[1] Immanuel Kant, in *Foundations of the Metaphysics of Morals,* wrote: "So act as to treat humanity, whether in your own person or in that of another, in every case as an end in itself, never as a means."

ress toward self-determination and self-government for all peoples is truly an encouraging translation into political action of the concept of human rights and the underlying ethical ideas. But let us not forget that there is a colonialism of the heart and of the mind, which no political decision can overcome and against which the battle must be waged within ourselves, without any exception.

To honor in this spirit and in this wider perspective Human Rights Day may help us to give life and reality to what is handed to us by legislators, diplomats, and politicians and what otherwise would be but empty form.

❧ 1961 ❧

"A New Look at Everest"
Article Written For the National Geographic
Magazine

JANUARY 1961

WHAT FOLLOWS is the text of an article written by Hammarskjöld for the *National Geographic Magazine* to accompany some very beautiful photographs he had taken from an airplane of Everest, Annapurna, and other Himalayan peaks during a visit to Nepal in March 1959. Although not published until the January 1961 issue the article had been completed before the beginning of the Congo crisis. In the light of what had happened since July 1960 his tribute in the article to those who had failed to conquer Everest is striking: ". . . their glory, written into the history of the mountain, is that they went to the limits of the humanly possible and were defeated only by circumstances beyond human mastery."

Hammarskjöld enclosed a copy of the magazine with a New Year's letter to Hans Engen, who was now state secretary for foreign affairs of Norway, in which he described his present mood in the following terms:

> The job has become a bit like fighting an avalanche; you know the rules—get rid of the skis, don't try to resist but swim on the surface and hope for a rescuer. (Next morning historians will dig up the whole rotten mess and see how many were buried.) A consolation is that avalanches, after all, automatically always come to a stop and that thereafter you can start behaving like an intelligent being again—provided you have managed to keep afloat.[1]

WE FLEW NORTH from Calcutta to Katmandu in the early afternoon. The season was beginning to change, and heavy clouds had already condensed over the mountains.

National Geographic Magazine, vol. 119, no. 1 (January 1961), © 1960 by National Geographic Society, pp. 87-93.

[1] Quoted in Brian Urquhart *Hammarskjöld* (New York: Knopf, 1972), p. 493.

I was sitting in the cockpit with the pilot—a man as able as he was pleasant—and he told me eloquently about what I did *not* see. He spoke with glowing enthusiasm about his flights into the Himalayas, during which he found a sense of freedom and elation that gave him the best moments of his life.

After a reception in Katmandu, a representative of the government, knowing of my interest in mountaineering, asked me whether I would like to fly into the eastern ranges of the Himalayas early the next morning before the start of official discussions that had brought me to Nepal. The King would put at our disposal his plane and pilot, the same young Sikh who had flown us from Calcutta.

I accepted eagerly. From then on I kept my fingers crossed, hoping that the weather would make its contribution to what promised to be a unique experience snatched from work in a couple of morning hours.

In the late evening we went strolling through the old city. The moon was bright, and over the narrow streets, lying in dark shadow, the roofs with their stern but festive architecture glimmered in the light.

It was the time when people went to bed. The shops were closing, and the street vendors, who had spent the afternoon selling and buying before their charcoal fires and spinning their long tales, were going home. Finally, we drifted practically alone among the temples and palaces with their fantastic multicolored wooden carvings, which seemed to come to life in the shimmering light.

Our Nepalese friend and guide suggested a visit to the great Buddhist shrine of Swayambhunath on a hill outside the city. Although it was late, I accepted, as I knew that the rest of our time would be mostly taken up by work. I did so not only because of my wish to see this famous place, but also because I hoped that in the clear moonlight we might get a view over the foothills toward the mountains.

We went as far as the car would take us. Then we walked the narrow, circular road up the steep hill on the top of which the stupa dreamed its dream of a world beyond pain and vicissitude in the shadow of the timeless mountains.

The air had the freshness of a spring night at Easter time in Burgundy. The association may seem farfetched, but the hills around led my thoughts to the land about Vézelay, where a shrine rises in the same way as a goal of pilgrimage.

The stillness was broken by chattering screams and noises, and soon we were surrounded by monkeys, surprised but seemingly also pleased to get this unexpected company at a late hour.

Two Tibetan monks in their high boots were walking around the stupa, turning the prayer wheels as they passed. At the side open toward Katmandu we stopped and looked out over the wide valley. A few lights still shone in the city and in Patan. For the rest, everything was asleep in a quiet that seemed to be in deep harmony with the spirit to which the shrine was dedicated. We were not far from the birthplace of the Buddha, and back of us the stupa rose against the night sky in a silence broken only by the light metallic sounds from the prayer wheels.

One of the monks opened the screen doors to a side chapel in which a big Buddha could barely be seen. Silently the monk invited us in and gave us candles and flowers. To share with him his reverence for the mystery of life was easy in this setting, so intensely reflecting the endlessness of man's search and the greatness of the world to which he belongs.

The clouds had disappeared, but a haze had arisen in the cool night and cut us off from the view of the high mountains. Although they were invisible, we could nonetheless strongly feel their presence in the deep blue behind the foothills.

I have described this evening because it gave me such a perfect introduction to our flight the next morning into the mountains. They are holy to the people as the dwelling of the gods, and for that reason they should be approached in the spirit into which our visit to the stupa had initiated us.

I learned later that because of this reverence for the mountains—but naturally also for more secular reasons—the government heretofore had permitted only a few persons to photograph the high ranges from the air.

After sunrise the next morning, the haze had gone and the sky was without a cloud. When we came down to the airstrip, the icy summits of the closest mountains stood out sharply over the green hills around the valley.

We flew through the valleys in the direction of Gauri Sankar and Everest. Even if we had never come to these mountains, it would have been a great experience just to see the beauty of the valleys and of the hillsides in the early morning light, the structure of the landscape, and the picturesque way in which cultivation and villages have developed.

The plane in which we were flying was a DC-3, nonpressurized and without oxygen. That naturally set an altitude limit for the flight; we flew at a height of twelve to fifteen thousand feet.

Our route took us first in under the overwhelming south wall of Gauri Sankar, with its beautiful double summit consecrated to the two Hindu deities that give the mountain its name. At our altitude we seemed to approach it at mid-height. Its vast size gave the impression that we were even closer to the mountainside than we were.

A somewhat lighthearted association was that this must be the way a fly feels as it approaches a house where it hopes to sit down on the wall for a nice quiet rest in the sun. Then, as we came closer, my climber's instincts were aroused and I started speculating—in vain—on possible routes of access for those who one day might brave this most inaccessible south mountain wall.

But planes move fast, and a few minutes later we had, so to speak, rounded a corner and were looking in over the icy wastes of the Himalayas. Forbidding in its bold, sculptural structure, it was a world far beyond human comprehension and of the harsh purity we are accustomed to find in the miniature world of crystals. But here it met the eye in proportions that reduced our human world to a microcosm.

Swinging southeast, we left these areas behind us and headed toward Everest. Over the highest green hills, which seemed to be clad in dark green moss, the Everest range stretched out in compact strength. The pilot pointed to a sharp peak behind the nearest ice-clad mountains. It wore a plume of snow, made by strong northwesterly winds. This was Everest, its special rank and position marked with a truly regal ornament.

From here on the route became somewhat confusing to me. The pilot found his way through valleys, over passes, and between mountains with an impressive familiarity that left me far behind in my effort to orient myself. It added to my confusion that I developed a kind of hunting fever with my camera; I felt I must try to get a chronicle in pictures of the constantly changing views and renewed experiences of stunning beauty.

Mount Everest? Is it heresy to say that it somewhat let me down? Beautiful in its clean outlines? Yes, both that and impressive. But it stood, from the angle at which we saw it, without that accent which separates one mountain from another and gives it a personality to stamp its mark on your mind.

Now I ranged Everest in the files of my memory in very much the same way as I could Mont Blanc—a mountain singled out by its proportions and by its history in human terms more than by other qualities. I thought of Hillary's gaunt stride and ruddy face, I remembered Tenzing's soft handshake and subtle smile.

Superficially, they were an oddly matched pair, but combining qualities that brought them to that summit we saw in front of us. There, expressing an attitude I have often met in the fraternity to which they belong, they displayed the flags not only of their countries but also of the United Nations.

However, while thinking of those who had succeeded, I could not forget those who had failed. They have been many, and their glory, written into the history of the mountain, is that they went to the limits of the humanly possible and were defeated only by circumstances beyond human mastery.

The first hour had flown away. It was necessary to return if we were to be back in time, and if we wished to avoid the assembling clouds. We came back to Gauri Sankar, and I decided to try to get a full picture of the south wall.

On my first attempt, I felt that I did not succeed, and, forgetting the situation, I asked the pilot to make a second round under the mountain. This time I succeeded. . . . Meanwhile, however, we had lost altitude, and I could not help smiling—perhaps a little apprehensively—when I saw the pilot looking down through a side window to judge if he would get safely over the range we had to pass.

The experiences of this first contact with the Himalayas from the air were such that I asked the authorities if, on our flight to Delhi somewhat later, we could follow the high mountains west of Katmandu for a distance, in order to cover at least Annapurna. In their generous hospitality, they at once agreed.

During short visits to a country for professional purposes, there is little time for sightseeing. Before we left Katmandu, however, I had another experience that, in its way, tied together the first visit to the Himalayas and what we were to see the next time. Linking the two flights, it also created a bridge to the night at Swayambhunath. Again, it was a visit made with friends, and on a moonlit night.

Just outside the city lies a meadow surrounded by high trees but with a view across the valley to Swayambhunath. It is called the Twenty-two Fountains, for just where a steep hillside breaks the plain, there is a long stone ramp through which the cold waters of a mountain stream burst forth in many openings. It is a place steeped in the atmosphere of the mountains and yet stamped with the mark of ancient, high civilization, as sure in its artistic sense as in its sense of how to create a harmonious interplay between the work of men and the surrounding landscape.

At the side of the ramp lies a small square pond built of stone, eroded by water and frost. Down into it lead worn steps. Resting in the pond lies a statue of the sleeping Vishnu, sunk so deep in the water that only the upper parts of the body break the surface.

The moonlight played on the wet figure, contrasting with the red glow from fires burning a short distance from where we stood. The silence was of the kind that is to be found only in the mountains, a silence that is audible.

The charcoal fires were burning at a rest site on one of the roads from the north. Round them were grouped pilgrims on their way to Swayam-bhunath, preparing their evening food without a word and without a glance at the strangers who passed.

The sleeping Hindu god and the silent Buddhist monks crystallized two of the great spiritual currents that have grown out of the meeting between man and the mountains. They were of the mountains and of one spirit with the mountains. But they fused into the scenery the soul and the human perspective without which our feeling for nature is sterile and empty aestheticism.

The morning of our flight to Delhi was perfect. The route took us first straight toward Tibet. Over the broad pass we could look from a great distance onto the high Tibetan plateau. Then we were in the mountains again, but with a great change of atmosphere. Here the peaks seemed to be isolated giants, each with its own personality.

The first new shock was the Machhapuchhare (the Fish's Tail), a Mat-terhorn in its bold, towering greatness and its pure balance of lines up to the sharp summit. But soon this impression was surpassed by another.

Climbing in a half circle over a lower range, we suddenly had before us Annapurna, with a beauty of structure and a majesty far surpassing that of Everest or Gauri Sankar. It seemed a Potala, built by the gods for their incarnation not as frail human beings but as giants. The contrast between the sovereign quiet of the mountaintop and the wild ranges leading in toward it added to the otherworldliness, the feeling that we had pene-trated into a world of cosmic purpose and character.

In spite of his long experience, the pilot was plainly moved by the sight. If it is possible in an airplane to simulate a tender stroke of affection, that is what he did, using the plane as his fingertips when rounding the gla-ciers and the rocks.

So we reached the final point, Dhaulagiri, a brutal mass, uninviting with its steep fields of ice and snow furrowed by innumerable ravines, as forbidding as a clenched fist. It is indeed appropriate that this is one of the latest of major Himalayan peaks to be conquered by man. A six-man Swiss team reached the top on May 13, 1960.

To someone who has learned to love the mountains and see in mountaineering one of the most satisfactory ways we can test our ability against nature—yet basically as a tribute to nature—it is somewhat shameful to approach the Himalayas by plane. My last words here should be a tribute to our pilot, who did his job with the deep insight and love of the mountains that characterize the true mountaineer. He managed to convey, at least to this passenger, a bit of the feeling of liberty, strength, and harmony we achieve when we fight a mountain and live with it, helped only by our body and our mind.

Protests to Belgium Over Use of Ruanda-Urundi Trust Territory for Expedition to Bukavu

NEW YORK   DECEMBER 1960-JANUARY 1961

LUMUMBA HAD considerable support among the population of Kivu Province. On Christmas Day, 1960, Gizenga sent from Stanleyville a few score soldiers to Bukavu, the capital of Kivu. They proceeded to arrest those provincial leaders who remained loyal to Leopoldville. A few days later Anicet Kashamura, former minister of information in the Lumumba government, arrived with a mission to consolidate Lumumbist control of the province. Word of these developments alarmed the Kasavubu-Mobutu régime. It secretly requested permission from the Belgian government to use the airfield at Usumbura in the UN trust territory of Ruanda-Urundi for the transit of about one hundred ANC soldiers dispatched to regain control of Bukavu, which lay just across the border from the trust territory. Hammarskjöld immediately addressed to the representative of Belgium the following notes of protest.

(a) Note verbale *dated December 30, 1960, to the Representative of Belgium*

The Secretary-General of the United Nations presents his compliments to the Permanent Representative of Belgium to the United Nations and wishes to draw his attention to the fact that he has today received the information, from a trustworthy source, that the Congolese authorities have addressed to the Belgian Ambassador at Brazzaville a request that the airfield at Usumbura, situated in the trust territory of Ruanda-Urundi, may be used by troops of the Armée nationale congolaise proceeding to the Bukavu area.

The Secretary-General feels certain that, in view of the status of the trust territory and the provisions of the Trusteeship Agreement, no such authorization will be granted to the Congolese authorities. Nevertheless, having regard to the seriousness of the problem, he considers it his duty to draw the attention of the representative of Belgium to the provisions of

Security Council Official Records, Sixteenth Year, Supplement for January, February, and March 1961, document S/4606, sections II, V and VI.

operative paragraph 6 of resolution 1474 (ES-IV) adopted by the General Assembly on September 20, 1960.

(b) Note verbale *dated January 1, 1961, to the Representative of Belgium*

The Secretary-General of the United Nations has the honour to refer to the *note verbale* dated December 31, 1960, of the permanent mission of Belgium to the United Nations concerning the landing of troops of the Armée nationale congolaise at the airport of Usumbura in the trust territory of Ruanda-Urundi.

The Secretary-General has noted the statement of the Belgian government that it had been informed of the request made by Mr. Kasavubu and Mr. Bomboko for authorization to land and effect transit of Congolese troops at the same time that the Belgian government learned of the actual landing at Usumbura. He further notes that the Belgian government then instructed its Resident-General in Ruanda-Urundi to dispatch without delay the contingents to the Congolese frontier.

The report received by the Secretary-General from his special representative in the Congo stated that the troops of the Armée nationale congolaise, which were permitted to land at Usumbura, were provided with trucks driven by Europeans in civilian dress which brought them some ninety miles from Usumbura to Shangugu, thus facilitating their transit to Bukavu in the Kivu province of the Republic of the Congo.

The conclusion that the Secretary-General is compelled to draw from this report is that the authorities of the administering power in the trust territory of Ruanda-Urundi failed to take action to ensure that the Congolese troops did not carry out a military operation through the trust territory. It is evident that persons in the trust territory must have lent support to the operation both at the landing and by facilitating the transit of the Congolese troops to their intended destination. The Secretary-General finds it difficult to believe that such support can have been furnished by persons in Ruanda-Urundi without the knowledge of the responsible authorities of Belgium in the trust territory.

In view of these facts, the events referred to above indicate the direct or indirect provision of assistance for military purposes to the Armée nationale congolaise by authorities under the Belgian government, in contravention of operative paragraph 6 of the resolution 1474 (ES-IV), adopted unanimously by the General Assembly on September 20, 1960. The gravity of the event is accentuated by the fact that assistance was rendered through the facilities and in the trust territory of Ruanda-Urundi, which is administered by Belgium under an agreement with the United Nations that includes a solemn obligation to further international peace and security.

The Secretary-General accordingly calls upon the Belgian government to take immediate and effective measures to ensure that there will be no possibility of Belgian authorities in the trust territory of Ruanda-Urundi or elsewhere lending support directly or indirectly to military action by Congolese troops. It is imperative that instructions be given to the officials of the Belgian government in Ruanda-Urundi that any attempt by Congolese troops to utilize that territory for transit purposes in support of military action must, in accordance with the duty of impartiality, require the disarming of such Congolese troops and if necessary guarding them in order to ensure that they do not engage in military action. This obligation, which is similar to that imposed upon neutrals under international law, follows from the duty of nonintervention contained in the resolutions of the General Assembly and the Security Council.

(c) Note verbale *dated January 2, 1961, to the Representative of Belgium*

The Secretary-General of the United Nations presents his compliments to the Permanent Representative of Belgium to the United Nations and, with reference to his *note verbale* of January 1, 1961, has the honour to make the following additional observations with regard to the question treated in the *note verbale.*

The Secretary-General has today received reports from United Nations representatives stating that the military operation recently launched by troops of the Armée nationale congolaise across the trust territory of Ruanda-Urundi has given rise to serious measures on the part of anti-army factions in Kivu province. The operation has also led to a rise in tension which may undermine law and order and, in particular, endanger the European population, as may be anticipated from the fact that the recent incident gives indication of Belgian participation. One of the psychological aspects of the situation consists of the rumours circulating in Kivu province that fresh troops are moving to Bukavu through the territory of Ruanda-Urundi and that arms for these troops are in the process of being shipped.

Although relative calm now prevails in the greater part of Bukavu, it is felt that any fresh incident of a similar nature might bring about a highly dangerous state of panic. The unit of the United Nations Force stationed at Bukavu consists at present of only one battalion of staff troops. Arrangements have been made, nevertheless, to ensure the greatest possible protection of human lives and of property in the event of a serious crisis. The local command of the Belgian parachute unit stationed at Shangugu, opposite Bukavu, has been asked to stop any possible entry of fresh detachments of Congolese troops into Kivu province and it has acceded to this request.

The above information and observation confirm the gravity of the question raised by the Secretary-General in his note of yesterday's date and the urgent need for a clarification by the Belgian government of the situation on the Ruanda-Urundi side, as already requested by the Secretary-General. Obviously the administering authority of Ruanda-Urundi must bear a very special responsibility in counteracting the present deterioration in the situation; indeed, its attitude is important not only in regard to the situation in general but also, more particularly, in regard to the influence it exerts on the situation of the Belgian and other non-African populations. Whatever the steps which the United Nations may take to maintain law and order, they will not be effective unless the other responsible parties give their support by observing strictly the principles set forth by the United Nations. It is evident that at present this task of protection can be assumed only by the United Nations; indeed, any attempt to afford protection from any other source would not only be contrary to the position adopted by the United Nations but would in every way seriously augment the present risks.

THE MOBUTU expedition to Bukavu was an immediate failure. His soldiers, who had apparently not realized that Lumumba's supporters already were in control, promptly surrendered or scattered. However the cooperation of the Belgian authorities in the attack caused tensions and rumors which threatened serious repercussions for European civilians in Bukavu. The Secretary-General's third *note verbale* referred to this aspect. The Belgian government, in its reply, maintained that it had acted correctly in transporting the ANC troops to the Congo frontier, once they had landed, rather than disarming them. However it gave assurances that future landings would not be permitted and that Belgian troops in the trust territory would not engage in any action outside it.

On January 7 a conference at Casablanca of the heads of state of Morocco, the United Arab Republic, Ghana, Guinea, Mali, and Algeria (with representatives of Libya and Ceylon also participating) adopted a declaration on the Congo. They reaffirmed the intention to withdraw from ONUC unless it acted to disarm Mobutu's soldiers, free Lumumba and all other imprisoned members of Parliament, reconvene the Parliament, eliminate all Belgian military and paramilitary personnel, turn over to the control of the legitimate government all airports and other establishments and prevent Belgium from using Ruanda-Urundi as a base to commit "aggression" against the Congo.

On January 11 the Government of the USSR issued a statement calling for an immediate meeting of the Security Council for the purpose of ending forthwith Belgium's trusteeship of Ruanda-Urundi and in order to carry out the recommendations of the Casablanca conference. Despite Hammarskjöld's vigorous protests over the Ruanda-Urundi affair the Soviet statement accused him of conspiring with the Belgians and other "colonialists" to crush "the national liberation movement in the Congo."[1]

The Security Council met four times on January 12, 13, and 14. Poland, Tunisia, Italy, and Argentina had been replaced as members at the first of the year by the United Arab Republic, Liberia, Turkey, and Chile. The UAR, Ceylon, and Liberia submitted a draft resolution accusing Belgium of violating its obligations as administering authority of Ruanda-Urundi and calling for withdrawal of all Belgian military and civilian advisers from the Congo. The debate was desultory and the meetings brief compared with the recent past. The resolution lost, receiving 4 affirmative votes (the sponsors' and the Soviet Union's) and no negative votes, while there were 7 abstentions. Hammarskjöld spoke briefly just before the vote, choosing to make his main theme an appeal for support of the efforts of the Conciliation Commission rather than another reply to the Soviet Union (next following text).

[1] Security Council Official Records, Supplement for January, February, and March 1961, document S/4622.

Appeal in the Security Council for Support of the Congo Conciliation Commission

NEW YORK   JANUARY 14, 1961

ALTHOUGH, IN THE DOCUMENTS now under consideration by the Security Council and in statements to the Council, some of the most violent attacks so far on the United Nations operations in the Congo and on the Secretary-General and his integrity have been made, there is no reason for me to take much of the Council's time for explanations, corrections, or defence.

The greatly disturbing but limited incident at Bukavu on New Year's Day provoked, as the Council knows, immediate and sharp counteraction from my side and from the United Nations representatives. However, in statements by the Soviet Union, especially in a press statement (S/4622), sharp accusations have been levelled against the way in which we treated the incident. I have nothing to add to the documents which I have placed before the Council since, to any reader of those documents, which are simple and clear, it is immediately obvious how groundless are the accusations against the United Nations and its agents. In the circumstances, it is difficult indeed to believe that they are addressed to this Council or to others who have access to the documents or who know the facts.

Why, then, have the accusations been made? I think that the substance of the line now taken by the USSR makes it clear. By trying to give the impression that the Secretariat and its representatives, in particular the Secretary-General, are inspired by racial prejudice, they want to drive a wedge into the collaboration, based on confidence, which has been established between the African states and the Secretariat in this operation. Why this is tried needs no explanation. I believe that the effort will be in vain, because I trust that the African representatives are well informed through their own firsthand observations and that they know how to regard with equally sober realism flattery and efforts to win them by sowing hate and distrust.

Security Council Official Records, Sixteenth Year, 927th meeting.

The representative of the Republic of the Congo, in his intervention a few moments ago, raised several points of a highly controversial nature. He imputed intentions to the United Nations operation which certainly are not justified, he accused the operation of omissions, and he gave advice on what we should do.

I believe that those various points could best be discussed directly between the delegation and the Secretariat. And I am strengthened in that belief by the fact that quite recently I had the opportunity to discuss similar matters, and in detail, with President Kasavubu whose accent was a different one.

There were also statements of fact in the intervention to which I feel it may be reasonable to revert in documents to be submitted to the Council.

As I thus see no reason to go into the substance of these most recent attacks on the United Nations operation in the Congo, I can limit myself to directing your attention to a point which I find of considerable immediate importance.

On January 5 the Conciliation Commission, established by the Advisory Committee on the Congo under General Assembly resolution 1474 (ES-IV) of September 20, arrived in Leopoldville. I had the privilege to meet with them; and I had repeated talks with the chairman, Mr. Wachuku, who, together with the other presiding officers, had already spent some few weeks in the Congo. It is my impression that this Commission— the third arm of the United Nations operation in assistance to the Republic, the third arm together with the military and civilian operation—has got off to a promising start and may render great service in the direction of political stabilization. This task, as is well known, has been outside the mandate and the competence of the civilian and military operations.

However, the work of the Commission is highly delicate. It requires tact, understanding, modesty and wisdom. It cannot succeed unless it is given a fair chance to do so both by the leaders in the Congo and by the United Nations itself, including all the Member states. It should be obvious that the presence of the Conciliation Commission in the Congo and the need to assure all possible success for its work should be very much in the mind of all here at Headquarters when the affairs of the Congo are being discussed and decisions passed. It would seem to me that this should apply specifically to those whose interest in the Conciliation Commission at an earlier stage was so great that they used the Commission as an added argument against the Secretary-General who was alleged not to have shown the proper energy in getting its work off the ground.

Certainly, nobody would now wish to give the African states the impression that they, or the Conciliation Commission in which they have nine members in Leopoldville, are regarded only as pawns to be moved to the right or to the left, or perhaps sacrificed, depending upon whether their activities seem to serve this or that external interest or this or that specific personality in the Congo.

Thus, in view of the task pursued by the United Nations in the Congo, for the sake of the country and the Organization, and also so as to help towards the success of its work in the country, in accordance with the target set, I appeal to Members to do what is in their power in order to protect and support the efforts now pursued through the Conciliation Commission. If that appeal is heeded, I believe that the very negative aspects in part apparent in the present meetings of the Security Council may not have done too much harm.

Letter Responding to President Kasavubu's Request for the Recall of Rajashwar Dayal

NEW YORK JANUARY 15, 1961

WITH THE TURN of the year Kasavubu's resentment over United Nations refusal to recognize Mobutu's College of Commissioners as the legal government focused increasingly on the person of Ambassador Dayal, whose reports had minced no words about the inadequacies of the régime and about the open hostility toward ONUC of the Belgian advisers who had been brought back. Furthermore, Dayal was on Indian, and India had become in December a leading sponsor in the Assembly of the Afro-Asian draft resolution calling for the return of Parliament, the release of Lumumba and other parliamentarians, and the withdrawal of Belgian military and civilian advisers. A press campaign was mounted in Leopoldville, charging that Dayal, though ostensibly serving as an international official, was in reality serving the policies of Nehru and the left-wing African governments. This campaign had considerable support from Belgian and other Western government officials.

In his letter of January 14 formally requesting Dayal's recall, Kasavubu chose as his principal complaint the fact that ONUC had not forcibly intervened at Bukavu on his side against the ANC soldiers sent by Gizenga, thus following, in this respect, the earlier example of Lumumba when he broke with Hammarskjöld in August over the latter's refusal to use force against Tshombé. Hammarskjöld's response, rejecting Kasavubu's request, follows.

I HAVE THE HONOUR to acknowledge receipt of your letter of January 14, 1961, [sect. I] about which I had received information through the news agencies several hours before it was transmitted, these news releases covering also a press conference given by Mr. Bomboko providing pertinent explanations of the background to the letter.

I wish to recall that I had the privilege of visiting you when I was in Leopoldville on January 5. I note that, on that occasion, you did not raise with me the question of a recall of Mr. Dayal, although practically all of the considerations which you now invoke as reasons for your demand for

Security Council Official Records, Sixteenth Year, Supplement for January, February, and March 1961, document S/4629, section II.

his withdrawal should have been before you at that time. Naturally, I would with pleasure have met with you alone if you had wished to discuss anything with me of that nature. It is regrettable that such an opportunity to exchange views personally about such a delicate and important matter was not utilized.

I further note that the memorandum to which you refer in the first paragraph of your letter was not mentioned by you at our meeting, although it was transmitted soon thereafter when, as was known, I had left for South Africa; in the circumstances it will not surprise you that I did not see your memorandum until Thursday night, January 12. A reply was dispatched to you [S/4630, sect. II] before the transmittal of your letter and, in fact, less than two days after I had first been able to see it. In this case I regret likewise the failure to use our meeting for a personal discussion of all the various points raised in your memorandum.

In your letter you refer specifically to two concrete cases regarding which you wish to put the blame on the United Nations authorities, in particular on the Special Representative of the Secretary-General in Leopoldville.

In the case of the alleged death of the minister of education of Kivu, you go so far as to speak about "complicity in the murder." However, the very same day that I received your letter, the representative of the United Nations in Stanleyville visited the minister of education. He found that the minister had been exonerated of all charges, was free, and is to return to Kivu as soon as there is a plane available. He was comfortably lodged at the Hotel des Chutes and was recovering from an attack of malignant malaria for which he had been treated at the hospital. He was still under medical care and did not show any visible marks of manhandling. While I take pleasure in informing you about these facts and about the falsity of statements to the effect that the minister had been killed, I must at the same time express my great surprise that an allegation such as this one, with which you link such serious political conclusions, had not been properly checked by your collaborators before it was presented in your letter.

As regards the incident at Bukavu, in which certain members of the provincial government were abducted, the facts of the matter were indeed discussed when we met on January 5, 1961. It was pointed out to you that the version that had been given to you by your sources was not correct and that when the question was submitted to United Nations authorities in Leopoldville, as the circumstances had then developed, these authorities acted in accordance with the general mandate of the ONUC and the precedents. You will also recall that it was explained at the meeting that Mr. Dayal was not a party to the instructions as he was away from Leopoldville. However, in spite of these clarifications given you at our meeting, you accuse him in your letter of having refused the necessary authorization to the Nigerian commander in Bukavu. For a more detailed account of the incident I refer to the reply to your memorandum as transmitted to you on January 14, 1961.

In your letter you further raise the question of the general policy of the United Nations, requesting, *inter alia,* that we assist the President of the Republic and the central authorities of the country to disarm "the rebellious bands of Gizenga and Lundula." In view of the question of principle to which this request gives rise, this cannot be done by me or the United Nations Force short of new instructions from the Security Council. Your criticism as well as your request should, therefore, be addressed to that body. Under no circumstances can any blame for a failure to disarm the Armée nationale congolaise groups under the control of Mr. Gizenga be placed on Mr. Dayal who has acted strictly in accordance with the general rules laid down by the Security Council in not taking action to that effect.

Let me finally add that, under instructions from Mr. Dayal, consistent and objective efforts have been made, through diplomatic means, to secure the release and, pending release, good treatment of personalities imprisoned by Mr. Gizenga and his supporters as well as by others.

I must in this context also draw your attention to Mr. Dayal's status which you, in your formal demand, seem to overlook.

Ambassador Dayal is not a diplomatic representative accredited to the Government of the Republic of the Congo and he can therefore not be subject to a declaration that he is *persona non grata* with the effect generally given in diplomatic practice to such declarations. He is a senior official of the United Nations Secretariat assigned as special representative of the Secretary-General to be in over-all charge of the United Nations operations in the Congo. His assignment is thus established under the special authority of the Secretary-General of the United Nations in accordance with Article 101 of the Charter. Further, Article 100 of the Charter stipulates that the Secretary-General shall not seek or receive instructions from any government and that each Member of the United Nations undertakes not to seek to influence him in the discharge of his responsibilities. You will appreciate that it is difficult to reconcile your formal demand regarding Mr. Dayal with the status of the Secretary-

General and of his special representative as established by the two Articles of the Charter to which I have thus referred.

In the circumstances, and taking into account the lack of facts in support of your accusation of Mr. Dayal for *inconscience et partialité* as well as his status, I find, as Secretary-General, that it is impossible to accede to your demand for his recall. You will remember that, in the course of your visit to New York, you presented a similar demand orally which, however, you dropped when I stated that I personally shouldered responsibility for the actions of Mr. Dayal on which you seemed to base your stand.

In view of the seriousness of this *démarche* from your side as regards both the general question of policy and as regards Mr. Dayal, I will put your letter and this reply before the Security Council for such action as the Council may find warranted.

At the end of your letter you express yourself in favour of close collaboration with the United Nations. May I, in this context, bring again to your attention my suggestion in a letter to you of December 21, 1960, [S/4606 and Add. I, sect. I] that you give publicly a clarification which would provide a basis for improved cooperation. I have not received any reply to this letter nor am I informed about any initiative from your side which would meet the need to which I drew your attention.

DAG HAMMARSKJÖLD
Secretary-General

KASAVUBU, in his reply to the Secretary-General's letter, maintained his request for Dayal's recall on the ground that he had lost the confidence of the Congolese people and that better cooperation between ONUC and the Congolese government would not be possible unless he left. This continued to be Kasavubu's position in the weeks that followed. He never did make any response to the suggestions in Hammarskjöld's letter of December 21.

Report on Certain Steps Taken in Regard to the Implementation of the Security Council Resolution of April 1, 1960, Concerning the Situation in the Union of South Africa

NEW YORK   JANUARY 23, 1961

THE SECRETARY-GENERAL finally was able to accomplish his visit to the Union of South Africa between January 6 and 12. He had first gone to Leopoldville on January 3 for three days of an intensive on-the-spot review of Congo developments. It had been his intention to extend his stay in South Africa for two more days and then visit Cairo and New Delhi for talks with Nasser and Nehru, but the insistence of the Soviet Union on another series of Security Council meetings on the Congo forced him to return immediately to New York.

His discussions with Prime Minister Henrik Verwoerd failed to budge that dogmatic and stubborn leader from the policies of segregation and Bantu "homelands" pursued simultaneously by the South African government. However they were extensive, frank and serious enough to cause the Secretary-General to conclude that it would be worthwhile to keep the lines open and make another effort at persuasion in due course. His intense preoccupation with the Congo, followed by his untimely death, prevented fulfillment of this intention.

---

1. BY THE RESOLUTION which the Security Council adopted on April 1, 1960, it requested the Secretary-General in consultation with the Government of the Union of South Africa, "to make such arrangements as would adequately help in upholding the purposes and principles of the Charter and to report to the Security Council whenever necessary and appropriate."

2. In his interim report of April 19, 1960,[1] the Secretary-General informed the Security Council that after an exchange of communications between the minister of external affairs of the Union of South Africa and himself, through the permanent representative of the Union government,

Security Council Official Records, Sixteenth Year, Supplement for January, February, and March 1961, document S/4635.

[1] See volume IV of this series.

he had accepted a proposal of the Union government that preliminary consultations between the prime minister and minister of external affairs and himself should be held in London after the conclusion of the Commonwealth Prime Ministers' Conference, probably in early May 1960.

3. It will be recalled that paragraph 5 of the interim report stated that:

The consultations rendered necessary by the provisions of paragraph 5 of the Security Council's resolution of April 1, 1960, will be undertaken on the basis of the authority of the Secretary-General under the Charter. It is agreed between the Government of the Union of South Africa and myself that consent of the Union government to discuss the Security Council's resolution with the Secretary-General would not require prior recognition from the Union government of the United Nations authority.

4. In his second interim report of October 11, 1960, (p. 222) the Secretary-General informed the Security Council that during the preliminary discussions which took place in London on May 13 and 14, 1960 between the Secretary-General and the minister of external affairs of the Union of South Africa, it was agreed that the basis for future discussions would flow from paragraph 5 of the first interim report and that agreement had also been reached on the character and course of the further consultations to take place in Pretoria. It was also stated that "during the contemplated visit to the Union of South Africa, while consultation throughout would be with the Union government, no restrictive rules were to be imposed on the Secretary-General."

5. In paragraphs 5 and 6 of the second interim report, the Secretary-General explained that:

Due to circumstances resulting from the mandate given to me by the Security Council by resolutions S/4387, S/4405, and S/4426 dated July 14 and 22 and August 9, 1960, in connection with the United Nations operation in the Republic of the Congo (Leopoldville), I have been unable to visit the Union of South Africa as envisaged in the interim report. On four occasions, precise plans were made for the visit but on each occasion it became necessary first to postpone, then to cancel those plans owing to developments in the Republic of the Congo.

During a meeting at Headquarters with the minister of external affairs of the Union of South Africa on September 28, 1960, a new invitation was extended to me by the prime minister of the Union government to visit the Union early in January 1961.

6. It will be recalled that I stated in the same report that it would be my hope to arrange for the visit at the time suggested for the purpose of the requested consultations with the prime minister of the Union of South Africa and that it would be my intention to explore with the prime min-

ister the possibility of arrangements which would provide for appropriate safeguards of human rights, with adequate contact with the United Nations

7. Accordingly I visited the Union of South Africa between January 6 and 12, 1961. It had been my plan to stay two additional days, but due to the convening of the Security Council on a question relating to the mandate given to me by the Council, I felt it necessary to hold myself available to members of the Council when the United Nations operation in the Republic of the Congo was being discussed.

8. While in the Union of South Africa, consultations took place between the Secretary-General and the prime minister of the Union at six meetings on January 6, 7, 10, and 11, 1961. In Cape Town, Umtata (Transkei), Johannesburg, and Pretoria, the Secretary-General had opportunities to have unofficial contacts with members of various sections of the South African community.

9. Having regard to paragraph 5 of Security Council resolution S/4300, the Secretary-General wishes to state that during the discussions between the Secretary-General and the prime minister of the Union of South Africa so far no mutually acceptable arrangement has been found. In the view of the Secretary-General this lack of agreement is not conclusive and he wishes to give the matter his further consideration.

10. The exchange of views in general has served a most useful purpose. The Secretary-General does not consider the consultations as having come to an end, and he looks forward to their continuation at an appropriate time with a view to further efforts from his side to find an adequate solution for the aforementioned problem.

11. The prime minister of the Union of South Africa has indicated that further consideration will be given to questions raised in the course of the talks and has stated that "the Union government, having found the talks with the Secretary-General useful and constructive, have decided to invite him at an appropriate time, or times, to visit the Union again in order that the present contact may be continued."

Communications Protesting the Transfer of Patrice Lumumba to Katanga

NEW YORK JANUARY 1961

SINCE HIS CAPTURE Lumumba had been kept prisoner in the ANC military camp at Thysville, along with two of his supporters, Joseph Okito, vice-president of the Senate, and Maurice Mpolo, minister of youth, who had been captured with him on the way to Stanleyville. Discipline was never reliable at Thysville and there was restlessness and then a mutiny in January. Kasavubu and Mobutu feared Lumumba might be freed at any moment by disgruntled soldiers and decided to send him, Okito and Mpolo to Katanga, where security would be better. When approached Tshombé was at first unwilling. but Kasavubu and Mobutu went ahead anyway and the three prisoners were secretly put aboard an Air Congo plane for Elisabethville on January 17 with an escort of Baluba ANC soldiers who remembered, of course, the August massacres of their people in Kasai.

ONUC headquarters at Leopoldville knew nothing of this move until after the plane landed at Elisabethville. There a Swedish UN detail of six men at the airport had a distant, fleeting view of three blindfolded prisoners, one of them with a small beard, being savagely beaten as they left the plane and then driven swiftly away. Next day the UN representative at Elisabethville obtained from Tshombé confirmation that it was indeed Lumumba and his supporters who had been spotted, but he refused any information about where they had been taken.

Hammarskjöld immediately dispatched the following protests and appeals to both Kasavubu and Tshombé.

I. Letter dated January 19, 1961, to the President of the Republic of the Congo (Leopoldville)

As you are no doubt aware, grave concern has been expressed here regarding the transfer of Mr. Lumumba to Katanga. I have, accordingly, despatched the attached communication to Mr. Tshombé.

In this connection, I should like to recall to you my communication of December 5, 1960, in which I made a strong appeal for the application of due process of law to every stage of legal action in the case of Mr. Lumumba, and your reply of December 7, 1960, in which you acknowl-

Security Council Official Records, Sixteenth Year, Supplement for January, February, and March 1961, document S/4637, sections I, II and III.

edged the obligations imposed upon the Republic of the Congo by the Charter in this respect, and expressed your concern in seeing that Mr. Lumumba's case would be conducted in accordance with the rules applied by civilized countries.

As stated in my communication to Mr. Tshombé, it seems evident that the transfer of Mr. Lumumba to Katanga necessarily involves a further interference of Mr. Lumumba's right to be tried without undue delay, to communicate with counsel, friends, and family, and generally to have adequate facilities for the preparation of his defence. It has, moreover, long been recognized as a fundamental rule by many countries that a defendant may not be removed, without his consent, from the competent jurisdiction; a principle which is obviously based upon the requirements of a fair and speedy trial.

In view of these considerations, I must urge upon you that you take immediate measures to have Mr. Lumumba return from Katanga and that, unless released, he be given the opportunity to answer the charges against him in a fair and public hearing by an impartial tribunal at which he will have all the guarantees necessary for his defence.

DAG HAMMARSKJÖLD
Secretary-General

*II. Message dated January 19, 1961, addressed, through his special
representative in the Congo, to Mr. Tshombé*

Mr. Berendsen, the United Nations representative in Elisabethville, has informed me about his conversation with you concerning the unannounced transfer of Messrs. Lumumba, Mpolo, and Okito from Thysville to Elisabethville. You will no doubt know that the transfer of Mr. Lumumba has caused widespread and grave concern because of all its implications and possible consequences, particularly since it appears to involve a further postponement of judicial proceedings to which Mr. Lumumba, after his long period of detention, is entitled under commonly accepted principles of law and human rights. It seems obvious, moreover, that this transfer and the consequent detention in Katanga would substantially interfere with certain minimum rights generally guaranteed to the accused, such as his right to have adequate facilities for the preparation of his defence, to communicate with counsel of his own choosing, to be tried without undue delay, and to obtain the attendance of witnesses on his behalf.

If, as I understand, you and the Katanga authorities have been presented by this transfer with a *fait accompli,* you will no doubt consider what steps can properly be taken so that Mr. Lumumba and his companions may be given the benefit of due process of law at the place of competent jurisdiction. I am sure that, pending a decision in this matter, you will see to it that they receive the humane and fair treatment to which they are entitled.

III. Letter dated January 20, 1961, addressed through his special representative in the Congo, to the President of the Republic of the Congo (Leopoldville)

In my letter of January 19, I have addressed to you my immediate observations on the transfer of Mr. Lumumba and others to Katanga. I wish to inform you that the same matter has today been discussed by the Advisory Committee on the Congo which, while unanimously and fully approving of the views I expressed in my letter, felt that important additional observations were in order.

The Advisory Committee has, as you know, under a mandate from the General Assembly, set up the Conciliation Commission which at present is in the Congo. In accordance with this mandate, the Committee takes special interest in, and feels a special responsibility for, efforts promoting the reunification and reconciliation within the Congo. They do so while fully recognizing that steps to that effect depend solely on the Congolese themselves and that their authority in the matter is limited by the fact that this, basically, is a matter of domestic concern although—as fully recognized by the General Assembly and the Security Council—of such international concern as to entitle the Organization to express views and give advice.

The Advisory Committee feels strongly that the incarceration of various political leaders is incompatible with successful efforts to achieve the aims which you yourself, Mr. President, have stated as being yours. They are of the strong conviction that negotiations cannot be conducted among political leaders as long as some of them are detained, and thus unable in freedom to express their views or to take part in deliberations. This general observation, which is amply justified by experience, has special application in the present situation where, as is well known, one of those incarcerated commands a position in wide sections of the public which would make any solution arrived at without proper contact with him unstable.

In these circumstances the Committee considers it appropriate to draw to your urgent attention the serious bearing on the efforts towards reconciliation and national unification which the continued imprisonment of Mr. Lumumba seems to it to have, especially as months have passed without any steps having been taken in order to clarify his position in accordance with the rules of due process of law. Obviously, the political significance of these observations is enhanced by the recent transfer of Mr. Lumumba which cannot but aggravate the complications created by his arrest and detention.

When bringing these serious and urgent considerations of the Advisory Committee, to which I fully subscribe, to your attention, I wish at the same time to mention that I have received confirmed and incontradictable reports regarding the brutal manhandling of Mr. Lumumba and his companions on the occasion of their transfer. These reports force me to reemphasize with all vigour my insistent appeal that they be given humane treatment, in accordance with generally accepted principles, and in line with what the United Nations and its representatives try to urge for all persons, irrespective of political orientation or race, as part of its duty to maintain the protection of life and property.

DAG HAMMARSKJÖLD
Secretary-General

HAMMARSKJÖLD'S protests and appeals brought only negative responses from both Kasavubu and Tshombé, the latter professing astonishment at so much concern over the fate of Lumumba, a man who "has been recognized as guilty of genocide by the international Organization." Efforts to visit Lumumba by representatives of ONUC, the Red Cross, and the UN Conciliation Commission were all rebuffed.

On January 23 the Secretary-General turned his attention to Stanleyville where both European and Congolese civilians continued to suffer harassments and brutalities in which undisciplined bands of ANC soldiers joined and where a number of opponents of Lumumba were held as political prisoners. The text of his protest to Gizenga follows.

Message of Protest Addressed to Mr. Gizenga Against Violations of Human Rights in Orientale Province

NEW YORK   JANUARY 23, 1961

DURING THE LAST few weeks, I have received several confirmed reports from representatives of the United Nations in Orientale Province indicating that a very large number of violations of the most basic human rights of both Congolese and non-Congolese elements of the population have taken place. My special representative, in his note dated January 19, 1961, which I entirely approve, has already drawn your attention to the many arbitrary acts committed by members of the provincial régime.

I am aware that you have informed my representative at Stanleyville that you intend to issue appeals to the population prohibiting any act of violence. I sincerely trust that these appeals will eliminate the serious injustices which have been committed and by that very fact will eliminate the occasions for friction and tension, the results of which cannot but be detrimental to the welfare of all the inhabitants of the province.

I should like in particular to ask you, as a matter of urgency, to take the most vigorous steps to ensure that the ANC units operating in the Stanleyville area assume the very function they should in fact assume, since it has essentially devolved upon them; that is, the maintenance of internal security. This amounts to saying that they should endeavour to ensure the protection of innocent persons against any mistreatment, instead of acting as a force instigating disorder and agitation.

I should like to further remind you that it is obviously unacceptable for ANC units to allow themselves to interfere directly in the protective functions of the United Nations Force, as has happened on many occasions, and more particularly on January 21, 1961.

Security Council Official Records, Sixteenth Year, Supplement for January, February, and March 1961, document S/6437, section V.

I sincerely hope that you will use all the influence you may have to ensure that local order is fully maintained in the area now under your control, with the serious responsibilities for you, both national and international, which follow from that fact.

DAG HAMMARSKJÖLD
Secretary-General

Report on the Intended Withdrawals of Certain Contingents from the United Nations Force in the Congo

NEW YORK   JANUARY 26, 1961

THE DELIVERY OF Lumumba into the hands of Tshombé's régime caused the governments of Morocco, Indonesia, and the United Arab Republic to order the withdrawals of their contingents from the United Nations Force, as they had been threatening to do since early December. This serious development, which the Secretary-General had been trying to prevent, caused him to make the following report to the Security Council.

---

1. THE DEFINITE decisions of three governments to withdraw their contingents of troops from the United Nations Force in the Congo, which have been conveyed to the Secretary-General in recent days, have implications for the future of that Force so serious as to need to be called to the attention of the Security Council.

2. The projected withdrawals, without replacements, are the following.

3. The Government of Indonesia has notified its intention "to repatriate the Indonesian contingent at the earliest possible date, since in February next it will in any case have to finish its six months' field duty." The Indonesian contingent numbers approximately 1,150 officers and men.

4. The Government of Morocco has communicated its intention to "repatriate, before January 31, 1961" the troops of the Moroccan contingent serving in the Congo, numbering approximately 3,240 officers and men.

5. The Government of the United Arab Republic has made an oral request for the repatriation of its contingent, numbering approximately 510 officers and men, by February 1.

Security Council Official Records, Sixteenth Year, Supplement for January, February, and March 1961, document S/4640.

6. Previous reductions of the Force have occurred as a result of the withdrawal, now in process, of the contingent of Guinea, approximately 749 officers and men, and of the 21 Yugoslav members, who left at the end of December.

7. Messages dated December 14, 1960, and January 25, 1961, from the Secretary-General to certain governments concerning the proposed withdrawals are appended as annexes I and II of this report.

ANNEX I

Telegraphed Message of December 14, 1960, to the Governments of Ceylon, Guinea, Indonesia, Morocco, Yugoslavia, and the United Arab Republic

I am sure that you have been fully informed by your representative in New York concerning the statements which I made before the Security Council on December 7 and 13, 1960, and particularly the general appeal which I felt it my duty to address to those governments which had announced their intention to withdraw from the United Nations Force.

As Secretary-General, I feel obliged to underline these public appeals by a personal approach to you. While it is superfluous to reiterate what has already been said publicly in the Security Council, permit me to express to you my deep anxiety about the consequences of a liquidation of the United Nations operation such as may be forced upon the Organization by the threatened withdrawals. Whatever opinion may be held with regard to the extent of the functions of the United Nations operation in the Congo, the elimination or the weakening of the United Nations Force from the Congo would inevitably lead to the situation which in the course of the last five months we have with all our means attempted to forestall, namely a disintegration within the country provoking open and active involvement of major powers. The threat of such an involvement is likely quickly to become a reality if present intentions to withdraw from the United Nations Force should materialize.

In the light of these very serious prospects, I regard it as the clear obligation of the Secretary-General to appeal to you and to your government to reconsider the intended withdrawal of your troops from the United Nations Force in the Congo in the light of such further steps as the General Assembly may take for a strengthening of the possibilities of the United Nations to further a peaceful development in democratic forms. I am personally firmly convinced that the threat to peace and security of a substantial part of the world is vitally involved in this question.

ANNEX II

Telegraphed Message of January 25, 1961, to the Governments of Indonesia, Morocco, and the United Arab Republic

I learn with great regret of your Government's definite decision to repatriate the troops of your country now serving in the United Nations Force in the Congo, with no replacements to be provided for them. In this regard, I must express my disappointment that my appeal to you of December 14, [annex I] to reconsider the intended withdrawal of your troops has been unavailing. I must now again point out to you that the decision to withdraw your contingent results in a serious weakening of the Force, for the consequences of which the responsibility is clearly assumed by those countries which, for whatever reason, have found it indicated to withdraw. In this context may I refer to my statement of December 13, 1960 to the Security Council [920th meeting], in which I warned of the likelihood in the Congo of immediate civil war degenerating into uninhibited tribal conflict and the complete disintegration of the remaining fabric of national unity, should the United Nations Force and operations in the Congo be forced to cease. Nevertheless, the fact must be faced that severe weakening of the Force by reason of withdrawals may make it impossible for it to function effectively and would thus make necessary a proposal for the liquidation of the Force, and in consequence the entire United Nations operation in the Congo.

You will realize, of course, that the attention of the Security Council will need to be drawn in some appropriate manner to the serious threat thus posed to the continued existence of the Force, and this in a context in which it is not at all easy to comprehend what interests are really served by the withdrawals. Obviously, those who now take the decision must bear the responsibility for the resulting developments which, to the best of my understanding, are likely to prove to be, in time, against the interests and wishes they intend to serve.

ON JANUARY 26 Ceylon, Ghana, Guinea, Mali, Morocco, the United Arab Republic, and Yugoslavia formally requested an early meeting of the Security Council and the Soviet Union followed suit on January 29. In an exchange of private letters with Nehru, Hammarskjöld again urged India to contribute a substantial contingent of troops to help restore the strength of the UN Force. He also upheld the restrictive principles that had been applied in the conduct of the UN operation against Nehru's criticism that it was too passive. However he agreed with Nehru's view that a new effort to reduce the intensity of the East-West rivalry in support of opposing factions in the Congo was essential to the prevention of wider civil war, accompanied by an escalating cold war confrontation.

Adlai Stevenson had just become the U.S. Representative to the United Nations. His presence and the desire of the new Kennedy administration to gain the confidence of the nationalist African leaders provided an opportunity for a fresh attempt at reestablishing some sort of consensus behind the Congo operation. The Secretary-General engaged in a series of talks with Stevenson and other delegates directed toward exploring the possibilities in this direction.

Meanwhile in the Congo, two attempts to patch up a truce among the warring political factions were launched against a background of recurrent resorts to violence. The United Nations Conciliation Commission began consultations with the political leaders in Leopoldville, Stanleyville, Elisabethville, Luluabourg, and Bakwanga. Its chairman was Jaja Wachuku of Nigeria and its members included representatives of Ethiopia, Malaya, Ghana, India, Liberia, Morocco, Pakistan, Senegal, the Sudan, and Tunisia. President Kasavubu had never liked the Conciliation Commission, most of whose members he considered hostile and he moved independently to call a round-table conference in Leopoldville to which all factions were invited. Joseph Iléo was entrusted with the task of organizing the conference with the understanding that he would later attempt to form a coalition government to replace Mobutu's commissioners. However both Gizenga and Tshombé and their supporters refused to attend, though some of the more moderate Lumumbists were present, as well as delegates from South Kasai.

This conference was in its early stages when the Security Council reconvened on February 1. First there was a series of welcoming speeches by Council members, including Zorin of the USSR, for Adlai Stevenson when, for the first time, he took his seat as the U.S. representative. Hammarskjöld then opened the debate. He proposed a new move by the Council to neutralize all factions of the ANC, pending its reorganization into a disciplined instrument of law and order and to get the decision "enforced with the cooperation of the leaders concerned" (first following text).

Appeal in the Security Council for Support of New Efforts to Avert Widening Civil War in the Congo

NEW YORK   FEBRUARY 1, 1961

ON THE AGENDA of the Security Council figures a telegram from President Kasavubu with a complaint against the United Arab Republic, a letter from seven Member governments, now eight, about the treatment of Mr. Lumumba and related matters, and finally a letter from the USSR delegation. However, there are before the Council also other documents regarding which no debate at the present stage has been requested, but which all the same require the most serious attention of the Council. I have in mind various documents which I, as Secretary-General, have submitted to the Council, such as the exchange of communications with President Kasavubu regarding United Nations representation in the Congo, the exchange of communications with President Kasavubu regarding action required by him in relation to Orientale and Kivu provinces, a letter from the Secretary-General regarding the status of the bases in the Congo and, in particular, my report on the withdrawal of troops from the United Nations Force.

I believe that the Council may wish to have some comments on important elements in the present situation, as reflected in the various documents mentioned, before embarking upon a debate on the specific aspects put before the Council for its consideration at this meeting. In fact, as all the various elements in the Congo situation naturally are linked together, it is difficult to discuss any one of them without fitting it into the total picture.

In presenting my observations on the present situation, I would like to deal, first of all, with the domestic political development in order to turn later to the problem of interference from outside and, finally, to the problem of the various units of the Armée nationale congolaise (ANC) and their role both in relation to the domestic political development and as an element in the interplay between foreign powers and groups within the country.

Security Council Official Records, Sixteenth Year, 928th meeting.

On the political front, the rift between the authorities in Leopoldville and groups in control in the Orientale and Kivu provinces seems to have been widened through the transfer of Mr. Lumumba to Katanga regarding which I have presented my objections in two letters to President Kasavubu. To what extent this development is counterbalanced or—in other respects—reinforced by a realignment between Leopoldville, Elisabethville, and Bakwanga, or between Stanleyville and groups in the adjoining provinces, is at present difficult to say. At the preparatory round table conference, which is at present meeting in Leopoldville, not one of the three provinces, Orientale, Kivu, and Katanga, is represented by spokesmen for the responsible authorities. How far the Congo is from reconciliation in the interest of national unity is clearly illustrated by the threatening possibility of civil war, were present trends to continue, fanned by new incidents and unrestrained by the presence of the United Nations Force.

This is the setting in which the Conciliation Commission has had to pursue its efforts. So far no report from them has been received, but their work continues, and I am certain that the Commission will wish to report on its work through the Advisory Committee to the General Assembly in time for the opening of the resumed session. What I say is stated with reservation for the views which may later be expressed by the Conciliation Commission. It would, however, surprise me if my assessment of the political situation and theirs would prove to be far apart.

With the continued divisions of the Congo and the splits which, as indicated, may recently even have been deepened and widened, it may well be asked where we are heading and what the possibilities are to achieve the aims of the United Nations in the Congo, that is, to provide protection to the country against outside military interference and to assist in maintaining law and order so as to enable the Congolese people to find their way to the establishment of a stable government, in constitutional and democratic forms, giving substance to the independence of the country and maintaining its integrity.

Let it first be stated again that it is not the task of the United Nations to act for the Congolese people and to take political or constitutional initiatives aiming at the establishment of such a government. This is true not only in the sense that the United Nations has no right to try to impose on the Congo any special régime but also in the sense that the Organization cannot support the effort of any faction to impose such a régime. No, the duty of the United Nations is only the one which has just been recalled. It has to deal only with interference from outside the country and with the maintenance of law and order within the country. It cannot go beyond any one of these points. And even in its efforts to insulate the country from outside interference and to maintain law and order, the Organization must stay strictly within the limits established by the Charter just as the Secretary-General and the Force must, in their turn, stay strictly within the limits of the mandate established by the Security Council and the General Assembly.

It is my conviction that if an effective insulation from outside interference had been achieved, and if, likewise, the internal problems of law and order had been more completely resolved, the way would have been paved to a reconciliation of various factions and leaders, and the Congo would today have been much closer to the establishment of a constitutional government with sufficient authority to function effectively all over the country.

From what I have said it may seem that, to a certain degree, I agree with those who wish to put the blame for the lack of progress on the inefficiency of the United Nations operation. That is, as we know, a very popular line, and for those working for the United Nations it sometimes seems that the Organization is appreciated by many especially as a convenient scapegoat for shortcomings for which the responsibility should properly be borne by Member governments and by leaders within the Congo. However, in my view the Organization cannot be blamed for an attitude in the past which has been clearly dictated by its wish to avoid any interference in domestic affairs and which would have been of sufficient strength to cope with a situation with greater initial cohesion among leaders and factions.

On the other hand, the Organization could well be blamed if, at the present juncture, it did not reassess its policy in the light of experience and consider whether, in the interest of peace and security, for which it carries primary responsibility, more far-reaching measures are not now called for in order to overcome this continued and increasing lack of cohesion, even if such measures by some might be felt as coming close to a kind of interference.

The immediate aim of the United Nations operation was to provide for the withdrawal of all Belgian combat troops. That target was met at the end of August. Later on, however, outside interference has recurred in new and subtler but not less dangerous forms. Although it is difficult to determine the extent of such interference in concrete terms and to substantiate the findings, its existence is an incontrovertible fact and its effects are strongly negative. Thus we know for certain that, both as regards arms and men, the military potential of various factions has been reinforced from the outside and that foreign mercenaries have been recruited on an increasing scale. Recent bombings speak their shocking language. This development may in some cases have come about without the active cooperation of this or that foreign government, but it must be assumed that it has at least been tolerated by some foreign governments.

Volunteers or sales of arms from private companies are time-honoured forms for military assistance maintaining a seeming neutrality for the governments most directly concerned. It is my firm conviction that such interference must be stopped, but I have not so far found a sufficient legal basis in the resolutions for effective countermeasures by the United Nations. Such countermeasures would not have been, or be, necessary if the Organization had been or were now able to count on the loyal cooperation and assistance from all its Member governments. Such cooperation has not always been forthcoming. Is it too much to hope that at the present serious phase of the development the United Nations will be able to count on all its Members so that they would not only avoid giving any military assistance themselves but, furthermore, take the necessary steps, which undoubtedly are within their power, to stop any such assistance in other forms, less accessible for counteraction through the United Nations and its organs?

However, outside interferences need not take the form of military assistance, or merely omission of measures against such assistance on a nongovernmental basis. The radio is a powerful weapon and so is the press. Comments made from various sources, attitudes maintained in various quarters have had and continue to have a strong influence on the domestic political situation in the Congo. Heroes are made of some. Others are maligned. Solutions are imposed. The motives of other approaches are discredited. I wonder if any other country and its political leaders have ever to the same degree found themselves converted by others into actors in an international drama with very little respect for their true positions and the true interests of the country concerned.

Is it too much to expect that governments in this respect will try to exercise and ask for restraint, thus providing the leaders of the Congo with a setting in which their true ambitions and ideals can be tested in democratic debate with other leaders without having the outcome prejudged by outsiders who are only partly informed and pursue interests of their own? The United Nations itself has but modest means to influence such planned or unplanned propaganda. However, it would seem to be a minimum requirement that it be not itself used as a platform for such interference.

This brings me to the internal situation as regards law and order. I have already on a previous occasion characterized the present conditions and the role of the Armée nationale congolaise. I have drawn attention to the fact that the old Force publique has broken up into factions claiming allegiance to this or that leader and thus, in fact, providing various political groups with small private armies. However, the disintegration has gone even further. Recent examples can be given both from the Leopold-ville area and from Stanleyville or Kivu of groups of the military force having acted in a way clearly indicating that they were not under the control of the leader to whom they were supposed to owe allegiance. Thus even the loyalties of the various private armies must be put in question. At all events they may be assumed to include groups which can scarcely be regarded as elements of an organized military force under a responsible command.

What I have said should be enough to indicate why military assistance in men or matériel, on a governmental or nongovernmental basis, given to any one of the various factions of the army at present is a dangerous and negative element leading not in the direction of a solution of the Congo problem in any lasting terms but away from conciliation and the creation of national unity. When it must be said that, in this way, the army itself has been and continues to be the main threat to law and order, it is obviously the last thing that can be justified to strengthen the hands of that same army by military supplies or men.

The United Nations Force is now threatened by serious reductions of its strength through repatriation. I have pointed out that a further reduction may lead us to a point where I would have to put before the Security Council, or the General Assembly, the question whether the Force should continue or should be liquidated as no longer being able to tackle its tasks due to its reduced strength. We may not be there yet. But we are in my view so close as to render it necessary to see under what conditions the Force with its reduced strength can continue to function. Were outside support to the various factions of the ANC to continue—indeed, even without such support, were the present development to continue—with various factions of the army functioning as private armies in actual or potential conflict among themselves, breaking loose from their own command and threatening the population, it can be seriously questioned whether the situation any longer would permit a useful United Nations contribution unless the Force were to be strengthened.

Were the answer to this question to be negative, it would not be only the United Nations Force that would have to be withdrawn. If the United Nations were to become incapable of giving minimum protection, the civilian operation which the Organization has brought into being as part of its technical assistance may well become ineffective. Therefore I believe that this operation also might have to be brought to an end.

In the circumstances, and for these reasons, I feel that the Council should give serious consideration especially to what the United Nations line should be regarding the ANC, in all its factions. It seems to me that the time has come when the Council must provide a basis for arrangements which would eliminate the present threat from the army, or units thereof, against efforts to reestablish normal political life and against law and order.

The members of the Council will remember that at an early stage of the operation the approach that I outlined to the problem of the ANC, was as follows: The army, which was the instrument of the government both for the protection of the integrity of the country and for the maintenance of law and order, had lost its cadre of officers and become disorganized. It had to be rebuilt from the bottom by adequate training and by the schooling of officers. Naturally, during this phase of reorganization, up to the stage when it would be able to function in a satisfactory way, the army should be unburdened from its tasks both as regards the protection of the integrity of the country and as regards the maintenance of law and order. In the reorganization operation the United Nations should be instrumental in giving the necessary technical assistance and, for that purpose, obviously would have to be in a position to check that the assistance given be not put to uses contrary to the very aims of the Organization.

What was thus said in July and August is, if I understand the situation correctly, still the accepted position of the United Nations. I believe that it is more valid today than when it was first presented.

The United Nations did what it could along the line thus indicated, but its efforts came to nothing when early in September the army broke into the political field and, at the same time, split up in factions going beyond the division already caused by the claim of Katanga to secession. What thus happened in the beginning of the fall stands as a main cause of the continued deterioration of the internal situation in the Congo.

I believe, therefore, that a most important contribution in the direction of conciliation in the interest of national unity would be to revert to the initial stand of the United Nations and get it enforced with the cooperation of the leaders concerned. This would mean to return the army to its proper role and to give it as quickly and effectively as possible a chance to fulfill it. If the effort proved successful, it would mean that the army had stepped out of the present political conflicts and had devoted itself to its own reorganization in order to become, again, an effective, integrated, disciplined, and well-organized national instrument of a government, accepted in constitutional and democratic forms as the central authority of the Republic.

In fact, for the United Nations to revive this initial concept and to put its moral pressure back of it would be to express in positive terms its neutrality in relation to all domestic conflicts in the Congo—in positive terms which are the natural counterpart to the negative terms which, under the pressure of present conflicts, all too often have come to dominate the picture in the last few months. It would also be an effective contribution towards reconciliation, which is stated by the General Assembly to be one of the aims of the Organization. Is it too much to expect that the Organization, thus firmly adhering to the line it took from the very beginning and now urgently asking for its implementation with the support of the full cooperation needed from the leaders in the country, should be able to count on such cooperation?

As a clarification of the basis and aim of the policy which I thus find strongly indicated, I would welcome a decision by the Council requesting the Secretary-General to take urgently appropriate measures for assistance in the reorganization of the national army, preventing it, or units thereof, from intervening in the present political conflicts in the Congo.

As is well known, the mandate of the United Nations Force does not permit it to take military initiative. This limitation has repeatedly been challenged and demands have been raised for a revision of the mandate to include such military initiative. In a couple of the documents now before the Security Council, demands are made that the United Nations resort to the use of force for certain specific purposes. Thus, President Kasavubu wants the United Nations to use force against the units of the ANC which are serving Mr. Gizenga, and he threatens to ask for military assistance from other countries if the request is not met, thus neglecting the stand of the General Assembly at its fourth emergency special session in its resolution of September 20 [1474 (ES-IV)] which should exclude other countries from granting such assistance. Further, the Belgian government requests the use of force for protection of its nationals in Orientale and Kivu, including obviously eight Belgian soldiers detained in Stanleyville.

The Security Council will remember that similar requests for the use of force have previously been made for other purposes. Thus, the question was raised by members of the Organization with a view to the liberation of Mr. Lumumba, and, at a still earlier stage, the central government asked for the use of force against the units of the army which were loyal to Mr. Tshombé.

I believe that a look at the four cases of requests for armed intervention which I have recalled, and their different purposes, will bring out clearly to everybody what problems would arise were the mandate to be widened as proposed. Certainly such a widening of the mandate could not be considered without a much clearer and fuller definition of the objectives to be pursued by the United Nations. Nor, of course, could the mandate be changed in relation to earlier decisions short of giving countries which have contributed troops on the basis of those first decisions an opportunity to withdraw were they not to approve of the new stand.

I have tried to outline in this intervention a few problems which seem to me to be of special importance in the consideration of the United Nations operation in the Congo. I have not dealt at any length with the background. It should be well known. But, all the same, I may in concluding sum it up again.

The serious divisions of the Congo continue and have in some respects been widened and reinforced. The army remains broken up in factions with varying loyalties and partly outside the control of any responsible authority. Foreign backing and support have led to a strengthening of the military potentials. Offensive steps are taken and alliances between groups discussed. In these circumstances the risk of a civil war, tearing the country to pieces and bringing civilian life to a standstill, has come closer. It could easily be triggered through such incidents as those to which recent military initiatives have led.

Civil war would indeed in my view be unavoidable if the United Nations Force were withdrawn under present circumstances. Were it to break out in spite of the restraining influence of the presence of the United Nations, I consider that the right thing to do would be for the United Nations Force to withdraw, as it cannot interpose itself effectively and permit itself to become a third party between contending forces.

In a situation of this gravity several member countries have withdrawn, or have stated their intention to withdraw, their contingents in the Force. Naturally, such withdrawals bring us closer to the stage where the United Nations Force would be clearly insufficient. That also would be a reason for withdrawal unless a fundamental change could be brought about in the situation which would permit us to continue. Such a change would result if the various factions of the ANC were brought back to their normal role as parts of a unified, disciplined army, outside politics, and under the ultimate control of a functioning constitutional government. This would also be an effective step in support of national reconciliation. It may also be a necessary step if new withdrawals are to be prevented.

Certainly nobody overlooks the difficulties ahead of the United Nations along the lines which circumstances now seem to point out, but the alternative is forbidding, as a breakdown would open the door to a wider conflict and might well threaten all with the dangers against which this Organization and its Members have mobilized their best efforts since July 14, 1960, when this Council unanimously decided to step in in order to avert the developing threat to peace and security.

THE SECURITY COUNCIL met again twice on February 2 and twice on February 7. It then adjourned until either Friday, February 10, or Monday, February 13, at the suggestion of the President, Sir Patrick Dean of the United Kingdom, to provide time for further consultations. No draft resolutions had been introduced.

Most of the speeches were by representatives of the Casablanca powers—Ceylon, Mali, Guinea, Indonesia, Morocco, and the United Arab Republic—who called upon the Council to take the measures proposed in the Casablanca declaration. Zorin supported them, but his langauge was notably less abusive than usual and he expressed hope for the new leaders of the United States "to look the facts soberly in the face and to advocate strict implementation of the security Council resolutions on the Congo for which the United States and the Soviet Union both voted."[1]

After his response to the welcome given him Stevenson did not speak again during this period. Ambassador C. S. Jha of India expressed Nehru's attitude when he declared that "the suggestions of the Secretary-General are well worth consideration, but only in conjunction with other measures . . . the release of all political leaders and members of Parliament, in particular Mr. Lumumba and his supporters, the immediate reconvening of Parliament and the immediate with-

[1] Security Council Official Records, Sixteenth Year, 930th meeting.

drawal of all Belgian military and paramilitary personnel and other such personnel."[2]

Hammarskjöld also supported the latter three objectives but he continued to believe they should be sought by diplomatic and political means and not forcibly imposed. In the discussions outside the Council chamber he worked for commitments from the West to stop helping Mobutu and Tshombé, from the Soviet Union to stop helping Gizenga, from the Afro-Asians to stop helping one or another faction in the political struggle. If the Congo could be better insulated from all outside pressures and all units of the ANC neutralized and reorganized under United Nations supervision the hope for maintaining the unity of the Congo by peaceful, constitutional and democratic means might again be within reach.

In Leopoldville on February 9 the formation was announced of a new provisional government of politicians to replace Mobutu's College of Commissioners. Iléo was named prime minister and Adoula minister of the interior, with Bomboko continuing as foreign minister. The new government would exercise legislative powers until Parliament could be recalled, Kasavubu declared, and some seats in the cabinet were reserved for regions not represented at the round-table conference. Though the new cabinet was still a far cry from the broadly based coalition that was needed it might, in other circumstances, have been a first step toward a return to constitutional and parliamentary rule. But the failure to obtain any information about Lumumba's whereabouts and condition had now given rise to growing suspicions that he had been killed.

[2] Ibid., 929th meeting.

THE DEATH OF LUMUMBA AND ITS CONSEQUENCES

ON FEBRUARY 10 Tshombé's minister of the interior, Godefroid Munongo, announced that Lumumba, Mpolo, and Okito had escaped from detention in an isolated farmhouse the night before, that an extensive search was under way and a large reward was offered for their recapture. Three days later Munongo spoke again. This time he reported that the three fugitives had been massacred by the inhabitants of a village he refused to name. Munongo and two other members of Tshombé's cabinet had gone to identify the bodies, which were then buried at a location he also refused to reveal. The villagers would receive the promised reward, he said, and could not be blamed "for having rid Katanga, the Congo, Africa, and the world of a problem . . . which threatened to be a source of trouble to mankind." Munongo was defiant about the inevitable reaction. The following excerpts are representative of the line of self-justification in his remarks:

> We shall be accused of having murdered them. My reply is: prove it. . . . I refuse in advance to recognize any right on the part of the United Nations to take a position on this question. . . . Did the defunct League of Nations and the United Nations concern themselves with the fate of the millions of Russians exterminated in the concentration camps of the USSR? What has the United Nations done to protect the life of the brave General Maleter or that of Imre Nagy, the standard-bearer of the Hungarian patriots? Did not the Allies, who established the United Nations, calmly abandon their companion in arms, General Mihailovič, executed by his rival Tito?[1]

From the first there were few who believed Munongo's version of how Lumumba and his associates met their end. The true circumstances have never been finally established but months later the UN Commission of Investigation concluded that they were probably killed during the night of January 17, only hours after their arrival in Elisabethville, in the presence of high officials of the Katanga government who almost certainly included Munongo and perhaps Tshombé and two Belgian mercenaries as well.

When the Security Council convened in the morning of February 13, Dayal's report of the day before on the story of Lumumba's alleged escape was on the table[2] and the later word confirming his death had just been received. After the Secretary-General made his brief statement (first following text) the Council adjourned until February 15 to give the Member governments time to digest the tragic news.

[1] Security Council Official Records, Supplement for January, February, and March 1961, document S/4688/Add. 1.
[2] Ibid., documents S/4688 and Add. 1 and 2.

1. First Statement in the Security Council

NEW YORK   FEBRUARY 13, 1961

AFTER THE CIRCULATION of the report from the special representative in the Congo regarding Mr. Lumumba, the Secretariat has this morning received information from Elisabethville of a most serious and tragic nature, the substance of which is already well known to the Members. In view of this new information, I would propose that the aforementioned report be added to the agenda.

Limiting myself to one immediate observation regarding the steps now called for from the United Nations, I would express the view that the matter is of such a character and significance as to render necessary a full and impartial investigation. The representatives of the United Nations, in the first place, General Iyassu, have still not been received by Mr. Tshombé. I have instructed the General to stay either until he is received and can proceed with his task, with the necessary assistance from the authorities, or until he receives new instructions in the light of the position of the Council. I feel that an international investagation in an appropriate form is indicated.

The importance of recent tragic events is such that I shall for a moment leave aside the so-called offensive of the Katanga *gendarmerie* against civilian population of the Baluba tribes, covered in another report this morning. However, I wish to reserve my right to revert later in an appropriate context to this question, which merits the most urgent attention of the Council, as well as to the question of measures that may have to be taken by the United Nations in order to counter to the limits of its possibilities the various serious developments which may be released by yesterday's events.

Security Council Official Records, Sixteenth Year, 933rd meeting.

THE DEATH OF Lumumba produced shock waves around the world. His murder was condemned almost everywhere, including the Western countries where he had been generally regarded with profound distrust. The African nationalist leaders—and many in Asia too—reacted with high emotion and sometimes bitter anger. The reaction of the USSR was the most extreme of all and Hammarskjöld was its principal target. The Soviet government evidently concluded that blaming the West and the Secretary-General for what had happened to Lumumba might open new chances to win support in Africa and Asia for replacing the office of Secretary-General by the "troika." A Soviet government statement issued on February 14 employed such unbridled language as the following:

> The murder of Patrice Lumumba and his comrades-in-arms in the dungeons of Katanga is the culmination of Hammarskjöld's criminal activities. It is clear to every honest person throughout the world that the blood of Patrice Lumumba is on the hands of this henchman of the colonialists and cannot be removed. The states which cherish the authority and future of the United Nations cannot acquiesce in a situation where a sorry lackey of the colonialists speaks in the international arena on behalf of the Organization. His actions place a dark stain on the whole United Nations. Not only can such a man not enjoy any confidence; he deserves only the contempt of all honest people. There is no place for Hammarskjöld in the high office of Secretary-General of the United Nations and his continuance in that office is intolerable.[1]

The statement concluded by demanding sanctions against Belgium, the arrest and trial of Tshombé and Mobutu, the liquidation of ONUC and departure of all foreign troops within a month and the dismissal of Hammarskjöld as Secretary-General. For its part, the Soviet government, it declared, "will not maintain any relations with Hammarskjöld and will not recognize him as an official of the United Nations." Finally, the Soviet government pledged "all possible help and support to the Gizenga régime in Stanleyville as "the lawful government of the Congo."

Adlai Stevenson was the first speaker at the Security Council meeting Wednesday morning, February 15. His speech was interrupted by a prolonged and violent demonstration in the public gallery. Many of the unarmed UN guards were injured before they were able to round up the demonstrators and eject them from the building. The rioters had gained admission with protocol passes issued to delegations for their guests. After the gallery was cleared Stevenson resumed his speech, which gave full support to the Secretary-General and also reflected the desire of the Kennedy administration to go further toward meeting Afro-Asian concerns than the Eisenhower administration had been willing to go in its final weeks in power.

---

[1] Security Council Official Records, Sixteenth Year, Supplement for January, February, and March 1961, document S/4704.

Zorin spoke next, repeating the extreme language used in the USSR government statement and submitting a draft resolution to carry out all its demands, including the dismissal of the Secretary-General. When the Council reconvened after luncheon Hammarskjöld was the first speaker (first following text).

---

2. Second Statement After Soviet Demand for His Dismissal

NEW YORK   FEBRUARY 15, 1961

BEFORE ENTERING ON the subject matter under consideration, I wish to express our deep regret at the assassination of Mr. Lumumba, Mr. Okito, and Mr. Mpolo. What has happened is a revolting crime against principles for which this Organization stands and must stand.

It is vain to argue with those for whom truth is a function of party convenience and justice a function of party interest. But for others it may be essential that some facts are recalled and clearly and simply put on record. The points which may be useful to cover are those which should determine the judgement regarding the relations of the United Nations to the fate of Mr. Lumumba and, in consequence, the responsibility of the Organization and of its various organs.

Together with Mr. Kasavubu, Mr. Lumumba asked for United Nations military assistance. When such assistance had been granted, he wanted the United Nations Force, on his behalf, to fight down the secessionist group in Katanga. In keeping with the stand taken unanimously by the Council, I was obliged to turn down this request as contrary to the status and functions of the Force. My stand on this issue came before the Security Council, and it was upheld by the Council.

In view of the desperate necessity to get the United Nations Force into Katanga in order to achieve the withdrawal of Belgian troops from all over the Congo, I managed a breakthrough for the Force to Katanga, which made it possible to reach this result. As this move had not been discussed with Mr. Lumumba personally, he accused me bitterly of by-

Security Council Official Records, Sixteenth Year, 935th meeting.

passing the legitimate government. However, the move had been discussed with the delegation of that government in New York consisting of, among others, Mr. Gizenga, the vice-prime minister, Mr. Mpolo, and Mr. Kanza. Again, the matter was brought before the Security Council, and again my stand was upheld by the Council. No member even introduced a resolution which would have involved disapproval of the action.

In early September, President Kasavubu and Mr. Lumumba each declared the mandate of the other null and void, and both positions were disapproved in a session of Parliament. Somewhat later, Colonel Mobutu, basing himself on units of the Armée nationale congolaise in the Leopoldville area, declared that he had, as he said, "neutralized" both the chief of state and Mr. Lumumba. In the light of the principles applied by the United Nations as regard domestic conflicts, the instruction to the command and the special representative was that they should stand aside from the conflict that had developed and avoid any actions which could make them a party to the conflict or involve support to any one side in it. These instructions were challenged on the basis that Mr. Lumumba remained the head of government and should be treated as such by the United Nations. The matter came up both before the Security Council and the General Assembly, and the General Assembly adopted on September 20, 1960, without any dissenting vote, a resolution which must be interpreted as upholding the line taken by me in the instructions to the United Nations Command. Thus, whatever is said about "the failure of the United Nations to uphold legality in the Congo," it is something for which the responsibility is shared by all Members of this Organization.

While staying in his official residence, Mr. Lumumba requested United Nations protection. He got such protection at the place of his residence, in keeping with the principles upheld by the Organization. While he was under protection, attempts to arrest Mr. Lumumba were stopped by the United Nations. At a later stage of this period, on November 7, Mr. Lumumba issued a statement in which he called the United Nations Organization the "guardian of democracy." With reference to passages in the Secretary-General's report that dealt with a variety of political questions in the Congo, Mr. Lumumba also declared that "the Government which I represent and the Congolese parliament fully endorse these statements of the United Nations Secretary-General because they are in keeping with the truth and the reality which we have lived through during these past few weeks." And he concluded his statement by referring to "the United Nations Assembly and its Secretary-General in whom we place our full confidence to save this country from the anarchy and the collapse which today gravely threaten it." That is the end of the quotation from Mr. Lumumba's statement of November 7, while he was under what Mr. Zorin this morning called "house arrest."

Mr. Lumumba escaped from his residence in a way unknown to the United Nations and travelled east, without any possibility for the United Nations to know where he was and thus without possibility for the Organization to give him protection. He was arrested out in the country without any possibility for the United Nations to stop this action, as it was not in control of the situation. This may be the point to remind the Members of the simple fact that a force of, at its maximum, twenty thousand men spread over a country not far from five times the size of France, is not in a position to check what is going on everywhere in the country or in a position to protect individuals of whom the whereabouts are unknown.

When brought for imprisonment to Thysville, Mr. Lumumba was in the custody of the Armée nationale congolaise. The United Nations had neither the power nor the right to liberate Mr. Lumumba from his captors by force—I say the United Nations, because to my knowledge not even this Council or the General Assembly would have such a right. Much less did it exist for the United Nations representatives in the Congo under their mandate. The action of the Organization had therefore to concentrate on efforts to give Mr. Lumumba all possible legal and humanitarian protection. I, together with the United Nations representatives in the Congo, exercised all the pressure I possibly could for that purpose. We received assurances from the president. The prisoners were visited by Red Cross personnel. No steps were taken, however, by the authorities in Leopoldville with regard to the observance of due process of law for Mr. Lumumba, which I had requested and which obviously applied to all stages of his arrest and detention.

Mr. Lumumba was brought to Katanga. His departure was entirely outside the control of the United Nations organs. His arrival in Elisabethville was witnessed from some distance by a few United Nations soldiers, far outmanned by the Katanga forces and without any possibility of interference. Immediately, in *démarches* to Mr. Kasavubu and Mr. Tshombé, I exercised all the influence possible for the return of Mr. Lumumba to Leopoldville and for application of normal legal rules in protection of his interests. Members will recall that this, as so many of the previous steps to which I referred, was regarded by various Congolese authorities as interference in Congolese internal affairs.

I did not make any special efforts for our own representatives to see Mr. Lumumba while at Katanga, as at that stage the United Nations Conciliation Commission for the Congo and its members had solicited a promise from Mr. Kasavubu to see him and were going to do so when they visited Katanga. When Mr. Tshombé refused the contact with Mr. Lumumba, I protested to Mr. Kasavubu. For more than two weeks the Conciliation Commission made several representations to Mr. Kasavubu with a view to arranging a visit to Mr. Lumumba; they did not succeed in securing his cooperation.

That is where we stood when on the morning of February 10 the authorities in Elisabethville announced that Mr. Lumumba had, as they said, escaped from his place of detention. As it appears from the report, steps were immediately taken in order to find out all the facts, and in various ways it was impressed on the authorities that the Organization attached the greatest importance to the protection of the life of Mr. Lumumba; as reported by the Katanga authorities, the escape took place from a house far from any United Nations detachment and whose location was unknown to the United Nations. When no response had been received, on February 11 further steps were taken in order to establish objectively the facts and, of course, also thereby to get guidance as to whether the United Nations could intervene and give protection; the instruction was that if Mr. Lumumba were to seek protection from any United Nations unit, he would immediately be granted asylum. As is well known, in spite of repeated *démarches,* no response has been received from the authorities and General Iyassu, who was sent especially for the purpose to Elisabethville, has not been received by Mr. Tshombé.

These are the main steps on the road, and it does not seem to me to be asking too much if those who now talk about the responsibility of the United Nations, and more especially of its Secretary-General—in language which only emotion could excuse but which may be inspired by cold calculation—are requested to state clearly when and how representatives of the Organization did not use all the means put at their disposal, in accordance with the mandate as established by the Members of the United Nations and the Security Council. I know that it will be said, as it was said a week ago by the representative of the Soviet Union, that I maintain that we in the Secretariat have made no mistakes and that all responsibility rests with others. Members are all aware of the fact that I did not say so then, and that I do not say so now. But if those who have established the mandate and those who have decided on the means by which the mandate should be fulfilled attack the representatives of the Organization because they have not exceeded the mandate, thus established, or acted against it, and because they have not used means which have never been put at their disposal, then it seems to me to be fair to point out that it is not the Secretary-General who has determined the mandate, nor is it the Secretariat which has decided on what means they should use to fulfill it. There is no escape from the responsibility which flows from this—in statements to which we have listened to the effect that this or that Member gives the mandate another interpretation, often even forgetting the Charter, and claims that we have had or have rights that are not ours. A single voice does not change the decision of a major organ and no single Member is above the Charter.

In the present effort in some quarters to blacken the Organization and discredit its representatives, irrespective of the validity of the reasons and irrespective of the facts of the case, the real victim is the future. To gain a short advantage, nationally or for a party, those who act in that way sacrifice the legacy which future generations should have in this Organization. It is ironic for us, who have been guided solely by the interest of the Congo and solely by the wish to develop the practices of this Organization in a way which may lay a foundation for future international cooperation, to be attacked by those who pursue entirely different aims, mostly only too easily discernible, and for that purpose find it useful to undermine confidence in the Organization by claiming that we act against the interest of the Congo and against the principles of the Charter.

The facts as recalled, and as easily verified from the records of the United Nations, obviously do not provide a basis for the attacks of the Soviet Union in the statement of the Government released to the press yesterday, in the draft resolution, and in the speech of Mr. Zorin this morning. And why should they? In fact, what we are witnessing is in part a follow-through of an attempt which the General Assembly witnessed during the general debate—a vain attempt to break through the present United Nations setup so as to open the road to such a change of the structure of the Organization and its Secretariat as would give the Soviet Union the kind of influence it wants beyond that which follows from the rules of the Charter.

On October 3 of last year, Chairman Khrushchev said in the General Assembly: "I should like to repeat: we do not, and cannot place confidence in Mr. Hammarskjöld. If he himself cannot muster the courage to resign in, let us say, a chivalrous way, we shall draw the inevitable conclusions from the situation."

What we have heard today is nothing but a repetition of the same thesis with one added argument, the assassination of Mr. Lumumba— supported by the preposterous allegation that this crime can be laid at the doorstep of the Secretary-General.

In reply to what Mr. Khrushchev said, I stated:

I said the other day that I would not wish to continue to serve as Secretary-General one day longer than such continued service was considered to be in the best interests of the Organization. The statement this morning seems to indicate that the Soviet Union finds it impossible to work with the present Secretary-General. This may seem to provide a strong reason why I should resign. However, the Soviet Union has also made it clear that if the present Secretary-General were to resign now, it would not wish to elect a new incumbent but insist on an arrangement which—and this is my firm conviction based on broad experience— would make it impossible to maintain an effective executive. By resigning I would, therefore, at the present difficult and dangerous juncture throw the Organization to the winds. I have no right to do so because I have a responsibility to all those Member states for which the Organization is of decisive importance—a responsibility which over-rides all other considerations.[1]

What I thus said in reply to Chairman Khrushchev I can restate today. And so as to leave no ambiguity, I want to point out that in line with what I stated during the Suez crisis, I would consider the withdrawal of the confidence of one of the permanent members of the Security Council as a reason why the Secretary-General should resign, were it not for the fact that in this case the Soviet Union, while refusing its confidence to the Secretary-General, has at the same time taken a stand which makes it absolutely clear that, were the present Secretary-General to resign, no new Secretary-General could be appointed, and the world would have to bow to the wish of the Soviet Union to have this Organization, on its executive side, run by a triumvirate which could not function and which most definitely would not provide the instrument for all the uncommitted countries of which they are in need. And this would happen at a time of great tension and unprecedented demands on the Organization. Thus, while taking a stand which would without any hesitation cause me to resign under normal circumstances, the Soviet Union has at the same

[1] See pp. 199-201.

time created a situation in which I could not do so, unless it were to be the wish of the uncommitted nations that I do so in their own interest and in the interest of the United Nations. In the language of the Soviet Union, I have the "chivalry" to respect the view of the vast majority of Members who are uncommitted and—although I use the word with hesitation—I can assure the Soviet Union that I have the "courage" to take the full consequences of this attitude, even if it means being forced to continue in my post without the support needed and with means desperately weak in the face of enormous demands.

I hope that my language is clear enough. It is all I have to say about the matter and it is all I need to say about it. The decision is thus in the hands of all those for whom the Soviet Union pretends to speak. Whatever the Members of this Organization may decide on the subject will, naturally, be my law.

I said in the intervention in the General Assembly to which I have referred that I deplored that the attitude of the Soviet Union had tended to personalize an issue which, in fact, concerns an institution. In doing so again, the Soviet Union has again forced me to speak about my own attitude. I regret that I have had to do so, as the issue remains one concerning the institution and not the man. And I regret it even more in a situation in which much more is at stake than this or that organization of the United Nations or this or that organ of the United Nations. Indeed, the United Nations has never been and will never be more than an instrument for Member governments in their effort to pave the way towards orderly and peaceful coexistence. It is not the man, it is not even the institution, it is that very effort that has now come under attack. That this is so is clear if we look at the realities of the problem. In putting aside further comments on the questions to which so far in this intervention I have been forced to devote attention, I should now, before concluding, like to say a few words about the realities of the present situation.

For seven or eight months, through efforts far beyond the imagination of those who founded this Organization, it has tried to counter tendencies to introduce the Big-Power conflict into Africa and put the young African countries under the shadow of the cold war. It has done so with great risks and against heavy odds. It has done so at the cost of very great personal sacrifices for a great number of people. In the beginning the effort was successful, and I do not now hesitate to say that on more than one occasion the drift into a war with foreign-power intervention of the

Korean or Spanish type was avoided only thanks to the work done by the Organization, basing itself on African solidarity. We effectively countered efforts from all sides to make the Congo a happy hunting ground for national interests. To be a roadblock to such efforts is to make yourself the target of attacks from all those who find their plans thwarted. In the case of some, the opposition to the United Nations line was for a while under the surface, but it was not long before it broke out in the open. In other cases, the disappointment at meeting this unexpected obstacle broke out at once in violent and vocal attacks on the Organization. From both sides the main accusation was a lack of objectivity. The historian will undoubtedly find in this balance of accusations the very evidence of that objectivity we were accused of lacking, but also of the fact that very many Member nations have not yet accepted the limits put on their national ambitions by the very existence of the United Nations and by the membership of that Organization.

Now, under basically identical, although superficially more dramatic, circumstances, we have again reached the point where a local armed conflict is threatening in forms which are only too likely to lead to a widening of the conflict into the international arena. I have no new solutions to offer you. Still, I firmly believe that, as in July and August of last year, the only way in which the continent of Africa and its countries can counter a tragic development into an international conflict, perhaps on a world-wide scale, is by rallying around common aims within the framework of the United Nations. African solidarity within the United Nations was the reply to the threats last summer; I am firmly convinced that it still is the only reply.

However, it is not enough to state in general terms such a line of policy as the solution to the problem. We are all in duty bound to be concrete both as to the aims and as to the means to achieve those aims. Again, on this point, I have little new to offer, but I should all the same like to sum up briefly what seem to me to be measures which must be pursued with vigour and courage.

First, I have already suggested an international investigation of the circumstances surrounding the assassination of Mr. Lumumba and his colleagues. Is there any other way to determine responsibility? Is there any other way to lay the basis for appropriate counteraction? It may be said to be on the outer margin of what the Security Council can decide, but the Council can point to at least one important precedent established by the General Assembly.

Secondly, instructions have already been given to the Force to protect the civilian population against attacks from armed units, whatever the authority under which they are acting. Again, it may be said that this is on the outer margin of the mandate of the United Nations, but already in September I said that I felt that it must be considered as a natural part of the duties of the Organization, and I did not meet with any objections.

Thirdly, instructions have already been given that, in case a clash between armed units is threatening, the United Nations should use all means, short of force, to forestall such clashes through negotiations, through the establishment of neutralized zones, through cease-fire arrangements and through similar measures. Negotiations to those ends can be conducted on the basis of the military force at the disposal of the United Nations. The chance of success is greater the bigger the force. If this method of preventing civil-war risks by peaceful means is to be successful, it is indeed desirable that the United Nations Force should be strengthened. The weakening of the Force through withdrawal may make the efforts useless. I have also already stated that, were clashes between armed units to develop, the United Nations could not permit itself to become a third party to such a conflict. But the use of force in support of cease-fire arrangements should not therefore be excluded.

Fourthly, on February 1, I proposed that the United Nations reactivate its basic attitude on the Armée nationale congolaise and take appropriate steps for its reorganization for its normal purposes in the service of the national government, thus withdrawing all its various factions from their present engagement in the political strife.

Fifthly and lastly, already on October 8 of last year, as is clear from documents circulated to the Security Council, I addressed myself to the Government of Belgium and to Mr. Tshombé, pointing out the necessity to eliminate the Belgian political element in the Congo. I do not remember that I got any active support from any Member country or from any organ of the United Nations for that stand at that time. I was attacked violently by Belgium and by various leaders in the Congo. I still hold the same view, for which I have been trying to get respect all through these months, alas without effect. It is still, in my opinion, as essential a need as it was in the early autumn. May I now hope that it my gain the moral support of this Council?

What I have recalled here are five points on which I have, thus, already taken a stand and for which I should like to have an endorsement that only in part has been forthcoming in the past. Taken together, they do not represent a "plan," but they are all, in my view, essential elements of a constructive policy for the Congo.

I could, however, go further. Money is as important as men. Arms are essential for any military operation. It can be put in question whether the United Nations has the right to inspect trains and aircraft coming to the Congo so as to see to it that no arms are imported. The legal advice I have sought and obtained indicates that we may have no such right to search. Is it under such circumstances surprising that so far we have not been able to counter arms imports, when Member countries outside the Congo have not shown hesitation to export arms to the Congo?

But further, movements of funds and capital are definitely outside the control of the United Nations. To the extent that such movements are not for the purposes of economic development or for humanitarian purposes they are certainly not desirable in the present situation. What authority, if any, is the Council prepared to give its representatives in this field?

There is also the constitutional question. Already in the fall I pointed out the essential importance of getting Parliament together as a basis for the reorganization of the political life of the nation. This attitude had wide support, but what can the Organization do in this respect as obviously it has not so far claimed a right itself to convene Parliament? I am certain that the Conciliation Commission with its nine African members has used its best endeavours in the direction indicated. If they have not succeeded by means of persuasion, is the Council prepared to override the sovereign rights of the Republic of the Congo, and, in the interest of peace and security, to order the reconvening of Parliament?

The five points on which, as previously mentioned, I have already taken action, are all of them such that no new legal mandate is required while, definitely, there is a need for moral and political support. The three last mentioned points are of a different nature. They are points on which it is for this Council and only for this Council to decide what it feels entitled to do and what it wants to do. The Secretary-General cannot act short of a clear decision by the Council. In this case, at least, there is no question about where the responsibility lies. As regards arms imports, as regards the transfer of funds, as regards enforced constitutional measures, it is for the Security Council to determine the ends and to decide on the means, in full awareness of its responsibility for the maintenance of peace and security, but also of its duty to respect the sovereignty of a Member nation. It cannot shirk its responsibilities by expecting from the Secretariat action on which it is not prepared to take decisions itself.

Were the Security Council to reaffirm and redefine, perhaps even to widen, the mandate for the United Nations operation, I am certain that Members would realize that nothing had been achieved—or worse, that the Council had misled world opinion—unless at the same time the Council provided satisfactory means for the fulfilment of the established purposes of the United Nations action. If those means remain insufficient, we shall see the prolongation of a situation from which the United Nations has suffered for too long: a sharp discrepancy between aims, which have rallied general support, and means so inadequate as to make it impossible to realize those same aims. We have seen, and we would see again, that such a discrepancy will serve as a basis for attacks on the Organization and on its servants, attacks which certainly do not serve the interests of the Congo nor the interests of this Organization.

IN THE ENSUING DEBATE over the next two days only Guinea and Mali among the Afro-Asians gave any support to the Soviet demand for Hammarskjöld's resignation. Representatives of such countries as the United Arab Republic and Yugoslavia declared that the Security Council and the General Assembly must share blame with the Secretary-General for mistakes and failures. The West maintained its solid backing for the Secretary-General. Outside the formal sessions negotiations were resumed in search of language that might command a majority and avoid a veto in a draft resolution to be sponsored by the Council's three Afro-Asian members, Ceylon, Liberia, and the UAR.

Meanwhile in Leopoldville Dayal learned that a number of Lumumba supporters had been secretly arrested and that at least six of them had been flown to Bakwanga in South Kasai, where they would be at the mercy of Kalonji and his Baluba supporters. Dayal and the Secretary-General immediately made strong representations to Kasavubu, Iléo, and Kalonji and informed the Security Council. On February 20, however, it was confirmed that all six had been summarily executed soon after their arrival.

Despite all the anarchy and brutalities that had prevailed for months in the Congo, the deaths of Lumumba, Okito, and Mpolo were the first political assassinations that had occurred. Now, within a few days, here were six more, also arranged in a cold-blooded manner by some of Kasavubu's men in Leopoldville. Western supporters of Kasavubu were horrified at these acts, as of course was the Secretary-General (next two following texts). The prompt reprisal executions by a firing squad in Stanleyville of fifteen Kasavubu and Mobutu supporters who had been held in prison for some time did not become known in New York until after the Security Council ended its meetings on February 21.

3. Letter to Kasavubu Protesting Secret Arrests and Deportation to Bakwanga of Political Opponents

NEW YORK   FEBRUARY 19, 1961

WE HAVE BEEN INFORMED by Mr. Dayal on February 18, in a report which I am circulating to the Security Council, that during the last week there has been a series of secret arrests in Leopoldville and elsewhere of persons of prominence in the political life of the country, followed by the deportation of these persons to Bakwanga, an area which through certain spokesmen has proclaimed that it does not consider itself to be under the jurisdiction of the Leopoldville authorities. The individuals deported include Messrs. Finant, Elengenza, Nzuzi, Lumbala, Yangara, Major Fataki, and possibly others.

Those known to have been arrested are alleged to be political opponents of the Leopoldville authorities. Moreover, it has been rumoured, although verification has not been possible, that several of the deported persons have been killed after their arrival in Bakwanga. In the light of the recent murder of Mr. Lumumba and his colleagues in Katanga, these arrests and deportations of political personalities cannot but give rise to the gravest concern.

The situation is one of the utmost seriousness and it is imperative that you, as the chief of state, take immediate action to bring about the return of these individuals and to permit them, with the cooperation of the United Nations Force, to obtain due protection as to their persons and their rights. It is obvious that even if there should be criminal charges against some of the individuals—I note, however, that to my knowledge no such charges have been presented, at least not in legally acceptable form—their secret and arbitrary arrests and transfers to South Kasai constitute a flagrant violation of the minimum rights guaranteed to the accused under the commonly accepted principles of law and human rights.

Security Council Official Records, Sixteenth Year, Supplement for January, February, and March 1961, document S/4727, annex III.

I am compelled to address this appeal to you in the strongest possible terms, particularly in view of the fact that my special representative has received no reply from Mr. Iléo and from Mr. Kalonji to his communications, urgently requesting information regarding the fate of the arrested persons and offering United Nations cooperation in providing for their security. I need hardly emphasize that acts of lawless violence such as those taken or feared in the cases mentioned are acts violating the basic principles for which the United Nations stands and shocking the conscience of the world. Those principles must be observed by any Member nation. I must also emphasize that such acts clearly make it impossible to carry on the task of political conciliation and stabilization to which you are committed.

DAG HAMMARSKJÖLD
Secretary-General

4. Statement in the Security Council After Summary Executions in Bakwanga

NEW YORK   FEBRUARY 20, 1961

ON FEBRUARY 16 the special representative, Mr. Dayal, reported to me about rumours that various personalities in Leopoldville had been deported to South Kasai. The rumours also indicated a possibility that the persons in question had been executed in Bakwanga. I requested immediately the fullest possible information and that protective steps should be taken so that no harm to the lives of the people concerned would occur.

Last Saturday night, February 18, I received the report of the findings of the special representative, which was immediately circulated. To the document are annexed three letters, to Mr. Iléo, Mr. Kalonji, and Mr. Kasavubu. I wish to draw attention especially to my letter to Mr. Kasavubu.

I have now to inform the Security Council that I have this morning received a short cable from the special representative informing me that the so-called Minister of Justice of South Kasai has just confirmed that

Finant, Fataki, Yangara, Muzungu, Elengenza, and Nzuzi have been executed. Mr. Dayal adds that he will transmit the text of the message with an additional report from himself.

I bring this news to the knowledge of the Council with revolt and shock. My words in the letter to Mr. Kasavubu indicate my reaction, but in the light of what has now been brought out, I would use much stronger language. It should be inconceivable for personalities with whom the United Nations has to deal—in a country to which it has tried its utmost to bring assistance—to flout in this way basic values upheld by the Organization. For the Organization, itself, it is humiliating and corroding to be confronted with such acts wherever they happen, but this reaction is reinforced when the Organization has also to recognize its powerlessness in the face of policies coldly disregarding its efforts and the principles on which they must be based.

It is for the Council to judge how this latest development, following the assassination of Mr. Lumumba and others, should influence United Nations action in relation to the Congo and the various groups in the Congo.

FOLLOWING IS THE TEXT of the resolution sponsored by Ceylon, Liberia, and the United Arab Republic as finally revised before its adoption in the early morning hours of February 21:

A

The Security Council,

Having considered the situation in the Congo,

Having learnt with deep regret the announcement of the killing of the Congolese leaders, Mr. Patrice Lumumba, Mr. Maurice Mpolo, and Mr. Joseph Okito,

Deeply concerned at the grave repercussions of these crimes and the danger of widespread civil war and bloodshed in the Congo and the threat to international peace and security,

Noting the report of the Secretary-General's special representative (S/4691) dated February 12, 1961, bringing to light the development of a serious civil war situation and preparations therefore,

1. *Urges* that the United Nations take immediately all appropriate measures to prevent the occurrence of civil war in the Congo, including arrangements for cease-fires, the halting of all military operations, the prevention of clashes, and the use of force, if necessary, in the last resort;

2. *Urges* that measures be taken for the immediate withdrawal and evacuation from the Congo of all Belgian and other foreign military and paramilitary personnel and political advisers not under the United Nations command, and mercenaries;

3. *Calls upon* all states to take immediate and energetic measures to prevent the departure of such personnel for the Congo from their territories, and for the denial of transit and other facilities to them;

4. *Decides* that an immediate and impartial investigation be held in order to ascertain the circumstances of the death of Mr. Lumumba and his colleagues and that the perpetrators of these crimes be punished;

5. *Reaffirms* the Security Council resolutions of July 14, July 22, and August 9, 1960, and the General Assembly resolution 1474 (ES-IV) of September 20, 1960, and reminds all states of their obligation under these resolutions.

B

The Security Council,

Gravely concerned at the continuing deterioration in the Congo, and the prevalence of conditions which seriously imperil peace and order, and the unity and territorial integrity of the Congo, and threaten international peace and security,

Noting with deep regret and concern the systematic violations of human rights and fundamental freedoms and the general absence of rule of law in the Congo,

Recognizing the imperative necessity of the restoration of parliamentary institutions in the Congo in accordance with the fundamental law of the country, so that the will of the people should be reflected through the freely elected Parliament,

Convinced that the solution of the problem of the Congo lies in the hands of the Congolese people themselves without any interference from outside and that there can be no solution without conciliation,

Convinced further that the imposition of any solution, including the formation of any government not based on genuine conciliation would, far from settling any issues, greatly enhance the dangers of conflict within the Congo and threat to international peace and security,

1. *Urges* the convening of the Parliament and the taking of necessary protective measures in that connection;

2. *Urges* that Congolese armed units and personnel should be reorganized and brought under discipline and control, and arrangements be made on impartial and equitable bases to that end and with a view to the elimination of any possibility of interference by such units and personnel in the political life of the Congo;

3. *Calls upon* all states to extend their full cooperation and assistance and take such measures as may be necessary on their part, for the implementation of this resolution.[1]

As a concession to the Soviet Union the resolution made no mention of the Secretary-General's responsibility for carrying out its provisions. The representatives of the United Kingdom, the United States, and other Western members of the Council announced they would vote for the resolution, despite some reservations, on the understanding that the Secretary-General's continuing role was implicit under the Charter and covered also by the resolution's reaffirmation of the earlier Council and Assembly resolutions of July 14 and 22, August 9 and September 20. They also said they understood that the authorization for "the use of force, if necessary, in the last resort" to prevent civil war was limited to preventing clashes between rival Congolese troops and did not extend to the use of force in order to promote a political settlement favorable to one side or another.

After the Soviet draft resolution had been defeated by 8 votes to 1 (the Soviet Union), with Ceylon and the United Arab Republic abstaining, the Afro-Asian resolution was adopted by 9 votes to none, with 2 abstentions (USSR and France).

A second Afro-Asian draft resolution condemning political assassinations, calling for measures to prevent their recurrence, and deciding on an impartial investigation of the crimes already committed failed to pass because of a dispute over a preambular paragraph which mentioned Leopoldville, Katanga, and South Kasai as the scenes of "atrocities and assassinations" but omitted mention of Stanleyville. As noted earlier, confirmed reports of the political executions in the latter city had not yet reached New York, but rumors were widespread and there had already been many instances of arbitrary arrests and brutalities. An amendment to replace the words "in Leopoldville, Katanga, and South Kasai" by "in various parts of the Congo" received 8 affirmative votes but was vetoed by the Soviet Union. The draft resolution itself then failed of adoption, there being 6 affirmative votes, none against and 5 abstentions, the latter including the United States, the United Kingdom, France, Turkey, and China.

After the voting the Secretary-General made the statement that follows.

[1] Security Council resolution 161 (1961) of February 21, 1961 (S/4741).

5. *Statement in the Security Council After Adoption of Afro-Asian Resolution*

NEW YORK   FEBRUARY 21, 1961

I STRONGLY WELCOME the first three-power resolution adopted today by the Council as giving a stronger and clearer framework for United Nations action although, as so often before, it does not provide a wider legal basis or new means for implementation.

I note the reaffirmation of previous resolutions which entrusted the Secretary-General with execution of the decisions of the Security Council in the Congo affairs. On that basis I shall urgently avail myself of the valuable assistance of the Advisory Committee. It is from its members, fifteen of whom are from African and Asian countries, that I will seek guidance in the implementation.

The resolution adds to the duties of the United Nations Force, and I am certain that the states backing it, many of which have troops in the Congo, fully realize that these duties will necessitate the strengthening of the Force by further generous contributions from their side. I do not believe that such additions to the troops—or at least their maintenance— will require renegotiation since I understand the reaffirmation of the earlier resolutions as clearly indicating that those additions to the troops would be on the same legal basis as previous contributions.

The second three-power draft resolution was not adopted, and I regret it. Its adoption would have strengthened the hand of the United Nations representatives in the Congo. However, I note that there has been no difference of opinion, if I understand the situation correctly, as regards the operative paragraphs. Under such circumstances I feel entitled to use those operative paragraphs with the full moral value which they have in our efforts in the Congo.

Thus I shall bring to the attention of those concerned the strong condemnation of unlawful arrests and other actions of a similar kind, and I shall also bring to their attention the wish of all members of the Council

Security Council Official Records, Sixteenth Year, 942nd meeting.

that an end be put immediately to such practices. And finally, as a matter of course, the standing instructions to the United Nations authorities in the Congo to take all possible measures to prevent occurrences of outrages will be reaffirmed and even, if possible, strengthened.

As regards the fourth point, the impartial investigation to determine responsibility, it will have to be done within the means of the Secretariat, or rather at the initiative of the Secretariat, but I see in the stand taken on operative paragraph 4 an acceptance of the fact that such an investigation be made.

I hope that the Council will bear with me if I say a word about some interventions which were addressed to me very personally and which, for that reason, seem to require a reaction from me on the record.

Speaking after the representative of the Soviet Union on February 15, I put on record what seem to me to be the main points regarding the relationship of the United Nations to the fate of Mr. Lumumba. The same representative has later renewed his personal attacks and he has, in this, been followed at the table by four nonmembers, as well as in some messages addressed to the Council.

This is not the time for detailed comments on these attacks—nor do I believe that there is much reason for such comments here—whatever the bitterness of the accusations, whatever the gross distortions on which they are based, whatever especially the unprecedented and immoderate language used and whatever, finally, the emotional impact of this language on the uninformed, to whom, of course, it is addressed.

Therefore, I shall only recall a couple of facts which usefully should be kept in mind together with those I mentioned in my intervention on February 15. Some have found it proper to label me the "organizer of the murder of Mr. Lumumba." Regarding the long series of developments finally leading to the tragedy, may I first refer to the fact that Mr. Lumumba, on November 7, made a statement in which, in unequivocal terms, he expressed his appreciation for the assistance of the United Nations and his confidence in the Secretary-General. With respect to later events, the arrest and detention and, subsequently, the transfer to Katanga, it does appear necessary for me to draw attention to certain facts which have been ignored.

The accusations addressed to me suggest that the action I took upon learning of Mr. Lumumba's arrest was inadequate. In fact, what must be implied is that I should have ordered the United Nations Force in the

Congo to take military initiative in order to liberate Mr. Lumumba from the custody of the Armée nationale congolaise at Thysville. But could there be any question that the use of such military force against the authorities in Thysville would have constituted a clear departure from the mandate and its clear Charter framework? What I should like to recall here is that this conclusion represents not merely my judgement but conforms to the views of most Member states. That this is so is demonstrated by the fact that seven Members—Ghana, India, Indonesia, Iraq, Morocco, the United Arab Republic, and Yugoslavia—introduced a draft resolution in the General Assembly on December 16, which would have had the Assembly urge "the immediate release of all political prisoners under detention . . . ." These Member states strongly desired the release of Mr. Lumumba and his colleagues, yet in their resolution they did not request the Secretary-General to take other measures than he had indeed already taken nor, *a fortiori*, did they authorize him to use the United Nations Force to effect their release. The proposed resolution "urged" the release, and did not go beyond that. In short, the seven states were in fact asking the General Assembly to add its authority in support of measures which I did take immediately, in order to exert the pressure of the United Nations on the authorities to accord to Mr. Lumumba his full legal rights, including the recognition of his parliamentary immunity and, of course, his release, unless generally accepted legal steps for a fair trial were taken within a short time.

When it became known that Mr. Lumumba and his colleagues had been transferred to Katanga and held *incommunicado*, again I took immediate action to urge the authorities concerned, and in particular Messrs. Kasavubu and Tshombé to return Mr. Lumumba and apply normal legal rules, with the implications I mentioned a moment ago. In addition, I immediately took the matter to the Advisory Committee on the Congo in order to ask them what, if any, further steps they would recommend.

At this meeting on January 20, the members of that Committee expressed their objections to the illegal detention of Mr. Lumumba, but laid emphasis on the need for steps for reconciliation and, in consequence, for calling on the authorities to release him. This led, from my side, to an urgent additional message to Mr. Kasavubu which certainly did not understate the unanimous view of the Advisory Committee—I referred this question to the members. What should be underscored at this stage is that the members of the Advisory Committee did not, at any time, propose that the Secretary-General take further action, specifically military action, against the Katanga authorities to bring about his release. While it was the unanimous view of these members that all possible pressure should be brought to bear on the responsible officials, it was not suggested that the Secretary-General was in a position to order military measures against the authorities for that purpose.

This attitude of the Member states most directly concerned with the Congo, and with the fate of Mr. Lumumba, coincided with the position of the Secretary-General. That this was so is not surprising, for it had always been clearly recognized that the resolutions of the Security Council, authorizing the United Nations Force to assist in the maintenance of law and order, did not constitute an "enforcement" measure calling for coercive military action against governmental authorities. The fact that the Council did not take any action under Article 41 and Article 42 of the Charter had been expressly pointed out to the Council at an earlier stage, and no government expressed any dissent.

It is telling that in the second three-power draft resolution considered by the Council today, there was a reference to the use of force which, obviously, was regarded by the sponsors as a new departure giving new rights, presumably with Article 42 as a basis. That being so, it is clear *a contrario* that such a right to military intervention to liberate prisoners detained by local authorities, *de facto* or *de jure*, was not considered as having existed in previous resolutions, and the draft thus confirmed the interpretation maintained so far.

The stand in the draft resolution, as well as the interpretation by the main organs of previous resolutions, therefore, supports the position that whatever differences there might be regarding the interpretation of the Charter it could hardly be doubted that military action by the United Nations to free prisoners charged with crime must be regarded as prohibited by the Charter except when such military action constitutes part of an enforcement measure and is expressly adopted by the Council under Chapter VII of the Charter.

The representative of Czechoslovakia in a speech on February 17 talked about my "procolonialist policies" and more specifically said that we had "condoned and abetted" the return of the Belgian colonialists to the Congo. It seems appropriate in this context simply to quote a couple of paragraphs of my letters to the Belgian government, and to Mr. Tshombé, of October 8, 1960, to which I have already briefly referred but which seem to have been forgotten. First is a short quotation from the letter to Mr. Tshombé:

> The dangers, as they appear at present, seem in my opinion to derive from three factors: the confused and disquieting situation which still prevails at Leopoldville, the continued presence of a considerable number of Belgian nationals—soldiers, paramilitary personnel and civilians—and, lastly, the unresolved constitutional conflict, threatening the unity of the Congo, which is symbolized by the name Katanga. Among these factors, I regard the last two as of crucial importance, even from the standpoint of the first: that is to say that, if we could fully circumscribe the Belgian factor and eliminate it—I meant, of course the military and political factor—and if we could lay the groundwork for a reconciliation between Katanga and the rest of the Territory of the Republic of the Congo, the situation at Leopoldville might very well be rectified.
>
> ... You will fully realize that if the Belgians also withdrew all their technicians, under whatever title they are now serving in the Congo, and if, in addition, they channelled all their assistance through the United Nations, the result would be a situation in which all the parties in the Congo would have to give urgent reconsideration to their policies regarding the future of the country. I am certain that, with that in view, you yourself would wish to review your policy, in view of the fact that Katanga might find itself cut off from all outside assistance, with the exception of what you could receive within the framework of the assistance furnished through the United Nations to the Republic of the Congo.

That should be read together with the following quotation from the *note verbale* sent simultaneously to the Government of Belgium, in which I discussed the resolution adopted by the General Assembly on September 20, 1960:

> On the basis of this conclusion, the Secretary-General would request the Belgian government to withdraw all the military, paramilitary or civil personnel which it has placed at the disposal of the authorities in the Congo and henceforth to follow the example of many other states by channelling all aid to the Congo, or to any authorities in the Congo, through the United Nations.

Certainly, this is the language and these are the demands of a colonialist "condoning and abetting" the return of Belgian colonizers to the Congo. As Mr. Kurka so rightly said, "Facts are stubborn things . . . you may distort them as you like, but you cannot get away from them."

And certainly this is the language of the man, whose collaboration with Mr. Tshombé was so spectacularly demonstrated by Mr. Zorin, with the picture showing that, in order to get the United Nations troops into Katanga and the Belgian troops out of Katanga, as requested by the Security Council, the Secretary-General had to deal with the man whose resistance he had to break, if the Council were to get its decisions implemented with all the necessary speed. A full record of the events was considered by the Council in August 1960. The conclusions now drawn from it are new. Even the implementation of a request of the Council can obviously now be held against me.

EFFORTS TO CARRY OUT THE SECURITY COUNCIL RESOLUTION OF FEBRUARY 21, 1961

As the Secretary-General had remarked to the Security Council after the vote, the February 21 resolution, while employing stronger and clearer language in some respects, did not provide "a wider legal basis or new means for implementation." Furthermore it came at a time when the UN position in the Congo was being further weakened by the withdrawal of contingents from the Force as well as by dissension among the African states and by worsening political conflicts among the rival Congolese authorities on the one hand and between each of them and ONUC on the other.

Hammarskjöld was undeterred by all this and engaged in a vigorous diplomatic offensive over the next weeks during which he directed a stream of letters and *notes verbales* to Belgium, Kasavubu, Tshombé, and various African governments. He mingled exhortation, explanation, and warning in this campaign, the first stage of which is given in the first of the following texts, his report of February 27 and later addenda. First reactions were very discouraging. Under the influence of their Belgian advisers Kasavubu and Tshombé had both immediately denounced the February 21 resolution as an attempt to impose a UN trusteeship on the Congo. The Belgian government also continued its evasions and excuses for delay on the question of withdrawing the Belgian military and political advisers. However, as we shall see, the tide began to turn in March.

1. Report to the Security Council on Steps Taken in Regard to Implementation

NEW YORK   FEBRUARY 27-MARCH 8, 1961

1. In pursuance of the statement which the Secretary-General made in the Security Council on February 21, 1961, following the adoption of the resolution on the Congo, the Secretary-General has consulted the Advi-

Security Council Official Records, Sixteenth Year, Supplement for January, February, and March 1961, documents S/4752 and Add. 1 and 4.

sory Committee on the Congo with regard to questions relating to the implementation of that resolution.

2. The members of the Advisory Committee, while asserting that the initiative with respect to the implementation of this resolution remained, as before, with the Secretary-General, expressed for the guidance of the Secretary-General their views concerning concrete steps to be initiated by him.

3. As to the urgent matters emanating from part A, operative paragraphs 2 and 3 of the resolution, the Secretary-General sent, on February 22, 1961, the day following the adoption of the resolution, a letter to the Government of Belgium which is reproduced in annex I of this report. The reply of the Government of Belgium was received on February 27, 1961; it is reproduced as annex II.

4. In further implementation of part A, paragraphs 2 and 3 of the resolution, the Secretary-General sent on February 23, 1961, to all Members of the United Nations, a letter, which is reproduced in annex III of this report. Thus far the Secretary-General has received no replies for transmission to the Security Council.

5. Concerning part A, paragraph 1 of the resolution, the Secretary-General, after consultation with the Advisory Committee, instructed the United Nations command in the Congo to take appropriate steps in the direction and in the spirit of the resolution, in respects indicated by the command itself, taking into account, on the one side, the availability of troops and the likely developments in that respect and, on the other side, the stands taken by the governments of Ethiopia, Sudan, and Tunisia, to the effect that they do not wish to become third parties in any conflict between opposing sides in the Congo.

6. For the purpose of securing the full cooperation of the Congo authorities in the implementation of this paragraph of the resolution, and also in order to prepare the groundwork for the implementation of the provisions of part B of the same resolution, the Secretary-General addressed, on February 27, 1961, a letter to the President of the Republic of the Congo which is reproduced in annex IV. The Secretary-General has also requested his special representative [in the Congo] to bring the substance of this letter to the immediate attention of other authorities in the Congo.

7. The Secretary-General has received from his special representative

in the Congo advice that the implementation of the resolution adopted by the Security Council would require a substantial increase in the strength of the Force under the United Nations command. The Secretary-General thereupon, on February 23, 1961, approached the Government of Morocco, which had previously announced the repatriation of its contingent from the United Nations Force—a repatriation which is not yet completed. The telegram is reproduced in annex V. He also approached the Government of Indonesia, which had previously requested that its contingent under the United Nations command should be repatriated upon completion of its six months' tour of duty. This telegram is reproduced in annex VI.

8. The Secretary-General further addressed to certain African states requests for troops to be attached to the United Nations command. These letters are reproduced in annex VII. The governments of Libya and Togo were not approached for this purpose, since they had previously informed the Secretary-General that they had no military units available for overseas service.

9. In the discussion relating to the implementation of part A, paragraph 4 of the Security Council resolution, it was the opinion of the members of the Advisory Committee that a certain lack of precision in the paragraph made "immediate" implementation, as decided by the Security Council, difficult to carry out. It was thought necessary that, as a first step, a panel of three independent judges—an African serving as chairman, an Asian, and a Latin American—be appointed to undertake an impartial investigation to ascertain the circumstances of the death of Mr. Lumumba and his colleagues. Members of the Advisory Committee wished, however, to give the matter further consideration and to undertake consultations. On the advice of the Committee, the Secretary-General addressed a telegram to the Acting President of the International Court of Justice, in his private capacity, for the purpose of securing names of suitable candidates. The Secretary-General wishes to inform the Security Council that as soon as the Advisory Committee has concluded this stage of the consideration of the question, the Security Council will be informed.

10. With reference to the discussion in the Security Council of a draft resolution relating to deportations and executions of Congolese political leaders, the Secretary-General sent a letter dated February 21, 1961 to Mr. Kasavubu, and requested his special representative to despatch simi-

lar messages to certain other Congolese leaders. The letter to the President of the Republic of the Congo is reproduced in annex VIII.

ANNEX I

Note Verbale *Dated February 22, 1961, to the Representative of Belgium*

The Secretary-General of the United Nations presents his compliments to the permanent representative of Belgium to the United Nations and has the honour to refer to the resolution S/4741 adopted by the Security Council on February 21, 1961, and in particular to part A, operative paragraphs 2 and 3 of that resolution, which read:

Urges that measures be taken for the immediate withdrawal and evacuation from the Congo of all Belgian and other foreign military and paramilitary personnel and political advisers not under the United Nations command, and mercenaries;

Calls upon all states to take immediate and energetic measures to prevent the departure of such personnel for the Congo from their territories, and for the denial of transit and other facilities to them.

The reports received by the Secretary-General from his special representative in the Congo indicate that there are in the Congo at present a considerable number of Belgian nationals who fall within the categories referred to in the resolution, namely, military and paramilitary personnel and political advisers not under the United Nations command, and mercenaries. The Belgian personnel in question include several hundred officers in the military and paramilitary forces of Katanga and South Kasai. There are in addition a number of Belgian political advisers attached to the authorities in these areas as well as those attached to Congolese officials in Leopoldville and certain other cities.

The terms of the above-mentioned paragraphs of the Security Council resolution are general in character, and addressed to all concerned. However, it is apparent from the reference to Belgian personnel and natural in the light of the facts just mentioned, that the request has particular reference to the Belgian government. As regards Belgian military and paramilitary personnel, it will be recalled that in previous communications the Secretary-General has pointed out that it must be assumed, in view of customary military regulations, that such personnel could not be serving in the armed forces or police of the local authorities without the assent, in one form or another, of the Belgian authorities.

The Belgian government will also in this connexion undoubtedly take full account of the legal character of the Security Council resolution of February 21, which, like the earlier resolutions on the Congo, must be regarded as a mandatory decision that all Members of the United Nations are legally bound to accept and carry out in accordance with Article 25 of the Charter. The juridical consequence is that all Member states concerned are under a legal obligation to adapt their national legislation to the extent necessary to give effect to the decision of the Council. In the circumstances and whatever the legal provisions thus far prevailing the Secretary-General must conclude that with respect to military personnel as well as with regard to Belgian political advisers in the Congo, the Government of Belgium will be able to take action to bring about their immediate withdrawal from the Congo.

In view of the peremptory character of the Security Council resolution in question and its immediate importance in the Congo crisis, the Secretary-General must now request, in keeping with the responsibility imposed on him by the Council, that the Belgian government take the steps called for by part A, paragraphs 2 and 3. In this regard and in the event of a positive response the Secretary-General is prepared to designate a senior officer of the Secretariat to meet immediately with representatives of your government in order to further the implementation of the resolution and to assist in obtaining information as to the specific details for the members of the Security Council and the other Members of the United Nations.

The Secretary-General desires to conclude by emphasizing once again the critical importance at this juncture of removing Belgian military personnel and political advisers from the Congo. Immediate and effective action by the Belgian government to this end is an indispensable condition for meeting the purposes of the resolution, which, it will be recalled, was adopted by the Security Council without a negative vote.

It is essential that the members of the Council be informed within the next few days of the specific steps that have been or will be taken, as well as any other measures that are legally possible, by the Government of Belgium to comply with the resolution. If the position of the Belgian government does not satisfy the requirements of the resolution this will require the immediate attention of the Security Council.

The Secretary-General would be obliged if the representative of Belgium would reply to this note at the earliest possible date.

Editor's Note—The Belgian government replied in *notes verbales* dated February 27 that the remaining Belgian military personnel at the Kamina and Kitona bases and certain other Belgian army officers made available to the Congolese authorities would be withdrawn in March. However it denied any responsibility for securing the withdrawal of individual Belgians serving in the Force publique or of Belgian civilian advisers and officials serving on the invitation of Congolese authorities. Hammarskjöld rejected this stand in *notes verbales* dated March 2 and 8 (see Add. 1. and 4. to this report).

[ANNEX II OMITTED]

ANNEX III
Letter Dated February 23, 1961, Addressed to All States Members of the Organization

The Secretary-General of the United Nations presents his compliments to the permanent representative . . . . . . and requests him to transmit this note to his government regarding the resolution adopted by the Security Council at its 942nd meeting, on February 20 and 21, 1961, a copy of which is attached.

In part A, operative paragraph 2, of the resolution, the Security Council "*Urges* that measures be taken for the immediate withdrawal and evacuation from the Congo of all Belgian and other foreign military and paramilitary personnel and political advisers not under the United Nations command, and mercenaries." Naturally, this paragraph addresses itself only to governments of those countries which have military and paramilitary personnel as well as political advisers and mercenaries in the Congo.

In part A, operative paragraph 3, the Council "*Calls upon* all states to take immediate and energetic measures to prevent the departure of such personnel for the Congo from their territories, and for the denial of transit and other facilities to them."

With reference to this paragraph, the representative of Liberia, one of the cosponsors of the draft which was subsequently adopted by the Council, stated it as an interpretation that the text should also be construed as applicable to matériel. This interpretation by one of the sponsors did not meet with any objection by any member of the Council.

In part B, operative paragraph 3, the Council "*Calls upon* all states to extend their full cooperation and assistance and take such measures as may be necessary on their part, for the implementation of this resolution."

Furthermore, the Council, in part A, operative paragraph 5, "reaffirms the Security Council resolutions of July 14, July 22, and August 9, 1960, and the General Assembly resolution 1474 (XV) of September 20, 1960, and reminds all states of their obligation under these resolutions."

Your government will undoubtedly take full account of the legal character of the Security Council resolution of February 21 which, like the other resolutions on the Congo, must be regarded as a mandatory decision that all Members of the United Nations are legally bound to accept and carry out in accordance with Article 25 of the Charter.

The Secretary-General wishes to bring to the notice of all Member states the relevant parts of the resolution adopted by the Security Council. He expects that the governments of states which are concerned will initiate, where applicable, suitable action with a view to giving effect to the provisions of the resolution of the Security Council, and requests them to inform him, for transmission to the Council, with regard to any actions taken.

DAG HAMMARSKJÖLD
Secretary-General

ANNEX IV
Letter Dated February 27, 1961, to the President of the Republic of the Congo (Leopoldville)

In a letter to you of February 21, 1961 [annex VIII], drawing attention to the strong position taken by the members of the Security Council on certain acts of political lawlessness and violence, I mentioned that I would revert to observations on the resolution adopted. You will have received it at once and, therefore, are well acquainted with its content, as appears also from statements through Mr. Iléo and through Mr. Bahizi. I shall later revert to questions of substance, but wish first to make some general observations, the weight and seriousness of which I am sure that you will fully appreciate.

The United Nations undertook last summer, at your request and that of the prime minister, Mr. Patrice Lumumba, a very heavy task. It did so in the interest of the Congolese people as a whole and indirectly in order to safeguard international peace and security. We who have been working for the Congo have, to the best of our understanding, done all we could within the limits set by the Charter, the mandate, and our limited resources to provide for its people a chance to develop its life in peace, harmony, and full independence. We have also done our best, in all directions, in order to safeguard the Congo against outside interference, irrespective of its source, and to protect its territorial integrity. In these various respects the Organization has had to strain its resources to the utmost. The result is that the work of the United Nations has been kept down to a difficult holding operation while, with loyalty and cooperation, it could long ago have been a full success in the best and widest interest of the people of the Congo and of the world. The deterioration and the complications have continued up to and beyond the point of the assassination of various political leaders; I need not repeat to you here the feelings to which this has given rise and the serious jeopardy in which the United Nations has been put by the failure of those with whom we have had to deal to heed our demands and warnings. May I, in this context, remind you of the many approaches I made to you at the time of the arrest of Mr. Lumumba and later of his transfer—approaches which echoed strong convictions and deep concern which you have found expressed also in communications from the Special Representative.

This is the background against which one has to judge the resolution of the Security Council of February 21. This is what gives it its utter seriousness, representing, as it does, a unanimous decision to cut through all that so far has hampered the United Nations effort. The resolution is in this respect the strongest and most decisive expression of the concern of the Security Council to maintain standards, without which sound and harmonious political development is impossible, and to put an end to conditions which threaten the world community and the United Nations, even as they represent a mortal danger to the Congo itself.

It is my evaluation of the stage reached that the world is no longer willing nor in a position to accept the consequences of the continued splits, abetted by outside interests, which divide the country. Reconciliation on a nation-wide scale is, therefore, imperative, and anyone in a responsible position refusing to make his full and selfless contribution to such a reconciliation, shoulders a heavy responsibility. But further, we are now at a point where even the sincere wish of the representatives of the Organization to take fully into account views and wishes of the leaders of the Congo, and to respect fully what follows from the stand of the United Nations troops, as a foreign group invited to the country, cannot be permitted to hamper effective efforts to prevent developments towards civil war and to counteract all forces which upset law and order. The Organization, in taking this attitude, is not acting out of any wish to exercise power to establish itself; it is therefore shocking to see the repeated allegations of a desire in the United Nations to infringe upon the sovereignty of the Congo—most recently repeated even by you—or even to establish some kind of "trusteeship," when the aim of the Organization is the opposite one, namely, to give to the sovereignty and independence of the country its full meaning and to eliminate any reason for others to try to exercise their influence over it.

In order to render effective the operation in its present phase, I have appealed for reinforcements for the United Nations Force, and I have reason to believe in a quick response. Behind the words and the will of the Security Council, therefore, stands not only the firm determination of the representatives of the Organization, but also the strength needed. I am sure that you will agree that it would be idle to expect world opinion to accept things to continue as they have been. Either the will manifested by the world community will be respected, or chaos will come about.

With these words, which I hope convey to you the full weight that has to be given to the position of the Security Council, to our determination to carry through and to our means to do so, I turn to some comments on the various points of the resolution.

In the words of the resolution itself, the solution of the problem of the Congo lies in the hands of the Congolese themselves without any interference from the outside, and there can be no solution without conciliation. Action by the United Nations—and this is a point which I wish to emphasize—is precisely intended to create the conditions in which such a solution can be achieved.

No solution can be expected in a situation of developing civil war, with armed groups engaged in partisan clashes and seeking a military solution to political goals. Preventing the further deterioration of the situation in this respect must clearly be the task of the United Nations command, especially in view of the fact that armed groups have frequently tended to escape from the control of any authorities and to engage in private warfare. The question is one of preventive and pacifying measures, not coercion, but those engaged in these measures on behalf of the United Nations cannot allow themselves to be forcibly deterred from carrying them out. Therefore, I feel confident in proceeding on the assumption that the United Nations can count on the cooperation of all Congolese authorities concerned, military and civilian, in arranging cease-fires, halting all military operations, and preventing clashes. This must surely be a common goal of all those who feel that conciliation is the necessary approach to the country's political problems.

Special attention was devoted in the Security Council debate to the problem of the immediate withdrawal and evacuation of all Belgian and other foreign military and paramilitary personnel, political advisers, and mercenaries. This is not an attempt to deprive the Congo of the technical assistance which it admittedly requires; nor could it be further removed from any attempt to impose an alleged "trusteeship" over a Member state. It is rather the expression of the Council's determination to deal with foreign military and political elements which have repeatedly tended, not only to frustrate the goals of the United Nations, but also to foster secessionist tendencies in the Congo and create grave international political complications for the country. You may rest assured that the United Nations will continue to place its facilities at the disposal of the Republic to assist in the recruitment of the necessary technical and other trained personnel.

The problem dealt with in part A, operative paragraph 3, of the resolution will be tackled immediately, and the active cooperation of all states concerned, especially Belgium, is being urgently sought. The Security Council will be kept fully informed of steps taken by all those concerned to ensure in this manner that the Congo's problems shall be solved by the Congolese themselves, without foreign interference. In this connection you will, I am sure, have noted the peremptory terms in which both this paragraph and the related paragraph 3 are couched. It is my firm hope that I shall in the very near future learn of urgent and comprehensive steps being taken by you in regard to paragraph 2.

Part A, paragraph 4, of the resolution has acquired additional significance in view of the fact that political deportations and assassinations have continued after Mr. Lumumba's death. It is my duty to draw to your attention that the Council's decision in this respect sprang from a unanimous feeling of international concern and revulsion, and that the Council is entitled to expect that full cooperation will be forthcoming from all Congolese authorities. This should include all necessary facilities and assistance, such as the making available of material evidence and of witnesses, so that those responsible shall be duly punished.

I am of course aware of your continued and declared readiness to abide by the provisions of, and United Nations actions under, the resolutions adopted by the Security Council on July 13 and 22 and August 9, 1960, and by the General Assembly on September 20. The importance and continued validity of these resolutions is undiminished since they were reaffirmed in the Security Council's resolution of February 21, even while the scope of United Nations action as delineated in them has been extended. But the goal of the United Nations remains the achievement of an independent and united Congo, free from foreign interference, and whose sovereignty, unity, and territorial integrity will be secure.

In regard to part B, paragraph 1, urging the convening of Parliament and the taking of necessary protective measures in that connection, it is, I believe, understood that the convening of Parliament will be undertaken in accordance with the provisions of the Loi fondamentale. That law imposes an obligation upon specified Congolese authorities to initiate speedy action in this direction—an obligation not only in regard to the world at large. I may personally add that such action is essential, if the Congo desires to emerge as a democratic nation. The United Nations command will, of course, undertake the protection of all parliamentarians, irrespective of political affiliation.

The provision of part B, paragraph 2, which urges that Congolese armed units and personnel should be reorganized and brought under discipline and control, and arrangements be made on impartial and equitable bases to that end and with a view to the elimination of any possibility of interference by such units and personnel in the political life of the Congo, is, of course, a logical corollary to the provisions of part A, paragraph 1. It is in my opinion intolerable for the internal, as well as external, security of any state to have its security forces act as the chief agents in the political life of the country; even more intolerable is a situation in which armed units act on their own initiative, as has only too frequently occurred in the last six months or so. I am familiar with the argument that the units under the control of General Mobutu are legal units of the Republic of the Congo, whereas those owing allegiance to other authorities now functioning in the Congo are not. You are no doubt familiar with the statements which have been made which reverse the position and give legal status only to the authorities in Stanleyville. For the United Nations, the task is of course described by the resolution alone. I am personally convinced, as I have stated in the Security Council, that no political conciliation is possible without the elimination of armed units from the political life. I may add that only those who hope for a military solution in the Congo—in my view an indefensible stand—and consequently wish to impress their own will on the people by force are likely to express themselves in opposition to this provision of the resolution. I trust that the United Nations can count on your support and thus lay the foundation for a Congo army which, like that of other democratic countries, serves the country and no political or geographical sections thereof.

DAG HAMMARSKJÖLD
Secretary-General

ANNEX V
Telegram Dated February 23, 1961, to H.M. the King of Morocco

You have no doubt noted the resolution concerning the Congo adopted by the Security Council on February 21, 1961. As you know, this important resolution establishes new responsibilities for the United Nations Force in the Congo. After consulting the Advisory Committee on the Congo, I shall soon take the liberty of communicating to you a request that Morocco reexamine its attitude as regards its contribution to the United Nations Force. Such a reexamination is necessary in view of the new requirements which the resolution has created, and the resolution will, I hope, provide a new basis for Morocco's cooperation in the efforts of the United Nations. I should be grateful if, pending receipt and study of this communication, your Majesty would consider postponing the departure of the Moroccan contingents which are still part of the United Nations Force in the Congo.

ANNEX VI
Telegram Dated February 23, 1961, to the President of the Republic of Indonesia

You will no doubt have taken note of the resolution of the Security Council regarding the Congo adopted on February 21, 1961. As you know, this important resolution establishes new tasks for the United Nations Force in the Congo. After consultations with the Advisory Committee, I shall shortly take the liberty to address to you a request for the reconsideration of the stand of Indonesia on its contribution to the

United Nations Force, called for in the light of the new needs to which the resolution has given rise, and, I hope, giving a new basis for the collaboration of Indonesia in the United Nations effort. Pending the receipt and consideration of this communication, and in view of the present weakness of the Force in the face of new demands, I would ask you to consider delaying for a short time the departure of the Indonesian troops which form part of the United Nations Force in the Congo.

ANNEX VII

*Text of Message Dated February 24, 1961, to Certain African States
Concerning the Need for Troops and the Function of the Force*

(With variations for individual countries)

I know your deep concern for the effectiveness of the United Nations operations in the Congo and for the attainment of the United Nations objectives of peace and stability in that country. I wish, therefore, to bring directly to your attention certain considerations affecting the United Nations Force in the Congo which assume a new significance in the light of recent developments.

At present the Force commands a strength of approximately 17,500 all ranks, comprising twenty battalions. That strength is threatened with an early reduction to some 14,500 officers and men, or about fifteen battalions, if the decisions of the governments of Indonesia and Morocco to repatriate their troops without replacement are implemented.

In view of the new demands on the Force envisaged in the resolution adopted without negative vote by the Security Council on February 21, 1961, the reduction of the strength of the Force at this time would be paradoxical and most inopportune. Operative paragraph 1 of part A of that resolution "*Urges* that the United Nations take immediately all appropriate measures to prevent the occurrence of civil war in the Congo, including arrangements for cease-fires, the halting of all military operations, the prevention of clashes, and the use of force, if necessary, in the last resort." In all such measures, the presence of a strong United Nations Force is indispensable. Thus, the United Nations Force must continue to have a sufficient number of troops deployed to prevent armed conflict and to protect life and property. The threats, now increasing, of civil war must be met; the withdrawal and evacuation of all Belgian and other foreign military, paramilitary personnel, and mercenaries in the Congo will have to be arranged; the ingress of further military personnel and material to the Congo has to be checked upon and stopped. All this requires more troops.

In order to meet the needs created by the new resolution, the military command of the Force perceives a required strength for it numbering about 23,000 or twenty-five battalions.

You will agree, I am sure, that the countries of Africa should be looked to principally for the new components needed by the Force. Thus, I trust that it will be possible for your government to respond favorably to this new appeal for troops to serve in the Congo, [and to provide at an early date a contingent of your troops of not less than a battalion in strength. (*All African states except Ethiopia, Ghana, Liberia, Morocco, Nigeria, Sudan, and Tunisia*)] [and to provide an addition to your contingent of a battalion or more. (*Ethiopia, Ghana, Liberia, Nigeria, Sudan, and Tunisia*)] [and to permit the Moroccan contingent to remain in the Congo and if possible to reinforce it; but as the minimum, to defer for some time its repatriation. (*Morocco*)]

Permit me, in this context, to add a few thoughts about the function of the Force. Previous contributions of troops to the United Nations Force have been based on the Security Council resolutions of July 14 and 22, 1960, the latter one supplemented by explanations regarding the character and mandate of the Force contained in my report to the Security Council of July 18, 1960, which was commended by the Council in the resolution of July 22, 1960, and thus—together with later stands taken by the Security Council and the General Assembly—represents an authoritative interpretation of the position of the United Nations. New contributions in troops obviously have the same basis, but must also take into account the resolution of February 21, which, without any change of the United Nations mandate, widens its scope and application. I draw attention especially to the reference to the use of force for prevention of civil war, "as an ultimate resort." Regarding the interpretation of this last mentioned clause, I have to refer to the debate that took place in the Council.

However, I may here draw attention to the attitude of some governments of African states, contributing considerable elements to the Force. Three governments in that position have made it clear that they cannot permit their units to become parties to an armed conflict in the Congo.

[As you have said in a message to me: "The United Nations Forces in the Congo must not be found third party to any dispute which might arise." (*Ethiopia*)]

[From a statement of Mr. Adeel, I understand that you share this view. (*Sudan*)]

[As you have said in a message to me: "In any case the Tunisian government has no intention of engaging one or other of the parties concerned." (*Tunisia*)]

Without intending this to be an interpretation of the relevant clause in the resolution and with a view only to assisting in the clarification of the assumptions on which governments base their contribution, I would like to make the following observations on the positions to which I have just referred.

The latest resolution, adopted by the Security Council, does not seem to me to derogate from the position that United Nations troops should not become parties to armed conflict in the Congo. The basic intention of the resolution is, in my opinion, the taking of all appropriate measures for the purposes mentioned, resort being had to force only when all other efforts such as negotiation, persuasion, or conciliation were to fail. If, following such efforts—or measures taken in support of their result—United Nations troops engaged in defensive action, when attacked while holding positions occupied to prevent a civil-war risk, this would not, in my opinion, mean that they became a party to a conflict; while the possibility of becoming such a party would be open, were troops to take the initiative in an armed attack on an organized army group in the Congo.

If the position taken by the governments referred to above, as I believe, does not derogate from the stand taken by the Security Council in the resolution, and if those governments agree with the distinction just made, this distinction would obviously have to be observed in any instructions that have to be given to the troops by the United Nations command.

[As you have yourself raised this question, I would appreciate your guidance in the form of comments on the observations just made. *(Ethiopia, Sudan, and Tunisia)*]

That I address you on this general subject and to this length is a measure of the gravity of the situation and the urgency of the United Nations need. I would appreciate a reply at your earliest convenience.

DAG HAMMARSKJÖLD
Secretary-General

ANNEX VIII

Letter Dated February 21, 1961, to the President of the Republic of the Congo (Leopoldville)

You are certainly aware of the Security Council's consideration of recent arrests, deportations, and executions of political personalities in the Congo. I shall send a further communication regarding the resolution adopted by the Council, but I at once wish to draw your attention urgently to another resolution which was not adopted by the Security Council but which is of the greatest significance and deserves serious consideration.

The nonadoption of the resolution was due to a difficulty in drafting, but does not affect in any way the substance of the text submitted to the Council. It is clear from the discussion that all the members of the Council supported the essential parts of the text and that these may be considered as expressing *de facto* the unanimous views of the Council, including of course those of its permanent members.

The draft resolution to which I refer was based on the report concerning the assassination of Mr. Finant and other personalities in Southern Kasai; they had been deported from Leopoldville after being held in detention, in some cases for very long periods of time.

In the parts of this draft resolution which may be considered as representing their unanimous views, the members of the Council, profoundly shocked "at the continuance of large-scale assassinations of political leaders in complete disregard of human rights and fundamental freedoms, world public opinion, and the Charter of the United Nations, strongly condemn the unlawful arrests, deportations, and assassinations of political leaders of the Congo." In addition, the members of the Council call upon "all concerned in the Congo immediately to put an end to such practices" and call upon "the United Nations authorities in the Congo to take all possible measures to prevent the occurrence of such outrages including, if necessary, the use of force as a last resort."

I am sure you understand the extreme seriousness of this reaction, in particular the sharp condemnation of acts like those which were the immediate cause of the Council's concern. That the Council thereby condemns what has already happened is one thing; what is more important for the future is of course the clear-cut attitude unanimously taken by the members of the Council with regard to such acts. This attitude implies a unanimous decision that such acts should be considered serious crimes at the international level also.

I have nothing to add, in my capacity as Secretary-General, to the views of the members of the Council as expressed in the parts of the text to which I have referred. I share them personally with the strongest conviction. I therefore deem it my duty to bring these reactions to your attention in the firm hope that you will bear them fully in mind and accordingly comply immediately and entirely with the demand that an end be put to such acts. Although the draft resolution was not adopted, any repetition of such acts, wherever they may occur in the Congo, cannot but entail the gravest consequences for those responsible for them. In any case, I am certain that you will consider it your manifest duty to adopt in their entirety the standards which have now been so clearly expressed. That means, of course, not only that you will not excuse such acts in any way and will not be a party to them, but that you will at once take effective measures to prevent their repetition. With regard to this last point, you will be expected to see to it that appropriate penalties are devised and firmly applied to those responsible for such crimes.

I should be grateful if you would reply to this letter through my special representative at Leopoldville, so that I can report on your reactions and those of other personalities in the Congo to whom I am sending a similar communication.

DAG HAMMARSKJÖLD
Secretary-General

DOCUMENT S/4752/ADD. 1

Subsequent to the publication of this report and of the correspondence annexed to it (especially annexes I, II, IV, and VIII), the Secretary-General dispatched the following communications after consultation with the Advisory Committee on the Congo.

I. Note verbale *dated March 2, 1961, to the Representative of Belgium*

The Secretary-General of the United Nations presents his compliments to the Permanent Representative of Belgium to the United Nations and has the honour to acknowledge the receipt of the *notes verbales* dated February 27 [S/4752, annex II].

The Secretary-General takes note of the Belgian government's statement as to its intention, expressed before receiving the Secretary-General's letter, to "collaborate for the successful outcome of the United Nations action for the restoration of order and prosperity in the Congo." He therefore feels entitled to voice the firm hope that the indications, in that letter, of measures required for the implementation of the Security Council's resolution of February 21, 1961, will be fully accepted by the Government of Belgium, which surely is aware of the peremptory and unconditional nature of the Security Council's decision. He hopes that indications in the Belgian government's note as to reservations in the views it holds about the resolution will not be permitted by it to hinder or delay full compliance with it, although the measures indicated in its present reply, in the view of the Secretary-General, fall short of such compliance. In view, moreover, of the urgency of implementation, the Secretary-General hopes to receive, without delay, information as to the dates envisaged by the Government of Belgium for the prompt and unconditional implementation of the various provisions of the resolution that are applicable to, or require action from, that government. The Secretary-General also hopes to receive precise information as to the steps taken in implementation of the resolution.

As a matter of clarification with reference to a question raised by the Permanent Representative in his first note of February 27, the Secretary-General wishes to point out that the provisions of the resolution refer to "Belgian and other foreign" personnel to be withdrawn and evacuated, and that accordingly such withdrawal and evacuation obviously have to be implemented without any discrimination as to nationality.

The Secretary-General further wishes to assure the Permanent Representative that he is keenly aware of the rightful concern of foreign governments for the security of their nationals who are in the Congo on legitimate business. ONUC has been given appropriate instructions in this respect, and these will be implemented, for the sake of the security of Congolese and non-Congolese alike, with all the vigour permitted under the broadened United Nations mandate pursuant to the Security Council resolution.

The allegation in the Belgian government's note to the effect that Mr. Dayal, the Secretary-General's special representative in the Congo, has made "inaccurate" or "gratuitous" statements in his reports, or has inaccurately analysed responsibilities for the difficulties encountered by the United Nations in the execution of its task, is noted with regret by the Secretary-General, who must emphatically reject it as baseless. The Secretary-General, assumes full responsibility for Mr. Dayal's execution of his assignment, which has been carried out consistently in thorough conformity with the Secretary-General's instructions, the Charter, and the mandate of the Security Council.

The Secretary-General has examined the views of the Belgian government about foreign political advisers, and regrets that he is unable to accept the position that methods of selection can be invoked to justify, on the part of the Government of Belgium, a claim of inability to control its nationals in such posts, whatever the procedures under which they may have been appointed to them. After consultations with his Advisory Committee, the Secretary-General maintains that bilateral arrangements for the placement of Belgian officials and agents under the provision of article 250 of the Loi fondamentale cannot override the obligations of Belgium under the peremptory decisions of the Security Council for the maintenance of international peace and security, calling for the withdrawal and evacuation of the Belgian nationals specified in the Security Council resolution. The applicability of Article 103 of the Charter in this respect will assuredly have been noted by the Government of Belgium.

With regard to part A, operative paragraph 2, of the resolution in respect of which the Security Council, as the Government of Belgium is aware, urged "immediate" implementation, the Secretary-General has examined carefully the comments of the Permanent Representative concerning the three categories of military and paramilitary personnel under (a), (b), and (c).

As regards group (a), the Secretary-General wishes to recall that under the provisions of part A, operative paragraph 1, of the resolution, which urges immediate measures to prevent civil war in the Congo, including arrangements for cease-fires, the halting of all military operations, the prevention of clashes, and the use of force, if necessary, in the last resort, ONUC is prepared to assume legitimate and necessary protective tasks. The United Nations is further initiating steps to be taken in conjunction with the Congolese authorities concerned for the replacement and relief, to the extent necessary, of the Belgian officers and noncommissioned officers. On the other hand, such action by the United Nations derives from its own responsibilities in the Congo, and should in no way be construed as suggesting that compliance by Belgium with its obligations under the resolution would be conditional on such United Nations action.

As regards group (b), the Secretary-General notes that steps are already being taken by the Belgian military authorities to recall such personnel to Belgium. He must assume that these steps will be undertaken forthwith so as to comply with the Security Council's request for "immediate withdrawal and evacuation."

As regards group (c), the Secretary-General has taken note of the steps listed in the two *notes verbales* of the representative of Belgium. It is imperative that the measures envisaged are taken with all the efficiency and speed called for by the resolution. On the other hand, the Security Council's requirement is not to be construed as being applicable solely "to the extent that some [of these persons] still have military obligations in Belgium." All Belgian and other foreign mercenaries are covered, and it is the firm position of the United Nations that, in the circumstances of the present threat to peace and security, as declared by the Security Council, a Member state should take immediate measures to the full extent of its power to bring about the withdrawal and evacuation of its nationals.

The Secretary-General has noted the readiness of the Belgian government to receive the senior official, whom the Secretary-General proposes to send to enter in contact with that government. It is the conviction of the Secretary-General that in the implementation of the Security Council resolution problems are likely to arise which, in view of that resolution's urgent terms and the requirements of immediate and speedy action, can only be resolved through direct contact on this level. Measures will have to be devised which will be both detailed and effective, and the United Nations must and will be ready to extend all the assistance it can to ensure that the resolution will be translated into reality.

This official will, *inter alia*, have the responsibility for arrangements under which the United Nations can be kept fully and currently informed of progress achieved in the implementation of the Security Council resolution. The Secretary-General expects to name this official shortly.

In addition to measures to be undertaken by the Government of Belgium in its own behalf, however, there is other action which lies within its power and the importance of which, for the speedy implementation of the resolution, is apparent. This refers to the use of the Belgian government's influence with the authorities in the Congo, and with economic groups and institutions which have played no minor role in the developments in various parts of the Congo, so as to ensure that all the relevant provisions of the Security Council's resolution may be carried out promptly and fully by all concerned.

II. Letter dated March 2, 1961, to the President of the Congo
(Leopoldville)

With further reference to the letter which I had the honour to address to you on February 27 in connection with the implementation of the resolution adopted by the Security Council on February 21, I wish to draw to your attention certain specific points relating to the implementation of part A, operative paragraphs 2 and 3, which, as you know, concern other governments as well as the Republic of the Congo.

In pursuance of the Council's resolution I addressed on February 22, 1961, to the Government of Belgium a letter which has now been published as a United Nations document. I hereby wish to draw your attention to this letter, as well as to the reply sent by the representative of Belgium on February 27, 1961, which has likewise been published. Copies of these documents are attached for your convenience. I wish to draw to your special attention, however, the further communication which I addressed to the Government of Belgium, dated March 2, 1961, a copy of which is also attached.

May I first bring to your notice the Belgian government's comments on the officers and noncommissioned officers whom it had made available to the former Force publique before July 1, 1960, under article 250 of the Loi fondamentale. The Government of Belgium states that it "asks" that the Congolese authorities "shall relieve these officers and noncommissioned officers from their tasks as soon as the latter can be assumed with equal effectiveness, and in agreement with those authorities, by the United Nations forces."

Under provisions of the Security Council resolution urging measures for the prevention of civil war, the halting of all military operations, the prevention of clashes, and the use of force, if necessary, as a last resort (part A, paragraph 1), ONUC is prepared to make available within the required limits to the Armée nationale congolaise personnel to assume legitimate and necessary protective functions. Having further regard to other provisions of the resolution, urging that Congolese armed units and personnel should be reorganized and brought under discipline and control and removed from interference in the Congo's political life, you will appreciate, I trust, that in connection with the implementation of this provision, any reasons that may have been thought to stand in the way of the relief of Belgian and other foreign personnel, not under the United Nations, should be recognized as having fallen away.

In the case of officers and noncommissioned officers, who, members of the Belgian Army until the time when they were made available to the Congolese authorities, after July 1, 1960, to assist the officers of the former Force publique in their task of officering and training—you will have noted that "steps are being taken by the Belgian military authorities to recall them to Belgium." It must clearly be assumed that you will assist so that this provision will be implemented immediately.

There are, finally, the mercenaries recruited by various Congolese authorities in the Congo, in Belgium, or abroad. You will have noted the statement of the Belgian government that it has no interest in these nationals and disapproves of their venture. According to the note, the Government of Belgium indicated that persons in this category who have military obligations in Belgium will be requested to return; that recruitment will be stopped, and that proceedings will be instituted against promoters of recruitment who have contravened the law. I wish it to be noted that the enclosed *note verbale,* dated March 2, to the Government of Belgium makes it clear that this interpretation of the Belgian government has not been accepted as in conformity with the Security Council resolution.

An examination of the resolution of the Security Council will make it clear that, in addition to the steps to be taken by the Government of Belgium and, where applicable, by other foreign countries, urgent measures are likewise required of the Congolese authorities. The United Nations, which fully expects that all necessary action to comply with the resolution will be duly and speedily taken by all concerned, is prepared to assist in the implementation of that resolution within the terms of its strengthened mandate.

In this respect, and as a first step, I hereby request you to make immediately available to the United Nations representative accurate and comprehensive information concerning personnel in the Congo under the authority of Leopoldville who fall under the provisions of the Security Council resolution. Such information will also assist in assessing the personnel needs required to replace prohibited personnel.

I further request you to advise the United Nations representative at the earliest possible moment what steps will be taken under your authority to comply with the Security Council resolution, including time limits where applicable, and to continue to keep the United Nations representative informed of progress in implementation until the programme is promptly completed.

The above procedures should, of course, also be made to apply to the political advisers who, under the Security Council resolution, must likewise be withdrawn and evacuated, and the United Nations is prepared in this connection to extend similar assistance to the Congolese authorities.

DAG HAMMARSKJÖLD
Secretary-General

*III. Message dated March 2, 1961, addressed to Mr. Tshombé through
the special representative of the Secretary-General in the Congo*

I have previously drawn your attention to the fact that on February 21, 1961, the Security Council adopted a resolution in regard to the Congo. You will recall that in part A, operative paragraph 2, of this resolution the Council: "*Urges* that measures be taken for the immediate withdrawal and evacuation from the Congo of all Belgian and foreign military and paramilitary personnel and political advisers not under the United Nations command, and mercenaries." In view of the importance of this paragraph for the paragraph just quoted, I also quote part A, paragraph 3: "*Calls upon* all states to take immediate and energetic measures to prevent the departure of such personnel for the Congo from their territories, and for the denial of transit and other facilities to them."

In pursuance of this resolution I addressed on February 22, 1961, to the Government of Belgium a letter which has now been published as a United Nations document. I hereby wish to draw your urgent attention to this letter, as well as to the reply sent by the representative of Belgium on February 27, 1961, which has likewise been published. Copies of these documents are attached for your convenience. I wish to draw to your special attention, however, the further communication which I addressed to the Government of Belgium on March 2, 1961, a copy of which is also attached.

May I first bring to your notice the Belgian government's comments on the officers and noncommissioned officers whom, before July 1, 1960, it had made available to the former Force publique under article 250 of the Loi fondamentale. The Government of Belgium states that it "asks" that the Congolese authorities—and this includes the authorities of Katanga—"shall relieve these officers and noncommissioned officers from their tasks as soon as the latter can be assumed with equal effectiveness, and in agreement with those authorities, by the United Nations forces."

Under the provisions of the Security Council resolution urging measures for the prevention of civil war, the halting of all military operations, the prevention of clashes, and the use of force, if necessary, as a last resort (part A, paragraph 1), ONUC is prepared to make available within the required limits personnel to assume legitimate and necessary protective functions. Having further regard to other provisions of the resolution, urging that Congolese armed units and personnel should be reorganized and brought under discipline and control and removed from interference in the Congo's political life, you will appreciate, I trust, that in connection with the implementation of this provision any reasons that may have been thought to stand in the way of the relief of Belgian and other foreign personnel not under the United Nations should be recognized as having fallen away.

In the case of officers and noncommissioned officers who were members of the Belgian army until the time when they were made available to the Congolese authorities, after July 1, 1960, to assist the officers of the former Force publique in their task of officering and training—you will have noted that "steps are being taken by the Belgian military authorities to recall them to Belgium." It must clearly be assumed that you will assist so that this provision will be implemented immediately and fully.

There are, finally, the mercenaries recruited by various Congolese authorities in the Congo, in Belgium, or abroad. You will have noted the statement of the Belgian government that it has no interest in these nationals and disapproves of their venture. According to the note, the Government of Belgium indicates that persons in this category who have military obligations in Belgium will be requested to return; that recruitment will be stopped, and that proceedings will be instituted against promoters of recruitment who have contravened the law. I wish it to be noted that the enclosed communication, dated March 2, to the Government of Belgium makes it clear that this interpretation of the Belgian government has not been accepted as in conformity with the Security Council resolution.

An examination of the resolution of the Security Council will make it clear that, in addition to the steps to be taken by the Government of Belgium and, where applicable, by other foreign countries, urgent measures are likewise required of the Congolese authorities, including those of Katanga. The United Nations, which fully expects that all necessary action to comply with the resolution will be duly and speedily taken by all concerned, is prepared to assist in the implementation of that resolution within the terms of its strengthened mandate.

In this respect, and as a first step, I hereby request you to make immediately available to the United Nations representative accurate and comprehensive information concerning personnel in Katanga who fall under the provisions of the Security Council resolution. Such information will also assist in assessing the personnel needs required to replace prohibited personnel.

I further request you to advise the United Nations representative at the earliest possible moment what steps will be taken under your authority to comply with the Security Council resolution, including time limits where applicable, and to continue to keep the United Nations representative informed of progress in implementation until the programme is promptly completed.

The above procedure should, necessarily, also be made to apply to the political advisers who, under the Security Council resolution, must likewise be withdrawn and evacuated, and the United Nations is prepared in this connection to extend similar assistance to the Congolese authorities.

DAG HAMMARSKJÖLD
Secretary-General

DOCUMENT S/4752/ADD. 4

Note Verbale *Dated March 8, 1961, to the Representative of Belgium*

The Secretary-General of the United Nations presents his compliments to the Permanent Representative of Belgium to the United Nations and has the honour to acknowledge receipt of his *note verbale* dated March 4, 1961. The Secretary-General wishes to state that the United Nations continues to adhere to the position clearly set out in the resolution adopted by the Security Council on February 21, 1961, concerning the implementation of which he has already addressed several communications dated February 22, February 23, and March 2 to the representative of Belgium.

The Secretary-General notes with regret that in the latest note from the representative of Belgium there are again indications which allow of some doubts about whether the Belgian government is fully prepared to implement some of the provisions explicitly laid down in the Security Council resolution. It is clear that only if the resolution is implemented fully and promptly will it be possible to consider that the obligations imposed by the Security Council resolution are being carried out. The Secretary-General therefore deems it necessary to express the firm hope that, whatever views may have been expounded, the Belgian government will, as a matter of urgency, formulate and carry out vigorous measures for the full implementation of all the provisions of the Security Council resolution which relate to Belgium, to Belgian nationals, and, in general, to foreign countries.

The Secretary-General has taken note of the Belgian government's observations concerning the three groups referred to in the *note verbale* dated February 27, 1961, from the representative of Belgium. In that connection, he would like additional information, with a view to the implementation of operative paragraph 2 of part A of the resolution, on the following points:

Group (a): number of persons concerned, according to the information or estimates available to the Belgian government;

Group (b): number of persons concerned, if any, over and above the persons already recalled;

Group (c): number of persons, among those noted by the Belgian consular services as belonging to this group, who would be subject to recall under the military regulations which the Belgian government proposes to apply.

In the light of the foregoing, the Secretary-General feels he can conclude from the *note verbale* of the Permanent Representative that the Belgian government thinks it advisable to examine in detail, with the representative of the Secretary-General, the ways and means of applying the Security Council resolution, the terms of which can obviously not be the subject of negotiations. The Secretary-General attaches particular importance, as he has already said, to the mission of the United Nations representative, who will endeavour in Brussels to work out the necessary arrangements, in cooperation with the Belgian government, and through whom the United Nations will be kept fully informed of the progress made in the application of the resolution.

The Secretary-General has the honour to inform the representative of Belgium that he has appointed to represent him Ambassador Taieb Sahbani of Tunisia, who will leave for Brussels at the beginning of next week. Mr. Taieb Sahbani will be accompanied by Mr. Mahmoud Mestiri of Tunisia.

Editor's note—Because of difficulties raised by Belgium, Ambassador Sahbani's departure for Brussels was delayed until March 21 (see p. 400).

THE FIRST POSITIVE development since February 21 came from New Delhi, and it was an important and timely one. After extensive correspondence with Hammarskjöld and over considerable opposition in the Indian parliament, Nehru finally agreed to contribute a brigade of five thousand men to the UN Force. This was by far the biggest national contingent to be offered by any government. The Tunisian government of Habib Bourguiba also agreed at this time to add six hundred men to its contingent. These developments reversed in decisive fashion the downward trend of recent weeks in the strength of the Force. Hammarskjöld's letter of March 4 to the Indian representative (first following text) expressed his appreciation of Nehru's move and confirmed certain understandings of the Indian government on the conditions applying to the participation of its contingent.

2. Letter in Response to India's Decision to Provide a Brigade for the United Nations Congo Force

NEW YORK   MARCH 4, 1961

The following is the text of a letter dated March 4, 1961, from Secretary-General Dag Hammarskjöld to C. S. Jha, permanent representative of India to the United Nations, in reply to the latter's letter dated March 3 addressed to the Secretary-General:

Dear Ambassador Jha,

Your letter of March 3 brings encouraging and important news, and I acknowledge it with thanks. The action of your government in responding favorably to the appeal for additional strength for the UN Force in the Congo, by providing a brigade, is most helpful and comes at a time when the need is keenly felt. Moreover, it is of particular importance to the Force that the incoming Indian brigade is immediately available.

Please convey to the prime minister and to your government my deep appreciation of the understanding and timely support thus given to the UN effort. This is said in full realization that it is difficult for India to

UN Press Release SG/1016-CO/135.

spare for service with the UN so large a number of troops under existing circumstances. The generosity is, therefore, doubly appreciated.

Your assumption is correct that transport will be provided by the United Nations. This is already being arranged and you will shortly be informed of the details for transmission to New Delhi.

Careful note is taken of the views and position of the Government of India with regard to the use of armed Indian troops in the Congo, and I take the liberty to make brief comments on them.

You are, of course, fully aware, from my numerous and persistent communications and statements on the subject—dating back to the first stages of the operation—of my complete agreement with the position that the prompt withdrawal of Belgian military and paramilitary personnel and political advisers is of decisive importance. I hope that the clear stand now taken by the Security Council will finally make it possible to meet this imperative need.

The wish will be firmly respected that except for Congolese armed units, and Belgian and other foreign military personnel and mercenaries in the Congo, the troops of India will not be called upon to fight troops or nationals of other Member states of the United Nations. In any case, it is, in my view, a problem which is most unlikely to arise.

It is clearly understood, of course, that the Indian troops now provided are in reinforcement of the Indian military establishment already in the Congo and in no sense are to be regarded as replacements for the withdrawn units of any other countries. The objective sought in my appeal is to strengthen the Force above even its previous peak numbers and to widen participation in it.

The Government of India may be assured that their troops in the Congo will never be used for the suppression of any popular movements or in support of any parties or factions which are challenging the United Nations authority. Indeed, neither the troops of India nor of any other country participating in the UN Force in the Congo can, under the mandate of the Security Council, be used to further any partisan political ends.

As to the matter of command, the normal practice in the UN Force is to keep contingents under their own commands. However, certain operational situations occasionally necessitate the detachment of a company or more to other areas, functions, or contingents for limited periods. On such occasions, however, detachments are kept in recognized military size under command of their own officers.

We are in complete accord, also, on the question of Belgian military equipment. The only such equipment left in the Congo is on their ex-military bases of Kamina, Kitona, and Banana, which are under United Nations custody and where detailed inventories are kept of all matériel. Belgian military and paramilitary personnel are now providing the cadres for the Katanga gendarmerie and some officers, instructors, and advisers to the Congolese army and Kalonji's army. Therefore military equipment in such units is the property of the Congolese and the question of taking it over from Belgian military and paramilitary personnel who are withdrawing does not arise.

The principle applicable to the Force in the Congo with regard to costs is that the United Nations accepts responsibility for all extraordinary expenses incurred by the contributing country in providing its troops. This, of course, applies to replacement of personnel and equipment.

I trust that the foregoing observations will prove helpful.

DAG HAMMARSKJÖLD
Secretary-General

INDIA'S OFFER of a brigade to the UN Force came at a time when relations between the Kasavubu régime and the United Nations were deteriorating to their lowest point. The Belgian advisers to the president, Iléo and Bomboko, easily played their tune on the suspicions, frustrations, and fears of the Leopoldville leaders about Lumumba's followers, both in Stanleyville and among their African neighbors. Their dislike of Dayal was assiduously stoked by the British and American embassies. And they were frightened by penetrations into Kivu, Equateur, and Kasai provinces by ANC detachments loyal to Gizenga. Although the United Nations commander had managed to prevent a major clash late in February in the Orientale-Equateur-Kasai border area by interposing between rival ANC forces under Generals Lundula, for Gizenga, and Mobutu, for Kasavubu, the latter blamed ONUC for not supporting him against the Gizenga régime.

At the end of February Iléo, Tshombé, and Kalonji of South Kasai agreed to work together, on both military and political levels, against both Stanleyville and the demands of the United Nations under the Security Council's February 21 resolution. They decided to call a conference of Congolese leaders early in March to seek some sort of political agreement that might forestall further United Nations intervention. Iléo yielded to Tshombé's insistence that the conference meet in Tananarive, the capital of Madagascar, a former French colony friendly to Tshombé and his aspirations.

Hammarskjöld instructed Dayal and his UN mission chiefs to do all they could to persuade Gizenga and other leaders in Stanleyville, as well as the more moderate Lumumbists and other provincial leaders, to attend the conference so that it might be broadly representative. Gizenga was at first receptive, provided the conference was moved to a more neutral African capital. When this was turned down he refused to attend.

The conference met at Tananarive from March 8 to 12 and was dominated from start to finish by Tshombé rather than by the Leopoldville delegation led by Kasavubu and Iléo. They agreed on a plan to transform the Congo into a confederation of virtually independent states, with Kasavubu as titular president and a joint council to act as a coordinating body but without effective central authority. A resolution was also adopted declaring the Security Council resolution a violation of both the sovereignty of the Congo and the United Nations Charter.

As we shall see the Leopoldville leaders, who favored a federation with real sovereign powers, not a confederation, soon had second thoughts about what they had agreed to at Tananarive, but first the hostility that had been generated toward the United Nations over recent weeks resulted in a succession of ugly confrontations and serious clashes during the first days of March in Leopoldville and the port of Matadi.

On March 1 Bomboko demanded that the UN Force evacuate the air force installations at Leopoldville's Ndjili Airport and the next day protested the establishment by ONUC of "neutral" or protected areas in Leopoldville, serving as refuges for those fearing arbitrary arrest or worse. The same day Kasavubu replied to the Secretary-General's February 21 letter about political arrests and assassinations with a denunciation of Dayal for allegedly treating the political executions at Stanleyville more lightly than those at Bakwanga. On March 3 a military bulletin was posted at ANC headquarters alleging that the United Nations intended to expel all foreign technicians from the Congo and to disarm the ANC. It called upon the soldiers to resist, for "it is better to die than again to fall under foreign domination" via a UN trusteeship.

Incendiary agitation of this sort among the ANC soldiers helped provoke serious armed clashes, first at Banana on March 3 and the next day at Matadi, the port of entry for ONUC supplies coming by sea. At Matadi the lightly armed UN Sudanese garrison of one hundred and thirty men was overwhelmed by a large ANC force using heavy armaments and forced to evacuate the base.

In the first two of the following messages to President Kasavubu the Secretary-General replied to the latter's allegations in his letter of March 2 and gave his first reactions to the ANC attacks at Banana and Matadi.

3. First Messages to Kasavubu on Matadi Incident and Relations with ONUC

NEW YORK   MARCH 3 and 5, 1961

(a) Letter dated March 3, 1961, to the President of the Republic of the Congo (Leopoldville)

I have the honour to acknowledge receipt of your letter dated March 2, 1961. I note with regret that this message, which concludes with an expression of firm intention to cooperate with ONUC authorities, contains a series of allegations which I must reject.

It is difficult to reconcile this intention to cooperate with incidents in which United Nations troops are subjected to a violent attack as at the base of Banana, and in which United Nations personnel are subjected to indignities and physical assault in Leopoldville, or with announcements such as those issued by the ANC headquarters in Leopoldville on March 3, 1961.

Your statement of willingness to cooperate is made contingent on the ONUC authorities' respect for the Congolese authorities and sovereignty. To an increasing extent, and especially since the adoption of the recent resolution by the Security Council, the United Nations has been confronted by what seems to be a determination on the part of persons under your authority to frustrate efforts to create conditions in which respect for these authorities would be ensured.

The reference to the condemnation by your spokesmen of the murders of political prisoners must be judged in the light of the fact that those in question were as a rule deported to their deaths by action of Leopoldville authorities. It would not have been for me to pass judgement on the charges which might have been made against them if they had been brought to justice before the Congolese courts; the point is precisely that,

Security Council Official Records, Sixteenth Year, Supplement for January, February, and March 1961, documents S/4758, section IV, and S/4758/Add. 4.

after having been held for months without any such charges being preferred, they were surrendered into the hands of persons known as their political enemies.

I note with particular suprise your references to the establishment of United Nations protected areas in Leopoldville. I deeply regret that conditions in Leopoldville have compelled ONUC to take there too protective measures which had previously been necessary in other places. These areas, as indicated in the report dated March 2, 1961 to the Secretary-General from his special representative, have been established by ONUC whenever this became inescapable in order to protect individuals from arbitrary arrest and violation of fundamental human rights, including such localities as Stanleyville, Bukavu, Goma, and Kindu, and various places in Katanga and Kasai provinces. The principles delineated in paragraph 8 of the special representative's report are strictly observed in giving United Nations protection in asylum; no such protection is granted to persons under lawful prosecution for common crimes; no political activities are permitted to the persons granted asylum; nor is anybody admitted unless in real danger of assassination, arbitrary arrest, ill-treatment, or other persecution on account of race, tribal origin, nationality, religion, political convictions, or associations.

The setting up of protected areas in various parts of the Congo is in fact an example of the humanitarian motivation of the United Nations operation. This action in no way infringes upon Congolese sovereignty and authority, and it must be continued until—and I hope that this will be soon—conditions are restored in which it will no longer be necessary.

The allegation in your letter that the special representative is using United Nations protected camps to muster "rebel elements" to be concentrated at Stanleyville does not even merit any rejoinder.

I must refer to your mention of the "massacre of fifteen innocent persons at Stanleyville," since the situation in that city has manifestly been a matter of deep concern to the special representative and myself. Mr. Dayal has kept me fully and continually informed of rumours about the alleged murder of Mr. Songolo and his associates; the special representative's report on this matter was submitted to the Security Council on February 22. Like myself, the special representative believes that there exists strong circumstantial evidence that a repulsive crime may in fact have been committed. But in the absence of some more concrete proof— of the kind which became available in the case of Mr. Lumumba or Mr.

Finant and their colleagues—no responsible United Nations official can take it upon himself to report as facts rumours which, despite their unremitting efforts, United Nations representatives have been unable to verify beyond doubt.

I have already referred to the statement which appeared in the bulletin of the ANC headquarters in Leopoldville. This statement depicts the United Nations effort in the Congo in a fanciful and distorted fashion, in sharp contradiction to what we have repeatedly explained, most recently in my letter to you of February 27, 1961. Statements of this kind, with their serious misrepresentation of the views of the Security Council, may well lay the groundwork for action directly at variance with your assurances of intentions to cooperate with ONUC. It should not be necessary to point out that the Security Council never envisaged the expulsion of foreign technicians from the country; its resolution of February 21, only refers to foreign military and paramilitary personnel, political advisers, and mercenaries, as was fully explained in my letter of March 2, 1961. In the second place, the Security Council decision does not call for the disarming of the ANC. On the contrary, it speaks of reorganizing it, bringing it under discipline and control, and making arrangements with a view to eliminating interference by its units and personnel in the Congo's political life—an aim which most recent events have fully justified.

With this background the Banana incident of today takes on a special significance. I must protest in the strongest terms against this deplorable incident, in which ANC soldiers without any provocation or justification attacked Sudanese members of the United Nations Force who were engaged in a peaceful activity. This occurrence must be added to the string of incidents in which ANC units have behaved in a manner that adds weight to the feeling expressed by so many members of the Security Council, and reflected in its resolution, that urgent action is required to turn units of that force again into an agency that supports peace, law, and order. This, surely, must be a primary consideration of the authorities themselves.

It is indeed essential that discipline and observance of the will to maintain good relations with the United Nations Force be restored to armed units lest incidents followed by even graver political repercussions ensue. Nothing would be more tragic than to see the soldiers of many countries that have come to the Congo in order to help that country find themselves compelled, in self-defence and as a last resort, to use force, under the decisions of the Security Council, in the last analysis, to save the country to which they have been invited, but whose citizens have displayed such lack of understanding and even hostility towards them.

It is not yet too late, Mr. President, despite everything that has happened, to turn a new page in relations between the Congo and the international community as represented by the United Nations, an organization the sole aim of which in the Congo is to help the people to form its country into a peaceful, prosperous and fully independent member of that community.

(b) Telegram dated March 5, 1961, to the President of the Republic of the Congo (Leopoldville)

In the light of the grave events of the past few hours and with further reference to my letter to you dated March 3, 1961, I have the honour to protest to you most strongly concerning the unlawful acts which since March 3 have been perpetrated by the ANC, with the apparent involvement of Ministers of the Iléo régime, in the region of the Lower Congo against units serving under the United Nations command. These developments raise the most serious questions of principle regarding the operation which the United Nations has undertaken, after an appeal from the Government of the Republic, upon the decision of the Security Council, in pursuance of its function of maintaining international peace and security.

After grave developments, first at Banana and then, graver yet, at Matadi, in which ANC soldiers without provocation attacked units of the United Nations Force engaged in their assigned activity, there occurred an inadmissible threat of the use of force to compel evacuation of the Sudanese unit of the United Nations force from Matadi. In this connection I must draw your urgent attention to the following points:

First, the United Nations, under the Security Council mandate, must keep complete freedom of decision as regards the deployment of national contingents in performance of the United Nations operation. In the exercise of its responsibility the placement of specific contingents will, of course, always be made with due regard to all the pertinent circumstances. I am bound to consider unacceptable any attempt by force or otherwise to influence ONUC in this respect, including the setting of conditions as to the selection of units for Matadi. The forced withdrawal of the Sudanese detachment from Matadi today cannot be interpreted as derogating from this position of principle.

Secondly, the presence of the United Nations Force in Matadi is a vital condition for the carrying out of the United Nations operation in the Congo, especially for the prevention of civil war and the halting of military operations, for which, as you know, the Security Council resolution authorizes the use of force, if necessary, in the last resort. This point is necessarily subject, as regards placement of specific contingents, to the principles laid down in the preceding paragraph in the implementation of which the United Nations, on its own responsibility, takes into account all factors essential for the fulfilment of the task of the Force.

There is scarcely any need to emphasize that the decisions taken by the Leopoldville authorities within the next few hours will be crucial if the Leopoldville authorities are to convince the world that they continue to be committed, as you have assured me, to cooperation with, rather than defiance of the United Nations. I request you to initiate urgent action for immediately locating and returning to their units the one Canadian, one Tunisian, and seven Sudanese soldiers missing, as well as for the observance of the cease-fire that has been ordered. In this connection also the next few hours will provide the Congolese authorities with a major opportunity to demonstrate that they are prepared to repudiate deplorable acts and attitudes and, with United Nations cooperation and assistance, to reassert control over unruly and irresponsible ANC and civilian elements. In any case full responsibility for the past events must attach to you and to these authorities.

In concluding I must reiterate the importance of the principles established in the paragraphs above. If, against my firm expectation, the situation in Matadi should not be redressed forthwith, the matter will of course become an urgent concern of the Security Council.

THERE FOLLOW the texts of additional messages addressed by the Secretary-General to President Kasavubu on March 8,10,12,16, and 26.

With respect to Matadi he carefully explained why it was necessary to station there a small detachment of the UN Force to guard supplies arriving by sea and why the Congolese government was in violation both of its obligations under Chapter VII of the Charter and its commitment in the status of forces agreement of July 27, 1960, in refusing to agree to the return of UN troops to the port.

Justin Bomboko, who held the title of foreign minister in the provisional Iléo cabinet, replied on behalf of Kasavubu. He was on weak legal ground and so he tried to argue that a return of the UN soldiers would cause riot and bloodshed because of the anger of the ANC and the people over the Security Council resolution of February 21. Since this reaction, to the extent that it existed at all, was due to misunderstandings and falsifications of the intent of the resolution, which had been assiduously spread about by the government itself, the Secretary-General rejected the argument with a measure of indignation (see especially the letters of March 12 and 26). Discussions continued in Leopoldville but it was to prove impossible for some time to come to restore the UN position at Matadi.

Hammarskjöld did make some progress on the questions of removing Belgian military personnel and political advisers and the reorganization and training of the ANC. The way was opened in part by the explanations he reiterated in his communications to Kasavubu and in part by the departure of Ambassador Dayal from Leopoldville where the bitter hostility to him had made his position increasingly untenable. For three months the Secretary-General had sharply rebuffed Kasavubu's repeated demands for Dayal's resignation but it was now evident that it would be impossible for him to conduct the negotiations on both the Belgian presence and the ANC that were required with Kasavubu's régime.

Much against his will Hammarskjöld therefore resorted to the device of a temporary recall of Dayal to Headquarters for consultations. Mekki Abbas, the Sudanese executive secretary of the UN Economic Commission for Africa, was appointed acting special representative of the Secretary-General in Leopoldville. Hammarskjöld hoped that Dayal could return later if the political climate calmed down enough to make it possible for him to work effectively with the régime.

This move immediately improved the atmosphere. It was followed on March 21 by the dispatch to Leopoldville of a delegation of two African members of the Secretariat, Robert Gardiner of Ghana and Francis Nwokedi of Nigeria, and to Brussels of Ambassador Taieb Sahbani of Tunisia as the Secretary-General's representative, all with the mandate of consulting on the best means to give effect to the Security Council's resolutions on Belgian personnel and on the ANC (see following letter of March 16 to Kasavubu and, for later developments, report to the Security Council of May 17).

4. Further Messages to Kasavubu on Matadi and Relations with ONUC

NEW YORK   MARCH 8 to 26, 1961

(a) *Message dated March 8, 1961, to the President of the Republic of the Congo (Leopoldville)*

In discussions following the deplorable incidents at Matadi, according to the information I have received, there have been put forward certain conditions regarding United Nations activities in the Congo, freedom of movement, deployment of troops, use of certain facilities, etc. I wish in this context to draw your attention to some legal aspects of the United Nations presence in the Congo.

We are, of course, strongly aware of the fact that the initial action of the United Nations was undertaken in response to a request of the Government of the Republic of the Congo. But I am certain that you, on your side, are also aware of the fact that this action was taken because it was considered necessary in view of an existing threat to international peace and security. Thus, in its resolution of July 22, 1960, and subsequent resolutions, the Security Council expressly linked the maintenance of law and order in the Congo to the maintenance of international peace and security, and made it clear that the primary basis of the Security Council decision was the maintenance of international peace and security. The considerations ruling the relationship between the Republic of the Congo and the United Nations, therefore, should not be seen solely in the light of the request of the government and what flows from that request. The status, rights, and functions of the United Nations are basically determined by the fact that the action was taken in order to counteract an international threat to peace.

This becomes important especially to an interpretation of the undertak-

Security Council Official Records, Sixteenth Year, Supplement for January, February, and March 1961, documents S/4775, sections I, II, IV, V and VII.

ing entered into by the Government of the Republic of the Congo on July 27, 1960, in which the government agreed that

> . . . in the exercise of its sovereign rights with respect to any question concerning the presence and functioning of the United Nations Force in the Congo, it will be guided, in good faith, by the fact that it has requested military assistance from the United Nations and by its acceptance of the resolutions of the Security Council of July 14 and 22, 1960; it likewise states that it will ensure the freedom of movement of the Force in the interior of the country and will accord the requisite privileges and immunities to all personnel associated with the activities of the Force.

You will observe that the government undertook "in the exercise of its sovereign rights with respect to any question concerning the presence and functioning of the United Nations Force" to be guided in good faith by its acceptance of the resolutions of the Security Council of July 14 and 22, 1960, and, specifically, to ensure the freedom of movement of the Force. This undertaking has obviously continued in legal force, and must be considered as precluding any actions of the government which would make it impossible for the United Nations Force to function, under the resolutions, in the way called for as a means of eliminating the threat to international peace and security. This in particular refers to its freedom of movement.

As a further element of the legal situation you will have noted the explicit declaration by the Security Council in its resolution of August 9, 1960, that all Member states are bound in accordance with Articles 25 and 49 of the Charter to accept and carry out the decisions of the Council and, in particular, to afford mutual assistance in carrying out measures decided by the Council. This obviously precludes all Member states, including in this case the host state, from actions which render the United Nations operation ineffective for its declared purposes or hamper its successful continuation. In fact, Member states are under the obligation positively and actively to assist in the operation.

You will see from the references made that the relation between the United Nations and the Government of the Republic of the Congo is not merely a contractual relationship in which the Republic can impose its conditions as host state and thereby determine the circumstances under which the United Nations operates. It is rather a relationship governed by mandatory decisions of the Security Council. The consequence of this is that no government, including the host government, can by unilateral action determine how measures taken by the Security Council in this context should be carried out. Such a determination can be made only by the Security Council itself or on the basis of its explicit delegation of authority. It is of special importance that only the Security Council can decide on the discontinuance of the operation, and that, therefore, conditions which, by their effect on the operation, would deprive it of its necessary basis, would require direct consideration by the Security Council, which obviously could not be counted upon to approve of such conditions unless it were to find that the threat to peace and security had ceased.

I am sure that the fundamental legal points which I have recalled here will be taken fully into account by you in your consideration of the present situation.

Approaching you in this way, I feel that I should bring to your attention also another fact of relevance in this context. In the ceasefire talks in Matadi, after the incident of March 5, 1961, Mr. Delvaux acknowledged, according to the reports available to me, that the United Nations Force requires for the free movement of its personnel and supplies that United Nations troops be stationed at Matadi. The only reservation made by Mr. Delvaux referred to the undesirability of deployment of Sudanese troops in Matadi; on this reservation I have already expressed my views in my message to you of March 5, 1961, indicating this reservation cannot be accepted as a condition by the United Nations as it would mean an interference in what must be solely a United Nations responsibility. The recognition of the need for the UN to be in a satisfactory military position in Matadi was again recognized clearly and unconditionally in the message communicated to me by the permanent mission of the Republic of the Congo on March 7, 1961. However, I wish to draw your attention to the fact that in other and later contacts we have understood that there was a wish to introduce conditions going considerably beyond the one mentioned by Mr. Delvaux in Matadi, on March 5, 1961, and already rejected by us. If such an effort is or were to be made, it obviously would mean that the Congolese authorities would go back on their previous word, which I am convinced cannot be your intention.

There is one final point on which it seems appropriate to make some short comments. It apparently has been assumed by some Congolese units that the recent resolution of the Security Council demands the "disarming of the ANC" and authorizes the use of force for that purpose. On this point, I should like to note that part B, paragraph 2 of the Security Council resolution of February 21, 1961, relating to Congolese armed units and personnel does not aim at a disarming of the troops but urges a resumption of the organization and training of the ANC, apart from political involvements. I am sure you have understood that clearly yourself, as is apparent from your message of March 5, 1961, to which I wish to reply as soon as I have had an opportunity to study your suggestions more closely. Nor does this operative paragraph of the resolution authorize the use of armed force to carry out even that limited end. Moreover, part A, operative paragraph 1, which authorizes the use of force "if necessary, in the last resort" indicates that such use shall be in support of cease-fire arrangements and similar measures for the prevention of civil war; there is no reference in this paragraph which indicates that the authorization to use force "as a last resort" applies to the assistance in the reorganization of the army. You will recall that, in my statements to the Council concerning the control and discipline of the ANC, I suggested only that the United Nations Force might have to be used with respect to such units as might have broken loose from their own command and threatened the population. On the more general problem, I made it entirely clear that the reorganization of the ANC would have to be undertaken in cooperation with the Congolese authorities. It is my opinion that this principle remains the accepted position of the United Nations.

Mr. President, the matters which are here brought to your attention all refer to a question of basic significance for the possibilities of the United Nations to continue its assistance to the Republic of the Congo. I am certain that you wish to see this assistance continue in a spirit of collaboration and confidence, and I am therefore also certain that you will see to it that no new and harmful developments are precipitated in the present sensitive situation by any rash action but that, to the extent that there is a need for it, full opportunity is given for the elaboration of practical and workable formulae for the continued activities of the United Nations, taking fully into account the legal aspects I have explained in this telegram, as well as our needs for a successful operation.

I trust that you will exercise all your personal influence to that effect, and I can, from my side, assure you that we remain animated by the same intentions, while, naturally, being obliged to maintain firmly those principles with which all Member states have to comply in the interest of their joint efforts through the Organization.

DAG HAMMARSKJÖLD
Secretary-General

(*b*) *Message dated March 10, 1961, to the President of the Republic of the Congo (Leopoldville)*

Further to my message of March 8, 1961, having received a report on the conditions put forward by your representatives at Leopoldville, I wish to make the following observations.

You have already taken cognizance of the legal situation with reference to the possibility of subjecting the United Nations operation in the Congo to conditions which conflict with the purposes of that operation. I do not wish to repeat myself. I must, however, emphasize that such conditions would call into question the assistance rendered by the United Nations to the Republic of the Congo. It is my firm opinion, supported by the unanimous reaction of the nineteen members of the Advisory Committee for the Congo, that the conditions laid before the United Nations during the negotiations at Leopoldville are such as to make the operation impossible, and this applies to the civil as well as the military aspect. Accordingly, you will, I am sure, give your representatives at Leopoldville instructions to reconsider their attitude, having regard to the status of the United Nations operation, the circumstances in which the operation can be continued, and the consequences which would ensue should the Security Council be forced to decide that the operation could not be continued under the conditions stipulated.

What has been said here, in general terms, applies particularly to the United Nations position at Matadi. Without a satisfactory position at Matadi—and this includes not only a military presence in sufficient strength but also freedom of movement and action—a vital line of communication would be cut, thus raising the question whether the operation could be continued. Mr. Delvaux himself has recognized that it is necessary for the United Nations to have such a presence at Matadi, and this position has been repeated, unconditionally, as your own by your spokesmen here in New York. A retreat on the Congolese side from the position thus taken—a position which is obviously essential—could not but arouse the most unfavourable reactions, and I am sure you do not intend to make any such retreat.

But time is passing swiftly. The troops urgently need supplies. The departure of the Indonesian contingent has already been postponed. For these reasons we must reach a quick solution, and one which takes the needs of the United Nations operation fully into account, to the problems which have arisen, especially as regards the United Nations position at Matadi.

Allow me to sum up. The legal basis of the United Nations position is clear. The practical needs of the operation are also plain. It disturbs me to think what the probable reaction will be if your representatives should maintain an attitude which is indefensible, either from the standpoint of legal basis, or from that of the needs of the operation as envisaged by the Security Council. The problem of Matadi is particularly pressing. This problem is in itself a limited one, but it reflects the essential features of the present situation and calls for rapid solution. For these reasons I turn to you again with an urgent appeal to exercise your great influence as chief of state so that a solution may be found very quickly to the immediate problems, without the complications involved in the attitude hitherto taken by the Congolese spokesmen—complications which, I greatly fear, would have very widespread and very dangerous consequences.

In making this appeal, I rely on your wish, so eloquently expressed, to see fruitful cooperation develop with the United Nations, and on your will, which I share, to act solely in the best interest of the Congolese people who have already been so sorely tried by events.

DAG HAMMARSKJÖLD
Secretary-General

(c) *Message dated March 12, 1961, to the President of the Republic of the Congo (Leopoldville)*

Through our representatives in Leopoldville I have received your reply of March 11 to my message of March 5, delivered on March 6, in which Mr. Bomboko, on your behalf, presented your comments on various aspects of the present problem. After receipt of the message to which you now have sent a reply, you received two further messages of March 8 and 10 to which I wish to refer as they partly cover the same ground; you will observe that in my message of the 8th I express my intention to get back to your suggestions in the letter of March 5 as soon as I have had an opportunity to study them more closely.

I have read your message of March 11 with concern, because it seems to me to reflect some continued misunderstanding of the principles which must apply to the United Nations operation. You should not doubt our sincerity when I say that the United Nations is animated solely by the interest to assist the Congolese people but realizes that that must be done in such a way as to safeguard not only the Congo, but Africa and the world, against the present threat to peace and security, while fully protecting the independence and integrity of the country. Part of the difficulty in the present situation derives from the fact that, in these conditions, assistance to the Congo cannot be detached from the much wider international problem of peace, which may sometimes seem to lead to reactions on the United Nations side running counter to Congolese views; naturally, there is not, and there cannot be, any such conflict of interest as the primary concern of the Congolese people also must be the maintenance of peace around the Congo and the prevention of possible military intervention on the part of foreign powers. Thus, when the Congo has to adjust itself to circumstances and accept decisions of the Security Council in conformity with Chapter VII of the Charter, like any other Member state, there is no impairment of the wider interests of the country, as these can best be judged by the Council with its high authority under the Charter; nor is there any impairment of the sovereign rights of the Congo, other than within the limits accepted by all other Member states under a resolution like that adopted on February 21. Therefore, to the extent that the resolutions are binding on all Member states, I feel that the Congo should not, when it has to adjust itself to a decision in the overriding interest of peace for the world and for the Congo, see any obstacle to true cooperation with the United Nations in the wide area where such cooperation is necessary.

In the present case, what I have said applies specifically to the United Nations Force. Its size, its composition, and its deployment cannot be subordinated to the will of any one government, be it a contributing government or the host government. If the United Nations organizes the Force, the Force must remain exclusively under the command of the United Nations, guided by the judgement of the military command of the United Nations as to what is necessary for the mission of the Force in order to enable it to fulfil its purpose as jointly endorsed by all governments concerned. This must be accepted by the Congolese government.

There naturally remains a wide area for cooperation aimed at the best and mutually most satisfactory arrangements. In this respect the basic notion that the Force is in the Congo in the first instance for the assistance of the Congo takes on its full significance. The situation is similar in other fields, as for example in the administrative field. The Security Council has the right to decide, with binding effect in relation to all governments, that all foreign military or paramilitary personnel outside the United Nations command should leave the country, and the authorities of the Congo are then, like the governments of countries from which such personnel may have come, bound by the decision. But there remains an important question, that of the way in which the decision should be carried out, so as to achieve the desired end without any harm being done to legitimate Congolese interests, and consultations are therefore desirable regarding, for example, replacements through the good offices of the United Nations, once a basis is established by acceptance by the Congo of the decision of the Security Council.

I apologize for discussing these matters at such length, but some of your reactions, Mr. President, make me feel strongly that misunderstandings have arisen not only as to the significance in substance of the Security Council resolutions, in particular the last one, but also regarding their juridical significance for Member states, including the Congo. Just as I tried in my message of March 8 to explain what the resolution meant and did not mean with respect to, for example, the Armée nationale congolaise, I therefore consider it necessary now to point out in which area and for what reasons the United Nations must claim autonomy in its operation and, on the other hand, within what spheres active and, I firmly hope, fruitful consultations are called for and will be welcomed by the Organization.

I note also with concern your observations on the atmosphere in Matadi and the conclusions which you seem to wish to draw from this alleged atmosphere. I need not repeat what I have already stated regarding the vital significance of Matadi for the whole United Nations operation, civilian as well as military, nor is it necessary to stress once again the extreme urgency of an arrangement which reestablishes this lifeline for the operation. But I must comment briefly on your observations. First, let me emphatically reject the comparison with the reaction in relation to the Belgians. I am surprised that you have found it possible to make such a comparison, with the full knowledge which you have of the happenings in July, with the full knowledge which you must have regarding what happened on March 4 and 5, as proved by the testimony of entirely trustworthy witnesses. It is difficult to believe that the presence of a small group of Canadian signal personnel and of some 130 Sudanese, who had never to my knowledge taken any unfriendly action against the population and have never tried to exercise any authority over the population or the ANC, could have given rise to feelings such as those you refer to, unless emotions had been whipped up by irresponsible statements against the United Nations, of which there are many examples, and by misinterpretations of the purpose of the presence of the United Nations. I note what you say in this context with some personal bitterness, in view of the fact that, as you know, Matadi was reopened, the pilot service reorganized, and traffic made to flow again only as a result of efforts and sacrifices of the United Nations. It is difficult to believe that the memory of the population is so short that this striking evidence of the purposes of the United Nations assistance has been forgotten within six months.

Given these circumstances, I am convinced that, if you were to use your great personal influence in the region to explain to the population what the United Nations has done to help it, to indicate the real reasons for the presence of the United Nations contingent in Matadi, and to explain the purposes of the operation in progress which you, yourself, wish to continue, the psychological background would be changed so quickly as to permit the resumption of regular United Nations services at Matadi without any delay. I am afraid that you would find that nobody would understand it if the Congo, for the time being at least, bows to a supposedly hostile attitude and shows itself unwilling to do its utmost to change that attitude quickly, the more so as this attitude—to the extent that it may exist—has undoubtedly been influenced by the misleading information recently circulated.

I wish to address to you a special message regarding the release of prisoners and related matters.

DAG HAMMARSKJÖLD
Secretary-General

(d) Message dated March 16 1961, to the President of the Republic of the Congo (Leopoldville)

Further to my letter of February 27, 1961, and the subsequent exchange of correspondence concerning the implementation of the resolution adopted by the Security Council on February 21, 1961, I now wish to take further measures, with your cooperation, in respect of the part of the resolution dealing with the withdrawal and evacuation from the Congo of Belgian and other foreign military and paramilitary personnel and political advisers, part A, operative paragraph 2 of the resolution. I also wish to refer to the question of the reorganization of the Armée nationale congolaise, part B, operative paragraph 2 of the resolution, a matter concerning which you made certain observations in your letter of March 5, 1961 (S/4752/Add.3).

It is most regrettable that the meaning of the resolution of February 21 and the very purpose of the presence of the United Nations in the Congo are still being misinterpreted in certain quarters, despite our repeated explanations and assurances. It should hardly be necessary to reaffirm that the Organization's sole purpose is to help to restore and maintain public order, to safeguard the Congo's independence and territorial integrity, and to promote the well-being of its 14 million inhabitants. I know you have always understood that to be so and I therefore make the following proposals:

To ensure the speedy implementation of part A, paragraph 2 of the resolution, particularly with regard to political advisers, I propose to send to Leopoldville next week a delegation consisting of Mr. R. Gardiner and Mr. F. C. Nwokedi to discuss with you and your advisers the best means of giving effect to the Security Council's decision. I am sure that you will give this delegation your full cooperation. The delegation will be assisted by Mr. Khiari who occupies the post of consultant on public administration for ONUC's civilian operations at Leopoldville. In a few days I propose to send Mr. Taieb Sahbani to Brussels in connection with the obligations imposed by the aforementioned resolution on the Belgian government, with which, as you know, I have exchanged letters emphasizing the principal responsibility incumbent upon it under the terms of the resolution. After his initial discussions in Brussels, Mr. Sahbani may join Mr. Gardiner and Mr. Nwokedi at Leopoldville.

Within the framework of United Nations technical assistance to the Congo, the Organization's resources, including its recruitment facilities, will as far as possible be placed at the disposal of the Congolese authorities to help them to replace, where necessary, those officials who will have to be relieved of their duties. I am sure you will appreciate that the implementation of the Security Council's resolution is not subject to such replacement. Nevertheless, in the spirit of the United Nations operation, every effort will be made to provide the personnel needed to avoid disrupting public services and enable the administration to continue to function unimpaired.

I hope that the delegation and any advisers you may wish it to consult will study the position with regard to civil service personnel in the Congo and decide, with particular reference to any measures taken in that respect by the Belgian government, the posts to which the Security Council's decision is applicable.

With regard to the other matter raised in the Security Council's resolution, namely, the reorganization of the Armée nationale congolaise, I have noted the reorganization measures suggested in your letter of March 5, 1961, which could to some extent serve as the starting point for a joint study of the question. Those proposals are now being urgently considered by the United Nations military command in the Congo and at the Organization's Headquarters. I shall address a further communication to you on the subject as soon as possible. Meanwhile, I have asked the delegation to consult with you and notify me of any further information it may obtain on your views in the matter. I also hope that the delegation's visit will help to dispel any misunderstanding or misconception which may still exist concerning the resolution. I need hardly repeat that at no time did the Security Council intend to disarm the Armée nationale congolaise.

I should like to add that your approach to this matter leads me to believe that a joint programme can be drawn up which will serve the best interests of the Republic of the Congo.

Lastly, I would inform you that, in view of the special nature and scope of this particular operation, I have asked the delegation to communicate my views and proposals directly to you and your advisers. In taking this decision, I considered it unnecessary to burden my special representative in the Congo with this particular mission, as he must devote all his time to the day-to-day problems raised by ONUC's operation in the Congo. The special representative and his assistants will, of course, be available to give the delegation and yourself every assistance you may need.

DAG HAMMARSKJÖLD
Secretary-General

(e) *Message dated March 26, 1961, to the President of the Republic of the Congo (Leopoldville)*

With reference to the message dated March 25, 1961, which Mr. Bomboko sent to me through my special representative, and in connection with my recent communications to you concerning the situation at Matadi, I have the honour to make the following comments.

I noted with interest the offer of cooperation contained in Mr. Bomboko's letter and the recognition, implicit in that letter, of the importance of Matadi for the maintenance of the United Nations operation in the Congo. I would have hoped to see the logical conclusion drawn from this premise—a conclusion which had previously been reached by all responsible Congolese spokesmen, including Mr. Delvaux, but which was lost sight of and even refuted in subsequent statements—namely that the presence at Matadi of a limited number of units of the United Nations Force is indispensable to United Nations operation, in view of the need to ensure the safety of United Nations consignments. Unfortunately, the alternative solutions proposed in Mr. Bomboko's letter are by no means adequate to meet that need.

Since the apprehensions of the population of the Lower Congo were adduced as an argument against the return of United Nations military units to Matadi, I find it hard to understand the suggestion that, in order to eliminate those apprehensions, supplies intended for the United Nations should be left without any protection whatsoever, instead of the minimum normal protection being guaranteed by units which could scarcely be considered to constitute a threat to the ANC in the area. I would emphasize in this connection that a violent reaction from the population would be more readily attributable to fears concerning the "disarmament" of ANC, fears which—as United Nations representatives have repeatedly pointed out—are by no means warranted by the Security Council resolution of February 21, 1961 and which your spokesman could easily dispel.

It may be recalled that, in order to meet the requirements of the United Nations Emergency Force stationed on the demarcation line between Israel and the United Arab Republic, a small United Nations military detachment has been maintained for a number of years at Port Said (United Arab Republic). It has given rise to no problems of sovereignty and to no friction, and thus furnishes a useful precedent to follow.

I am sure that you will readily agree that, as long as the United Nations is unable freely to exercise effective control over the movement of the supplies necessary for the maintenance of the operation, and is therefore likely to be prevented from carrying out the task entrusted to it under the Security Council resolutions, the basic question of the good faith of the Congolese authorities in complying with the terms of the undertaking given on July 27, 1960, cannot be considered settled. The arrangements suggested by Mr. Bomboko would appear impossible to reconcile with those terms so long as he insists that the United Nations should temporarily suspend all shipments of military matériel or ammunition through the port of Matadi.

Towards the end of his letter, Mr. Bomboko points out that in the last resort it is imperative to avoid one contingency which cannot be contemplated without grave anxiety. I sincerely endorse that view. In light of those considerations, those responsible must do all in their power to induce the public to correct certain mistaken views which would make it impossible to reinstate the United Nations presence at Matadi in the appropriate form. Your spokesmen would do well to make it clear to the public that they realize how important the success of the United Nations operation is for the future of the country, thus using their influence to further this operation in the interests of the authorities of the Republic and of the people.

It is above all the interests of the Congo that would be served by an agreement on these points, and on others which I have mentioned in earlier communications to you. I have every confidence that, in the light of this fact, the negotiations which my special representative is now conducting for the dispatch of a Tunisian unit to Matadi will be successful.

DAG HAMMARSKJÖLD
Secretary-General

THE FIRST OF the following texts is self-explanatory. On April 15 the General Assembly adopted a resolution establishing a Commission to investigate Lumumba's death with the membership and terms of reference recommended by the Advisory Committee (see also p. 435). The second document—the *note verbale* to Belgium—was written in response to a Belgian complaint that ONUC was failing to provide sufficient protection to Belgian civilians from the anarchy and violent disorder into which much of Kivu province had fallen.

5. *Report on Plan for Commission to Investigate Lumumba's Death*

NEW YORK   MARCH 20, 1961

IN THE REPORT of the Secretary-General to the Security Council "on certain steps taken in regard to the implementation of the Security Council resolution adopted on February 21, 1961," the Security Council was informed of the consideration by the Advisory Committee on the Congo of part A, operative paragraph 4, of the above-mentioned resolution. The Advisory Committee has now concluded its discussions concerning the implementation of this paragraph. The Secretary-General wishes to inform the Security Council that the Advisory Committee has made the following recommendation regarding the terms of reference of the Investigation Commission envisaged in part A, paragraph 4, of the Security Council resolution:

1. The terms of reference of the Commission, as indicated in the above-mentioned Security Council resolution, will be to hold an impartial investigation in order to ascertain the circumstances of the death of Mr. Patrice Lumumba and his colleagues, Mr. Maurice Mpolo and Mr. Joseph Okito. In particular, the Commission will endeavour to ascertain the events and circumstances relating to and culminating in the death of Mr. Lumumba and his colleagues and to fix responsibility therefor;

2. For the fulfilment of the task entrusted to it, the Commission may call upon the assistance of Member states of the United Nations, and of the authorities in the Republic of the Congo (Leopoldville). In addition to the normal methods of investigation the Commission may, at its discretion and to the extent considered necessary for the implementation of its mission, call upon the United Nations or any authorities in the Republic of the Congo to furnish any information or documents which may, in its opinion, be related to its terms of reference. The Commission may also, at

Security Council Official Records, Sixteenth Year, Supplement for January, February, and March 1961, document S/4771.

its discretion, invite or receive oral or documentary testimony from any person within or outside the republic of the Congo.

3. The Commission shall be entitled to receive from all Member states of the United Nations full cooperation and assistance as laid down in part B, paragraph 3, of the above-mentioned Security Council resolution. It shall also have the right to ask for and receive any assistance from the authorities in the Republic of the Congo and the local machinery of the United Nations Operation in the Congo.

4. The Commission shall carry out its task with promptness and despatch and submit a report to the Security Council by ———————— .

The Advisory Committee has further recommended that this Commission be composed of four members, nominated by the governments of Burma, Ethiopia, Mexico, and Togo.

---

6. *Note Verbale to Belgium on Protection for Civilians in Kivu Province*

NEW YORK   MARCH 22, 1961

THE SECRETARY-GENERAL presents his compliments to the Permanent Representative of Belgium to the United Nations and has the honour to acknowledge receipt of his *note verbale* dated March 20, 1961, the contents of which he has carefully examined.

He wishes to remind him in that connection that, as stated in the report of February 22, 1961, from his special representative, "the protection that the United Nations can afford to the civilian population is, despite its most strenuous efforts, limited to the means presently available." There is no doubt that owing to the weakening of the Force through the withdrawal of several national contingents during January–February 1961, and taking into account other urgent obligations, the United Nations Force did not have a sufficient number of troops to deploy them across the whole of Kivu province, some parts of which are difficult of access and infested by undisciplined bands. As indicated in the report of March 13, 1961, unceasing efforts are being made to remedy the situation and it

Security Council Official Records, Sixteenth Year, Supplement for January, February, and March 1961, document S/4768, section IV.

is hoped that when sufficient reinforcements have been sent in, more effective action can be taken. At the same time, ONUC is endeavouring to secure the cooperation of the local authorities, both civilian and military, which may exert some influence in Kivu on the armed bands and the civilian population.

The collapse of all authority in Kivu province, which explains the arbitrary acts of local leaders and the wave of violence directed against foreigners and Congolese, was described in the report dated February 22, 1961, from the special representative of the Secretary-General on the situation in Orientale and Kivu provinces. According to the latest reports, the concerted efforts of ONUC representatives in Bukavu, Kindu, and Stanleyville have brought about an improvement in the situation and curbed the lawlessness of the local leaders, some of whom have apparently been arrested by the provincial authorities. ANC elements, which obey the commands of their officers, have been assigned to security duty and are cooperating with patrols of the United Nations Force to afford better protection to the peaceful population against outbreaks of violence and the brutality of the undisciplined bands. For example, a strong patrol has just been sent to Kasongo where the Congolese and foreign population had been terrorized by marauders. Nevertheless, the security situation in Kivu, particularly in the outlying districts cut off from the mining communities, is far from satisfactory and United Nations efforts to improve it are limited by the factors cited in paragraph 15 of the report of March 13, 1961.

Whenever possible, the United Nations Force assists in the evacuation of persons wishing to leave Kivu, whether they are Belgians, other foreign nationals, or Congolese. For example, as noted in paragraph 15 of the report of February 22, over one thousand persons were able to leave the area by convoys arranged either by the United Nations or otherwise, and a number of others left the province by their own means. The greatest number left on January 17 after elements of the local population had been driven to violence by the announcement that Lumumba and his colleagues had been deported to Katanga. At present, as stated in the report of March 13, fewer than three hundred foreigners remain in the province, and, since then, it has become possible for the United Nations also to begin the evacuation of persons wishing to leave the Maniema district, including, in addition to employees of the Belgian mining companies, American and Dutch missionaries. It has been noted, however, that in the last few weeks at least forty foreigners had returned to Bukavu and

Goma where living conditions have become relatively stable owing to the presence of United Nations troops.

With regard to the matter of the three Belgian nationals whose names appear in the report of March 13, there can be no doubt that United Nations authorities, both in Kivu and Leopoldville, have received many visits from persons representing foreign firms, communities, or other private interests. The three gentlemen mentioned by the representative of Belgium in his *note verbale* of March 20 were among those visitors. At no time, however, was ONUC made aware that some of those visitors represented the interests of the foreign population of Kivu as a whole, especially as each visitor spoke only of individual interests. Moreover, the United Nations was not in a position to verify or recognize any claim to represent the foreign community of the province, even if such a claim had been made. In any event, the United Nations staff has always been willing to see anyone seeking help and to do its best within its means to evacuate, protect, or assist in one way or another any individual in difficulty no matter what his nationality or who the person appealing on his behalf.

STATEMENTS DURING RENEWED CONGO DEBATE IN THE GENERAL ASSEMBLY

THE GENERAL ASSEMBLY began the second part of its fifteenth annual session on March 7, when it heard President Kwame Nkrumah of Ghana call once again for African control of a new UN command in the Congo and other measures to make possible an "African solution" to the problem based on "positive neutralism" and the elimination of interference from both sides in the cold war.

The general debate on the Congo was resumed on March 21, when Soviet Foreign Minister Andrei Gromyko attempted to revive the USSR campaign for the dismissal of Hammarskjöld and replacement of the Secretary-General by a troika (see pp.194-95). Contrary to his recent custom Hammarskjöld withheld a reply until he could gauge the reactions of a representative cross-section of the Members. Debate continued at plenary meetings on March 24, 27, and 28. The last speaker on the 28th was Mario Cardoso, the representative of President Kasavubu's Leopoldville régime. He complained, as often before, of United Nations failures to consult and cooperate with the Congo's authorities and of lack of respect for Congolese sovereignty. In the course of his remarks he misinterpreted a passage in the "good faith" agreement of July 1960, in a way which the Secretary-General felt called for immediate correction (first following text).

1. First Statement

NEW YORK   MARCH 29, 1961

THE LAST INTERVENTION yesterday afternoon, made by the spokesman of the Republic of the Congo (Leopoldville), contains one substantive point which, in my view, requires an immediate clarification so as to avoid unnecessary misunderstanding. I therefore wish to avail myself of the possibility of replying on this specific point, reserving my right, if necessary, to revert to other points of the intervention and to other speakers at a later stage.

The speaker referred to point 3 in the so-called basic agreement with

General Assembly Official Records, Fifteenth Session, 970th plenary meeting.

the Central Government of the Republic of the Congo, of July 27, 1960, and quoted the third paragraph of this basic agreement in full. Obviously the representative had not been properly informed by his advisers about the sense of the passage he quoted, which says that: ". . . the Government of the Republic and the Secretary-General state their intention to proceed immediately . . . to explore jointly specific aspects of the functioning of the UN Force."

The representative read into this a commitment to prior cooperation and consultation on all United Nations operations. However, the text quoted is in substance something much more limited and much more precise: the passage is simply a declaration of intention to conclude a so-called status agreement. I suppose that, just as the speaker had not been informed about the sense of the text he quoted, he was not aware of the fact that a draft of such a status agreement was presented to the government on September 2, 1960, but that thereafter nothing was done by the Congo to get negotiations under way for the well-known reason that for months the authorities were not in a position to negotiate, the central government having broken up, Parliament being suspended, and no constitutional authority functioning with the right to commit the republic in international negotiations.

A few days ago, from the United Nations side, in consultation with the Advisory Committee, I renewed the invitation to the Congo to negotiate the substance of a status agreement. I hope that the Congolese authorities will be able and willing finally to implement the passage quoted by the representative in accordance with the stated intention—although obviously the form of a status agreement now would have to be adjusted to the constitutional difficulties which still prevail.

The reasons why the Congolese authorities have never followed up point 3 in the basic agreement are only part of an aspect of the Congo picture, omitted in the speech to which the General Assembly listened yesterday. Thus, in the attempt at an evaluation of the United Nations contribution made in that statement, did the Assembly find any reference to the fact that the authorities in Leopoldville, even at the time when the United Nations came to the Congo, were not recognized all over the republic, that soon thereafter the central government broke up, that later the administration claiming authority in Leopoldville was extraconstitutional, that the Congolese National Army instead of contributing to the maintenance of law and order was used by various leaders to further other political objectives, that too many in the Congo saw fit to demonstrate their nationalism by attacks on the United Nations and by trying to render its aims suspect, and, finally, that too many accepted or even furthered this or that kind of continued foreign intervention in support of their own aims and ambitions?

However, all this is well known to the Members of the General Assembly, and I have no reason to discuss such aspects of this intervention any more than similar aspects of other interventions which, for entirely different purposes, have also found it convenient to try to put the blame for all that happened in the Congo on the United Nations. Such efforts lead, indeed, to strange alliances.

It has been said that the United Nations operation in the Congo is disappointing or even a failure. It seems reasonable to ask those who say so whether the reason for their disappointment is that the Organization has done anything less than it could do, or that elements beyond the control of the Organization have created difficulties which at the present stage of its development are insuperable for the instrument for international cooperation which Members have created in the United Nations, even when that instrument is strained to its utmost capacity. One can blame a mountain climber for his failure to reach the summit when his road has been blocked by an avalanche, but to do so is an irresponsible play on words.

In ending, I would, without any other comments than those provided by facts as they can be evaluated by all Members, like to quote the first of the three points of the basic agreement of July 27, 1960, a point to which the speaker yesterday did not refer. There, the Government of the Republic of the Congo states that: ". . . in the exercise of its sovereign rights with respect to any question concerning the presence and functioning of the United Nations Force in the Congo, it will be guided, in good faith, by the fact that it has requested military assistance from the United Nations and by its acceptance of the resolutions of the Security Council of July 14 and 22, 1960; . . . " And, further, that: ". . . it will ensure the freedom of movement of the Force in the interior of the country and will accord the requisite privileges and immunities to all personnel associated with the activities of the Force."

THE DEBATE continued through six more plenary meetings between March 29 and April 5. By then it was clear that Gromyko's attempt to revive the "troika" had drawn a total blank outside the Soviet bloc and halfway support from Guinea.

Hammarskjöld felt some bitterness, however, that a stronger rebuke had not been given to Gromyko's use of unbridled language and personal abuse and, as we shall see, he frankly expressed his feelings on this aspect of the matter. The Secretary-General began his statement (next following text) by brief references to military developments in the Congo—the arrival of the first Indian troops, the occupation of the Baluba town of Manono by a force of Katanga gendarmerie led by Belgians and other white mercenaries, and a hostile demonstration at Elisabethville.

2. Second Statement

NEW YORK   APRIL 5, 1961

I MAY BEFORE the end of this debate be permitted to revert to the military and political situation in the Congo. Present developments do not invite any detailed comments from me today.

You will have observed that we are at present in the favourable position that the Indian reinforcements are brought in and deployed, thus to some extent restoring the Force to its original and intended numerical strength; the remainder of the Indian troops will arrive in Dar es Salaam on April 8, and arrangements are made for an immediate airlift to Kamina. Together with other units the Indian troops are used in support of the policy laid down by the Security Council in prevention of civil war. We have strengthened considerably United Nations positions in Katanga on the basis laid when the United Nations presence in that province was brought about in August last year.

The practical problem facing us remains the foreign element which, although slight in number, is important in the military situation. I need not repeat what the Members of the General Assembly have already learned of that element, most recently through the press and its news on Manono and, yesterday, on the airport in Elisabethville where the group sent out against the United Nations unit was led by an officer of Belgian nationality. Therefore, we must continue to devote all attention to a satisfactory implementation of part A, paragraph 2 of the Security Council

General Assembly Official Records, Fifteenth Session, 977th plenary meeting.

resolution of February 21, 1961, asking for the withdrawal and evacuation of the foreign military and political elements. Our means, in this respect, remain on the very modest side in view of the lack of cooperation which we face, and we have to try to make up for that in other ways. Let us hope that, firmly continuing on the lines followed so far, the desired results will be achieved before long even if irresponsible elements have now even resorted to attempts to whip up the emotions of the people against the United Nations.

On this occasion I ask for permission to make some necessary comments for the record regarding a side issue brought to the fore in this debate by a group of delegations.

On Tuesday, March 21, 1961, the foreign minister of the Soviet Union said in the Assembly, in words which merit to be put again on record:

The Soviet Government has already declared that it considers Hammarskjöld to be responsible for the murder of Patrice Lumumba and his comrades. Today we are reiterating this accusation from the rostrum of the United Nations. For we cannot reconcile ourselves to this villainy which was perpetrated with the connivance of the international Organization of which our country is a member, perpetrated with the sanction and assistance of the highest official in the United Nations executive body. We cannot reconcile ourselves to the fact that a prominent post in the United Nations is held by a man who has sullied himself by this murder. It is not only he who wields the knife or revolver that is the murderer: the main criminal is the one who placed the weapon in his hand.

Later the foreign minister requested the removal of the present incumbent from the post of Secretary-General "as an accomplice and organizer of the slaughter of the leading statesmen of the Republic of the Congo."

Following up the same theme, the foreign minister of the Byelorussian Soviet Socialist Republic said:

"Having betrayed the interests of the Congolese people, having entered into a plot with the colonialists, having become a coparticipant in the murder of Patrice Lumumba and his colleagues, Mr. Hammarskjöld has lost all the confidence and has brought upon himself the condemnation and contempt of all decent human beings. He has placed himself outside the United Nations."

Members of the Assembly will have noted that these accusations, couched in the most general and condemning terms, were put forward without attempts to give them credence by the indication of any single substantive fact on which they might be based.

I have no reason to comment on these accusations in personal terms. The record is there. It proves that the Secretariat and the United Nations command have acted loyally in support of the interest of the whole of the Congolese people, that they have taken a completely independent, in fact, defiant, stand against so-called colonialists—as well as against others who have tried to intervene in the Congo—and have done what could be done for the protection of Mr. Lumumba by the means at the disposal of the Secretary-General. However, the statements I quoted, and some others of the same character, require comments from another viewpoint.

Where, in any parliament, jealous of its democratic traditions, its integrity, and its respect for the human person, could such allegations be made without those making them trying to justify their case or, especially, without the parliamentary body requesting them to do so? The United Nations General Assembly has been called a parliament of nations. Are the peoples of the world less jealous of the integrity of the General Assembly than the members of a nation are of the integrity of its democratic institutions?

We, all of us, who give what we may have to give to the work of this Organization, do so because of our faith in what it stands for and in the vital necessity of this experiment in organized international cooperation for mutual aims. We do so with pride in the integrity of the efforts made. When we come under responsible criticism, we accept it as a valuable contribution to the common effort, aimed at improving its quality. However, when criticism takes such a direction as to negate the very ideals for which the Organization stands and for which we consider it a privilege to work, one may be led to ask whether the spirit of this Organization will justify for long the faith on which the efforts are and must be based.

As an international civil servant entitled to express his views on the development of international cooperation in the forms provided by the United Nations and related agencies, I consider it my duty to voice these concerns. I would have expressed them with equal conviction but with a greater sense of freedom if the developments to which I refer had not, as in this case, happened to refer also to me as a person.

As regards the Secretary-Generalship and my way of conducting my office, the critics have in this debate brought forward one new viewpoint, a viewpoint which seems to reveal awareness of the weakness of the arguments previously used, and to show also what the basic considerations are which, over the last few months, have led to the repeated and increasingly violent attacks. In the same speech on March 21, Mr. Gromyko said:

> Having without any legitimate grounds taken the whole affair into his own hands, Hammarskjöld began to decide on his own what should and what should not be done. . . . He began to determine on his own choice which countries should send their troops to the Congo and in what numbers; he placed those troops under his own command and became, indeed, some sort of United Nations field marshal.

Further he said:

> An intolerable situation has, indeed, taken shape in the United Nations at present where Hammarskjöld, taking advantage of his office of Secretary-General, is usurping the prerogatives of its bodies, one after another, and in some cases has acted for these bodies trying to supplant them by his own person. . . .
> If Hammarskjöld is allowed to follow this course, he may assume himself to be the prime minister of a world government. . . .

From the context, it is to be assumed that also these latter remarks mainly refer to the Congolese operation.

It is with some hesitation that I take your time for comments on this new element in the continued attack, since I am certain that all members, who have followed the development of the Congo operation, are aware of the groundlessness of the allegations, and since I also believe that they give a realistic interpretation to the motives for the introduction of this new point. However, a short reminder of the facts may be in order.

The resolution of July 14, 1960, for which the Soviet Union voted, authorizes "the Secretary-General to take the necessary steps." It was thus the Security Council which on its own independent initiative gave me a general authorization, obviously implying a request for immediate action. In the early morning hours of July 14, after the end of the Security Council meeting, I had to go ahead on the basis of the authorization without the privilege of any prior consultations.

However, in a report put before the Council July 18—four days later—a very full account was given not only of my interpretation of the mandate and the tasks of the Force, but also of the requests for troops made, the accepted offers, the composition of the Force, the assignment of a commander, and related matters. This report was considered by the Security Council a few days later and "commended"—I repeat, the word was "commended"—by the Council in its resolution of July 22, again with the concurrent vote of the Soviet Union.

When, soon thereafter, units from the United Nations were stopped from going into Katanga, because of armed resistance, although, in the language of the resolution of August 9, the Organization "was ready, and in fact attempted, to do so," I brought the matter at once to the attention of the Security Council for consideration and instructions. By that time I had already continued consultations with an informal group composed of heads of all African delegations, which advised me on the implementation of the resolutions. The approach to the Security Council to which I just referred had as its background such consultations with the Member states which, from a regional viewpoint, were most directly concerned. In the resolution of August 9 the Council, for the third time with the concurrent vote of the Soviet Union, confirmed the authority given on July 14 and 22 to the Secretary-General and requested him to continue to carry out the responsibility placed on him thereby.

Again, when my interpretation of the resolution of August 9 had been challenged by Congolese authorities, I went directly to the Security Council, which, after some delay, met on August 21. I gave the Council a very full account of what had happened, of what steps I had taken and what interpretation I had given to the mandate. The deliberations of the Council ended this time without any resolution, a draft resolution which had been put forward by the Soviet Union being withdrawn by the delegation before the voting; this draft resolution did not criticize the actions but proposed the establishment of a consultative group for the special representative in the Congo.

On my own suggestion, but without any decision of the Security Council, I formalized, after this fourth meeting of the Security Council on the Congo question, an arrangement for standing consultations with a group including representatives of all states participating in the military operation. As is well known, the group had a very strong African-Asian majority. The Assembly later itself used this group for special tasks.

I would have preferred if at this stage, or earlier, the Security Council itself, realizing the enormous and delicate task they had put on the Secretary-General, had found reason and taken the initiative to establish a consultative committee or some similar organ, with proper authority, for sharing of the responsibilities, as in fact the General Assembly had done in the very first resolution on the United Nations Emergency Force during the Suez crisis. The initiative to such an arrangement should naturally have come from the Council and its members, as it would have implied a certain delegation of authority from the Council.

On my initiative, the Congo question was considered again by the Security Council a few days after the so-called *coup d'état* early in September. The problem was then finally transferred to an emergency special session of the General Assembly. As is well known, the outcome was the General Assembly resolution of September 20, on which the Soviet Union abstained, in which the Assembly, fully supporting the three resolutions of the Security Council—including obviously the authorization given to the Secretary-General to take the necessary steps for implementation without any arrangements for consultations with any United Nations organ—requested the Secretary-General "to continue to take vigorous action in accordance with the terms of the aforesaid resolutions."

I can end this condensed review of the constitutional issue, as raised by Mr. Gromyko, with a reminder that, in the General Assembly in December, I invited the General Assembly to make arrangements for the sharing of responsibility, an invitation later repeated but never acted upon by the General Assembly or the Security Council.

I believe that every Member of this Assembly knows why over the years, and again in the Congo crisis, the Security Council or the General Assembly have found it convenient to entrust, in very general terms, executive action on highly explosive problems to the Secretary-General. If the Soviet Union regrets its participation in these decisions, that is its right, but is it its opinion now that the Secretary-General, in anticipation of its own afterthoughts, should have refused to respond to requests for which it had voted?

The same theme has been taken up and further elaborated also by another member of the Soviet group, the foreign minister of the Ukrainian SSR. He brought out four quotations from the Secretary-General's reports to the General Assembly which he considers as evidence of my "usurpation" of power, against the Charter, and as supporting the theses of the foreign minister of the Soviet Union.

The first two quotations are from the reports of 1954 and 1956. It may surprise some that the significance of these statements of mine had not been discovered until March 1961 and, especially, that they were not noted at my reelection in 1957.

However, the most important quote or, as the spokesman said, "the most blatant expression" of my "authoritative tendencies" is, according to him, to be found in my report to the General Assembly in 1959.[1] The way in which the text is treated in the intervention may suffice as comment on all the observations of the speaker in this context. He said that the Secretary-General was "compelled to recognize that in the United Nations Charter there was no basis for his unilateral actions." Let us compare this with the text the speaker discussed. I quote the passage to which he seems to refer, in full:

There have been, in the first place, various decisions taken in recent years by the General Assembly or the Security Council under which the Secretary-General has been entrusted with special diplomatic and operational functions, which he is responsible for carrying out within the wide framework of general terms of reference laid down in the resolutions and, naturally, in the Charter itself. This, also, represents an evolution of the procedures of the United Nations for which no explicit basis is to be found in the Charter. . . .[2]

The Members of the General Assembly will thus see that the text referred to discusses action taken by the Secretary-General at the direct request of the General Assembly or the Security Council, and that the statement regarding the lack of an explicit Charter basis for such action refers not to the Secretary-General's response to the requests but to the decisions of the General Assembly and the Security Council.

I would invite the Members to make for themselves a comparison between what I ha e said and what I have now been said to have said. The speaker was kind enough to provide the Assembly with the necessary references, so I need not repeat them here. If the texts are studied, Members will find that also in this context it is now one of the main accusations against the Secretary-General that he has acted in accordance with requests for which the accusers have voted.

It is with regret that I have found it necessary to take the time of the General Assembly for comments on some points raised, as they have no relation to the situation in the Congo, although they have figured broadly in the speeches of one group of delegates.

Naturally, the methods illustrated by the points discussed have been applied also to the writing of the history of the Congo operation. One can admire the ingenious way in which, with a skilful combination of unrelated facts, a careful choice of data, and appropriate changes of emphasis

[1] See volume IV of this series, Introduction to the Fourteenth Annual Report.
[2] Ibid., p. 451.

and lighting, the representative of Romania, for example, has built up history which to the uninformed may have a semblance of veracity. But such admiration cannot hide the fact that the skill shown has no application to the way in which United Nations organs must deal with a serious international problem, however effective they may have proven for political purposes in this or that national setting.

At this point it may be appropriate for me to give a few comments of a mainly legal and technical nature regarding the two specific questions raised before the Assembly by the representative of the Soviet Union in his intervention last Monday.

The Soviet Union insists that expenditure for an operation like the one undertaken in the Congo and, of course, previously the operation started during the Suez crisis, from the financial point of view should fall under Articles 43 and 48 of the Charter: the principle is supposed to be that all expenditure for the maintenance of peace and security should be decided upon by the Security Council. Members of the General Assembly will undoubtedly have noted the implications of this principle.

A decision on action, be it for the maintenance of peace and security or for other aims within the Council's competence, is governed by the unanimity rule in the Security Council. No one can question the right of the Security Council to take decisions in pursuance of Articles 43 or 48 or any other provisions under which it has competence. However, once the Council has taken a valid decision which imposes responsibilities on the Organization and requires implementation by the Secretary-General, then the costs which are involved are clearly expenses of the Organization within the meaning of Article 17, paragraph 2, of the Charter and therefore must be apportioned by the General Assembly. True, the Council retains the right to revoke or change its decisions, but as long as the decisions require expenditures by the Organization then Article 17, paragraph 2, must be considered applicable.

If this provision of the Charter were to be disregarded and the apportionment of expenses left to the Security Council, this would obviously involve an extension of the unanimity rule in that the approval of all the permanent members would be required for the continued financing of peace and security operations. In short, each permanent member would then have a continuing veto over the implementation decided on by the Council. This would enable each such member to prevent operations, even though the Council itself did not adopt a new decision revoking or modifying its previous action. I leave it to the Members of the General

Assembly to draw their own conclusions regarding what this new line would have meant, for example, in the Suez crisis, or would mean for the future development of the Organization and its possibilities to render service in the essential area of international peace and security.

The complaint has also been made that the Congo operation has not been run by the Department of Political and Security Council Affairs, allegedly because the department now is headed by a Soviet citizen.

In this context I wish to bring to your attention the following: The request for action was, in this as in other similar cases, addressed to the Secretary-General, which obviously means the Secretary-General and not another member of the Secretariat, however qualified. The Secretary-General is the only member of the administration in which Members have chosen, by election, to vest political responsibility; he cannot and does not delegate such responsibility, be it to a citizen of the Soviet Union or a citizen of the United States or, indeed, a citizen of any other Member country. The Secretary-General naturally must have the freedom to choose the collaborators who, among those available, he finds can best assist him in a special task. Nationality has to be taken into account, but the resources of the Secretariat are not such that nationality can be permitted to be decisive. Nor does the choice automatically follow from the posts normally held by those assigned. Through the fifteen years of existence of the United Nations this has been the rule applied.

Were the under-secretary in charge of the Political Affairs Department, whoever he is, to be considered as automatically in charge of field operations, on his own personal responsibility, the logical conclusion would seem to be that he should be appointed with the approval of the main organs of the United Nations, in analogy with the principle established in Article 97.

The new stands on financing and on administration to which these short observations refer are obviously entirely consistent with the objectives of the proposal to put a group of three in the place of the Secretary-General.

All the various efforts of members of the Soviet group to build up a case against me have one and the same purpose, that is to try to achieve some progress in the direction indicated by Mr. Khrushchev's demand that I leave the post of Secretary-General. My position regarding this demand is well known from previous debates, especially from the recent debate in the Security Council. It can be summed up briefly as follows. I do not consider that I am entitled to present the General Assembly with a *fait accompli* by resigning because I have been requested to do so by a Big Power and its like-minded supporters. On the other hand, I regard the will of the General Assembly in this respect as my law, and the General Assembly may thus consider itself as seized with a standing offer of resignation, were the Assembly to find it to be in the best interest of the Organization that I leave.

Members of the Assembly, in determining their position regarding this question, will undoubtedly wish to take into account the reduction of the usefulness of the Secretary-General caused by the withdrawal of cooperation with him by one of the permanent members of the Security Council. But they may also wish to consider the possibility to reconcile the view that a Big Power, by withdrawing its cooperation, at any time should be able to break the term of office of the Secretary-General—thus *de facto* extending its right of veto from the election, as based on Article 97, to his conduct of business through the whole of his established term of office— to reconcile this with the spirit of Article 100 of the Charter and its demand that the Secretary-General, in order to preserve the international and independent charter of the office, should be protected against pressures. In doing so, they will have to look at the reasons given for the withdrawal of cooperation as, obviously, the question of Article 100 does not arise if those reasons are found to be valid in terms of the Charter, while, on the other hand, the question does arise in a very pointed form if the reasons for withdrawal of confidence are found to be of a partisan nature, contrary to the principles of the Organization.

With this clear and unambiguous background, responsibility for the impact and consequences of the Soviet demand that the Secretary-General be dismissed rests where it should be, with the General Assembly and in particular with that vast majority of Members who have an overriding interest in the proper functioning of this Organization and who cannot be suspected of reflecting any bloc interests.

So far the Assembly has not been seized with the issue in a form requiring its formal consideration. If the Assembly does not, on such a basis or otherwise, give expression to its wish for action in accordance with the Soviet demand I must, with my standing offer of resignation before it, conclude that it neither expects me to proceed on the basis of that offer nor desires in any other way to avail itself of the possibility it opens.

I have said this in order to clarify the situation and to indicate on the basis of what considerations I will have to draw my conclusions from this debate and the vote that may follow it. Naturally I must reserve my right, if necessary, to revert also to this issue when the General Assembly has concluded its consideration of the Congo question.

TWO AFRO-ASIAN draft resolutions were introduced on April 5 and 6. One was directed against Belgium's failure to comply with the February 21 Security Council resolution on withdrawal of Belgian military personnel and political advisers. Its twenty-one sponsors were Burma, Cambodia, Ceylon, Ethiopia, Ghana, Guinea, India, Indonesia, Iraq, Liberia, Libya, Malaya, Mali, Morocco, Nepal, Saudi Arabia, Sudan, Togo, the United Arab Republic, Yemen, and Yugoslavia. When introduced it set a twenty-one-day deadline for completing the Belgian withdrawal but this provision failed to win the necessary two-thirds majority when put separately during the voting (see p. 434).

The second Afro-Asian draft resolution noted the report of the Conciliation Commission, called for further efforts at political conciliation in the Congo instead of attempts to find a military solution and urged the reconvening of Parliament under UN protection. It was sponsored by the following seventeen Afro-Asian members: Burma, Chad, Ethiopia, Iran, Japan, Liberia, Libya, Malaya, Nigeria, Pakistan, the Philippines, Senegal, Somalia, Sudan, Tunisia, Turkey, and Upper Volta. The sponsorship of this text included the moderates among the Africans and Asians, some of whom had joined in sponsoring the first resolution, as well as some Asians aligned with the West and a few of the former French colonies. It did not include any of the more radical neutralists and nationalists who were the principal sponsors of the first resolution.

Gromyko had gone home but Zorin was there to speak again on April 7. He renewed Soviet criticism of Hammarskjöld's conduct of the Congo operation but did not introduce any resolution calling for his dismissal. Instead he indicated that the Soviet Union would vote for the first Afro-Asian resolution, despite its "defects," and oppose the second. He also introduced a separate Soviet resolution that simply called for reconvening the Congolese parliament under UN protection and for the preservation of the territorial integrity, unity, and independence of the Republic of the Congo.

Immediately after Zorin had spoken the Secretary-General made a brief reply (first following text).

3. Third Statement

NEW YORK   APRIL 7, 1961

I THANK THE PRESIDENT for giving me an opportunity to give a short reply right away to a few of the observations to which the Assembly has just listened. I will limit myself to some very brief factual comments.

The spokesman of the Soviet Union attacked again the erroneous and arbitrary, or the inefficient, way in which various decisions of the Security Council and the General Assembly have been implemented. He found his worst fears confirmed in view of the way in which the February 21 resolution has been implemented, and naturally the responsibility was put on me. I wish only to draw attention to the fact that the distinguished delegate of the Soviet Union in the Security Council, regarding this resolution, said that it contained no mandate for the Secretary-General nor any mandate addressed to the Secretary-General.

I would also like to draw attention to the fact that the implementation of the February 21 resolution has been carried out in very close contact with the Advisory Committee, or—if, in spite of a previous decision of this General Assembly, the representative of the Soviet Union does not regard it as constitutional—let me say that it was in close contact with sixteen Members of this Organization from African and Asian countries representing all factions in those regions of the world. Those contacts and those consultations were for some time practically daily, and I do not remember any case regarding the implementation where we did not reach a consensus.

Further, there was a reference to the history of the case, as reflected in the records, as proof of the fact of severe criticism of the way in which this matter has been handled. Well, I do not think that anybody needs to go to the record to know that there has been very severe criticism. But we are acting in a constitutional organization with parliamentary forms of work, and it is one thing when something is said from the floor and

General Assembly Official Records, Fifteenth Session, 980th plenary meeting.

another thing if the same view is reflected in a decision of a responsible organ.

I would like the representative of the Soviet Union in this light to explain the resolution of the Security Council of July 22, 1960, the resolution of the Security Council of August 9, the outcome of the debate in the Security Council on August 22, and the resolution of the General Assembly of September 20. Obviously the executive must be guided by the majority view as expressed in constitutional form, not by views held by minorities.

Finally, it was said that what has been done by way of implementation of part A, paragraph 2, of the resolution of February 21 was mainly—and I hope I noted the words correctly—"useless correspondence with usurpers." The two usurpers in question are the Government of Belgium and the chief of state of the Republic of the Congo, as elected and recognized by Parliament and recognized by all the leaders of the Congo until March 31, 1961, when Mr. Gizenga changed his stand. He has also, as we know, been recognized as the chief of state by this Assembly and seated in the Assembly. That much about the "usurpers."

As regards the "uselessness," I would be very interested to know what alternatives there are to correspondence and talks when there is a question of pressing on people and authorities the necessity to implement resolutions. Is the alternative military means? If so, what troops would the Secretary-General have been able to use and with what legal authorization?

ON APRIL 15, during a lengthy series of votes on the two Afro-Asian draft resolutions and amendments thereto, an opportunity arose for the Assembly to deliver a rebuff of sorts to the Soviet Union's assertions of "no confidence" in Hammarskjöld. The first of the draft resolutions, directed against Belgium and sponsored by twenty-one Members, made no mention of the Secretary-General. The second, however, included a paragraph considering "it essential that necessary and effective measures be taken by the Secretary-General" against shipment of arms into the Congo. Diallo Telli of Guinea proposed an amendment to replace the words "the Secretary-General" by "all the authorities concerned" but then withdrew it on the urging of his fellow African delegates. However, a request for a separate roll-call vote on retaining the words "by the Secretary-General" was made and the reference was endorsed by 83 votes to 11, with 5 abstentions. Only the Soviet bloc, Guinea, and Cuba voted "no." The abstainers were France, Mali, Morocco, Portugal, and Yugoslavia.

The first Afro-Asian draft resolution as a whole was adopted by 61 votes to 5, with 33 abstentions, after the provision for a twenty-one-day deadline for the withdrawal of Belgian personnel was deleted because it fell short of a two-thirds majority on a separate vote (40 to retain, 36 to delete, with 23 abstentions). In the vote on the resolution as a whole Belgium, Nepal, Portugal, South Africa, and Uruguay voted "no". Most of the West abstained, with the notable exceptions of Canada and the Nordic bloc, who joined the affirmative.

The text of the resolution, as adopted, read as follows (resolution 1599 (XV)):

The General Assembly,

Recalling its resolution 1474(ES-IV) of September 20, 1960, and the Security Council resolutions of July 14, July 22, and August 9, 1960, and, more particularly, that of February 21, 1961, urging the immediate withdrawal and evacuation of all Belgian and other foreign military and paramilitary personnel and political advisers not under the United Nations command, and mercenaries,

Deploring that despite all these requests the Government of Belgium has not yet complied with the resolutions and that such noncompliance has mainly contributed to the further deterioration of the situation in the Congo,

Convinced that the central factor in the present grave situation in the Congo is the continued presence of Belgian and other foreign military and paramilitary personnel and political advisers, and mercenaries, in total disregard of repeated resolutions of the United Nations,

1. *Calls upon* the Government of Belgium to accept its responsibilities as a Member of the United Nations and to comply fully and promptly with the will of the Security Council and of the General Assembly;

2. *Decides* that all Belgian and other foreign military and paramilitary personnel and political advisers not under the United Nations command, and mercenaries, shall be completely withdrawn and evacuated;

3. *Calls upon* all states to exert their influence and extend their cooperation to effect the implementation of the present resolution.

The second Afro-Asian draft resolution as a whole was adopted by 60 votes to 16, with 23 abstentions, after a series of votes on separate parts and paragraphs. The negative votes were provided by an unnatural partnership of the Soviet bloc with some of the former French African colonies. The abstentions were provided by an equally unnatural combination of the more radical "Third Force" Asians and Africans with Belgium, South Africa, Portugal, Spain, and France.

The text of the resolution, as adopted, was as follows (resolution 1600 (XV)):

The General Assembly,

Having considered the situation in the Republic of the Congo,

Gravely concerned at the danger of civil war and foreign intervention and at the threat to international peace and security,

Taking note of the report of the Conciliation Commission appointed in pursuance of paragraph 3 of its resolution 1474(ES-IV) of September 20, 1960,

Mindful of the desire of the Congolese people for a solution of the crisis in the Congo through national reconciliation and return to constitutionality without delay,

Noting with concern the many difficulties that have arisen in the way of effective functioning of the United Nations operation in the Congo,

1. *Reaffirms* its resolution 1474(ES-IV) and the Security Council resolutions on the situation in the Congo, more particularly the Council resolution of February 21, 1961;

2. *Calls upon* the Congolese authorities concerned to desist from attempting a military solution to their problems and resolve them by peaceful means;

3. *Considers it essential* that necessary and effective measures be taken by the Secretary-General immediately to prevent the introduction of arms, military equipment, and supplies into the Congo, except in conformity with the resolutions of the United Nations;

4. *Urges* the immediate release of all members of Parliament and members of provincial assemblies and all other political leaders now under detention;

5. *Urges* the convening of Parliament without delay, with safe conduct and security extended to the members of Parliament by the United Nations, so that Parliament may take the necessary decisions concerning the formation of a national government and on the future constitutional structure of the Republic of the Congo in accordance with the constitutional processes laid down in the *Loi fondamentale*;

6. *Decides* to appoint a Commission of Conciliation of seven members to be designated by the President of the General Assembly to assist the Congolese leaders to achieve reconciliation and to end the political crisis;

7. *Urges* the Congolese authorities to cooperate fully in the implementation of the resolutions of the Security Council and of the General Assembly and to accord all facilities essential to the performance by the United Nations of functions envisaged in those resolutions.

A third draft resolution was introduced by Ceylon, Ghana, India, and Morocco to provide for establishing a commission of investigation into the death of Lumumba as proposed in the Secretary-General's report of March 20 to the Security Council (p. 414). It was also adopted by the Assembly on April 15 by 45 votes to 3 (the Congo-Leopoldville, Spain, and Portugal), with 49 abstentions, the latter including most of the West, the Soviet bloc, and the former French African colonies.

The text of the resolution, as adopted, read as follows (resolution 1601 (XV)):

The General Assembly,

Recalling part A, paragraph 4, of the Security Council resolution of February 21, 1961,

Taking note of documents S/4771 and Add.1,

1. *Decides* to establish a Commission of Investigation consisting of the following members: Justice U Aung Khine (Burma), Mr. Teschome Haile-

mariam (Ethiopia), Mr. Salvador Martínez de Alva (Mexico), Mr. Ayité d'Almeida (Togo);

2. *Requests* the Commission to proceed as early as possible to carry out the task entrusted to it.

During the explanations of vote on April 18 Zorin again charged Hammar- skjöld with failing to implement the Security Council's February 21 resolution. The Secretary-General immediately responded (first following text). The incidents to which he refers were, first, the capture by UN soldiers at Kabalo of thirty mercenaries, mostly South Africans, who had been recruited for Tshombé's forces and came in by plane expecting to seize the airfield and, second, the detention of a West German plane chartered by Sabena which had managed to unload a cargo of arms at Kolwezi for the Katanga forces before it was stopped at another airport, where ONUC had troops.

---

4. Fourth Statement

NEW YORK   APRIL 18, 1961

I AM SORRY INDEED to have to take time from the deliberations of the General Assembly, but one or two observations made by the representa- tive of the Soviet Union make it necessary for me to reply. The represen- tative of the Soviet Union saw fit to repeat all the previous accusations against the Secretary-General. I have already replied. I will not discuss them now and I can easily take them; but he went much further, and that is the point which calls for a reply.

He said again that the February 21 resolution of the Security Council has not been implemented, and he found that natural in view of the fact that implementation was in the hands of the Secretary-General. First of all, let us note that if it is, it is at the request of the Security Council and of the General Assembly, recently repeated by this General Assembly on Saturday, in a vote to which the representative of the Soviet Union did not refer.

Moreover, what are the facts? The fact is, first, that implementation of this resolution has, as I have said before in the Assembly, been carried out in very intimate and close cooperation with the Advisory Committee

General Assembly Official Records, Fifteenth Session, 987th plenary meeting.

on the Congo. The composition of this Advisory Committee is well known to the Assembly. Further, negotiations concerning implementation of part A, paragraph 2, to which the representative of the Soviet Union attaches special importance, have been carried out in Brussels by Ambassador Sahbani of Tunisia, and in Leopoldville by Mr. Gardiner of Ghana and Mr. Nwokedi of Nigeria.

My special representative in the Congo is still Mr. Dayal, and acting for him is Mr. Abbas of Sudan. You also know the composition of the command. The commander is an Irishman; the deputy commander is an Ethiopian. All these people are now called acolytes of the colonialists, and that is the reason why I take the floor. That is the point on which it is my duty as Secretary-General to protest.

In order to prove his case, this time the representative of the Soviet Union referred to two recent reports. He did so in a way which I think is significant. He referred to the report on certain interrogations of mercenaries whom we had detained. He did not see in that report any sign of the fact that we take vigorous action against mercenaries. He saw only a sign of the fact that there are mercenaries. Likewise, he referred to the reports on our impounding a German aircraft. He saw in that not any sign of our intervening in the spirit of the resolutions, but only a sign of the fact that there has been some arms running.

Those who have studied the case of the German aircraft may have observed that it went from Forty Lamy to Kolwezi in Katanga. We have at present some fifteen thousand men in the Congo over a territory which, as you know, is five times as large as France. We cannot be, and we are not, at all air strips, and for that reason I think that there can be no accusation against us if this aircraft, coming from outside the Congo, landed there without our being able to impound it at the time of unloading. It was impounded on its way back, when it happened to pass a point where we were represented.

In considering the whole question of the implementation of the resolutions, I think it would be appropriate to make a distinction between demands, authority, and means. I believe that all through the history of the Congo operation demands have gone far beyond authorization and authorization far beyond means. That is the only comment I would like to make on the new complaints.

STATEMENTS ON FINANCING UNITED NATIONS OPERATIONS IN THE CONGO

THE DIFFICULTIES in the way of raising the money to pay for the Congolese operations had become worse since the Assembly's action on the question in December 1960 (see p. 236).

De Gaulle had disliked from the start the United Nations intervention in the Congo and the French government now decided to join the Soviet bloc in refusing to pay its share as assessed by the General Assembly or to recognize that the obligations under Article 17, paragraph 2, of the Charter applied.

The Soviet Union restated its constitutional position—only the Security Council had the power under the Charter to raise and dispatch UN armed forces and to decide how they should be paid for. India and some other Afro-Asians also considered that the obligations of Article 17 did not apply but thought the Assembly should make special arrangements for funding such operations. Mexico led a Latin American revolt against United States insistence on the applicability of both Article 17 and the penalties for nonpayment provided in Article 19. Its representative argued that the records of the 1945 San Francisco conference showed that Articles 17 and 19 had not been intended to apply to expenditures for the use of armed forces. He proposed that 70 per cent of the costs of ONUC be borne by the five permanent members of the Security Council, 25 per cent by those states whose investments in the Congo exceeded $1 million and only 5 per cent apportioned on the basis of the regular scale of assessments.

With only four days remaining before the end of the Assembly session the Fifth Committee remained unable to reach a decision when the Secretary-General came before it on April 17 to address the constitutional issue (first following text).

1. Statement in the Fifth Committee

NEW YORK   APRIL 17, 1961

I HAVE FOLLOWED with close attention the recent discussions of this Committee on the expenditures in the Congo and I welcome this opportunity

General Assembly Official Records, Fifteenth Session, Annexes, agenda items 49–50, document A/C.5/864.

to make some observations on one or two points of fundamental importance that have arisen in the discussion. In particular, I should like to address myself to the constitutional issue raised by some members that the costs of the Congo operation should not properly and legally be treated as expenses of the Organization within the meaning of Article 17, paragraph 2 of the Charter. In support of this, it has been suggested—notably by the distinguished representative of Mexico—that the records of the United Nations Conference on International Organization, held at San Francisco, require an interpretation that expenditures of the kind incurred in the Congo cannot come within the terms of Article 19 of the Charter relating to arrears and therefore are not to be treated as "expenses" in the obligatory sense of Article 17.

I have given careful consideration to his argument because, as the members know, I believe it of the utmost importance that the Organization adhere strictly to the law and principle laid down in the Charter. My conclusion—and it seems to me, with all respect, to be the only possible conclusion—is that Article 17 must apply to the expenses in question. The records of the conference which I have looked into do not contradict this or even cast any doubt on it; I shall indicate specifically why this is so in order that the record in this General Assembly will be entirely clear.

Before doing so, I should like to make it clear that my conclusion as to Article 17 would not in any way prejudge or restrict the right of this Committee and the General Assembly to apportion the expenses as it considers appropriate and equitable. Certainly these costs have been heavy and extraordinary and they present a grave problem for many states. But it seems to me that this problem can be dealt with adequately within the framework of Article 17 and without departing from the clear provisions of the Charter.

May I now turn to the arguments put forth in detail by the representative of Mexico. In his statement he drew two main conclusions from his analysis of the discussion at San Francisco. The first of these was that "all expenses of the Organization within the meaning of Article 17, paragraph 2, were subject, without exception, to the sanctions provided for in Article 19."

On this, I am fully in agreement. I might only note that Article 19 also empowers the General Assembly to permit a defaulting Member to vote if it is satisfied that the failure to pay is due to conditions beyond the control of the Member.

The second conclusion stated by the representative of Mexico was that expenses resulting from the use of armed forces as in the Congo operation had been deliberately excluded by the San Francisco conference from the application of the sanctions provided for in Article 19. I stress the words "use of armed forces." Here I regret to say we are not in agreement. In my opinion, his conclusion rests on a mistaken premise as to the nature of the United Nations operations in the Congo, and is not, in fact, supported by the arguments and quotations from the San Francisco conference which were cited.

The representative of Mexico particularly stressed an Australian proposal made at the conference to introduce the following amendment to Chapter V of the Dumbarton Oaks Proposals: "A Member shall have no vote if it has not carried its obligations as set forth in Chapter VIII, section B, paragraph 5" (this latter provision being the paragraph which later became Article 43 of the Charter).

The representative of Mexico sought to show that the introduction and discussion of this amendment—on which no decision was taken, and which was later conditionally withdrawn—shows conclusively that the sanctions provided for in Article 19 of the Charter could not have been intended to apply to the expenses of enforcement measures taken involving the use of armed force.

The first point to note in this connection is that the Australian amendment referred to by the representative of Mexico referred specifically and exclusively to obligations under Article 43 of the Charter (formerly Chapter VIII, section B, paragraph 5, of the Dumbarton Oaks Proposals) but it did not refer in any general sense to operations involving the use of armed forces. This distinction between action taken under Article 43 and the use of armed force in other contexts and under other Charter provisions is of crucial importance to the question now under discussion and I shall need to refer to it again.

The representative of Mexico himself acknowledged that the Australian amendment referred expressly to Article 43, and it was with reference to this Article that he then proceeded to draw conclusions. To quote here from his statement, he said:

The competent Committee took a first decision approving the text of what was to become Article 17, paragraphs 1 and 2, of the Charter. It then voted to add an amendment incorporating the penal provision which is at present contained in Article 19 of the Charter and which is applicable to all the expenses referred to in Article 17, paragraph 2. Immediately thereafter, the Committee voted to postpone discussion of an Australian amendment under which the penal provision in Article 19, which the Committee had just approved, would have been extended to Members failing to carry out the obligations laid down in the provision that has since become Article 43 of the Charter; in other words, to Members which, *inter alia,* failed to contribute their assessed share of the costs of operations involving the use of armed forces, carried out under that Article.

I repeat, "under that Article."

It is thus clear that whatever significance may be attributed to this Australian amendment at the San Francisco conference in regard to the nonfulfilment of obligations under Article 43, it has no relevance to the action taken under other Articles of the Charter. Accordingly, since United Nations operations in the Congo have at no time been carried out under Article 43 of the Charter, it follows that the argument of the representative of Mexico concerning the nonapplicability of the sanctions provided for in Article 19, is really not relevant to the question of these expenses.

To make this clear I should like to amplify a little further the legal basis under the Charter for the United Nations operations in the Congo. In the first place, one must bear in mind the fundamental difference between the use of armed force under Article 43 or 42 of the Charter and the use of military personnel or contingents for essentially internal security functions in the territory of a Member state at the invitation of the government of that state. The operation in the Congo is clearly of the latter type. The function of the United Nations Force—as stated initially—was to assist in maintaining law and order; this was later expanded by the Security Council resolution of February 21, 1961, to include the objectives of preventing civil war. The Security Council considered these measures necessary to counteract the threat to international peace, but the measures themselves did not constitute "sanctions" or enforcement action directed against a State as contemplated by Articles 42 and 43 of the Charter.

The records of the Security Council leave no doubt about this. No one ever suggested that its decisions regarding the Congo were in any way related to Article 43 of the Charter, and no proposal was made that agreements for this purpose should be concluded between the Security Council and Members as contemplated by that Article. Even more significant is the fact that no single member of the Security Council and indeed not a single Member who took part in the debates in the Security Council or the General Assembly on this subject stated, or even intimated that the Council had acted on the basis of Article 43.

On the contrary, it was explicitly stated in the Security Council that the resolutions did not constitute an enforcement measure in the sense referred to in Article 42 of the Charter. On various occasions in the Security Council and the General Assembly, I drew attention to this point and expressed the view that the Security Council resolutions in this respect could be considered as implicitly taken under Article 40, but certainly did not involve the type of coercive action directed against governments envisaged by the enforcement measures of Article 41, or Article 42.

You will find these statements in my interventions in the Security Council on December 13/14, 1960, in the General Assembly on December 17, 1960, and in the Security Council meeting on February 20/21, 1961. No objection was voiced against this conclusion. Several members of the Security Council, in fact, made it clear in their own statements that they did not consider the Council resolutions as involving the enforcement actions or sanctions provided for in Article 42 of the Charter. I do not want to take the time of the Committee by lengthy quotations but those interested might wish to refer to the remarks of the delegate of Ceylon at meetings of the Council on December 10, 1960, and December 13/14, 1960, those of the representatives of France on February 7, 1961, of the United States of America on February 20, 1961. It may be recalled that the representative of the United Arab Republic stated at the meeting on February 17, 1961, that if the necessary cooperation were not given, then "we will be forced to go back to the Security Council once again and ask that measures falling within the framework of Chapter VII of the Charter be taken in order to obtain this objective. I am speaking of sanctions."

In the light of these statements and the record of the Security Council resolutions, one cannot avoid the conclusion that the quotations and argument put forward by the representative of Mexico rests on a mistaken assumption. In short, the action taken by the Security Council was not the type of action which he referred to as having been discussed by the United Nations Conference on International Organization in San Francisco in connection with Article 19. Whatever the merits of his argument, it is simply not applicable to the case before us. The fact that military contingents were used for the maintenance of law and order and to prevent civil war did not mean that Article 43 was being applied, either in letter or spirit, or that military enforcement action was being taken as contemplated by that Article. For these reasons, it seems clear to me that the references made by the representative of Mexico to the San Francisco discussions, and indeed the entire record of those discussions, contain nothing to suggest that expenses of the Organization of the kind now incurred in the Congo are not fully within the meaning of Article 17, paragraph 2, of the Charter.

I come now to another point. Several of the representatives have naturally laid emphasis on the size of the Congo expenditures and on their "extraordinary" character. But how, from a legal and constitutional point of view, can these factors lead to a conclusion that they are not expenses of the Organization? The fact that these expenses have been substantial and unusual—indeed, unforeseeable at the time of the San Francisco conference—cannot mean that the Charter provision must now be disregarded. Nor would there appear to be any practical necessity to do so. For under Article 17, the Assembly has a broad discretion to deal with the apportionment of expenses; it may provide—and in fact it has provided—for different methods of apportionment to meet the necessities in particular cases. Certainly it is free to take into account the special considerations which have been alluded to and to ensure a just and equitable distribution of the burdens assumed by the Organization in maintaining international peace and security. This can be done, with full respect for the legal principles prescribed in the Charter and without departing from the clear and specific rule that these costs constitute expenses of the Organization within the meaning of the Charter.

As I have had this opportunity to intervene in the debate in the Fifth Committee, you may perhaps permit me to add another observation. Members of the Committee may remember that on November 21, 1960, I addressed the Committee and on that occasion reminded it of the fact that, as had been stated in the General Assembly, the daily cost to the world for current armaments amounts to some $320 million. Let us assume that this figure is on the high side. It all the same remains true, and it should be registered, that the total annual cost for the Congo operation is less than a half of the daily cost for present armaments. I think the conclusions can easily be drawn by anybody.

A COMPROMISE draft resolution sponsored by Ghana, Liberia, Pakistan, and Turkey finally came to a vote on April 20 in the Fifth Committee. Unlike the resolution of December 20, 1960, it did not include an explicit affirmation of the applicability of Articles 17 and 19 to the Congo costs, though it did provide for the appropriation of $100 million "as expenses of the Organization." These were to be apportioned in principle in accordance with the regular scale of assessments, but with reductions of 75 percent for Member states whose contributions to the regular budget were less than 1.25 percent of the total and by 50 percent for any Member state receiving technical assistance. The short-fall would be made up by voluntary contributions requested of the Big Five, Belgium, and other more affluent Members. The United States announced that it would contribute $15 million in addition to its regular assessment provided the principle of collective responsibility for meeting the costs was maintained. Even so the resolution carried by only 43 votes to 26, with 14 abstentions. This was less than the two-thirds majority that would be required in plenary the next day and prompted the following statement by the Secretary-General.

2. Further Statement in the Fifth Committee

NEW YORK   APRIL 20, 1961

I AM GRATEFUL to the Chairman for granting me the floor to make a few observations on the result of this vote.

Five days ago the General Assembly adopted two resolutions regarding the Congo operation which confirmed previous decisions of the Security Council and the General Assembly, and in particular the Security Council resolution of February 21, 1961, which in important respects even widened the tasks of the United Nations Force. Also one of the resolutions adopted on April 15, 1961, added a new task for the Force. Resolution 1599 (XV) was adopted by 61 votes in favour, 5 against, and 33 abstentions. Resolution 1600 (XV) was adopted by 60 votes in favour, 16 against, and 23 abstentions.

Were the General Assembly now to fail to provide the funds necessary for the carrying out of the various resolutions on the Congo operation, the General Assembly would within a few days have taken two irreconcilable stands on one of the major political questions with which it has ever had to deal. The Secretary-General is neither entitled nor able to carry out political decisions for which funds have been refused. Conversely, he is not entitled to stop a political operation he has been ordered to carry out by the Security Council. Thus, there would remain nothing for him to do but to report the situation to the Security Council. Thereafter, the Coun-

General Assembly Official Records, Fifteenth Session, Annexes, agenda items 49-50, document A/C. 5/867.

cil would urgently have to consider whether it would reverse its stand and take a decision to the effect that, because of the financial decision of the General Assembly, the Congo operation should be stopped. Were the Council to find that it could not take such a decision in view of its responsibilities and in view also of the recent substantive decisions of the General Assembly itself, it would, all the same, be impossible to carry out the Security Council and General Assembly decisions unless, in some way, through an appropriate initiative the necessary means were to be made available.

How could the continued impossibility to carry out such decisions, required for peace and security, be justified by anyone who cares for the dignity of this Organization as it reflects on all its Member nations or, in fact, be reconciled with the responsibilities of this Organization as laid down in the Charter?

THE FINAL MEETING of the Assembly began in the evening of April 21 and continued through the night until 6 o'clock the next morning. When the resolution was first put to the vote it failed of the necessary two-thirds majority, receiving 45 affirmative votes to 25 against, with 27 abstentions. No fewer than seventeen Latin American states failed to support the United States position, with nine voting "no" and eight abstaining. Then followed a period of confusion with various procedural proposals on how to meet the situation. For the Soviet Union A. A. Roshchin urged that the question be referred to the Security Council and said this was the solution proposed the day before by Hammarskjöld himself. The Secretary-General quickly corrected Roshchin's misinterpretation of what he had said (first following text).

---

3. Statement in the General Assembly

NEW YORK   APRIL 21, 1961

I AM SORRY, but I must correct the reference made by the representative of the Soviet Union to my stand in the Fifth Committee.

General Assembly Official Records, Fifteenth Session, 995th plenary meeting.

The representative of the Soviet Union said that I had taken the line that if this draft resolution were not adopted the natural thing for me to do would be to go to the Security Council. That is not what I said. What I said was that if funds were not provided I would face the following situation: On the one hand, I would have no possibility of continuing the operation; on the other hand, I was under the obligation, in relation to the Security Council, to continue it. In such circumstances I could do nothing but report to the Security Council that the General Assembly had failed to take any action which permitted such continuance.

Obviously, this stand in no way precludes the General Assembly from continuing its consideration of this issue until it has reached a decision. The action which I would be forced to take would be action coming only when the General Assembly had said its last word—and I understand from the present debate that the Assembly has not yet said its last word.

THE ASSEMBLY then agreed to a suggestion by the United States representative Philip M. Klutznick, that the question be left open for a time, while the Assembly proceeded to consider several other items that had to be disposed of at this meeting. This maneuver made room for off-the-floor discussions which finally produced a solution of the impasse. Just before dawn the representative of Pakistan, Said Hasan, announced that the sponsors had agreed to increase the reductions provided in the resolution for the smaller states from 75 to 80 percent and moved reconsideration. The motion carried by 67 votes to 12, with 14 abstentions. The amendments to increase reductions to 80 per cent were then approved by 51 votes to 17, with 24 abstentions, and the draft resolution, as amended, was adopted as a whole by 54 votes to 15, with 23 abstentions (resolution 1619 (XV)). Seven Latin Americans who had abstained the first time shifted to the affirmative and six who had voted "no" shifted to abstentions. Four of the former French African colonies who abstained the first time also shifted to the affirmative. These and a few other switches of position proved more than sufficient to carry the day.

Second Report to the Security Council on Certain Steps Taken in Regard to the Implementation of the Council Resolution of February 21, 1961

NEW YORK   MAY 17, 1961

WHEN HAMMARSKJÖLD circulated the following report to the Security Council there was some progress to register on the military, diplomatic, and political fronts. In northern Katanga reinforced units of the UN Force had succeeded, by interposing themselves, in frustrating the offensive mounted by Tshombé's foreign-led *gendarmerie* against the Balubas. In Belgium Paul-Henri Spaak had become foreign minister late in April in a coalition government established after new elections and prolonged negotiations among the parties. Spaak's views, record, and influence nourished hope for some improvement in Belgium's attitude but the strong pro-Katanga influences upon Belgian public opinion restricted his freedom of maneuver and he had to move very slowly.

In the Congo a dramatic turnabout in the attitude of President Kasavubu and the other Leopoldville leaders was under way. Hammarskjöld was able to report that they now accepted the Security Council's February 21 resolution (161 (1961)) and had initialed on April 17 a compromise agreement on carrying out their responsibilities under the resolution. The texts were included in his report, but he did not discuss the conference of Congolese political leaders which met from April 24 to May 28 at Coquilhatville, capital of Equateur Province.

This conference had been planned as a sequel to the earlier meeting at Tananarive (pp. 393-94). Once again Tshombé came and Gizenga stayed away, but any similarity between the two conferences ended there. Tshombé immediately demanded that Kasavubu abrogate the April 17 agreement with the United Nations. When Kasavubu refused and Tshombé failed to win support from other conferees for his demand he walked out. However, ANC soldiers at the airport refused to let him fly back to Elisabethville, insisting that no one should leave until a coalition government for a united Congo had been agreed. The soldiers perhaps acted on their own in the beginning but Kasavubu then decided to put Tshombé under house arrest. He also ordered that the Belgian advisers who had accompanied Tshombé be detained and expelled from the Congo by the United Nations and this was done (paragraph 8 of the following text). The conference then voted to endorse the April 17 agreement with the United Nations and before it adjourned annulled the decisions of Tananarive, supported a federal solution with a fairly strong central government, and called for the reconvening of Parliament under UN protection without delay (see p. 497 for later developments).

Security Council Official Records, Sixteenth Year, Supplement for April, May, and June 1961, documents S/4807 and Add. 1.

1. SINCE THE PUBLICATION of the report of the Secretary-General on certain steps taken in regard to the implementation of the Security Council resolution S/4741 of February 21, 1961 (161 [1961]), the Secretary-General has continued to consult regularly with the United Nations Advisory Committee on the Congo concerning the implementation of the Security Council resolutions, especially that of February 21, 1961, as well as the resolutions adopted by the General Assembly with regard to the Congo (Leopoldville).

2. With reference to part A, operative paragraph 1, of the resolution of February 21, 1961, the United Nations command in the Congo, having received substantial increases in the strength of its Force, has taken measures designed to prevent the occurrence of civil war, particularly in the areas of northern Katanga and South Kasai. As a result of actions taken by United Nations forces in the localities of Kabalo and Nyunzu and as a result of the redeployment of United Nations forces in other localities of northern Katanga, the danger of emerging civil war has been substantially lessened. In this connection, it may be noted that in the course of the ONUC actions in northern Katanga, United Nations forces have taken into custody a total of thirty-seven mercenaries. A report relating to thirty mercenaries apprehended at Kabalo has been distributed to the Security Council. In actions at Nyunzu on May 6 and 7, 1961, seven additional mercenaries were apprehended. All of these mercenaries have now been evacuated. With a view to reducing the possibility of civil war in South Kasai, a redeployment of United Nations forces has recently been undertaken.

3. In regard to measures to be taken in pursuance of part A, paragraph 2, of the Security Council resolution of February 21, the Secretary-General, after an exchange of letters with the representative of Belgium and the president of the Republic of the Congo and after consultation with the United Nations Advisory Committee on the Congo, appointed Ambassador Sahbani of Tunisia to proceed to Brussels in order to make arrangements with the Government of Belgium concerning the immediate withdrawal and evacuation from the Congo of all Belgian military and paramilitary personnel, as well as Belgian political advisers and mercenaries. At the same time, the Secretary-General, in consultation with the Advisory Committee on the Congo, dispatched two members of the

United Nations Secretariat, namely Mr. Nwokedi and Mr. Gardiner, to the Republic of the Congo for the purpose of eliciting the assistance of the President of the Republic, as well as that of other Congolese authorities, in the implementation of part A, paragraph 2, and part B, paragraph 2, of the Security Council resolution of February 21, 1961.

4. Mr. Sahbani went to Brussels on March 20, 1961, and, as a result of a government crisis of unexpectedly long duration, was compelled to stay there until May 11, on which date he returned to report to the Secretary-General and to the Advisory Committee on the Congo on that first stage in the talks. In the conversations held by the representative of the Secretary-General at Brussels, the Belgian government repeatedly asserted its willingness to accept and implement the resolution of February 21. That willingness was expressed once again in a note from Mr. Wigny, minister for foreign affairs of the former government, to the Secretary-General, dated April 1, 1961. Unfortunately, as regards definition of the methods of implementing the resolution, the Belgian government has shown a reluctance which, on some occasions, came close to putting in doubt its very acceptance of the resolution in principle. The Secretary-General and his representative at all times firmly opposed this attitude and recalled that the resolution of February 21 could in no circumstances be subject to negotiation. On the other hand, the representative of the Secretary-General at Brussels obtained useful information from the Belgian government on the distribution of Belgian military personnel in the different provinces of the Congo as well as on its distribution by rank. Continuing his conversations with the new government, the representative held a number of talks with Mr. Spaak, the minister for foreign affairs. In the course of these talks, a slight change in the position of the Belgian government became apparent. Nevertheless, Belgium's position still falls far short of what is required by the Security Council resolution; in fact, the Belgian minister for foreign affairs, in a communication to the representative of the Secretary-General dated May 6, takes an attitude which, in the view of the Secretary-General and of the Advisory Committee on the Congo, is not in accord with either the letter or the spirit of the resolution of February 21. This communication, to which the Secretary-General replied by making, through his representative, the objections and clarifications which were required, nevertheless gives some hope that in the future Belgium will adopt a more constructive attitude and one more in keeping with its obligations. For this reason the representative of the Secretary-General went back to Brussels on May 16, equipped with adequate in-

structions, in order to resume his conversations with the Belgian government, and it is expected that these conversations will be concluded shortly.

5. The United Nations Secretariat mission to the Congo held consultations between March 21 and April 17 not only with the president of the republic but also with representatives of the authorities in Stanleyville, Elisabethville, and Bakwanga.

6. For the purpose of implementing both part A, paragraph 2, and part B, paragraph 2, of the Security Council resolution of February 21, Mr. Kasavubu, president of the Republic of the Congo, together with Mr. Bomboko, and Mr. Nwokedi and Mr. Gardiner, signed on April 17, 1961, an agreement of general principles which is reproduced in annex I. In this document, the president accepted the resolution of the Security Council of February 21 and, in particular, the two paragraphs mentioned above.

7. After consultations and comments by the Advisory Committee on the Congo concerning the agreement, the Secretary-General addressed a letter dated April 26, 1961, to President Kasavubu, which is reproduced in annex II.

8. For the purpose of discussing with Congolese authorities the further implementation of part A, paragraph 2, and also part B, paragraph 2, of the resolution, the Secretary-General asked Mr. Gardiner to return to the Congo, where he is at present holding discussions with the president of the republic and his representatives. In this connection, it may be noted that, at the request of President Kasavubu, ONUC held and later evacuated five Belgian nationals and one stateless person who had accompanied Mr. Tshombé to Coquilhatville.

9. Following the adoption by the General Assembly of resolution 1601 (XV) of April 15, 1961, which provided for the appointment of a commission of investigation in implementation of part A, paragraph 4, of the Security Council resolution of February 21, 1961, the Secretary-General invited the members of the commission to convene in New York. Although the Secretary-General had hoped that the first meeting could be convened on April 28, three members of the commission, namely Justice U Aung Khine (Burma), Mr. Teshome Hailemariam (Ethiopia), and Mr. Ayité d'Almeida (Togo) assembled formally on May 11, 1961. It is expected that the Mexican member of the commission will be appointed shortly. The commission is presently holding private meetings. The Secretariat transmitted to the commission all the information at its disposal.

10. In regard to part B, paragraph 2, of the resolution, reference is

made to the agreement of April 17, 1961, by which the Republic of the Congo recognizes the need to reorganize the Armeé nationale congolaise, it being understood that this reorganization is to be carried out under the authority of the president of the republic, with United Nations assistance, and on the basis of the proposals made by the chief of state in his letter of March 5, 1961, to the Secretary-General. Discussions are presently taking place between a representative of the Secretary-General and the president of the republic concerning the implementation of this provision on a basis which would apply to the Republic of the Congo as a whole.

ANNEX I

Agreement on General Principles Between the President of the Republic of the Congo (Leopoldville) and the Secretary-General of the United Nations

As a Member of the United Nations, the Republic of the Congo (Leopoldville), whose sovereignty should not be in doubt, is under an obligation to respect the Charter of the Organization and to carry out the resolution of the Security Council.

The Republic of the Congo accepts the resolution S/4741 of February 21, 1961, taking into account:

(1) That the United Nations reaffirms its respect for the sovereignty of the Republic of the Congo in the implementation of the resolution;

(2) That the aim of the resolution of February 21, part A, paragraph 2, and part B, paragraph 2, is to eliminate all deleterious foreign influence. To this effect the president of the Republic of the Congo will receive all possible assistance of the United Nations;

(3) That the United Nations is to assist the president of the republic so that all foreign personnel, whether civilian, military, or paramilitary and all mercenaries and political advisers who have not been recruited or recalled under the authority of the president, be repatriated from the Congo within the shortest possible period of time. To implement the above and taking into account the recognition of the sovereign rights of the republic and the constitutional powers which he holds, the president of the republic will reexamine the appointments of foreign civilian, military, and paramilitary personnel made under his authority and will take the necessary decisions compatible with the interests of the Republic of the Congo;

(4) That the United Nations is to give to the president of the republic all possible assistance in:

(a) Recruiting the technicians needed by the Republic of the Congo, without however having a monopoly of such recruitments;

(b) Training the administrative and technical cadres by granting fellowships and establishing specialized institutes.

The Republic of the Congo recognizes the need to reorganize the national army, it being understood that this reorganization is to be carried out under the authority of the president of the republic, with United Nations assistance and on the basis of the proposals made by the chief of state in his letter of March 5, 1961, to the Secretary-General of the United Nations.

The detailed application of the basic agreement outlined above shall be subject, in each case, to a careful study on the part of the Government of the Republic of the Congo and the United Nations.

Leopoldville, April 17, 1961

[For the United Nations] [For the Republic of the Congo (Leopoldville)]

F.C. Nwokedi   J. Kasavubu
R. Gardiner   J. Bomboko

Annex II

Final Text of a Letter Dated April 26, 1961, from the Secretary-General to the President of the Republic of the Congo (Leopoldville) Concerning the Agreement Relating to Security Council Resolution S/4741

I have the honour to refer to the agreement on general principles relating to the Security Council resolution S/4741 of February 21, 1961, the text of which, for confirmation, is annexed to this letter. You will recall that it was necessary for my representatives, in view of their terms of reference, to reserve to me the right of final approval of the agreement on the side of the United Nations.

I have now heard from my representative a full account of the discussions leading to the agreement and have considered with them and with my other advisers all of its provisions and implications. May I say that I have been encouraged by the results of the discussions which took place between you and your colleagues and my representatives in terms not only of the substance of the agreement itself, but also of the spirit of constructive cooperation and mutual trust which my representatives have reported to me as having characterized the discussions.

I understand and appreciate that the agreement represents, on the side of the Republic of the Congo, the full and free exercise of the sovereign rights of the republic including the recognition of its obligations as a Member state of the United Nations, particularly in respect of the resolution concerned. On the side of the United Nations, the agreement indicates the intention of the Organization to afford assistance to the Republic of the Congo in meeting those same obligations. It is worth noting that in striking the balance between your obligations and the intention of the United Nations, nothing has been included in the agreement that could be construed as being at variance with the terms and meaning of the Security Council resolution concerned. Thus the agreement, without derogating from the resolution, represents a valuable first step towards its implementation in cooperation between you, Mr. President, and the United Nations.

The text of the agreement leaves a considerable measure of initiative for the discharge of the obligation of the Republic of the Congo under the Security Council resolution to you, Mr. President. The execution of the relevant parts of the resolution, which is by its very nature mandatory, is in that sense, therefore, dependent on your determination to cooperate fully with the United Nations. I have no doubt that you intend to do so. This assumption enables me to interpret the provisions of the agreement, which call for United Nations assistance, to mean that such assistance will be given in order to facilitate your wholehearted cooperation in the implementation of the resolution. The above observation has particular reference to paragraph 3 where, in recognition of the constitutional powers which you hold, you have undertaken to reexamine the appointments of foreign civilian, military, and paramilitary personnel made under your personal authority and to take the necessary decisions compatible with the interest of the Republic of the Congo. In this connection, I wish to recall that subsequent to the initialling of the agreement, the General Assembly adopted resolution 1600 (XV) on April 15, 1961, in which, among other things, it "*urges* the Congolese authorities to cooperate fully in the implementation of the resolutions of the Security Council and of the General Assembly and to accord all facilities essential to the performance by the United Nations of functions envisaged in those resolutions."

With this understanding I am pleased to signify my approval of the text as initialled, which together with this letter of approval will constitute our definitive agreement.

DAG HAMMARSKJÖLD
Secretary-General

Document S/4807/Add. 1

With reference to paragraph 9 of the report, the Secretary-General wishes to note that Ambassador Salvador Martínez de Alva has been appointed by the Mexican government as a member of the Commission of Investigation under General Assembly resolution 1601 (XV), and that Mr. Martínez de Alva arrived in New York on May 18, 1961.

As PREVIOUSLY NOTED the Secretary-General, when he recalled Ambassador Dayal to Headquarters for consultations, had hoped that the hostility toward him in Leopoldville might diminish sufficiently after a short time to make it feasible to return him to duty there. This hope was disappointed. When Hammarskjöld sounded out the Kasavubu régime the reaction was violently negative and it was apparent that the recent progress toward a constructive cooperation with ONUC would be lost if the Secretary-General insisted. Dayal then eased matters by himself requesting to be relieved and Hammarskjöld issued the statement that follows. The post of special representative was not filled again. Stüre Linnér was named officer-in-charge.

Statement on Conclusion of Ambassador Dayal's Service as Special Representative in the Congo

NEW YORK   MAY 25, 1961

FOLLOWING CONSULTATIONS at Headquarters regarding the Congo operation and in particular a reorganization of the administrative arrangements for this operation, which has been in planning for some time, the Secretary-General announces that Ambassador Dayal, at his own request, is now returning to his office as India's high commissioner to Pakistan.

Responding to an immediate request from the Secretary-General, the prime minister of India kindly agreed, at very short notice, in August 1960 to release Mr. Dayal for a limited period from his duties as high commissioner of India to Pakistan. Mr. Dayal accepted the assignment as special representative in the Congo on the understanding that its duration would be determined in the light of the extent of his ability to remain away from his regular post and of the need for his service in the Congo.

In the course of the Secretary-General's visit to Leopoldville early in January of this year, he asked Mr. Dayal to agree to continue as special representative until progress in the UN operation in the Congo would indicate the advisability of other administrative arrangements.

In view of recent developments, Mr. Dayal, referring to his initial undertaking of August 1960, and to his discussion with the Secretary-General last January, has now asked to be relieved from UN service in order to return to his duties in his government's service. In the circumstances, the Secretary-General, to his regret, has found it necessary to accede to the request of Mr. Dayal. In so doing he takes the occasion to express his full gratitude to Mr. Dayal for his services, both in the Congo and at Headquarters. Mr. Dayal's work for the UN as special representative has been marked by the highest ability and level of performance, equalled by his loyalty to the purposes of the UN and his unfailing integrity.

An announcement will be made later concerning the administrative arrangements in the Congo to prevail henceforth. The emphasis in the

UN Press Release SG/1019.

tasks for the special representative there is now shifting from being principally in the diplomatic field to the administrative field, the main need now being for coordination on the UN side of its growing activities in the assistance field to the Congo. This coordination has to be largely undertaken at UN Headquarters in New York. Pending the intended changes in the administrative arrangements, no new special representative will be appointed and activities in the Congo will be coordinated by the senior UN officer in Leopoldville, as officer-in-charge.

ON MAY 26 the Secretary-General held his first press conference in more than a year. The questions and answers covered a wide range on the Congo, including administrative arrangements for ONUC following Dayal's departure; prospects for agreement with Gizenga on reconvening Parliament; UN financial assistance for the Congo; prospects for better cooperation from Belgium; the UN role in relation to Tshombé's continued detention; the forthcoming appointment of Conor Cruise O'Brien, a former member of the delegation of Ireland to the United Nations, who later in the summer was to play a controversial role as the UN representative in Elisabethville. A question related to the upcoming Kennedy-Khrushchev meeting in Vienna evoked some interesting observations by Hammarskjöld on the problems of finding the right balance in the United Nations between the responsibilities of the Great Powers and the rights and interests of the majority of Members. Another question provided an opportunity to put on record the frustration of his hopes for a constructive UN presence in Laos caused by the continuing political and military struggle there (next following text).

From Transcript of Press Conference

NEW YORK   MAY 29, 1961

THE SECRETARY-GENERAL: Well, Ladies and Gentlemen, we have not met for quite a while. In fact, I think the last time we were facing each other across this hall was in June of last year. When we met that time we did not foresee what was ahead of us. We had in July the very difficult operations around the Congo, which made it impossible for me to find even the minimum of time necessary for press conferences, and from then on we got straight into the General Assembly, where the rule, of course, is that we have no press conferences. There have been intervals when it would have been possible to have them for formal reasons, but I guess you understand that there have also been some substantive reasons. I would have liked to meet with you. I would have liked to help you, to the extent I can, to get a better understanding of the background of certain things, and perhaps explain a little bit what we are trying to do, but again and again I felt that the questions you had to put, which were natural and indicated questions, were questions on which I could not give you any replies which really would have been helpful.

The reason was not any reluctance to give you such replies but the fact that, to an unusual extent, what I could tell would have been the property of others, of governments and government representatives; and as you know, I have to impose on myself very strict discipline in that respect. I can give you what is mine; I cannot give you what is the property of others. So, I was sitting back.

Now, however, time runs and it is impossible to have this gap between us. For that reason I have been rather eager to get back to press conferences now. I hope that it will prove that I am right. That will depend not on you but much more on myself and on circumstances, because I am not quite sure that the way in which I characterized my difficulties when I was thinking of press conferences at an earlier stage is not still valid so as to make the press conference from your angle less than helpful. But let us try it, and I will do my best.

UN Note to Correspondents No. 2339.

I hope you will understand if there are points on which I will be perhaps a little bit more reticent than you complained of my being before. Anyway, there is no need for any further explanations. I think you have, even without my assistance, understood me; and I just give you the floor for whatever questions you wish to put.

QUESTION: Allow me to express our joy at the resumption of these conferences, which we value so highly. Now that the United Nations will not have a special representative on the spot in the Congo, is it possible to give us some ideas of the new Secretariat setup regarding the direction of operations?

THE SECRETARY-GENERAL: I would rather start with the developments on the Congolese side. We already have the civilian operation. We have the Force. We have negotiations going on concerning implementation of paragraph A-2 of the Security Council resolution, which, as you may remember, is the one that talks about withdrawal and evacuation of military and paramilitary personnel, mercenaries, and political advisers. Parenthetically, I would say that these negotiations are going on in Leopoldville and in Brussels, with discussions of a less formal nature also in other places in the Congo. Further, we have under way implementation of paragraph B-2, which is the question of reorganization of the army, arrangements for retraining, and so on and so forth. We have not got far, but I hope we will make progress soon. We also have a commission for the investigation of the circumstances relating to the assassination of Mr. Lumumba and others. Finally, we have the Conciliation Commission.

Over and above that, I think that there are one or two operations which may become necessary very shortly within the civilian field in the Congo.

These things are, as you see, rather heterogeneous. There is a common denominator—the Congo—and there is another common denominator in the policy-making here. I think it is clear to you that it is unreasonable to expect anybody to sit in the Congo and be the coordinator for those activities, because they would go beyond what anyone can bring within his own sphere of competence. We have to activate our best resources here and give directives from here to those in charge of the various operations, and see to it that it all fits together within the framework of the resolutions and the general United Nations policies.

For that reason, I had intended to build up a special quasi-executive office. I have found it very difficult to recruit broadly the people I would have liked to have for it, and for that reason we are continuing a somewhat intensified activity with the people whom we have already engaged on the Congo operation. We have our daily meetings, we have current contacts on it, and I believe that, putting our best efforts into this matter here, we will be able very well to keep these operations together within a pattern of planned coordination.

There is also a coming and going, as you know. At present, for example, on the financial side, Mr. de Seynes, from this Headquarters, is out there with experts; Mr. Gardiner, who really belongs now to the executive office, is out there for A-2; and so on and so forth. But I do not have in mind to put a formal hat, so to speak, on the operation here as a substitute for what we have had on another level so far in the Congo.

QUESTION: I was wondering whether, as a result of your talk with Premier Ben-Gurion yesterday, you see any new or immediate approach to the problem of peace in the Middle East. I wonder whether you would care to comment on your meeting with him.

THE SECRETARY-GENERAL: We covered a very wide range of problems. Very few words were said about the Middle East because we are at a juncture where political interest fortunately has drifted away, leaving that area a little bit more in peace, and we have had to concentrate more on other regions. For that reason there is nothing to say about the matter you raised.

QUESTION: Mr. Secretary-General, we are all, I believe, aware of the widened responsibilities throughout this whole year which have held you close to a dawn-to-midnight schedule: the continuous waves of crisis in the Congo, the necessity to defend the UN under siege, and a long extraordinary Assembly. Yet this is a year marked by the emergence of Dag Hammarskjöld in other fields: as translator of Nobel Prize winner St. John Perse's volume *Chronique;* as cotranslator of the English play in verse, *The Antiphon,* which had a world première in Stockholm in February; as author of *A New Look at Mt. Everest,* complete with some strikingly beautiful pictures by photographer Hammarskjöld. My question is: How did you manage it all and what about sharing with us this magical formula for extension in time?

THE SECRETARY-GENERAL: Well, frankly all this was done before the Congo crisis. There was a happy period in May and June last year when things looked much better and when I could indulge in some activities of another type. But with your permission, Mrs. Gray [*Greenwich* (Conn.) *Time*], I think we should not indulge in those matters now but should get back to the tasks of the United Nations proper.

QUESTION: To get back to political subjects, do you see any likelihood of any major crises or major developments that would occupy the United Nations in the near future such as those we have had in other summers, aside from the Congo?

THE SECRETARY-GENERAL: All of us can certainly enumerate possible centres of crises, but why look at it in dramatically negative terms? If you look at the tasks ahead of the United Nations, I would hope that we would be able to forestall crises-like developments in a few places. We should do that, as I see it, first of all by trying to get into the constructive fields in Africa. generally. The Congo has taken on aspects which have been rather dramatic. But do not forget that the underlying philosophy on our side and the underlying philosophy in what I have tried to do is a purely constructive one, to help them to help themselves toward peace and progress. The same can be done in other places. We may come in under more fortunate circumstances. We may do a job which is essential without getting those overtones which have been unavoidable in the case of the Congo.

Thus, in the first place, in looking at Africa I would say that you and I can easily point out this or that territory where things may go wrong and perhaps even may go very wrong. But the main task for the United Nations, as I see it, is in the direction I indicate to forestall such developments by speedy action in cooperation with the Africans and in cooperation with others interested. If we succeed in that, there will not be a crisis but a very major task.

QUESTION: Sir, can you tell us whether you have any plans for a further approach to South Africa in pursuance of your mandate from the Security Council, especially because of the increasing racial tension created by the proclamation of the Republic?

THE SECRETARY-GENERAL: You remember the outcome of the talk which at long last came about in January. We did not manage to agree on any arrangements, but on the other hand the Union Government in a most official form indicated its wish to continue consultations for the purposes which brought me there.

Naturally, in a situation so full of problems and so full of risks, if I may say so, as the African one in general and especially the South African one, in this case, such a standing invitation cannot be taken lightly. I have every intention in the world to keep it under constant review, and if I see that, on the basis of that invitation, new consultations could be taken up which would be likely to straighten things out, I would not hesitate to give such consultations a very high priority. But for the moment I am keeping the matter under consideration. I have to judge first of all about the chances that such consultations might yield results, because, of course, consultations are not and cannot be an end in themselves.

QUESTION: Sir, in recent months we have had, just checking the record, a plethora of charges and accusations in this building, some of them directed against yourself. To some extent we can ascertain the effect these charges and accusations may have on the solution of a problem, by the past developments and what is yet to come. But I am curious for some information, some indication, concerning the extent to which these charges and accusations affect the day-to-day operations of quiet diplomacy.

THE SECRETARY-GENERAL: If the question is put in the way you now put it, I would say that such accusations, etc., do not affect quiet diplomacy at all. All the contacts I have to pursue have been pursued in very much the same atmosphere, in very much the same way as if we had not had the discussions in public which have been going on. As to the day-to-day work, I think you can see very clearly that this kind of debate takes a lot of time from other tasks, because you must reply, you must do this, and you must do that because of it. But, otherwise, I do not think that you should fear that it influences either the direction of action or the spirit in which action is undertaken.

QUESTION: To pursue just this one point further, when public opinion in a particular country seems influenced by these matters, does it not have some sort of effect on the position and the problems of the diplomats with whom you must discuss these problems?

THE SECRETARY-GENERAL: I would say less than you believe, because public opinion and direct private diplomacy are somewhat separate. There is a more stable trend in diplomacy than you can have in public opinion, which may be carried away by emotion or carried away by propaganda statements which do not apply behind closed doors.

QUESTION: Mr. Secretary-General, what are the prospects of a meeting soon of the Congo parliament, which I would assume would require some sort of understanding between Mr. Gizenga and President Kasavubu? And in the second place, is the Kamina Base a possible site, a logical site, or anything like that, for such a meeting of Parliament, regardless of the auspices under which the Parliament would be summoned?

THE SECRETARY-GENERAL: It is practically impossible to make any safe forecast as to the likelihood of a meeting. However, there is one important development at least, and that is the parallel expressions of the wish to see Parliament get together which we have had from Mr. Gizenga and Mr. Kasavubu. You know our stand on it; it has been said again and again by the Security Council and the General Assembly that we must get Parliament back in order to reestablish legality and in order to get a central government the legality of which cannot be disputed. Naturally, those expressions have had a parallel in as solid efforts as we have been able to make on the Secretariat level in the same direction, efforts which will continue on the basis which now is established by these two declarations. However, there is a lot of work to be done, because parallel declarations of intention are not enough; there must also be common ground on which the meeting can be arranged. I think you hinted at it, and I am quite agreed that a meeting in which at least those two sides are not fully represented and do not take part does not make sense. That is to say, common ground must be found between Leopoldville and Stanleyville in order to get Parliament together in a form that really is constructive and helps the Congo, and thereby helps us all.

We have various means, direct and indirect, by which we can further the finding of what I call the common ground, and we shall certainly do all we can in that direction. But, in the final analysis, it is of course for the Congolese themselves to decide the circumstances under which they will meet. We cannot impose anything. We can help them with whatever professional training we have in smoothing out what may sometimes prove to be rather unnecessary differences of opinion. We should also give them all practical assistance in getting people together, making security arrangements, and so forth.

That brings me to the other question that has been raised. In our view, Kamina is perfectly possible. The conveniences there are perhaps not the best, because, after all, the entire place is a military installation. But I do not think that we need worry about that. Security-wise, we can arrange matters there. In fact, since Kamina is a rather isolated place, it would be easier for us to provide what would come close to 100 per cent security there than in most other places.

. . . QUESTION: Most journalists find high finance very difficult to understand—and particularly, I believe, the high finance in the Congo. I should like to ask you, Mr. Secretary-General, to clarify some of these questions of high finance: Whatever happened to the money belonging to the Congo which Belgium is purported to have had? How much money has the United Nations advanced to the Congo? What does President

Kasavubu mean when he refers in his letter of May 26 to "this substantial assistance" by the United Nations? What is the general situation, in terms that a journalist can interpret?

THE SECRETARY-GENERAL: You have raised one of those questions which are difficult in principle and extremely complicated as to the facts. Thus, I am simply not competent, off the cuff, to give you a well-reasoned and well-documented reply to your question. Sir Alexander MacFarquhar is here, and I would ask him to say a few words on the subject.

SIR ALEXANDER MACFARQUHAR: The general financial situation is this: The Congo has had some small advances from the United Nations and has also had some projects based on the contributions to the United Nations Fund for the Congo. Apart from that, it has been living very largely on its own Central Bank advances. There is a limit in the neighborhood of $150 million on Central Bank advances, and the Congolese are getting very close to that limit. The Central Bank has indicated that it is unwilling to increase the limit. The president has therefore appealed to the Secretary-General for assistance. This has been agreed to, in principle, but no money has actually been given. This week, Mr. de Seynes is investigating with the Congolese authorities what budgetary disciplines can be imposed if assistance is to be given.

In regard to the debt and the Congolese portfolio, those matters are still in abeyance because there was no financial settlement between the Congo and Belgium at the time of independence and there has been none subsequently.

QUESTION: Might I follow that up? I should like to ask what form the applications of the Congo take to the United Nations, and what is meant by the statement made by President Kasavubu on May 26 as follows: "The assistance we are being given must be used to reduce the deficit in the budget and also to combat unemployment, and with this substantial assistance. . . ." What kind of money are we talking about?

SIR ALEXANDER MACFARQUHAR: I do not think that either party knows at this stage. We have some estimates of what the budget deficit will be if it goes on at the present level, which is about $9 million a month. But that does not necessarily determine the answer. Things are in a very bad way. There is a rate of unemployment of about 50 per cent and, naturally, if and when that improves there will be an increase in expenditures. But at the same time we would hope to reduce the deficit by improvements in revenues.

THE SECRETARY-GENERAL: There is one restraining factor, and that is that, whatever financial arrangements we make, they cannot be made in a way which would prejudge a question of a constitutional nature or of a political nature within the country. That is to say, in that, as in other respects, we have to see to it that our operation is one which avoids so-called interference in internal affairs. In this specific case that is a badly restraining influence, because who is at the receiving end? What position does he hold under the constitution? And so on and so forth. These are questions which we can never leave out of account.

There is one important element in this picture and that is that our limited financial operations have been, for all practical purposes, with the Central Bank which, as central banks in most countries, has an independent position.

. . . QUESTION: Could you give us a bird's-eye view of the cooperation with the various Security Council and General Assembly resolutions regarding the Congo now by countries in Europe, Africa, and elsewhere, as far as cooperating with the United Nations under the terms of the various resolutions is concerned?

THE SECRETARY-GENERAL: The question of cooperation has arisen in fairly few cases in a form which gives me a basis for any kind of judgment. We have had repatriations, as you know, of mercenaries and some other people—some civilians—and I must say that the countries concerned in those repatriations have acted quickly and efficiently to help us. That is the case in the two countries most concerned, as you have seen from the publication of nationalities of mercenaries—that is to say, the United Kingdom and the Union of South Africa. In other fields the need for cooperation has been much more limited and much more sporadic. I would say that, for the most part, we have, without too much difficulty, got the kind of reaction we needed. I suppose, however, that you had in mind specifically the problem of Belgium. There we have discussions going on in Brussels. They are discussions which have been fairly slow, partly due to the Cabinet crisis there. They are at present showing much more speed of progress, and I hope that when the books are closed we shall be able to say that we got all the assistance needed from the Belgians in implementation of the resolutions. As I said in the recent report on negotiations with Belgium, we are not there yet, but you should not pass judgment until the story is at a close.

QUESTION: One other point on that same question: how about the matter of sending aid outside United Nations channels into any part of the Congo?

THE SECRETARY-GENERAL: There is not much of that, and there are not very many initiatives either. It seems that the fervor, which was shown in some quarters in the beginning, to make this and that kind of bilateral approach has somewhat abated, and for that reason this does not represent a basic problem for us at present.

QUESTION: Mr. Secretary-General, the United Nations suffered a loss of dignity and respect during the last Assembly session as a result of gallery demonstrations in both the Assembly and the Security Council chambers. My question concerns steps by this house to stop such propagandizing. Specifically, is anything being done about the apparent practice of certain delegations in packing the visitors' gallery with visitors who are obviously, at least partly, professional agitators?

THE SECRETARY-GENERAL: We leave it to delegations to judge for themselves what is proper and not proper to do, and I would not like to interfere with their freedom of action in any respect. As to the galleries, this is a democratic institution where in principle the public should have free access, and it was only under the pressure of obvious abuses that I for my part accepted, for a short time, restrictions. I hope that the trust which we have in the public, and which certainly in 999 cases out of a thousand is fully justified, will be, so to say, honored by the other side and that we will not see any new abuses. You may feel that this is blue-eyed and overoptimistic, but I would rather be that than indulge in some kind of restrictions.

QUESTION: Sir, do you see any time-limit on the fully efficient functioning of the Organization if the present financial limitations are continued at the present level?

THE SECRETARY-GENERAL: I fail to believe that we are living in a world and dealing with governments that would permit financial considerations to put a time-limit on political operations which are considered necessary. I have every reason to believe that, in whatever form they approach the United Nations and whatever philosophy they have about the United Nations, they will not let the United Nations sink because of lack of funds.

. . . QUESTION: Mr. Secretary-General, it seems to be an open secret that President Kennedy next weekend will bring up all sorts of veto questions in his talks with Premier Khrushchev: the veto in regard to nuclear test talks and the veto in the structure of the United Nations. Although I know that you have no influence on either of the participants—particularly not on one—I would like to ask you what you would like to see as the outcome of these discussions on the veto in general and the structure of international organizations.

THE SECRETARY-GENERAL: That is a very big problem and my reply will not refer to the forthcoming discussions; I think that that would be most improper for me. But I may say something in general terms.

There is a real veto problem and there is an artificial one. The real veto problem, for which in fact the word "veto" is a misnomer, is based on the fact that there are questions which cannot be solved without agreement between the Big Powers, especially in this case between the predominant military powers.

There is the artificial veto problem, that is to say, the attempt by this or that power to make its consent essential for questions which naturally should be solved, let us say, on a majority basis.

On the first point neither you nor I can change anything because there we are up against a hard fact. It is a real problem and it can be solved only by agreement and by the will to agree among the Big Powers.

As regards the other question, what I call the artificial veto problem, it is my firm and strong feeling that the introduction and development of such a problem is harmful to international cooperation because it stymies a development which could take place on majority decisions here in this Organization or on some other kind of objective basis.

As to the work of international organizations generally, I think I can draw certain conclusions from what I have said. We are of course in the United Nations basing ourselves very largely on two principles which we find reflected also in other international organizations, the principle being on the one side that decisions are taken by a majority and on the other side that execution is, so to say, lifted outside the sphere of political influence. The latter point has come up for debate, as you know, by a certain stress on the use of, so to say, governmental influences also on execution, whether that is done formally or whether it is done *de facto*. As regards majority, of course the whole question has arisen because of the fact that we now have majorities here which are partly rather incalculable in relation to Big-Power politics and therefore may represent a hampering or complicating problem in Big-Power thinking. I think that we must try to find our way to a new balance where on the one side the Big Powers give all the respect due to a majority but where, on the other hand, the majorities do recognize that there are problems which simply cannot be solved by voting but where what I call the real veto does apply.

I guess that in San Francisco one tried to strike a balance by having the unanimity rule in the Security Council and the simple majority rule or qualified majority rule in the General Assembly. For reasons which we all know, this system has not worked very well. It has led to curious shifts in the balance of responsibility between the two organs, and at present there is obviously some kind of dissatisfaction both on, so to say, the Small-Power majority side and on the Big-Power side. Whether it is possible to work out a new balance with mutual recognition of the special position and responsibility of the Big Powers and of the rights of the majority, I do not know. I would hope so and I think that one of the most constructive efforts that could be made at present by politicians, whether they come from Big Powers or others, would be to try, within the framework of the Charter as it stands, to arrive at this kind of equilibrium. I think that what is required is less this or that kind of formal change than a real understanding on the two sides of the table, so to say, of the needs of the other side and the rights of the other side.

To repeat myself, the weight that should be given to a majority, even if it is a Small-Power majority, on the one side, must be balanced against the crucial significance, on the other hand, of the consent of the Big Powers, necessary in many cases to give sense to a majority decision.

QUESTION: Mr. Secretary-General, I understand that Dr. Conor O'Brien of Ireland is to be given an assignment in the Secretariat. Can you explain to us what that assignment is, Sir?

THE SECRETARY-GENERAL: I can refer to an earlier question. I hope to be able to use Dr. Conor O'Brien's services, which I am very, very happy to get, in the coordination to which I referred, the coordination of the various activities in the Congo; but he will formally join, so to say, the Secretary-General's more or less personal staff in the Secretariat.

QUESTION: Mr. Secretary-General, the United Nations has not well protected political leaders like Mr. Patrice Lumumba. What is the United Nations doing to protect Mr. Tshombé?

THE SECRETARY-GENERAL: This brings up the whole question of protection which is one of the most misunderstood questions we have had in the Congo operation.

First of all, no protection is given unless a person asks for it. Naturally, we can never promise to give protection anywhere and under all circumstances.

In the case of Mr. Lumumba, we gave him, at his request, protection at his residence in Leopoldville. He left it without our knowledge, and he was arrested outside our control. From then on what we could do was to intervene by direct diplomatic means in relation to those in power.

In the case of Mr. Tshombé, when he came to Coquilhatville he had not asked for any protection. He had no protection, and we were not equipped for that kind of protection for him if he had asked for it at that stage. If he had asked beforehand, we simply would have had to say that our resources are limited in such and such a way, and you must take that fully into account. However, his detention arose also in a situation entirely outside our control.

As in the case of Mr. Lumumba our activity, therefore, has to be limited to such intervention as we can make diplomatically and politically within the limits of our competence.

QUESTION: Sir, the General Assembly and the Security Council has a vested interest, I would suppose you could say, in what happens in Korea because of many things and the nominal use of the United Nations name. You yourself have carried certain responsibilities in connection with Laos, as does the whole Organization. The question is: Can you give us some idea of the participation, the penetration, and the responsibility now carried in those two places by the Organization?

THE SECRETARY-GENERAL: In the formal setup in Korea there is no change and the reports from UNCURK are not of a nature which I think would interest you here. There is nothing really to put on record.

As regards Laos, our mission was basically a mission which depends for its success on reasonably peaceful conditions. We were setting up teams for work in the villages, for an integration of the villages with bigger markets, and similar things. This operation, which would have done much, I believe, to mold the various areas into one nation, had not really started when the trouble on the political level began. From then on, the situation has been one which increasingly has made it difficult to get anything useful out of what we tried to do.

For the moment, and pending a solution of the purely political problem, the operation is therefore kept, so to say, in abeyance, in a kind of icebox, with its potentialities maintained but without any real activity.

You should remember what this operation was from the very beginning. It started in September 1959. United Nations interest in Laos started earlier, but formally in September 1959 with a debate in the Security Council, which led to a subcommittee going to Laos.

However, before the Security Council discussed the report of the subcommittee, I had discussions with the government at its invitation, and we then agreed on an approach which attacked the problem substantively and from the roots, so to speak, since very much of the difficulty was explained by the fact that the country had never been really integrated, that there were great tensions between the countryside and the cities, great social differences, bad marketing conditions, and what not. This had to be, on our side, a coordinated operation in which practically all the specialized agencies and we were to be together. At the same time, it had to have very close links with the government.

We started that operation and, because of the coordination problems arising there and the whole nature of the question, we felt—and especially the government felt—that it would be very useful to have a high-powered special representative, a kind of technical assistance resident representative with special rights. Thus, we switched at that stage from a political to an economic approach, recognizing however that the economic approach had special value for its possible stabilizing political consequences.

You can well see that therefore the United Nations operation, the United Nations activities, can very well be separated from the political aspects as now debated. But they are influenced by them in the sense that, short of some kind of national reconciliation, short of peaceful conditions, what we tried to do cannot be done in a way that is useful. That is really where we are.

. . . QUESTION: You spoke earlier of the United Nations' trying to forestall crises around the world. It seems to me that there is one United Nations body that has been sadly neglected over the past years—the United Nations Peace Observation Commission. Could not this body function as a sort of watchdog of peace, with observers sent out to these various places, so that you would have a direct connection, as a matter of course, with what is happening?

THE SECRETARY-GENERAL: Somehow, that ship has never been properly launched, and I do not know how it would sail. It is really not a question for the Secretariat; it is a question for the participating members. There seems to have been some kind of disenchantment with it because, as you say, they have not used it, and it has very rarely been mentioned even in debate.

. . . .

SOON AFTER this press conference the Secretary-General left for England to deliver at Oxford University his famous exposition of the importance for a constructive evolution in international affairs of an international civil service led by a

Secretary-General with exclusively international responsibilities (first following text). His lecture was prepared with very great care and was partly an elaboration of drafts dictated during the Assembly session in case the Soviet Union should formally submit for the agenda Khrushchev's proposal for a three-man executive, each of whom could veto the other two. The "troika" as such attracted little support, but the controversy spawned other reactions among the Afro-Asians and in the West that were less extreme in form but might have been no less regressive in their effect. Oscar Schachter, the best legal mind in the Secretariat, worked closely with the Secretary-General in the preparation of his Oxford lecture.

"The International Civil Servant in Law and in Fact" Lecture Delivered in Congregation at Oxford University

OXFORD, ENGLAND   MAY 30, 1961

I

In a recent article Mr. Walter Lippmann tells about an interview in Moscow with Mr. Khrushchev. According to the article, Chairman Khrushchev stated that "while there are neutral countries, there are no neutral men," and the author draws the conclusion that it is now the view of the Soviet government "that there can be no such things as an impartial civil servant in this deeply divided world, and that the kind of political celibacy which the British theory of the civil servant calls for, is in international affairs a fiction."

Whether this accurately sums up the views held by the Soviet government, as reflected in the interview, or not, one thing is certain: The attitude which the article reflects is one which we find nowadays in many political quarters, communist and noncommunist alike, and it raises a problem which cannot be treated lightly. In fact, it challenges basic tenets in the philosophy of both the League of Nations and the United Nations, as one of the essential points on which these experiments in international cooperation represent an advance beyond traditional "conference diplomacy" is the introduction on the international arena of joint permanent organs, employing a neutral civil service, and the use of such organs for executive purposes on behalf of all the members of the organizations. Were it to be considered that the experience shows that this radical innovation in international life rests on a false assumption because "no man can be neutral," then we would be thrown back to 1919, and a searching reappraisal would become necessary.

II

The international civil service had its genesis in the League of Nations but it did not spring full-blown in the Treaty of Versailles and the Cov-

UN Press Release SG/1035.

enant. The Covenant was in fact silent on the international character of the Secretariat. It contained no provisions comparable to those of Article 100 of the Charter and simply stated: "The permanent Secretariat shall be established at the Seat of the League. The Secretariat shall comprise a Secretary-General and such secretaries and staff as may be required."

In the earliest proposals for the Secretariat of the League, it was apparently taken for granted that there could not be a truly international secretariat but that there would have to be nine national secretaries, each assisted by a national staff and performing, in turn, the duties of Secretary to the Council, under the supervision of the Secretary-General. This plan, which had been drawn up by Sir Maurice Hankey, who had been offered the post of Secretary-General of the League by the Allied powers, was in keeping with the precedents set by the various international bureaus established before the war which were staffed by officials seconded by Member countries on a temporary basis.

It was Sir Eric Drummond, first Secretary-General of the League, who is generally regarded as mainly responsible for building upon the vague language of the Covenant a truly international secretariat. The classic statement of the principles he first espoused is found in the report submitted to the Council of the League by its British member, Arthur Balfour:

> By the terms of the Treaty, the duty of selecting the staff falls upon the Secretary-General, just as the duty of approving it falls upon the Council. In making his appointments, he had primarily to secure the best available men and women for the particular duties which had to be performed; but in doing so, it was necessary to have regard to the great importance of selecting the officials from various nations. Evidently, no one nation or group of nations ought to have a monopoly in providing the material for this international institution. I emphasize the word "international," because the members of the Secretariat once appointed are no longer the servants of the country of which they are citizens, but become . . . servants only of the League of Nations. Their duties are not national but international (League of Nations, *Official Journal*, June 1920, p. 137.)

Thus, in this statement, we have two of the essential principles of an international civil service: (1) its international composition and (2) its international responsibilities. The latter principle found its legal expression in the regulations subsequently adopted which enjoined all officials "to discharge their functions and to regulate their conduct with the interests of the League alone in view" and prohibited them from seeking or receiving "instructions from any government or other authority external to the Secretariat of the League of Nations."

Along with the conception of an independent, internationally responsible staff, another major idea was to be found: the international Secretariat was to be solely an administrative organ, eschewing political judgments and actions. It is not at all surprising that this third principle should have originated with a British Secretary-General. In the United Kingdom, as in certain other European countries, a system of patronage, political or personal, had been gradually replaced in the course of the nineteenth century by the principle of a permanent civil service based on efficiency and competence and owing allegiance only to the state which it served. It followed that a civil service so organized and dedicated would be nonpolitical. The civil servant could not be expected to serve two masters and consequently he could not, in his official duties, display any political allegiance to a political party or ideology. Those decisions which involved a political choice were left to the government and to parliament; the civil servant was the nonpartisan administrator of those decisions. His discretion was a limited one, bound by the framework of national law and authority and by rules and instructions issued by his political superiors. True, there were choices for him, since neither legal rules nor policy decisions can wholly eliminate the discretion of the administrative official, but the choices to be made were confined to relatively narrow limits by legislative enactment, government decision, and the great body of precedent and tradition. The necessary condition was that there should exist at all times a higher political authority with the capacity to take the political decisions. With that condition it seemed almost axiomatic that the civil service had to be "politically celibate" (though not perhaps politically virgin). It could not take sides in any political controversy and, accordingly, it could not be given tasks which required it to do so. This was reflected in the basic statements laying down the policy to govern the international Secretariat. I may quote two of them:

We recommend with special urgency that, in the interests of the League, as well as in its own interests, the Secretariat should not extend the sphere of its activities, that in the preparation of the work and the decisions of the various organizations of the League, it should regard it as its first duty to collate the relevant documents, and to prepare the ground for these decisions without suggesting what these decisions should be; finally that once these decisions had been taken by the bodies solely responsible for them, it should confine itself to executing them in the letter and in the spirit.[1]

Une fois les décisions prises, le rôle du Secrétariat est de les appliquer. Ici encore, il y a lieu de faire une distinction entre application et interprétation, non

[1] Report of Committee Four, records of the Second Assembly.

pas, à coup sûr, que je demande au Secrétariat de ne jamais interpréter; c'est son métier! Mais je lui demande, et vous lui demanderez certainement tous, d'interpréter le moins loin possible, le plus fidèlement possible, et surtout de ne jamais substituer son interprétation à la vôtre.[2]

Historians of the League have noted the self-restraining role played by the Secretary-General. He never addressed the Assembly of the League and in the Council "he tended to speak . . . as a secretary of a committee and not more than that."[3] For him to have entered into political tasks which involved in any substantial degree the taking of a position was regarded as compromising the very basis of the impartiality essential for the Secretariat.

True, this does not mean that political matters as such were entirely excluded from the area of the Secretariat's interests. It has been reported by Sir Eric Drummond and others that he played a role behind the scenes, acting as a confidential channel of communication to governments engaged in controversy or dispute, but this behind-the-scenes role was never extended to taking action in a politically controversial case that was deemed objectionable by one of the sides concerned.

III

The legacy of the international Secretariat of the League is marked in the Charter of the United Nations. Article 100 follows almost verbatim the League regulations on independence and international responsibility—barring the seeking or receiving of instructions from states or other external authority. This was orginally proposed at San Francisco by the four sponsoring powers—China, the USSR, the United Kingdom, and the United States, and unanimously accepted. The League experience had shown that an international civil service, responsible only to the Organization, was workable and efficient. It had also revealed, as manifested in the behavior of German and Italian Fascists, that there was a danger of national pressures corroding the concept of international loyalty. That experience underlined the desirability of including in the Charter itself an explicit obligation on officials and governments alike to respect fully the independence and the exclusively international character of the responsibilities of the Secretariat.

[2] Statement by M. Noblemaire, Second Assembly, October 1, 1921.
[3] Proceedings, Conference on Experience in International Administration, Washington, D.C., Carnegie Endowment, 1943, p. 11.

It was also recognized that an international civil service of this kind could not be made up of persons indirectly responsible to their national governments. The weight attached to this by the majority of members was demonstrated in the Preparatory Commission, London, when it was proposed that appointments of officials should be subject to the consent of the government of the Member state of which the candidate was a national. Even in making this proposal, its sponsor explained that it was only intended to build up a staff adequately representative of the governments and acceptable to them. He maintained that prior approval of officials was necessary, in order to obtain the confidence of their governments which was essential to the Secretariat, but once the officials were appointed, the exclusively international character of their responsibilities would be respected. However, the great majority of Member states rejected this proposal, for they believed that it would be extremely undesirable to write into the regulations anything that would give national governments particular rights in respect of appointments and thus indirectly permit political pressures on the Secretary-General.

Similarly in line with Article 100, the Preparatory Commission laid emphasis on the fact that the Secretary-General "alone is responsible to the other principal organs for the Secretariat's work," and that all officials in the Organization must recognize the exclusive authority of the Secretary-General and submit themselves to rules of discipline laid down by him.

The principle of the independence of the Secretariat from national pressures was also reinforced in the Charter by Article 105, which provides for granting officials of the Organization "such privileges and immunities as are necessary for the independent exercise of their functions in connection with the Organization." It was in fact foreseen at San Francisco that in exceptional circumstances there might be a clash between the independent position of a member of the Secretariat and the position of his country, and consequently that an immunity in respect of official acts would be necessary for the protection of the officials from pressure by individual governments and to permit them to carry out their international responsibilities without interference.

In all of these legal provisions, the Charter built essentially on the experience of the League and affirmed the principles already accepted there. However, when it came to the functions and authority of the Secretary-General, the Charter broke new ground.

In Article 97 the Secretary-General is described as the "chief administrative officer of the Organization," a phrase not found in the Covenant, though probably implicit in the position of the Secretary-General of the League. Its explicit inclusion in the Charter made it a constitutional requirement—not simply a matter left to the discretion of the organs—that the administration of the Organization shall be left to the Secretary-General. The Preparatory Commission observed that the administrative responsibility under Article 97 involves the essential tasks of preparing the ground for the decisions of the organs and of "executing" them in cooperation with the Members.

Article 97 is of fundamental importance for the status of the international Secretariat of the United Nations, and thus for the international civil servant employed by the Organization, as, together with Articles 100 and 101 it creates for the Secretariat a position, administratively, of full political independence. However, it does not, or at least it need not represent an element in the picture which raises the question of the "neutrality" of the international civil servant. This is so because the decisions and actions of the Secretary-General as chief administrative officer naturally can be envisaged as limited to administrative problems outside the sphere of political conflicts of interest or ideology, and thus as maintaining the concept of the international civil servant as first developed in the League of Nations.

However, Article 97 is followed by Article 98, and Article 98 is followed by Article 99. And these two Articles together open the door to the problem of neutrality in a sense unknown in the history of the League of Nations.

In Article 98 it is, thus, provided not only that the Secretary-General "shall act in that capacity" in meetings of the organs, but that he "shall perform such other functions as are entrusted to him by these organs." This latter provision was not in the Covenant of the League. It has substantial significance in the Charter, for it entitles the General Assembly and the Security Council to entrust the Secretary-General with tasks involving the execution of political decisions, even when this would bring him—and with him the Secretariat and its members—into the arena of possible political conflict. The organs are, of course, not required to delegate such tasks to the Secretary-General but it is clear that they *may* do so. Moreover, it may be said that in doing so the General Assembly and the Security Council are in no way in conflict with the spirit of the Charter—even if some might like to give the word "chief administrative officer" in Article 97 a normative and limitative significance—since the Charter itself gives to the Secretary-General an explicit political role.

It is Article 99 more than any other which was considered by the drafters of the Charter to have transformed the Secretary-General of the United Nations from a purely administrative official to one with an explicit political responsibility. Considering its importance, it is perhaps surprising that Article 99 was hardly debated: most delegates appeared to share Smuts' opinion that the position of the Secretary-General "should be of the highest importance and for this reason a large measure of initiative was expressly conferred." Legal scholars have observed that Article 99 not only confers upon the Secretary-General a right to bring matters to the attention of the Security Council but that this right carries with it, by necessary implication, a broad discretion to conduct inquiries and to engage in informal diplomatic activity in regard to matters which "may threaten the maintenance of international peace and security."

It is not without some significance that this new conception of a Secretary-General originated principally with the United States rather than the United Kingdom. It has been reported that at an early stage in the preparation of the papers that later became the Dumbarton Oaks proposals, the United States gave serious consideration to the idea that the Organization should have a President as well as a Secretary-General. Subsequently, it was decided to propose only a single officer, but one in whom there would be combined both the political and executive functions of a President with the internal administrative functions that were previously accorded to a Secretary-General. Obviously, this is a reflection in some measure, of the American political system, which places authority in a chief executive officer who is not simply subordinated to the legislative organs but who is constitutionally responsible alone for the execution of legislation and in some respects for carrying out the authority derived from the constitutional instrument directly.

The fact that the Secretary-General is an official with political power as well as administrative functions had direct implications for the method of his selection. Proposals at San Francisco to eliminate the participation of the Security Council in the election process were rejected precisely because it was recognized that the role of the Secretary-General in the field of political and security matters properly involved the Security Council and made it logical that the unanimity rule of the permanent Members should apply. At the same time, it was recognized that the necessity of such unanimous agreement would have to be limited only to the selection of the Secretary-General and that it was equally essential that he be protected against the pressure of a Member during his term in office.

Thus a proposal for a three-year term was rejected on the ground that so short a term might impair his independent role.

The concern with the independence of the Secretary-General from national pressures was also reflected at San Francisco in the decision of the conference to reject proposals for Deputies Secretary-General appointed in the same manner as the Secretary-General. The opponents of this provision maintained that a proposal of this kind would result in a group of high officials who would not be responsible to the Secretary-General but to the bodies which elected them. This would inevitably mean a dilution of the responsibility of the Secretary-General for the conduct of the Organization and would be conducive neither to the efficient functioning of the Secretariat nor to its independent position. In this action and other related decisions, the drafters of the Charter laid emphasis on the personal responsibility of the Secretary-General; it is he who is solely responsible for performing the functions entrusted to him for the appointment of all members of the Secretariat and for assuring the organ that the Secretariat will carry out their tasks under his exclusive authority. The idea of a "cabinet system" in which responsibility for administration and political functions would be distributed among several individuals was squarely rejected.

It is also relevant in this connection that the provision for "due regard to geographical representation" in the recruitment of the Secretariat was never treated as calling for political or ideological representation. It was rather an affirmation of the idea accepted since the beginning of the League Secretariat that the staff of the Organization was to have an international composition and that its basis would be as "geographically" broad as possible. Moreover, as clearly indicated in the language of Article 101, the "paramount consideration in the employment of the staff" should be the necessity of securing the highest standards of efficiency, competence, and integrity. This terminology is evidence of the intention of the drafters to accord priority to considerations of efficiency and competence over those of geographical representation, important though the latter be.

To sum up, the Charter laid down these essential legal principles for an international civil service:

It was to be an international body, recruited primarily for efficiency, competence, and integrity, but on as wide a geographical basis as possible;

It was to be headed by a Secretary-General who carried constitutionally the responsibility to the other principal organs for the Secretariat's work;

And finally, Article 98 entitled the General Assembly and the Security Council to entrust the Secretary-General with tasks going beyond the *verba formalia* of Article 97—with its emphasis on the administrative function—thus opening the door to a measure of political responsibility which is distinct from the authority explicitly accorded to the Secretary-General under Article 99 but in keeping with the spirit of that Article.

This last mentioned development concerning the Secretary-General, with its obvious consequences for the Secretariat as such, takes us beyond the concept of a nonpolitical civil service into an area where the official, in the exercise of his functions, may be forced to take stands of a politically controversial nature. It does this, however, on an international basis and, thus, without departing from the basic concept of "neutrality"; in fact, Article 98, as well as Article 99, would be unthinkable without the complement of Article 100 strictly observed both in letter and spirit.

Reverting for a moment to our initial question, I have tried to emphasize the distinction just made. If a demand for neutrality is made, by present critics of the international civil service, with the intent that the international civil servant should not be permitted to take a stand on political issues, in response to requests of the General Assembly or the Security Council, then the demand is in conflict with the Charter itself. If, however, "neutrality" means that the international civil servant, also in executive tasks with political implications, must remain wholly uninfluenced by national or group interests or ideologies, then the obligation to observe such neutrality is just as basic to the Charter concept of the international civil service as it was to the concept once found in the Covenant of the League. Due to the circumstances then prevailing the distinction to which I have just drawn attention probably never was clearly made in the League, but it has become fundamental for the interpretation of the actions of the Secretariat as established by the Charter.

The criticism to which I referred at the beginning of this lecture can be directed against the very Charter concept of the Secretariat and imply a demand for a reduction of the functions of the Secretariat to the role assigned to it in the League and explicitly mentioned in Article 97 of the Charter; this would be a retrograde development in sharp conflict with the way in which the functions of the international Secretariat over the years have been extended by the main organs of the United Nations, in response to arising needs. Another possibility would be that the actual developments under Articles 98 and 99 are accepted but that a lack of confidence in the possibility of personal "neutrality" is considered to render necessary administrative arrangements putting the persons in question under special constitutional controls, either built into the structure of the Secretariat or established through organs outside the Secretariat.

IV

The conception of an independent international civil service, although reasonably clear in the Charter provisions, was almost continously subjected to stress in the history of the Organization. International tensions, changes in governments, concern with national security, all had their inevitable repercussions on the still fragile institution dedicated to the international community. Governments not only strove for the acceptance of their views in the organs of the Organization, but they concerned themselves in varying degrees with the attitude of their nationals in the Secretariat. Some governments sought in one way or another to revive the substance of the proposal defeated at London for the clearance of their nationals prior to employment in the Secretariat; other governments on occasion demanded the dismissal of staff members who were said to be inappropriately representative of the country of their nationality for political, racial, or even cultural reasons.

In consequence, the Charter Articles underwent a continual process of interpretation and clarification in the face of pressures brought to bear on the Secretary-General. On the whole the results tended to affirm and strengthen the independence of the international civil service. These developments involved two complementary aspects: first, the relation between the Organization and the Member states in regard to the selection and employment of nationals of those states, and second, the relation between the international official, his own state, and the international responsibilities of the Organization. It is apparent that these relationships involved a complex set of obligations and rights applying to the several interested parties.

One of the most difficult of the problems was presented as a result of the interest of several national governments in passing upon the recruitment of their nationals by the Secretariat. It was of course a matter of fundamental principle that the selection of the staff should be made by the Secretary-General on his own responsibility and not on the responsibility of the national governments. The interest of the governments in placing certain nationals and in barring the employment of others had to be subordinated, as a matter of principle and law, to the independent determination of the Organization. Otherwise there would have been an abandonment of the position adopted at San Francisco and affirmed by the Preparatory Commission in London.

On the other hand, there were practical considerations which required the Organization to utilize the services of governments for the purpose of obtaining applicants for positions and, as a corollary of this, for information as to the competence, integrity, and general suitability of such nationals for employment. The United Nations could not have an investigating agency comparable to those available to national governments, and the Organization had therefore to accept assistance from governments in obtaining information and records concerning possible applicants. However, the Secretary-General consistently reserved the right to make the final determination on the basis of all the facts and his own independent appreciation of these facts.

It may be recalled that this problem assumed critical proportions in 1952 and 1953 when various authorities of the United States government, host to the United Nations Headquarters, conducted a series of highly publicized investigations of the loyalty of its nationals in the Secretariat. Charges were made which, although relating to a small number of individuals and largely founded upon inference rather than on direct evidence or admissions, led to proposals which implicitly challenged the international character of the responsibilities of the Secretary-General and his staff. In certain other countries similar proposals were made and in some cases adopted in legislation or by administrative action.

In response, the Secretary-General and the Organization as a whole affirmed the necessity of independent action by the United Nations in regard to selection and recruitment of staff. The Organization was only prepared to accept information from governments concerning suitability for employment, including information that might be relevant to political considerations such as activity which would be regarded as inconsistent with the obligation of international civil servants. It was recognized that there should be a relationship of mutual confidence and trust between international officials and the governments of Member states. At the same time, the Secretary-General took a strong position that the dismissal of a staff member "on the basis of the mere suspicion of a government of a Member state or a bare conclusion arrived at by that government on evidence which is denied the Secretary-General would amount to receiving instructions in violation of his obligation under Article 100, paragraph 1, of the Charter "not to receive in the performance of his duties instructions from any government." It should be said that, as a result of the stand taken by the Organization, this principle was recognized by the United States government in the procedures it established for hearings and submission of information to the Secretary-General regarding U.S. citizens.

A risk of national pressure on the international official may also be introduced, in a somewhat more subtle way, by the terms and duration of his appointment. A national official, seconded by his government for a year or two with an international organization, is evidently in a different position psychologically—and one might say, politically—from the permanent international civil servant who does not contemplate a subsequent career with his national government. This was recognized by the Preparatory Commission in London in 1945 when it concluded that members of the Secretariat staff could not be expected "fully to subordinate the special interests of their countries to the international interest if they are merely detached temporarily from national administrations and dependent upon them for their future." Recently, however, assertions have been made that it is necessary to switch from the present system, which makes permanent appointments and career service the rule, to a predominant system of fixed-term appointments to be granted mainly to officials seconded by their governments. This line is prompted by governments which show little enthusiasm for making officials available on a long-term basis, and, moreover, seem to regard—as a matter of principle or, at least, of "realistic" psychology—the international civil servant primarily as a national official representing his country and its ideology. On this view, the international civil service should be recognized and developed as being an "intergovernmental" secretariat composed principally of national officials assigned by their governments, rather than as an "international" secretariat as conceived from the days of the League of Nations and until now. In the light of what I have already said regarding the provisions of the Charter, I need not demonstrate that this conception runs squarely against the principles of Articles 100 and 101.

This is not to say that there is not room for a reasonable number of "seconded" officials in the Secretariat. It has in fact been accepted that it is highly desirable to have a number of officials available from governments for short periods, especially to perform particular tasks calling for diplomatic or technical backgrounds. Experience has shown that such seconded officials, true to their obligations under the Charter, perform valuable service but as a matter of good policy it should, of course, be avoided as much as possible to put them on assignments in which their status and nationality might be embarrassing to themselves or the parties concerned. However, this is quite different from having a large portion of the Secretariat—say, in excess of one-third—composed of short-term officials. To have so large a proportion of the Secretariat staff in the seconded category would be likely to impose serious strains on its ability to function as a body dedicated exclusively to international responsibilities. Especially if there were any doubts as to the principles ruling their work in the minds of the governments on which their future might depend, this might result in a radical departure from the basic concepts of the Charter and the destruction of the international civil service as it has been developed in the League and up to now in the United Nations.

It can fairly be said that the United Nations has increasingly succeeded in affirming the original idea of a dedicated professional service responsible only to the Organization in the performance of its duties and protected insofar as possible from the inevitable pressures of national governments. And this has been done in spite of strong pressures which are easily explained in terms of historic tradition and national interests. Obviously, however, the problem is ultimately one of the spirit of service shown by the international civil servant and respected by Member governments. The International Secretariat is not what it is meant to be until the day when it can be recruited on a wide geographical basis without the risk that then some will be under—or consider themselves to be under—two masters in respect of their official functions.

V

The independence and international character of the Secretariat required not only resistance to national pressures in matters of personnel, but also—and this was more complex—the independent implementation of controversial political decisions in a manner fully consistent with the exclusively international responsibility of the Secretary-General. True, in some cases implementation was largely administrative; the political organs stated their objectives and the measures to be taken in reasonably specific terms, leaving only a narrow area for executive discretion. But in other cases—and these generally involved the most controversial situations—the Secretary-General was confronted with mandates of a highly general character, expressing the bare minimum of agreement attainable in the organs. That the execution of these tasks involved the exercise of political judgment by the Secretary-General was, of course, evident to the Member states themselves.

It could perhaps be surmised that virtually no one at San Francisco envisaged the extent to which the Members of the Organization would assign to the Secretary-General functions which necessarily required him to take positions in highly controversial political matters. A few examples of these mandates in recent years will demonstrate how wide has been the scope of authority delegated to the Secretary-General by the Security Council and the General Assembly in matters of peace and security.

One might begin in 1956 with the Palestine armistice problem, when the Security Council instructed the Secretary-General "to arrange with the parties for adoption of any measures" which he would consider "would reduce existing tensions along the armistice demarcation lines." A few months later, after the outbreak of hostilities in Egypt, the General Assembly authorized the Secretary-General immediately to "obtain compliance of the withdrawal of foreign forces." At the same session he was requested to submit a plan for a United Nations Force to "secure and supervise the cessation of hostilities," and subsequently he was instructed "to take all . . . necessary administrative and executive action to organize this Force and dispatch it to Egypt."

In 1958 the Secretary-General was requested "to dispatch urgently an Observation Group . . . to Lebanon so as to insure that there is no illegal infiltration of personnel or supply of arms or other matériel across the Lebanese borders." Two months later he was asked to make forthwith "such practical arrangements as would adequately help in upholding the purposes and principles of the Charter in relation to Lebanon and Jordan."

Most recently, in July 1960, the Secretary-General was requested to provide military assistance to the Central Government of the Republic of the Congo. The basic mandate is contained in a single paragraph of a resolution adopted by the Security Council on July 13, 1960, which reads:

. . . . . *The Security Council* . . . . .

2. *Decides* to authorize the Secretary-General to take the necessary steps, in consultation with the Government of the Republic of the Congo, to provide the government with such military assistance, as may be necessary, until, through the efforts of the Congolese government with the technical assistance of the United Nations, the national security forces may be able, in the opinion of the government to meet fully their tasks; . . .

The only additional guidance was provided by a set of principles concerning the use of United Nations forces which had been evolved during the experience of the United Nations Emergency Force. I had informed the Security Council before the adoption of the resolution that I would base any action that I might be required to take on these principles, drawing attention specifically to some of the most significant of the rules applied in the UNEF operation. At the request of the Security Council I later submitted an elaboration of the same principles to the extent they appeared to me to be applicable to the Congo operation. A report on the matter was explicitly approved by the Council, but naturally it proved to leave wide gaps; unforeseen and unforeseeable problems, which we quickly came to face, made it necessary for me repeatedly to invite the Council to express themselves on the interpretation given by the Secretary-General to the mandate. The needs for added interpretation referred especially to the politically extremely charged situation which arose because of the secession of Katanga and because of the disintegration of the central government which, according to the basic resolution of the Security Council, was to be the party in consultation with which the United Nations activities had to be developed.

These recent examples demonstrate the extent to which the Member states have entrusted the Secretary-General with tasks that have required him to take action which unavoidably may have to run counter to the views of at least some of these Member states. The agreement reached in the general terms of a resolution, as we have seen, no longer need obtain when more specific issues are presented. Even when the original resolution is fairly precise, subsequent developments, previously unforeseen, may render highly controversial the action called for under the resolution. Thus, for example, the unanimous resolution authorizing assistance to the Central Government of the Congo offered little guidance to the Secretary-General when that government split into competing centers of authority, each claiming to be the central government and each supported by different groups of Member states within and outside the Security Council.

A simple solution for the dilemmas thus posed for the Secretary-General might seem to be for him to refer the problem to the political organ for it to resolve the question. Under a national parliamentary régime, this would often be the obvious course of action for the executive to take. Indeed, this is what the Secretary-General must also do whenever it is feasible. But the serious problems arise precisely because it is so often not possible for the organs themselves to resolve the controversial issue faced by the Secretary-General. When brought down to specific cases involving a clash of interests and positions, the required majority in the Security Council or General Assembly may not be available for any particular solution. This will frequently be evident in advance of a meeting and the Member states will conclude that it would be futile for the organs to attempt to reach a decision and consequently that the problem has to be left to the Secretary-General to solve on one basis or another, on his own risk but with as faithful an interpretation of the instructions, rights, and obligations of the Organization as possible in view of international law and the decisions already taken.

It might be said that in this situation the Secretary-General should refuse to implement the resolution, since implementation would offend one or another group of Member states and open him to the charge that he has abandoned the political neutrality and impartiality essential to his office. The only way to avoid such criticism, it is said, is for the Secretary-General to refrain from execution of the original resolution until the organs have decided the issue by the required majority (and, in the case of the Security Council, with the unanimous concurrence of the permanent members) or he, maybe, has found another way to pass responsibility over on to governments.

For the Secretary-General this course of action—or more precisely, nonaction—may be tempting; it enables him to avoid criticism by refusing to act until other political organs resolve the dilemma. An easy refuge may thus appear to be available. But would such refuge be compatible with the responsibility placed upon the Secretary-General by the Charter? Is he entitled to refuse to carry out the decision properly reached by the organs, on the ground that the specific implementation would be opposed to positions some Member states might wish to take, as indicated, perhaps, by an earlier minority vote? Of course the political organs may always instruct him to discontinue the implementation of a resolution, but when they do not so instruct him and the resolution remains in effect, is the Secretary-General legally and morally free to take no action, particularly in a matter considered to affect international peace and security? Should he, for example, have abandoned the operation in the Congo because almost any decision he made as to the composition of the Force or its role would have been contrary to the attitudes of some Members as reflected in debates, and maybe even in votes, although not in decisions?

The answers seem clear enough in law; the responsibilities of the Secretary-General under the Charter cannot be laid aside merely because the execution of decisions by him is likely to be politically controversial. The

Secretary-General remains under the obligation to carry out the policies as adopted by the organs; the essential requirement is that he does this on the basis of his exclusively international responsibility and not in the interest of any particular state or groups of states.

This presents us with the crucial issue: Is it possible for the Secretary-General to resolve controversial issues on a truly international basis without obtaining the formal decisions of the organs? In my opinion and on the basis of my experience, the answer is in the affirmative; it is possible for the Secretary-General to carry out his tasks in controversial political situations with full regard to his exclusively international obligation under the Charter and without subservience to a particular national or ideological attitude. This is not to say that the Secretary-General is a kind of delphic oracle who alone speaks for the international community. He has available for his task varied means and resources.

Of primary importance in this respect are the principles and purposes of the Charter which are the fundamental law accepted by and binding on all states. Necessarily general and comprehensive, these principles and purposes still are specific enough to have practical significance in concrete cases.

The principles of the Charter are, moreover, supplemented by the body of legal doctrine and precepts that have been accepted by states generally, and particularly as manifested in the resolutions of United Nations organs. In this body of law there are rules and precedents that appropriately furnish guidance to the Secretary-General when he is faced with the duty of applying a general mandate in circumstances that had not been envisaged by the resolution.

Considerations of principle and law, important as they are, do not of course suffice to settle all the questions posed by the political tasks entrusted to the Secretary-General. Problems of political judgment still remain. In regard to these problems, the Secretary-General must find constitutional means and techniques to assist him, insofar as possible, in reducing the element of purely personal judgment. In my experience I have found several arrangements of value to enable the Secretary-General to obtain what might be regarded as the representative opinion of the Organization in respect of the political issues faced by him.

One such arrangement might be described as the institution of the permanent missions to the United Nations, through which the Member states have enabled the Secretary-General to carry on frequent consultations safeguarded by diplomatic privacy.

Another arrangement, which represents a further development of the first, has been the advisory committees of the Secretary-General, such as those on UNEF and the Congo, composed of representatives of governments most directly concerned with the activity involved, and also representing diverse political positions and interests. These advisory committees have furnished a large measure of the guidance required by the Secretary-General in carrying out his mandates relating to UNEF and the Congo operations. They have provided an essential link between the judgment of the executive and the consensus of the political bodies.

VI

Experience has thus indicated that the international civil servant may take steps to reduce the sphere within which he has to take stands on politically controversial issues. In summary, it may be said that he will carefully seek guidance in the decisions of the main organs, in statements relevant for the interpretation of those decisions, in the Charter and in generally recognized principles of law, remembering that by his actions he may set important precedents. Further, he will submit as complete reporting to the main organs as circumstances permit, seeking their guidance whenever such guidance seems to be possible to obtain. Even if all of these steps are taken, it will still remain, as has been amply demonstrated in practice, that the reduced area of discretion will be large enough to expose the international Secretariat to heated political controversy and to accusations of a lack of neutrality.

I have already drawn attention to the ambiguity of the word "neutrality" in such a context. It is obvious from what I have said that the international civil servant cannot be accused of lack of neutrality simply for taking a stand on a controversial issue when this is his duty and cannot be avoided. But there remains a serious intellectual and moral problem as we move within an area inside which personal judgment must come into play. Finally, we have to deal here with a question of integrity or with, if you please, a question of conscience.

The international civil servant must keep himself under the strictest observation. He is not requested to be a neuter in the sense that he has to have no sympathies or antipathies, that there are to be no interests which are close to him in his personal capacity or that he is to have no ideas or ideals that matter for him. However, he is requested to be fully aware of those human reactions and meticulously check himself so that they are not permitted to influence his actions. This is nothing unique. Is not every judge professionally under the same obligation?

If the international civil servant knows himself to be free from such personal influence in his actions and guided solely by the common aims and rules laid down for, and by the Organization he serves and by recognized legal principles, then he has done his duty, and then he can face the criticism which, even so, will be unavoidable. As I said, at the final last, this is a question of integrity, and if integrity in the sense of respect for law and respect for truth were to drive him into positions of conflict with this or that interest, then that conflict is a sign of his neutrality and not of his failure to observe neutrality—then it is in line, not in conflict with his duties as an international civil servant.

Recently, it has been said, this time in Western circles, that as the international Secretariat is going forward on the road of international thought and action, while Member states depart from it, a gap develops between them and they are growing into being mutually hostile elements; and this is said to increase the tension in the world which it was the purpose of the United Nations to diminish. From this view the conclusion has been drawn that we may have to switch from an international Secretariat, ruled by the principles described in this lecture, to an intergovernmental Secretariat, the members of which obviously would not be supposed to work in the direction of an internationalism considered unpalatable to their governments. Such a passive acceptance of a nationalism rendering it necessary to abandon present efforts in the direction of internationalism symbolized by the international civil service—somewhat surprisingly regarded as a cause of tension—might, if accepted by the Member nations, well prove to be the Munich of international cooperation as conceived after the First World War and further developed under the impression of the tragedy of the Second World War. To abandon or to compromise with principles on which such cooperation is built may be no less dangerous than to compromise with principles regarding the rights of a nation. In both cases the price to be paid may be peace.

THERE WERE several questions arising from his Oxford University lecture at Hammarskjöld's next press conference on June 12. His replies are of interest. He also spelled out more definitely than before the conditions under which he would be willing to stay on as Secretary-General. Having lost Soviet support he could not continue to function, he said, without the support of at least two-thirds of the General Assembly (following text).

From Transcript of Press Conference

NEW YORK   JUNE 12, 1961

THE SECRETARY-GENERAL: Ladies and Gentlemen, permit me to start on a personal note, and I hope the person in question will excuse me. Last week our friend, Max Beer, celebrated his seventy-fifth birthday. I would like to go on record with my congratulations to him and to us. To us, for having with us a veteran of international journalism, knowing the League of Nations as well as the United Nations, but yet the youngest in spirit among us all. I do not want to elaborate, because I do not want to embarrass you, Max. But I wanted to have on record this expression of my very warmest feelings. And when I speak here in this way, I speak, of course, for all my colleagues.

MR. MAX BEER: Thank you very much, Mr. Hammarskjöld. I thank you from the bottom of my heart.

. . . QUESTION: The Kennedy-Khrushchev meeting in Vienna left quite a few doors open for wider talks. I was wondering if in that light you would welcome a possible gathering of heads of state here at the next Assembly?

THE SECRETARY-GENERAL: I have no comments on that suggestion at all.

. . . QUESTION: In the Soviet memorandum on Germany and Berlin, reference was made to the possible use of United Nations troops in West Berlin as an additional guarantee. In your view and in terms of what you know about the feelings of many of the delegations here, is that not likely to be more acceptable if you have an efficient central executive?

THE SECRETARY-GENERAL: The views on what is an efficient central executive vary, as you know, quite a good deal. I guess everybody would agree with what you say. It is essential to have the right kind of executive in order to get this operation going. But, alas, they are likely to mean very different things by it.

QUESTION: In your widely commented-upon Oxford University speech

UN Note to Correspondents No. 2347.

about two weeks ago you warned that to abandon or compromise with the principles on which international cooperation is based, as symbolized in an independent international civil service, might well prove to be the Munich of international cooperation. You also pointed out two basic principles in the Charter: that decisions were to be political and that the administration and implementation were to be lifted out of the realm of the political. I want to ask you whether you consider these principles applicable to any political decisions taken on nuclear tests, on disarmament, or on any possible arrangement for the United Nations in Berlin.

THE SECRETARY-GENERAL: I believe that the principles do apply whenever you want an impartial implementation or execution of a decision which has been reached or an agreement which has been established. You may remember that at the last press conference I made a distinction between what I called a natural veto, which is based on substance, and an artificial and imposed veto. I believe one could develop the theme further in the light of your question and say that, as regards agreements, or basic decisions, of course, the cooperation of all parties concerned is necessary, and, for that reason, to a greater or lesser extent, a political element enters basically into the operation. On the other hand, once an agreement is reached or a decision taken with the necessary support—that is to say, when you reach the stage of execution—it is just as essential that all parties should be able to feel that the execution will not give rise to new negotiations or, so to speak, tear up the agreement or decision.

Therefore, my conclusion is that the principles I tried to develop, especially the principle of the international character of an executive, do apply to all operations in which parties to an agreement or decision should feel assured that the decision will be carried out in a way which is not partisan.

I believe very strongly that the basic principle of internationalism, as established especially in Article 100, is decisive, because if it were not applied, if it were not respected, what would we have? We would have executives or secretariats which in fact were a lower-level government and party representation. That being so, of course, you would have not an impartial execution of a decision or an agreement, but you would have, in a sense, a continued negotiation or a continued effort to reach decisions. And there you can see how the very logic of the situation indicates the need of the international character which I mentioned. If we were to lose the international character of the executive part of the operation, of the

Secretariat, I think that it would mean a very serious slowing-down of the execution of agreements and the carrying through of decisions. And, when I talked about those principles in somewhat dramatic terms, it was because of the fear which I feel for what we may risk if in this way the whole process of international cooperation were to be slowed down.

QUESTION: Mr. Secretary-General, in connection with what you have just said, I would like to ask you a question on a sort of broader aspect. We have seen during the past few months the emergence of a theory of international relations which actually goes back behind the theory of Thomas Hobbes, namely, that objectivity or neutrality is irreconcilable with the working of the human mind and that there is not a single neutral person on this globe. Now, in connection with this new theory, I would like to ask you two questions. First, as a man who was a neutral even in a neutral country, what do you think about the possibility of the freedom of the individual from dependence on ideologies or loyalties to one particular country? And second, what do you think can be done to counter this new theory in order to make possible the theoretical and practical working of international organizations?

THE SECRETARY-GENERAL: In a sense, I have said what I feel can be said about the neutrality of an executive and the neutrality of an international civil servant in the speech at Oxford to which reference has been made. But you put the question in more personal terms, and I may try to explain myself in personal terms.

It may be true that in a very deep, human sense there is no neutral individual, because, as I said at Oxford, everyone, if he is worth anything, has to have his ideas and ideals—things which are dear to him, and so on. But what I do claim is that even a man who is in that sense not neutral can very well undertake and carry through neutral actions, because that is an act of integrity. That is to say, I would say there is no neutral man, but there is, if you have integrity, neutral action by the right kind of man. And "neutrality"—may develop, after all, into a kind of *jeu de mots*. I am not neutral as regards the Charter; I am not neutral as regards facts. But that is not what we mean. What is meant by "neutrality" in this kind of debate is, of course, neutrality in relation to interests; and there I do claim that there is no insurmountable difficulty for anybody with the proper kind of guiding principles in carrying through such neutrality one hundred percent.

QUESTION: There have been reports from Cairo that leaders of uncommitted nations are considering plans for united action at the United Nations to increase their influence in the Organization, and also possibilities of revising the United Nations structure. In view of your own emphasis on the role of the uncommitted countries in the United Nations, and your experience in the Organization, can you tell us how you envisage the creation of a more effective Secretariat, independent of the Big Powers and under a single executive? Do you feel, for instance, that the quota system and national preserves stand in the way of a more effective Secretariat? Are you in favor of greater representation of uncommitted countries in the higher levels? Also, I would like to ask you whether you feel that the Soviet criticism of the United Nations structure has seriously affected the utilization of the United Nations machinery by other nations?

THE SECRETARY-GENERAL: Your question could easily launch me on another fifty-minute speech and I do not think that we should enter upon that kind of thing, so you will excuse me for replying briefly.

As regards representation, I would favor much broader representation in the Secretariat of the new countries in the parts of the world which are fairly new on the world stage. We have had difficulties the nature of which is well known: an inherited setup, and also some lack of persons easily available for use because the countries need them for themselves. Those are only two of the difficulties; there are others which come into play. But to the fullest extent possible, I should like to see development in that direction. I think that would, in general terms, strengthen the Secretariat. I do not think that it puts in question, in any sense, the international character of the Secretariat. It really all depends on the spirit of those who come, the spirit in which they work, and the spirit in which they are permitted to work, and I have no reason to believe that that spirit will not be the right one.

As regards the attitude of noncommitted countries, I, for one, have not checked, but I would believe their view of this whole story and this whole matter, this problem, is rather close to the one which I have tried to express. I believe so because it seems to be natural from their viewpoint to trust to this kind of independent and objective execution. Naturally, they would like to have as much influence in it as possible, not in terms of policy-making, but in the sense that they want to feel part of the body; and that is an attitude which I find not only natural and justified but an attitude which I, for my part, will try to meet as much as I can.

As regards the structure of the Secretariat and the organization of it, I would not like to enter here upon any discussion, especially in view of the fact that the Committee of Eight for review of the Secretariat[1] is likely to issue its report shortly, and then I shall have to make comments on the report for the use of the General Assembly. You will understand that, this being so, I feel that there is the right place and time for me to try to develop whatever ideas I may have on the subject.

. . . QUESTION: A part of the discussion this morning seems to have centred on an interpretation I was looking for of the statement made on page 10 of your Oxford speech. There you raised the question that once the possibility of the impartiality of an international civil servant is raised there may be—and you go into a sentence which implies a need for changes, constitutional or otherwise to meet the possibility, if it is acknowledged or accepted that an international civil servant may be impartial. I wondered—whereas you have previously indicated that a resignation would be forthcoming if the majority of the Assembly should vote against you on a crucial issue—does this represent a sort of *de facto* evolution of the Charter as a constitution or would such an interpretation be beyond what you were saying on page 10 of the Oxford speech?

THE SECRETARY-GENERAL: I think that in fact you mix two problems here. What I meant on page 10—I really do not remember where it was—is covered by the trite expression, "Caesar's wife must not even be suspected." Under such circumstances any international service should be willing to submit itself to all checks and controls which are found constitutionally advisable. That is one thing and I would be quite happy to have it. You may remember that I have at various stages during the Congo operation, for example, invited decisions to the effect that there would be what I called a sharing of responsibilities. You can also say that such a sharing of responsibilities means that the people will have the chance to look at the spirit, the way in which decisions are carried out so as to ascertain that there is this neutrality of action to which I referred. That is really what I had in mind here.

You bring up the other question, the question of, so to say, the standing offer of resignation. That represents a *de facto* development. It does not have any precedent. There is nothing in the Charter indicating that form. You may perhaps say that it is built on a kind of parliamentary theory in the interpretation of the Charter, a parliamentary theory which, however,

---

[1] Committee of Experts on the Review of the Activities and Organization of the Secretariat.

I have never, so to say, spelled out. We have a situation where one of the permanent members has ceased cooperation. What should the consequences be? Obviously the General Assembly comes into the picture, too. The Security Council is not the only one to decide in such matters. I am not in the position to extend Article 97 to cover the whole period of the service of the Secretary-General. That certainly would be absolutely preposterous for the Secretary-General to do. But he must, on the other hand, take into account the hard facts of the situation. Bringing the General Assembly into the question the way I did, I think that, if you want to translate it into constitutional terms—I should not like to formalize it myself but you may want to do so—it is reasonable to say that if the Secretary-General has lost the support of one of the permanent members of the Security Council, which presumably is one of the conditions for his functioning, and if, moreover, he does not have the support of at least two-thirds of the General Assembly, he is no longer in a position to function.

. . . . .

REFERENCE WAS made during the Secretary-General's May 29 press conference to the financial chaos in the Congo and the need for emergency assistance from the United Nations. Hammarskjöld had dispatched a special mission to Leopoldville headed by Philippe de Seynes, Under-Secretary-General for Economic and Social Affairs, to examine the situation with President Kasavubu and his ministers. They reached agreement on certain immediate measures on June 7, some to be taken by the Leopoldville régime and some by the United Nations. The agreement was confirmed in an exchange of letters between Kasavubu and Hammarskjöld. The Secretary-General's letter is the first following text.

Letter to President Kasavubu on Conclusion of Agreement on United Nations Economic and Financial Aid to the Congo

NEW YORK   JUNE 10, 1961

I THANK YOU FOR your letter of June 7 concerning the conversations you and your representatives have had with Mr. de Seynes and his colleagues about the economic and financial problems now facing your country and the financial assistance which might be given to it.

I am glad that these discussions have made it possible to reach certain important conclusions to which all the participants were able unreservedly to subscribe.

I note with great interest that you have decided to take a number of practical steps to put the state's finances on a sound footing and to bring about normal economic conditions. Certainly, without an effort at internal reform, the external assistance you may receive will not solve any of your problems. I am convinced that as part of your proposed programme, this aid can be extremely helpful in reducing substantially the impact of the measures which the state of the public finances and the shortage of foreign exchange make imperative.

As Mr. de Seynes told you, the United Nations is prepared to provide additional technical assistance in support of the efforts you proposed to make to strengthen the administrative structure of the state and the provinces, and more particularly the machinery for supervising the expenditure of public funds. I intend to take action, with all due speed, on the request you have seen fit to make in this matter.

There is one point in your letter on which I feel I must lay particular emphasis, the action of the United Nations is designed to benefit the whole country through the channel of the treasury. Any discrimination in the use of the financial assistance made available to you would be con-

UN Press Release CO/153.

trary to the spirit in which it is extended and would jeopardize the chances of further action. I am glad that you saw fit to record clearly your agreement with this view.

I have today authorized Mr. Linnér to sign the agreement, the draft of which you found acceptable, between the Monetary Council and the United Nations, and I have taken the necessary steps to transfer the sum of ten million dollars to the Monetary Council's account at the Irving Trust Bank.

International financial assistance nowadays is as a rule repayable under terms—often very favourable as a matter of fact—such as those contemplated by the International Development Association affiliated to the International Bank for Reconstruction and Development. In view of the special difficulties facing your country at the present time, the conditions of a possible reimbursement would have to be studied later in the light of the economic rehabilitation of the Congo and of the progress made in the negotiations you propose to initiate for dealing with the public debt.

I sincerely hope that the agreement reached at Leopoldville—a milestone in cooperation between the Republic of the Congo and the United Nations—may prove an effective contribution to your progress on the long and difficult road towards economic and financial recovery.

Dag Hammarskjöld
Secretary-General

THE REPORT to the Security Council that follows recounts the success of the mediating efforts of Robert Gardiner, Francis Nwokedi, and Mahmoud Khiari, which were undertaken on Hammarskjöld's instructions, in winning agreement between Stanleyville and Leopoldville on terms for reconvening the Congolese parliament under UN protection. The session would be convened at the University of Lovanium on July 15. It was at first believed that Katanga's representatives would also attend the parliamentary session. Tshombé was released from detention in Leopoldville on June 22 and two days later signed the protocol of agreement with the Leopoldville régime that is included as addendum 2 in the following report. However, Tshombé repudiated the agreement as soon as he returned to Elisabethville, claiming that he had signed under duress. For later developments see pp. 538-41.

Report to the Security Council on Convening the Parliament of the Congo

NEW YORK   JUNE 20—JULY 6, 1961

1. PART B, OPERATIVE paragraph (1), of the resolution which the Security Council adopted on February 21, 1961, "Urges the convening of Parliament and the taking of necessary protective measures in that connection," and operative paragraph 5 of General Assembly resolution 1600 (XV) of April 15, 1961,

Urges the convening of Parliament without delay, with safe conduct and security extended to the members of Parliament by the United Nations, so that Parliament may take the necessary decisions concerning the formation of a national government and on the future constitutional structure of the Republic of the Congo in accordance with the constitutional processes laid down in the Loi fondamentale.

2. In pursuance of these resolutions the Secretary-General requested his representative in the Congo to explore, by discussions with the various Congolese authorities, the possibility of an early meeting of Parliament.

3. After preliminary explorations with various authorities, Mr. Gardiner, on the instructions of the Secretary-General, visited Stanleyville on June 9, 1961, for discussions with Mr. Gizenga and his collaborators concerning the meeting of Parliament. As a result of these discussions, Mr. Gizenga proposed that he would send to Leopoldville a mission of three persons for the purpose of discussing with representatives of the Leopoldville authorities the modalities for an early reconvening of Parliament. The United Nations undertook to give to the members of this mission all facilities and full protection.

4. On June 12, 1961, after discussions with Mr. Khiari and Mr. Gardiner, the Leopoldville authorities agreed to appoint three representatives to meet with the representative of the Stanleyville authorities.

Security Council Official Records, Sixteenth Year, Supplement for April, May, and June 1961, documents S/4841 and Add. 1-3.

5. On June 13, the representatives named by the Leopoldville authorities, namely Mr. Cyrille Adoula, Mr. Jean Bolikango, and Mr. Marcel Lihau, met with the representatives of the Stanleyville authorities, namely Mr. Jacques Massena, Mr. Etienne Kihuyu, and Mr. Mapago, at the headquarters of the United Nations in Leopoldville.

6. On June 19, 1961, following meetings in which, at the request of both delegations, Mr. Khiari, Mr. Gardiner, and Mr. Nwokedi, acting on behalf of the Secretary-General, gave occasional assistance, agreement on the modalities for the convening of Parliament was reached. The statement of the representative of the Leopoldville authorities is reproduced in annex I, the statement of the representative of the Stanleyville authorities is reproduced in annex II, and the agreement itself is reproduced in annex III.

7. The Secretary-General has informed the authorities concerned that he accepts all the responsibilities which, under this agreement, devolve upon the United Nations, and will continue to render all possible assistance to facilitate the meeting of Parliament at the place and date agreed upon.

ANNEX I

Statement Made by Mr. Bolikango

My dear compatriots, men, women, and children of the Congo.

After a year of crisis, dissension, and misunderstanding, we are now on the eve of national reconciliation.

The Tananarive and Coquilhatville conferences were steps towards an understanding between the various parties in the Congo, which unfortunate circumstances had separated. Those conferences could only bring about a political solution of the country's problems. They were certainly useful in bringing together some of our political leaders who would not otherwise have met.

The final solution, however, can be based only on law. For that reason, we must have recourse to Parliament. We hope that your representatives will provide the country with a solution which will enable us once and for all to emerge from the impasse in which we find ourselves.

Dear compatriots, special circumstances make it necessary for your elected representatives to have certain safeguards if they are to exercise in full safety and freedom the mandate with which you have entrusted them. A delegation representing the Stanleyville authorities, consisting of Mr.

Massena, Mr. Kihuyu, and Mr. Mapago, has just concluded a very important agreement with a delegation from the Leopoldville authorities, of which I was the leader and which included Mr. Adoula and Mr. Lihau.

Dear compatriots, in order to give you irrefutable evidence of the understanding which has been reached between the authorities, I yield the floor to Mr. Massena, the leader of the Stanleyville delegation.

ANNEX II

Statement Made by Mr. Massena

The two Congolese delegations have again found peace and understanding, following the fraternal contacts and talks which they had from June 12 to 19, 1961. They both recognized that their aim was the same: i.e., national unity and respect for national law, integrity, and independence.

The two delegations have agreed on the following measures to restore normal life throughout the Republic:

1. They have accepted the University of Lovanium as the site for a meeting of Parliament on June 25, 1961, on the basis of an agreement between them, one copy of which has been handed to the representative of the Secretary-General of the United Nations in the Congo;

2. During the talks between the two delegations, particular emphasis was placed on the need to avoid external influences, which have been one of the primary causes of the sufferings of our young republic. Effective measures are planned to preserve the freedom of action and integrity of the parliamentary representatives throughout the entire session of Parliament;

3. The two delegations ask their respective authorities to remove all restrictions on freedom of movement, trade, communications, etc. which might impair the fundamental freedoms and the economic life of the Congolese people. They appeal to those authorities to renew their sincere friendship forthwith, before the forthcoming meeting of Parliament;

4. The two delegations urgently appeal to the military authorities to stand aloof from all political activity and to submit unconditionally to whatever government will be constituted at the present session of Parliament;

5. The two delegations pay a particular tribute to the Secretary-General of the United Nations and his representatives in the Congo for the attention and help they have continually given the various Congolese political factions with a view to enabling them to settle their differences

by peaceful means. They request ONUC to use its influence and good offices in order to persuade the authorities of the province of Katanga to join them in finding a solution to the Congolese problem once and for all.

ANNEX III

Agreement of June 19, 1961, Between the Leopoldville Authorities and the Stanleyville Authorities

On Monday, June 19, 1961, Mr. J. Bolikango, Mr. C. Adoula, and Mr. M. Lihau, representing the Leopoldville authorities, on the one hand, and Mr. J. Massena, Mr. E. Kihuyu, and Mr. S. P. Mapago, representing the Stanleyville authorities, on the other, agreed as follows:

1. The typed records of the meetings of June 13 to 16 and 19, 1961 shall be signed by the two parties, who will thereby indicate their approval, and shall serve as basic documents for the arrangements listed hereinafter;

2. After the inspection of the premises by United Nations military authorities, the two parties agree that Parliament shall meet at the University of Lovanium, which place fulfils the conditions required to ensure the absolute safety of the members of Parliament;

3. Armée nationale congolaise forces and police at Leopoldville and the adjoining zones shall not circulate in the city and the said adjoining zones carrying arms, which must be deposited beforehand in armouries under guard of the respective forces. It shall be the responsibility of ONUC to exercise supervision to ensure that no soldier or policeman carries arms in the city or in the adjoining zones, throughout the entire period of the parliamentary session;

4. During the session all the members of Parliament shall be housed in Lovanium itself and shall have no contacts with the outside world;

5. The administrative personnel servicing the assemblies, who will be given special permits issued by the officers of the two chambers, shall be compelled to stay at Lovanium for the duration of the parliamentary session, under the conditions referred to in the preceding paragraph;

6. It shall be the duty of the United Nations to ensure that the members of Parliament, the administrative personnel of the assemblies and the United Nations civilian personnel placed at the disposal of Parliament shall not have with them any weapons, any money, or any other negotiable instruments of any kind, either when entering Lovanium or upon their departure;

7. All telephone lines to Lovanium shall be cut off;

8. The free passage of members of Parliament through the Congo shall be ensured by ONUC at the request in writing of the members concerned;

9. United Nations civilian personnel placed at the disposal of members of Parliament during the session shall be required to reside at the seat of Parliament for periods of a fortnight at a time. During each period such personnel shall have no contact with the outside world and shall also be subject to the conditions stipulated in paragraphs 6 and 7 above;

10. The two delegations propose June 25, 1961 as the latest possible date for the opening of Parliament and the United Nations shall take all the necessary steps to ensure that Parliament may open on the date agreed upon by the two delegations;

11. The two delegations propose to Parliament that the vote of confidence in the Government should be taken by secret ballot;

12. The President of the Republic shall convene Parliament on the date appointed by the two delegations;

13. In order that the meeting of Parliament may be the reflection of national opinion, the United Nations shall be requested to invite all the other political factions in the Congo to subscribe to this agreement;

14. The United Nations shall also be requested to continue to accord its good offices to the parties concerned in seeking a real and satisfactory solution to the Congolese crisis and to that end it shall be authorized to arrange all the necessary contacts between the Congolese political leaders.

DOCUMENT S/4841/ADD.1
Statement Made by Mr. Gizenga on June 23, 1961

We are approaching the end of our first year of independence. These twelve months have been marked by a good many tragic incidents which have stained the history and the name of the Congo with blood. All this must stop. We who followed Patrice Lumumba until his death were and remain determined to see the Congo as a whole return to legality in a healthy atmosphere of national reconciliation.

It was in this spirit that I, several weeks ago, proposed the convening of Parliament in the neutral zone of Kamina. To this statement of my position Mr. Kasavubu replied by suggesting that Parliament should meet at Leopoldville. Still motivated by the desire for general harmony and a calming of passions, I sent a delegation to Leopoldville, under the auspices of the United Nations, to discuss with the authorities and the United Nations conditions regarding the possibility of convening Parliament at Leopoldville. I also asked, as a prior condition, for further information regarding rhe complete safety which the United Nations must guarantee our parliamentary representatives. On these conditions we are prepared to go to Leopoldville. It was also suggested that before the meeting of Parliament, talks should be held concerning the formation of a government of national reconciliation. To this we reply simply that the government formed by Patrice Lumumba is a government of national union and, guided by that wisdom and by the supreme interests of the Congo, we are determined to continue in the way already laid down, within the limits of legality and parliamentary procedure. We are ready to go even further, for we are prepared to meet the Congolese who now share this view. We have always been of the opinion that so long as the Armée nationale congolaise remains divided there can be no peace and security throughout the republic. While ensuring the citizens of legality, it is our duty at the same time to guarantee them total safety. It is to this end that I propose to all the leaders of the Congo a general amnesty for all our troops, so that our military leaders can meet and discuss the problems of the *Armée nationale* in peace and security.

After these various statements of position, no one can question our sincerity and our desire to continue to be governed by legality. Our only ambition, our only desire, is to see order restored by the government of national union.

At this critical moment in the history of the Congo, I make this solemn declaration as a gesture in honour and memory of our great leader, the national hero Patrice Lumumba.

Considering the foregoing,

1. The government has decided to free the eight imprisoned Belgian soldiers;

2. It has further requested the effective cooperation of the United Nations in reestablishing the national institutions;

3. The government has decided to continue its efforts to restore legality, understanding, and national harmony;

4. The government proposes that a general amnesty for all Congolese soldiers shall be established throughout the Republic;

5. Our parliamentary representatives are prepared to go to Leopoldville as soon as the conditions for complete safety are fulfilled by the United Nations;

6. The government is convinced of the desire of all citizens to safeguard at all costs national independence, the unity of the country, and its territorial integrity.

DOCUMENT S/4841/ADD.2

Protocol of Agreement Dated June 24, 1961, Signed by Mr. Tshombé and by the Representatives of the Leopoldville Authorities

Article 1

Parliament shall convene at Leopoldville as soon as possible. The central government, assisted by the United Nations, shall ensure the safety of the members of Parliament.

Article 2

A new government shall be constituted and shall come before the Chambers for a vote of confidence. This new government shall remain in power until the adoption of the new constitution. The new constitution shall be adopted within a period not exceeding three months.

Article 3

All custom barriers between Katanga and the rest of the Congo shall be abolished. Goods from Katanga shall be carried along the national route. The central government shall ensure the protection of the goods.

Article 4

All entry and exit dues levied on goods shall be payable in their entirety to the national exchequer. All dues levied at Matadi shall be payable to the central government at Leopoldville, and those levied in Katanga shall be payable to the Katanga treasury.

Article 5

A commission of national experts, assisted if necessary by foreign experts, shall be established for the purpose of settling the disputes of parastatal companies and those enjoying special status, such as CSK, CNKI, INEAC, OTRACO.

Article 6

Currency—During the transitional period, a single currency shall be legal tender, but shall bear two monetary symbols. The two monetary symbols shall be gradually replaced by a single monetary symbol. During this period, Katanga shall be represented on the Currency Council.

Article 7

Social, educational, and administrative problems—In the educational sphere, curricula at secondary, higher, and university levels shall be unified, in order that academic grades, established and organized by the central power, may be conferred. In the administrative sphere, the respective states shall be represented in the Commission to be established under the agreement of April 17, 1961 (S/4807, annex I). The states shall propose that the commission approve technicians selected by them. In reaching its decisions on such proposals, the Commission shall be guided solely by the interests of the states. Where a proposal is rejected, the state concerned shall be requested to submit further proposals.

Article 8

Diplomatic representation—Representation abroad is within the exclusive competence of the head of state. During the transitional period, practical measures shall be taken to ensure that there shall henceforth be only a single diplomatic representation abroad.

Article 9

Muluba problem—The delegation of Katanga undertakes to release all political prisoners immediately and unconditionally. A commission of inquiry assisted by representatives of both parties shall be established by the central government. The president of the Government of Katanga agrees to meet Mr. Sendwe outside Leopoldville and in the presence of the Commission of Inquiry.

Article 10

Military problems—With regard to military problems, the two delegations shall refer to the agreement concluded between the headquarters of the Armée nationale congolaise and the authorities of Katanga. This agreement shall be implemented immediately.

Article 11

The two parties undertake on their honour to ensure the complete implementation of these agreements.

The agreement between Leopoldville and Katanga has been signed on behalf of Leopoldville by: Bolikango, Bomboko, Lihau, Nkayi, Dérico-yard, Kabangui, Massa, Kimvayi, Kisolokela, Mahamba, and on behalf of Katanga by: Tshombé and Kimba.

DOCUMENT S/4841/ADD.3
Order No. 41 of July 5, 1961, convening the Legislative Chambers

The President of the Republic,

Considering the Loi fondamentale, concerning the structure of the Congo of May 19, 1960, and more particularly articles 15, 17, 55, and 69 thereof;

Considering the constitutional legislative decree of February 9, 1961, concerning the exercise of the legislative and executive powers at the central level, particularly article 2 thereof;

Considering the order of June 24, 1961, declaring the closure of the parliamentary session opened in September 1960;

On the proposal of the Council of Ministers;

Orders:

Article 1

The Legislative Chambers shall be convened at Leopoldville on July 15, 1961.

Article 2

The former Presidents of the Chambers shall agree upon the actual date of the first meeting of the Chambers.

Article 3

The Minister of the Interior is responsible for carrying out this order, which shall enter into force immediately.

Done at Leopoldville, July 5, 1961

J. KASAVUBU
President of the Republic

(The order is countersigned by Mr. J. Iléo, Mr. C. Adoula, Mr. J. Bomboko, and Mr. M. Lihau.)

From Transcript of Press Conference

NEW YORK   JUNE 26, 1961

In 1960 a greatly increased number of Members, principally from the third world, were admitted to the United Nations. The Secretary-General and his Executive Assistant, Andrew W. Cordier, had numerous discussions of the political and administrative implications of this enlarged membership. Cordier came to the conclusion that despite the theory that his post was outside geographical distribution the major contribution to an adjustment to the nationals of the third world would come through his resignation from his post.

In May 1961 Mr. Hammarskjöld proposed to Cordier a division of the post in which he, Cordier, would assume responsibility for General Assembly affairs, while the other post, renamed Chef de Cabinet, would be assigned to a national of the third world. Cordier did not look with favor upon this arrangement and replied that he would prefer to resign from the Secretariat. Hammarskjöld refused to accept his resignation and terminated the conversation at that point. Cordier's motives in resigning from the Secretariat arose not alone from distaste for the split arrangement but were dictated by his age and the prospect of adding a useful career in the years remaining. Cordier, sixty years of age, had played a leading role in enforcing the sixty-year retirement rule upon others in the Secretariat and could not see himself violating a rule which he asked others to accept.

Several days after the above conversation between the two men, Cordier, in London en route to Jerusalem, despatched a letter to Hammarskjöld pressing the conviction that his resignation from the Secretariat was the correct course to follow and expressing the hope that the Secretary-General would respond to his desire to resign (see pp. 513-16).

Hammarskjöld reluctantly accepted Cordier's resignation but in the month of June 1961 asked that Cordier accept the post of Under-Secretary for General Assembly Affairs on a temporary and transitional basis, which in effect meant the continuation of Cordier's service through the next session of the General Assembly.

Cordier's resignation from the Secretariat was colored to some degree by the acute political pressures being brought by the Soviet bloc upon the Secretary-General's office and some of the senior posts in the Secretariat. Hammarskjöld's insistence that Cordier remain, although in a different post, demonstrated his nonacquiescence to such pressures.

UN Note to Correspondents No. 2358.

THE SECRETARY-GENERAL: Ladies and Gentlemen, I have first a couple of announcements.

I shall go for a little bit less than a week to the Economic and Social Council meeting in Geneva. I should be there from the 10th onwards. In connection with the visit to Geneva, I hope to pay a visit to Cairo. The date is still to be fixed. And somewhat later in the summer I shall go to New Delhi. The date will be announced later in that case also. As regards Cairo, you know we have so many irons in the fire in that part of the world generally, so it has been rather exceptional that I have not been more closely in touch with our operations and with that area in such a long time.

I would also like to say one word about reorganization in my own executive office. It is a question of a redistribution of responsibilities on the 38th floor. Recently, Mr. Cordier informed me of his wish to resign as executive assistant in order to assist in the adjustment of posts at the under-secretary level, taking into account the much enlarged and revised geographical character of the membership of the United Nations. I understood that this wish also reflected Mr. Cordier's views regarding the disposition of his personal efforts during forthcoming years. I asked Mr. Cordier kindly to continue to help me, in the first place, with the tasks relating to the work of the General Assembly—to do that as a special assignment. Mr. Cordier agreed, and thus, effective from August 1, Mr. Cordier will be under-secretary in charge of General Assembly and related affairs. The remaining part of the tasks which so far have fallen on the executive assistant will be taken care of by Mr. Narasimhan, who will then be, on an *ad hoc* basis, as an additional assignment, something which I might perhaps, in European terminology, most properly call *chef de cabinet.*

Those are the announcements that I would like to make on this occasion, and now the floor is yours.

QUESTION: The three former presidents of the Assembly who were consulted proposed the appointment of an under-secretary with special qualifications and experience in military matters, but the Committee of Experts on the Organization of the Secretariat seems to have ignored the suggestion. What are your views on the need for a military adviser to the Secretary-General?

I have a second question: Under the new formula proposed by the Committee on the Organization of the Secretariat, it would seem that the quota of the nonaligned countries would be slightly raised, but the number would be less than at present. Also it seems to me that they would have far less representation than the members of the other two blocs. Do you not feel that this would make the Secretariat even less effective in promoting international cooperation?

THE SECRETARY-GENERAL: As regards the military expert, that is a detail of the whole problem. For my part, I would feel that it would be a good thing, if we can afford it, to have one of the men on an under-secretary level as somebody who is especially in charge of the military aspects of the United Nations operations. However, as I say, it is a detail of a much wider problem, and I would like to subordinate it to whatever is the outcome of the deliberations of the General Assembly concerning the whole question of the structure of the under-secretary level.

Regarding the second point you raised, it brings us rather deep into the details of the proposals of the Committee of Eight.

In a short while—I expect before the end of the week—I shall present to the Advisory Committee on Administrative and Budgetary Questions my observations on the report of the Committee of Eight, and that, of course, will be the proper occasion to comment on such special matters as the one to which you have referred. I can anticipate my own comments by saying that the line which I shall try to follow myself is one which would give countries outside the group of the Big Five—I would not say "nonaligned countries"—a definite increase in representation in the Secretariat on the under-secretary level. That is to say, whatever may be the effect of this or that proposal which has been made by members of the Committee of Eight, I would have my own proposals; and your worries would not apply to those proposals as they now stand.

I noted—it may have been a slip of the tongue—a phraseology on your side which rather amused me. You said that the Secretariat in that case would become "even less effective."

QUESTION: In connection with your visit to Cairo, you spoke of "the area." May I ask, first, if you could give us details as to the date on which you will be visiting Cairo and how long you will stay there and, secondly, whether you intend to visit any other states in the area, particularly Israel?

THE SECRETARY-GENERAL: The most I can squeeze in is a couple of days as matters stand. I have no plan to visit any other country. As you well know, the United Arab Republic has a very special position because we have a big operation still going on on its territory.

.... QUESTION: In the past you have expressed hope that the negotiations between the Algerians and the French would be fruitful, especially during your conference when the Melun talks were taking place. Now again the talks have collapsed. Would you be able to give us your comment on this question now?

THE SECRETARY-GENERAL: With the enormous patience and enormous energy which has been shown so far in order to bring those talks about and to reach the point which after all has been reached—and I think you will agree with me that progress has been registered—I feel that unless there is a change of mind on either one of the two sides, or on the two sides, these talks in one way or another will be resumed and will not be dropped. That would go against the underlying trend which I think we have been able to register. This is one of the cases where, if you permit me a somewhat literary association, one is rather tempted to quote Shelley when he says, if I remember correctly, that one should "hope 'til Hope creates from its own wreck the thing it contemplates."[1] I would like to make that the motto in quite a few United Nations operations and also for a few operations outside the United Nations, including these talks.

.... QUESTION: Mr. Secretary-General, it is always a pleasure to see you back here with us. I have been very quiet, like yourself, for almost a year; and I have the feeling that I have completely lost this habit of the question and answer period. Since you are generous enough to let me try again, I should like to ask you a question—just an easy one—on the United Nations Organization itself.

Sir, while a great number of United Nations Members are against the proposal of a "troika" to replace the Secretary-General, many of us, especially among the uncommitted countries, believe that in all fairness there must be a change in the United Nations Charter which will take into account the increase of Afro-Asian Members. Would you care to give us your comments on this matter, Sir?

THE SECRETARY-GENERAL: Whether the question is to be considered easy or difficult is something we can leave aside entirely. But the reply is quite clear.

[1] *Prometheus Unbound.*

There is very much that can be done in order to adjust this Organization better to the present geographical picture. Very much can be done without any change of the Charter or revision of the Charter. I have several times in press conferences stressed that I am not particularly inclined to think of Charter revision as long as we have not used the possibilities of the Charter. And that would be my reply also to your question.

I have already stressed, and stress it again, that from my point of view adjustments should be made within all reasonable limits so as to make the Organization in various ways a proper picture of its present membership.

QUESTION: On this topic, how do you run a "troika" without a coachman?

THE SECRETARY-GENERAL: Well, I have never tried a "troika" and I do not think I ever will.

QUESTION: Mr. Secretary-General, judging from what you announced today on a change in the Secretariat and on your travel plans and on what may be your forthcoming comments on the proposals of the Committee of Eight, would it be right to assume that your present philosophy about the future of this Organization lies in the belief that the hope of this Organization lies outside the Big Five, or the Big Four, if you want to put it this way, and that the chance for survival of the United Nations lies in all nations outside the Big Powers forcing the Big Powers to remain in and to heed to the United Nations?

THE SECRETARY-GENERAL: I think you put it in too extreme a form, if you permit me to say so. It is not, and it can never be, a question of the United Nations living, so to say, outside the Big Five or being maintained somehow independently of the Big Five. It is necessarily a question of "both-and." I have already, I think, on some occasion indicated the need to have a balance between the recognition of the crucial role of the major powers, on the one side, and the rights and responsibilities of the majority of nations, on the other side. What I see as the future of the United Nations lies in the direction of such a balance.

The vast majority of Members must, so to say, come into their own positively in relation to the permanent members of the Security Council. Their significance, their importance, their responsibilities, and their rights must be fully recognized. But on the other hand, the majority should, of course, look realistically at the world as it stands today and see clearly what is the role and what must be the role of the Big Powers. Under such circumstances, my reply to your question is not one which I can give with your own terminology. I would rather say that I see the future of this Organization very much as one of an organ which primarily serves the interests of smaller countries which otherwise would not have a platform in world affairs—these smaller countries, however, within the Organization intimately cooperating with the Big Powers.

. . . .

Correspondence Between the Secretary-General and Andrew W. Cordier

*Excerpts from letter dated May 23 from Mr. Cordier to the
Secretary-General*

Dear Dag,

I have devoted the fullest and most serious reflection to the matter we discussed together last Wednesday. I have pondered deeply over all aspects and implications of the total situation—both politically and organizationally. I hope that you will believe me when I say that in my review I have given first consideration to the serious problems that you face organizationally and to the steps that, in full justice, you must take to safeguard and further the interests of the Organization.

•　　•　　•　　•

In thinking this matter over countless times since Wednesday I have always come to the same conclusion. With very deep regret, therefore, I hereby submit my resignation from the Secretariat and hope that, in full understanding, you will accept it. As the first link in the chain of reorganization, I would further hope that my successor would take on the functions of my post at once, so that you could proceed expeditiously with the rest of the plan.

•　　•　　•　　•

Outside the Secretariat I shall continue to support you and the work of the Organization with full heart and enthusiasm.

There are no words that would adequately express my feelings for the priceless privilege it has been to have had you as my chief for more than

Mr. Cordier's private papers.

eight years. The many expressions of confidence in me and of generosity toward me will always be warmly treasured. To have worked so closely with you and, thus, to have been inspired by the wide and profound range of your interests, has been an experience which I have often wished could be enjoyed by people everywhere. . . . .

Letter dated June 19 from the Secretary-General to Mr. Cordier

Dear Mr. Cordier,

You have recently informed me of your wish to resign as executive assistant to the Secretary-General in order to assist in the adjustment of posts at the under-secretary level, taking into account the much enlarged and revised geographical character of the membership of the United Nations. You have also indicated that this action would be in accord with your view regarding the disposition of your personal efforts during the coming years.

In view of the outstanding contribution you have made to the development of the United Nations and your most distinguished record as an international civil servant, carrying the greatest responsibilities, it would be for me a source of great regret to see you leave the Organization. It would also be a serious loss for the Organization not to be able to rely any longer on your wide experience and deep knowledge of its problems. On the other hand, I appreciate your motives, and I have therefore given careful thought to how, while meeting your viewpoints, the interests of the work of the Organization can best be met.

In our talks on this matter you have been responsive to my request that you might continue for a temporary and transitional period to assist us in some aspects of our work. I refer particularly to your willingness to assume responsibility for General Assembly affairs and related matters as a special assignment, at least over the sixteenth session of the General Assembly. In due course, and as necessary, we could revert to the question of adjusting our needs and your anticipated outside obligations.

Naturally this assignment would maintain you on the basis of your present contract with the United Nations as senior official on the under-secretary level.

UN Press Release SG/1404.

In case you confirm your acceptance of the post of Under-Secretary for General Assembly Affairs on a temporary and transitional basis, I would entrust one of the other under-secretaries, with the probable title of chef de cabinet, to assume the responsibilities—aside from General Assembly affairs matters—which you have carried in the past as executive assistant to the Secretary-General.

As I sincerely hope that this arrangement will be agreeable to you, I will not on this occasion express what I otherwise would have liked to say concerning the unique quality of your work and the invaluable assistance which you have given so generously to the Organization and from which I have profited so much as Secretary-General.

Letter dated June 26 from Mr. Cordier to the Secretary-General

Dear Mr. Hammarskjöld,

I thank you for your letter of June 19 which reflects the talks that we have had regarding my relations with the Secretariat. I will be glad to accept the post of Under-Secretary for General Assembly Affairs on the basis outlined in your letter.

I am most grateful for your kindly remarks regarding my work as a member of the Secretariat. Although I shall revert to the matter at the time of my actual separation from the Secretariat, I take the occasion now to tell you that it has been a priceless privilege to have had you as my chief during these years.

THE COMMITTEE OF EIGHT, or more correctly the Committee of Experts, to whose recommendations on organization of the Secretariat at the top level reference was made during the June 26 press conference, was composed of the following members: Guillaume Georges-Picot, France, chairman; Francisco Urrutia, Colombia, rapporteur; A. A. Roschin, USSR; Omar Loutfi, United Arab Republic; Sir Harold Parker, United Kingdom; Alex Quaison-Sackey, Ghana; C. S. Venkatachar, India; and L. M. Goodrich, United States.

As was to be expected this committee issued a divided report on June 14, 1961. The representatives of France, Colombia, the United Kingdom, and the United States suggested reducing to not more than eight the number of officials at the level immediately below the Secretary-General. The three Afro-Asian representa-

UN Press Release SG/1040.

level immediately below the Secretary-General. The three Afro-Asian representatives proposed replacing the two existing under-secretaries for special political affairs by three deputy secretaries-general—a bow in the direction of tripartite political representation at the top level for the West, the Communist bloc, and the "third world." The Soviet representative wanted three secretaries-general of equal rank on the "troika" formula and added a denunciation of the present geographical distribution of senior staff in general because "an overwhelming majority" were nationals of countries belonging to Western military alliances.

The Secretary-General disagreed with all three approaches by the committee members and on June 30 issued a separate document giving his comments on the report and his own recommendations. Parts I, II, and III of the document, dealing with top level organization and with the question of geographical distribution, are reproduced in the text that follows.

From Comments on the Report of the Committee of Experts on the Review of the Activities and Organization of the Secretariat

NEW YORK   JUNE 30, 1961

I

1. In making his observations and comments on the report of the Committee of Experts on the Review of the Activities and Organization of the Secretariat (A/4776), the Secretary-General would like to draw attention once again to the terms of General Assembly resolution 1446(XIV) requesting the Secretary-General to appoint such a committee. The committee was expected "to work together with the Secretary-General in reviewing the activities and organization of the Secretariat of the United Nations, with a view to effecting or proposing further measures designed to ensure maximum economy and efficiency in the Secretariat." Thus the committee was expected to work in close contact with the Secretary-General, and to suggest measures designed to ensure maximum economy and efficiency in the Secretariat.

2. Discussions between the Secretary-General and the committee were, in fact, limited to one meeting at the very beginning of the committee's work (see paragraph 2 of the report), and another meeting towards the very end of its work. On the former occasion, the question of the relationship between the work of this committee and that of the Advisory Committee on Administrative and Budgetary Questions was discussed. At the latter meeting, the Secretary-General made his observations on the various tentative approaches to the question of the reorganization of the Secretariat at the top level. Chapter III of the report, however, does not reflect in any sense the views that the Secretary-General expressed to the committee on the latter occasion.

3. In regard to the criteria of efficiency and economy, the Secretary-General observes that the committee felt "that the problem of the organi-

General Assembly Official Records, Sixteenth Session, agenda item 6, document A/4794, sections I, II and III.

zation at the top level is not solely, or even primarily, a matter of administrative organization," and that there were important political considerations which the committee felt it could not ignore, even though it recognized that they were outside the strict terms of reference of the committee (paragraph 26). As a result the Secretary-General finds himself obliged, in his comments on the committee's report, especially chapter III, to pay special attention to the political considerations to which the committee's approach gives rise.

4. The Secretary-General would like to state here that the efforts of the Secretariat to achieve efficiency and economy, which, in the circumstances, will be subordinated in these comments to other aspects of the problem, will naturally continue, independently of the discussion of the report of the Committee of Experts. These efforts have been and will be reflected in the Secretary-General's own proposals in the budget of the Organization, as also for the reorganization at the senior level.

5. The detailed comments of the Secretary-General on chapters III to VI of the report follow.

II

6. The Secretary-General has the following comments and observations to make on chapter III of the report entitled "Organization of the Secretariat at the top level."

7. These comments are made on the basis of the present Charter provisions governing the Secretariat. It may be recalled that Article 100 of the Charter provides for an international civil service with one chief administrative officer (Article 97). Thus, the Secretary-General does not take up for consideration proposals which would either, directly or indirectly, infringe upon the responsibilities of the Secretary-General, as established in the Charter, or contrary to the Charter, introduce the notion that members of the Secretariat are representatives, in the work of the Organization, of the governments of their home countries or of the ideologies or policies to which these countries may be considered to adhere. Such proposals would assume a fundamental change in the character of the Organization, requiring a Charter revision.

8. The Secretary-General is fully in accord with the view that the Secretariat, especially at the top level, should be progressively adapted to a changing membership and changing needs. Therefore, he feels that a special effort should be made to secure adequate participation in the work of

the Secretariat, particularly in the higher levels, by staff members recruited from new Member countries, side by side with improved participation by the older Member countries which continue to be underrepresented in the Secretariat. In passing, it may be stated that the situation in regard to these older Member countries has developed for historical reasons over the last fifteen years; recently the Secretary-General has initiated a special effort to secure the services of more staff members from these countries. This effort has been rendered necessary by the continued difficulties encountered.

9. While there will be almost unanimous support for the view that changes should be made to suit such changing conditions as those mentioned, differences of opinion are bound to arise when a determination has to be made as to what these changes should be. There are two proposals in the report of the committee on which some comments are called for here.

10. In paragraph 37 of the report it is stated that three members of the committee "favoured the maintenance of the present structure at the under-secretary level, subject to an important change in the handling of political affairs. They proposed that, in order to enable the Secretary-General to discharge his political responsibilities, there should be at the top level three deputy secretaries-general, who would be primarily concerned with political, diplomatic, and *ad hoc* functions of a special character, including administrative and budgetary functions." In paragraph 38 it is stated that "other members of the committee considered that there would be practical advantages in a grouping of activities which would reduce to not more than eight the number of officials in the grade immediately below the Secretary-General." In paragraph 74(iii) the majority of the committee of Experts has emphasized "the desirability of securing over-all geographical balance for the seven main geographical regions of the world."

11. It is not clear whether those members of the committee whose views have been quoted in paragraph 38 of the report had in mind the maintenance of two levels of senior officials. It is stated in paragraph 40 that "the title of senior officials should reflect the importance of their responsibilities." As for paragraph 37 of the report, the three members of the Committee who held the views reported therein would seem to contemplate a double echelon.

12. With regard to paragraph 38 of the report, the Secretary-General is of the opinion that from the point of view of strict administrative needs it

is possible to arrange the work of the Secretariat so as to "reduce to not more than eight the number of officials in the grade immediately below the Secretary-General." However, for adequate representation of the seven broad geographical regions—recognized by the committee—at the level immediately below the Secretary-General, some fourteen posts would be necessary. The Secretary-General considers that, with the re-grouping of tasks proposed by him in paragraphs 16–24 below, this would not mean that he would have to deal directly with too large a number of officials.

13. A split of the group of fourteen into two echelons, for the purpose of easing the burden of the Secretary-General, would lead to a devalu-ation of the second level, making it less acceptable for purposes of geo-graphical distribution. With a limitation of the higher echelon to, say, three to five officials, a satisfactory solution to the problem of balanced distribution would again become impossible. As developed here, on the contrary, the manning table would satisfy both the needs of equitable geographical distribution and a properly organized administrative system. In taking this stand against a double echelon system, the Secretary-Gen-eral has also in mind its administrative weaknesses, as clearly revealed in the initial years of the Organization. The system proved cumbersome, and of little value to the Secretary-General in reducing the number of officials whom he had to consult, with the result that it was eventually abolished.[1]

14. The Secretary-General notes that, in his separate statement (A/ 4776, appendix, section 2), the rapporteur of the committee has observed that

. . . under the Charter the Secretary-General is the only elected official of the Secretariat. He alone, therefore, bears the responsibility for the manner in which the decisions of the principal organs are implemented by him and by the staff under his direction. The Secretary-General cannot delegate this responsibility without assuming, in turn, full personal responsibility for the actions of his ap-pointees. The consequence of this responsibility is that the views of the Secretary-General himself on the organization of the top level staff who work directly under him, whom he selects and appoints, and to whom he assigns the specific tasks involved in the discharge of his responsibility, must be decisive.

The Secretary-General notes in this context that under the Charter, Arti-cles 97 and 101, the organization of the work of the Secretariat is the exclusive responsibility of the Secretary-General, naturally within limits set by the financial decisions of the General Assembly.

[1] See volume II of this series, pp. 169–192, for the Secretary-General's 1953 proposals on this matter.

15. In line with the above observation, the Secretary-General wishes to make his own proposals as follows.

16. One senior level would be maintained corresponding to the present one.

17. The senior officials would be grouped in two categories: one with "political," and one with primarily "administrative" functions, who may be designated as assistant secretary-general and under secretary-general respectively. There would be no difference in rank between the two categories. Nor would the administrative under-secretaries-general be subordinated to the assistant secretaries-general, except in such cases where specific authority is specially delegated to one or another of them by the Secretary-General.

18. "Geographical distribution" would apply, separately, both to the assistant secretaries-general and to the whole group of assistant and under-secretaries-general.

19. As regards assistant secretaries-general, it would be an established principle that they would, individually, serve only for one term (of three to five years). The under-secretaries-general might serve for up to two terms.

20. There would be five assistant secretaries-general selected on a broad regional basis. They would be responsible for advising the Secretary-General on political problems. All the members of the group would be available for special assignments entrusted to them by the Secretary-General on his own responsibility and at his discretion. The Secretary-General will entrust General Assembly affairs and Security Council affairs, respectively, to two of the assistant secretaries-general.

21. It will be noted that, in paragraph 20 above, provision has been made for a separate assistant secretary-general to be in charge of General Assembly affairs. This responsibility is at present discharged by the executive assistant. The Secretary-General proposes to separate the two functions of the executive assistant, namely those of a chef de cabinet and those of a senior official responsible for General Assembly affairs. In consequence, the post of chef de cabinet will be in the "administrative" category of under-secretary-general, while the post of assistant secretary-general for General Assembly affairs will be in the "political" category.

22. In the "administrative" category there is, at present, a director of personnel in charge of all personnel matters and a controller in charge of the budget and financial matters. The Secretary-General feels that a repeated demand for greater integration between these two departments

could adequately be met by combining the policy responsibility of the two posts in a new post of under-secretary-general for administrative affairs. In addition, however, there would be a director of personnel who would be responsible for the implementation of the policy of the Secretariat in regard to individual cases. As his work will bring him into close and frequent contact with the permanent representatives, the director should rank as an under-secretary-general. The relationship between the under-secretary-general for administrative affairs and the director of personnel would be somewhat similar to the present relationship between the under-secretary for economic and social affairs and the commissioner for technical assistance. Thus, although the director of personnel will have the rank of an under-secretary-general, the under-secretary-general for administrative affairs will be in overall charge of the two offices at present directed by the controller and the director of personnel.

23. There would thus, in the offices of the Secretary-General, be four posts of under-secretary-general, namely the chef de cabinet, the under-secretary-general for administrative affairs, the director of personnel and the legal counsel. Of these only three would report directly to the Secretary-General, because of the special position held by the director of personnel.

24. In addition, there would be five under-secretaries-general, whose functions would be as follows: one for trusteeship, one in over-all charge of economic and social affairs, with one under-secretary-general as commissioner of technical assistance, one under-secretary-general for conference services and general services together (against two separate posts of under-secretary at present), and one under-secretary-general for the office of public information. Of these five, four would report directly to the Secretary-General.

25. These arrangements would require the following formal changes in the present manning table:

(a) The addition of one post in the senior level;

(b) The division of the present post of executive assistant into a post of assistant secretary-general for General Assembly affairs and a post of under-secretary-general to serve as chef de cabinet;

(c) A merger of the two posts now provided for conference services and general services into one.

26. Within this reorganization, there will be full opportunity for geographical distribution on an equitable basis of the seven main geographi-

cal areas of the world, including one or at least one from each of the permanent members of the Security Council.

27. Specifically, the Secretary-General envisages that, of the five permanent members, nationals of two would be appointed to the category of assistant secretary-general, and nationals of the other three would be appointed to the category of under-secretary-general. Following present traditions, two of the assistant secretaries-general would thus be nationals of the United States of America and of the Union of Soviet Socialist Republics. For a variety of reasons, the remaining three assistant secretaries-general should be nationals from countries outside any power-blocs. The established pattern of participation of nationals of the other three permanent members may be followed in the assignments of the under-secretaries-general.

28. To a certain extent, considerations similar to those developed here would apply to the category of officials at the D-2 level. However, it is not possible to deal with them solely on the basis of the regional principle adopted with regard to the category of assistant secretaries-general and of under-secretaries-general, as, in the case of officials at the D-2 level also, the rules adopted as guidance for geographical representation within the Secretariat in general must be given due weight. Adjustments of the D-2 level are under consideration so as to satisfy the geographical principle in adequate form.

29. The manner in which the arrangements outlined here can be implemented, were they to meet with the approval of the General Assembly, will depend on the following considerations.

30. With the established principle that contracts within the Secretariat are not cancelled solely for reasons of geographical adjustment, the timing of such adjustments will depend largely on the rotation of officials within the framework of existing contracts. In the light of experience it is also clear that recruitment from some areas may take some time. Naturally, recruitment should be conducted with strict adherence to the criteria laid down in Article 101 of the Charter, that is, without a lowering of the professional standard required. Finally, responsible development of the administration will make it necessary to provide for continuity and an orderly take-over. Having fully considered these various aspects, the Secretary-General is of the view that, were his proposals to meet with the approval of the General Assembly, they can, to a considerable extent, be implemented in the early part of 1962, and become fully effective some time in the course of 1963.

III

31. With regard to chapter IV of the report of the Committee of Experts on the subject of "geographical distribution," the Secretary-General observes that the Committee rightly began its discussion of the subject by reviewing the relevant provisions of the Charter and especially of Article 101, paragraph 3. The Secretary-General wishes to emphasize that, while due regard is to be paid to the importance of recruiting the staff on as wide a geographical basis as possible, the "paramount consideration . . . shall be the necessity of securing the highest standards of efficiency, competence, and integrity." This fundamental principle is and must remain basic in the recruitment policies pursued.

32. Judged on this basis, it cannot be doubted that the Charter requirements have been faithfully pursued in recruitment to the Secretariat. In seeking the widest possible geographical distribution there has been an active effort to extend recruitment to new countries as soon as they become Members of the Organization. These efforts have been described in earlier reports to the General Assembly. They have resulted in widening the composition of the Secretariat to include nationals from seventy-six Member countries. With appointments now in process, which include ten additional nationalities, eighty-six Member countries will be represented in the Secretariat by the time the General Assembly meets for its sixteenth session, and possibly ninety by the end of the year.

33. However, in spite of the best efforts in this direction, it may not be possible in the near future to recruit qualified nationals from all Member countries. Some of the new Members have such pressing need, in the early stage of their independence, for trained people that they are unable to release anyone for service in the Secretariat. Towards meeting this situation, arrangements have been made for taking on in the Secretariat trainees who may join the Secretariat for a few years and return to their national services at the end of the period with the benefit of a better knowledge of the work and methods of the United Nations. The Secretary-General notes that the Committee of Experts has expressed its support of this scheme in paragraph 87 of its report.

34. The Secretary-General also draws attention to the fact that the principle of the widest possible geographical distribution has been reduced by the General Assembly to a formula which applies to certain prescribed groups of posts. Even when the present formula was suggested

by the Secretariat in 1948, it was emphasized that it should be used only as an indicator or guide, and applied in a flexible manner. This element of flexibility was reflected by indicating a range of posts rather than a precise figure. No doubt the formula that has been used in the past can be improved, provided again that the formula is regarded not as a precise expression of the goal, but rather as a general indicator of the road by which the goal is to be reached.

35. On this basis, the Secretary-General feels that there is merit in the suggestion that population be included as a factor in the geographical distribution formula. Any formula which is based exclusively on the contribution of a Member country to the United Nations budget would have the effect of penalizing countries which may be economically weak but which may be able, nevertheless, to make a good contribution to the work of the Secretariat. In respect of some of these countries, there is also the training aspect to which reference has already been made. The inclusion of the population factor would therefore give some recognition to these factors.

36. As to the proposal that the Secretariat be composed of equal numbers of nationals of three political groups of states, the Secretary-General observes that many of the states included in one or the other category may not wish to be thus labelled. Apart from this, it is obvious that such a proposal runs counter to the Charter. Secretariat representation that would be determined by political or ideological groupings would be unrelated to geographical distribution. Nor could it be justified on grounds of equity.

37. In paragraph 80 of its report the Committee has referred to the "existing imbalance and inequality in geographical distribution of staff." In fact, there are only two regions from which staff representation is significantly below the desired level. The first is Africa, with particular reference to the newly independent states. Here, however, recruitment is proceeding at a rate which will ensure an adequate minimum representation before the end of the year, including some representation at the senior levels.

38. The other such region is Eastern Europe. In earlier reports to the General Assembly, the Secretary-General has acknowledged that the number of staff members in the Secretariat from this region is considerably less than he would wish. From the beginning of 1961, intensive efforts have been made by the Secretary-General to increase this number. Much of the time of the director of personnel and his staff is devoted to

the recruitment and placement of staff from this area, particularly from the Union of Soviet Socialist Republics, the Byelorussian Soviet Socialist Republic, and the Ukrainian Soviet Socialist Republic. In addition, the Secretary-General has requested an under-secretary for special political affairs to give special attention to this subject. Here again, progress is slower than the Secretary-General would wish, but he believes that over a period of two or three years satisfactory results can be achieved without resorting to drastic measures which would have the effect of lowering the morale of the Secretariat.

39. As for the proposal that the categories of posts subject to geographical distribution should include the executive chairman of the Technical Assistance Board and his staff, as also the managing director of the Special Fund and his staff, the Secretary-General would urge that this be the subject of careful reflection. These programmes have their own governing bodies. The contributions supporting them are provided by Members on a voluntary basis, which may not bear any relationship to the contribution ratios which are used as one indicator for geographical distribution in the Secretariat proper. Further, some non-member states are important contributors to these programmes. Finally, in the case of the Technical Assistance Board, the specialized agencies have a voice in the selection of some of the field staff, who have also to be acceptable to the governments with which they will work.

40. Concerning the inclusion of posts at the G-5 level in the geographical distribution formula, the Secretary-General observes that this would appear to be inconsistent with the principles on which recruitment for this category is based. Further, international recruitment to fill G-5 posts is bound to bring a substantial additional charge to the budget.

. . . .

THE BIZERTA AFFAIR

1. Messages to the Secretary of State for Foreign Affairs of Tunisia and the Representative of France

NEW YORK   JULY 21, 1961

WHEN TUNISIA WON its independence in 1956 France had held on to its naval base at Bizerta and thereafter resisted efforts by President Bourguiba to negotiate for the withdrawal of French forces. After several earlier rebuffs Bourguiba on July 6 demanded immediate talks aimed at total evacuation. De Gaulle refused, declaring France would not negotiate under pressure and threats. Bourguiba's response was to declare a blockade of the naval base. Tunisian troops and civilians surrounded the base and French planes were forbidden to enter the air space in the Bizerta region as well as over a disputed zone at the southern frontier. Shooting broke out, French reinforcements were flown in, and French armored units went on the offensive and occupied much of the city in bloody fighting which resulted in heavy casualties among Tunisian soldiers and civilians.

The Security Council convened on July 21 to hear Tunisia's charges of aggression by France and the latter's reply that Tunisia had provoked the trouble and France had been compelled to take steps to ensure the safety of its base and its freedom of communications. The first of the following texts reflects the Secretary-General's concern over the casualties suffered in the street-fighting and his high regard for the Tunisian government's leaders, in particular, Bourguiba and Mongi Slim.

(a) Telegram to the Secretary of State for Foreign Affairs of Tunisia

Have the honour to acknowledge receipt of your telegram of last night in which you draw my attention to the worsening of the situation at Bizerta. I wish to express to you my most grave concern, my sincere desire to do what I can to find a solution to this dispute and my hope that through prompt action by the Security Council a basis for such a solution will be found, which will safeguard the rights involved while affording protection for human lives and restoring friendly relations between two

Security Council Official Records, Sixteenth Year, Supplement for July, August, and September 1961, documents S/4874 and S/4875.

states Members of the United Nations. The present situation places a grave responsibility on the United Nations particularly in view of the loyal and generous cooperation which the Government of Tunisia has always given the United Nations. I am sure that for its part the government will do its utmost to help to find a solution in the spirit of the Charter.

DAG HAMMARSKJÖLD
Secretary-General

(b) Letter to the Representative of France

I have the honour to transmit to you herewith a copy of a message sent in reply to a telegram received this morning from the Government of Tunisia.

The aims set out therein naturally reflect my general attitude which I desire to bring to your notice and to that of the French government.

DAG HAMMARSKJÖLD
Secretary-General

WHEN THE SECURITY COUNCIL met again on July 22 to continue its consideration of the charges and countercharges, reports from Bizerta indicated an intensification of the fighting and mounting casualties. The Secretary-General decided to speak at once in support of an appeal by the Council for an immediate cease-fire (next following text).

---

2. Statement in the Security Council

NEW YORK   JULY 22, 1961

NEWS REACHING US from Tunisia indicates that the serious and threatening development which the Council took up for consideration yesterday

Security Council Official Records, Sixteenth Year, 962nd meeting.

continues, with risks of irreparable damage to international peace and security. In view of the obligations of the Secretary-General under Article 99 of the Charter, I consider it my duty in the circumstances to make an urgent appeal to this Council. Whatever the problems which may arise in an effort to get a complete and definitive resolution, there is need for immediate action which cannot wait for the more time-consuming consideration necessary in order to reach an agreed conclusion to this debate.

I therefore take the liberty to appeal to the Council to consider, without delay, taking an intermediary decision pending the further consideration of the item and conclusion of the debate. Such a decision should not prejudge the final outcome of the deliberations of the Council, as it should, in my view, only request of the two sides concerned an immediate cessation, through a cease-fire, of all hostile action. Naturally, this demand should be combined with a demand for an immediate return to the *status quo ante,* as otherwise the cease-fire would be likely to prove too unstable to satisfy the urgent needs of the moment. I repeat that this is an appeal which is related exclusively to the immediate dangers and does not pretend to indicate the direction in which a solution to the wider conflict should be sought.

LIBERIA RESPONDED to Hammarskjöld's statement by introducing a draft resolution by which the Security Council would call for an immediate cease-fire and a return of all armed forces to their original position pending the conclusion of its debate. The resolution was adopted by 10 votes to none (resolution 164 (1961). France refused to participate in the vote, claiming that France had from the start been calling for a cease-fire. Two other draft resolutions introduced during the day fell short of the majority required for passage. Liberia and the United Arab Republic proposed a call for immediate withdrawal of French reinforcements and immediate negotiations aimed at the speedy evacuation of all French forces from Tunisia. This resolution received 4 affirmative votes, with 7 members abstaining. The United States and the United Kingdom sponsored a draft resolution calling upon both sides to refrain from any action likely to make the situation worse and urging them to negotiate promptly a peaceful settlement of their differences. This resolution received 6 affirmative votes, while 5 members abstained. Thus there was a stalemate. However, the Liberian resolution had included a decision to continue the debate, with its call for an immediate cease-fire and a return of forces to the *status quo ante.* Thus the matter remained before the Council pending further consultations.

After the Council adjourned on Saturday afternoon, July 22, Slim asked Hammarskjöld if he could send UN observers to help secure the cease-fire. The Secretary-General replied that such a move would require a joint request from

France and Tunisia and probably further Council action as well even if France should unexpectedly agree. However he himself could go in his capacity as Secretary-General in response to an invitation from Bourguiba for a personal exchange of views. On Sunday, July 23, Bourguiba cabled such an invitation on an urgent basis. The Secretary-General replied as follows:

I have received your communication in which you state that you feel it necessary to have a direct and personal exchange of views with me. Such a request on your part imposes upon me the clear duty to place myself at your disposal for such a personal exchange of views, which, I hope, might help to lead towards peace. I would point out, however, that the problem is still before the Security Council, which has decided to continue its discussion of the matter, and that, that being so, the substance of the problem is outside my personal competence.[1]

After informing the French delegation of his intentions Hammarskjöld left for Tunis on Sunday night. He met with Bourguiba the next day and found the relationship between France and Tunisia so dangerously strained as to call for an immediate effort on his part to break the deadlock. The French, having occupied strong positions in Bizerta and placed armored units in a threatening manner on the road to Tunis, proclaimed their own cease-fire but ignored the Security Council resolution and showed no intention of withdrawing to their previous positions as the Council had demanded. In this situation Hammarskjöld decided to send the following telegram to the French foreign minister, Maurice Couve de Murville, in an attempt to start discussions between the two sides on the basis of the Council resolution.

[1] Security Council Official Records, Sixteenth Year, Supplement for July, August, and September 1961, document S/4885.

---

3. Messages to the Foreign Minister of France

NEW YORK JULY 25 AND 27, 1961

(a) Letter dated July 25, 1961

By telegram dated Saturday, July 22, 1961, I informed you of the interim resolution adopted by the Security Council [S/4882]. Although I have received no reply, you have, I am sure, given your urgent attention to this decision and to the obligations for both parties deriving from it.

During the debate, the French representative informed the Council of

Security Council Official Records, Sixteenth Year, Supplement for July, August, and September 1961, documents S/4894 and Add.1.

the French government's order for a cease-fire. If I understood the French attitude rightly, this order was not regarded by the French government as having been taken in compliance with the Council's decision, but as an action indicated by the position already established by the French forces. Apart from this information, no official communication from the French government on the action taken by France to carry out the resolution had reached me before my departure from New York on Sunday evening, and I have not received any indication that such information was transmitted to the United Nations later.

Upon my arrival here yesterday afternoon, I was informed by the Tunisian authorities of efforts to establish contact between Tunisian and French representatives with a view to enabling the resolution to be carried out. I note that no such contact has yet been established at Bizerta, but that after contact had been made in the south of Tunisia at the initiative of the French, the Tunisian authorities withdrew their armed forces, as the resolution requests, to the positions they held before the crisis.

The present situation at Bizerta causes me the most serious concern in view of the fact that, more than two days after the Security Council's decision, no progress has been reported regarding the withdrawal of armed forces requested by the Council as an essential sequel to the cease-fire itself.

In view of the responsibilities incumbent upon the Secretary-General for the execution of this resolution, as of any other decision by the Security Council or the General Assembly, I consider it my duty to explore the possibilities of improving this disturbing situation by making an effort, at least, to establish immediately the necessary contact between the two parties, the basis for which must obviously be strict compliance with the terms of the resolution and respect for Tunisian sovereignty.

Having heard the Tunisian authorities' account of the situation, I should now like to have corresponding information on the French attitude regarding the conditions under which the necessary contact can take place and its immediate purpose. I should be grateful for any relevant information which you could send me forthwith. I hope to be able to take advantage of my stay in Tunisia to initiate full implementation of the resolution on the basis indicated above.

You will share, I am sure, my strong desire to see the present situation, with all the serious risks it entails, develop in a favourable direction, with the Security Council decision as the natural point of departure which must be given stability through the speedy fulfilment of the resolution's terms.

Dag Hammarskjöld
Secretary-General

While waiting for a reply to his cable to Couve de Murville Hammarskjöld drove from Tunis to Bizerta on July 26 for a first-hand look. His car was stopped and searched by French paratroops on the outskirts of the city despite his protests. Eventually he was permitted to proceed into the city, where French tanks and troops were strongly in evidence. The French commander, Admiral Amman, then refused to see him. These discourtesies had been deliberately committed on instructions from Paris. That evening Couve de Murville's reply arrived. It dismissed the Security Council's resolution as irrelevant, ignored Hammarskjöld's request for information on the views of the French government and accused him of taking the side of the Tunisian government in his letter. The rebuff was sharp and complete. Hammarskjöld had greatly underestimated the depth of De Gaulle's displeasure with the United Nations in general and the Secretary-General in particular over the UN Congo operations and now over the intervention in France's relations with a former colony. He dispatched the following reply to Couve de Murville and returned directly to New York.

(b) Letter dated July 27, 1961

I thank you for your reply to my letter of July 25. I have also taken note of the statement referred to in your reply.

I think it hardly necessary to embark on an exchange of views by correspondence concerning the points you have raised, since I shall soon be able to discuss matters with your representative to the United Nations personally. I think, however, that a simple clarification is called for.

I have noted with some surprise that what I said in my letter appears to you to set out the views of the Tunisian government. This remark of yours might be interpreted as meaning that I have acted as the spokesman of one of the parties to the present conflict. I am sure, however, that such is not your intention, and it must have been apparent to you that my attitude, as presented in my letter, is based solely on the interpretation of the duties of the Secretary-General and of the principles of the Charter adopted by the Organization in the past, and also on the intentions, I venture to believe, of all the members of the Council who voted for the interim resolution of July 22, 1961.

You refer in your letter to only one part of that resolution. However, without in any way usurping the right to interpret the resolution—a right which belongs to the Council alone—I must point out that the cease-fire and the withdrawal of armed forces were linked together by the Council as two integrated phases of a peace-making operation. In the light of United Nations practice, the request must be regarded as being addressed to each of the two parties to the conflict, separately. I also note that, since no conditions were attached by the Council, the normal interpretation is that the implementation of the measures requested cannot be regarded as conditional on any acts which the other party might perform outside the scope of the resolution. Nevertheless, it is clear that the Council, in this case as with other decisions of a similar nature, acts on the assumption that the reciprocity of the measures adopted by the parties will be ensured by the respect of all the parties concerned for the Council's decision.

You will have noted that in my reply to President Bourguiba's invitation I observed that the basic problem which the Council has decided to continue debating is in my view outside my personal competence— which in no way affects the fact that it is my duty, as usual, to do everything possible to further the implementation of the decision already taken, as set forth in operative paragraph 1 of the resolution. It was with that end in view that I thought it useful to make contact with you to see whether, on the basis of clarification of the attitudes of both parties, it might not be possible to overcome the difficulties which have been encountered hitherto in attempts to establish the contact desirable for an exchange of views on the withdrawal of armed forces.

I regret that this initiative on my part has not yielded any result. If the establishment of contact continues to prove impossible, it seems clear to me that the execution of the Council's request must not be further delayed by the difficulty of achieving coordination, by agreement between both parties, of the measures indicated.

Since it rests with the Council to interpret its decisions, the right to do so not being delegated to any organ, and since it also rests with the Council to take the necessary decisions with a view to their implementation, I shall limit myself to this brief explanation of the way in which I have had to interpret my duties under the Charter in the present case.

DAG HAMMARSKJÖLD
Secretary-General

WHEN THE SECURITY COUNCIL resumed consideration of the Bizerta affair on July 28 France refused to take part. The representative of Liberia requested that the Secretary-General be invited to make a statement on his recent visit to Tunisia. Hammarskjöld then made the oral report that follows.

4. Oral Report to the Security Council on His Initiative

NEW YORK   JULY 28, 1961

I AM HAPPY TO MEET the request of the representative of Liberia. He has recalled that I have paid a short visit to Tunisia in the last few days at the invitation of the president of Tunisia. I arrived there in the afternoon of Monday, July 24, and left in the afternoon of Thursday, July 27, that is to say, yesterday afternoon. In the course of my visit I had the opportunity of having extensive personal contacts with President Bourguiba and with senior members of the Tunisian government. I think that you, Mr. President, and the members of the Council will appreciate that both the character of this visit at the invitation of President Bourguiba and the limits which naturally impose themselves on me in a situation where a matter is pending before the Security Council restrict the field that I should cover in any reply to the question of the representative of Liberia, but I shall say what I feel I can say at this time.

As the invitation of President Bourguiba and my reply have been circulated as Security Council documents [S/4885], the Council will have noted that the aim of the visit was defined by President Bourguiba as a direct and personal exchange of views regarding the developments following the interim resolution of the Security Council of Saturday, July 22. The Council will also remember that I noted in my reply that the question of substance—to which operative paragraph 2 of the resolution may be

Security Council Official Records, Sixteenth Year, 964th meeting.

considered to refer—was considered by me as falling outside my personal competence in view of the fact that it was pending before the Council. The scope and character of my visit are thus clearly defined by these two documents. Quite apart from the fact that it is naturally the duty of the Secretary-General to put himself at the disposal of the government of a Member state, if that government considers a personal contact necessary, my acceptance of the invitation falls within the framework of the rights and obligations of the Secretary-General, as Article 99 of the Charter authorizes him to draw to the attention of the Security Council what, in his view, may represent a threat to international peace and security, and as it is obvious that the duties following from this Article cannot be fulfilled unless the Secretary-General, in case of need, is in a position to form a personal opinion about the relevant facts of the situation which may represent such a threat.

My discussions in Tunis, as well as the visit to Bizerta on which I decided, fell entirely within the framework thus outlined. I had the advantage of getting from the chief of state and his collaborators a full picture of their views on the situation and their problems—specifically as regards the implementation of the resolution of July 22. I also was in a position through personal observation to become acquainted with the circumstances relevant to the implementation of the resolution.

Without, of course, in any way assuming the role of mediator—a role for which obviously neither the terms of the Tunisian invitation nor the invitation of itself could provide a basis—but with a view to getting a better understanding of the difficulties with which efforts to establish a direct contact between the parties have met, difficulties which might be explained by a lack of communication, I took the initiative of expressing to the French government my hope that it would inform me about its views regarding the questions on which I had been informed of the Tunisian viewpoint. The letter I addressed on July 25 to the foreign minister of France with that in view has been circulated to the Security Council, along with the foreign minister's reply [S/4894 and Add. 1], and I have therefore no reason to go further into this aspect of the matter.

As is well known, and as appears also from my letter to the French foreign minister, the implementation of the Security Council resolution of last Saturday remains so far incomplete. It is true that the cease-fire has been established, but that does not seem to have led to an immediate cessation of all actions which, under such a cease-fire, should be ruled out; nor, as the Council knows, does it mean that the integral demand by the

Council for a return of the armed forces to their original positions has been met.

In view of the need for coordination of steps to be taken from the two sides, various efforts have been made to establish a contact between the two parties prior to the full implementation of the resolution. The two delegations most directly concerned have both referred to those efforts. The Council is of course aware of the fact that so far the efforts have not met with success. The situation is unprecedented, and that may in part explain the difficulties which have arisen. In part it may, as already explained, have been a question of a lack of communication. But there are questions of substance involved regarding the place for the contact, and perhaps also its objective. As stated to the parties, it seemed obvious to me from the resolution and from the general principles of the Charter, that the objective of such a contact should be the coordination of steps needed for the implementation of the resolution, and that the choice of modalities should take into account the prevailing legal situation.

By personal observation I can confirm the already well-known fact of the presence in the city of Bizerta, and at a fairly considerable distance from Bizerta on the main road to Tunis, of French military units at the time of my visit; in the city itself, I observed a number of French tanks; the main part of the troops which I observed were French paratroopers. By personal experience I can also confirm that these troops, at the time of the visit, exercised functions for the maintenance of law and order in the city which normally belong to organs of the sovereign government.

Regarding the facts of the situation, I should perhaps add that testimony given in personal contacts—testimony which I have reason to regard as trustworthy—appears to confirm that actions difficult to reconcile with the principle of a ceasefire have also occurred after the time of the cease-fire, and that French military personnel have been involved in these actions. I must, however, repeat here that, since I have no information from the French side regarding these same matters, my statement should be evaluated with that in mind.

It is not for me here to pass any judgment on the situation either in terms of what it may involve by way of risks of a breakdown in the ceasefire in case of an incident, or in terms of the resolution, or in terms of international law. I felt that I should limit myself to a factual statement, and I feel that it is for the members of the Security Council to make comments and draw conclusions.

In view of the aims of the present meeting of the Security Council, and in view also of my interpretation of the limitations of the competence of the Secretary-General in the present phase of the work of the Council, I have naturally not touched upon the wider problem of substance involved.

TWO DRAFT RESOLUTIONS were introduced by Ceylon, Liberia, and the United Arab Republic. The first called upon France to comply immediately with all the terms of the interim resolution of July 22. The second called upon France to enter immediately upon negotiations for the rapid evacuation of all French forces from Tunisia. Both resolutions received only 4 affirmative votes. There were 6 abstentions, including the United Kingdom and the United States. Turkey introduced a third draft resolution not aimed at France but simply calling for full implementation of the July 22 interim resolution. This also fell short of the required majority. There were 6 affirmative votes, including the United States and the United Kingdom, but Ceylon, Liberia, and the UAR joined the Soviet Union in abstaining because the resolution did not, in their view, put the blame where it belonged.

On August 7, thirty-eight African-Asian Members requested the Secretary-General to convene a special session of the General Assembly on "the grave situation in Tunisia" because of the Security Council's failures to take appropriate action. The nine Soviet bloc Members, which did not recognize the Secretary-General, addressed a similar request to "the Secretariat." After polling the Members Hammarskjöld announced that a majority favored a special session. It met between August 21 and 25. Once again France refused to take part.

A draft resolution sponsored by thirty African-Asian Members, joined by Yugoslavia and Cyprus, was adopted on August 25 by 66 votes to none, with 30 abstentions (resolution 1622 [S-III]). The resolution reaffirmed the Security Council's interim resolution, recognized Tunisia's sovereign right "to call for the withdrawal of all French armed forces present on its territory without its consent" and called upon both governments to enter immediately into negotiations aimed at achieving such a withdrawal by peaceful measures. The United States, the United Kingdom, and most of the other Western Members abstained, but the four Nordic states voted for the resolution.

Five weeks later the French began the withdrawal of their troops from positions in the city of Bizerta to the naval base. Diplomatic relations between France and Tunisia were not restored until July 1962 and the French withdrawal from the base itself was not finally completed until October 15, 1963.

Letter to Prime Minister Adoula After Confirmation of His Government by the Congolese Parliament

NEW YORK   AUGUST 10, 1961

DEPUTIES AND SENATORS began arriving on July 15 at Lovanium for the reconvening of the Congolese parliament under UN protection. Gizenga himself was absent, but his parliamentary supporters all came, as did the factions from South Kasai and Bakwanga. By the time the two chambers organized late in July all provinces of the Congo, except Katanga, were fully represented. Despite repeated efforts by UN representatives and by moderates among the Congolese leaders Tshombé and his Conakat deputies refused to take part. Both Gardiner and Khiari were active in the exercise of good offices during negotiations between the Stanleyville and Leopoldville parties on the formation of a new government. When these were successfully concluded, President Kasavubu nominated Cyrille Adoula as *formateur* on August 1 and his government won a unanimous vote of confidence the next day. Gizenga was named the first deputy prime minister and Jason Sendwe of the Balubakat the second. Christophe Gbenye, a leader of the Lumumbist-Gizenga party returned to his old post as minister of the interior. On August 6 Gizenga announced his acceptance of the new government but delayed coming to Leopoldville to take up the duties of his office. This was the situation when the Secretary-General sent the reply that follows to Adoula's formal message to him about the new government and its intentions.

I HAVE THE HONOUR to acknowledge receipt of your letter dated August 10 [sect. I] for which I thank you. I note that the Congolese parliament which met recently at Lovanium has given a unanimous vote of confidence to a government of national unity and political reconciliation presided over by you as prime minister. I also note that, in the resolution adopted unanimously on August 2, 1961, the two chambers of Parliament declared that the new government of national unity would be the legal successor to the first Central Government of the Republic of the Congo. It is further noted that in the same resolution Parliament declared that no

Security Council Official Records, Sixteenth Year, Supplement for July, August, and September 1961, document S/4923, section II, August 13, 1961.

other government can claim to act as the Government of the Republic of the Congo.

As you are aware, the Security Council and the General Assembly have always attached the greatest importance to the convening of the Parliament and the establishment of a constitutional government. It is, therefore, a matter of great satisfaction to me that such a government has now been formed and I have no hesitation in confirming to you that the United Nations, in the activities with which the Secretary-General has been charged by the Security Council, will, in response to the decisions of Parliament, deal with your government as being the Central Government of the Republic of the Congo. I thus agree that whatever aid and support the United Nations is in a position to give to the Congo, within the limits of this mandate, should be rendered exclusively to your government.

My colleagues and I await the indication promised by you of the details of the programme of assistance which your government intends to request of the United Nations. Please be assured, Mr. Prime Minister, that we shall do all we can to assist within the limits of our capacity.

My representatives in the Congo have instructions to keep your government informed of the activities of the United Nations mission in the Congo in the civilian field, as also in regard to the United Nations Force which, as you have recognized, has only one goal, namely, to aid your government in the maintenance of public order.

DAG HAMMARSKJÖLD
Secretary-General

ADOULA FLEW to Stanleyville for talks with Gizenga on August 16. He persuaded the latter to accompany him early in September to Belgrade, where Tito planned to host a conference of nonaligned nations, but Gizenga remained unwilling to join the government in Leopoldville until decisive action was taken to end the secession of Katanga. Pressure was building for stronger steps in this direction, including the use of force if necessary, both within the Adoula government and among many of the African and Asian nations represented on the UN Congo Advisory Committee at Headquarters.

Hammarskjöld had talked with Spaak in Geneva during July and the Belgian foreign minister showed much more willingness than had his predecessor to press for the evacuation of Belgian officers and political advisers serving the Tshombé régime. However, the attitude of the Belgians in Elisabethville was more defiant than ever. The number of white mercenary officers of various nationalities in the

Katanga *gendarmerie* was now over five hundred, and revenues received from the Union Minière supplied plenty of money to pay them and to buy more arms as well as to support an able, unscrupulous, and lavishly financed propaganda campaign in the United States, Great Britain, France, Belgium, and other Western states in support of Katanga's independence and against United Nations objectives. Northern Rhodesia was a geographically convenient ally and the great copper interests there were linked with the Union Minière, the two together generating politically powerful financial and business support in the West, especially in Great Britain and France.

Despite the formation of the Adoula government the European "ultras" in Katanga, who used Tshombé and his ministers as easily influenced front men, believed their international position was strong enough to give them a good chance to carry the day. Thus, whenever Tshombé gave signs of a willingness to compromise with Leopoldville, he was promptly persuaded to resume an attitude of intransigence. During August it became apparent that hope for bringing Tshombé and Adoula together depended in the first instance on new steps to secure the removal of the Belgian officers and mercenaries.

At Hammarskjöld's suggestion President Kasavubu issued on August 24 an ordinance for the immediate expulsion of all non-Congolese officers and mercenaries in the Katanga forces who had not entered into a contractual engagement with the central government. On the same day Prime Minister Adoula formally requested United Nations assistance in the execution of the ordinance. This provided legal authority for United Nations action within the Congo in accordance with the evacuation provision of the Security Council's February 21 resolution. The next day Hammarskjöld sent a new request to Spaak for the withdrawal of Belgian political advisers in Katanga.

After the failure of a final effort by Conor Cruise O'Brien to persuade Tshombé to go to Leopoldville under UN protection for talks with Adoula, UN troops on August 28 moved swiftly to take up positions at *gendarmerie* headquarters, the radio station, the post office and other key points in Elisabethville and then proceeded to search out and arrest Belgian officers and foreign mercenaries. Similar steps were taken in other parts of Katanga. The ultras were taken by surprise and there was no resistance, no fighting. In a few hours almost one hundred officers had been arrested. Tshombé then announced his agreement to dismiss all foreign officers from the Katangese armed forces and to their evacuation.

The Belgian consul, in company with his colleagues in the consular corps, offered to take responsibility for ensuring the surrender and repatriation of all the remaining foreign officers if the United Nations would suspend its search and arrest operations. O'Brien accepted, but this quickly proved to have been a mistake. Most of the regular Belgian army officers were repatriated under orders from their government and the mercenaries already arrested by the UN Force were expelled, but the others went into hiding and then began reinfiltrating units of the *gendarmerie* and *sureté* (secret police). They included the most extreme and lawless of the white mercenaries and were joined by armed ultras among the European residents of Elisabethville. Demonstrations were organized against the United Nations, there were reports of planning for guerrilla warfare and acts of sabotage against the UN Force, and Radio Katanga engaged in inflammatory broadcasts. Panic spread among the Baluba population and by September 9 the number of refugees seeking protection in United Nations camps had grown to thirty-five thousand, thus increasing the danger of tribal war and massacre.

Linnér, Khiari, and O'Brien thought that prompt and drastic countermeasures by the United Nations were now required. All three were recently appointed international officials who were either impatient with or did not fully understand Hammarskjöld's reminders of the constitutional restraints upon the extent of United Nations reaction to the crisis. They proceeded to develop a plan for action which went considerably beyond the scope of the authority given them from Headquarters (see pp. 567-72 for later developments).

Introduction to the Sixteenth Annual Report

NEW YORK   AUGUST 17, 1961

THIS TURNED OUT to be the last of Hammarskjöld's annual statements on the role and future of the United Nations given in his introductions to the Secretary-General's Annual Reports to the General Assembly. As in his Oxford University lecture he pointed out to Member governments that they were confronted with a choice between two views of the United Nations—either a "static conference machinery" or a "dynamic instrument" of evolution toward more effective forms of international cooperation. This last introduction was Hammarskjöld's definitive statement of the reasons, as he saw them, why the second alternative should be pursued. After dictating it he took the draft to Cordier with the remark, "I don't see what I can write after this one." Though completed on August 17, it was not distributed to delegations and released to the press until August 24.

I

Debates and events during the year since the publication of the last report to the General Assembly have brought to the fore different concepts of the United Nations, the character of the Organization, its authority, and its structure.

On the one side, it has in various ways become clear that certain Members conceive of the Organization as a static conference machinery for resolving conflicts of interests and ideologies with a view to peaceful coexistence, within the Charter, to be served by a Secretariat which is to be regarded not as fully internationalized but as representing within its ranks those very interests and ideologies.

Other Members have made it clear that they conceive of the Organization primarily as a dynamic instrument of governments through which they, jointly and for the same purpose, should seek such reconciliation but through which they should also try to develop forms of executive action, undertaken on behalf of all Members, and aiming at forestalling conflicts and resolving them, once they have arisen, by appropriate diplomatic or political means, in a spirit of objectivity and in implementation of the principles and purposes of the Charter.

General Assembly Official Records, Sixteenth Session, Supplement No. 1A (A/4800/Add.1).

Naturally, the latter concept takes as its starting point the conference concept, but it regards it only as a starting point, envisaging the possibility of continued growth to increasingly effective forms of active international cooperation, adapted to experience, and served by a Secretariat of which it is required that, whatever the background and the views of its individual members, their actions be guided solely by the principles of the Charter, the decisions of the main organs, and the interests of the Organization itself.

The first concept can refer to history and to the traditions of national policies of the past. The second can point to the needs of the present and of the future in a world of ever-closer international interdependence where nations have at their disposal armaments of hitherto unknown destructive strength. The first one is firmly anchored in the time-honoured philosophy of sovereign national states in armed competition of which the most that may be expected in the international field is that they achieve a peaceful coexistence. The second one envisages possibilities of intergovernmental action overriding such a philosophy, and opens the road towards more developed and increasingly effective forms of constructive international cooperation.

It is clearly for the governments, Members of the Organization, and for these governments only, to make their choice and decide on the direction in which they wish the Organization to develop. However, it may be appropriate to study these two concepts in terms of the purposes of the Organization as laid down in the Charter and, in this context, also to consider the character and the significance of the decisions of the Organization as well as its structure.

II

The purposes and principles of the Charter are set out in its Preamble and further developed in a series of articles, including some which may seem to be primarily of a procedural or administrative nature. Together, these parts of the Charter lay down some basic rules of international ethics by which all Member states have committed themselves to be guided. To a large extent, the rules reflect standards accepted as binding for life within states. Thus, they appear, in the main, as a projection into the international arena and the international community of purposes and principles already accepted as being of national validity. In this sense, the Charter takes a first step in the direction of an organized international community, and this independently of the organs set up for international cooperation. Due to different traditions, the state of social development and the character of national institutions, wide variations naturally exist as to the application in national life of the principles reflected in the Charter, but it is not too difficult to recognize the common elements behind those differences. It is therefore not surprising that such principles of national application could be transposed into an agreed basis also for international behaviour and cooperation.

In the Preamble to the Charter, Member nations have reaffirmed their faith "in the equal rights of men and women and of nations large and small," a principle which also has found many other expressions in the Charter.

Thus, it restates the basic democratic principle of equal political rights, independently of the position of the individual or of the Member country in respect of its strength, as determined by territory, population, or wealth. The words just quoted must, however, be considered as going further and imply an endorsement as well of a right to equal economic opportunities.

It is in the light of the first principle that the Charter has established a system of equal votes, expressing "the sovereign equality of all its Members," and has committed the Organization to the furtherance of self-determination, self-government, and independence. On the same basis, the Charter requires universal respect for and observance of human rights and fundamental freedoms for all "without distinction as to race, sex, language or religion."

It is in the light of the latter principle—or, perhaps, the latter aspect of the same basic principle—that the Charter, in Article 55, has committed the Members to the promotion of higher standards of living, full employment, and conditions of economic and social progress and development as well as to solutions of international economic and related problems. The pledge of all Members to take joint and separate action, in cooperation with the Organization, for the achievement of these purposes has been the basis for the far-reaching economic and technical assistance channelled through or administered by the Organization, and may rightly be considered as the basic obligation reflected also in such economic and technical assistance as Member governments have been giving, on a bilateral basis, outside the framework of the Organization.

It would seem that those who regard the Organization as a conference machinery, "neutral" in relation to the direction of policies on a national or international basis and serving solely as an instrument for the solution of conflicts by reconciliation, do not pay adequate attention to those essential principles of the Charter to which reference has just been made. The terms of the Charter are explicit as regards the equal political rights of nations as well as of individuals and, although this second principle may be considered only as implicit in the terms of the Charter, they are clear also as regards the demand for equal economic opportunities for all individuals and nations. So as to avoid any misunderstanding, the Charter directly states that the basic democratic principles are applicable to nations "large and small" and to individuals without distinction "as to race, sex, language and religion," qualifications that obviously could be extended to cover other criteria such as, for example, those of an ideological character which have been used or may be used as a basis for political or economic discrimination.

In the practical work of the Organization these basic principles have been of special significance in relation to countries under colonial rule or in other ways under foreign domination. The General Assembly has translated the principles into action intended to establish through self-determination a free and independent life as sovereign states for peoples who have expressed in democratic forms their wish for such a status. Decisive action has in many cases been taken by Member governments, and then the United Nations has had only to lend its support to their efforts. In other cases, the main responsibility has fallen on the Organization itself. The resolution on colonialism, adopted by the General Assembly at its fifteenth session, may be regarded as a comprehensive restatement in elaborated form of the principle laid down in the Charter. Results of developments so far have been reflected in the birth of a great number of new national states and a revolutionary widening of the membership of the Organization.

The demand for equal economic opportunities has, likewise, been—and remains—of special significance in relation to those very countries which have more recently entered the international arena as new states. This is natural in view of the fact that, mostly, they have been in an unfavourable economic position, which is reflected in a much lower *per capita* income, rate of capital supply, and degree of technical development, while their political independence and sovereignty require a fair measure of economic stability and economic possibilities in order to gain substance and full viability.

In working for the translation into practical realities in international life of the democratic principles which are basic to the Charter, the Organization has thus assumed a most active role and it has done so with success, demonstrating both the need and the possibilities for such action.

Further, in the Preamble to the Charter it is stated to be a principle and purpose of the Organization "to establish conditions under which justice and respect for the obligations arising from treaties and other sources of international law can be maintained." In these words—to which, naturally, counterparts may be found in other parts of the Charter—it gives expression to another basic democratic principle, that of the rule of law. In order to promote this principle, the Charter established the International Court of Justice, but the principle permeates the approach of the Charter to international problems far beyond the sphere of competence of the Court. As in national life, the principle of justice—which obviously implies also the principle of objectivity and equity in the consideration of all matters before the General Assembly or the Security Council—must be considered as applicable without distinction or discrimination, with one measure and one standard valid for the strong as well as for the weak. Thus, the demand of the Charter for a rule of law aims at the substitution of right for might and makes of the Organization the natural protector of rights which countries, without it, might find it more difficult to assert and to get respected.

The principle of justice can be regarded as flowing naturally from the principles of equal political rights and equal economic opportunities, but it has an independent life and carries, of itself, the world community as far in the direction of an organized international system as the two first-mentioned principles. It has deep roots in the history of the efforts of man to eliminate from international life the anarchy which he had already much earlier overcome on the national level, deeper indeed than the political and economic principles which, as is well known, were much later to get full acceptance also in national life. Long before the United Nations and long before even the League of Nations, governments were working towards a rule of justice in international life through which they hoped to establish an international community based on law, without parliamentary or executive organs, but with a judicial procedure through which law and justice could be made to apply.

The Charter states and develops the three principles mentioned here as a means to an end: "to save succeeding generations from the scourge of war." This adds emphasis to the concept, clearly implied in the Charter, of an international community for which the Organization is an instrument and an expression and in which anarchic tendencies in international life are to be curbed by the introduction of a system of equal political rights, equal economic opportunities, and the rule of law. However, the Charter goes one step further, drawing a logical conclusion both from the ultimate aim of the Organization and from the three principles. Thus, it outlaws the use of armed force "save in the common interest." Obviously, the Charter cannot, on the one side, establish a rule of law and the principle of equal rights for "nations large and small," and, on the other hand, permit the use of armed force for national ends, contrary to those principles and, therefore, not "in the common interest." Were nations, under the Charter, to be allowed, by the use of their military strength, to achieve ends contrary to the principle of the equality of Members and the principle of justice, it would obviously deprive those very principles of all substance and significance. One practical expression of this approach, which may be mentioned here, is that the organs of the United Nations have consistently maintained that the use of force, contrary to the Charter as interpreted by those organs, cannot be permitted to yield results which can be accepted as valid by the Organization and as establishing new rights.

In the Charter, the right to the use of force is somewhat more extensive than may seem to be the case from a superficial reading of the phrase "save in the common interest." Thus, apart from military action undertaken pursuant to a decision of the Security Council for repression of aggression—that is, for upholding the basic Charter principles—the Charter opens the door to the use of armed force by a nation in exercise of its inherent right to resist armed attack. This is a point on which, both in theory and in practice, the development of international law is still at a very early stage. As is well known, no agreement has been reached on a definition of aggression, beyond that found in Article 2, paragraph 4, of the Charter, and the Organization has several times had to face situations in which, therefore, the rights and wrongs in a specific case of conflict have not been clarified. It would be a vitally important step forward if wider agreement could be reached regarding the criteria to be applied in order to distinguish between legitimate and illegitimate use of force. History is only too rich in examples of armed aggression claimed as action in self-defence. How could it be otherwise, when most cases of armed conflict are so deeply rooted in a history of clashes of interests and rights, even if, up to the fatal moment of the first shot, those clashes have not involved recourse to the use of armed force?

In recognition of this situation and in the light of historical experience, the Charter makes yet another projection into international life of solutions to conflicts tested in national life, and establishes the final principle that the Organization shall "bring about by peaceful means and in conformity with the principles of justice and international law, adjustment or settlement of international disputes or situations which might lead to a breach of the peace." This principle, as quoted here from Article 1 of the Charter, is further developed specifically in Article 33, which requires parties to any dispute, the consequence of which is likely to endanger the maintenance of international peace and security, to "seek a solution by negotiation, enquiry, mediation, conciliation, arbitration, judicial settlement, resort to regional agencies or arrangements, or other peaceful means of their own choice." It is in this sphere that the Security Council has had, and is likely to continue to have, its main significance, both directly as a forum before which any dispute threatening peace and security can be brought up for debate and as an organ which directly, or through appropriate agents, may assist the parties in finding a way out and, by preventive diplomacy, may forestall the outbreak of an armed conflict. It seems appropriate here to draw attention especially to the right of the Security Council under Article 40 to "call upon the parties concerned to comply with such provisional measures as it deems necessary or desirable" for the prevention of any aggravation of a situation threatening peace and security, and to the obligation of Members to comply with a decision on such measures.

It is in the light of the approach to international coexistence in our world today, which is thus to be found in the Charter, that judgement has to be passed on the validity of the different conceptions of the Organization which in recent times have become increasingly apparent. As already pointed out, the basic principles regarding the political equality of nations and their right to equal economic opportunities are difficult to reconcile with the view that the Organization is to be regarded only as a conference machinery for the solution, by debate and joint decisions, of conflicts of interest or ideology. It seems even more difficult to reconcile these principles with a view according to which equality among Members should be reflected in the establishment of a balance between power-blocs or other groupings of nations. The same difficulty is apparent as regards the principle of justice and the principle prohibiting the use of armed force. It is easier to apply the conference concept to the principle of prevention of conflict through negotiation, but also on this point the difficulties become considerable if it is recognized that such solutions as may be sought by the Organization should be solutions based on the rules of equality and justice.

III

The General Assembly, the Security Council, and other collective organs of the United Nations have features in common with a standing international diplomatic conference, but their procedures go beyond the forms of such a conference and show aspects of a parliamentary or quasi-parliamentary character.

While decisions of a conference, in order to commit its participants, must be based on their subsequent acceptance of the decisions, the organs of the United Nations act on the basis of voting, with the decisions being adopted if supported by a majority. However, the decisions of the Assembly have, as regards Member States, only the character of recommendations (except for financial assessments and certain other types of organizational action) so that obligations like those arising out of an agreement, coming into force after a conference, do not normally flow from them. But although the decisions, legally, are only recommendations, they introduce an important element by expressing a majority consensus on the issue under consideration.

Naturally, such a formula leaves scope for a gradual development in practice of the weight of the decisions. To the extent that more respect, in fact, is shown to General Assembly recommendations by the Member states, they may come more and more close to being recognized as decisions having a binding effect on those concerned, particularly when they involve the application of the binding principles of the Charter and of international law.

Both those who regard a gradual increase in the weight of decisions of the General Assembly as necessary, if progress is to be registered in the direction of organized peaceful coexistence within the Charter, and those who oppose such a development, have to recognize that, with certain variations in individual cases, the practice still is very close to the restrictive Charter formula. Experience shows that even countries which have voted for a certain decision may, later on, basing themselves on its character of merely being a recommendation, refuse to follow it or fail to support its implementation, financially or in other respects.

What has been said applies generally to the collective organs of the

Organization, but, as is well known, the Charter has gone one step further beyond the conference concept, in the direction of the parliamentary concept, in the case of the Security Council. In Article 25, Member states of the United Nations have agreed to "accept and carry out the decisions of the Security Council in accordance with the present Charter," thus by agreement, making the decisions of the Council mandatory, except, of course, when such decisions take the form of "recommendations" within the terms of Chapter VI or certain other articles of the Charter. They have further, in Article 49, undertaken to "join in affording mutual assistance in carrying out the measures decided upon by the Security Council."

This agreed mandatory nature of certain Security Council decisions might have led to a demand for unanimity in the Council, a unanimity which was the rule for the Council of the League of Nations. Even so, however, the arrangement would have gone beyond the conference principle with its requirement that no decision reached in an international organ should be binding on an individual Member short of his agreement. With the present arrangements, requiring a majority of seven and the concurring votes of the permanent members, a bridge between the traditional conference approach and a parliamentary approach is provided by the commitment in Article 25 to agree to the carrying out of the decisions in the Council which should be considered as giving the Council its authority by general delegation as indeed stated in Article 24, paragraph 1.

What clearly remains within the Council of the traditional conference and agreement pattern is the condition that its decisions of a nonprocedural character must be supported by the unanimous vote of the five permanent Members, thus avoiding for those members the risk of being bound by a decision of the Council which has not met with their agreement. It may be observed that this special position for the permanent members, apart from other reasons, has the justification that, without such a rule, the other Members of the Organization, in complying with a Security Council decision, might find themselves unwillingly drawn into a Big-Power conflict.

In spite of the delegated authority which the Council may be considered as exercising, and the condition that decisions must be agreed to by the permanent members, the experience of the Organization, as regards the implementation of Council decisions, is uneven and does not indicate full acceptance in practice of Article 25. In this case also, examples can be given of a tendency to regard decisions, even when taken under Chapter

VII, as recommendations binding only to the extent that the party concerned has freely committed itself to carry them out; there is here a clear dichotomy between the aims of the Charter and the general political practice at its present stage of development. Such cases refer not only to Members outside the Council, or, perhaps, Members inside the Council, who have not supported a specific decision, but also to Members within the Council who have cast their votes in favour of a decision but who later on are found to reserve for themselves at least a right to interpret the decision in ways which seem to be at variance with the intentions of the Council. The ambiguity of this situation emerges with special force in cases where such attitudes have been taken by permanent members of the Council, who are considered to shoulder the responsibility for the maintenance of peace and security which is reflected in the special position they hold within the Council. Obviously, the problem whether the intended legal weight is given to decisions of the Security Council arises in practice not only in cases of noncompliance but also in cases of a refusal to shoulder the financial consequences of a decision of the Council.

These observations—which have been limited to a reminder of the Charter rules and a factual reminder also of the experiences in practice— point to a situation which in any evaluation of the United Nations must be given the most serious consideration by Members. For the judgement on the various concepts of the United Nations which are put forward, it is one thing to note what the Charter stipulates; it is an entirely different but ultimately more important question as to what the situation is in practice and what, in fact, is the weight given to decisions of the Organization when they go beyond the conference pattern of agreement.

For those who maintain the conference concept of the Organization, it is natural to side-step the mandatory nature of decisions by the Security Council. For those who take a different view, it is equally natural and essential to work for a full and general acceptance of the Charter rules. Were those to be right who hold that the Charter on the points discussed here, and, maybe, also as regards the five basic principles discussed in the first part of this introduction, is ahead of our time and the political possibilities which it offers, such a view still would not seem to justify the conclusion that the clear approach of the Charter should be abandoned. Rather, it would indicate that Member nations jointly should increase their efforts to make political realities gradually come closer to the pattern established by the Charter.

In the light of such considerations, the significance of the outcome of every single conflict on which the Organization has to take a stand, and the weight given to its decisions in such a conflict stand out very clearly. A failure to gain respect for decisions or actions of the Organization within the terms of the Charter is often called a failure for the Organization. It would seem more correct to regard it as a failure of the world community, through its Member nations and in particular those most directly concerned, to cooperate in order, step by step, to make the Charter a living reality in practical political action as it is already in law.

Were such cooperation, for which the responsibility naturally rests with each single Member as well as with all Members collectively, not to come about, and were the respect for the obligations flowing from Article 25 of the Charter, to be allowed to diminish, this would spell the end of the possibilities of the Organization to grow into what the Charter indicates as the clear intention of the founders, as also of all hopes to see the Organization grow into an increasingly effective instrument, with increasing respect for recommendations of the General Assembly as well.

What this would mean for the value of the Organization as protector of the aims, principles, and rights it was set up to further and safeguard, is obvious. The effort through the Organization to find a way by which the world community might, step by step, grow into organized international cooperation within the Charter, must either progress or recede. Those whose reactions to the work of the Organization hamper its development or reduce its possibilities of effective action, may have to shoulder the responsibility for a return to a state of affairs which governments had already found too dangerous after the First World War.

IV

The growth of the United Nations out of the historic conference pattern—which, as observed earlier in this introduction, at all events naturally remains the starting point in all efforts of the Organization—is clearly reflected in what, in the light of experience, may seem to be a lack of balance in the Charter. While great attention is given to the principles and purposes, and considerable space is devoted to an elaboration of what may be called the parliamentary aspects of the Organization, little is said about executive arrangements. This does not mean that the Charter in any way closes the door to such arrangements or to executive action, but only that, at the stage of international thinking crystallized in the Charter, the conference approach still was predominant, and that the needs for executive action, if the new Organization was to live up to expectations and to its obligations under the Charter, had not yet attracted the attention they were to receive in response to later developments.

The key clause on the executive side may be considered to be Article 24 in which it is said that "in order to assure prompt and effective action by the United Nations, its Members confer on the Security Council primary responsibility for the maintenance of international peace and security." On that basis the Security Council is given the right, under Article 29, to establish such subsidiary organs as it deems necessary for the performance of its functions, the right under Article 40 to decide on so-called provisional measures, the right to use, for the purposes of the Charter, under certain conditions, armed forces made available to the Council, the right under Article 48 to request from governments action on the Council's behalf, as well as the right to request of the Secretary-General to "perform such ... functions as are entrusted to him" by the Council.

The various clauses here briefly enumerated open a wide range of possibilities for executive action undertaken by, and under the aegis of, the Security Council. However, no specific machinery is set up for such action by the Council, apart from the Military Staff Committee, with planning responsibilities in the field of the possible use of armed force by the Security Council under Chapter VII of the Charter. In fact, therefore, the executive functions and their form have been left largely to practice, and it is in the field of the practices of the Organization that cases may be found in the light of which it is now possible to evaluate the ways in which the Organization may develop its possibilities for diplomatic, political, or military intervention of an executive nature in the field.

The forms used for executive action by the Security Council—or when the Council has not been able to reach decisions, in some cases, by the General Assembly—are varied and are to be explained by an effort to adjust the measures to the needs of each single situation. However, some main types are recurrent. Subcommittees have been set up for fact-finding or negotiation on the spot. Missions have been placed in areas of conflict for the purpose of observation and local negotiation. Observer groups of a temporary nature have been sent out. And, finally, police forces under the aegis of the United Nations have been organized for the assistance of the governments concerned with a view to upholding the principles of the Charter. As these, or many of these, arrangements require centralized administrative measures, which cannot be performed by the Council or the General Assembly, Members have to a large extent used the possibility to request the Secretary-General to perform special functions by instructing him to take the necessary executive steps for implementation of the action decided upon. This has been done under Article 98, as quoted above, and has represented a development in practice of the duties of the Secretary-General under Article 97. The character of the mandates has, in many cases, been such that in carrying out his functions the Secretary-General has found himself forced also to interpret the decisions in the light of the Charter, United Nations precedents, and the aims and intentions expressed by the Members. When that has been the case, the Secretary-General has been under the obligation to seek guidance, to all possible extent, from the main organs; but when such guidance has not been forthcoming, developments have sometimes led to situations in which he has had to shoulder responsibility for certain limited political functions, which may be considered to be in line with the spirit of Article 99 but which legally have been based on decisions of the main organs themselves, under Article 98, and thus the exclusive responsibility of Member states acting through these organs. Naturally, in carrying out such functions the Secretariat has remained fully subject to the decisions of the political bodies.

This whole development has lately become a matter of controversy, natural and, indeed, unavoidable in the light of differences of approach to the role of the Organization to which attention has been drawn earlier in this introduction. While the development is welcomed by Member nations which feel a need of growth as regards the possibilities of the Organization to engage in executive action in protection of the Charter principles, it is rejected by those who maintain the conference concept of the Organization. The different opinions expressed on the development are only superficially related to this or that specific action and the way in which it is considered to have been carried through. They are also only superficially related to the choice of means used for translating decisions into action. The discussion regarding the development of executive functions is basically one confronting the same fundamentally different concepts of the Organization and its place in international politics, which could be seen also in the different attitudes towards the legal weight of decisions of the Organization.

It is in this context that the principle embodied in Article 100 of the Charter is of decisive significance. This principle, which has a long history, establishes the international and independent character of the Secretariat. Thus, it is said that the Secretary-General and the staff of the Secretariat "shall not seek or receive instructions from any government or from any other authority external to the organization," and that they "shall refrain from any action which might reflect on their position as international officials responsible only to the Organization." In the same Article, the Members of the United Nations undertake to respect "the exclusively international character of the responsibilities of the Secretary-General and the staff and not to seek to influence them in the discharge of their responsibilities."

The significance of the principle stated in Article 100 is a dual one. It envisages a Secretariat so organized and developed as to be able to serve as a neutral instrument for the Organization, were its main organs to wish to use the Secretariat in the way which has been mentioned above and for which Article 98 has opened possibilities. But in doing so, the principle also indicates an intention to use the Secretariat for such functions as would require that it have an exclusively international character.

In the traditional conference pattern, participants in a meeting are mostly serviced by a secretariat drawn from the same countries as the participants themselves, and constituting a mixed group regarding which there is no need to demand or maintain an exclusively international character. It is therefore natural that those who favour the conference approach to the United Nations tend to give to Article 100 another interpretation than the one which the text calls for, especially in the light of its historical background and its background also in other clauses of the Charter.

There is no reason to go more deeply into this special problem here. Suffice it to say that, while the Organization, if regarded as a standing diplomatic conference, might well be serviced by a fully international Secretariat but does not need it, the other approach to the Organization and its role cannot be satisfied with anything less than a Secretariat of an exclusively international character, and thus cannot be reconciled with a secretariat composed on party lines and on the assumption that the interests represented in the main organs in this manner should be represented and advocated also within the Secretariat. Thus, again, the choice between conflicting views on the United Nations Secretariat is basically a choice between conflicting views on the Organization, its functions, and its future.

In order to avoid possible misunderstandings, it should be pointed out here that there is no contradiction at all between a demand for a truly international Secretariat and a demand, found in the Charter itself, for as wide a "geographical" distribution of posts within the Secretariat as possible. It is, indeed, necessary precisely in order to maintain the exclusively international character of the Secretariat, that it be so composed as to achieve a balanced distribution of posts on all levels among all regions. This, however, is clearly something entirely different from a balanced representation of trends or ideologies. In fact if a realistic representation of such trends is considered desirable, it can and should be achieved without any assumption of political representation within the ranks of the Secretariat, by a satisfactory distribution of posts based on geographical criteria.

The exclusively international character of the Secretariat is not tied to its composition, but to the spirit in which it works and to its insulation from outside influences as stated in Article 100. While it may be said that no man is neutral in the sense that he is without opinions or ideals, it is just as true that, in spite of this, a neutral Secretariat is possible. Anyone of integrity, not subjected to undue pressures, can, regardless of his own views, readily act in an "exclusively international" spirit and can be guided in his actions on behalf of the Organization solely by its interests and principles, and by the instructions of its organs.

V

After this brief review of the principles of the Organization, of the character of its decisions and of its structure, especially as regards arrangements for executive action, presented only as a background for the consideration of what basic concepts and approaches should guide the development of the Organization, it may be appropriate, in conclusion, to give attention to the activities of the Organization and their relevance to the current international situation.

For years the Organization has been a focal point for efforts to achieve disarmament. This may still be considered as the main standing item on the agenda of the General Assembly. However, in recent years these efforts of the Organization have been running parallel to other efforts which are either outside of it or only loosely tied to the work of the United Nations. This may be justified on the basis that a very limited number of countries hold key positions in the field of armaments, so that any effort on a universal basis and by voting, to reach a decision having practical force, would be ineffective, unless founded on a basic agreement between those few parties mostly concerned. Therefore, direct negotiations between those countries are an essential first step to the solution, through the United Nations, of the disarmament problem, and do not in any way derogate from the responsibilities or rights of the Organization.

The situation may serve as an example of a problem which has become increasingly important in the life of the Organization: the right way in which to balance the weight of the Big Powers and their security interests against the rights of the majority of Member nations. Such a majority naturally cannot expect the Big Powers, in questions of vital concern to them, with their superior military and economic strength, automatically to accept a majority verdict. On the other hand, the Big Powers cannot, as Members of the world community, and with their dependence on all other nations, set themselves above, or disregard the views of, the majority of nations. An effort to balance the Big Power element and the majority element is found in the Charter rules regarding the respective competence of the General Assembly and the Security Council and regarding the special position of the Big Powers within the Council. Other efforts to solve the same problem are reflected in the way in which the disarmament problem has been attacked in recent years. No fully satisfactory or definitive formula has been found, but it must be sought, and it is to be hoped that when the time comes for a Charter revision, agreement may be reached on a satisfactory solution.

What is true of the disarmament problem is, of course, true also of those more specific questions in which security interests of Big Powers are or may be directly involved, as for example the Berlin problem. The community of nations, represented in the United Nations, has a vital interest in a peaceful solution, based on justice, of any question which— like this one—unless brought to a satisfactory solution, might come to represent a threat to peace and security. However, the problem of the balance to be struck between the rights and obligations of the Big Powers and the rights and obligations of all other nations applies, in a very direct way, also to this problem which is now so seriously preoccupying the minds of all peoples and their leaders. The United Nations, with its wide membership, is not, and can, perhaps, not aspire to be a focal point in the debate on an issue such as the Berlin question, or in the efforts to solve it, but the Organization cannot, for that reason, be considered as an outside party which has no right to make its voice heard should a situation develop which would threaten those very interests which the United Nations is to safeguard and for the defence of which it was intended to provide all Member nations with an instrument and a forum.

Reference has already been made in this introduction to the work of the Organization devoted to furthering self-determination, self-government, and independence for all peoples. In that context it was recalled that the General Assembly, at its last session, adopted a resolution regarding the colonial problem which elaborates the basic principles of the Charter in their application to this problem.

This is, likewise, a question which for years has been before the General Assembly and it is likely to remain a major item until a final result is achieved which reflects full implementation of the basic principles in the direction indicated by last year's resolution. Experience has shown that peaceful progress in that direction cannot be guaranteed solely by decisions of the General Assembly or the Security Council, within the framework of a conference pattern. Executive action is necessary, and neither the General Assembly nor the Security Council—which has had to deal with situations in which the liquidation of the colonial system has led to acute conflict—has abstained from such action in support of the lines upheld. As in the past, executive action by the Organization in the future will undoubtedly also be found necessary if it is to render the service expected from it under the terms of the Charter.

It is in conflicts relating to the development towards full self-government and independence that the Organization has faced its most complicated tasks in the executive field. It is also in the case of executive action in this context that different concepts of the Organization and of its decisions and structure have their most pointed expressions. As regards this specific aspect of the work of the United Nations, the front line has not been the usual one between different bloc interests, but more one between a great number of nations with aims natural especially for those which recently have been under colonial rule or under other forms of foreign domination, and a limited number of powers with other aims and predominant interests. This seems understandable if one takes into account that a majority of nations wishes to stand aside from the Big-Power conflicts, while power blocs or Big Powers tend to safeguard their positions and security by efforts to maintain or extend an influence over newly emerging areas. The United Nations easily becomes a focal point for such conflicting interests as the majority looks to the Organization for support in their policy of independence also in relation to such efforts, while power blocs or countries with other aims may see in the United Nations an obstacle in the way of their policies to the extent that the Organization provides the desired support. How this is reflected in the attitude towards the development of the executive functions of the United Nations can be illustrated by numerous examples. It may be appropriate in this context to say in passing a word about the problem of the Congo and the activities of the United Nations in that country.

Different interests and powers outside Africa have seen in the Congo situation a possibility of developments with strong impact on their international position. They have therefore, naturally, held strong views on the direction in which they would like to see developments in the Congo turn and—with the lack of political traditions in the country and without the stability which political institutions can get only by being tested through experience—the doors have been opened for efforts to influence developments by supporting this or that faction or this or that personality. True to its principles, the United Nations has had to be guided in its operation solely by the interest of the Congolese people and by their right to decide freely for themselves, without any outside influences and with full knowledge of facts. Therefore, the Organization, throughout the first year of its work in the Congo, up to the point when Parliament reassembled and invested a new national government, has refused—what many may have wished—to permit the weight of its resources to be used in support of any faction so as thereby to prejudge in any way the outcome of a choice which belonged solely to the Congolese people. It has also had to pursue a line which, by safeguarding the free choice of the people, implied resistance against all efforts from outside to influence the outcome. In doing so, the Organization has been put in a position in which those within the country who felt disappointed in not getting the support of the Organization were led to suspect that others were in a more favoured position and, therefore, accused the Organization of partiality, and in which, further, such outside elements as tried to get or protect a foothold within the country, when meeting an obstacle in the United Nations, made similar accusations. If, as it is sincerely to be hoped, the recent national reconciliation, achieved by Parliament and its elected representatives of the people, provides a stable basis for a peaceful future in a fully independent and unified Congo, this would definitely confirm the correctness of the line pursued by the United Nations in the Congo. In fact, what was achieved by Parliament early in August may be said to have done so with sufficient clarity. It is a thankless and easily misunderstood role for the Organization to remain neutral in relation to a situation of domestic conflict and to provide active assistance only by protecting the rights and possibilities of the people to find their own way, but it remains the only manner in which the Organization can serve its proclaimed purpose of furthering the full independence of the people in the true and unqualified sense of the word.

The United Nations may be called upon again to assist in similar ways. Whatever mistakes in detail and on specific points critics may ascribe to the Organization in the highly complicated situation in the Congo, it is to be hoped that they do not lead Members to revise the basic rules which guide the United Nations activities in such situations, as laid down in the first report of the Secretary-General to the Security Council on the Congo question, which the Council, a year ago, found reason, unanimously, to commend.

Closely related to a policy aiming at self-government and independence for all is the question of economic and technical assistance, especially during the first years of independence of a new Member state. The United Nations and its agencies and affiliated organs have at their disposal only very modest means for the purpose, but a rich experience has been gathered and the personnel resources are not inconsiderable.

Last year the Economic and Social Council and the General Assembly had to consider proposals designed to open up new possibilities for the Organization to respond to the demands of Member governments facing all the problems of newly achieved independence. Naturally, the problems which are of special importance for such countries are basically the same as those which face all countries which have been left behind in economic development. Therefore, the urgent attention required by newly independent countries in this respect can in no way justify a discrimination in their favour against other countries with similar difficulties.

This year the General Assembly will have before it proposals initiated by the Scientific Advisory Committee and endorsed by the Economic and Social Council, for a conference under United Nations aegis, intended to provide possibilities for a breakthrough in the application of the technical achievements of present times to the problems of the economically less-developed countries. It is sincerely to be hoped that, in the interest of international cooperation and the acceleration of the economic progress of those countries, this proposal will meet with the approval of the General Assembly.[1]

---

[1] *Editors' note*—After Hammarskjöld's death the Assembly voted the necessary funds for the conference, to be held in Geneva, if possible in August 1962. The conference was subsequently deferred until February 1963.

So far, the economic and technical activities of the United Nations have been less influenced by the conflict between different concepts of the role of the Organization than its activities in other fields. However, it is impossible to isolate the economic and technical problems from the general question discussed in this introduction. While receiving countries should have full freedom to take assistance from whatever source they find appropriate, they should not be barred, if they so wish, from getting all the assistance they need through United Nations channels or under United Nations aegis. The Organization is far from being able to meet all such demands, as donor nations continue to show a strong preference for bilateral approaches on a national or group basis. Again, the problem arises of the basic concept of the United Nations. With the conference approach to the work of the Organization a choice is made also in favour of bilateral assistance, while the alternative approach opens the door to a development under which international assistance, in implementation of the principle of equal economic opportunities for all, would be channelled through the Organization or its related agencies to all the extent that this is desired by the recipient countries and is within the capacity of the Organization.

Basic to the United Nations approach to economic and technical assistance is the principle, under all circumstances, that, although the Organization has to follow its own rules and maintain its own independence, its services are exclusively designed to meet the wishes of the recipient government, without the possibility of any ulterior motives and free from the risk of any possible influence on the national or international policies of that government. Whatever development the executive activities of the Organization may show in the field, there should never be any suspicion that the world community would wish or, indeed, could ever wish to maintain for itself, through the United Nations, a position of power or control in a member country. Were political groups in a country really to believe in such a risk, the explanation would seem to be that, as had indeed happened in the case of governments of Member countries with long established independence, they may find it difficult to accept the judgement of the majority of the nations of the world as to what in a specific situation is necessary in order to safeguard international peace and security, when such a judgement appears to be in conflict with the immediate aims of the group. With growing respect for the decisions of the Organization and growing understanding of its principles, the risks for such misinterpretations should be eliminated.

This introduction has limited itself to general observations on questions of principle, leaving all problems of detail to the report itself. This has seemed appropriate in view of the fact that the Organization has now reached a stage in its development where Member nations may find it timely to clarify their views on the direction in which they would like to see the future work of the Organization develop.

DAG HAMMARSKJÖLD
Secretary-General

August 17, 1961

Last Words to the Staff—from Remarks on Staff Day

NEW YORK   SEPTEMBER 8, 1961

I AM HAPPY TO have this opportunity to meet with you today. Both in the world at large, and by way of repercussion of world events on the Organization, much has happened during the two years which have elapsed since the last Staff Day.

During this period the General Assembly has met under most exacting circumstances and the Organization has had to undertake a major operation which in its magnitude and complexity has been quite unique in its history. As a result, the resources of the Secretariat have been heavily taxed, and I know that all of you have had to work under considerable pressure and that many of you have had to put in very long hours.

Those of you who have responded to the call to go out to the Congo, mostly at short notice, have displayed your readiness often despite considerable personal and family inconvenience. Quite a few of those who went out to the Congo are now back in New York and their place has been taken by others. I hope that those of you who have had this opportunity of participating in the Congo operation feel as enriched by your experience as the Organization has been enriched by your contribution.

I have publicly paid tribute to all those who have participated directly in the Congo operation; but tribute is due equally to those who stayed behind and did the backstopping from Headquarters. I therefore take this opportunity to record, and express, a deep gratitude to all of you for the way in which you have responded to the demands of the Organization.

The general world situation and its repercussions on the Organization have unavoidably left their mark on the Secretariat. In particular the discussions in the last session of the General Assembly have raised far-reaching questions on the nature of the Secretariat. What is at stake is a basic question of principle: Is the Secretariat to develop as an international secretariat, with the full independence contemplated in Article 100 of the Charter, or is it to be looked upon as an intergovernmental—not

Unnumbered mimeographed circular.

international—secretariat providing merely the necessary administrative services for a conference machinery? This is a basic question and the answer to it affects not only the working of the Secretariat but the whole of the future of international relations.

If the Secretariat is regarded as truly international, and its individual members as owing no allegiance to any national government, then the Secretariat may develop as an instrument for the preservation of peace and security of increasing significance and responsibilities. If a contrary view were to be taken, the Secretariat itself would not be available to Member governments as an instrument, additional to the normal diplomatic methods, for active and growing service in the common interest.

I have dealt with this question at some length in various statements, most recently and fully in the introduction to the Annual Report. It is a question which the Secretariat itself cannot answer as it is up to the Member governments to decide what kind of Secretariat they want. But the quality and spirit of our work will necessarily greatly influence the reply.

In a situation like the one now facing all peoples of the world, as represented in this Organization, it is understandable that staff members should sometimes feel frustrated and even depressed. In that they are not different from their fellow beings in other positions influenced by the trend of world events. There is only one answer to the human problem involved, and that is for all to maintain their professional pride, their sense of purpose, and their confidence in the higher destiny of the Organization itself, by keeping to the highest standards of personal integrity in their conduct as international civil servants and in the quality of the work that they turn out on behalf of the Organization. This is the way to defend what they believe in and to strengthen this Organization as an instrument of peace for which they wish to work. Dejection and despair lead to defeatism—and defeat.

During this period of two years, one of the major changes affecting the Organization has been the introduction of many new Members, especially from Africa. The presence of these new Members is welcome, as it reflects the spread of independence and greater freedom, and as it greatly strengthens the Organization and its capacity for service. These new Members are entitled to get their fair share in the staff of the Organization. At the same time some of the older Members have shown greater interest than heretofore in the representation of their nationals in the Secretariat.

These two factors have lent added urgency to a problem which affects every one of you, namely the problem of adjusting geographical distribution. It has been obvious to me that adjustments should be made as quickly as possible to the new situation on the basis of the present formula, and without waiting for the consideration by the General Assembly of a new one. It has been our concern to ensure that these changes should be carried out with the least possible adverse effect on the promotion prospects and other service rights of the existing staff. I have the feeling that on the whole it has been possible to strike an equitable balance. Special hardship aspects are still under study.

• • • •

You are also aware that a number of important proposals dealing with salaries and allowances will be considered by the forthcoming session of the General Assembly. Some of these proposals have been based on the conclusions reached by the International Civil Service Advisory Board. Some others arise out of the recommendations submitted by the Expert Committee on Post Adjustments.

Elements like salaries and promotion naturally are very close to all of us and their significance for the feeling of security and quiet of staff members is obvious. But the spirit of a corps like the United Nations Secretariat, as it develops within the framework set by working conditions, is finally determined by other factors.

We all know that if we feel that what we do is purposeful, not to say essential for the progress of men and human society in a broader sense— yes, even if we believe that what we do is essential only for a small group of people and its future happiness—we are willing to accept hardships and serve gladly for the value of serving.

This common truth naturally applies to this Secretariat as to any other group in which people work together for a common aim. Of course, this does not justify those who decide on the conditions of service of the Secretariat to take advantage of the international spirit of service and of the idealism which may be found within its ranks by maintaining less than fair conditions of work. A good worker should be treated on a basis of equity whatever the motives which guide or inspire him. But it does mean that for the staff members themselves, given the proper conditions of work, the ultimate satisfaction they derive from the work will depend on their personal engagement in it and on their understanding of the collective aim which the work is intended to serve and its significance for the world in which we want to live and which we want to see built for future generations.

This leads me back to the international situation and to the role of the United Nations. It is true that we are passing through a period of unusual threats to human society and to peace. The dangers are too well known for me to add any comments here. If anything, you hear and see too much about them in the headlines of every paper. It is also true that the role of the Organization is necessarily a modest one, subordinated as it must be to governments, and through governments to the will of the peoples.

But, although the dangers may be great and although our role may be modest, we can feel that the work of the Organization is *the* means through which we all, jointly, can work so as to reduce the dangers. It would be too dramatic to talk about our task as one of waging a war for peace, but it is quite realistic to look at it as an essential and—within its limits—effective work for building dams against the floods of disintegration and violence.

Those who serve the Organization can take pride in what it has done already in many, many cases. I know what I am talking about if I say, for example, that short of the heavy work in which you, all of you, have had his or her part, the Congo would by now have been torn to pieces in a fight which in all likelihood would not have been limited to that territory, but spread far around, involving directly or indirectly many or all of the countries from which you come. I also know what the activities of the Organization in the economic and social fields have meant for the betterment of life of millions, and for the creation of a basis for a happier future.

This is not said in a spirit of boastful satisfaction with what this Organization has been able to do—which, alas, falls far short of the needs—but as a realistic evaluation of the contribution we all of us, individually, have been permitted to make through our work for this Organization. It is false pride to register and to boast to the world about the importance of one's work, but it is false humility, and finally just as destructive, not to recognize—and recognize with gratitude—that one's work has a sense. Let us avoid the second fallacy as carefully as the first, and let us work in the conviction that our work *has* a meaning beyond the narrow individual one and *has* meant something for man.

•   •   •   •

FINAL MISSION TO THE CONGO

1. Letter to Prime Minister Adoula

SEPTEMBER 10, 1961

HAMMARSKJÖLD had decided to go to Leopoldville before the opening on September 19 of the sixteenth annual session of the General Assembly. One purpose was a personal effort to persuade Tshombé to a reconciliation with Adoula and thus bring a peaceful end to the secession of Katanga and provide the central government of the Congo with the strongest and widest political base it had enjoyed since independence. Hammarskjöld also intended to explore with Adoula possibilities for progressive reductions in the scope of UN participation in civil administration and in the size and expense of the UN Congo Force.

It would be the Secretary-General's first visit to the Congo since Lumumba's break with him in August 1960. Thus the letter sent by Prime Minister Adoula on September 10 took care to specify that the invitation was at the unanimous request of the members of the government, thereby including Gizenga, who had finally taken up his post as first vice-prime minister, as well as other ministers belonging to the Lumumba party. The Secretary-General replied the same day (first following text). It was announced that he would leave on September 12, arriving in Leopoldville the next day, and plan to return to Headquarters on September 18, just in time for the beginning of the Assembly session.

I HAVE THE HONOUR to acknowledge receipt of your kind letter of September 10 [sect. I] which was sent at the unanimous request of the central government and in which you invite me to come to Leopoldville for an exchange of views with your ministers and yourself with regard to United Nations aid and support to the Republic of the Congo on the basis of the Organization's intentions as confirmed to you in my letter of August 13.

As you say, it is true that there are practical difficulties in the way of making such a visit just before the opening of the General Assembly, but

Security Council Official Records, Sixteenth Year, Supplement for July, August, and September 1961, document S/4937, section II.

I hasten to accept the government's invitation, since I am convinced that direct personal contact with you and all your ministers at the present moment would be of the greatest value in connection with the establishment on a firm and clear basis of the development of United Nations aid to the central government. The excellent relations which exist, and the fruitful consultations initiated by your government with the representatives of the Organization, are a subject for congratulation. By going to Leopoldville at your invitation, I hope to be able to make some small contribution towards strengthening the relationship which you have so auspiciously begun.

In extending to you my warm thanks for this invitation, I also desire to convey to you my deep appreciation of the kind references to the United Nations which you were good enough to make in your letter.

DAG HAMMARSKJÖLD
Secretary-General

DURING THE LAST FEW DAYS before he left Headquarters the Secretary-General had been pressed by his principal lieutenants in the Congo to authorize forceful measures of one kind or another to complete the evacuation of the remaining foreign officers and mercenaries and to cope with the growing threat of violence by the ultras against the UN forces and civilian personnel in Katanga. Hammarskjöld's inclination, as he cabled to Linnér, was "to remain strong but to sit tight and to let the medicine do its work without, if possible, new injections." As the situation in Elisabethville grew more ominous just before his departure he indicated approval, in principle and as a last resort, of a plan for repeating the steps taken on August 28 if further efforts to persuade Tshombé to cooperate failed. However, he thought Linnér and the others understood that no major action should be launched before consulting him after his arrival during the afternoon of September 13 at Leopoldville.

His lieutenants, however, went ahead early in the morning of that day, apparently on the assumption that they could repeat in a couple of hours and without bloodshed the successful surprise operation of August 28, thus dealing a crippling and probably decisive blow to the Katanga independence movement. This time, however the *gendarmerie* and armed ultras drawn from the white population of Elisabethville were ready. The UN troop units immediately came under fire and sporadic fighting and sniping in and around Elisabethville continued through the day. Tshombé, after first offering to arrange a cease-fire, disappeared from his home and could not be located. There were mercenary-led attacks on UN troops in Kamina, Jadotville and Albertville. A single *Fouga Magister* jet fighter, flown by a mercenary pilot, bombed and strafed UN troop positions and transport planes. Since the United Nations did not have a single military aircraft it dominated the skies.

O'Brien compounded the difficulties by announcing to correspondents in Elisabethville during the day that "the secession of Katanga is ended," thus reinforcing the impression that the United Nations had decided to use force on behalf of the central government to unify the country. This went against a basic principle that the Secretary-General had upheld from the very beginning.

Hammarskjöld first learned that something had gone wrong during a refueling stop at Accra where he read a Reuters dispatch about the fighting and quoting O'Brien. After reaching Leopoldville he wasted no time in recriminations or rebukes and set about trying to retrieve the situation.

There was no turn for the better during the next three days. Attacks on the UN troops continued in Katanga and efforts to make contact with Tshombé were unavailing. In Leopoldville the parliament unanimously voted in favor of launching an invasion of Katanga.

Strong protests, partly based on misinformation about UN intentions, were directed to the Secretary-General from London, Washington, and Brussels. Finally, on September 16 O'Brien received word through the British consul in Elisabethville that Tshombé would talk with him the next day in Bancroft, Northern Rhodesia, across the border from Katanga. Hammarskjöld transmitted at once the message that follows proposing that he himself fly to meet Tshombé on September 17 at Ndola instead, where there was an airport.

2. First Message to Mr. Tshombé

SEPTEMBER 16, 1961

(1) THE MANDATE OF the United Nations force in the Congo is, broadly speaking, to help maintain public order. The resolution of February 21 [S/4741] defined further two aspects of this mandate which are binding on the Organization and on all Member states and their nationals. I quote the two relevant paragraphs:

1. *Urges* that the United Nations take immediately all appropriate measures to prevent the occurrence of civil war in the Congo, including arrangements for cease-fires, the halting of all military operations, the prevention of clashes, and the use of force, if necessary, in the last resort;

Security Council Official Records, Sixteenth Year, Supplement for July, August, and September 1961, document S/4940/Add.4.

2. *Urges* that measures be taken for the immediate withdrawal and evacuation from the Congo of all Belgian and other foreign military and paramilitary personnel and political advisers not under the United Nations command, and mercenaries.

(2) In the same resolution the Security Council declares that it is convinced that the solution of the problem of the Congo lies in the hands of the Congolese people themselves without any interference from outside and that there can be no solution without conciliation. The Council adds that it is convinced further that the imposition of any solution not based on genuine conciliation would, far from settling any issues, greatly enhance the dangers of conflict within the Congo and the threat to international peace and security.

(3) A principle of the United Nations which is absolutely binding upon all is the maintenance of peace and, to that end and in order to protect human life, they are bound to cease all hostilities and to seek solutions to the conflict by means of negotiation, mediation, and conciliation.

(4) You have yourself accepted the objectives of the United Nations mission as defined in paragraph (1), that is to say, the maintenance of public order, the prevention of civil war, and the evacuation of all the personnel referred to by the Security Council. There should therefore be no difference of opinion between the Organization and you as to the framework within which ways must be sought of putting an end to the present armed conflict.

(5) As regards the idea that a solution to the problem of the Congo should be sought through reconciliation which would naturally have to be achieved within the framework of the constitution of the republic you have several times given us clear indications that you also accepted this point of view. I am therefore convinced that you do not share the opinion of certain elements who reject the idea of reconciliation, which leads me to the conclusion that your views and those of the United Nations are identical with respect to the principles on which the attempt to find a solution to the political problem should be based.

(6) On the morning of September 13, you yourself requested a cease-fire and I understand that you made efforts to bring it about. Since the United Nations desires without reservation to avoid hostilities and the shedding of blood, your request was accepted in advance, on condition, of course, that you could establish an effective cease-fire on your side. In so doing, you would remain faithful to the position you have taken, which I mentioned in paragraphs (4) and (5) above. The efforts to bring about a

cease-fire have failed for reasons which we do not know, but which seem to derive from the opposition of certain of those responsible for military operations in Katanga. We have unceasingly sought to make contact with you and you even promised us that you would meet United Nations representatives for discussions on Friday evening, but you did not come to the meeting place chosen by common consent. The United Nations, faithful to its principles, still wishes to see established, without delay, the cease-fire which you yourself requested and which it should be possible for you to achieve, given your position of principle as I have described it.

(7) I have been informed of the message received by Mr. O'Brien from Mr. Dunnett, the British consul, inviting him to meet you tomorrow at 11:30 a.m. at Bancroft in Northern Rhodesia. I suggest that I should meet you personally, so that together we can try to find peaceful methods of resolving the present conflict, thus opening the way to a solution of the Katanga problems within the framework of the Congo. The proposed meeting obviously requires that orders should be given beforehand for an immediate and effective cease-fire. I therefore propose to you that such a cease-fire should be firmly imposed by both sides, so as to make a meeting possible and to come nearer to a solution of the present conflict within the framework established by the Security Council and already accepted by you. As I shall have to go to the meeting place by air, I suggest that the meeting should be at Ndola. I am dependent on our transport facilities and for this reason the hour which you propose is impossible for me. I shall inform you as early as possible tomorrow morning of my time of arrival, allowing for the fact that before I leave I must have your reply to this message, including your decision regarding the cease-fire. The cease-fire will occur automatically on the United Nations side, in view of the fact that according to the instructions given and the rules followed by the Organization, it only opens fire in self-defence.

(8) I am awaiting your urgent reply to this proposal for a meeting and for an immediate cease-fire.

DAG HAMMARSKJÖLD
Secretary-General

TSHOMBÉ replied during the morning of September 17 that he agreed in principle to an immediate cease-fire but demanded that UN troops be confined to their camps and that all troop movements and reinforcements by ground or air be suspended. These conditions were, of course, unacceptable and the Secretary-General sent the following immediate response, via O'Brien and the British consul.

---

3. Second Message to Mr. Tshombé

SEPTEMBER 17, 1961

KINDLY INFORM Mr. Tshombé that the Secretary-General finds it impossible to accept the conditions for a cease-fire and a meeting which have been conveyed to him.

According to the terms of the letter from the Secretary-General, in the existing circumstances, there can be no question of anything but an unconditional cease-fire and an agreement of both parties to meet together, all other modalities obviously to be discussed in the course of the meeting. The Secretary-General cannot agree to meet Mr. Tshombé unless this preliminary agreement, which is fully in accord with normal practice, is accepted.

The Secretary-General regrets that by introducing conditions, Mr. Tshombé has delayed the taking of measures to protect human life. He sincerely hopes that a favourable reply to his observations by Mr. Tshombé will make possible a meeting without further delay.

As regards military movements and maintaining the positions of the various military groups, the cease-fire order should naturally be interpreted as having no effect on the status quo, which is to be maintained in all respects throughout the period during which an agreement is being sought.

WHEN O'BRIEN passed on this message to the British consul he was told that Tshombé was about to leave his Northern Rhodesian refuge for Ndola. Hammarskjöld then decided to go himself without waiting for a reply in order not to lose any more time. His DC-6B plane took off just before 5 p.m. local time. With the

Security Council Official Records, Sixteenth Year, Supplement for July, August, and September 1961, document S/4940/Add.4.

Secretary-General were Heinrich Wieschhoff, his principal adviser on Africa, William Ranallo, his personal aide, Vladimir Fabry, Linnér's legal adviser, a secretary and three security officers borrowed from ONUC, and two Swedish UN soldiers. There was a six-man Swedish crew.

Because of the *Fouga* jet no flight plan was filed beyond Luluabourg and the plane observed radio silence for most of the trip. Late in the evening it made radio contact with the Ndola control tower and at ten minutes after midnight local time informed the tower that the airfield lights were in sight and it was descending. An instruction to report when it reached 6,000 ft. above sea level was acknowledged. Thereafter there was silence. Not until the next afternoon, fifteen hours later, was the wreckage sighted, about ten miles from the airport. The plane had crashed and disintegrated in flames in a wooded area. The rescue party found only one man alive, Harold Julien, one of the UN security men. He had been terribly burned and died a few days later without being able to give any information on the circumstances of the disaster.

Hammarskjöld had been thrown clear of the wreckage and was the only victim not burned at all, but he had suffered massive and surely fatal internal injuries. Because of the circumstances in which the flight had been undertaken there were widespread suspicions of sabotage or some other form of foul play. A UN investigation commission later found no evidence to support such theories but also reported its inability definitely to exclude any of four possible causes—sabotage, attack from ground or air, aircraft failure, or pilot failure.[1] One fact was clear. The plane was on a normal landing approach to the airport, with wheels and wing flaps lowered. For whatever reason, it had been a few feet too low to clear the trees on rising ground beneath it.

The Secretary-General's chair on the podium stood empty when the General Assembly began its sixteenth annual session on September 19. In Ndola the next day Tshombé concluded with Khiari a cease-fire agreement after first laying a wreath on Hammarskjöld's coffin. (The cease-fire did not last long and there were to be further episodes of violence before the secession of Katanga finally came to an end in January 1963).

It was a week before identification of the remains of all the victims could be completed, while expressions of grief and tribute poured in from every quarter. A chartered plane then began the last flight home, with brief stops along the way at Leopoldville and Geneva. Sweden was in full mourning and on September 28 the King and Queen led a throng of notables from all over the world at a state funeral in the Cathedral of Uppsala and then to the Hammarskjöld family plot in the old graveyard where the Secretary-General found his resting place. A few weeks later the Norwegian parliament announced the posthumous award of the Nobel Peace Prize to Dag Hammarskjöld.

After the plane crash Hammarskjöld's briefcase was found intact near his body. Besides the small copy of the United Nations Charter and an English edition of the New Testament and Psalms which were always with him when he traveled

[1] For the report of the commission, see General Assembly Official Records, Seventeenth Session, Annexes, agenda item 22, document A/5069.

was a copy of a new edition of Martin Buber's *Ich und Du* (*I and Thou*) and a legal size yellow writing pad which Hammarskjöld used during the flight to continue work on a Swedish translation of the Jewish philosopher's book that he had begun only a few days earlier. Just a month before his death he had written to Buber, renewing the contact between them that had lapsed since 1959.[2] His letter included the following passage: "I still keep in mind the idea of translating you so as to bring you closer to my countrymen, but it becomes increasingly difficult to choose. . . . Also, the more I sense the nuances of your German, the more shy I become at the thought of a translation. . . ."

Buber had responded at once, writing from Jerusalem on August 23 that "Were I asked which of my books a Swede should read first, I should answer: 'The most difficult of them all, but the most apt to introduce the reader into the realm of dialogue, I mean *I and Thou.*'" Buber sent along a copy of the new German edition, to which he had added a "Postscript", as well as a paper on language he had recently given. Hammarskjöld decided not only to accept the suggestion but to go right ahead with it. On September 12, the day before he left New York for the Congo, he wrote Buber that the Swedish publisher, Bonnier's, had welcomed the idea of publishing the translation and that he intended to start work at once. Buber received the letter an hour after he had heard the news of Hammarskjöld's death over the radio.[3]

Among the effects the Secretary-General had left in his room in Linnér's house at Leopoldville when he departed on the flight to Ndola were the first twelve typed pages of his translation of *Ich und Du* with handwritten corrections on the first page. There was also a typed copy of an article he had written during the summer of 1961 for publication in the 1962 Yearbook of the Swedish Tourist Association.[4] It was entitled *Slottsbacken* (*Castle Hill*) and was written in response to a request for his recollections of the Uppsala of his student days, when his father was governor of the province and he lived in the castle on the hill. He set down his memories of those days in the order of the four seasons, a series of sensitive word pictures evoking the cycle of nature and the life of the town and its people through the year—by turns gay, compassionate, reflective. Of the time just before New Year's he wrote: "The Lutheran hymns' reminder of time's bitter flight and the transience of all things captures the mood in which the Castle has sunk back while winter darkness has deepened. When the wind sweeps in from the plain against the walls one remembers the words of the old, that a windy new year's eve bodes the death of great men."[5]

---

[2] See volume IV of this series.

[3] The correspondence is quoted in Audrey Hodes, *Martin Buber—An Intimate Portrait,* Viking, 1971.

[4] See volume IV of this series, pp. 545-553, for earlier references to this organization and the Secretary-General's interest in its work.

[5] *Castle Hill,* in English translation, was published in 1971 as a pamphlet by The Dag Hammarskjöld Foundation, Uppsala. © 1962 by Svenska Turistföreningen.

Index

Abbas, Mekki: acting special representative of Secretary-General, in Congo, 400, 437
Accra, Ghana, 84, 569
Adeel, Mr., 379
Administration: Conference on Experience in International Administration, 474n
Administrative and Budgetary Committee (Fifth Committee, GA), 12, 259, 294
——Hammarskjöld statements in: financing ONUC, 226-36, 438-45; United Nations personnel policies, 208-13
Adoula, Cyrille, 14, 154, 176, 339, 499, 500, 501, 507, 540; forms government after reconvening of Congolese Parliament, 538; Hammarskjöld efforts for reconciliation between Adoula and Tshombé, 567-74; Hammarskjöld letter, following confirmation of Adoula's government by Congolese Parliament, 538-39
Advisory Committee on Administrative and Budgetary Questions, 227, 228, 234, 235, 236, 510, 517
Advisory Committee on the Congo, 120, 181, 191, 267, 273, 276, 286, 291, 311, 322, 323, 331, 359, 361, 365-66, 376, 381, 405, 413, 414, 415, 419, 432, 437, 448, 449, 450; Conciliation Commission appointed, 221; establishment of, 107-8, 152
Afghanistan: Congo operation, 69
Africa: in the international community, 122-26; United Nations role in, 460; see also United Nations Operation in the Congo; names of countries
Aggression, armed: United Nations Charter and, 547
Albertville, Congo, 145, 146, 147, 568
Alexander, Gen. H. T., 41
Algeria: Congo operation, 308
Algerian situation, 511

d'Almeida, Ayité, 436, 450
Amman, Adm., 532
ANC, see Congolese Army
Annual Reports: Introductions: 14th (1959), 427; 15th (1960), 14, 122-41; 16th (1961), 14, 542-62
Argentina: Congo operation, 26, 49, 255, 268, 309
Armée nationale congolaise (ANC), see Congolese Army
Astrid (Queen of the Belgians), 97n
Aung Khine, U, 435, 450

Bahizi, Mr., 371
Bakwanga, Congo, 142, 151, 167, 329, 331, 353, 394, 450, 538; deportation and execution of Kasavubu opponents in, 354-56
Balfour, Arthur, 472
Baluba tribe, 180, 353, 421, 447, 541; massacres of, 142, 153, 154, 160, 167, 320, 341
Banana base, Congo, 393, 394, 395, 397, 398
Bancroft, Northern Rhodesia, 569, 571
Bandung treaty powers, 19
Barnes, Djuna: The Antiphon, 459
Baudouin (King of the Belgians), 97n
Beer, Max (correspondent, Neue Zürcher Zeitung), 490
Beethoven, Ludwig van, 15, 224, 225
Belgian Congo, 3; see also United Nations Operation in the Congo
Belgium: in Congo crisis, 1-10 passim, 13, 16-20, 22, 23-24, 25-27, 37-38, 39, 40, 43-46, 50, 56, 57-66, 68, 69, 70-71, 73-74, 75-77, 79, 80, 81, 82, 87, 89-90, 98-100, 101, 103, 104, 105-7, 109, 111, 112, 113, 115, 121, 142-50, 153, 168, 169, 189-90, 255, 258-60, 268-69, 271, 280, 281, 282, 313, 338-39, 351, 357, 362-63, 365, 374, 385-86, 392-93, 400, 413, 421, 431, 433-34,